3D GAME
PROGRAMMING
ALL IN ONE

SECOND EDITION

KENNETH C. FINNEY

THOMSON

COURSE TECHNOLOGY

Professional ■ Technical ■ Reference

ISBN-10: 1-59863-266-3
ISBN-13: 978-1-59863-266-8
Library of Congress Catalog Card Number: 2006927129
Printed in the United States of America
07 08 09 10 11 TW 10 9 8 7 6 5 4 3 2 1

Publisher and General Manager, Thomson Course Technology PTR:
Stacy L. Hiquet

Associate Director of Marketing:
Sarah O'Donnell

Manager of Editorial Services:
Heather Talbot

Marketing Manager:
Heather Hurley

Acquisitions Editor:
Mitzi Koontz

Marketing Coordinator:
Adena Flitt

Project Editor:
Jenny Davidson

Technical Reviewer:
Jacqueline Finney

PTR Editorial Services Coordinator:
Erin Johnson

Copy Editor:
Laura Gabler

Interior Layout Tech:
Interactive Composition Corporation

Cover Designer:
Mike Tanamachi

CD-ROM Producer:
Brandon Penticuff

Indexer:
Sharon Shock

Thomson Course Technology PTR,
a division of Thomson Learning Inc.
25 Thomson Place
Boston, MA 02210
http://www.courseptr.com

For all we have and are,
For all our children's fate,
Stand up and take the war.
The Hun is at the gate!
Our world has passed away,
In wantonness o'erthrown.
There is nothing left to-day
But steel and fire and stone!

—Rudyard Kipling
"For All We Have And Are", 1914

This book is dedicated to my students, past, present and future.

—Ken Finney,
Bowmanville, Ontario

Acknowledgments

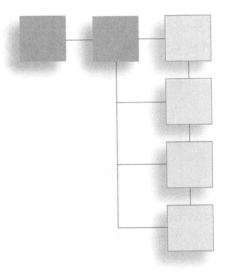

I'm absolutely humbled by how well received this book has been by the independent computer game development folks: certainly in the GarageGames development community, but more significantly, by the larger reader base in countries all over the world. And I am grateful to each and every one of those who have allowed me into their dens, basements, living rooms, garages, and yes, even classrooms.

I want to thank my editors Laura, Jenny, and Mitzi, without whom this book wouldn't be possible. I want to extend special thanks to my wife, Jacquie, who spent hours and hours immersed in both Torque's C++ engine source code and TorqueScript double-checking things. To be edited by one's spouse is an educational experience in and of itself.

As usual, my boys, Indy and Luc, were veritable fonts o' gamer wisdom and ideas. And they kept me on my toes with their late-night ninja Airsoft sneak attacks on me in the gazebo during the summer when I was working on this book. They only got me once. However, the many, many paintball bruises and welts I had on my body all summer are indications that they're no slouches, tactically speaking.

It almost seems that it should go without saying (because I keep saying it over and over), but a great deal of thanks, gratitude, and respect go to those guys in the greasepit at GarageGames, and the greater GG community. It would be a great disservice to them to not express my gratitude publicly yet again, no matter how repetitive I risk sounding.

Special thanks go to Josh Williams (The Kid) who, along with Jay Moore, helped me out of a serious bind that I inadvertently constructed for myself about a half a year ago. Mark Frohnmayer had no small part to play also, and to him go my thanks as well.

Tip o' the hat to Dave Wyand, Matt Fairfax, Tom Brampton, John Kabus, and the rest of the Constructor development team. You guys are kickin' and takin'.

I want to thank the crew at AiTO for their thoughtfulness and support, and for continuing to help make my job there the most enjoyable and rewarding one I've ever had. Special thanks go to Jan Czechowicz, the Gnome of Bay Street. Also, shout outs and props go to David Smith, Predrag Peshikan, and Lisa Delorme for their guidance, the latitude they grant me, and for paying me to come to the school and have fun, day in and day out. Paul Armstrong keeps everything held together with duct tape or something, and doesn't kick me out of his office whenever I come whining to him about some problem.

Last but certainly not least, I want to acknowledge these great people, GAD students all:

Ali Rafati, Calvin Lee, Colin Dyer, Corrie Ramsey, Cory Phillips, Craig Twigg, David Dick, Feras Jaber, James Thuss, Jason Cabral, Jim Wray, John Montegro, Jonathan Gidney, Joseph Pendon, Josh Edgar, Juan Pinzon, Juan Rodriguez, Karl Nevill, Kyle Kokocinski, Laura Genova, Marlon Tyson, Nathan Tillotson, Patricia Rossi, Paul Da Silva, Peter Bruce, Randy Abbot, and Shawn Corney.

Future big names in computer games. You just watch and see!

Regards,
Ken

About the Author

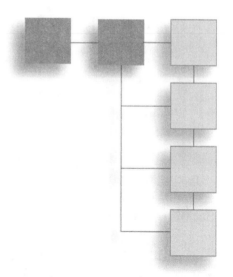

Kenneth C. Finney is the lead faculty member for the Game Art & Design program at the Art Institute of Toronto. He began programming in 1974 and his career as a software engineer included work on high-speed trading systems technology, armored fighting vehicle systems design, nuclear reactor safety and testing technology, robotic pharmaceutical systems, and 3D game engine technology. In 1997 Ken was a recipient of the prestigious Conference Board of Canada ITX (Innovation in Technology Excellence) Award for his work on InScan—a high-speed document scanning system.

At the turn of the millennium, Ken decided to pursue his passion for computer games, and began gradually moving out of the world of commercial and industrial technology and into the game development arena. Ken is the creator of the popular *Tubettiworld* online game and the 'QuicknDirty' game management tools for Novalogic's *Delta Force 2* game series.

Ken is currently working on the new and unique *Return to Tubettiworld* action/adventure game (www.tubettiworld.com) using the Torque Game Engine. The *Return to Tubettiworld* design includes integrated episodic single-player, polyplayer, and Internet multi-player combat with distributed player-hosted servers in a persistent game world.

CONTENTS

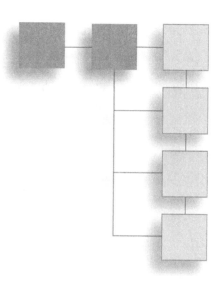

INTRODUCTION

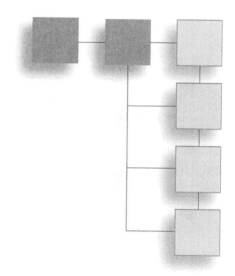

Beginnings

"Hi, I'm using your software and I was wondering—can you tell me how I can make a computer game? I don't have much money, but I have this terrific idea for a shooter like XYZ game, except I'll make it do . . ."

During the years bracketing the millennium changeover, while working on the Tubettiland "Online Campaign" software and more recently while working on the *Return to Tubettiworld* game, I figure I've received more than a hundred queries from people of all ages about how to get started making games. There were queries from 40-year-olds and 13-year-olds and every age in between. Most e-mails were from guys I would estimate to be in their late teens or early 20s.

After about the 30th response or so, I gave up trying to help these people out in detail and started to just point them to Web sites where they could gather the information they needed. Finally I stopped responding completely. But this bugged me to no end (I still get several of these e-mails in a month), so every now and then I will respond with the Web links or some pointers. However, whenever I do answer, I often get drawn into long e-mail exchanges for which I just don't have the time. Eventually I have to beg out of the exchange, usually by being nonresponsive at some point. Then I feel bad again.

This book started out as a sort of e-mail to everyone I hadn't responded to. It had been rattling around in my head for several years, and I finally managed to get it out!

This Second Edition is two things: an effort to bring the book up-to-date with the latest version of Torque, from GarageGames, and an attempt to bring the very best tools available to the Indie game maker. And of course, a number of errors and omissions in the first edition are corrected, as well.

About This Book

If you want to, you will be able to take this book and a computer, go into a room without Internet access, and emerge with a completed, ready-to-play first-person shooter game within weeks. You will then be able to spend as much time as you want to dream up your game play concepts, and you will have the ability to add them to *your* game.

You might think this is a bold claim, but you can see for yourself. Go ahead and turn to the Table of Contents, or take a quick flip-through skim of the chapters. It's all there. If you follow through and do the exercises and work, you will arrive at the other end of the journey with experience, not just book learnin'.

But keep this in mind: you must start at the beginning and work your way through to the end. As the book advances, it builds on your efforts in earlier chapters. This is not the sort of book to leap around in, until you've been through it at least once.

Believe in Yourself

Computer games are a $9 billion per year industry, and that number increases every year. A growing part of this industry is people like you—part of an expanding segment of the gamer population that doesn't just want to *play* the games but believes that you can *make* them better than the game companies can. Your problem may be that you lack the right combination of training, experience, and tools needed to turn dreams into reality. This book is for you.

Every year more and more colleges offer game development programs, and every few months a new online indie game developer site launches on the Web. There is no lack of training available for those with the money to pay, and there is no lack of books for those of you who want to create your own engines or other specialized parts of a game.

The key element missing is a resource that takes the inspired and aspiring game developer by the hand and walks him through all the steps and tools required to make a fully featured game. This book is that resource. With the exception of game music composition (which itself could be a complete book series), you, the

Gentle Reader, will *learn how to create every part of the game yourself* by using a well-defined toolkit of programs, knowledge, skills, and ideas. Sound, music, art, and code libraries are included on the companion CD for you to use if you lack a certain artistic or creative flair.

What You Bring to the Party

I assume that you have more than a passing familiarity with computer games, especially the first-person shooter genre. Throw in some computer savvy, add a reasonably capable computer system, sprinkle with desire, spice it with passion, and you should be good to go!

Skills

You are probably fully able to deal with all aspects of Microsoft Windows-based computing. You don't need to be a programmer, but you do need to be aware that some programming will be required in creating a computer game. The first few chapters will introduce you to all the programming concepts that you will encounter in the course of using the book. You will not be expected to learn advanced 3D math in detail, but you will learn enough about 3D to accomplish your goals.

I'm going to show you how to create your own artwork, but you don't need to be an artist. The companion CD features a collection of art you can use in your game, distributed throughout the game engine demo and RESOURCES folders.

System

All of the development tools, including the engine, are also included on the companion CD. All of these tools are priced such that even though the shareware version may be included on the CD, the actual registered versions are less than $100.

You will need a Windows-based computer to use this book. (See below for minimum system requirements.) It is possible for Macintosh and Linux users to use this book to create a game, because the game engine used—Torque—is also available for those platforms. However, not all of the required development tools are available on Mac and Linux, so the book's focus will be on Windows on Intel.

System Requirements
Windows 98/SE/ME/2000/XP

Pentium III 500, 128 MB RAM

OpenGL or DirectX Compatible 3D Graphics Accelerator, DirectX compatible sound card

Mac OS X

G4 +, 128 MB RAM

OpenGL Compatible 3D Graphics Accelerator

Linux

Pentium 500, 128 MB RAM

NVIDIA TNT2 or better 3D Graphics Accelerator, Linux-supported sound card

XFree86 4.0 or newer with NVIDIA OpenGL drivers

glibc 2.2 or newer (e.g.: Redhat 7.x+, Mandrake 8.x+, Debian 3.0+)

SDL version 1.2 or newer (1.2.3 or later is recommended)

OpenAL Runtime or SDK Installation

Mesa3D version 3.4 or newer (3.4.2 or later recommended)

What the Book Offers

In this book we are going to look at all aspects of game development, a journey from first principles to the completed game.

Concepts

We are going to take a look at various aspects of the game industry to give you the opportunity to see where you might fit in and what sort of opportunities there are. We'll also examine the elements of a 3D game, game design issues, and game genres.

Programming

Next, you'll be introduced to the programming concepts that you will need to understand in the course of using the book. You will see how to structure program code, create loops, call functions, and use globally and locally scoped variables. We'll use a subset of an object-oriented programming language called TorqueScript, which is built into the Torque Engine. Hands-on sample programs are available on the companion CD. We'll move on to examining the 3D concepts that you will need to understand some of the more sophisticated activities later in the book. This will provide a foundation for both the programming and the modeling tasks that you will take on later.

Torque

Once you've been powered up with sufficient knowledge and understanding of the main concepts in 3D game development, we'll get into using the Torque Engine in detail. You will learn how to handle client/server programming, how to control the player-character, how to send messages between players, and much more. Concepts will be presented with exercises and sample programs that are available on the CD. Although we will cover some of the more intricate low-level workings of the Torque Engine in order to understand it better, it's important to realize that as an independent game developer you'll benefit more from mastering the higher-level functions that utilize the engine for us, so you can worry about other stuff—like game play. Without game play, you won't have a game.

Textures

Next, the book will show you everything you need to know about game textures: how to create them, how to modify and manipulate them, and how to use them in the game. The coverage is comprehensive; all of the texture types and their uses are discussed: skins, tiles, terrain, skyboxes, height maps, GUI widgets, and more. You will be guided through exercises in creating each of the texture types. A library of textures is available on the companion CD to fill in any gaps in your texture needs.

Models

Then we get to the meat of a 3D game—the models. In these chapters we will be delving into the world of low-poly modeling. We'll talk about the general principles involved in ways that can be applied to other tools, such as the expensive 3D Max or Maya. But the practical focus will be geared toward using MilkShape, UVMapper, and other low-cost tools that are included on the companion CD.

I will show you the various model types, such as polysoup and CSG models. You will create models for all aspects of the game in the exercises: player-characters, vehicles, weapons, powerups, decorations or clutter, buildings, and structures. You will walk through each step in the creation of the different model types so that you can create your own unique game look, if you want. All of the models in these chapters, plus many more, are available on the companion CD to round out your model library.

Sound and Music

After modeling, you will encounter the icing on the game cake: sound and music. You will discover how to select, create, and modify sounds for use in your game. You will also get some advice about selecting musical themes and how to integrate music into your game.

Integration

After picking up the required programming skills, and learning how to use the art creation and modeling tools, you will learn how to knit all the parts together to create a game, populate your game world, and then test and troubleshoot your game. Finally, we look at where you can go with your shiny new 3D game developer's toolkit of ideas, knowledge, skills, and software tools.

The Companion CD

The companion CD contains quite a few resources.

Source Code

The book's CD contains all of the TorqueScript source code in sample form and final form. The samples will be aligned with the exercises in each chapter. The scripts for the final completed game will be included in its own directory tree. The game will be usable immediately upon installation from the CD so that you can have an instant and extensive preview of what is to come.

Game Engine

The CD will contain the complete Torque Game Engine version 1.4 with its executable, DLLs, and all required GUI and support files. It is a fully featured game engine that includes advanced networking capabilities, blended animations, built-in server-side anticheat capabilities, a strong and complete object-oriented C++-like scripting language, and many other advanced features.

Tools

The following shareware tools are included on the CD:

- Torque ShowTool Pro for reviewing 3D player and item models

- MilkShape 3D for 3D player and item modeling

- Constructor for 3D interior modeling

- The Gimp 2 for texture and image manipulation

- Audacity for sound editing and recording

- UVMapper to perform UV unwrapping tasks

- UltraEdit-32 as the text or programming editor

Goodies

The CD also includes a few extras that aren't mentioned in the book or that are only briefly touched on:

- Retail games created with Torque: *Orbz, ThinkTanks, Marble Blast, Chain Reaction, Tube Twist*

- Additional image and audio resources

- Open Source utility source code

Go Get 'em!

The most important asset you have as an independent, and the key to any success, is your enthusiasm. Remember to use this book, and other books and training you acquire, as resources that will help you do what you want to do; they are not vouchers that you can trade in for a nice big pot of success. You have to do the work in the learning, and you have to do the work in the creating. And if you believe you can, then I know you can! Go get 'em!

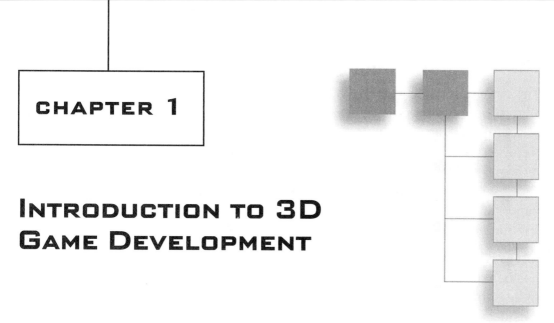

CHAPTER 1

INTRODUCTION TO 3D GAME DEVELOPMENT

Before we get into the nitty-gritty details of creating a game, we need to cover some background so that we can all work from the same page, so to speak. In the first part of this chapter, we will establish some common ground regarding the 3D game industry in the areas that matter—the types of games that are made and the different roles of the developers that make them. In the second part of the chapter, we'll establish what the essential elements of a 3D game are and how we will address them.

Throughout the book you will encounter references to different *genres,* or types, of games, usually mentioned as examples of where a particular feature is best suited or where a certain idea may have originally appeared. In this chapter we will discuss the most common of the 3D game genres. We will also discuss game development roles; I will lay out "job descriptions" for the roles of producer, designer, programmer, artist, and quality assurance specialist (or game tester). There are various views regarding the lines that divide the responsibilities, so my descriptions are fairly generic.

Finally, we will discuss the concept of the 3D game engine. If ever there is going to be an area of dispute between a writer and his readers in a book like this, a discussion of what constitutes a 3D game engine will be it. I do have a trump card, though. In this book we will be using the Torque Game Engine as our model of what constitutes a fully featured 3D game engine. We will use its architecture as the framework for defining the internal divisions of labor of 3D game engines.

The Computer Game Industry

The computer game industry is somewhat different from other high-tech fields. With properties, producers, artists, and distributors, as well as its own celebrities, the computer game business operates more like Hollywood than the traditional commercial or industrial software development company. It is quite a bit more informal and relaxed than other high-tech fields in many ways but is quicker paced with a higher burnout rate. There are independent game developers, or indies, and big-name studios, but the computer game industry tends to be more entrepreneurial in spirit.

Just as is true of indies in the motion picture industry, an indie game developer is not beholden to other businesses in the industry that can direct their efforts. Indies fund their own efforts, although they sometimes can get funding from outside sources, like a venture capitalist (good luck finding one, however). The key factor that makes them independent is that the funding does not come from *downstream* industry sources that would receive the developer's product, like a major game development house, publisher, or distributor.

Indies sell their product to distributors and publishers after the product is complete, or nearly so. If a developer creates a product under the direction of another company, they are no longer independent.

A good measure of the "indie-ness" of a developer is found in the answer to the following two questions:

- Can the developer make any game he wants, in whatever fashion he wants?

- Can the developer sell the game to whomever he wants?

If the answer is yes in both cases, then the developer is an indie.

Of course, another strong similarity with movies is that, as I pointed out earlier, games are typically classified as belonging to different genres.

3D Game Genres and Styles

Game development is a creative enterprise. There are ways to categorize the *game genres*, but I want you to keep in mind that while some games fit each genre like a glove, many others do not. That's the nature of creativity. Developers keep coming up with new ideas; sometimes they are jockeying for an advantage over the competition, and sometimes they are just scratching an itch. At other times, calculating marketing departments decide that mixing two popular genres is a surefire path to a secure financial future.

The first rule of creative design is that there are no rules. If you are just scratching an itch, then more power to you. If you are looking to make a difference in the gaming world, you should at least understand the arena. Let's take a look at the most common 3D genres around today and a few that are interesting from an historical perspective. When you are trying to decide what sort of game you want to create, you should try understanding the genres and use them as guides to help focus your ideas.

It's important to note that all of the screen shots in this chapter are of games by indie game developers. Some of the games are currently being shipped as retail games, and some are still in development. Almost all of them use the same Torque Game Engine we will use in this book to develop our own game.

By no means is this a definitive list; there are many genres that don't exist in the 3D gaming realm, and the number of ways of combining elements of genres is just too large to bother trying to enumerate. If you take pride in your creativity, you might resist attempts to pigeonhole your game idea into one of these genres, and I wouldn't blame you. When trying to communicate your ideas to others, however, you will find it useful to use the genres as shorthand for various collections of features, style, and game play.

Action Games

Action games come in several forms. The most popular are the *First-Person Point-of-View* (1st PPOV) games, where your player-character is armed, as are your opponents. The game play is executed through the eyes of your character. These sorts of games are usually called *First-Person Shooter* (FPS) games. Game play variations include *Death Match, Capture the Flag, Attack & Defend,* and *King-of-the-Hill.* Action games often have multiplayer online play, where your opponents are enemies controlled by real people instead of by a computer. Success in FPS games requires quick reflexes, good eye-hand coordination, and an intimate knowledge of the capabilities of your in-game weapons. Online FPS games are so popular that some games have no single-player game modes.

Some action games are strictly 3rd PPOV, where you view your player-character, or *avatar,* while also viewing the rest of the *virtual world* your avatar inhabits (see Figure 1.1).

Figure 1.1
ThinkTanks—a 3rd PPOV action game made by BraveTree Productions using the Torque Game Engine.

Half-Life 2, F.E.A.R., and *Doom 3* are popular examples of FPS-style action games.

Adventure Games

Adventure games are basically about exploring, where player-characters go on a quest, find things, and solve puzzles. The pioneering adventure games were text based. You would type in movement commands, and as you entered each new area or room, you would be given a brief description of where you were. Phrases like "You are in a maze of twisty passages, all alike" are now gaming classics. The best adventure games play like interactive books or stories, where you as the player decide what happens next, to a certain degree.

Text adventures evolved into text-based games with static images giving the player a better idea of his surroundings. Eventually these merged with 3D modeling technology. The player was then presented with either a first- or third-person point of view of the scene his character was experiencing.

Adventure games are heavily story based and typically very linear. You have to find your way from one major accomplishment to the next. As the story develops, you soon become more capable of predicting where the game is going. Your success derives from your ability to anticipate and make the best choices.

Figure 1.2
Tubettiworld—an action-adventure-FPS hybrid game being developed by Tubetti Enterprises using the Torque Game Engine.

Some well-known examples of adventure games are golden oldies like *The King's Quest* series and more recent fare like *The Longest Journey* and *Syberia 2*.

Online adventure games have not really come into their own yet, although some games are emerging that might fit the genre. They tend to include elements of FPS action games and *Role-Playing Games* (RPGs) to fill out the game play, because the story aspect of the game is more difficult to accomplish in an online environment. Players advance at different speeds, so a monolithic linear story line would become pretty dreary to a more advanced player. An example of an online action-adventure-FPS hybrid game is *Tubettiworld* (see Figure 1.2), being developed by my all-volunteer team at Tubetti Enterprises.

Role-Playing Games

Role-playing games are very popular; that popularity can probably find its roots in our early childhood. At younger than age six or seven, we often imagined and acted out exciting adventures inspired by our action figures and other toys or children's books. As was also true for strategy games, the more mature forms of these games first evolved as pen-and-paper games, such as *Dungeons & Dragons*.

Figure 1.3
Minions of Mirth—a *Dungeons & Dragons*–style RPG made with Torque and created and sold by Prairie Games.

These games moved into the computer realm with the computer taking on more of the data-manipulation tasks of the game masters. In role-playing games the player is usually responsible for the development of his game character's skills, physical appearance, loyalties, and other characteristics. Eventually the game environment moved from each player's imaginations onto the computer, with rich 3D fantasy worlds populated by visually satisfying representations of buildings, monsters, and creatures (see Figure 1.3). RPGs are usually science fiction or fantasy based, with some historically oriented games being popular in certain niches.

Maze and Puzzle Games

Maze and puzzle games are somewhat similar to each other. In a maze game you need to find your way through a "physical" maze in which your routes are defined by walls and other barriers. Early maze games were 2D, viewed from the top; more recent ones play more like 3D adventure or FPS games.

Puzzle games are often like maze games but with problems that need to be solved, instead of physical barriers, to find your way through.

Mazes also make their appearance in arcade pinball–style games, such as *Marble Blast* (see Figure 1.4) by GarageGames. It is a maze-and-puzzle hybrid game

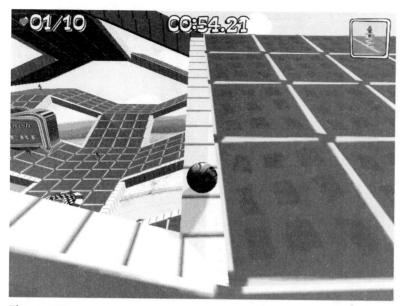

Figure 1.4
Marble Blast—a maze-and-puzzle hybrid game by GarageGames using its Torque Game Engine.

where you compete against the clock in an effort to navigate a marble around physical barriers. The puzzle aspect lies in determining the fastest (though not necessarily the most direct) route to the finish line.

Puzzle games sometimes use puzzles that are variations of the shell game or that are more indirect problem-solving puzzles where you must cause a series of things to happen in order to trigger some further action that lets you advance. Many puzzle games utilize direct problem-solving modes where the puzzle is presented visually. You then need to manipulate on-screen icons or controls in the correct sequences to solve the problem. The best puzzles are those where the solution can be deduced using logic. Puzzles that require pure trial-and-error problem-solving techniques tend to become tedious rather quickly. An historic example of a puzzle game is *The Incredible Machine* series by Dynamix. The latest variation of this type is the new game *Tube Twist* by 21-6 Productions (see Figure 1.5).

Simulator Games

The goal of a simulator (or *sim*) game is to reproduce a real-world situation as accurately as possible. The measure of the simulation accuracy is usually called

Figure 1.5
Tube Twist—a puzzle game made by 21-6 Productions using the Torque Game Engine.

its *fidelity*. Most simulators put a heavy emphasis on the fidelity of the visual appearance, sounds, and physics of the game.

The point is total immersion in the game environment, so that you get the feeling you are actually there. You may be flying a jet fighter or driving a thoroughbred Grand Prix racing car. The game mirrors the real-life experience to the maximum the developers can manage.

Simulators usually require specialized input devices and controllers, such as aircraft joysticks and rudder pedals. Many simulator enthusiasts build complete physical cockpit mockups to enhance the immersion experience.

Silent Steel, NASCAR Sim Racing, and *Air Ace* (see Figure 1.6) are examples of simulator games.

Sports Games

Sports games are a variation of the simulator class of games in which the developer's intent is to reproduce the broad experience of the game as accurately as possible. You can participate in a sports game at various levels and watch the action play out in a realistic 3D environment (see Figure 1.7).

Figure 1.6
Air Ace—a flight combat sim in development by Phil Carlisle, an independent game developer, using the Torque Game Engine.

Figure 1.7
Maximum Football—a football sports game by David A. Winter, an independent game developer, and sold by MatrixGames.

Unlike the action-oriented flight and driving simulators, sports games usually have a manager or season angle. While playing the game you can also take on the role of coach, owner, or team manager. You can execute draft picks and trades or groom new players like any major league ball organization would. In a modern sports simulator you could be managing budgets, and you might play or race a regular year's schedule, playing in different stadiums or arenas or racing on different tracks.

Strategy Games

Strategy games began as pen-and-paper games, like war games, and have been around for centuries. As computer technology evolved, computer-based tables and random-number generators replaced the decision-making aspects of strategy games traditionally embodied by lookup charts and dice rolls.

Eventually the tabletop battlefields (or sandbox battlefields) with their cardboard markers or die-cast military miniatures moved into the computers as well. The early tabletop games were usually turn based: each player would in turn consider his options and issue "orders" to his units. Then he would throw the dice to determine the result of the orders. The players would then modify the battlefield based upon the results. After this the players would observe the new shape of the battlefield and plot their next moves. The cycle then repeated itself.

The advent of computer-based strategy games brought the concept of *real time* to the forefront. Now the computer determines the moves and results and then structures the battlefield accordingly. It does this on a time scale that reflects the action. This has given birth to the *Real-Time Strategy* (RTS) genre. Sometimes the computer will compress the time scale, and other times the computer will operate in real time, where one minute of time in the game action takes one minute in the real world. The player issues orders to his unit as he deems them to be necessary. Recently, strategy games have moved into the 3D realm, where players can view the battlefield from different angles and perspectives as they plot their next moves (see Figure 1.8).

There are strategy games that exist outside the world of warfare. Examples include business strategy games and political strategy games. Some of these games are evolving into *strategic simulations,* like the well-known *SimCity* series of games.

Figure 1.8
Tribal Trouble—a 3D real-time strategy game created by indie-developer Oddlabs.

Some Popular Retail 3D Games and Their Genres

If you are still unclear about what a particular genre is, take a look at the following table. It is a list of current "big-name" game titles (including one or two that are not yet released). Be aware that you may find a Web site or magazine somewhere that classifies these games in a slightly different way. That's cool—don't worry about it.

Game	Publisher	Genre
Age of Empires III	Microsoft	Strategy
Battlefield 2	Electronic Arts	Action-FPS
Call of Duty 2	Activision	Action-FPS
Civilization IV	2K Games	Strategy
Command & Conquer (various)	Electronic Arts	RTS
Delta Force Xtreme	Novalogic	Action-FPS
Diablo III	Blizzard	RPG
Doom 3	Activision	Action-FPS
Duke Nukem Forever	Gathering of Developers	Action-FPS
Dungeon Siege	Microsoft	Action-RPG
Enter the Matrix	Infogrames	Action-FPS
Everquest II	Sony	RPG
Far Cry	Ubisoft	Action-FPS

continued

continued

Game	Publisher	Genre
Ghost Recon: Advanced Warfighter	Ubisoft	Action-FPS
Grand Theft Auto: San Andreas	Rockstar Games	Action-Sim
Half-Life 2	Sierra	Action-FPS
Homeworld 2	Vivendi Universal	RTS
Medal of Honor: Allied Assault	Electronic Arts	Action-FPS
Myst III: Exile	Ubisoft	Adventure
PlanetSide	Sony	Action-FPS
Rainbow Six 3: Raven Shield	Ubisoft	Action-FPS
Return to Castle Wolfenstein	Activision	Action-FPS
Rome: Total War	Activision	RTS
SimCity 4	Electronic Arts	Strategy-Sim
Star Wars: Knights of the Old Republic 2	LucasArts	Action-RPG
Syberia 2	Microids	Adventure
Tom Clancy's Splinter Cell: Chaos Theory	Ubisoft	Action-FPS
Unreal II: The Awakening	Infogrames	Action-FPS
Unreal Tournament 2004	Infogrames	Action-FPS
WarCraft III: Reign of Chaos	Blizzard	RTS
World War II Online: Battlefield Europe	Playnet/Cornered Rat Software	FPS-RPG-Sim-Strategy

Game Platforms

This book is about computer games written for personal computers. There are three dominant operating systems: Microsoft Windows, Linux, and Macintosh. For some of these systems there are quite a few different flavors, but the differences within each system are usually negligible, or at least manageable.

Another obvious game platform type is the home game console, such as the Sony PlayStation or the Nintendo GameCube. These are indeed important, but because of the closed nature of the development tools and the expensive licenses required to create games for them, with one bright exception, they are beyond the scope of this book.

That exception is the Xbox and its more recent state-of-the-art descendent, the Xbox 360. It is now possible to create your Torque-based game with the Xbox as the target system. If you think you are interested in doing this, you should contact GarageGames directly (http://www.garagegames.com). Your approximate development plan will involve two large phases: (1) make your game on the PC, and then (2) convert your game to Xbox.

Other game platforms include *Personal Digital Assistants* (PDAs), such as Palm-based computers, and cell phones that support protocols that permit games to be played on them. Again, these platforms are also beyond the scope of this book.

Now that those little disclaimers are out of the way, let's take a closer look at the three game platforms of interest. It's important to note that by using the Torque Game Engine, you will be able to develop what amounts to a single code base for a game that you can ship for *all three platforms:* Windows, Linux, and Macintosh!

Microsoft Windows

Windows has various historical versions, but the current flavors are Windows 2000, Windows XP, and the specialized Windows CE. In this book the expectation will be that you are developing on or for a Windows XP target system, because that is the version that Microsoft is now selling to the home computer market.

Within Windows XP we will be using OpenGL and Direct3D (a component of DirectX) as our low-level graphics *Application Programming Interfaces* (APIs). These APIs provide a means for our engine to access the features of the video adapters in our computers. Both OpenGL and Direct3D provide basically the same services, but each has its own strengths and weaknesses. With Torque you will have the choice of letting your end users use either API.

OpenGL's greatest strength lies in its availability with different computer systems. An obvious benefit is that the developer can create a game that will work on most computers. OpenGL is an open-source product. In a nutshell this means that if there is a particular capability you want that OpenGL lacks, you can get access to the OpenGL source code and rebuild it the way you want. This assumes you have the skills, time, and tools necessary to get the job done, but you *can* do it.

DirectX is proprietary—it is the creation and intellectual property of Microsoft Corporation. Its biggest advantage is that it tends to support more features than OpenGL, and the 3D video adapter manufacturers tend to design their hardware to work with DirectX as much as they can. With DirectX you get a much more complete and the most advanced feature set. Unfortunately, you are limited to Windows-based systems if you put all your eggs in the DirectX basket.

The Torque Game Engine uses both APIs and gives you a rather straightforward set of techniques to set up your game with either API. This means that in a Windows version of your game, you can offer your users the option of using the API that best suits their video adapter.

Linux

For most people the single most important reason to use Linux is the price—it's free. You may have to pay to get a distribution of Linux on CD with manuals at a store, but you are paying for the cost of burning the CD, writing and printing the manuals, and distributing the end product. You don't have to pay for the operating system itself. In fact, you can download Linux from many different locations on the Internet.

As a game developer, you will have a threefold interest in targeting Linux:

- Linux is a growing marketplace, and any market that is growing is a good target. Although the market is growing, it is still smaller than the Windows market. The place where Linux is growing is in universities, colleges, and other postsecondary institutions—and this is probably where your best computer gaming audience is.

- Few computer games are available for Linux desktops; most developers focus on Windows because it is the biggest market. If you ship a game for Linux, you will be a bigger fish in a smaller ocean. That gets you exposure and a reputation that you can build on. And that's nothing to sneeze at.

- Linux offers a more configurable and secure environment for unattended Internet game servers. Linux servers can be run in a console mode that requires no fancy graphics, buttons, or mice. This allows you to utilize slower computers with less memory for servers and still get the computing power you need for your game server.

Unlike other operating systems, Linux comes in a variety of flavors known as *distributions*. There are many ongoing arguments about the merits of one distribution or another. Some of the more popular distributions are Red Hat, SuSE, Mandrake, Turbolinux, Debian, and Slackware. Although they may be organized differently in some cases and each has its own unique graphical look and feel, they are all based on the same kernel. It is the kernel that defines it as Linux.

Macintosh

The Macintosh is used a great deal in art-related fields and in the art departments of many businesses. Although the price point might not be as good as Linux (where the OS and most software is free), the Macintosh operating system is typically more accessible to the less tech-savvy users among us.

As with Linux, there has also traditionally been a dearth of computer games available for the Mac. So the big fish–small ocean factor applies here as well. Go ahead and make a splash!

Note

One minor disadvantage of working with cross-platform software like Torque is the issue of naming conventions. In this book, wherever possible, I will head off the potential conflicts with a note that will cast a particular naming approach in stone for the duration of the book.

An example that will probably become obvious pretty quickly is the concept of *directories* or *folders*. The latter is shorter and easier to type, and the term will be used often. To save my editors the hassle, I will use *folders*. If you are a *directories* person, please just play along, okay?

Game Developer Roles

In the context of the game we will develop during our journey together through this book, you will wear all of the different game developer hats. The thing to remember is that oftentimes the lines between the roles will blur, and it might be hard to tell which hat you are wearing. So wear them all. Many indies wear multiple hats throughout the life of a game project, so it's just as well to get used to it!

Producer

A game producer is essentially the game project's leader. The producer will draw up and track the schedule, manage the people who do the hands-on development work, and oversee the budget and expenditures. The producer may not know how to make any part of a game at all, but he is the one person on a game project who knows everything that is happening and why.

It's the producer who needs to poke the other developers in the ribs when they seem to be lagging. The producer must be aware when different members of the team are in need of some tool, knowledge, or resource and arrange to provide the team members with what they need.

Sometimes producers just need to spray a liberal dose of Ego-in-a-Can to refresh a despondent developer who keeps smashing into the same brick wall over and over while the clock ticks down.

The producer will also be the team's interface with the rest of the world, handling media queries, negotiating contracts and licenses, and generally keeping the big noisy bothersome world off the backs of the development team.

Designer

If you are reading this, I have no doubt that you want to be a game designer. And why not? Game designers are like fun engineers—they create fun out of their imaginations. As a game designer, you will decide the theme and rules of the game, and you will guide the evolution of the overall feel of the game. And be warned—it had better be fun!

There are several levels of designers: lead designer, level designer, designer-writer, character designer, and so on. Large projects may have more than one person in each design role. Smaller projects may have only one designer or even a designer who also wears a programmer's or artist's hat! Or both!

Game designers need to be good communicators, and the best ones are great collaborators and persuaders. They need to get the ideas and concepts out of their heads and into the heads of the rest of the development team. Designers not only create the concept and feel of the game as a whole but also create levels and maps and help the programmers stitch together different aspects of the game.

The lead designer will put together a design document that lays out all the aspects of the game. The rest of the team will work from this document as a guide for their activities. A design document will include maps, sketches of game objects, descriptions of plot devices, flow charts, and tables of characteristics. The designer will usually write a narrative text that describes how all of these parts fit together. A well-written and thorough game design completely describes the game from the player's perspective.

Unlike the producer, a designer needs to understand the technical aspects of the game and how the artists and programmers do what they do.

Programmer

Game programmers write program code that turns game ideas, artwork, sound, and music into a fully functional game. Game programmers control the speed and placement of the game artwork and sound. They control the cause-and-effect relationships of events, translating user inputs through internal calculations into visual and audio experiences.

There can be many different specializations in programming. In this book you will be doing a large amount of programming of game rules, character control, game event management, and scoring. You will be using TorqueScript to do all of these things.

For online game programming, specialization may also be divided between client code and server code. It is quite common to specify character and player behavior as a particular programmer specialty. Other specialty areas might be vehicle dynamics, environmental or weather control, and item management.

Other programmers on other projects might be creating parts of the 3D game engine, the networking code, the audio code, or tools for use with the engine. In our specific case these specializations aren't needed because Torque looks after all of these things for us. We are going to focus on making the game itself.

Visual Artist

During the design stages of development, game artists draw sketches and create storyboards to illustrate and flesh out the designers' concepts. Figure 1.9 demonstrates a conceptual design sketch created by a visual artist and used by the development team as a reference for modeling and programming work. Artists will later create all the models and texture artwork called for by the design document, including characters, buildings, vehicles, and icons.

The three principal types of 3D art are models, animations, and textures—and the artists who create these types of art are 3D modelers, animators, and texture artists, respectively.

- 3D modelers design and build player-characters, creatures, vehicles, and other mobile 3D constructs. In order to ensure that the game gets the best performance possible, 3D modelers usually try to make the least complex model that suits the job. A 3D modeler is very much a sculptor working with digital clay.

- Animators make those models move. The same artist quite often does both modeling and animation.

- Texture artists create images that are wrapped around the constructs created by 3D modelers. Texture artists take photographs or paint pictures of various surfaces for use in these texture images. The texture is then

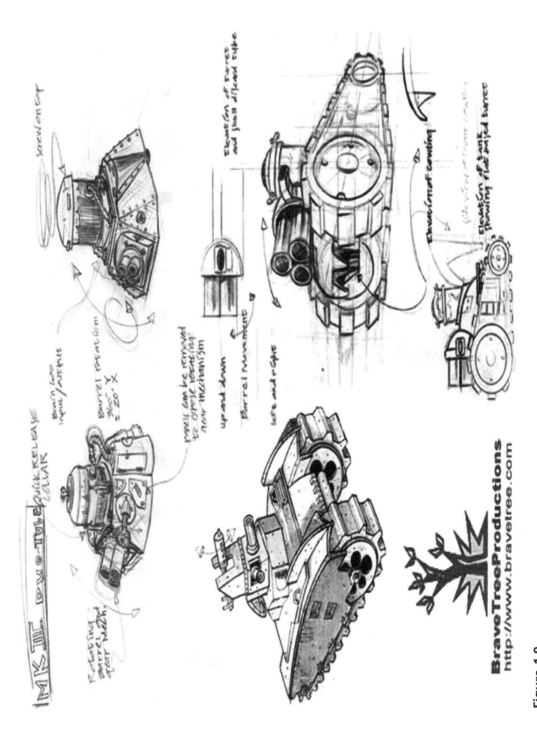

Figure 1.9
A conceptual design sketch.

wrapped around the objects in question in a process called *texture mapping.* Texture artists help the 3D modelers reduce the model complexity by using highly detailed and cleverly designed textures. The intent is to fool the eye into seeing more detail than is actually there. If a 3D modeler molds a sculpture in digital clay, the texture artist paints that sculpture with digital paint.

Audio Artist

Audio artists compose the music and sound in a game. Good designers work with creative and inspired audio artists to create musical compositions that intensify the game experience.

Audio artists work closely with the game designers to determine where the sound effects are needed and what the character of the sounds should be. Audio artists often spend quite a bit of time experimenting with sound-effect sources, looking for different ways to generate the precise sound needed. Visit an audio artist at work and you might catch him slapping rulers and dropping boxes in front of a microphone. After capturing the basic sound, an audio artist will then massage the sound with sound-editing tools to vary the pitch, to speed it up or slow it down, to remove unwanted noise, and so on. It's often a tightrope walk balancing realistic sounds with the need to exaggerate certain characteristics in order to make the right point in the game context.

Quality Assurance Specialist

Quality Assurance (QA) is a somewhat fancy name for *testing.* The general field of QA is more extensive than that, of course, but in the game business game testers take the brunt of the QA load. The purpose of testing is to ensure that a finished game is really finished, with as few bugs or problems as humanly possible. QA testing requires the quality assurance specialist, or game tester, to play each part of a game, trying to flush out all glitches and bugs.

Most of the problems QA testing will find are visual or behavioral: text that doesn't properly wrap on an edge, characters that don't jump correctly, or a level that has buildings misplaced. Testing can find game play problems; these are usually related more to the design than the programming. An example could be that the running speed of a player might not be fast enough to escape a particular enemy when it should be more than fast enough.

QA specialists need to be methodical in order to increase the chances of finding a bug. This might mean replaying a certain part of a game many times to the point of boredom. QA specialists need to be able to communicate well in order to write useful and meaningful bug reports.

Publishing Your Game

You can self-publish, of course. Whip up a Web site, add a shopping cart system, get your site added to various search engines, and sit back to wait for the dough to roll in, right? Well, it *might* work.

If you really think you have the next killer game and want it to sell, however, you need to hook up with someone who knows what they are doing. That would be a publisher. If you are an independent game developer, you will probably have difficulty attracting the attention of the big-name publishers. They usually know what they are looking for, are normally only interested in developers with proven track records, and probably already know whom they want to deal with anyway.

But all is not lost—there are options available for the indie. The one I recommend is GarageGames (http://www.garagegames.com). Besides offering competitive publishing terms for indie developers, GarageGames also created the Torque Game Engine, which it has graciously agreed to allow me to include on the CD for this book. Torque is the technology behind the popular and successful *Tribes* series of games. I'm going to help you learn how to use Torque as an enormous lever in creating your game.

But wait—there's more! If you really need to, you can buy a license from GarageGames for the Torque Game Engine that will give you (under the terms of the license) all of the source code for the engine, so you can turn any game dream into a reality—for only $100! That's a hundred bucks for full access to the inner workings of an award-winning AAA 3D game engine. As Neo would say, "Whoa!"

I have no qualms about suggesting that you go to GarageGames. They are the guys behind the *Tribes* franchise, which is now owned by Sierra. They know their stuff, but they are not some big faceless corporate entity. They're basically a handful of guys who've made their splash in the corporate computer game industry, and now they're doing their level best to help the independent game developers of the world make their own splashes.

And no, they aren't paying for this book!

Elements of a 3D Game

The architecture of a modern 3D game encompasses several discrete elements: the engine, scripts, GUI, models, textures, audio, and support infrastructure. We're going to cover all of these elements in detail in this book. In this section I'll give you some brief sketches of each element so you'll have a sense of where we are going.

Game Engine

Game engines provide most of the significant features of a gaming environment: 3D scene rendering, networking, graphics, and scripting, to name a few. See Figure 1.10 for a block diagram that depicts the major feature areas.

Game engines also allow for a sophisticated rendering of game environments. Each game uses a different system to organize how the visual aspects of the game will be modeled. This becomes increasingly important as games are becoming more focused on 3D environments, rich textures and forms, and an overall realistic feel to the game. Textured polygon rendering is one of the most common forms of rendering in FPS games, which tend to be some of the more visually immersive games on the market.

By creating consistent graphic environments and populating those environments with objects that obey specific physical laws and requirements, gaming engines allow games to progress significantly along the lines of producing more and more plausible narratives. Characters are constrained by rules that have realistic bases that increase the gamer's suspension of disbelief and draw him deeper into the game.

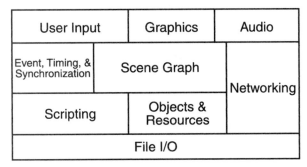

Figure 1.10
Elements of a game engine.

By including physics formulas, games are able to realistically account for moving bodies, falling objects, and particle movement. This is how FPS games such as *Tribes 2, Quake 3, Half-Life 2,* or *Unreal II* are able to allow characters to run, jump, and fall in a virtual game world. Game engines encapsulate real-world characteristics such as time, motion, the effects of gravity, and other natural physical laws. They provide the developer with the ability to almost directly interact with the gaming world created, leading to more immersive game environments.

As mentioned earlier, this book will employ the Torque Game Engine from GarageGames (http://www.garagegames.com). The Torque Game Engine is included on the CD with this book. Later on we will discuss Torque in more detail—and you will understand why Torque was chosen.

Scripts

As you've just seen, the engine provides the code that does all the hard work, graphics rendering, networking, and so on. We tie all these capabilities together with scripts. Sophisticated and fully featured games can be difficult to create without scripting capability.

Scripts are used to bring the different parts of the engine together, provide the game play functions, and enable the game world rules. Some of the things we will do with scripts in this book include scoring, managing players, defining player and vehicle behaviors, and controlling GUI interfaces.

Following is an example of a TorqueScript code fragment:

```
// Beer::RechargeCompleteCB
// args: %this    - the current Beer object instance
//       %user    - the player connection user by id
//
// description:
//   Callback function invoked when the energy recharge
//   the player gets from drinking beer is finished.
//   Note: %this is not used.
function Beer:: RechargeCompleteCB (%this,%user)
{
    // fetch this player's regular recharge rate
    // and use it to restore his current recharge rate
    // back to normal
    %user.setRechargeRate(%user.getDataBlock().rechargeRate);
}
```

```
// Beer::OnUse
// args: %this    - the current Beer object instance
//       %user    - the player connection user by id
//
// description:
//    Callback function invoked when the energy recharge
//    the player gets from drinking beer is finished.
//
function Beer::OnUse(%this,%user)
{
   // if the player's current energy level
   // is zero, he can't be recharged, because
   // he is dying
  if (%user.getEnergyLevel() != 0)
  {
      // figure out how much the player imbibed
      // by tracking the portion of the beer used.
      %this.portionUsed += %this.portion;
      // check if we have used up all portions
      if (%this.portionUsed >= %this.portionCount)
      {
         // if portions used up, then remove this Beer from the
         // player's inventory and reset the portion
         %this.portionUsed = 0;
         %user.decInventory(%this,1);
      }
      // get the user's current recharge rate
      // and use it to set the temporary recharge rate
      %currentRate = %user.getRechargeRate();
      %user.setRechargeRate(%currentRate +%this.portionCount);

      // then schedule a callback to restore the recharge rate
      // back to normal in 5 seconds. Save the index into the schedule
      // list in the Beer object in case we need to cancel the
      // callback later before it gets called
      %this.staminaSchedule = %this.schedule(5000,"RechargeCompleteCB",%user);

      // if the user player hasn't just disconnected on us, and
      // is not a 'bot.
      if (%user.client)
      {
         // Play the 2D sound effect signifying relief ("ahhhhh")
         %user.client.play2D(Relief);
```

```
    // send the appropriate message to the client system message
    // window depending on whether the Beer has been finished,
    // or not. Note that whenever we get here portionUsed will be

    // non-zero as long as there is beer left in the tankard.
    if (%this.portionUsed == 0)
      messageClient(%user.client, 'MsgBeerUsed', '\c2Tankard polished off');
    else
      messageClient(%user.client, 'MsgBeerUsed', '\c2Beer swigged');
  }
 }
}
```

The example code establishes the rules for what happens when a player takes a drink of beer. Basically, it tracks how much of the beer has been consumed and gives the player a jolt of energy for five seconds after every mouthful. It sends messages to the player's client screen telling him what he's done—had a sip or polished off the whole thing. It also plays a sound effect of the player sighing in relief and contentment with every drink.

Graphical User Interface

The *Graphical User Interface* (GUI) is typically a combination of the graphics and the scripts that carries the visual appearance of the game and accepts the user's control inputs. The player's *Heads Up Display* (HUD), where health and score are displayed, is part of the GUI. So are the main start-up menus, the settings or option menus, the dialog boxes, and the various in-game message systems.

Figure 1.11 shows an example main screen using the *Tubettiworld* game. In the upper-left corner, the text that says "Client 1.62" is an example of a GUI text control. Stacked along the left side from the middle down are four GUI button controls. The popsicle-stick snapper logo in the lower right and the *Tubettiworld* logo across the top of the image are GUI bitmap controls that are overlaid on top of another GUI bitmap control (the background picture). Note that in the figure the top button control (Connect) is currently highlighted, with the mouse cursor over top of it. This capability is provided by the Torque Game Engine as part of the definition of the button control.

In later chapters of this book we will spend a good deal of time contemplating, designing, and implementing the GUI elements of our game.

Figure 1.11
An example of a main menu GUI.

Models

3D models (see Figure 1.12) are the essential soul of 3D games. With one or two exceptions, every visual item on a game screen that isn't part of the GUI is a model of some kind. Our player's character is a model. The world he tromps on is a special kind of model called *terrain*. All the buildings, trees, lampposts, and vehicles in our game world are models.

In later chapters we will spend a great deal of time creating and texturing models, animating them, and then inserting them into our game.

Textures

In a 3D game, textures are an important part of rendering the models in 3D scenes. Textures (in certain cases called *skins*—see Figure 1.13) define the visually rendered appearance of all those models that go into a 3D game. Proper and imaginative uses of textures on 3D models not only will enhance the model's appearance but will also help reduce the complexity of the model. This allows us to draw more models in a given period of time, enhancing performance.

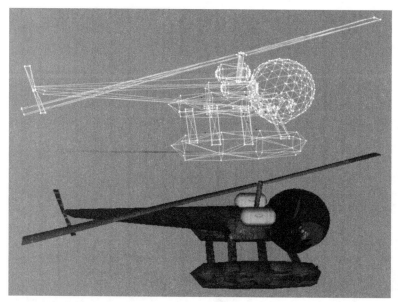

Figure 1.12
A 3D wire-frame model and a textured model of an old-style helicopter.

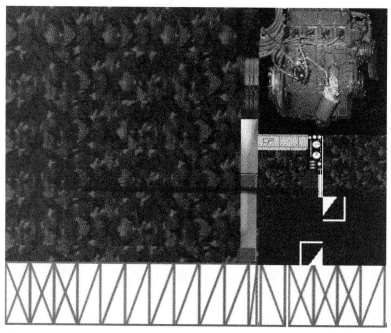

Figure 1.13
The textures used as the skin of the old-style helicopter.

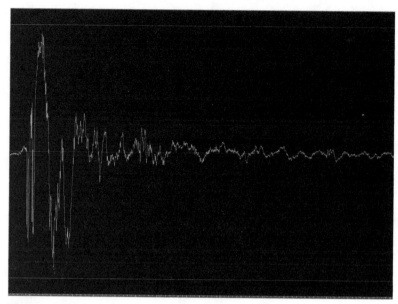

Figure 1.14
A graphical view of a gunshot sound-effect waveform.

Sound

Sound provides the contextual flavoring in a 3D game, providing audio cues to events and background sounds that imply environments and context, as well as 3D positioning cues for the player. Judicious use of appropriate sound effects is necessary for making a good 3D game. Figure 1.14 shows a sound-effect waveform being manipulated in a waveform-editing program.

Music

Some games, especially multiplayer games, use little music. For other games, such as single-player adventure games, music is an essential tool for establishing story line moods and contextual cues for the player.

Composing music for games is beyond the scope of this book. During the later chapters, however, I will point out places where music might be useful. It is always helpful to pay attention to your game play and whatever mood you are trying to achieve. Adding the right piece of music just might be what you need to achieve the desired mood.

Support Infrastructure

This is more important for persistent multiplayer online games than single player games. When we ponder game infrastructure issues, we are considering such things as databases for player scores and capabilities, auto-update tools, Web sites, support forums, and, finally, game administration and player management tools.

The following infrastructure items are beyond the scope of this book, but I present them here to make you aware that you should spend time considering what you might need to do.

Web Sites

A Web site is necessary to provide people with a place where they can learn news about your game, find links to important or interesting information, and download patches and fixes for your game.

A Web site provides a focal point for your game, like a storefront. If you intend to sell your game, a well-designed Web site is a necessity.

Auto-Update

An auto-update program accompanies your game onto the player's system. The updater is run at game start-up and connects via the Internet to a site that you specify, looking for updated files, patches, or other data that may have changed since the user last ran the program. It then downloads the appropriate files before launching the game using the updated information.

Many games, like *Delta Force: Blackhawk Down, World War II Online,* and *Everquest,* have an auto-update feature. Web-based distribution systems, like Steam from Valve, also have such capability. When you log in to the game, the server checks to see if you need to have any part of your installation upgraded, and if so it automatically transfers the files to your client. Some auto-updaters will download a local installer program and run it on your machine to ensure that you have the latest files.

Support Forums

Community forums or bulletin boards are a valuable tool for the developer to provide to customers. Forums are a vibrant community where players can discuss your game, its features, and the matches or games they've played against each other. You can also use forums as a feedback mechanism for customer support.

Administrative Tools

If you are developing a persistent online game, it will be important to obtain Web-based tools for creating and deleting player accounts, changing passwords, and managing whatever other uses you might encounter. You will need some sort of hosted Web service with the ability to use CGI-, Perl-, or PHP-based interactive forms or pages. Although this is not strictly necessary, you really should invest in a database to accompany the administrative tools.

Database

If you intend your game to offer any sort of *persistence* where players' scores, accomplishments, and settings are saved—and need to be protected from fiddling by the players on their own computers—then you probably need a database back end. Typically, the administrative tools just mentioned are used to create player records in the database, and the game server communicates with the database to authenticate users, fetch and store scores, and save and recall game settings and configurations.

A common setup would include MySQL or PostgreSQL or something similar. Again, you will probably need to subscribe to a hosted Web service that offers a database.

The Torque Game Engine

I've mentioned the Torque Game Engine (TGE) several times already. I think now would be a good time to take a little deeper look at the engine and how you will be using it.

Appendix A provides a reference for the Torque Game Engine, so look there if you really need more detail.

Descriptions

The following descriptions are by no means exhaustive, but a cup of coffee would go well with this section. Go ahead and make some—I'll wait. Black with two sweeteners, please.

Moving right along, you should note that the main reason for including this section is to give you, the gentle reader, the right sense of how much behind-the-scenes work is done for you by the engine.

Basic Control Flow

The Torque Game Engine initializes libraries and game functions and then cycles in the main game loop until the program is terminated. The main loop basically calls platform library functions to produce platform events, which then drive the main simulation.

Torque handles all of the basic event procession functions as follows:

- Dispatches Windows mouse movement events to the GUI

- Processes other input-related events

- Calculates elapsed time based on the time scale setting of the simulation

- Manages processing time for server objects

- Checks for server network packet transmission

- Advances simulation event time

- Processes time for client objects

- Checks for client network packet transmission

- Renders the current frame

- Checks for network timeouts

Platform Layer

The platform layer provides a cross-platform architecture interface to the engine. The platform layer is responsible for handling file and network operations, graphics initialization, user input, and events.

Console

The console library provides the foundation for Torque-based games. The console has both a compiler and an interpreter. All GUIs, game objects, game logic, and interfaces are handled through the console. The console language is called TorqueScript and is similar to a typeless C++, with some additional features that facilitate game development. You can load console scripts using a command from the console window as well as automatically from files.

Input Model

Input events are translated in the platform layer and then posted to the game. By default the game checks the input event against a global action map that supersedes all other action handlers. If there is no action specified for the event, it is passed on to the GUI system. If the GUI does not handle the input event, it is passed to the currently active (nonglobal) action map stack.

Platform-specific code translates Win32, X Windows, or Mac events into uniform Torque input events. These events are posted into the main application event queue.

Action maps translate platform input events to console commands. Any platform input event can be bound in a single generic way—so in theory, the game doesn't need to know if the event came from the keyboard, the mouse, the joystick, or some other input device. This allows users of the game to map keys and actions according to their own preferences.

Simulation

A stream of events drives the game from the platform library: `InputEvent`, `MouseMoveEvent`, `PacketReceiveEvent`, `TimeEvent`, `QuitEvent`, `ConsoleEvent`, `ConnectedReceiveEvent`, `ConnectedAcceptEvent`, and `ConnectedNotifyEvent`. By journaling the stream of events from the platform layer, the game portion of the simulation session can be deterministically replayed for debugging purposes.

The simulation of objects is handled almost entirely in the game portion of the engine. Objects that need to be notified of the passage of time can be added to one of the two process lists: the global server or global client process list, depending on whether the object is a server object or a client ghost.

Server-side objects are only simulated at certain times, but client objects, in order to present a smooth view when the frame rate is high, are simulated after each time event.

There is a simulator class that manages all of the objects and events in the simulation. Objects are collected in a hierarchy of simulator classes and can be searched for by name or by object ID.

Resource Manager

The Torque Game Engine uses many game resources. Terrain files, bitmaps, shapes, material lists, fonts, and interiors are all examples of game resources.

Torque has a resource manager that it uses to manage large numbers of game resources and to provide a common interface for loading and saving resources. Under the auspices of Torque's resource manager, only one instance of a resource will ever be loaded at a time.

Graphics

The Torque Game Engine does not perform its own graphics rasterization; instead, it uses the OpenGL graphics API. Torque includes a utility library that extends OpenGL to support higher-level primitives and resources.

TGE has a collection of utility functions that add support for complex primitives and resources like fonts and bitmaps and that add simple functions for more easily managing textures and 2D rasterization.

There is also a texture manager that tracks the loading and unloading of all textures in the game. Only one instance of a texture is ever loaded at a given time; after loading it is handed off to OpenGL. When the game switches graphics modes or video devices, the texture manager can transparently reload and redownload all the game's textures.

Torque supports several bitmap file types: PNG, JPEG, GIF, BMP, and the custom BM8 format, an 8-bit color texture format used to minimize texture memory overhead.

The GUI library manages the user interface of Torque games. It is designed specifically for the needs of game user interface development. The Canvas object is the root of the active GUI hierarchy. It dispatches mouse and keyboard events, manages update regions and cursors, and calls the appropriate render methods when it is time to draw the next frame. The Canvas keeps track of content controls, which are separate hierarchies of controls that render from bottom to top. The main content control is a screen in the shell that can be covered by any number of floating windows or dialog boxes.

A Profile class maintains common instance data across a set of controls. Information such as font face, colors, bitmaps, and sound data are all stored in instances of the Profile class, so that they don't need to be replicated on each control.

A Control class is the root class for all the GUI controls in the system. A control can contain any number of child controls. Each control maintains a bounding rectangle in the coordinate system of its parent control. The Control class processes input events, rendering, and mouse focus and coordinates automatic sizing.

3D Rendering

The Torque library has a modular, extensible 3D world rendering system. Game subclasses first define the camera orientation and field of view and then draw the 3D scene using OpenGL drawing commands. A class manages the setting up of the viewport as well as the model view and projection matrices. A function returns the viewing camera of the current control object (the object in the simulation that the player is currently controlling), and then the engine calls the client scene graph object to render the world.

On the client, a scene graph library is responsible for traversing the world scene and determining which objects in the world should be rendered given the current camera position, while on the server, it determines what objects should be sent to each client based on that client's position in the world. The world is divided into zones, which are volumes of space bounded by solid areas and portals. The outside world is a single zone, and interior objects can have multiple interior zones. The engine finds the zone of a given 3D point and which object owns that zone. The engine then determines which zone or zones contain an object instance. At render time the scene is traversed starting from the zone that contains the camera, clipping each zone's objects to the visible portal set from the zones before it. The engine also performs the scoping of network objects, deciding whether a given object needs to be dealt with by a client.

Every world object in the scene that can be rendered is derived from a single base class. As the world is traversed, visible objects are asked to prepare one or more render images that are then inserted into the current scene. Render images are sorted based on translucency and then rendered. This system permits an interior object with multiple translucent windows to render the building first, followed by other objects, and then followed by the building's windows. Objects can insert any number of images for rendering.

Terrain

The terrain library deals with objects that render a model of the outside world. It contains a sky object that renders the outside skybox, animates and renders cloud layers, and applies the visible distance and fog distance settings for when the world as a whole is rendered. The sky object also generates the vertical fog layers and sends them into the SceneGraph object for rendering. The TerrainBlock class provides a single 256×256 infinitely repeating block of heightfield terrain.

Heightfield data is stored and loaded by the resource manager so that a single terrain data file can be shared between server and client.

The terrain is textured by blending base material textures with program code into new material textures and then mapping those across multiple terrain squares based on the distance from the square. The Blender class performs the blending of terrain textures and includes a special assembly version to speed things up when executing on x86 architectures.

Water is dynamically rendered based on distance, making nearby water more tessellated and detailed. Water coverage of an area can be set to seed fill from a point on the surface, allowing the water to fill a depression to form a lake without leaking outside the corners.

Interiors

The interior library manages the rendering, collision, and disk-file services for interior objects, such as buildings. An interior resource class manages the data associated with a single definition of an interior, and multiple instances may exist at any one time. Interiors manage zones for the scene graph and may have sub-objects that render a mirrored view. A light manager class generates lightmaps for all currently loaded interiors. Lightmaps are shared among instances whenever possible. Interior resources are built and lit by an interior importer utility. The source files are Quake-style .map files that are little more than lists of convex physical constructive solid geometry "brushes" that define the solid areas of the interior. Special brushes define zone portal boundaries and objects like lights.

Shapes and Animation

A library manages the display and animation of shape models in the world. This library's shape resource class can be shared between multiple shape instances. The shape class manages all the static data for a shape: mesh data, animation key-frames, material lists, decal information, triggers, and detail levels. An instance class manages animation, rendering, and detail selection for an instance of a shape. The instance class uses the thread class to manage one of the concurrently running animations on an instance. Each thread can be individually advanced in time or can be set on a time scale that is used when all threads are advanced. A thread can also manage transitions between sequences.

Animation sequences can be composed of node/bone animation (for example, joints in an explosion), material animation (a texture animation on an explosion), and mesh animation (a morphing blob; note that most mesh animations can be accomplished with node scale and rotation animations). Animations can also contain visibility tracks so that some meshes in the shape are not visible until an animation is played.

Networking

Torque was designed from the foundation to offer robust client/server network simulation support. The networking design of Torque was driven by the need for superior network performance over the Internet. Torque addresses three fundamental problems of real-time network programming: limited bandwidth, packet loss, and latency. For a more detailed, if somewhat outdated, description of the Torque network architecture, see "The Tribes II Engine Networking Model," an article by Tim Gift and Mark Frohnmayer, at the GarageGames site (http://www.garagegames.com). An instance of a Torque game can be set up as a dedicated server, a client, or both client and server. If the game is both client and server, it still behaves as a client connected to a server, but the netcode has a short-circuit link to other netcode in the same game instance, and no data goes out to the network.

Bandwidth is a problem because of the large, open terrain environments Torque supports, as well as the large number of clients Torque can handle—up to 128 or more per server, which means that there is a high probability that many different objects can be moving and updating at the same time. Torque uses several strategies to maximize available bandwidth.

- It sends updates to what is most important to a client at a greater frequency than it updates data that is less important.

- It sends only the absolute minimum number of bits needed for a given piece of data.

- It only sends the part of the object state that has changed.

- It caches common strings and data so that they need only be transmitted once.

Packet loss is a problem because the information in lost data packets must somehow be retransmitted, yet in many cases the data in the dropped packet, if sent again directly, will be stale by the time it gets to the client.

Latency is a problem in the simulation because the network delay in data transmission makes the client's view of the world perpetually out of sync with the server. Twitch-style FPS games, for which Torque was initially designed, require instant control response in order to feel anything but sluggish. Also, fast-moving objects can be difficult for highly latent players to hit. In order to solve these problems, Torque employs the following strategies:

- *Interpolation* is used to smoothly move an object from where the client thinks it is to where the server says it is.

- *Extrapolation* is used to guess where the object is going based on its state and rules of movement.

- *Prediction* is used to form an educated guess about where an object is going based on rules of movement and client input.

The network architecture is layered. At the bottom is the OS/platform layer, above that the notify protocol layer, which is followed by the `NetConnection` object and event management layer.

Using Torque in This Book

As you've seen, the Torque Game Engine is powerful, feature rich, flexible, and controllable. What we will do in this book is create all of the different elements of the game that we'll need and then write game control script code to tie it all together.

Program code, artwork, and audio resources you will need are included on the companion CD, along with the tools to manipulate them and create your own.

At first glance that may not seem to be too daunting a task. But remember, we will be wearing *all* of the game developer hats. So we will be creating our own models (players, buildings, decorations, and terrains), recording our own sound effects, placing all of these things in a virtual world of our own fabrication, and then devising game rules and their scripted implementations to make it all happen.

Daunted yet?

Hey, it's not going to be *that* hard. We've got Torque!

Installing Torque

The companion CD contains all the materials you will need to follow the chapters: the Torque executable, the Torque Game Engine demos and tutorial base, any required art and script resources, plus useful tools. Everything you need will be in the folder called \3D2E.

Some of the tools, which will be located in the \3D2E\TOOLS folder, may require installation before you use them. Not all of the supplied tools are required in order for you to follow along in the book. Some are provided as a courtesy in case you do not have another suitable tool for a particular task.

If the text absolutely requires you to use a specific tool to complete a procedure outlined in the book, the text will tell you where to find and install it or otherwise use it for that task.

To install Torque for use with the book, insert the companion CD into your CD drive, and follow the on-screen instructions. When you have finished, the layout of the hard drive will match the layout of the companion CD, so anywhere you see the folder \3D2E or any of its subfolders described in the text, you will be able to find it on your hard drive or on the companion CD. The \EXTRAS folder on the CD is *not* needed in order to use the book, however.

For Macintosh and Linux Users

For readers using an operating system other than one of the Windows variants, the companion CD's installation procedure will likely not work for you. The Torque demo executable in \3D2E will also not work for you. However, the scripts and artwork from the book's examples *will* work on Macintosh and Linux systems, provided you have the correct demo installation from the \EXTRAS folder on the companion CD installed for your operating system.

When using the installers described in the following, please make sure that your destination directory or folder during the installation is /3D2E and not the default installer path. This is to ensure that your installation paths match the paths described in the book. You might need to create the /3D2E folder manually before running an installer.

To do this, first look in the /EXTRAS folder on the companion CD, and locate and install the demo for your operating system:

For **Macintosh**, use /EXTRAS/Macintosh/TorqueGameEngineDemo_1_4.dmg.

For **Linux**, use /EXTRAS/Linux/TorqueGameEngineDemo-1.4.bin.

After installing the appropriate Torque demo variant on your system, you must then copy the contents of the companion CD's /3D2E folder into the new /3D2E directory you created where you've just installed the Torque demo on your system.

After that you can then delete the files demo.exe, getdxver.exe, glu2d3d.dll, OpenAL32.dll, and opengl2d3d.dll from your new /3D2E folder if you like—they are Windows files that you won't be able to use anyway.

In the book you will sometimes see references to folders that use full path names (like \3D2E\demo\client\init.cs, for example) and other times you will see partial path names (like RESOURCES\ch2). The drive letter will never be included. This means that the path to the folder will be appropriate no matter which hard drive or volume you install to. With the partial paths it will be obvious where the folders are. RESOURCES is always a subfolder of \3D2E, for instance, as are the TOOLS, EXTRAS, demo, common, creator, and show folders.

Note

Throughout the book you will see references to the fps demo or the racing demo. These are the Torque Game Engine demo programs, set to run the fps or racing missions.

Run the fps demo by double-clicking demo.exe in the \3D2E folder. After the splash screen disappears, in the main menu click the Example: FPS Multiplayer button near the center. On the next screen make sure the Create Server box is checked, then click the right-facing arrow button in the lower-left part of the screen.

In addition to the fps first-person shoot-'em-up demo, there is a racing dune buggy demo for you to distract yourself with. On the main menu in the demo, click the Example: Multiplayer Racing button (the bottom button). When the screen changes check the Create Server box, and finally click the right-facing arrow button at the bottom.

Moving Right Along

There you go. You now have the basic Torque Game Engine plus some sample games installed. Enjoy!

Of course, if you are following along with the game development in this book, you will need to return to the CD and install all the other components when they are needed.

In this chapter we've looked at computer games from many different angles—the industry, the genres, and the different roles of developers. And we've explored the kinds of things that make a game engine work and how they relate to each other.

In the next chapter we'll get into the basics of programming. We'll use the Torque Engine itself to run our example programs as we work through the chapter. This will develop skills you'll need in later chapters when we start delving into real game programming scripts.

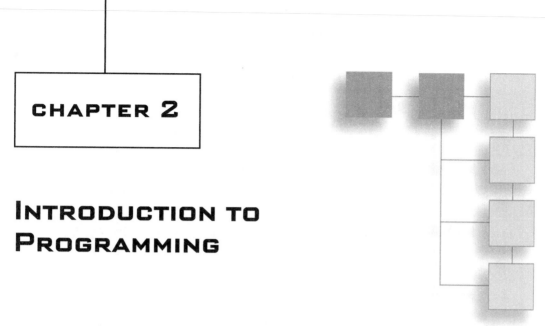

CHAPTER 2

INTRODUCTION TO PROGRAMMING

My intent with this chapter is to help you understand programming concepts and techniques and leave you with a foundation upon which you can build more advanced skills. By the end of this chapter, you will be proficient with a powerful programming editor; understand how to create, compile, and run programs you've written yourself; have a reasonable sense of programming problem-solving methods; and be familiar with valuable debugging tips and techniques.

UltraEdit-32

To write our programs, we will need to use a *text editor,* or *programming editor.* This kind of editor differs from a word processor, which is what most people use for writing documents, books, memos, and church bulletins.

A good programming editor has several useful features:

- A project feature that allows you to organize your source files
- A fully featured grep (find, search and replace) capability
- Syntax highlighting
- A function finder or reference
- Macro capability
- Bookmarks
- Text balancing or matching

I use a shareware editor called *UltraEdit-32* (UltraEdit), written by Ian D. Meade, included on the companion CD for this book. It also has several other useful features that I'll demonstrate later in this chapter.

grep? What Kind of Name Is That?

The name *grep* comes from the UNIX world, where strange and wonderful names and incantations for programs abound. The word *grep* is derived from the command string g/re/p, which first appeared in old line-editor programs on early UNIX systems. The *g* meant "global," the *re* meant "regular expression," and the *p* meant "print," as in print to the screen. If you entered that command into the editor's command line, you were telling the editor to globally search, using regular expression syntax, and then to print the results—and the expression would then follow those characters. Eventually that command string was migrated outside of the editor program and incorporated into a command that was usable from the UNIX command shell as a way of specifying how to look and what to look for when you were searching files that contained a particular piece of text. Over time, the name *grep* has become synonymous with searching files for embedded text and is a common term in the programming world, even in non-UNIX environments. Now it is often used as a verb meaning "search for text in files."

Program Setup and Configuration

If you haven't already installed the companion CD per the instructions near the end of Chapter 1, it might be a good idea to go back and review that section. Briefly: after you insert the companion CD into your computer's CD drive, use Explorer to browse the CD and locate the folder called 3D2E. Drag this folder from your CD to your hard drive, which will presumably be C:, though you can use whatever hard drive you want. Make sure you have about 500MB of disk space available, to hold both the CD contents you copy and the installed versions of the software tools that you will be installing as you work through this book. When you've finished copying, you are free to remove the CD and store it in a safe place. For instance, setting it on a windowsill in the hot sun is *not* a safe place. I'm just sayin'. . .

Now, browse your way into the new \3D2E folder on your hard drive and into the folder called TOOLS. In there you will see a folder called ULTRAEDIT-32. Inside *that* folder you will find uedit32.zip, which contains setup.exe; open the zip and double-click on uesetup.exe, and follow the installation instructions that appear. Finally, also in the TOOLS folder, locate the UESAMPLEPROJECT folder, and drag and drop the folder into the \3D2E folder.

Setting Up Projects and Files

Like any decent editor environment, UltraEdit-32 allows us to organize the files we want to work with using a *projects* concept. You can create, in UltraEdit-32, virtual folders and save links to your files in these folders. By doing this, you can make a quick and convenient access channel to files that are stored anywhere, even somewhere on the network! Setting up your projects takes a wee bit of effort, however, depending on your needs. Let's dive in and set up a project.

Configuring UltraEdit

To configure UltraEdit, follow these steps:

1. Launch UltraEdit by selecting Start, Program, UltraEdit, UltraEdit-32 Text Editor.

2. Close any open files or windows you may have in UltraEdit by selecting Window, Close All Files.

3. In UltraEdit, select View, Views/Lists, File Tree View. A new docked window will appear on the left side (see Figure 2.1). This is the File Tree View, also called the File View.

4. The File View has three tabs, which are used to select different ways of viewing files. Normally we work with the project files, so click on the tab that says Project, and this will bring the Project tab to the forefront in the File View, as depicted in Figure 2.2.

Figure 2.1
The File View.

Figure 2.2
The Project tab.

5. If the File View is free-floating (not docked), click and hold (grab) the colored bar at the top of the File View window where it says "File View" and drag it to the left side of your UltraEdit window such that the colored bar remains in the dark gray space, but the left side of the view window disappears off the left side of the UltraEdit window. You should see the outline of the view window change from a wide gray line to a thin black line. Let go of the mouse button and the view will be docked on the left side.

6. Select the menu item Project, New Project/Workspace. A Specify Project File dialog box will appear. Browse your way to \3D2E. Type in the project name (**myscripts**), and make sure you have the Project Files type selected in the drop-down list of the dialog box. Click Save, and the Project Settings dialog box will appear. If you are given an alert that tells you the file already exists and asks if you want to replace it, click Yes.

7. In the Folder Options section at the bottom, select the Include sub folders in folder check box if it isn't already set with a check mark.

8. Click Add Folder and select the Group check box.

9. Click the ellipsis button to the right of the empty text box.

10. Locate the folder that contains all the files you want to include in your project—in our case, it's the \3D2E folder on your hard drive. Locate and select that folder, then click OK.

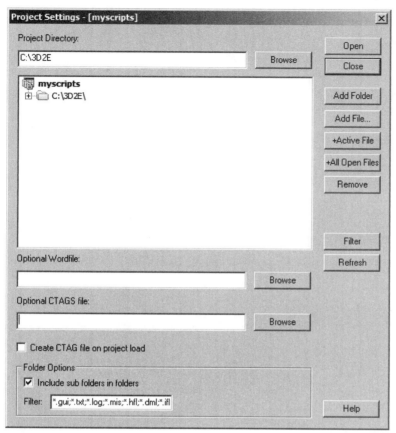

Figure 2.3
The Project dialog box with folder.

11. When you return to the New Folder dialog box, click OK again.

12. Down in the Folder Options section again, type the following into the Filter text box: *.cs;*.gui;*.txt;*.log;*.mis;*.hfl;*.dml;*.ifl. Each of these is a different file type, specified by extension. We are doing this in order to allow only files of these types to appear in our project. Don't worry about what they mean right now; we'll get into them in later chapters of the book. Your Project dialog box should look like the one in Figure 2.3.

13. Click the Close button.

14. Take a look at your Project tab of the File View, and click the plus sign (the *expand* symbol) to the left of the folder there (which should be \3D2E, if all went according to plan).

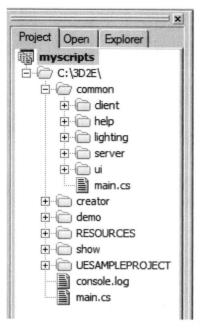

Figure 2.4
The myscripts Project tab of the File View.

You should now have a Project tab that shows the contents of the \3D2E folder, which contains several more folders: common, creator, demo, and show, to name a few, as well as the file main.cs (you might also have the files console.log and a README.txt as well, but if you don't, that's okay).

Your Project tab of the File View should look something like Figure 2.4. You can click on the plus sign in front of the folder entries in order to expand the folders to match the view in the figure.

As the saying goes, there is more than one way to skin a cat, and in this case there are other ways to set up your project. You can do it all from within the Project Settings dialog box using the Add File button. You can also use the + Active File button to add whatever file is currently the one being edited in UltraEdit. You can experiment and find the method that works best for you. I tend to use a combination of + All Open Files and + Active File, depending on my needs at the time.

Go ahead and open a few files and close them again, to get a feel for how the Project tab of the File View works.

After setting up the project, exit UltraEdit. This ensures that the project settings are properly saved. Then you can go ahead and reopen the project by double-clicking the myscripts.prj icon in the \3D2E folder. If you don't take this extra step of quitting and then relaunching UltraEdit, you may find that the settings haven't properly taken, and some functions might not work. Searching through project files for certain words is one capability that probably will not work correctly until you close and reopen the project.

Search and Replace

The search capabilities of UltraEdit are quite extensive and thorough. I'm going to focus on the few most important capabilities: finding specific text, finding specific text and replacing it, jumping to a line number, and advanced searching using wildcards and patterns. To practice the various features, open the UESAMPLEPROJECT folder, and open the file called sample_file_1.txt. Do this by browsing through the Project tab. The file called sample_file_1.txt has some text extracted from an early revision of Chapter 1 that we can hack away at.

Find

Select the Search, Find menu item, and you should get the Find dialog box (see Figure 2.5). Make sure the option check boxes match the ones in Figure 2.5. Now, type in the word you want to find, then click the Find Next button. The Find dialog box will go away, your text insertion point will jump to the first found instance of the word you want, and the word will be highlighted. Try this using the word *indie*. See that?

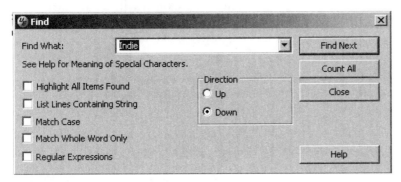

Figure 2.5
The Find dialog box set for a basic search.

Okay, now get your Find dialog box back and try doing this with the various options. Notice that the Find operates on the currently active file in the editor. Check out the various options, like searching "down" the file and then searching back "up" the file. Change your search word to *INDIE* (all capital letters) and then try your search again. Note that the Find still locates the word. Now try it with the Match Case option checked. Notice that you get an error message: Search String Not Found!

When searching, you will often have more than one match to your search criteria. If you are not using the List Lines option, then you can move through each match in the text by using Search, Find Next to continue to find matching strings as you move toward the end of the file (down). Using Search, Find Prev will do the same thing, though moving toward the start of the file (up). However, you will probably want to quickly get acquainted with using the keyboard shortcut F3 for Find Next and Ctrl+F3 for Find Prev.

Tip

A quick and convenient way to search for other occurrences of a word that is already written and visible in the active window is to highlight the word (double-click it), press Ctrl+F (the shortcut for Find), and then press Enter. The insertion point will jump to the next occurrence of the word. Then keep pressing F3 to move to the next, and the next, and the next, ad infinitum. UltraEdit will keep starting over from the beginning of the file until you die of boredom.

A feature of the Find dialog box that I think is particularly useful is the List Lines Containing String option. With this checked, all instances of the word you are looking for will be listed as complete lines in a separate window. Try it by searching for the word *action* with case sensitivity turned off. This should give you a window with a list of lines in it. Each line contains at least one instance of the search term you specified. If you double-click a line, you will see the text and insertion point in your edit window jump to where that line is located and the line will become highlighted.

Special Find Characters

When using Find, there are some things you may want to search for that are not normal alphanumeric characters or punctuation marks—the end of a line, for example.

These are handled by using special characters that are a combination of an *escape* character and a symbol. The caret ("^"; you get this when you hold down the Shift key and type the number "6" on North American keyboards) is the escape character. It is paired with a symbol that is a normal character. Whenever Find sees the combination of the caret in front of a character, the program knows it is doing a special character search.

Of course, the first special character is the caret itself; otherwise, we would never be able to do a search for a caret in text. Look at the following table for a list of the most common special Find characters.

These do *not* require you to turn on the Regular Expressions switch in the Find dialog box, although they are the same as some of the regular expression entries.

Special Characters Used in a Basic Find Function

Special Symbol	What the Program Looks For
^^	caret character ("^"; sometimes called Up Arrow)
^s	highlighted text (only while a macro is running)
^c	contents of the Clipboard (only while a macro is running)
^b	page break
^p	newline (carriage return and line feed) (Windows/DOS files)
^r	newline (carriage return only) (Macintosh files)
^n	newline (line feed only) (UNIX files)
^t	tab character

Replace

Select the Search, Replace menu item, and you should get the Replace dialog box (see Figure 2.6). This dialog box is similar to the Find dialog box, though the Replace dialog box has more options and a field in which to enter the replacement text.

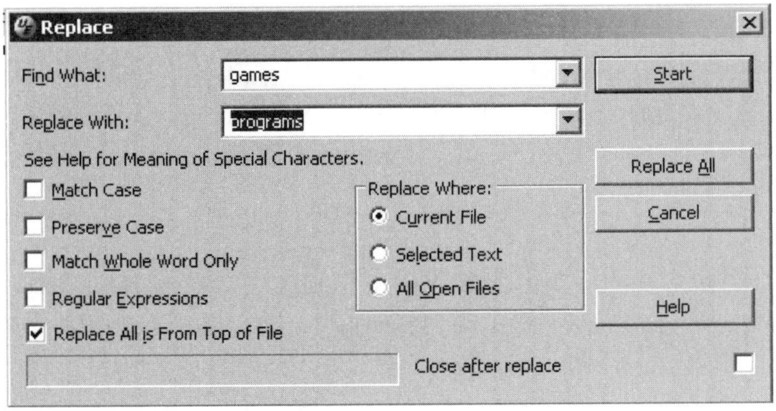

Figure 2.6
The Replace dialog box set for a basic search-and-replace operation.

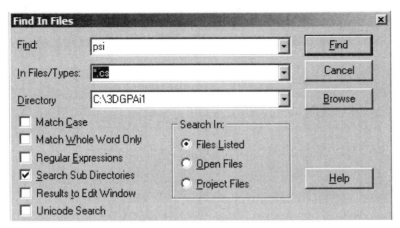

Figure 2.7
The Find In Files dialog box.

Find In Files

The Find In Files feature is UltraEdit's closest implementation of grep, which I mentioned earlier in the chapter. The basic Find In Files capability allows you to specify what word or phrase you are looking for and where to look for it in files other than the one you are currently editing (the *active* file). Figure 2.7 shows the Find In Files dialog box. You'll notice that you can specify one of three different sets of files to search.

First, you can search through the Files Listed. This means you can specify a file name search pattern with extension and a folder to look in. This is quite similar to the built-in Windows Search or Find feature. You can use wildcards to fine-tune which files will be checked. Searching with the In Files/Types box set to "new*.txt", for example, will search inside files with the names newfile.txt, new_data.txt, and so on. Setting the pattern to "*.*" will cause the program to search inside every file it finds in the specified folder. If you have the Search Sub Directories box checked, then it will also look inside every file inside every folder contained in the specified folder.

When the program finds a match in the file with the word you are looking for, it will print a listing at the bottom of the UltraEdit window containing a reference to the file where the word was found, plus the line in which it was found. If you double-click the line in the bottom window, UltraEdit will open the file and position the line in your window for viewing.

Next, you can search in the Open Files—that is, only within the files that are currently open in the editor. If you click the Open Files radio button in the Search

In: box, you see that now you only enter the word to search for; you don't need to specify file names or a folder.

Finally, the method I use the most is to search in Project Files. With this option selected, the program will search through all of the files in the project you currently have open—and only those files. It doesn't matter whether the files themselves are open or not.

grep

The grep capability in UltraEdit (also see the sidebar earlier in this chapter) is an advanced way of finding text within files and replacing it with other text when desired. You can use it in Search-related topics covered so far by putting a check mark in the Regular Expressions box; then Find will operate using standard UNIX-like grep or the older UltraEdit-specific form of grep.

You can configure UltraEdit to use its own grep syntax or the UNIX-style syntax in the configuration menu. Select the Advanced, Configuration menu item, and then select the Find tab. Change the check box labeled UNIX style Regular Expressions to suit your taste.

UltraEdit-Style grep Syntax

Table 2.1 shows the available UltraEdit-style grep functions. Let's do a few example grep searches to get a feel for how it works. Use the file sample_file 1.txt from the UESAMPLEPROJECT project to do the searches. For this section make sure you have the UltraEdit configuration setting for UNIX style Regular Expressions turned off.

Let us suppose that we want to find some reference to dungeons in games in the sample file. We'll grep (notice that I'm verbing the noun here!) for the term *game*dungeon*.

Press Ctrl+F to bring up the Find dialog box, and then make sure the Regular Expressions box is checked. Type in the search term **game*dungeon**, and click the Find Next button. The string it finds starts with "game" and ends with "dungeon". The words that appear in between were inconsequential to the search, because the asterisk means that the search program will match any string of characters of any length between the words *game* and *dungeon,* as long as it doesn't encounter a newline character or a carriage return. Try it again, but this time type in the term **computer*game** and see what you find. Remember that you can use F3 as a shortcut to find the next match.

Table 2.1 UltraEdit-Style grep Syntax

Symbol	Purpose
%	Matches the start of line. Indicates the search string must be at the beginning of a line but does not include any line terminator characters in the resulting string selected.
$	Matches the end of line. Indicates the search string must be at the end of a line but does not include any line terminator characters in the resulting string selected.
?	Matches any single character except newline.
*	Matches any number of occurrences of any character except newline.
+	Matches one or more instances of the preceding character. At least one occurrence of the character must be found. Does not match repeated newlines.
++	Matches the preceding character/expression zero or more times. Does not match repeated newlines.
^b	Matches a page break.
^p	Matches a newline (CR/LF) (Windows/DOS files).
^r	Matches a newline (CR only) (Mac files).
^n	Matches a newline (LF only) (UNIX files).
^t	Matches a tab character.
[ ]	Matches any single character or range in the brackets.
^{A^}^{B^}	Matches expression A or B.
^	Overrides the following regular expression character.
^(...^)	Brackets or tags an expression to use in the Replace command. A regular expression may have up to nine tagged expressions, numbered according to their order in the regular expression. The corresponding replacement expression is ^x, for x in the range 1–9. Example: If ^(h*o^) ^(f*s^) matches "hello folks", ^2 ^1 would replace it with "folks hello".

The operator that is the same as the asterisk, only different, is the question mark ("?"). Instead of matching any number of any characters, it will match only one instance of any character. For example, "s?n" matches "sun", "son", and "sin" but not "sign" or "soon".

Here are some more examples of how the matching criteria work:

be + st	will find "best", "beest", "beeeest", and so on *but not* "bst"
[aeiou]	will find every lowercase vowel
[,.?]	will find a literal ",", ".", or "?"
[0-9a-z]	will find any digit or lowercase letter
[~0-9]	will find any character *except* a numeral (the tilde ["~"] means to *not* include whatever follows)

UNIX-Style Syntax

The UNIX-style syntax is used in the same way as the UltraEdit style but is different in many ways. The advantages of using the UNIX style are:

- It is somewhat of a standard, so you may be familiar with it from elsewhere.

- It has more capabilities than the UltraEdit syntax.

- At some point in the future it may be the only syntax for grep supported by UltraEdit, when the program's author decides to stop supporting the old UltraEdit style.

You can see the differences by checking out Table 2.2. The first obvious difference is that the escape character has changed from the caret to the backslash. Our example searches would be a little different. The asterisk doesn't match any character anymore; now it matches any number of occurrences of the character that appears just before it. Also, now we use the period ("..") to match any single character instead of the question mark.

Before proceeding, make sure you have your editor set to use the proper UNIX-style syntax in the Advanced, Configuration menu under the Find tab.

Now, to go back to our dungeon games example, the way the search term in UNIX-style grep syntax would look is "game.*dungeon".

Compare these examples with the ones for the UltraEdit style:

be+st	matches "best", "beest", "beeeest", and so on *but not* "bst"
be*st	matches "best", "beest", "beeeest", and so on *and* "bst"
[aeiou]	matches every lowercase vowel
[,.?]	matches a literal ",", ".", or "?"
[0-9a-z]	matches any digit or lowercase letter
[^0-9]	matches any character *except* a digit (^ means *not* the following)

Bookmarks

One feature I use quite frequently is the Bookmark capability. Its purpose is to help you quickly find your way around large files. When you are working in an area that you think you may need to come back to later, just set a bookmark, and then when you are working in another place in your document, you can use the Goto Bookmark command to jump through each bookmark you've set until you

Table 2.2 UNIX-Style grep Syntax

Symbol	Purpose
\	Indicates the next character has a special meaning. "n" on its own matches the character "n". "\n" matches a linefeed or newline character. See examples below (\d, \f, \n).
^	Matches or anchors the beginning of line.
$	Matches or anchors the end of line.
*	Matches the preceding character zero or more times.
+	Matches the preceding character one or more times. Does not match repeated newlines.
.	Matches any single character except a newline character. Does not match repeated newlines.
(expression)	Tags an expression to use in the Replace command. A regular expression may have up to nine tagged expressions, numbered according to their order in the regular expression. The corresponding replacement expression is \x, for x in the range 1–9. Example: If (h.*o) (f.*s) matches "hello folks", \2 \1 would replace it with "folks hello".
[xyz]	A character set. Matches any characters between brackets.
[^xyz]	A negative character set. Matches any characters *not* between brackets.
\d	Matches a number character. Same as [0-9].
\D	Matches a nonnumeric character. Same as [^0-9].
\f	Matches a form-feed character.
\n	Matches a linefeed character.
\r	Matches a carriage return character.
\s	Matches any white space including space, tab, form-feed, and so on but not newline.
\S	Matches any non–white space character but not newline.
\t	Matches a tab character.
\v	Matches a vertical tab character.
\w	Matches any word character, including underscore.
\W	Matches any non-word character.
\p	Matches CR/LF (same as \r\n) to match a DOS line terminator.

find the one you want. This sure beats scrolling through all your open files looking for that one spot you worked on two hours ago!

To set a bookmark, click your mouse on a line of text, and then select the menu item Search, Toggle Bookmark. The line where the bookmark is set will be indicated by a lozenge-shaped cyan box around the line number on the left side (see Figure 2.8)—this is also a user-configurable parameter. In the figure, lines 11 and 13 are the bookmarked lines.

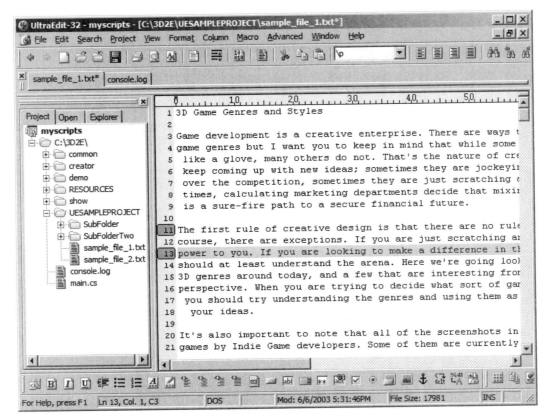

Figure 2.8
Bookmarked text.

To remove a bookmark, click your mouse in the bookmarked line, and select Search, Toggle Bookmark again. This will turn off the bookmark for that line.

To remove all bookmarks, select Search, Clear All Bookmarks, and all bookmarks that you previously set will vanish.

Tip

If you are using the Project tab when you close your documents, all the bookmarks you've set will be saved and restored the next time you open that document. This does not happen with documents that are not associated with the Project tab.

To navigate between the bookmarks, choose Search, Next Bookmark, and your insertion point will jump to the next bookmark in sequence. You can also choose Search, Previous Bookmark to jump in the reverse direction from bookmark to bookmark.

Tip

Most commands available in the menus have keyboard shortcuts available. Rather than listing them here, I'll just point you to the menu items. The keyboard shortcut for the command, if available, is written next to the menu selection. Some menu items, like Clear All Bookmarks, have no shortcut assigned, but don't despair. You can assign keyboard shortcuts by using the Key Mapping tab in the Advanced, Configuration menu and following the instructions. Note that the command names in the list are written with their main menu entry as the first part of the command. The Clear All Bookmarks command is written as SearchClearBookmarks. The commands are listed in alphabetical order.

Macros

Macro commands are like shortcuts. You can string together a whole series of tedious editing operations into a group, called a *macro,* that you can invoke at any time later by a simple keystroke, menu item, or toolbar button.

UltraEdit has two forms of macros: the standard and the Quick Record macro. Let's take a look at both, starting with the Quick Record macro.

Quick Record Macro

The *Quick Record macro* is a bare-bones macro function.

1. Select the Macro, Quick Record menu item (or press Shift+Ctrl+R).

2. Start performing all the editing actions you want recorded. In this case just type in the text **blah blah blah** somewhere.

3. Select Macro, Stop Quick Recording (or press Shift+Ctrl+R again).

Now replay your edit actions over again at any place in your text by simply placing your text insertion point where appropriate and typing Ctrl+M or selecting the Macro, Play Again menu item.

You can only ever have one Quick Record macro—each time you record one, it replaces the earlier recording.

Standard Macro

Standard macros are a bit more complex. The procedure for recording them is somewhat similar, but you can assign them to key combinations of your choice, to menus, or even to toolbar buttons. This gives you much more flexibility than the Quick Record macro, but at the cost of a bit of setup twiddling, of course.

Let's make a couple of standard macros. One will insert the words "This is cool" and the other will jump to the beginning of whatever line the insertion point is on, capitalize the first word, put a period at the end, and then insert the phrase "Capital Idea!" after the period.

1. Place your insertion point in a blank line somewhere.

2. Select the Macro, Record menu item.

3. In the Macro Name box, give it a name, something like "InsertCool".

4. Click the mouse in the HotKey edit box to the right of where it says "Press New Key", and then press and hold Alt+Ctrl+I.

5. Click the OK button.

6. Type in the phrase **This is cool.**

7. Select Macro, Stop Recording.

8. Place your insertion point at the end of the line with the phrase "This is cool" in it.

9. Select the Macro, Record menu item.

10. In the Macro Name box, give it a name, something like "MakeCapital".

11. Click the mouse in the HotKey edit box to the right of where it says "Press New Key", and then press and hold Shift+Ctrl+M.

12. Click the OK button.

13. Type the following key sequence, one at a time (don't type the text in parentheses):

Home
Shift+Ctrl+Right Arrow
F5
End
. (that's a period)
spacebar

14. Now type the phrase **Capital Idea!**

15. Finally, select the Macro, Stop Recording menu item.

There, that's done. So now let's test it out.

First, find or create a blank line, place your insertion point on it, and then press Shift+Ctrl+I. See the text that gets inserted? Okay, now leave your text insertion point in that new text, anywhere, and then press Shift+Ctrl+M. You should end with a line that says, "This is cool. Capital Idea!", with the same capitalization. Macros *are* cool!

UltraEdit Review

So now you've seen how to use what are, in my opinion, the most important editing features of UltraEdit—grep (find, search, and replace), macros, and bookmarks—and you've seen how UltraEdit can be configured in a project format to make it easy to use files in an organized fashion.

UltraEdit has a good Help feature that covers all aspects of the program, so I encourage you to use it.

Remember that UltraEdit is an *editor,* not a *word processor,* so there aren't a great deal of formatting features in the program, which is just as well because we are using it to write code and not to write documents or books. The focus is on the steak, not the sizzle.

Speaking of steak, it is now time to get to the meat of this chapter, coming up next!

Controlling Computers with Programs

When you create a computer program, you are creating a set of instructions that tell the computer exactly and completely what to do. Now before you jump all over me and hammer me with comments like, "Well, duh! Of course programming a computer is like telling it what to do," I want you to read the first sentence again. It is not an analogy, and it is not some kind of vague and airy all-encompassing cop-out.

Everything that a computer does, at any time, is decided by at least one programmer. In the vast majority of cases, the computer's instructions—contained in *programs*—are the work-product of hundreds, if not thousands, of programmers. All of the programs that a computer uses are organized and classified in many different ways. The organization helps us humans keep track of what they do, why we need them, how to link one program with another, and other useful things. The computer's operating system is a huge collection of programs designed to work in conjunction with other programs, or sometimes to work alone, but in the context created by other programs.

We leverage the efforts of other programmers when we sit down to program a computer for any purpose. One of the results of many that have gone before is the creation of *programming languages*. Computers operate using a language that is usually unique to each brand and model, called *machine code*. Machine code is designed to directly control the computer's electronics—the hardware. Machine code is *not* very friendly to humans.

To give you an idea, we'll look at an example of machine code that tells a computer using an Intel 80386 chip to add together two numbers and save the result somewhere. What we will do is add A and B together and leave the result in C. To start, A will equal 4 and B will equal 6.

So our formula will be a simple math problem:

```
A = 4
B = 6
C = A + B
```

The computer machine code looks like this:

```
11000111000001010000000000000000000000000000000000000010000000000000000000000
00000110001110000010100000000000000000000000000000000000000011000000000000000000
00000000001010000100000000000000000000000000000000000000011000001010000000000000
00000000000000000000010100011000000000000000000000000000000000000
```

Now go ahead and look carefully at that and tell yourself honestly whether you could work with a computer using machine code for longer than, oh, about 12 minutes! My personal best is somewhere around 30 seconds, but that's just me. The number system used here is the *binary* system.

Each one of those 1s and 0s is called a *bit* and has a precise meaning to the computer. This is all the computer actually understands—the 1s, the 0s, their location and organization, and when and how they are to be used. To make it easier for humans to read machine code at those rare times when it is actually necessary, we normally organize the machine code with a different number system, called *hexadecimal* (or *hex*), which is a base-16 number system (rather than base-10 like the *decimal* system we use in everyday work). Every 4 bits becomes a hex numeral, using the symbols from 0 to 9 and the letters A to F. We pair two hex numerals to carry the information contained in 8 bits from the machine code. This compresses the information into an easier-to-read and more manageable size. Here is the same calculation written in the hex form of machine code:

```
C7 05 00 00 00 00 04 00 00 00 C7 05 00 00 00 00 06 00 00 00 A1 00 00 00 00 03
05 00 00 00 00 A3 00 00 00 00
```

Much better and easier on the eyes! There are many people who work close to the computer hardware who work in hex quite often, but it still is pretty obscure. Fortunately, there is a human-readable form of the machine code for every microprocessor or computer, which in general is known as *assembly language*. In this case we use words and symbols to represent meaningful things to us as programmers. Tools called *assemblers* convert assembly language programs to the machine code we looked at earlier. Here is the Intel 80386 Assembler version of our little math problem:

```
mov    DWORD PTR a, 4     ; (1)
mov    DWORD PTR b, 6     ; (2)
mov    eax, DWORD PTR a   ; (3)
add    eax, DWORD PTR b   ; (4)
mov    DWORD PTR c, eax   ; (5)
```

Now we are getting somewhere! Let's take a closer look. Lines 1 and 2 save the numbers 4 and 6 in memory somewhere, referenced by the symbols a and b. The third line gets the value for a (4) and stores it in some scratch memory. Line 4 gets the value for b (6), adds it to the 4 in scratch memory, and leaves the result in the same place. The last line moves the result into a place represented by the symbol c. The semicolon tells the assembler tool to ignore what comes after it; we use the area after the semicolon to write commentary and notes about the program. In this case I've used the comment space to mark the line numbers for reference.

Now that, my friends, is a program! Small and simple, yes, but it is clear and explicit and in complete control of the computer.

As useful as assembly language code is, you can see that it is still somewhat awkward. It is important to note that some large and complex programs have been written in assembly language, but it is not done often these days. Assembly language is as close to the computer hardware as one would ever willingly want to approach. You are better served by using a *high-level language*. The next version of our calculation is in a powerful high-level language called *C*. No, really! That's the name of the language. Here is our calculation written in C:

```
a = 4;     // (1)
b = 6;     // (2)
c = a + b; // (3)
```

Now, if you're thinking what I think you're thinking, then you're thinking, "Hey! That code looks an awful lot like the original formula!" And you know what? I think you are right. And that's part of the point behind this rather long-winded introduction. When we program, we want to use a programming language that best represents the elements of the problem we want to solve. Another point is that quite a few things are done for the programmer behind the scenes—there is a great deal of complexity. Also, you should realize that there are even more layers of complexity "below" the machine code, and that is the electronics. We're not even going to go there. The complexity exists simply because it is the nature of the computer software beast. But be aware that the same hidden complexity can sometimes lead to problems that will need to be resolved. But it's not magic—it's software.

The C language you've just seen is what is known as a *procedural* language. It is designed to allow programmers to solve problems by describing the procedure to use and defining the elements that are used during the procedure. Over time, programmers started looking for more powerful methods of describing problems, and one such method that surfaced was called *Object-Oriented Programming* (OOP).

The simplest point behind OOP is that programmers have a means to describe the relationships between collections of code and variables that are known as *objects*. The C language eventually spawned a very popular variant called *C++*. C++ includes the ability to use the original C procedural programming techniques, as well as the new object-oriented methods. So we commonly refer to C/C++, acknowledging the existence of both procedural and object-oriented capabilities. From here on, in the book, I will refer to C/C++ as the general name of the language, unless I need to specifically refer to one or the other for some detailed reason.

Programming Concepts

For the rest of this chapter, we are going to explore basic programming techniques. We will be using TorqueScript for all of our code examples and running our little programs in the Torque Engine to see what they do.

Now, we just covered the simple math problem in the previous section. I showed you what the program looked liked in binary machine language, hex machine language, assembly language, and finally C/C++. Well, here is one more version—TorqueScript:

```
%a = 4;        // (1)
%b = 6;        // (2)
%c = %a + %b;  // (3)
```

Notice the similarity to C/C++? Even the comments are done the same way!

As demonstrated, TorqueScript is much like C/C++. There are a few exceptions, the most notable being that TorqueScript is *typeless* and does not require *forward declarations* of variables. Also, as you can see for yourself in the preceding code, TorqueScript requires *scope prefixes* (the percent signs) on its variable names.

Typeless? Forward Declarations? Huh?

In many languages, variables have a characteristic called *type*. In its simplest form, a type merely specifies how much memory is used to store the variable. TorqueScript doesn't require you to specify what type your variable has. In fact, there is no way to do it!

Forward declarations are a construct whereby the programmer must first indicate, usually at the beginning of a file or a subroutine block, what variables will be used and what their types are. TorqueScript also doesn't require this and again provides no mechanism for using forward declarations.

So now that you know what types and forward declarations are, you can forget about them!

The goal for you to achieve by the end of this chapter is the ability to put together simple programs to solve problems and have enough understanding of program techniques to make sensible decisions about the approaches to take.

How to Create and Run the Example Programs

There is an ancient and well-understood programming cycle called the *Edit-Compile-Link-Run* cycle. The same cycle applies with Torque, with the exception being that there is no link step. So for us, it can be thought of as the *Edit-Compile-Run* cycle. A further wrinkle to toss in is the fact that Torque will automatically compile a source file (that is, a program file that ends with .cs) into the binary byte code file (ends with .cs.dso), if there is no binary version of the file, or if the source file has changed since the last binary was created.

So I guess my point is, for us the cycle can now be regarded as the *Edit-Run* cycle.

- Put all user programs in the folder \3D2E\demo as filename.cs where "filename" is a name you've either made up yourself or one that I've suggested here in the book. So, for example, the first simple program in the next pages will be saved as \3D2E\demo\HelloWorld.cs.

- Run the demo by double-clicking \3D2E\demo.exe.

Hello World

Our first program is somewhat of a tradition. Called the *Hello World* program, it is used as an early confidence builder and test program to make sure that the gentle reader (that would be you, if you are reading this book!) has everything in place on his computer to successfully edit, compile, and run a program.

So, assuming that you have correctly copied the 3D2E folder from your CD to your hard drive, and you've installed UltraEdit-32, you can use your newly learned UltraEdit skills to create a new file with the name HelloWorld.cs and save it in the folder \3D2E\demo. Type into the file these lines of code:

```
// ==============================================================
// HelloWorld.cs
//
// This module is a program that prints a simple greeting on the screen.
//
// ==============================================================

function runHelloWorld()
// --------------------------------------------------------------
//    Entry point for the program.
// --------------------------------------------------------------
{
   echo("Hello World");
}
```

Save your work. Now, use the following procedure to run your program:

1. Browse to, and open, your \3D2E folder on your hard drive using Explorer (not UltraEdit-32!).

2. Locate the Torque Game Engine executable, demo.exe. If you can't find the file demo.exe, see the important note following this procedure.

3. Double-click demo.exe to launch the Torque default demo.

4. After the splash screen clears, you will see the main menu of the demo. Don't click any buttons; just press the Tilde ("~") key. This is the key that is normally to the left of the "1" (or shifted "!") key and above the Tab key. The Tilde key shares the keyspace with the Grave ("`") key. Get to know this key intimately—it is the console key.

5. The console will appear on your screen, looking something like Figure 2.9.

6. In the console window, type the following:

```
exec("demo/helloworld.cs");
```

You will see the following displayed in the console (the output):

```
Compiling demo/helloworld.cs...
Loading compiled script demo/helloworld.cs.
```

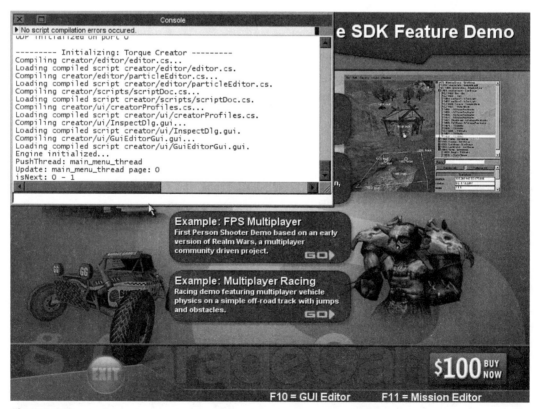

Figure 2.9
Output of the Hello World program.

7. Now type the following:

```
runhelloworld();
```

You will see the following output:

```
Hello World!
```

Tip

If you don't get the expected result on your screen, then look in the console. If there were any errors in your program, diagnostic information will be deposited there. It might be something as simple as a typo in the file name. Most error messages appear in red.

The contents of the console are also written to the file console.log, which you can view after you've quit Torque.

Also, if you see any errors regarding "onNeedRelight", or something from the future, missing PageGui, missing "inspect" object, a missing "license_other", or something called "SM_missionList" or an ammo bounding box, or a failed preload (whew!), *then ignore them.* They aren't yours, they're minor, and don't matter here.

IMPORTANT!

If you are using the Windows XP default desktop setup with the default folder settings, you may have trouble locating some files. This is because the default settings for Windows XP have the folder property that allows you to see file extensions turned off. You really, really should have this ability enabled (not only to use this book, but in all of your uses of Windows XP). Enable the ability to see file extensions by opening a window view to your computer (double-clicking the My Computer icon on your desktop is the quickest way), choosing the Tools menu for the window, and then choosing Folder Options.

When the Folder Options dialog box opens, choose the View tab. In the Advanced settings area, locate the Hide extensions for known files types check box, and remove the check mark. Do the same for the Hide protected operating system files check box. Now close the Folder Options dialog box, and get on with it!

Let's have a closer look at the code. The first thing you will notice is this stuff:

```
// ================================================================
// HelloWorld.cs
//
// This module is a program that prints a simple greeting on the screen.
//
// ================================================================
```

This is the *module header block.* It is not executable code—it's what we call a *comment.* The double-slash operator ("//") tells the Torque Engine to ignore everything from the slashes to the end of the line.

So if the engine ignores the module header block, why do we use it? Well, it's included in order to document what the module does so that later, when we've completely forgotten the details, we can easily refresh our memory. It also is included to help other programmers who may come along and need to understand the module so they can add new features or fix bugs.

Tip

> Whenever I tell you to open the console, you should immediately leap into action and press the Tilde ("~") key. Just making doubly sure you know, you know . . . now back to the action.

There are no real rules regarding the format of these headers, but most programmers or development shops have some sort of template that they want followed. At a minimum, the header should include the module file name, copyright notices, and a general description of what the code in the module is for. Sometimes we might include other details that are necessary for another person to understand how the module is used.

Then there is this part:

```
function runHelloWorld()
```

That is *executable code*. It is the declaration of the function block called runHelloWorld. This is the function we call from within the console. Following that, there is this:

```
// ----------------------------------------------------------
//    Entry point for the program.
// ----------------------------------------------------------
```

This is the *function header comment*. The function header comment is included in order to describe the specifics of a function—what it does, how it does it, and so on. In this case it is fairly simple, but function header comments can get to be quite descriptive, as you'll see later. Again, this is not executable code (note the double slash) and is not required to make your program work. The dashes could just as well be stars, equal signs, or nothing at all. It is good practice to always use function header comments to describe your functions.

Finally comes this:

```
{
  echo("Hello World");
}
```

That would be the *function body*—the guts of the function where the work is done. The function body is also sometimes called a *function block* and more generically (when used in other contexts that you'll see later) called a *code block*.

It is important to note the way a function block is made. It always begins with the keyword function followed by one or more spaces and whatever name you want it to have. After the name comes the argument list (or parameter list). In this case there are no parameters. Then comes the opening, or left, brace (or curly bracket). After the opening brace comes the body of the function, followed by the closing, or right, brace.

All functions have this same structure. Some functions can be several pages long, so the structure may not be immediately obvious, but it's there.

The actual code that does anything interesting is a single line. As you know by now, the line simply prints the text "Hello World" in the Torque console window.

Expressions

When we write program code, most of the lines, or *statements,* that we create can be evaluated. A statement can be a single TorqueScript line of any kind terminated by a semicolon, or it can be a *compound statement,* which is a sequence of statements enclosed in left and right braces that acts as a single statement. A semicolon does not follow the closing right brace. Here is an example of a statement:

```
echo("Hi there!");
```

Here is another example:

```
if (%tooBig == true) echo("It's TOO BIG!");
```

And here is one final example of a valid statement:

```
{
    echo("Nah! It's only a little motorcycle.");
}
```

Statements that can be evaluated are called *expressions.* An expression can be a complete line of code or a fragment of a line, but the important fact is that it has a value. In Torque the value may be either a number or text (a string)—the difference is in how the value is used. Variables are explained in the next section, but I'll sneak a few in here without detailed coverage in order to illustrate expressions.

Here is an expression:

```
5 + 1
```

This expression *evaluates* to 6, the value you get when 5 and 1 are added.

Here is another expression:

```
%a = 67;
```

This is an *assignment statement,* but more importantly right now, it is an expression that evaluates to 67.

Another:

```
%isOpen = true;
```

This expression evaluates to 1. Why? Because true evaluates to the value 1 in Torque. Okay, so I hadn't told you that yet—sorry about that. Also, false evaluates to 0. We can say the statements evaluate to true or false, instead of 1 and 0. It really depends on whatever makes sense in the usage context. You'll notice that the evaluation of the statement is determined by whatever expression is to the right of the equal sign. This is a pretty hard-and-fast rule.

Consider this code fragment:

```
%a = 5;
if (%a > 1 )
```

What do you figure that the (%a > 1) evaluates to, if %a has been set to 5? That's right—it evaluates to true. We would read the line as "if %a is greater than 1." If it was written as (%a > 10), it would have been false, because 5 is not greater than 10.

Another way we could write the second line is like this:

```
if ( (%a > 1 ) == true )
```

It would be read as "if the statement that %a is greater than 1 is true." However, the Department of Redundancy Department could have written that example. The first way I showed you is more appropriate.

Just for your information, in the preceding examples, %a and %isOpen are variables, and that's what is coming up next.

Variables

Variables are chunks of memory where values are stored. A program that reads a series of numbers and totals them up will use a variable to represent each number when it's entered and another variable to represent the total. We assign names to these chunks of memory so that we can save and retrieve the data stored there. This is just like high school algebra, where we were taught to write something like "Let *v* stand for the velocity of the marble" and so on. In that case *v* is the identifier (or name) of the variable. TorqueScript identifier rules state that an identifier have the following characteristics:

- It must not be a TorqueScript keyword.

- It must start with an alphabetical character.

- It must consist only of alphanumeric characters or an underscore symbol ("_").

A *keyword* is an otherwise valid identifier that has special significance to Torque. Table 2.3 gives a keyword list. For the purposes of Torque identifiers, the underscore symbol is considered to be an alphanumeric character. The following are valid variable identifiers:

```
isOpen  Today  X  the_result  item_234  NOW
```

These are not legal identifiers:

```
5input  miles-per-hour  function  true + level
```

Table 2.3 TorqueScript Keywords

Keyword	Description
break	Breaks execution out of a loop.
case	Indicates a choice in a switch block.
continue	Causes execution to continue at the top of a loop.
default	Indicates the choice to make in a switch block when no cases match.
do	Indicates the start of a do-while type loop block.
else	Indicates alternative execution path in an if statement.
false	Evaluates to 0, the opposite of true.
for	Indicates the start of a for loop.
function	Indicates that the following code block is a callable function.
if	Indicates the start of a conditional (comparison) statement.
new	Creates a new object datablock.
return	Indicates return from a function.
switch	Indicates the start of a switch selection block.
true	Evaluates to 1, the opposite of false.
while	Indicates the start of a while loop.

It's up to you as the programmer to choose the identifiers you want to use. You should always try to use meaningful identifiers—choose them to be significant to your program and what it is doing. Note that Torque is not case-sensitive. Lowercase letters are *not* treated as distinct from uppercase letters.

You assign values to variables with an assignment statement:

```
$bananaCost = 1.15;
$appleCost  = 0.55;
$numApples  = 3;
$numBananas = 1;
```

Notice that each variable has a dollar sign ("$") preceding it. This is a *scope* prefix. This means that the variable has *global* scope—it can be accessed from anywhere in your program, inside any function, or even outside functions and in different program files.

There is another scope prefix—the percent sign ("%"). The scope of variables with this prefix is *local.* This means that the values represented by these variables are valid only within a function, and only within the specific functions where they are used. We will delve into scoping in more detail later.

Using our fruit example, we can calculate the number of fruit as follows:

```
$numFruit = $numBananas + $numApples;
```

And we can calculate the total cost of all the fruit like this:

```
$numPrice = ($numBananas * $bananaCost) + ($numApples * $appleCost);
```

Here is a complete small program you can use to try it out yourself:

```
// ================================================================
// Fruit.cs
//
// This program adds up the costs and quantities of selected fruit types
// and outputs the results to the display
// ================================================================

function runFruit()
// ----------------------------------------------------------
//    Entry point for the program.
// ----------------------------------------------------------
{
  $bananaCost=1.15;// initialize the value of our variables
  $appleCost=0.55; //   (we don't need to repeat the above
```

```
$numApples=3;    //  comment for each initialization, just
$numBananas=1;   //  group the init statements together.)

$numFruit=0;     // always a good idea to initialize *all* variables!
$total=0;        // (even if we know we are going to change them later)

echo("Cost of Bananas(ea.):$"@$bananaCost);
            // the value of $bananaCost gets concatenated to the end
            // of the "Cost of Bananas:" string. Then the
            // full string gets echoed. same goes for the next 3 lines
echo("Cost of Apples(ea.):$"@$appleCost);
echo("Number of Bananas:"@$numBananas);
echo("Number of Apples:"@$numApples);

$numFruit=$numBananas + $numApples; // add up the total number of fruits
$total = ($numBananas * $bananaCost) +
            ($numApples * $appleCost);  // calculate the total cost
            //(notice that statements can extend beyond a single line)

echo("Total amount of Fruit:"@$numFruit); // output the results
echo("Total Price of Fruit:$"@$total@"0");// add a zero to the end
                            // to make it look better on the screen
}
```

Save the program in the same way you did the Hello World program. Use a name like Fruit.cs and run it to see the results. Note that the asterisk ("*") is used as the multiplication symbol and the plus sign ("+") is used for addition. These *operators*—as well as the parentheses used for evaluation precedence—are discussed later in this chapter.

Arrays

When your Fruit program runs, a variable is accessed in expressions using the identifier associated with that variable. At times you will need to use long lists of values; there is a special kind of variable called an *array* that you can use for lists of related values. The idea is to just use a single identifier for the whole list, with a special mechanism to identify which specific value—or *element*—of the list you want to access. Each value has numerical position within the array, and we call the number used to specify the position the *index* of the array element in question.

Let us say you have a list of values and you want to get a total, like in the previous example. If you are only using a few values (no more than two or three), then a different identifier could be used for each variable, as we did in the Fruit program.

However, if you have a large list—more than two or three values—your code will start to get awkwardly large and hard to maintain. What we can do is use a loop and iterate through the list of values, using the indices. We'll get into loops in detail later in this chapter. Following is a new version of the Fruit program that deals with more types of fruit. There are some significant changes in how we perform what is essentially the same operation. At first glance, it may seem to be more unwieldy than the original Fruit program, but look again, especially in the computation section.

```
// ============================================================
// FruitLoopy.cs
//
// This program adds up the costs and quantities of selected fruit types
// and outputs the results to the display. This module is a variation
// of the Fruit.cs module
// ============================================================

function runFruitLoopy()
// ------------------------------------------------------------
//    Entry point for the program.
// ------------------------------------------------------------
{
  //
  // --------------- Initialization ---------------------
  //

  %numFruitTypes = 5; // so we know how many types are in our arrays

  %bananaIdx=0;    // initialize the values of our index variables
  %appleIdx=1;
  %orangeIdx=2;
  %mangoIdx=3;
  %pearIdx=4;

  %names[%bananaIdx] = "bananas"; // initialize the fruit name values
  %names[%appleIdx] = "apples";
  %names[%orangeIdx] = "oranges";
  %names[%mangoIdx] = "mangos";
  %names[%pearIdx] = "pears";
```

```
%cost[%bananaIdx] = 1.15; // initialize the price values
%cost[%appleIdx] = 0.55;
%cost[%orangeIdx] = 0.55;
%cost[%mangoIdx] = 1.90;
%cost[%pearIdx] = 0.68;

%quantity[%bananaIdx] = 1; // initialize the quantity values
%quantity[%appleIdx]  = 3;
%quantity[%orangeIdx] = 4;
%quantity[%mangoIdx]  = 1;
%quantity[%pearIdx]   = 2;

%numFruit=0;    // always a good idea to initialize *all* variables!
%totalCost=0;   // (even if we know we are going to change them later)

//
// ---------------- Computation --------------------
//

// Display the known statistics of the fruit collection
for (%index = 0; %index < %numFruitTypes; %index++)
{
  echo("Cost of " @ %names[%index] @ ":$" @ %cost[%index]);
  echo("Number of " @ %names[%index] @ ":" @ %quantity[%index]);
}

// count up all the pieces of fruit, and display that result
for (%index = 0; %index <= %numFruitTypes; %index++)
{
   %numFruit = %numFruit + %quantity[%index];
}
echo("Total pieces of Fruit:" @ %numFruit);


// now calculate the total cost
for (%index = 0; %index <= %numFruitTypes; %index++)
{
  %totalCost = %totalCost + (%quantity[%index]*%cost[%index]);
}
echo("Total Price of Fruit:$" @ %totalCost);
}
```

Type this program in, save it as \3D2E\demo\FruitLoopy.cs, and then run it.

Of course, you will notice right away that I've used comments to organize the code into two sections, *initialization* and *computation*. This was purely arbitrary. But it is a good idea to label sections of code in this manner, to provide signposts, as it were. You should also notice that all the variables in the program are local, rather than global, in scope. This is more reasonable for a program of this nature, where having everything contained in one function puts all variables in the same scope.

Next you will see that I've actually created three arrays: name, cost, and quantity. Each array has the same number of elements, by design. Also, I have assigned appropriately named variables to carry the index values of each of the fruit types. This way I don't need to remember which fruit has which index when it comes time to initialize them with their names, prices, and counts.

Then it is just a simple matter of looping through the list to perform the operation I want.

Elegant, huh? But it could be better. See if you can find a way to reduce the number of lines of code in the computation section even more, and write your own version and try it out for yourself. I've written my own smaller version; you can find it in the \3D2E\RESOURCES\CH2 folder, named ParedFruit.cs.

Tip

If you haven't noticed, it's time you did: when we deal with paths in Windows, we use the backslash ("\"), as seen with C:\3D2E\demo. However, in TorqueScript (as in Linux and the Macintosh OS), we use the forward slash ("/") for the paths, as seen with demo/client/scripts. You'll run into a lot more of this later. Just keep this in mind if you are having path troubles.

For a further illuminating exercise, try this: rewrite FruitLoopy.cs to perform exactly the same operations, but without using arrays at all. Go ahead—take some time and give it a try. You can compare it with my version in the \3D2E\RESOURCES\CH2 folder, named FermentedFruit.cs.

Now, the final exercise is purely up to you and your mind's eye. Imagine that you have 33 types of fruit instead of 5. Which program would you rather modify—ParedFruit.cs or FermentedFruit.cs? Can you see the advantage of arrays now?

Another thing to point out is that the initialization section of the code would probably read in the values from a database or an external file with value tables in it. It would use a loop to store all the initial values—the names, costs, and quantities. Then the code would really be a lot smaller!

To review, an array is a data structure that allows a collective name to be given to a group of elements of the same type. An individual element of an array is identified by its own unique index (or subscript).

An array can be thought of as a collection of numbered boxes, each containing one data item. The number associated with the box is the index of the item. To access a particular item, the index of the box associated with the item is used to access the appropriate box. The index must be an integer and indicates the position of the element in the array.

Strings

We've already encountered strings in our earlier example programs. In some languages strings are a special type of array, like an array of single characters, and can be treated as such. In Torque, strings are in essence the only form of variable. Numbers and text are stored as strings. They are handled as either text or numbers depending on which operators are being used on the variables.

As we've seen, two basic string operations are *assignment* and *concatenation*, as illustrated here:

```
%myFirstName = "Ken";
%myFullName = %myFirstName @ " Finney";
```

In the first line, the string "Ken" is assigned to %myFirstName, then the string "Finney" is concatenated (or appended) to %myFirstName, and the result is assigned to %myFullName. Familiar stuff by now, right? Well, try this one on for size:

```
%myAge = 30;          // (actually it isn't you know !)
%myAge = %myAge + 12;  // getting warmer !
```

At this point, the value in %myAge is 42, the sum of 30 and 12. Now watch this trick:

```
%aboutMe = "My name is " @ %myFullName @ " and I am " @ %myAge @ " years old.";
```

I'm sure you can figure out what the value of the variable %aboutMe is. That's right, it's one long string—"My name is Ken Finney and I am 42 years old."—with the number values embedded as text, not numbers. Of course, that isn't my age, but who's counting?

What happened is that the Torque Engine figured out by the context what operation you wanted to perform, and it converted the number to a string value before it added it to the larger string.

Another form of string variable is called the *tagged string*. This is a special string format used by Torque to reduce bandwidth utilization between the client and the server. We'll cover tagged strings in more detail in a later chapter.

Operators

Table 2.4 is a list of operators. You will find it handy to refer back to this table from time to time.

Table 2.4 TorqueScript Operators

Symbol	Meaning
+	Add.
–	Subtract.
*	Multiply.
/	Divide.
%	Modulus.
++	Increment by 1.
--	Decrement by 1.
+=	Addition totalizer.
-=	Subtraction totalizer.
*=	Multiplication totalizer.
/=	Division totalizer.
%=	Modulus totalizer.
@	String append.
( )	Parentheses—operator precedence promotion.
[ ]	Brackets—array index delimiters.
{ }	Braces—indicate start and end of code blocks.
SPC	Space append macro (same as @ " " @).
TAB	Tab append macro (same as @ "\t" @).
NL	Newline append (same as @ "\n" @).
~	(Bitwise NOT) Flips the bits of its operand.
|	(Bitwise OR) Returns a 1 in a bit if either operand has a bit that is 1.
&	(Bitwise AND) Returns a 1 in each bit position if bits of both operands are 1s.
^	(Bitwise XOR) Returns a 1 in a bit position if bits of one but not both operands are 1.
<<	(Left-shift) Shifts its first operand in binary representation the number of bits to the left specified in the second operand, shifting in 0s from the right.
>>	(Sign-propagating right-shift) Shifts the first operand in binary representation the number of bits to the right specified in the second operand, discarding bits shifted off.

Symbol	Meaning
|=	Bitwise OR with result assigned to the first operand.
&=	Bitwise AND with result assigned to the first operand.
^=	Bitwise XOR with result assigned to the first operand.
<<=	Left-shift with result assigned to the first operand.
>>=	Sign-propagating right-shift with result assigned to the first operand.
!	Evaluates the opposite of the value specified.
&&	Requires both values to be true for the result to be true.
||	Requires only one value to be true for the result to be true.
==	Left-hand value and right-hand value are equal.
!=	Left-hand value and right-hand value are not equal.
<	Left-hand value is less than right-hand value.
>	Left-hand value is greater than right-hand value.
<=	Left-hand value is less than or equal to right-hand value.
>=	Left-hand value is greater than or equal to right-hand value.
$=	Left-hand string is equal to right-hand string.
!$=	Left-hand string is not equal to right-hand string.
//	Comment operator—ignore all text from here to the end of the line.
;	Statement terminator.
.	Object/datablock method or property delimiter.

Operators range from the familiar to the mighty weird. The familiar will be the ones like add (" + ") and subtract ("−"). A little strange for those who are adept with standard secondary school math but new to programming languages is the multiplication symbol—an asterisk ("*"). The division symbol, though not the regular handwritten one, is still a somewhat familiar slash ("/"). A mighty weird operator would be the vertical pipe ("|"), which is used to perform an OR operation on the bits of a variable.

Some of the operators are probably self-explanatory or understandable from the table. Others may require some explanation, which you will find in the following sections of this chapter.

You'll recall that strings and numbers are treated the same; there is, however, one exception, and that is when comparing strings to strings or numbers to numbers. We use different operators for those comparisons. For number comparisons, we use == (that's not a typo—it's two equal signs in a row; read it as "is identical to"), and for string comparisons, we use $= (read it as "string is identical to"). These operators will be discussed more in the sections called "Conditional Expressions" and "Branching."

Operator Precedence

An issue with evaluating expressions is that of *order of evaluation.* Should %a + %b * %c be evaluated by performing the multiplication first or by performing the addition first? In other words, as %a + (%b * %c) or as (%a + %b) * %c?

Torque and other languages (such as C/C++) solve this problem by assigning priorities to operators; operators with high priority are evaluated before operators with low priority. Operators with equal priority are evaluated in left-to-right order. The priorities of the operators seen so far are, in order of high to low priority, as follows:

```
( )
* / %
+ −
=
```

Therefore, %a + %b * %c is evaluated as if it had been written as %a + (%b * %c) because multiplication (*) has a higher priority than addition (+). If the + needed to be evaluated first, then parentheses would be used as follows: (%a + %b) * %c.

If you have any doubt, then use extra parentheses to ensure the correct order of evaluation. Note that two arithmetic operators cannot be written in succession.

Increment/Decrement Operators

There are some operations that occur so frequently in assignment statements that Torque has shorthand methods for writing them. One common situation is that of incrementing or decrementing an integer variable. For example,

```
%n = %n + 1;     // increment by one
%n = %n - 1;     // decrement by one
```

Torque has an increment operator (++) and a decrement operator (--). Thus

```
%n++;
```

can be used for the increment and

```
%n--;
```

can be used for the decrement.

The ++ and -- operators here have been written after the variable they affect; they are called the *postincrement* and *postdecrement operators,* respectively. Torque does not have preincrement and predecrement operators (which are written before the variable), as you would find in C/C++.

Totalizers

Totalizers are a variation on the increment and decrement theme. Instead of bumping a value up or down by 1, a totalizer does it with any arbitrary value. For example, a common situation that occurs is an assignment like this:

```
%total = %total + %more;
```

where a variable is increased by some amount and the result is assigned back to the original variable. This type of assignment can be represented in Torque by the following:

```
%total+= %more;
```

This notation can be used with the other arithmetic operators (+, -, *, /, and %), as you can see in the following:

```
%prod = %prod * 10;
```

which can be written as this:

```
%prod *= 10;
```

You can use totalizers in compound assignment statements quite easily as well. Here's an example:

```
%x = %x/(%y + 1);
```

becomes

```
%x /= %y + 1;
```

and

```
%n = %n % 2;
```

becomes

```
%n %= 2;
```

Be careful on that last one! The percent sign in front of the number 2 is the modulus operator, not a scope prefix. You can tell by the space that separates it from the 2— or in the case of the totalizer example, you can tell by the fact that the percent sign is adjacent to the equal sign on the right. They are certainly subtle differences, so make sure you watch for them if you work in code that uses these constructs.

In all cases, you must be performing these operations on numbers and not strings. That wouldn't make any sense!

Loops

Loops are used for repetitive tasks. We saw an example of a loop being used in the FruitLoopy sample program. This loop was used to step through the available types of fruit. The loop was a *bounded* one that had a specified start and end, a characteristic built into the loop construct we used, the `for` loop. The other kind of loop we are going to look at is the `while` loop.

The while Loop

The following piece of TorqueScript demonstrates a `while` loop. It gets a random number between 0 and 10 from the Torque Engine and then prints it out.

```
// ===========================================================================
//  WhilingAway.cs
//
//  This module is a program that demonstrates while loops. It prints
//  random values on the screen as long as a condition is satisfied.
//
// ===========================================================================

function runWhilingAway()
// --------------------------------------------------------------
//    Entry point for the program.
// --------------------------------------------------------------
{
   %value = 0;            // initialize %value
   while (%value < 7)     // stop looping if %n exceeds 7
   {
      %value = GetRandom(10);    // get a random number between 0 and 10
      echo("value="@%value );    // print the result
   }                              // now back to the top of the loop
                                  // ie. do it all again

}
```

Save this program as \3D2E\demo\WhilingAway.cs and run it. Note the output. Now run it again. Note the output again—and the fact that this time it's different. That's the randomness in action, right there. But the part that we are really interested in right now is the fact that as long as the number is less than 7, the program continues to loop.

The general form of a `while` statement is this:

```
while ( condition )
        statement
```

While the condition is `true` the statement is executed over and over. Each time the condition is satisfied and the statement executed is called an *iteration*. The statement may be a single statement (terminated by a semicolon) or code block (delimited by braces) when you want two or more statements to be executed. Note the following points. It must be possible to evaluate the condition on the first entry to the `while` statement or it will never be satisfied, and its code will never be executed. This means that all variables used in the condition must have been given values before the `while` statement is encountered. In the preceding example the variable `%value` was started at 0 (it was initialized) and it was given a random number between 0 and 10 during each iteration of the loop.

Now you have to make sure that at least one of the variables referenced in the condition can be changed in the statement portion that makes up the body of the loop. If you don't, you could end up stuck in an *infinite loop*. In the preceding example by making sure that the randomly chosen `%value` would always *eventually* cause the condition to fail (10 is greater than 7) we ensure that the loop will stop at some point. In fact, the random number code will return 7, 8, 9, and 10 at some point or other—any one of which will cause the code to break out of the loop.

Here is the important thing about `while` loops. The condition is evaluated *before* the loop body statements are executed. If the condition evaluates to `false` when it is first encountered, then the body is never entered. In the preceding example if we had initialized `%value` with 10, then no execution of the statements in the body of the `while` loop would have happened.

And now here's a little exercise for you. Write a program, saving it as \3D2E\demo\LoopPrint.cs. Make the program print all the integers starting at 0 up to and including 250. That's a lot of numbers! Use a `while` loop to do it.

The for Loop

When programming, we often need to execute a statement a specific number of times. Consider the following use of a `while` statement to output the numbers

1 to 10. In this case the integer variable count is used to control the number of times the loop is executed.

```
%count = 1;
while (%count <= 10)
{
  echo("count="@%count);
  %count++;
}
```

Three distinct operations take place:

- **Initialization.** Initializes the control variable %count to 1.

- **Evaluation.** Evaluates the value of an expression (%count <= 10).

- **Update.** Updates the value of the control variable before executing the loop again (%count++).

The for statement is specially designed for these cases—where a loop is to be executed starting from an initial value and iterates until a control condition is satisfied, meanwhile updating the value of the control variable each time around the loop. It has all three operations rolled up into its principal statement syntax. It's sort of the Swiss army knife of loop statements.

The general form of the for statement is

```
for (initialize; evaluate; update)
    statement
```

which executes the initialize operation when the for statement is first entered. The evaluate operation is then performed on the test expression; if it evaluates to true, then the loop statement is executed for one iteration followed by the update operation. The cycle of test, iterate, update continues until the test expression evaluates to false; control then passes to the next statement in the program.

Functions

Functions save work. Once you've written code to solve a problem, you can roll the code into a function and reuse it whenever you encounter that problem again. You can create functions in a manner that allows you to use the code with different starting parameters and either create some effect or return a value to the code that uses the function.

When solving large problems we often use a divide-and-conquer technique, sometimes called *problem decomposition*. We break a big problem down into smaller problems that are easier to solve. This is often called the *top-down approach*. We keep doing this until problems become small enough that a single person can solve them. This top-down approach is essential if the work has to be shared among a team of programmers; each programmer ends up with a specification for a small part of the bigger system that is to be written as a function (or a collection of functions). The programmer can concentrate on the solution of only this one problem and is likely to make fewer errors. The function can then be tested on its own for correctness compared to the design specification.

There are many specialized problem areas, and not every programmer can be proficient in all of them. Many programmers working in scientific applications will frequently use math function routines like sine and cosine but would have no idea how to write the code to actually perform those operations. Likewise, a programmer working in commercial applications might know little about how an efficient sorting routine can be written. A specialist can create such routines and place them in a public library of functions, however, and all programmers can benefit from this expertise by being able to use these efficient and well-tested functions.

In the "Arrays" section earlier in this chapter we calculated a total price and total count of several types of fruit with the FruitLoopy program. Here is that program modified somewhat (okay, modified a *lot*) to use functions. Take note of how small the entry point function—called runTwotyFruity—has become now that so much code is contained within the three new functions.

```
// ================================================================
// TwotyFruity.cs
//
// This program adds up the costs and quantities of selected fruit types
// and outputs the results to the display. This module is a variation
// of the FruitLoopy.cs module designed to demonstrate how to use
// functions.
// ================================================================

function InitializeFruit()
// ----------------------------------------------------------------
//     Set the starting values for our fruit arrays, and the type
//     indices
//
```

```
//      RETURNS: number of different types of fruit
//
// ----------------------------------------------------------------------
{
  %numTypes = 5; // so we know how many types are in our arrays
  $bananaIdx=0;    // initialize the values of our index variables
  $appleIdx=1;
  $orangeIdx=2;
  $mangoIdx=3;
  $pearIdx=4;

  $names[$bananaIdx] = "bananas"; // initialize the fruit name values
  $names[$appleIdx] = "apples";
  $names[$orangeIdx] = "oranges";
  $names[$mangoIdx] = "mangos";
  $names[$pearIdx] = "pears";

  $cost[$bananaIdx] = 1.15; // initialize the price values
  $cost[$appleIdx] = 0.55;
  $cost[$orangeIdx] = 0.55;
  $cost[$mangoIdx] = 1.90;
  $cost[$pearIdx] = 0.68;

  $quantity[$bananaIdx] = 1; // initialize the quantity values
  $quantity[$appleIdx]  = 3;
  $quantity[$orangeIdx] = 4;
  $quantity[$mangoIdx]  = 1;
  $quantity[$pearIdx]   = 2;

  return(%numTypes);
}

function addEmUp(%numFruitTypes)
// ----------------------------------------------------------------------
//    Add all prices of different fruit types to get a full total cost
//
//PARAMETERS: %numFruitTypes -the number of different fruit that are tracked
//
//    RETURNS: total cost of all fruit
//
// ----------------------------------------------------------------------
{
  %total = 0;
```

```
    for (%index = 0; %index <= %numFruitTypes; %index++)
    {
        %total = %total + ($quantity[%index]*$cost[%index]);
    }
    return %total;
}


// -----------------------------------------------------------------------
// countEm
//
//    Add all quantities of different fruit types to get a full total
//
//PARAMETERS: %numFruitTypes -the number of different fruit that are tracked
//
//    RETURNS: total of all fruit types
//
// -----------------------------------------------------------------------
function countEm(%numFruitTypes)
{
    %total = 0;
    for (%index = 0; %index <= %numFruitTypes; %index++)
    {
        %total = %total + $quantity[%index];
    }
    return %total;
}


function runTwotyFruity()
// -----------------------------------------------------------------------
//      Entry point for program. This program adds up the costs
//      and quantities of selected fruit types and outputs the results to
//      the display. This program is a variation of the program FruitLoopy
//
// -----------------------------------------------------------------------
{
    //
    // ---------------- Initialization ---------------------
    //

    %numFruitTypes=InitializeFruit(); // set up fruit arrays and variables
    %numFruit=0;        // always a good idea to initialize *all* variables!
    %totalCost=0;       // (even if we know we are going to change them later)
```

```
//
// ----------------- Computation --------------------
//

// Display the known statistics of the fruit collection
for (%index = 0; %index < %numFruitTypes; %index++)
{
echo("Cost of " @ $names[%index] @ ":$" @ $cost[%index]);
echo("Number of " @ $names[%index] @ ":" @ $quantity[%index]);
}

// count up all the pieces of fruit, and display that result
%numFruit = countEm(%numFruitTypes);
echo("Total pieces of Fruit:" @ %numFruit);

// now calculate the total cost
%totalCost = addEmUp(%numFruitTypes);
echo("Total Price of Fruit:$" @ %totalCost);
}
```

Save this program as \3D2E\demo\TwotyFruity.cs and run it in the usual way.
Now go and run your FruitLoopy program, and compare the output. Hopefully,
they will be exactly the same.

In this version all the array initialization has been moved out of the runFruitLoopy
function and into the new InitializeFruit function. Now, you might notice that I
have changed the arrays to be global variables. The reason for this is that Torque
does not handle passing arrays to functions in a graceful manner. Well, actually it
does, but we would need to use ScriptObjects, which are not covered until a later
chapter, so rather than obfuscate things too much right now, I've made the arrays
into global variables. This will serve as a useful lesson in contrast between global
and local variables anyway, so I thought, why not?

The global arrays can be accessed from within any function in the file. The local ones
(with the percent sign prefix), however, can only be accessed within a function. This is
more obvious when you look at the addEmUp and countEm functions. Notice that they
both use a variable called %total. But they are actually two *different* variables whose
scope does not extend outside the functions where they are used. So don't get mixed up!

Speaking of addEmUp and countEm, these functions have another construct, called
a *parameter*. Sometimes we use the word *argument* instead, but because we are all
friends here, I'll stick with parameter.

Functions with No Parameters

The function main has no parameters, so you can see that parameters are not always required. Because the arrays are global, they can be accessed from within any function, so we don't *need* to try to pass in the data for them anyway.

Functions with Parameters and No Return Value

Parameters are used to pass information into a function, as witnessed with the functions addEmUp and countEm. In both cases we pass a parameter that tells the function how many types of fruit there are to deal with.

The function declaration looked like this:

```
function addEmUp(%numFruitTypes)
```

and when we actually used the function we did this:

```
%totalCost = addEmUp(%numFruitTypes);
```

where %numFruitTypes indicates how many types of fruit there are—in this case, five. This is known as a *call* to the function addEmUp. We could have written it as

```
%totalCost = addEmUp(5);
```

but then we would have lost the flexibility of using the variable to hold the value for the number of fruit types.

This activity is called *parameter passing*. When a parameter is passed during a function call, the value passed into the function is assigned to the variable that is specified in the function declaration. The effect is something like %numTypes = %numFruitTypes; now this code doesn't actually exist anywhere, but operations are performed that have that effect. Thus, %numTypes (inside the function) receives the value of %numFruitTypes (outside the function).

Tip

Parameters are also called *arguments.*

Functions That Return Values

The function InitializeFruit returns a number for the number of different fruit types with this line:

```
return(%numTypes);
```

and the functions `addEmUp` and `countEm` both have this line:

```
return %total;
```

Notice that the first example has the variable sitting inside some parentheses, and the second example does not. Either way is valid.

Now what happens is that when Torque encounters a `return` statement in a program, it gathers up the value in the `return` statement and then exits the function and resumes execution at the code where the function was called. There isn't always a `return` statement in a function, so don't be annoyed if you see functions without them. In the case of the `InitializeFruit` function, that would have been the line near the start of `runTwotyFruity` that looks like this:

```
%numFruitTypes=InitializeFruit(); // set up fruit arrays and variables
```

If the function call was part of an assignment statement, as above, then whatever value was gathered at the `return` statement inside the function call is now assigned in the assignment statement. Another way of expressing this concept is to say that the function *evaluated* to the value of the `return` statement inside the function.

`Return` statements don't need to evaluate to anything, however. They can be used to simply stop execution of the function and return control to the calling program code with a return value. Both numbers and strings can be returned from a function.

Conditional Expressions

A conditional or logical expression is an expression that can only evaluate to one of two values: `true` or `false`. A simple form of logical expression is the conditional expression, which uses relational operators to construct a statement about a given condition. The following is an example of a conditional expression:

```
%x < %y
```

This reads as `%x` is less than `%y`, which evaluates to `true` if the value of the variable `%x` is less than the value of the variable `%y`. The general form of a conditional expression is

```
operandA relational_operator operandB
```

The operands can be either variables or expressions. If an operand is an expression, then the expression is evaluated and its value is used as the operand. The relational operators allowable in Torque are shown in Table 2.5.

Table 2.5 Relational Operators

Symbol	Meaning
<	less than
>	greater than
<=	less than or equal to
>=	greater than or equal to
==	equal to
!=	not equal to
$=	string equal to
!$=	string not equal to

Note

Another name for logic that involves only the values `true` or `false` is *Boolean* logic.

Note that equality is tested for using the operator == because = is already used for assigning values to variables. The condition evaluates to `true` if the values of the two operands satisfy the relational operator and `false` if they don't.

Here are some examples:

```
%i < 10
%voltage >= 0.0
%total < 1000.0
%count != %n
%x * %x + %y * %y < %r * %r
```

Depending on the values of the variables involved, each of the preceding expressions is `true` or `false`. If %x has the value 3, %y is 6, and %r is 10, the last expression evaluates to `true`, but if %x was 7 and %y was 8, then it would evaluate to `false`.

The value of a logical expression can be stored in a variable for later use. Any numerical expression can be used for the value of a condition, with 0 being interpreted as `false` and 1 as `true`.

This means that the value a logical expression evaluates to can be used in arithmetical operations. This is often done by programmers, but it is a practice not to be recommended. It can lead to code obscurity, creating a program that is difficult to understand.

Logical Expressions

We can create more complex conditions than those that can be written using only the relational operators described in the preceding section. There are explicit logical operators for combining the logical values true and false.

The simplest logical operator is NOT, which is represented in Torque by the exclamation point ("!"). It operates on a single operand and returns false if its operand is true and true if its operand is false.

The operator AND, represented by two ampersands ("&&"), takes two operands and is true only if both of the operands are true. If either operand is false, the resulting value is false.

The final logical operator is OR, which is represented by two vertical pipes ("||"). It results in true if either operand is true. It returns false only if both its operands are false.

The logical operators can be defined by truth tables as seen in Table 2.6. The "F" character is used for false and "T" is used for true in these tables.

Table 2.6 Logical Operator Truth Tables

NOT (!)

A	!A
F	T
T	F

OR (||)

A	B	A OR B
T	T	T
T	F	T
F	T	T
F	F	F

AND (&&)

A	B	A AND B
T	T	T
T	F	F
F	T	F
F	F	F

These tables show that NOT reverses the truth value of the operand A; that the AND of two operands is only `true` if both operands are `true`; and that the OR of two operands is `true` if either or both of its operands are `true`. Now we can write pretty complex logical operations.

If `%i` has the value 15, and `%j` has the value 10, then the expression `(i > 10) && (j > 0)` is evaluated by evaluating the relation `i > 10` (which is `true`), then evaluating the relation `%j > 0` (which is also `true`), to give `true`. If `%j` has the value −1, then the second relation would be `false`, so the overall expression would be `false`. If i has the value 5, then the first relation would be `false`, and the expression will be `false` irrespective of the value of the second relation. Torque does not even evaluate the second relation in this situation. Similarly, if the first relation is `true` in an OR (||) expression, then the second relation will not be evaluated. This short-circuit evaluation enables many logical expressions to be efficiently evaluated.

Examples Using Logical Operators

Note that in the last of the examples that follow, an actual truth value (0 or `false`) was used as one of the operands of `&&`. This means that whatever the value of `%i`, this logical expression evaluates to `false`. In these examples parentheses have been used to clarify the order of operator application.

```
(%i < 10) && (%j > 0)
((%x + %y) <= 15) || (%i == 5)
!((%i >= 10) || (%j <= 0))
(%i < 10) && 0
```

You've got to be careful not to confuse the assignment operator `=` with the logical equality operator `==`.

Using Table 2.6 with the following expression

```
x + y < 10 && x/y == 3 || z != 10
```

shows that the operators are evaluated in the order `/, +, <, ==, !=, &&,` and `||`. This is the same as using parentheses on the expression in this way: `((((x + y) < 10) && ((x/y) == 3)) || (z!= 10))`.

Similarly, the expressions given above could be written without parentheses as follows:

```
i < 10 && j > 0
x + y <= 15 || i == 5
```

```
!(i >= 10 || j <= 0)
i < 10 && 0
```

Now that we've covered the logical expressions (or conditions) in Torque, let's move on and take a look at the conditional control mechanisms in Torque.

Branching

The term *branching* refers to the idea that code can follow different execution paths depending on, well, something. What it depends on . . . ummm . . . depends. Well, let me try that again. It depends on what your program is doing and what you want it to do. Like this: say you are driving on a road, and you reach a T junction. The sign points left and says "Toronto 50 km." Another sign points right and says "Toronto (Scenic Route) 150 km." Which way are you going to go, left or right? Well, you see? It *depends*. The fastest way to Toronto might be to go left, but what if you aren't in a hurry—maybe you're interested in the scenic route? Just as we saw earlier with looping, there are conditions that will dictate what path your code will take.

That act of taking one path over others available is branching. Branching starts out with some sort of decision-making test. In addition to the two looping statements we've already covered—which employ branching of sorts—there are also two branch-specific statements: the if statement and the switch statement.

The if Statement

The simplest way to select the next thing to do in a program based upon conditions is to use the if statement. Check this out:

```
if (%n > 0)
  echo("n is a positive number");
```

This will print out the message "n is a positive number" only if %n is positive. The general form of the if statement is this:

```
if (condition)
    statement
```

where condition is any valid logical expression as described in the "Conditional Expressions" section we saw earlier.

This if statement adds % something to the variable %sum if % something is positive:

```
if (%something > 0)
  %sum += %something;
```

If %something isn't positive, then the program branches *past* the totalizer statement, and so %sum doesn't get incremented by %something.

This next piece of code similarly adds %something to %sum, but it also increments a positive number counter called %counter:

```
if (%something > 0)
{
  %sum += %something;
  %counter++;
}
```

Note how in the second example a compound statement has been used to carry out more than one operation if the condition is true. If it had been written like this:

```
if (%something > 0)
  %sum += %something;
  %counter++;
```

then if %something was greater than 0, the next statement would be executed—that is, %sum would be incremented by the amount of %something. But the statement incrementing %counter is now going to be treated as the next statement in the program and not as part of the if statement. The program execution is not going to branch around it. The effect of this would be that %counter would be incremented every time it is encountered, no matter whether %something is positive or negative.

The statements within a compound statement can be any Torque statements. In fact, another if statement could be included. For example, the following code will print a message if a quantity is negative and a further message if no overdraft has been arranged:

```
if ( %balance < 0 )
{
  echo ("Your account is overdrawn. Balance is: " @ %balance );
  if ( %overdraft <= 0 )
    echo ("You have exceeded your overdraft limit");
}
```

Now we could have done the same thing using two sequential if statements and more complex conditions:

```
if ( %balance < 0 )
  echo ("Your account is overdrawn. Balance is: " @ %balance );
```

```
if ( %balance < 0 && %overdraft <= 0 )
    echo ("You have exceeded your overdraft limit");
```

You should note that one of these versions will generally execute a little bit faster than the second when dealing with accounts that are not overdrawn. Before I tell you later in this chapter, see if you can figure out which one, and why.

The if-else Statement

A simple if statement only allows a single branch to a simple or compound statement when a condition holds. Sometimes there are alternative paths, some that need to be executed when the condition holds, and some to be executed when the condition does not hold. The two forms can be written this way:

```
if (%coffeeholic == true)
    echo ("I like coffee.");
if (%coffeeholic == false)
    echo ("I don't like coffee.");
```

This technique will work while the statements that are executed as a result of the first comparison do not alter the conditions under which the second if statement are executed. Torque provides a direct means of expressing these kinds of choices. The if-else statement specifies statements to be executed for both possible logical values of the condition in an if statement. The following example of an if-else statement writes out one message if the variable %coffeeholic is positive and another message if %coffeeholic is negative:

```
if (%coffeeholic == true)
    echo ("I like coffee.");
else
    echo ("I don't like coffee.");
```

The general form of the if-else statement is this:

```
if (condition)
    statementA
else
    statementB
```

If the condition is true, then statementA is executed; otherwise, statementB is executed. Both statementA and statementB may be either simple or compound statements.

The following `if-else` statement evaluates if a fruit is fresh or not, and if it is, the statement increments a fresh fruit counter. If the fruit isn't fresh, the statement increments the rotten fruit counter. I'm going to program my refrigerator's fruit crisper to do this one day and send me reports over the Internet. Well, I can wish, can't I?

```
if (%fruitState $= "fresh")
{
   %freshFruitCounter++;
}
else
{
   %rottenFruitCounter++;
}
```

Time for another sample program! Type the following program in, and save it as \3D2E\demo\Geometry.cs and then run it.

```
// ============================================================================
// Geometry.cs
//
// This program calculates the distance around the perimeter of
// a quadrilateral as well as the area of the quadrilateral and outputs the
// values.It computes whether the quadrilateral is a square or a rectangle and
// modifies its output accordingly. Program assumes that all angles in the
// quadrilateral are equal. Demonstrates the if-else statement.
// ============================================================================

function calcAndPrint(%theWidth, %theHeight)
// ----------------------------------------------------------------------------
//     This function does the shape analysis and prints the result.
//
//     PARAMETERS: %theWidth - horizontal dimension
//                 %theHeight - vertical dimension
//
//     RETURNS: none
// ----------------------------------------------------------------------------
{
  // calculate perimeter
  %perimeter = 2 * (%theWidth+%theHeight);

  // calculate area
  %area = %theWidth * %theHeight;
```

```
    // first, set up the dimension output string
    %prompt = "For a " @ %theWidth @ " by " @
              %theHeight @ " quadrilateral, area and perimeter of ";

    // analyze the shape's dimensions and select different
    // descriptors based on the shape's dimensions
    if (%theWidth == %theHeight)              // if true, then it's a square
      %prompt = %prompt @ "square: ";
    else                                      // otherwise it's a rectangle
      %prompt = %prompt @ "rectangle: ";

    // always output the analysis
    echo (%prompt @ %area @ " " @ %perimeter);
}

function runGeometry()
// ----------------------------------------------------------------------
//    Entry point for the program.
// ----------------------------------------------------------------------
{

    // calculate and output the results for three
    // known dimension sets
    calcAndPrint(22, 26); // rectangle
    calcAndPrint(31, 31); // square
    calcAndPrint(47, 98); // rectangle
}
```

What we've done here is analyze a shape. In addition to printing its calculated measurements, we modify our output string based upon the (simple) analysis that determines if it is a square or a rectangle. I realize that a square *is* a rectangle, but let's not get too picky, okay? Not yet, at least.

Nesting if Statements

You saw earlier in "The if Statement" section how an if statement can contain another if statement. These are called *nested if statements*. There is no real limit to how deep you can nest the statements, but try to be reasonable and only do it if it is absolutely necessary for functional reasons. It might be good to do it for performance reasons, and that's fine as well.

By the way, I had asked if you could tell which of the two examples would execute faster, remember that? The answer is that the nested version will execute faster when there is no overdraft condition. This is because only one condition is tested, resulting in less work for the computer to do. The sequential version will always perform both tests, no matter what the bank balance is.

The if and if-else statements allow a choice to be made between two possible alternatives. Well, sometimes we need to choose between more than two alternatives. For example, the following sign function returns −1 if the argument is less than 0, returns +1 if the argument is greater than 0, and returns 0 if the argument is 0.

```
function sign (%value)
//   determines the arithmetic sign of a value
//
//   PARAMETERS: %value - the value to be analyzed
//
//   RETURNS: -1  - if value is negative
//             0  - if value is zero
//             1  - if value is positive
{
  if (%value < 0) // is it negative ?
  {
    return -1;
  }
  else            // nope, not negative
  {
    if (%value == 0) // is it zero ?
    {
      return 0;
    }
    else            // nope, then it must be positive
    {
      return 1;
    }
  }
}
```

So there you go. The function has an if-else statement in which the statement following the else is also an if-else statement. If %value is less than 0, then sign returns −1, but if it is not less than 0, the statement following the else is executed. In that case if %value is equal to 0, then sign returns 0; otherwise, it returns 1. I used the compound statement form in order to make the nesting stand out more. The nesting could also be written like this:

```
if (%value < 0) // is it negative ?
  return -1;
else             // nope, not negative
  if (%value == 0) // is it zero ?
    return 0;
  else           // nope, then it must be positive
    return 1;
```

This is nice and compact, but it can sometimes be hard to discern where the nesting properly happens, and it is easier to make mistakes. Using the compound form formalizes the nesting a bit more, and personally, I find it more readable.

Newbie programmers sometimes use a sequence of if statements rather than nested if-else statements when the latter should be used. They would write the guts of the sign function like this:

```
if (%value < 0)
    %result = -1;
if (%value == 0)
    %result = 0;
if (%value > 0)
    %result = 1;
    return %result;
```

It would work and it's fairly easy to read, but it's inefficient because all three conditions are always tested.

If nesting is carried out to too deep a level and indenting is not consistent, then deeply nested if or if-else statements will be confusing to read and interpret. You should note that an else always belongs to the closest if without an else.

The switch Statement

We just explored how we can choose between more than two possibilities by using nested if-else statements. There is a sleeker and more readable method available for certain kinds of multiple-choice situations—the switch statement. For example, the following switch statement will set a game's weapon label based upon a numeric weapon type variable:

```
switch (%weaponType)
{
    case 1: %weaponName = "knife";
    case 2: %weaponName = "pistol";
    case 3: %weaponName = "shotgun";
    case 4: %weaponName = "bfg1000";
    default: %weaponName = "fist";
}
```

Here is what that would look like using if-else:

```
if (%weaponType == 1)
  %weaponName = "knife";
else if (%weaponType == 2)
  %weaponName = "pistol";
else if (%weaponType == 3)
  %weaponName = "shotgun";
else if (%weaponType == 4)
  %weaponName = "bfg1000";
else
  %weaponName = "fist";
```

It's pretty obvious from that simple example why the switch statement is so useful.

The general form of a switch statement is this:

```
switch ( selection-variable )
{
    case label1:
                statement1;
    case label2:
                statement2;
        ...
    case labeln:
                statementn;
    default:
                statementd;
}
```

The selection-variable may be a number or a string or an expression that evaluates to a number or a string. The selection-variable is evaluated and compared with each of the case labels. The case labels all have to be different. If a match is found between the selection-variable and one of the case labels, then the statements that follow the matched case until the next case statement will be executed. If the value of the selection-variable can't be matched with any of the `case` labels, then the statements associated with `default` are executed. The `default` is not required but should only be left out if it is certain that the selection-variable will always take the value of one of the `case` labels.

Here is another example, which writes out the day of the week depending on the value of the number variable %day.

```
switch (%day)
{
    case 1 :
            echo("Sunday");
    case 2 :
            echo("Monday");
    case 3 :
            echo("Tuesday");
    case 4 :
            echo("Wednesday");
    case 5 :
            echo("Thursday");
    case 6 :
            echo("Friday");
    case 7 :
            echo("Saturday");
    default :
            echo("Not a valid day number");
}
```

Debugging and Problem Solving

When you run your programs, the Torque Engine will automatically compile them and output a new .cs.dso file if it needs to. Therefore, Geometry.cs (the source code) will become Geometry.cs.dso (the compiled code). There is a gotcha though. If the script compiler detects an error in your code, it will abort the compilation but will not stop the program execution—rather, *it will use the existing compiled version if one exists.* This is an important point to remember. If you are changing your code, yet you don't see any change in behavior, then you should check the log file in console.log and look for any compile errors.

The log output is pretty verbose and should guide you to the problem area pretty quickly. It writes out a piece of code around the problem area and then inserts a pair of sharp characters ("##") on either side of the exact spot where the compiler thinks there is a problem.

Once you've fixed the first problem, don't assume you are done. Quite often, once one problem is fixed, the compiler marches on through the code and finds another problem. The compiler always aborts as soon as it encounters the first problem.

Of the large number of programming errors that the compiler catches and identifies, here are a few specific ones that frequently crop up:

- Missing semicolon at the end of a statement

- Missing a slash in double-slash comment operator

- Missing % or $ (scope prefix) from variable names

- Using uninitialized variables

- Mixing global and local scope prefixes

- Unbalanced parentheses or braces

In a later chapter we will cover how to use the console mode in Torque. That will give us access to three built-in Torque functions—echo, warn, and error—which are quite useful for debugging.

Without using those three functions, the best tool for debugging programs you've created is the echo statement. You should print out interim results throughout your code that will tell you how your program is progressing.

Tell you what—here is a different version of the TwotyFruity program. Type it in, and save it as \3D2E\demo\WormyFruit.cs. I've put five bugs in this version. See if you can spot them (in addition to any you might introduce while typing).

```
// =======================================================================
// WormyFruit.cs
//
// Buggy version of TwotyFruity. It has five known bugs in it.
// This program adds up the costs and quantities of selected fruit types
// and outputs the results to the display. This module is a variation
// of the FruitLoopy.cs module designed to demonstrate how to use
// functions.
// =======================================================================
```

```
function InitializeFruit()
// ------------------------------------------------------------------------
//    Set the starting values for our fruit arrays, and the type
//    indices
//
//    RETURNS: number of different types of fruit
//
// ------------------------------------------------------------------------
{
   numTypes = 5;    // so we know how many types are in our arrays
   $bananaIdx=0;    // initialize the values of our index variables
   $appleIdx=1;
   $orangeIdx=2;
   $mangoIdx=3;
   $pearIdx=3;

   $names[$bananaIdx] = "bananas"; // initialize the fruit name values
   $names[$appleIdx] = "apples";
   $names[$orangeIdx] = "oranges";
   $names[$mangoIdx] = "mangos";
   $names[$pearIdx] = "pears";

   $cost[$bananaIdx] = 1.15; // initialize the price values
   $cost[$appleIdx] = 0.55;
   $cost[$orangeIdx] = 0.55;
   $cost[$mangoIdx] = 1.90;
   $cost[$pearIdx] = 0.68;

   $quantity[$bananaIdx] = 1; // initialize the quantity values
   $quantity[$appleIdx]  = 3;
   $quantity[$orangeIdx] = 4;
   $quantity[$mangoIdx]  = 1;
   $quantity[$pearIdx]   = 2;

   return(%numTypes);
}

function addEmUp(%numFruitTypes)
// ------------------------------------------------------------------------
//    Add all prices of different fruit types to get a full total cost
//
//PARAMETERS: %numFruitTypes -the number of different fruit that are tracked
//
```

```
//    RETURNS: total cost of all fruit
//
// -----------------------------------------------------------------
{
  %total = 0;
  for (%index = 0; %index <= $numFruitTypes; %index++)
  {
    %total = %total + ($quantity[%index]*$cost[%index]);
  }
  return $total;
}



// -----------------------------------------------------------------
// countEm
//
//    Add all quantities of different fruit types to get a full total
//
//PARAMETERS: %numFruitTypes -the number of different fruit that are tracked
//
//    RETURNS: total of all fruit types
//
// -----------------------------------------------------------------
function countEm(%numFruitTypes)
{
  %total = 0;
  for (%index = 0; %index <= $numFruitTypes; %index++)
  {
    %total = %total + $quantity[%index];
  }
}

function runWormyFruit()
// -----------------------------------------------------------------
//    Entry point for program. This program adds up the costs
//    and quantities of selected fruit types and outputs the results to
//    the display. This program is a variation of the program FruitLoopy
//
// -----------------------------------------------------------------
{
  //
  // ---------------- Initialization ----------------
  //
```

```
%numFruitTypes=InitializeFruit(); // set up fruit arrays and variables
%numFruit=0      // always a good idea to initialize *all* variables!
%totalCost=0;    // (even if we know we are going to change them later)


//
// --------------- Computation --------------------
//

// Display the known statistics of the fruit collection
for (%index = 0; %index < %numFruitTypes; %index++)
{
echo("Cost of " @ $names[%index] @ ":$" @ $cost[%index]);
echo("Number of " @ $names[%index] @ ":" @ $quantity[%index]);
}

// count up all the pieces of fruit, and display that result
%numFruits = countEm(%numFruitTypes));
echo("Total pieces of Fruit:" @ %numFruit);

// now calculate the total cost
%totalCost = addEmUp(%numFruitTypes);
echo("Total Price of Fruit:$" @ %totalCost);
}
```

Run the program, and use the original TwotyFruity output as a specification to tell you whether or not this program is working correctly.

Best Practices

Programming is as much an art as it is anything else. There are often quite strenuous discussions between programmers about the best way to do certain things. However, there is consensus on a few practices that are considered to be good.

So take the following list as a guideline, and develop a style that is comfortable for you.

- Use module and function header comments to document your code.

- Sprinkle lots of commentary through your code, and make sure that it actually explains what is happening.

- Don't comment obvious things. Save the effort for the stuff that matters.

- Use white space (blank lines and spaces) to improve readability.

- Indent your code with readability in mind.

- Decompose large problems into small ones, and assault the small problems with functions.

- Organize your code into separate modules, and make sure the module file name is appropriate for the content, and vice versa.

- Restrict the number of lines of code you put in a module. Pick a size that suits you—about 1,000 lines should be near your upper limit.

- Use descriptive and meaningful variable names.

- While keeping your variable names descriptive, don't let the names get too long.

- Never embed tabs in code—use spaces instead. When you view your code later, you may have different tab settings, and therefore find the code hard to read. Using spaces guarantees that the visual appearance is consistent. Three spaces for an indent is a good number.

- Be consistent in your programming style decisions.

- Be alert to what programming decisions you make that work well for you, and try to consistently employ those techniques.

- Keep a change log of your work so you can keep track of the evolution of your programs.

- Use revision control software to manage your program versions.

Moving Right Along

You've now bitten off a fairly big chunk o' stuff. You've learned a new tool—in fact, a new *kind* of tool—the programmer's editor. After getting a handle on UltraEdit-32, we looked at how software does its thing bringing people and computer hardware together by using programming languages.

We then went off and started bullying the computer around using one of those programming languages called TorqueScript.

Coming up next, we'll delve into the world of 3D programming at a similar level and discover the basics of 3D objects and then how we can manipulate them with TorqueScript.

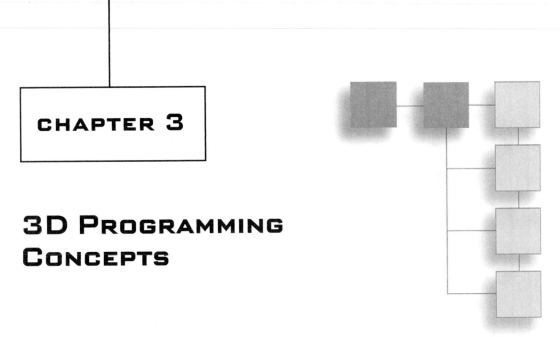

CHAPTER 3

3D PROGRAMMING CONCEPTS

In this chapter we will discuss how objects are described in their three dimensions in different 3D coordinate systems, as well as how we convert them for use in the 2D coordinate system of a computer display. There is some math involved here, but don't worry—I'll do the heavy lifting.

We'll also cover the stages and some of the components of the rendering pipeline—a conceptual way of thinking of the steps involved in converting an abstract mathematical model of an object into a beautiful on-screen picture.

3D Concepts

In the real world around us, we perceive objects to have measurements in three directions, or dimensions. Typically we say they have height, width, and depth. When we want to represent an object on a computer screen, we need to account for the fact that the person viewing the object is limited to perceiving only two actual dimensions: height, from the top to the bottom of the screen, and width, across the screen from left to right.

Note

> Remember that we will be using the Torque Game Engine to do most of the rendering work involved in creating our game with this book. However, a good understanding of the technology described in this section will help guide you in your decision making later on when you will be designing and building your own models or writing code to manipulate those models in real time.

Therefore, it's necessary to simulate the third dimension, depth "into" the screen. This on-screen three-dimensional (3D) simulation of a real (or imagined) object is called a *3D model*. In order to make the model more visually realistic, we add visual characteristics, such as shading, shadows, and textures. The entire process of calculating the appearance of the 3D model—converting it to an entity that can be drawn on a two-dimensional (2D) screen and then actually displaying the resulting image—is called *rendering*.

Coordinate Systems

When we refer to the dimensional measurement of an object, we use number groups called *coordinates* to mark each *vertex* (corner) of the object. We commonly use the variable names X, Y, and Z to represent each of the three dimensions in each coordinate group, or triplet. There are different ways to organize the meaning of the coordinates, known as *coordinate systems*.

We have to decide which of our variables will represent which dimension—height, width, or depth—and in what order we intend to reference them. Then we need to decide where the zero point is for these dimensions and what it means in relation to our object. Once we have done all that, we will have defined our coordinate system.

When we think about 3D objects, each of the directions is represented by an *axis*, the infinitely long line of a dimension that passes through the zero point. Width or left-right is usually the X-axis, height or up-down is usually the Y-axis, and depth or near-far is usually the Z-axis. Using these constructs, we have ourselves a nice tidy little *XYZ-axis system*, as shown in Figure 3.1.

Now, when we consider a single object in isolation, the 3D space it occupies is called *object space*. The point in object space where X, Y, and Z are all 0 is normally the *geometric center* of an object. The geometric center of an object is usually inside the object. If positive X values are to the right, positive Y values are up, and positive Z values are away from you, then as you can see in Figure 3.2, the coordinate system is called *left-handed*.

The Torque Game Engine uses a slightly different coordinate system, a *right-handed* one. In this system, with Y and Z oriented the same as we saw in the left-handed system, X is positive in the opposite direction. In what some people call *Computer Graphics Aerobics*, we can use the thumb, index finger, and middle finger of our hands to easily figure out the handedness of the system we are using

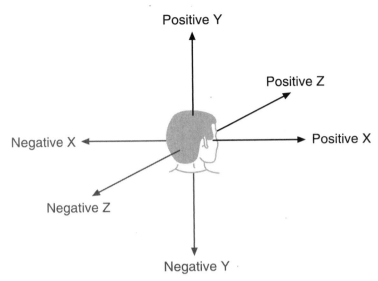

Figure 3.1
XYZ-axis system.

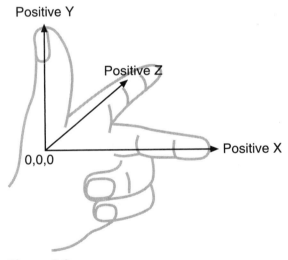

Figure 3.2
Left-handed coordinate system with vertical Y-axis.

(see Figure 3.3). Just remember that using this technique, the thumb is always the Y-axis, the index finger is the Z-axis, and the middle finger is the X-axis.

With Torque, we also orient the system in a slightly different way: the Z-axis is up-down, the X-axis is somewhat left-right, and the Y-axis is somewhat near-far (see Figure 3.4). Actually, *somewhat* means that we specify left and right in terms

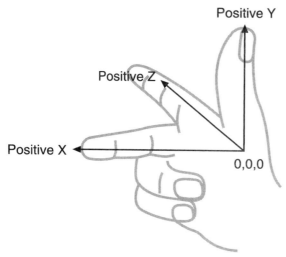

Figure 3.3
Right-handed coordinate system with vertical Y-axis.

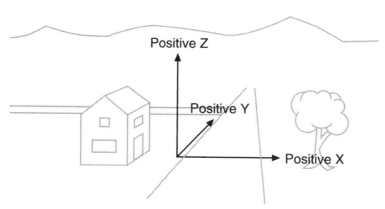

Figure 3.4
Right-handed coordinate system with vertical Z-axis depicting world space.

of looking down on a map from above, with north at the top of the map. Right and left (positive and negative X) are east and west, respectively, and it follows that positive Y refers to north and negative Y refers to south. Don't forget that positive Z would be up, and negative Z would be down. This is a right-handed system that orients the axes to align with the way we would look at the world using a map from above. By specifying that the zero point for all three axes is a specific location on the map, and by using the coordinate system with the orientation just described, we have defined our *world space*.

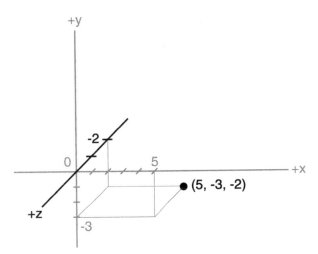

Figure 3.5
A point specified using an XYZ coordinate triplet.

Now that we have a coordinate system, we can specify any location on an object or in a world using a coordinate triplet, such as (5,−3,−2) (see Figure 3.5). By convention, this would be interpreted as X=5, Y=−3, Z=−2. A 3D triplet is always specified in XYZ format.

Take another peek at Figure 3.5. Notice anything? That's right—the Y-axis is vertical with the positive values above the 0, and the Z-axis positive side is toward us. It is still a right-handed coordinate system. The right-handed system with *Y-up* orientation is often used for modeling objects in isolation, and of course we call it *object space*, as described earlier. We are going to be working with this orientation and coordinate system for the next little while.

3D Models

I previously briefly touched on the idea that we can simulate, or model, any object by defining its shape in terms of its significant *vertices* (plural for *vertex*). Let's take a closer look, by starting with a simple 3D shape, or *primitive*—the cube—as depicted in Figure 3.6.

The cube's dimensions are two units wide by two units deep by two units high, or 2 × 2 × 2. In this drawing, shown in object space, the geometric center is offset to a position outside the cube. I've done this in order to make it clearer what is happening in the drawing, despite my statement earlier that geometric centers

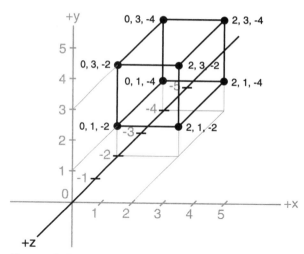

Figure 3.6
Simple cube shown in a standard XYZ-axis chart.

are usually located inside an object. There are times when exceptions are not only possible but necessary—as in this case.

Examining the drawing, we can see the object's shape and its dimensions quite clearly. The lower-left-front corner of the cube is located at the position where X=0, Y=1, and Z=−2. As an exercise, take some time to locate all of the other vertices (corners) of the cube, and note their coordinates.

If you haven't already noticed on your own, there is more information in the drawing than actually needed. Can you see how we can plot the coordinates by using the guidelines to find the positions on the axes of the vertices? But we can also see the actual coordinates of the vertices drawn right in the chart. We don't need to do both. The axis lines with their index tick marks and values really clutter up the drawing, so it has become somewhat accepted in computer graphics to not bother with these indices. Instead we try to use the minimum amount of information necessary to completely depict the object.

We only really need to state whether the object is in object space or world space and indicate the raw coordinates of each vertex. We should also connect the vertices with lines that indicate the edges.

If you take a look at Figure 3.7 you will see how easy it is to extract the sense of the shape, compared to the drawing in Figure 3.6. We specify which space definition we are using by the small XYZ-axis notation. The color code indicates the axis

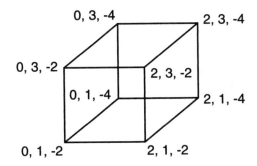

0, 3, -4   2, 3, -4

0, 3, -2   2, 3, -2

0, 1, -4   2, 1, -4

0, 1, -2   2, 1, -2

Figure 3.7
Simple cube with reduced XYZ-axis key.

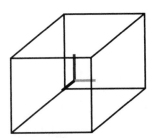

Figure 3.8
Simple cube with axis key at geometric center.

name, and the axis lines are drawn only for the positive directions. Different modeling tools use different color codes, but in this book dark yellow (shown as light gray) is the X-axis, dark cyan (medium gray) is the Y-axis, and dark magenta (dark gray) is the Z-axis. It is also common practice to place the XYZ-axis key at the geometric center of the model.

Figure 3.8 shows our cube with the geometric center placed where it reasonably belongs when dealing with an object in object space.

Now take a look at Figure 3.9. It is obviously somewhat more complex than our simple cube, but you are now armed with everything you need to know in order to understand it. It is a screen shot of a four-view drawing from the popular shareware modeling tool MilkShape 3D, in which a 3D model of a soccer ball was created.

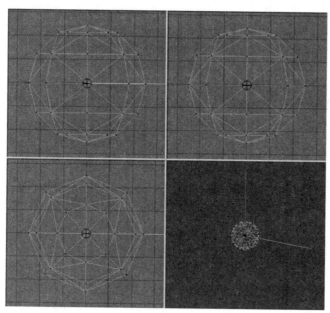

Figure 3.9
Screen shot of sphere model.

In the figure, the vertices are marked with red dots (which show as black in the picture), and the edges are marked with light gray lines. The axis keys are visible, although barely so in some views because they are obscured by the edge lines. Notice the grid lines that are used to help with aligning parts of the model. The three views with the gray background and grid lines are 2D construction views, while the fourth view, in the lower-right corner, is a 3D projection of the object. The upper-left view looks down from above, with the Y-axis in the vertical direction and the X-axis in the horizontal direction. The Z-axis in that view is not visible. The upper-right view is looking at the object from the front, with the Y-axis vertical and the Z-axis horizontal; there is no X-axis. The lower-left view shows the Z-axis vertically and the X-axis horizontally with no Y-axis. In the lower-right view, the axis key is quite evident, as its lines protrude from the model.

3D Shapes

We've already encountered some of the things that make up 3D models. Now it's time to round out that knowledge.

As we've seen, vertices define the shape of a 3D model. We connect the vertices with lines known as *edges*. If we connect three or more vertices with edges to create a closed figure, we've created a *polygon*. The simplest polygon is a triangle.

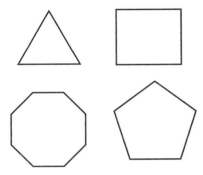

Figure 3.10
Polygons of varying complexity.

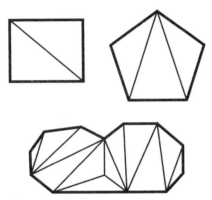

Figure 3.11
Polygons decomposed into triangle meshes.

In modern 3D accelerated graphics adapters, the hardware is designed to manipulate and display millions and millions of triangles in a second. Because of this capability in the adapters, we normally construct our models out of the simple triangle polygons instead of the more complex polygons, such as rectangles or pentagons (see Figure 3.10).

By happy coincidence, triangles are more than up to the task of modeling complex 3D shapes. Any complex polygon can be decomposed into a collection of triangles, commonly called a *mesh* (see Figure 3.11).

The area of the model is known as the *surface*. The polygonal surfaces are called *facets*—or at least that is the traditional name. These days, they are more commonly called *faces*. Sometimes a surface can only be viewed from one side, so when you are looking at it from its "invisible" side, it's called a *hidden surface* or

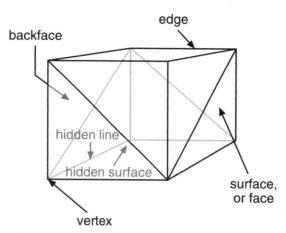

Figure 3.12
The parts of a 3D shape.

hidden face. A *double-sided face* can be viewed from either side. The edges of hidden surfaces are called *hidden lines*. With most models, there are faces on the backside of the model, facing away from us, called *backfaces* (see Figure 3.12). As mentioned, most of the time when we talk about faces in game development, we are talking about triangles, sometimes shortened to *tris*.

Displaying 3D Models

After we have defined a model of a 3D object of interest, we may want to display a view of it. The models are created in object space, but to display them in the 3D world, we need to convert them to world space coordinates. This requires three conversion steps beyond the actual creation of the model in object space.

1. Convert to world space coordinates.

2. Convert to view coordinates.

3. Convert to screen coordinates.

Each of these conversions involves mathematical operations performed on the object's vertices.

The first step is accomplished by the process called *transformation*. Step 2 is what we call *3D rendering*. Step 3 describes what is known as *2D rendering*. First we will examine what the steps do for us, before getting into the gritty details.

Transformation

This first conversion, to world space coordinates, is necessary because we have to place our object somewhere! We call this conversion *transformation*. We will indicate where by applying transformations to the object: a *scale* operation (which controls the object's size), a *rotation* (which sets orientation), and a *translation* (which sets location).

World space transformations assume that the object starts with a transformation of (1.0,1.0,1.0) for scaling, (0,0,0) for rotation, and (0,0,0) for translation.

Every object in a 3D world can have its own 3D transformation values, often simply called *transforms*, that will be applied when the world is being prepared for rendering.

Tip

Other terms used for these kinds of XYZ coordinates in world space are *Cartesian coordinates* or *rectangular coordinates.*

Scaling

We scale objects based upon a triplet of scale factors where 1.0 indicates a scale of 1:1.

The scale operation is written similarly to the XYZ coordinates that are used to denote the transformation, except that the scale operation shows how the size of the object has changed. Values greater than 1.0 indicate that the object will be made larger, and values less than 1.0 (but greater than 0) indicate that the object will shrink.

For example, 2.0 will double a given dimension, 0.5 will halve it, and a value of 1.0 means no change. Figure 3.13 shows a scale operation performed on a cube in

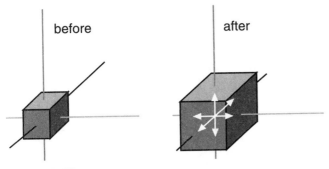

Figure 3.13
Scaling.

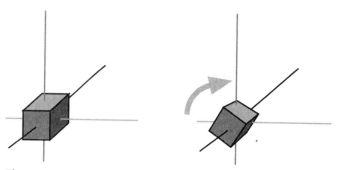

Figure 3.14
Rotation.

object space. The original scale values are (1.0,1.0,1.0). After scaling, the cube is 1.6 times larger in all three dimensions, and the values are (1.6,1.6,1.6).

Rotation

The rotation is written in the same way that XYZ coordinates are used to denote the transformation, except that the rotation shows how much the object is rotated around each of its three axes. In this book, rotations will be specified using a triplet of degrees as the unit of measure. In other contexts, radians might be the unit of measure used. Other methods of representing rotations are used in more complex situations, but this is the way we'll do it in this book. Figure 3.14 depicts a cube being rotated by 30 degrees around the Y-axis in its object space.

It is important to realize that the order of the rotations applied to the object matters a great deal. The convention we will use is the *roll-pitch-yaw* method, adopted from the aviation community. When we rotate the object, we roll it around its longitudinal (Z) axis. Then we pitch it around the lateral (X) axis. Finally, we yaw it around the vertical (Y) axis. Rotations on the object are applied in object space.

If we apply the rotation in a different order, we can end up with a very different orientation, despite having done the rotations using the same values.

Translation

Translation is the simplest of the transformations and the last that is applied to the object when transforming from object space to world space. Figure 3.15 shows a translation operation performed on an object. Note that the vertical axis is dark gray. As I said earlier, in this book, dark gray represents the Z-axis. Try to

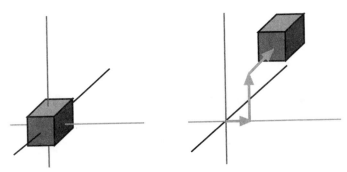

Figure 3.15
Translation.

figure out what coordinate system we are using here. I'll tell you later in the chapter. To translate an object, we apply a vector to its position coordinates. Vectors can be specified in different ways, but the notation we will use is the same as the XYZ triplet, called a *vector triplet*. For Figure 3.15, the vector triplet is (3,9,7). This indicates that the object will be moved three units in the positive X direction, nine units in the positive Y direction, and seven units in the positive Z direction. Remember that this translation is applied in world space, so the X direction in this case would be eastward, and the Z direction would be down (toward the ground, so to speak). Neither the orientation nor the size of the object is changed.

Full Transformation

So now we roll all the operations together. We want to orient the cube a certain way, with a certain size, at a certain location. The transformations applied are scale (s)=1.6,1.6,1.6, followed by rotation (r)=0,30,0, and then finally translation (t)=3,9,7. Figure 3.16 shows the process.

Note

The order that we use to apply the transformations is important. In the great majority of cases, the correct order is scaling, rotation, and then translation. The reason is that different things happen depending on the order.

You will recall that objects are created in object space and then moved into world space. The object's origin is placed at the world origin. When we rotate the object, we rotate it around the appropriate axes with the origin at (0,0,0) and then translate it to its new position.

If you translate the object first and then rotate it (which is still going to take place around (0,0,0)), the object will end up in an entirely different position, as you can see in Figure 3.17.

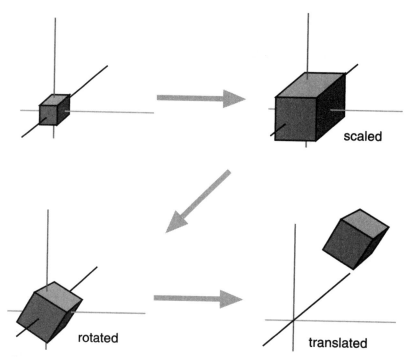

Figure 3.16
Fully transforming the cube.

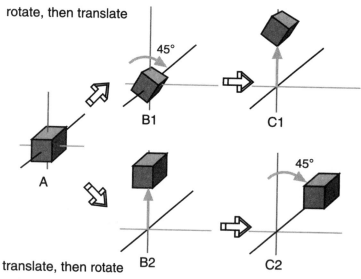

Figure 3.17
Changing the transformation order.

Rendering

Rendering is the process of converting the 3D mathematical model of an object into an on-screen 2D image. When we render an object, our primary task is to calculate the appearance of the different faces of the object, convert those faces into a 2D form, and send the result to the video card, which will then take all the steps needed to display the object on your monitor.

We will take a look at several different rendering techniques—those that are often used in video game engines or 3D video cards. There are other techniques, such as ray-casting, that aren't in wide use in computer games (with the odd exception, of course); we won't be covering the less-common techniques here.

In the previous sections our simple cube model had colored faces. In case you haven't noticed (but I'm sure you did notice), we haven't covered the issue of the faces, except briefly in passing.

A *face* is essentially a set of one or more contiguous coplanar adjacent triangles; that is, when taken as a whole, the triangles form a single flat surface. If you refer back to Figure 3.12, you will see that each face of the cube is made with two triangles. Of course, the faces are transparent in order to present the other parts of the cube.

Flat Shading

Figure 3.18 provides an example of various face configurations on an irregularly shaped object. Each face is presented with a different color (each visible as a

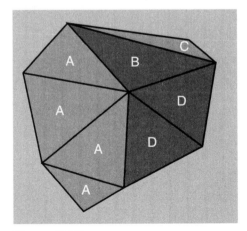

Figure 3.18
Faces on an irregularly shaped object.

different shade). All triangles with the label A are part of the same face; the same applies to the D triangles. The triangles labeled B and C are each single-triangle faces.

When we want to display 3D objects, we usually use some technique to apply color to the faces. The simplest method is *flat shading*, as used in Figure 3.18. A color or shade is applied to a face, and a different color or shade is applied to adjacent faces so that the user can tell them apart. In this case, the shades were selected with the sole criterion being the need to distinguish one face from the other.

One particular variation of flat shading is called *Z-flat shading*. The basic idea is that the farther a face is from the viewer, the darker or lighter the face.

Lambert Shading

Usually color and shading are applied in a manner that implies some sense of depth and lighted space. One face or collection of faces will be lighter in shade, implying that the direction they face has a light source. On the opposite side of the object, faces are shaded to imply that no light, or at least less light, reaches those faces. In between the light and dark faces, the faces are shaded with intermediate values. The result is a shaded object where the face shading provides information that imparts a sense of the object in a 3D world, enhancing the illusion. This is a form of flat shading known as *lambert shading* (see Figure 3.19).

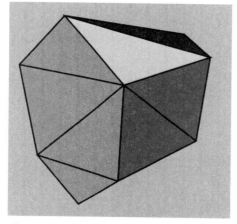

Figure 3.19
Lambert-shaded object.

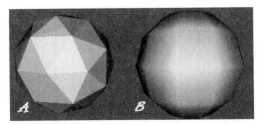

Figure 3.20
Flat-shaded (A) and gouraud-shaded (B) spheres.

Gouraud Shading

A more useful way to color or shade an object is called *gouraud shading*. Take a look at Figure 3.20. The sphere on the left (A) is flat shaded, while the sphere on the right (B) is gouraud shaded. Gouraud shading smoothes the colors by averaging the *normals* (the vectors that indicate which way surfaces are facing) of the vertices of a surface. The normals are used to modify the color value of all the pixels in a face. Each pixel's color value is then modified to account for the pixel's position within the face. Gouraud shading creates a much more natural appearance for the object, doesn't it? Gouraud shading is commonly used in both software and hardware rendering systems.

Phong Shading

Phong shading is a much more sophisticated—and computation-intensive—technique for rendering a 3D object. Like gouraud shading, it calculates color or shade values for each pixel. Unlike gouraud shading (which uses only the vertices' normals to calculate average pixel values), phong shading computes additional normals for each pixel between vertices and then calculates the new color values. Phong shading does a remarkably better job (see Figure 3.21), but at a substantial cost.

Phong shading requires a great deal of processing for even a simple scene, which is why you don't see phong shading used much in real-time 3D games where frame rate performance is important. However, there are games made where frame rate is not as big an issue, in which case you will often find phong shading used.

Fake Phong Shading

There is a rendering technique that looks almost as good as phong shading but can allow fast frame rates. It's called *fake phong shading*, or sometimes *fast phong*

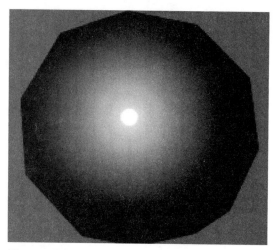

Figure 3.21
Phong-shaded sphere.

Figure 3.22
Example of a fake phong highlight map.

shading, or sometimes even *phong approximation rendering*. Whatever name it goes by, it is *not* phong rendering. It is useful, however, and does indeed give good performance.

Fake phong shading basically employs a bitmap, which is variously known as a *phong map*, a *highlight map*, a *shade map*, or a *light map*. I'm sure there are other names for it as well. In any event, the bitmap is nothing more than a generic template of how the faces should be illuminated (as shown in Figure 3.22).

As you can tell by the nomenclature, there is no real consensus about fake phong shading. There are also several different algorithms used by different people. This diversity is no doubt the result of several people independently arriving at the

Figure 3.23
Texture-mapped and gouraud-shaded cube.

same general concept at roughly the same time—all in search of better performance with high-quality shading.

Texture Mapping

Texture mapping is covered in more detail in Chapters 8 and 9. For the sake of completeness, I'll just say here that *texture mapping* an object is something like wallpapering a room. A 2D bitmap is "draped" over the object, to impart detail and texture upon the object, as shown in Figure 3.23.

Texture mapping is usually combined with one of the shading techniques covered in this chapter.

Shaders

When the word is used alone, *shaders* refers to *shader programs* that are sent to the video hardware by the software graphics engine. These programs tell the video card in great detail how to manipulate vertices or pixels depending on the kind of shader used.

Traditionally, programmers have had limited control over what happens to vertices and pixels in hardware, but the introduction of shaders allowed them to take complete control.

Vertex shaders, being easier to implement, were first out of the starting blocks. The shader program on the video card manipulates vertex data values on a 3D plane via mathematical operations on an object's vertices. The operations affect color, texture coordinates, elevation-based fog density, point size, and spatial orientation.

Pixel shaders are the conceptual siblings of vertex shaders, but they operate on each discrete viewable pixel. Pixel shaders are small programs that tell the video card how to manipulate pixel values. They rely on data from vertex shaders (either the engine-specific custom shader or the default video card shader function) to provide at least triangle, light, and view normals.

Shaders are used in addition to other rendering operations, such as texture and normal mapping.

Bump Mapping

Bump mapping is similar to texture mapping. Where texture maps *add* detail to a shape, bump maps *enhance* the shape detail. Each pixel of the bump map contains information that describes aspects of the physical shape of the object at the corresponding point, and we use a more expansive word to describe this—the *texel*. The name *texel* derives from *texture pixel*.

Bump mapping gives the illusion of the presence of bumps, holes, carving, scales, and other small surface irregularities. If you think of a brick wall, a texture map will provide the shape, color, and approximate roughness of the bricks. The bump map will supply a detailed sense of the roughness of the brick, the mortar, and other details. Thus bump mapping enhances the close-in sense of the object, while texture mapping enhances the sense of the object from farther away.

Bump mapping is used in conjunction with most of the other rendering techniques.

Environment Mapping

Environment mapping is similar to texture mapping, except that it is used to represent effects where environmental features are reflected in the surfaces of an object. Things like chrome bumpers on cars, windows, and other shiny object surfaces are prime candidates for environment mapping.

Mipmapping

Mipmapping is a way of reducing the amount of computation needed to accurately texture-map an image onto a polygon. It's a rendering technique that tweaks the visual appearance of an object. It does this by using several different textures for the texture-mapping operations on an object. At least two, but usually four, textures of progressively lower resolution are assigned to any given

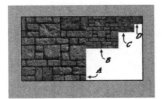

Figure 3.24
Mipmap textures for a stone surface.

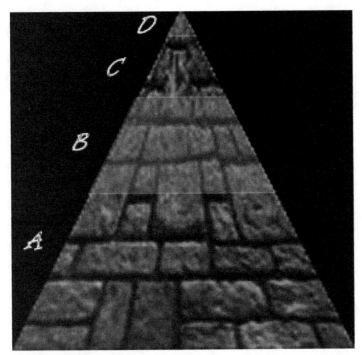

Figure 3.25
Mipmap textures in perspective view.

surface, as shown in Figure 3.24. The video card or graphics engine extracts pixels from each texture depending on the distance and orientation of the surface compared to the view screen.

In the case of a flat surface that recedes away from the viewer into the distance, for the nearer parts of the surface, pixels from the high-resolution texture are used (see Figure 3.25). For the middle distances, pixels from the medium-resolution textures are used. Finally, for the faraway parts of the surface, pixels from the low-resolution texture are used.

Normal Mapping

Normal mapping is a further enhancement of bump mapping. With normal mapping what we are doing, in essence, is transferring detail from a very high poly model to a low poly model using a bitmap gradient. This allows us to provide an astonishing sense of detail with very fast rendering speeds.

The basic procedure is to first create a very high polygon model of an object. Now, when I say very high, I mean just that: four or five _million_ polygons. Yeah, 5,000,000—_that_ high. We then make a rendered lighting pass on that object in our modeling tool and "bake" (preserve) the normals shading of the object in a bitmap very similar to the UV mapped texture bitmap for the object. Because what we are preserving is basically a graphical representation of the normals of all of the polygons in the high poly model, the data we save is called the _normal map_.

We then create a low poly (in the 2,000-polygon range, give or take 500 or 1,000 polygons) model and apply the normal map to the new model. The pixel values in the normal map are used to assign brightness values to the pixels of the texture map, with almost photorealistic results at times.

Parallax Mapping

Upping the ante even further, _parallax mapping_ is yet another evolutionary step beyond bump mapping.

With parallax mapping, we can create the illusion of holes and protrusions in flat surfaces, without adding polygons. A parallax map image is pretty well identical to a bump map, but it is used in rendering in a much more dramatic way.

Try this experiment. Set a drinking glass or cup on a table, and stand above it. Look straight down at the glass. You will obviously see the circular shape of the glass—in fact, you will probably see a series of concentric rings: the inside and outside of the opening rim, the inside and outside of the base, and so on. And in the background is the surface of the table. Now move your head to one side, while keeping your eyes on the glass. The shapes all change, even though the glass hasn't moved. The background is still the table. Eventually, as you move your head farther from the glass, the table stops being the background, starting at the top of the glass. The edge of the table "moves" down the glass toward the base. You can hasten this effect by moving your head toward the plane of the table.

Imagine now that those concentric rings that you started with were simply pixels on a bitmap, but whose values indicate a distance from the plane of a polygon (the table). Parallax-mapping software calculates *where* those pixels would be rendered as you move your head sideways, re-creating the changing appearance—in a 3D manner—of the glass. And yet there are no extra polygons involved! This is a simulation of the parallax effect—the apparent change of position of an object in space when viewed from a different location, even though the object hasn't moved. The apparent change becomes visible only when the object is viewed against a static background. In the case of the little experiment I told you to do (you did do it, right?), the table is the static background.

Now when you move your head closer to the table, off to one side, or you move your head far enough away from the glass, eventually you will see that the glass really does protrude up from the table. With parallax mapping and a rendered glass, if you do the same thing, you will see the pixels of the rendered glass get squashed together and never leave the bounds of the polygon on which they are mapped. Because they can't—they are part of the polygon! But this effect is really only visible in extreme situations that usually aren't noticeable when you are engaged in mortal combat with a room full of electro-ninjas.

The effect is most satisfying when the parallax-mapped objects are crossing the viewer's field of view, like when your character is walking past a series of large bullet holes or craters in a wall. Whole factories filled with pipes and machinery and valves and stuff can be rendered this way, with very little or no actual polygon budget penalties. In fact, large buckets of polygon budget can be recovered using this technique! And those polygons that were once used to create a maze of pipes and cables can now be better put to use in populating the scene with more nasty electro-ninjas.

Scene Graphs

In addition to knowing how to construct and render 3D objects, 3D engines need to know how the objects are laid out in the virtual world and how to keep track of changes in the status of the models, their orientation, and other dynamic

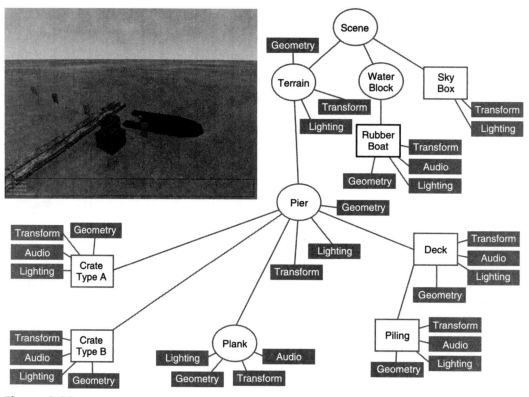

Figure 3.26
Simple scene graph.

information. This is done using a mechanism called a *scene graph*, a specialized form of a *directed graph*. The scene graph maintains information about all entities in the virtual world in structures called *nodes*. The 3D engine traverses this graph, examining each node one at a time to determine how to render each entity in the world. Figure 3.26 shows a simple seaside scene with its scene graph. The nodes marked by ovals are *group nodes*, which contain information about themselves and point to other nodes. The nodes that use rectangles are *leaf nodes*. These nodes contain only information about themselves.

Note that in the seaside scene graph, not all of the nodes contain all of the information that the other nodes have about themselves.

Many of the entities in a scene don't even need to be rendered. In a scene graph, a node can be anything. The most common entity types are 3D shapes, sounds, lights (or lighting information), fog and other environmental effects, viewpoints, and event triggers.

When it comes time to render the scene, the Torque Engine will "walk" through the nodes in the tree of the scene graph, applying whatever functions to the node that are specified. It then uses the node pointers to move on to the next node to be rendered.

3D Audio

Audio and sound effects are used to heighten the sense of realism in a game. There are times when the illusion is greatly enhanced by using position information when generating the sound effects. A straightforward example would be the sound generated by a nearby gunshot. By calculating the amplitude—based on how far away the shot occurred—and the direction, the game software can present the sound to a computer's speakers in a way that gives the player a strong sense of where the shot occurred. This effect is even better if the player is wearing audio headphones. The player then has a good sense of the nature of any nearby threat and can deal with it accordingly—usually by massive application of return fire.

The source location of a game sound is tracked and managed in the same way as any other 3D entity via the scene graph.

Once the game engine has decided that the sound has been triggered, it then converts the location and distance information of the sound into a stereo "image" of the sound, with appropriate volume and balance for either the right or left stereo channel. The methods used to perform these calculations are much the same as those used for 3D object rendering.

Audio has an additional set of complications—things like fade and drop-off or cutoff.

3D Programming

With the Torque Engine, most of the really grubby low-level programming is done for you. Instead of writing program code to construct a 3D object, you use a modeling tool (which we cover in later chapters) to create your object and a few lines of script code to insert the object in a scene. You don't even need to worry about where in the scene graph the object should be inserted—Torque handles that as well, through the use of information contained in the datablocks that you define for objects.

Even functions like moving objects around in the world are handled for us by Torque, simply by defining the object to be of a certain class and then inserting the object appropriately.

The kinds of objects we will normally be using are called *shapes*. In general, shapes in Torque are considered to be dynamic objects that can move or otherwise be manipulated by the engine at run time.

There are many shape classes. Some are fairly specific, like vehicles, players, weapons, and projectiles. Some are more general-purpose classes, like items and static shapes. Many of the classes know how their objects should respond to game stimuli and are able to respond in the game with motion or some other behavior inherent to the object's class definition.

Usually, you will let the game engine worry about the low-level mechanics of moving your 3D objects around the game world. However, there will probably be times while creating a game that you are going to want to cause objects to move in some nonstandard way—some method not defined by the class definition of the object. With Torque, this is easy to do!

Programmed Translation

When an object in 3D world space moves, it is *translating* its position in a manner similar to that shown earlier in the discussion about transformations.

You don't, however, absolutely need to use the built-in classes to manipulate shapes in your game world. For example, you can write code to load in an Interior (a class of objects used for structures like buildings) or an Item (a class of objects used for smaller mobile and static items in a game world, like signs, boxes, and powerups). You can then move that object around the world any way you like.

You can also write code to monitor the location of dynamic shapes that are moving around in the world, detect when they reach a certain location, and then arbitrarily move, or *teleport*, those objects to some other location.

Simple Direct Movement

What we are going to do is select an object in a 3D scene in Torque using the Mission Editor and then move it from one location to another using some script instructions entered directly into the game console. The first step is to identify the object.

1. Run the Torque demo by double-clicking the demo.exe file (the Torque demo executable) as you did for the exercises in Chapter 2, and click the mouse button once when the GarageGames splash screen appears.

2. When the main menu appears, press the Example: FPS Multiplayer button. It's the second one from the bottom.

3. On the next screen (Play Demo Game), make sure that the Create Server check box has a check mark in it. You can also put a name for your player in the Player Name box, but it isn't absolutely necessary.

4. Press the button with the right arrow in it, located at lower left of the screen. This will launch the demo. Note: the left arrow button will return you to the main menu.

Tip

You should make sure you remember steps 1 to 4 in the "Simple Direct Movement" section. These steps describe how to launch the Torque demo. At later points in the book when you see that I've written "launch the Torque demo" somewhere in a procedure, it's these four steps that I intend for you to follow. Yeah, I know. I'm lazy.

5. After you've spawned into the game, run over to where you can see the Great Hall structure (see Figure 3.27). Use Table 3.1 as a guide to the movement keys in the demo.

Table 3.1 Torque Demo Movement and Action Keys

Key	Description
w	Run forward
s	Run backward
a	Run (strafe) left
d	Run (strafe) right
spacebar	Jump
F11	Open Mission Editor
Tilde	Open console

Figure 3.27
The Great Hall.

6. Using the mouse, turn your player-character to the left or right a bit, if necessary, until you have a good view of the Great Hall.

7. Press F11. Torque's built-in World Editor will appear. As you move your cursor over the Great Hall, you'll notice it change to a hand icon.

8. Click the hand on the Great Hall to select it.

9. Move the cursor over to the right side, and click once on the plus sign to the left of the words "MissionGroup—SimGroup". You will see the list expand, and one of the folders that becomes visible will be called "Buildings— SimGroup". Expand this folder and you should see that the first entry, of the type InteriorInstance, will be highlighted with a padlock icon in green on the left. Take note of the number to the right of the padlock; this is the object's instance ID. See Figure 3.28 for help, if necessary. From the figure I get the object ID 1643, located just below and to the left of the key icon, and also in the highlighted entry in the list; your result might be the same but could very well be different.

10. After noting the Great Hall's entry highlighted in the upper-right panel, move your attention to the lower-right panel, where the properties of the

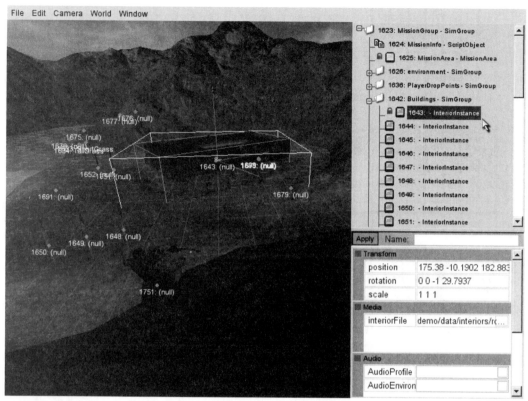

Figure 3.28
Finding the Great Hall object's instance ID.

Great Hall are located. Scroll this panel down until you come to a section called "Dynamic Fields". In here you will find a property called "locked" set to true. To the left of the property is a little trash can; click it, and the locked property will vanish. The Great Hall is now in a state where we can abuse it.

11. Press the Tilde ("~") key, and the console will pop open. The console interface allows us to directly type in program code and get immediate results.

12. In the console window, type **echo(1643.getTransform());** and then press the Enter key. Don't forget to include the semicolon at the end of the line before you press the Enter key.
    You should get a result like 175.38 −10.1902 182.883 0 0 −1 0.519998, which is the transform of the Great Hall. The first three numbers are the

XYZ coordinates of the geometric center of the structure. The next three are the axis normals, which in this case indicates that the Z-axis is pointing straight up. The final value indicates how much rotation is applied around the rotation axes. We'll look at rotation in more detail a little later. Here, the rotation amount (in radians) is applied to only the Z-axis.

Tip

You should note that when you read the rotation angle of an object in the World Editor Inspector, the value for the rotation is given in degrees. However, when you run the `getTransform` method for an object, the rotation value is returned in radians. To convert between the two, 1 radian equals 57.2957795 degrees, and 1 degree equals 0.017453293 radian.

13. In the console window, type **1643.setTransform("200 0 200 1 0 0 0");** and then press the Enter key.

14. Press the Tilde key to remove the console window, and take a look. You will notice that the Great Hall has moved.

15. Take the next several minutes to experiment with different transforms. Try rotating the structure around different axes or several axes at the same time.

16. When you are done, press the Tilde key to exit the console window, press Escape to exit the World Editor, and then press Escape one more time to exit the game.

Tip

In the little exercise in the "Simple Direct Movement" section, you saw a command that looked like this: `echo(1643.getTransform() );`. The number 1643 is an object ID, and the `getTransform()` part is what is called a *method* of that object. A method is a function that belongs to a specific object *class*. We'll cover these topics in more detail in a later chapter.

Programmed Movement

Now we are going to explore how we can move things in the 3D world using program code. We are going to use the StaticShape class to create an object based on a model of a stylized heart, insert the object in the game world, and then start it slowly moving across the terrain—all using TorqueScript.

Okay, now—so on to the program. Type the following code module into a file, and save the file as \3D2E\demo\moveshape.cs.

```
// ================================================================
// moveshape.cs
//
// This module contains a function for moving a specified shape.
// ================================================================

function MoveShape(%shape, %dist)
// ----------------------------------------------------------------
//     moves the %shape by %dist amount
// ----------------------------------------------------------------
{
  echo ("MoveShape: shape id: ", %shape);
  echo ("MoveShape: distance: ", %dist);
  %xfrm = %shape.getTransform();
  %1x = getword(%xfrm,0); // get the current transform values
  %1y = getword(%xfrm,1);
  %1z = getword(%xfrm,2);
  %1x += %dist;               // adjust the x axis position
  %shape.setTransform(%1x SPC %1y SPC %1z SPC "0 0 1 0");
  echo ("MoveShape: done.");
}
```

In this module there is one function that does all of the work. The function MoveShape accepts a shape handle (or instance ID number) and a distance as arguments. It then uses these to move whatever shape the handle points to.

First, there are a couple of echo statements that print, out to the console, the shape's handle and then the distance it will be moved.

Second, the code gets the current position of the shape using the %shape.getTransform method of the Item class.

Next, the program employs the getword function to extract the parts of the transform string that are of interest and store them in local variables. We do this because, for this particular program, we want to move the shape in the X-axis. Therefore, we strip out all three axes and increment the X value by the distance that the object should move. Then we prepend all three axis values to a dummy rotation and set the item's transform to be this new string value. This last bit is done with the %shape.setTransform statement.

Finally, another echo statement hurls out to the console the basic bit of information that the module is done.

This MoveShape function acts something like a wrapper folded around the other statements. Obviously, it saves us having to type the same set of statements over and over to move different shapes different amounts at different times.

To use the program, follow these steps:

1. Make sure you've saved the file as \3D2E\demo\moveshape.cs.

2. Run the Torque FPS demo.

3. Open the console and type in the following, making sure you press Enter after the semicolon:

```
exec("demo/moveshape.cs");
```

   You should get a response in the console window similar to this:

```
Compiling demo/moveshape.cs...
Loading compiled script demo/moveshape.cs.
```

   This means that the Torque Engine has compiled your program and then loaded it into memory. The function you defined is now in memory, waiting with barely suppressed anticipation for your next instruction.

Tip

About those slashes . . . I just want to re-emphasize that when you see the file names and paths written out, the backslash ("\") is used, and when you type in those same paths in the console window, the forward slash ("/") is used. This is not a mistake. Torque is a cross-platform program that is available for Macintosh and Linux as well as Windows. It's only on Windows-based systems that backslashes are used—everyone else uses forward slashes.

Therefore, the backslashes for Windows-based paths are the exception here. Just thought I'd point that out again, if it's not burned into your brain yet!

4. Next, make sure that the Great Hall object in the scene is unlocked. Whip on back to the "Simple Direct Movement" section to refresh your memory about locking and unlocking shapes, if necessary. You will also need to obtain the Great Hall's instance ID—again, the "Simple Direct Movement" section covers this.
   You should be familiar with opening and closing the console window by now, so I won't bother explaining that part in the instruction sequences anymore.

5. Type the following into the console window:

```
$gh=nnnn;
```

where nnnn is the instance ID number of the Great Hall. This will save that ID in the global variable $gh so that you don't have to remember the number. Note that the variable will be saved only as long as the engine is running. Once you quit Torque, the value and the variable are lost.

6. Type the following into the console window:
   ```
   MoveShape($gh,50);
   ```

7. Close the console window. You should see that the hall has moved away from its original location toward the "east" (positive Y).

Go ahead and experiment with the program. Try moving the Great Hall through several axes at once, or try changing the distance. Also attack some of the other items in the scene with your new software weapon.

Programmed Rotation

As you've probably figured out already, we can rotate an object programmatically (or directly, for that matter) using the same setTransform method that we used to translate an object.

Type the following program, and save it as \3D2E\demo\turnshape.cs.

```
// ================================================================
// turnshape.cs
//
// This module contains a function for turning a specified shape.
// ================================================================

function TurnShape(%shape, %angle)
// --------------------------------------------------------
//      turns the %shape by %angle amount.
// --------------------------------------------------------
{
  echo (";TurnShape: shape id: ", %shape);
  echo ("TurnShape: angle: ", %angle);
  %xfrm = %shape.getTransform();
  %lx = getword(%xfrm,0); // first, get the current transform values
  %ly = getword(%xfrm,1);
  %lz = getword(%xfrm,2);
  %rx = getword(%xfrm,3);
  %ry = getword(%xfrm,4);
```

```
    %rz = getword(%xfrm,5);
    %angle += 1.0;              // increment the angle (ie. rotate it a bit)
    %rd = %angle;              // Set the rotation angle
    %shape.setTransform(%lx SPC %ly SPC %lz SPC %rx SPC %ry SPC %rz SPC %rd);
    echo ("TurnShape: done.");
}
```

The program is quite similar to the moveshape.cs program that you were just working with. You can load and run the program in exactly the same way that you did with the moveShape module, except that you want to use TurnShape instead MoveShape.

Things of interest to explore are the variables %rx, %ry, %rz, and %rd in the TurnShape function. Try making changes to each of these, and then observe the effects your changes have on the item.

Programmed Scaling

We can also quite easily change the scale of an object using program code.

Type the following program, and save it as \3D2E\demo\sizeshape.cs.

```
// ========================================================================
// sizeshape.cs
//
// This module contains a function for scaling a specified shape.
// ========================================================================

function SizeShape(%shape, %scale)
// ----------------------------------------------------------------
//     moves the %shape by %scale amount
// ----------------------------------------------------------------
{
  echo ("SizeShape: shape id: ", %shape);
  echo ("SizeShape: angle: ", %scale);
  %shape.setScale(%scale SPC %scale SPC %scale);
  echo ("SizeShape: done.");
}
```

Ha! You thought there would be a ton o' typing in store, didn't you? Well, the program is obviously similar to the moveshape.cs and turnshape.cs programs, sort of. Except for all of the missing bits, that is. You can load and run this program in exactly the same way, except that you want to use SizeShape instead of MoveShape or TurnShape.

Why bother to write all this code to replace what is essentially a single line statement anyway (if you ignore the echo statements)? For the practice, of course!

You'll note that we don't call the object's %shape.getScale function (there is one), because in this case, we don't need to. Also notice that the three arguments to our call to %shape.setScale all use the same value. This is to make sure the object scales equally in all dimensions. Try making changes to each of these, and then observe the effects your changes have on the item.

Another exercise would be to modify the SizeShape function to accept a different parameter for each dimension (X, Y, or Z) so that you can change all three to different scales at the same time.

Programmed Animation

You can animate objects by stringing together a bunch of translation, rotation, and scale operations in a continuous loop. Like the transformations, most of the animation in Torque can be left up to an object's class methods to perform. However, you can create your own ad hoc animations quite easily by using the schedule function.

Type the following program, and save it as \3D2E\demo\animshape.cs.

```
// =============================================================
// animshape.cs
//
// This module contains functions for animating a shape using
// a recurring scheduled function call.
// =============================================================

function AnimShape(%shape, %dist, %angle, %scale)
// -------------------------------------------------------------
//    moves the %shape by %dist amount, and then
//    schedules itself to be called again in 1/5
//    of a second.
// -------------------------------------------------------------
{
  echo("AnimShape: shape:", %shape, " dist:",
        %dist, " angle:", %angle, " scale:", %scale);
```

```
  if (%shape $= "" ||
     %dist   $= "" ||
     %angle  $= "" ||
     %scale  $= "" )
  {
   error("AnimShape needs 4 parameters.syntax:");
   error("AnimShape(id,moveDist,turnAng,scaleVal);");
   return;
  }
  %xfrm = %shape.getTransform();
  %lx = getword(%xfrm,0); // first, get the current
  %ly = getword(%xfrm,1);        // transform values
  %lz = getword(%xfrm,2);
  %rx = getword(%xfrm,3);
  %ry = getword(%xfrm,4);
  %rz = getword(%xfrm,5);
  %lx += %dist;            // set the new x position
  %angle += 1.0;
  %rd = %angle;            // Set the rotation angle

  if ($grow)        // if the shape is growing larger
  {
   if (%scale < 5.0)  // and hasn't gotten too big
    %scale += 0.3;    // make it bigger
   else
    $grow = false; // if it's too big, then
  }                  // don't let it grow more
  else               // if it's shrinking
  {
   if (%scale > 3.0)  // and isn't too small
    %scale -= 0.3;    // then make it smaller
   else
    $grow = true;  // if it's too small,
  }                  // don't let it grow smaller

%shape.setScale(%scale SPC %scale SPC %scale);
%shape.setTransform(%lx SPC %ly SPC %lz SPC
                    %rx SPC %ry SPC %rz SPC %rd);
schedule(200,0,AnimShape, %shape, %dist, %angle, %scale);
}
```

```
function DoAnimTest(%shape)
{
 if (%shape $= "" && isObject(%shape))
 {
  error("DoAnimTest requires 1 parameter.");
  error("DoAnimTest syntax: DoAnimTest(shapeID);");
  return;
 }
 $grow = true;
 AnimShape(%shape, 0.2, 1, 2);
}
```

This module contains code from all of the three earlier modules and ties them together in a way that allows us to watch an absolutely nutso Great Hall gyrate and gambol about the countryside.

The function AnimShape accepts a shape handle as %shape, a distance step as %dist, an angle value as %angle, and a scaling value as %scale and uses these to transform the shape indicated by the %shape handle.

Before getting under way though, the function checks to make sure that it has values for all of the parameters.

First, it obtains the current position of the shape using the %shape.getTransform method of the Item class.

As with the earlier MoveShape function, the AnimShape function fetches the transform of the shape and updates one of the axis values.

Then it updates the rotation value stored as %rd.

Then it adjusts the scale value by determining if the shape is growing or shrinking. Depending on which way the size is changing, the scale is incremented, unless the scale exceeds the too large or too small limits. When a limit is exceeded, the change direction is reversed.

Next, the scale of the shape is changed to the new values using the %shape.-setScale method for the shape.

Finally, the function sets the item's transform to be the new transform values within the %shape.setTransform statement.

The DoAnimTest function accepts an object handle and verifies that it is valid, emitting an error message and exiting via the return statement if there is no valid object ID.

Then the global variable called $grow is set to true. This variable will determine whether the shape will start out by scaling up in size or not. This function then calls the AnimShape function, specifying which shape to animate by passing in the handle to the shape as the first argument and also indicating the discrete movement step distance, the discrete rotation angle, and the discrete size change value with the second, third, and fourth arguments.

To use the program, follow these steps:

1. Make sure you've saved the file as \3D2E\demo\animshape.cs.

2. Run the Torque FPS demo.

3. After spawning in, make your way over to the docks, near the Great Hall.

4. Bring up the console window.

5. Type in the following, and press Enter after the semicolon:

```
exec("demo/animshape.cs");
```

You should get a response in the console window similar to this:

```
Compiling demo/animshape.cs...
Loading compiled script demo/animshape.cs.
```

This means that the Torque Engine has compiled your program and then loaded it into memory. The datablock definition and the three functions are in memory, waiting to be used.

6. Now, type the following into the console, and close the console quickly afterward:

```
DoAnimTest($gh);
```

Remember that $gh is the variable that holds the instance handle of the Great Hall. You will probably need to assign the right value into this variable— check back in the "Programmed Movement" section for a quick refresher, if necessary.

What you should see now is the Great Hall start spinning and moving "inland" while growing and then shrinking.

Go ahead and experiment with the program. Try moving the item through several axes at once, or try changing the distance. I did not put any code in the animtest module to stop the animation. Review Chapter 2 and the preceding section in this chapter and see if you can add statements that will stop the animation when certain conditions are met.

3D Audio

Environmental sounds with a 3D component contribute greatly to the immersive aspect of a game by providing positional cues that mimic the way sounds happen in real life.

We can control 3D audio in the scene in much the same way we do 3D visual objects.

Type the following program, and save it as \3D2E\demo\animaudio.cs.

```
// =====================================================================
// animaudio.cs
//
// This module contains the definition of an audio emitter, which uses
// a synthetic water drop sound. It also contains functions for placing
// the test emitter in the game world and moving the emitter.
// =====================================================================

datablock AudioProfile(TestSound)
// ----------------------------------------------------------------
//      Definition of the audio profile
// ----------------------------------------------------------------
{
   filename = "~/data/sound/testing.ogg"; // wave file to use for the sound
   description = "AudioDefaultLooping3d"; // monophonic sound that repeats
      preload = false;  // Engine will only load sound if it encounters it
                        // in the mission
};

function InsertTestEmitter()
// ----------------------------------------------------------------
//      Instantiates the test sound, then inserts it
//      into the game world to the right and offset somewhat
//      from the player's default spawn location.
// ----------------------------------------------------------------
{
   // An example function which creates a new TestSound object
   %emtr = new AudioEmitter() {
     position = "0 0 0";
     rotation = "1 0 0 0";
```

```
        scale = "1 1 1";
        profile = "TestSound"; // Use the profile in the datablock above
        useProfileDescription = "1";
        type = "2";
        volume = "1";
        outsideAmbient = "1";
        referenceDistance = "1";
        maxDistance = "100";
        isLooping = "1";
        is3D = "1";
        loopCount = "-1";
        minLoopGap = "0";
        maxLoopGap = "0";
        coneInsideAngle = "360";
        coneOutsideAngle = "360";
        coneOutsideVolume = "1";
        coneVector = "0 0 1";
        minDistance = "20.0";
    };
    MissionCleanup.add(%emtr);

    // Player setup-
    %emtr.setTransform("200 -52 200 0 0 1 0"); // starting location
    echo("Inserting Audio Emitter " @ %emtr);
    return %emtr;
}

function AnimSound(%snd, %dist)
// ----------------------------------------------------------
//      moves the %snd by %dist amount each time
// ----------------------------------------------------------
{
  %xfrm = %snd.getTransform();
  %lx = getword(%xfrm,0); // first, get the current transform values
  %ly = getword(%xfrm,1);
  %lz = getword(%xfrm,2);
  %rx = getword(%xfrm,3);
  %ry = getword(%xfrm,4);
  %rz = getword(%xfrm,5);
  %lx += %dist;            // set the new x position
  %snd.setTransform(%lx SPC %ly SPC %lz SPC %rx SPC %ry SPC %rz SPC %rd);
  schedule(200,0,AnimSound, %snd, %dist);

}
```

```
function DoAudioMoveTest()
// -----------------------------------------------------
//    a function to tie together the instantiation
//    and the movement in one easy to type function
//    call.
// -----------------------------------------------------
{
  %ms = InsertTestEmitter();
  AnimSound(%ms,1);
}
DoAudioMoveTest();   // by putting this here, we cause the test to start
                     // as soon as this module has been loaded into memory
```

In this program, we also have a datablock that defines an *audio profile*. It contains the name of the ogg (sound) file that contains the sound to be played, a descriptor that tells Torque how to treat the sound, and a flag to indicate whether the engine should automatically load the sound or wait until it encounters a need for the sound. In this case, the engine will wait until it knows it needs the file.

Note

> Torque supports both wave (.wav) and Ogg Vorbis (.ogg) audio file formats. If you *do not* include the extension part of an audio file's name when specifying one in a datablock or an audio object, Torque will automatically tack the .wav extension onto the file name and then go look for the audio file. If Torque cannot find the file using the .wav extension, it will then add the .ogg extension instead and go look for the file again.
>
> If you *do* include an extension (.wav or .ogg) as part of the file name, then Torque will look for the specified file name with extension and give up if the file is not found.

The InsertTestEmitter function creates an audio object with a call to new AudioEmitter, and there are quite a few properties to be set. These properties will be explained in greater detail in Chapter 20.

A difference to note compared to the earlier modules you created is the last line, which is a call to DoAudioMoveTest. This allows us to load and run the program in one go, using the exec call. After the Torque Engine compiles the program, it loads it into memory and runs through the code. In our earlier program, like the AnimShape module, Torque would encounter only the datablock and function definitions. Because they are definitions, they aren't executed—they're just loaded into memory. The last line, however, is not a definition. It is a statement that calls a function. So when Torque encounters it, Torque looks to see if it has the function resident in memory, and if so, it executes the function according to the syntax of the statement. Statements in script modules that are not part of function definitions or datablock definitions are sometimes called *naked statements*, or more commonly, *inline statements*. They are "inline" because they are executed as soon as they are encountered (as if in a lineup), not saved elsewhere in memory prior to being used.

To use the program, follow these steps:

1. Make sure you've saved the file as \3D2E\demo\ animaudio.cs.

2. Run the Torque FPS demo.

3. After you spawn in, run down to the docks and out onto a dock, then turn around and face inland.

4. Press F11 to enter the Mission Editor, and then bring up the console window.

5. Type in the following, and press Enter after the semicolon:
   ```
   exec("demo/animaudio.cs");
   ```

   You should get a response in the console window similar to this:
   ```
   Compiling demo/animaudio.cs...
   Loading compiled script demo/animaudio.cs.
   ```

You should also begin to hear the dripping "test" sound off to the center-left side. If you wait without moving your player in any way, not even using the mouse to turn his head, you will notice the sound slowly approach you from the left, pass over to the right in front of you, and then go off into the distance to the left. Pretty neat, huh?

You'll also notice, while in the Mission Editor, a big black ball of "points" rolling from left to right. That is the construct that displays the presence and properties of an audio emitter.

Moving Right Along

So, we've now seen how 3D objects are constructed from vertices and faces, or polygons. We explored how they fit into that virtual game world using transformations and that the transformations are applied in a particular order—scaling, rotation, and then finally translation. We also saw how different rendering techniques can be used to enhance the appearance of 3D models.

Then we learned practical ways to apply those concepts using program code written using TorqueScript and tested with the Torque Game Engine.

In the next chapter, we will dive deeper into learning how to use TorqueScript.

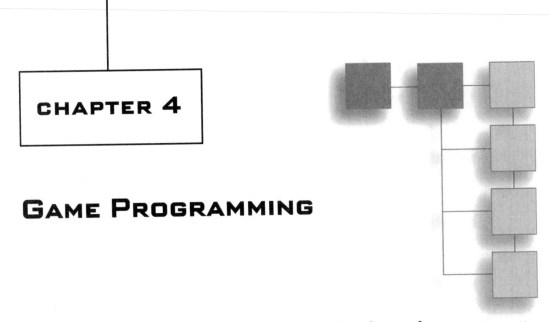

CHAPTER 4

GAME PROGRAMMING

In the preceding two chapters you were introduced to a few new concepts: programming, 3D graphics, 3D object manipulation, and stuff like that. Most of it was fairly broad, in order to give you a good grasp of what you can do to make your game.

The next bunch of chapters get down and dirty, so to speak. We're going to muck around with our own hands examining things, creating things, and making things happen.

In this chapter we're going to hammer at the TorqueScript for a while, writing actual code that will be used to develop our game. We'll examine in detail how the code works in order to gain a thorough understanding of how Torque works. The game we are going to create has the rather unoriginal name of *Emaga*, which is just *agame* spelled backward. The Chapter 4 version will be called *Emaga4*. Of course, you may—and probably should—substitute whatever name you wish!

TorqueScript

As I've said before, TorqueScript is much like C/C++, but there are a few differences. TorqueScript is typeless—with a specific exception regarding the difference between numbers and strings—and you don't need to preallocate storage space with variable declarations.

You can control all aspects of a game—from game rules and nonplayer character behavior to player scoring and vehicle simulation—through the use of TorqueScript. A script comprises *statements, function declarations,* and *package declarations.*

Most of the syntax in *Torque Game Engine* (TGE) Script language is similar to C/C++ language, with a high correlation of keywords (see Table A.3 in Appendix A) between the two, although, as is often the case in scripting languages, there is no type enforcement on the variables, and you don't declare variables before using them. If you read a variable before writing it, it will be an empty string or zero, depending on whether you are using it in a string context or a numeric context.

The engine has rules for how it converts between the script representation of values and its own internal representation. Most of the time the correct script format for a value is obvious; numbers are numbers (also called *numerics*), and strings are strings. The tokens true and false can be used for ease of code reading to represent 1 and 0, respectively. More complicated data types will be contained within strings; the functions that use the strings need to be aware of how to interpret the data in the strings.

Strings

String constants are enclosed in single quotes or double quotes. A single-quoted string specifies a *tagged* string—a special kind of string used for any string constant that needs to be transmitted across a connection. The full string is sent once, the first time. And then whenever the string needs to be sent again, only the short tag identifying that string is sent. This dramatically reduces bandwidth consumption by the game.

A double-quoted (or *standard*) string is not tagged; therefore, whenever the string is used, storage space for all of the characters contained in the string must be allocated for whatever operation the string is being used for. In the case of sending a standard string across connections, all of the characters in the string are transmitted, every single time the string is sent. Chat messages are sent as standard strings, and because they change each time they are sent, creating tag ID numbers for chat messages would be pretty useless.

Strings can contain formatting codes, as described in Table 4.1.

Table 4.1 TorqueScript String Formatting Codes

Code	Description
\r	Embeds a carriage return character.
\n	Embeds a newline character.
\t	Embeds a tab character.
\x*hh*	Embeds an ASCII character specified by the hex number (*hh*) that follows the *x*.
\c	Embeds a color code for strings that will be displayed on-screen.
\cr	Resets the display color to the default.
\cp	Pushes the current display color onto a stack.
\co	Pops the current display color off the stack.
\c*n*	Uses *n* as an index into the color table defined by GUIControlProfile.fontColors.

Objects

Objects are instances of object classes, which are a collection of properties and methods that together define a specific set of behaviors and characteristics. A Torque object is an *instantiation* of an object class. After creation, a Torque object has a unique numeric identifier called its *handle*. When two handle variables have the same numeric value, they refer to the same object. An *instance* of an object can be thought of as being somewhat like a *copy* of an object.

When an object exists in a multiplayer game with a server and multiple clients, the server and each client allocate their own handle for the object's storage in memory. Note that datablocks (a special kind of object) are treated differently—more about this a little later.

Note

Methods are functions that are accessible through objects. Different object classes may have some methods that are common between them, and they may have some methods that are unique to themselves. In fact, methods may have the same name, but work differently, when you move from one object class to another.

Properties are variables that belong to specific objects and, like methods, are accessed through objects.

Creating an Object

When creating a new instance of an object, you can initialize the object's fields in the new statement code block, as shown here:

```
%handle = new InteriorInstance()
{
    position = "0 0 0";
    rotation = "0 0 0";
    interiorFile = %name;
};
```

The handle of the newly created InteriorInstance object is inserted into the variable %handle when the object is created. Of course, you could use any valid and unused variable you want, like %obj, %disTing, or whatever. Note in the preceding example that %handle is a local variable, so it is only in scope—or valid—within the function where it is used. Once the memory is allocated for the new object instance, the engine then initializes the object's properties as directed by the program statements embedded inside the new code block. Once you have the object's unique handle—as assigned to %handle in this case—you can use the object.

Using Objects

To use or control an object, you can use the object's handle to access its properties and functions. If you have an object handle contained in the local variable %handle, you can access a property of that object this way:

```
%handle.aproperty = 42;
```

Handles are not the only way to access objects. You can assign objects by name, if you don't have a handle at hand. Objects are named using strings, identifiers, or variables containing strings or identifiers. For example, if the object in question is named MyObject, all of the following code fragments (A, B, C, D) are the same.

A

```
MyObject.aproperty = 42;
```

B

```
"MyObject".aproperty = 42;
```

C

```
%objname = MyObject;
%objname.aproperty = 42;
```

D

```
%objname = "MyObject";
%objname.aproperty = 42;
```

These examples demonstrate accessing a property field of an object; you invoke object methods (functions) in the same way. Note that the object name—MyObject—is a *string literal,* not a variable. There is no % or $ prefixed to the identifier. A string literal is a string embedded in the code, as you see in B and D above with "MyObject".

Object Functions

You can call a function referenced through an object this way:

```
%handle.afunction(42, "arg1", "arg2");
```

Note that the function afunction can also be referred to as a *method* of the object contained in %handle. In the preceding example, the function named afunction will be executed. There can be multiple instances of functions named afunction in a script, but each must be part of different *namespaces*. The particular instance of afunction to be executed will be selected according to the object's namespace and the namespace hierarchy. For more about namespaces, see the sidebar.

Namespaces

Namespaces are means of defining a formal context for variables. Using namespaces allows us to use different variables that have the same name without confusing the game engine or ourselves.

If you recall the discussion in Chapter 2 about variable scope, you will remember that there are two scopes: global and local. Variables of global scope have a "$" prefix, and variables of local scope have a "%" prefix. Using this notation, we can have two variables—say, $maxplayers and %maxplayers—that can be used side by side, yet whose usage and meaning are completely independent from each other. %maxplayer can only be used within a specific function, while $maxplayer can be used anywhere in a program. This independence is like having two namespaces.

In fact, %maxplayer can be used over and over in different functions, but the values it holds only apply within any given specific function. In these cases, each function is its own *de facto* namespace.

We can arbitrarily assign variables to a namespace by using special prefixes like this:

```
$Game::maxplayers
$Server::maxplayers
```

We can have other variables belonging to the namespace as well:

```
$Game::maxplayers
$Game::timelimit
$Game::maxscores
```

The identifier between the "$" and the "::" can be completely arbitrary—in essence, it is a *qualifier*. By qualifying the variable that follows, it sets a context in which the variable is meaningful.

Just as functions have a de facto namespace (the local scope), objects have their own namespaces. Methods and properties of objects are sometimes called *member functions* and *member variables*. The "member" part refers to the fact that they are members of objects. This membership defines the context, and therefore the namespace, of the methods and properties (member functions and member variables).

So, you can have many different object classes that have properties of the same name, yet they refer only to the objects that belong to that class. You can also have many different instances of an object, and the methods and properties of each instance belong to the individual instance.

In these examples:

```
$myObject.maxSize
$explosion.maxSize
$beast.maxSize
```

the maxSize property could have three entirely different meanings. For $myObject, maxSize might mean the number of items it can carry. For $explosion, it might mean how large the blast radius is. For $beast, it might mean how tall the creature is.

When an object's function is called, the first parameter is the handle of the object containing the function. Therefore, the function definition of the afunction method in the preceding example would actually have four parameters in its parameter list, the first of which will be the %this parameter. Note that only the last three parameters are used when you call the afunction method. The first parameter that corresponds to the %this parameter in the definition is automagically inserted by the engine when you call the function. You may be familiar with the this token in C/C++; however, in Torque there is nothing special about it. By prior convention, that variable name is often used when referring to an object's handle within one of its methods, but you could call that parameter anything you want.

If you want to access a field of an object, you always have to use something that evaluates to an object handle or a name followed by a dot followed by the field name, as in the A, B, C, and D code fragments seen earlier. The only exception to this rule is in the sequence of field initialization statements when creating an object with the new statement.

Datablocks

A *datablock* is a special kind of object containing a set of characteristics that are used to describe another object's properties. Datablock objects exist simultaneously on the server and all its connected clients. Every copy of a given datablock uses the same handle whether it is on the server or a client.

By convention, datablock identifiers have the form *NameData*. VehicleData, PlayerData, and ItemData are all examples of datablock identifiers. Although datablocks *are* objects, we typically don't explicitly call them objects when referring to them, in order to avoid semantic confusion with regular objects.

A VehicleData datablock contains many attributes describing the speed, mass, and other properties that can be applied to a Vehicle object. When created, a Vehicle object is initialized to reference some already-existing VehicleData datablocks that will tell it how to behave. Most objects can come and go throughout the course of the game, but datablocks are created once and are not deleted. Datablocks have their own specific creation syntax:

```
datablock ClassIdentifier(NameIdentifier)
{
     InitializationStatements
};
```

The value of this statement is the handle of the created datablock.

ClassIdentifier is an existing datablock class name, like PlayerData. NameIdentifier is the datablock name you've chosen. In both cases you must use valid identifiers. InitializationStatements is a sequence of assignment statements.

The assignment statements assign values to datablock field identifiers. It's possible for the contents of these fields to be accessible by both the script code and the engine code—and in fact that is often the case. In that situation you of course need to assign a value to the field that makes sense for the type of information it's supposed to be holding.

You don't have to restrict yourself to only initializing (and later using) fields that are accessible by the engine code. An object can have other fields as well; the engine code can't read them, but the scripts can.

Finally, note that there's a variation on the datablock creation syntax:

```
datablock ClassIdentifier(NameIdentifier : CopySourceIdentifier)
{
     InitializationStatements
};
```

CopySourceIdentifier specifies the name of some other datablock from which to copy field values before executing InitializationStatements. This other datablock must be of the same class as the datablock you are creating, or a *superclass* of it. This is useful if you want to make a datablock that should be almost exactly like a previously created datablock (with just a few changes) or if you want to centralize the definitions of some characteristics in one datablock that can then be copied by multiple other datablocks.

Game Structure

When you create your game, you can use pretty well any organizational structure you like. Your game will comprise script program modules, graphics images, 3D models, audio files, and various other data definition modules.

The only real limitation in how you structure your game folders is that the *root main module* must reside in the same folder as the Torque Engine executable, and this folder will be the *game root folder*.

The least you should do to sensibly organize your game folders is to have a subtree that contains *common* code, code that would be essentially the same between game types and variations, and another subtree that would contain the *control* code and specific resources that pertain to a particular game, game type, or game variation. GarageGames uses these two basic subtrees, common and control, in its sample games, although the company uses different names (such as *fps, rw, racing,* and *show*) for variations of the control subtree. See Figure 4.1 for a simple breakdown diagram.

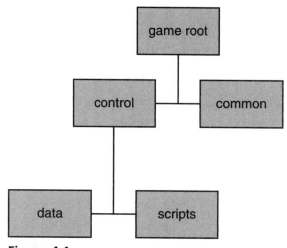

Figure 4.1
General game folder tree.

In the game we are creating, we will call the control subtree *control*.

Source files for TorqueScript have the .cs extension. After the source files are compiled, they have an extension of .cs.dso. There is no way to convert a .cs.dso file back into a .cs file, so you must make sure to hang on to your original source files and back them up regularly.

When you launch TGE, it looks for the module main.cs located in the same folder (the *game root folder,* shown in the following—the general tree format used for the Emaga set of tutorial sample games used in this book) as the TGE executable. In this chapter we will be using a simplified version of this tree. In the distribution of TGE you receive with the CD, the executable is called tge.exe. The particular main.cs file located in the game root folder can be thought of as the *root main module.* This expression is useful for distinguishing that particular main.cs module from others with the same name that aren't in the game root folder.

```
emaga (game root folder)
        common
                client
                        debugger
                        editor
                        help
                        lighting
                        server
                        ui
                                cache
        control
                client
                        misc
                        interfaces
                data
                        maps
                        models
                                avatars
                                items
                                markers
                                weapons
                        particles
                        sound
                        structures
                                docks
                                hovels
                                towers
```

```
server
        misc
        players
        vehicles
        weapons
```

These other main.cs modules are the root modules for the packages in the game. Although it isn't explicitly designated as such, the root main module functions as the root package of the game.

It's important to realize that the folder structure just outlined is not cast in stone. Note that although it is similar, it is still not exactly the same as the format used in the Torque sample games. As long as the root main module is in the same folder as the demo.exe executable, you can use whatever folder structure suits your needs. Of course, you will have to ensure that all of the hard-coded paths in the source modules reflect your customized folder structure.

Packages, Add-ons, Mods, and Modules

If you find the terminology confusing, don't fret—it *is* a little bit less than straightforward at first blush.

The first thing to understand is that the term *Mod* is an abbreviated, or truncated, form of the word *modification*. Mods are changes that people make to existing games, customizing the games to look or play differently. The term is often used in the independent game development scene. The word *Mod* is often capitalized.

What we are doing when we create the Emaga game is in many ways similar to creating a Mod—much like a certain kind of Mod that is often called a *Total Conversion*. Torque, however, is not a game; it is an engine. So we are in reality not modifying an existing game, but, rather, we are creating our own.

Also, there is a bit of an extra wrinkle here. When we create our game, we are going to provide some features that will allow other people to modify our game! To avoid total confusion, we are going to call this capability an *add-on* capability rather than a Mod capability. And we'll refer to the new or extra modules created by other people for our game as *add-ons*.

A *module* is essentially the melding of a program source file in text form with its compiled version. Although we usually refer to the source code version, both the source file version and the compiled (object code, or in the case of Torque, byte code) version are just different forms of the same module.

A *package* is a Torque construct that encapsulates functions that can be dynamically loaded and unloaded during program execution. Scripts often use packages to load and unload the different game types and related functions. Packages can be used to dynamically *overload* functions using the `parent::function` script mechanism in the packaged function. This is useful for writing scripts that can work with other scripts without any knowledge of those scripts.

To replace the graphical Help features in the Torque demo, for example, you could create one or more source code *modules* that define the new Help features and that together could compose a *Mod* to the graphical Help *package* and that could also be considered a *Mod* to the Torque demo game as a whole.

Clear as mud?

Figure 4.2 shows the simplified folder tree we will be using for this chapter's sample game, Emaga4. The rectangles indicate folder names, the partial rectangles with the wavy bottoms are source files, and the lozenge shapes indicate binary files. Those items that are not in gray are the items we will be dealing with in this chapter.

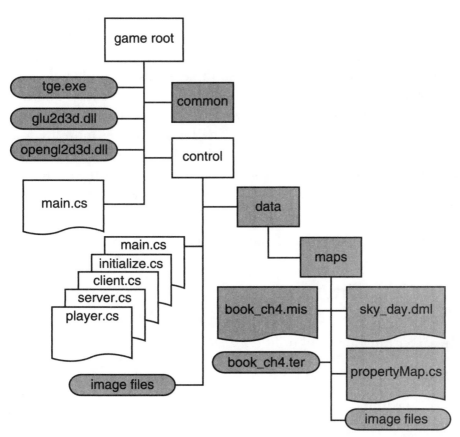

Figure 4.2
The Emaga4 folder tree.

Server Versus Client Design Issues

The Torque Engine provides built-in client/server capability. In fact, the engine is designed and built around the client/server model to such a degree that even if you are going to create a single-player game, you will still have both a server side and a client side to your code.

A well-designed online multiplayer game puts as much of the decision-making activity into the hands of the server as possible. This greatly reduces the chances that dishonest players could modify their clients to enable cheating or otherwise gain advantage over other, more honest players.

Conversely, a well-designed online multiplayer game only uses the client side to manage the interface with the human player—accepting input, displaying or generating output, and providing setup and game navigation tools.

This emphasis on server-side decisions has the potential to rapidly drain network bandwidth. This can lead to *lag,* a situation where a player's actions are not reflected on the server in a timely fashion. Torque has a highly optimized networking system designed to mitigate against these kinds of problems. For example, most strings of data are transmitted only once between clients and the game server. Anytime a string that has already been transmitted needs to be sent again, a *tag* is sent instead of the full string. The tag is nothing more than a number that identifies the string to be used, so the full string need not be sent again. Another approach is an update *masking* system that allows the engine to only provide updates from the server to its clients of data that has actually changed since the last update.

We will follow these guidelines when designing our sample game.

Common Functionality

The common subtree contains code and resources for the following capabilities:

- Common server functions and utilities, such as authentication
- Common client functions and utilities, such as messaging
- In-game world editor
- Online debugger
- Lighting management and lighting cache control code

- Help features and content files

- User interface definitions, widget definitions, profiles, and images

We will not be using all of these features in the code we'll be looking at in this chapter, but by the end of the book, we *will* be using all of it!

Preparation

In this chapter we will be concentrating on the control scripts found in the control subtree, as outlined in Figure 4.2. To prepare for this, you need to set up your development tree, as follows:

1. In your 3D2E\RESOURCES\CH4 folder, locate the EMAGA4 folder (*not* the EMAGA4 BOOK CODE folder).

2. Copy the EMAGA4 folder to your root folder on your hard drive, so that the path to the new folder is \EMAGA4 (you can use any hard drive you want; I won't be specifying the hard drives in the paths).

You probably won't use more than an additional 15MB of disk space, but you should have more available for backups and temporary files and so on.

You will note that there is no main.cs file in the same folder as tge.exe. This is by design, because that is one of the files you will be creating. Also note that there are no .cs files in the control folder either. Again, this is intentional—you will be creating them from this chapter.

The code in Emaga4 is pretty close to the bare minimum in terms of the game control code. In later chapters we will expand on this skeletal implementation as we add more and more useful features and flesh out the game.

Root Main

Once it has found the root main module, Torque compiles it into a special binary version containing *byte code,* a machine-readable format. The game engine then begins executing the instructions in the module. The root package can be used to do anything you like, but the convention established with the GarageGames code is that the root package carries out the following functions:

- Performs generic initialization

- Performs the command line parameter parsing and dispatch

■ Defines the command line help package

■ Invokes packages and add-ons (Mods)

Here is the root main.cs module. Type it in, and save it as Emaga4\main.cs. You can skip the comments if you like, in order to minimize your typing.

```
//---------------------------------------------------------------------------
//  ./main.cs
//
//  root main module for 3D2E emaga4 tutorial game
//
//  Copyright (c) 2003, 2006 by Kenneth C. Finney.
//---------------------------------------------------------------------------


// ===========================================================================
// ========================= Initializations =================================
// ===========================================================================

$usageFlag = false;  //help won't be displayed unless the command line
                     //switch ( -h ) is used

$logModeEnabled = true; //track the logging state we set in the next line.
SetLogMode(2);   // overwrites existing log file & closes log file at exit.


// ===========================================================================
// ======================= Function Definitions ==============================
// ===========================================================================

function OnExit()
//---------------------------------------------------------------------------
// This is called from the common code modules. Any last gasp exit
// activities we might want to perform can be put in this function.
// We need to provide a stub to prevent warnings in the log file.
//---------------------------------------------------------------------------
{
}

function OnStart()
//---------------------------------------------------------------------------
// This is called from the common code modules.
// We need to provide a stub to prevent warnings in the log file.
//---------------------------------------------------------------------------
{
```

```
}

function ParseArgs()
//-------------------------------------------------------------------
//  handle the command line arguments
//
//  this function is called from the common code
//
//-------------------------------------------------------------------
{
  for(%i = 1;  %i < $Game::argc ; %i++) //loop thru all command line args
  {
    $currentarg   = $Game::argv[%i];   // get current arg from the list
    $nextArgument    = $Game::argv[%i+1]; // get arg after the current one
    $nextArgExists = $Game::argc-%i > 1;// if there *is* a next arg, note that
    $logModeEnabled = false;        // turn this off; let the args dictate
                                // if logging should be enabled.

    switch$($currentarg)
    {
      case "-?": // the user wants command line help, so this causes the
        $usageFlag = true;   // Usage function to be run, instead of the game
        $argumentFlag[%i] = true;             // adjust the argument count

      case "-h":        // exactly the same as "-?"
        $usageFlag = true;
        $argumentFlag[%i] = true;
    }
  }
}

function Usage()
//-------------------------------------------------------------------
// Display the command line usage help
//-------------------------------------------------------------------
{
// NOTE: any logging entries are written to the file 'console.log'
  Echo("\n\nemaga4 command line options:\n\n" @
            "-h, -?        display this message\n" );
}

function  LoadAddOns(%list)
//-------------------------------------------------------------------
// Exec each of the startup scripts for add-ons.
```

```
//-------------------------------------------------------------------------
{
  if (%list $= "")
      return;
  %list = NextToken(%list, token, ";");
  LoadAddOns(%list);
  Exec(%token @ "/main.cs");
}


// ==========================================================================
// =============== Module Body - Inline Statements ==========================
// ==========================================================================
// Parse the command line arguments
ParseArgs();

// Either display the help message or start the program.
if ($usageFlag)
{
  EnableWinConsole(true);// send logging output to a Windows console window
  Usage();
  EnableWinConsole(false);
  Quit();
}
else
{

  // scan argument list, and log an Error message for each unused argument
  for ($i = 1; $i < $Game::argc; $i++)
  {
    if (!$argumentFlag[$i])
      Error("Error: Unknown command line argument:  " @ $Game::argv[$i]);
  }

  if (!$logModeEnabled)
  {
    SetLogMode(6);     // Default to a new log file each session.
  }
  // Set the add-on path list to specify the folders that will be
  // available to the scripts and engine. Note that *all* required
  // folder trees are included: common and control as well as the
  // user add-ons.
  $pathList=$addonList!$="" ? $addonList@ ";control;common" : "control;common";
  SetModPaths($pathList);
```

```
// Execute startup script for the common code modules
Exec("common/main.cs");

// Execute startup script for the control specific code modules
Exec("control/main.cs");

// Execute startup scripts for all user add-ons
Echo("-------- Loading Add-ons --------");
LoadAddOns($addonList);
Echo("Engine initialization complete.");

OnStart();
}
```

This is a fairly robust root main module. Let's take a closer look at it.

In the initializations section, the $usageFlag variable is used to trigger a simple Help display for command line use of tge.exe. It is set to false here; if the user specifies the -? or -h flags on the command line, then this flag will be set to true.

After the usage flag, we set the log mode and enable logging. Logging allows us to track what is happening within the code. When we use the Echo, Warn, or Error functions, their output is sent to the console.log file, in the root game folder.

The stub routines OnExit and OnStart are next. A *stub routine* is a function that is defined but actually does nothing. The common code modules have a call to this routine, but we have nothing for it to do. We could just leave it out, but a good policy is to provide an empty stub to avoid warning messages from appearing in our log file—when the Torque Engine tries to call a nonexistent function, it generates a warning.

Then there is the ParseArgs function. Its job is to step through the list of command line arguments, or parameters, and perform whatever tasks you want based upon what arguments the user provided. In this case we'll just include code to provide a bare-bones usage, or Help, display.

Next is the actual Usage function that displays the Help information.

This is followed by the LoadAddOns routine. Its purpose is to walk through the list of add-ons specified by the user on the command line and to load the code for each. In Emaga4 there is no way for the user to specify add-ons or Mods, but (you knew there was a *but* coming, didn't you?) we still need this function, because we treat our common and control modules as if they were add-ons. They are always added to the list in such a way that they get loaded first. So this function is here to look after them.

After the function definitions we move into the in-line program statements. These statements are executed at load time—when the module is loaded into memory with the Exec statement. When Torque runs, after the engine gets itself sorted out, it always loads the root main module (this module) with an Exec statement. All of the other script modules are loaded as a result of what this module does.

The first thing that happens is a call to the ParseArgs function, which we saw earlier. It sets the $usageFlag variable for us, you will recall.

Next is the block of code that examines the $usageFlag and decides what to do: either display the usage Help information or continue to run the game program. If we are not displaying the usage information, we move into the code block after the else.

The first thing we do in here is check to see if there are any unused arguments from the command line. If there are, that means the program doesn't understand the arguments and there was some kind of error, which we indicate with the Error function and a useful message.

After that we set the log mode, if logging has been enabled.

Next, we build the lists that help Torque find our add-ons. We notify Torque about the required folder paths by passing the list to the SetModPaths function.

Then we call the main module for the common code. This will proceed to load all the required common modules into memory, initialize the common functions, and basically get the ball rolling over there. We will talk about the common code modules in a later chapter.

After that we do the same thing for the control code modules, the details of which we will cover later in this chapter.

Then we actually start loading the add-ons using the previously defined Load-AddOns function.

Finally, we make a call to OnStart. This will call all versions of OnStart that appear in the add-on packages in order of their appearance in $addonList, with common being first, control next, and finally this root main module. If there is an OnStart defined in common, then it gets called. Next, the one in control, and so on.

When we get to the end of the module, the various threads initiated by the OnStart calls are ticking over, doing their own things.

So now what? Well, our next point of interest is the control/main.cs module, which we called with the Exec function just before we started loading the add-ons.

Control Main

The main.cs module for the control code is next on our tour. Its primary purposes in Emaga4 are to define the control package and to call the control code initialization functions. (In later chapters we will expand on the role of this module.) Following is the control/main.cs module. Type it in, and save it as Emaga4\control\main.cs.

```
//-----------------------------------------------------------------
// control/main.cs
//  main control module for 3D2E emaga4 tutorial game
//
// Copyright (c) 2003, 2006 by Kenneth C. Finney.
//-----------------------------------------------------------------
//
//-----------------------------------------------------------------
// Load up defaults console values.

// Defaults console values

//-----------------------------------------------------------------
// Package overrides to initialize the mod.
package control {

function OnStart()
//-----------------------------------------------------------------
// Called by root main when package is loaded
//-----------------------------------------------------------------
{
  Parent::OnStart();
  Echo("\n-------- Initializing control module --------");

  // The following scripts contain the preparation code for
  // both the client and server code. A client can also host
  // games, so they need to be able to act as servers if the
  // user wants to host a game. That means we always prepare
```

```
  // to be a server at anytime, unless we are launched as a
  // dedicated server.
  Exec("./initialize.cs");
  InitializeServer(); // Prepare the server-specific aspects
  InitializeClient(); // Prepare the client-specific aspects
}

function OnExit()
//------------------------------------------------------------
// Called by root main when package is unloaded
//------------------------------------------------------------
{

  Parent::onExit();
}

}; // Client package
ActivatePackage(control); // Tell TGE to make the client package active
```

Not a whole lot happens in here at the moment, but it is a necessary module because it defines our control package.

First, the *parent* OnStart function is called. This would be the version that resides in root main, which we can see doesn't have anything to do.

Then the initialize.cs module is loaded, after which the two initialization functions are called.

Finally, there is the OnExit function, which does nothing more than pass the buck to the OnExit function in the root main module.

All in all, control/main.cs is a fairly lazy, though important, little module.

Debugging Scripts Using the trace Function

The engine adds extra commentary to the log file. Extremely useful are the notations that tell you when the engine execution has just begun executing in a particular function or is just about to leave a particular function. The trace lines include the values of any arguments used when the function is entered and the contents of the return value when leaving a function.

Here is a fragmentary example of what the trace output can look like:

```
Entering GameConnection::InitialControlSet(1207)
Setting Initial Control Object
    Entering Editor::checkActiveLoadDone()
    Leaving Editor::checkActiveLoadDone - return 0
```

```
    Entering GuiCanvas::setContent(Canvas, PlayGui)
        Entering PlayGui::onWake(1195)
    Activating DirectInput ...
    keyboard0 input device acquired.
        Leaving PlayGui::onWake - return
        Entering GuiCanvas::checkCursor(Canvas)
            Entering (null)::cursorOff()
            Leaving (null)::cursorOff - return
        Leaving GuiCanvas::checkCursor - return
    Leaving GuiCanvas::setContent - return
Leaving GameConnection::InitialControlSet - return
Entering (null)::DoYaw(-9)
Leaving (null)::DoYaw - return -0.18
Entering (null)::DoPitch(7)
Leaving (null)::DoPitch - return 0.14
Entering (null)::DoYaw(-6)
```

To turn on the trace function, add the following statement to the first line of your root main.cs file:

```
trace(true);
```

To turn off the trace function, insert this statement at the place in the code where you would like to turn tracing off:

```
trace(false);
```

Initialization

The control/initialize.cs module will, in later chapters, become two different modules—one for the server code and one for the client code. Right now, we have a fairly limited amount of work to do, so we'll just house the initialization functions for the two ends in the same module. Here is the control/initialize.cs module. Type it in, and save it as Emaga4\control\initialize.cs.

```
//============================================================
// control/initialize.cs
//
// control initialization module for 3D2E emaga4 tutorial game
//
// Copyright (c) 2003, 2006 by Kenneth C. Finney.
//============================================================
```

```
function InitializeServer()
//------------------------------------------------------------------------
// Prepare some global server information & load the game-specific module
//------------------------------------------------------------------------
{
    Echo("\n-------- Initializing module: emaga server --------");

    // Specify where the mission files are.
    $Server::MissionFileSpec = "*/missions/*.mis";

    InitBaseServer(); // basic server features defined in the common modules

    // Load up game server support script
    Exec("./server.cs");

    createServer("SinglePlayer", "control/data/maps/book_ch4.mis");
}

function InitializeClient()
//------------------------------------------------------------------------
// Prepare some global client information, fire up the graphics engine,
// and then connect to the server code that is already running in another
// thread.
//------------------------------------------------------------------------
{
    Echo("\n-------- Initializing module: emaga client --------");

    InitBaseClient(); // basic client features defined in the common modules

    // these are necessary graphics settings
    $pref::Video::allowOpenGL  = true;
    $pref::Video::displayDevice = "OpenGL";

    // Make sure a canvas has been built before any gui scripts are
    // executed because many of the controls depend on the canvas to
    // already exist when they are loaded.

    InitCanvas("Emaga4 - 3D2E Sample Game"); // Start the graphics system.

    Exec("./client.cs");

    %conn = new GameConnection(ServerConnection);
    %conn.connectLocal();
}
```

First is the `InitializeServer` function. This is where we set up a global variable that indicates to the game engine the folder tree where the *map* (also called *mission*) files will be located.

Next, we prepare the server for operation by performing the common code initialization using the `InitBaseServer` function. This allows us to get the server code running full-bore, which we can do using the `createServer` call. We tell the function that this will be a single-player game and that we are going to load up the map control/data/maps/book_ch4.mis.

After that, we load the module that contains the game code, which is server-side code.

Then we do the client-side initialization in the `InitializeClient` function. This is a bit more involved. After performing the common code initialization with `InitBaseClient`, we set up some global variables that the engine uses to prepare the graphics system for start-up.

And that happens with the `InitCanvas` call. The parameter we pass in is a string that specifies the name of the window that the game will be running in.

Then we load the control/client.cs module, which we'll cover next in this chapter.

We're getting warm now!

Next, we create a connection object using the `GameConnection` function. This gives us an object that we will use from now on when referring to the connection.

Now we use that connection object to connect to the server using a local connection. We don't ever actually use the network or any network ports.

Client

The control/client.cs module is chock-full of good stuff. This is another module that will need to have some of its code divested when it grows in later chapters. The main activities taking place in here are as follows:

- Creation of a key map with key bindings

- Definition of a callback that gets called from Torque to generate a 3D view

- Definition of an interface to hold the 3D view

■ Definition of a series of functions that hook key commands to avatar motion

■ A series of stub routines

Here is the control/client.cs module. Type it in, and save it as Emaga4\control\client.cs.

```
//==============================================================
// control/client.cs
//
// This module contains client specific code for handling
// the setup and operation of the player's in-game interface.
//
// 3D2E emaga4 tutorial game
//
//  Copyright (c) 2003, 2006 by Kenneth C. Finney.
//==============================================================

if ( IsObject( playerKeymap ) )     // If we already have a player key map,
    playerKeymap.delete();          // delete it so that we can make a new one
new ActionMap(playerKeymap);

$movementSpeed = 1;                 // m/s  for use by movement functions

//--------------------------------------------------------------
// The player sees the game via this control
//--------------------------------------------------------------
new GameTSCtrl(PlayerInterface) {
  profile = "GuiContentProfile";
  noCursor = "1";
};

function PlayerInterface::onWake(%this)
//--------------------------------------------------------------
// When PlayerInterface is activated, this function is called.
//--------------------------------------------------------------
{
    $enableDirectInput = "1";
    activateDirectInput();

    // restore the player's key mappings
    playerKeymap.push();
}
```

```
function GameConnection::InitialControlSet(%this)
//----------------------------------------------------------------
// This callback is called directly from inside the Torque Engine
// during server initialization.
//----------------------------------------------------------------
{
  Echo ("Setting Initial Control Object");

  // The first control object has been set by the server
  // and we are now ready to go.

  Canvas.SetContent(PlayerInterface);
}


//================================================================
// Motion Functions
//================================================================

function GoLeft(%val)
//----------------------------------------------------------------
// "strafing"
//----------------------------------------------------------------
{
  $mvLeftAction = %val;
}

function GoRight(%val)
//----------------------------------------------------------------
// "strafing"
//----------------------------------------------------------------
{
  $mvRightAction = %val;
}

function GoAhead(%val)
//----------------------------------------------------------------
// running forward
//----------------------------------------------------------------
{
  $mvForwardAction = %val;
}
```

```
function BackUp(%val)
//---------------------------------------------------------------------
// running backwards
//---------------------------------------------------------------------
{
  $mvBackwardAction = %val;
}


function DoYaw(%val)
//---------------------------------------------------------------------
// looking, spinning or aiming horizontally by mouse or joystick control
//---------------------------------------------------------------------
{
  $mvYaw += %val * ($cameraFov / 90) * 0.02;
}


function DoPitch(%val)
//---------------------------------------------------------------------
// looking vertically by mouse or joystick control
//---------------------------------------------------------------------
{
  $mvPitch += %val * ($cameraFov / 90) * 0.02;
}


function DoJump(%val)
//---------------------------------------------------------------------
// momentary upward movement, with character animation
//---------------------------------------------------------------------
{
  $mvTriggerCount2++;
}



//=====================================================================
// View Functions
//=====================================================================


function Toggle3rdPPOVLook( %val )
//---------------------------------------------------------------------
// Enable the "free look" feature. As long as the mapped key is pressed,
// the player can view his avatar by moving the mouse around.
//---------------------------------------------------------------------
```

```
{
  if ( %val )
    $mvFreeLook = true;
  else
    $mvFreeLook = false;
}

function Toggle1stPPOV(%val)
//------------------------------------------------------------------------
// switch between 1st and 3rd person point-of-views.
//------------------------------------------------------------------------
{
  if (%val)
  {
    $firstPerson = !$firstPerson;
  }
}


//========================================================================
// keyboard control mappings
//========================================================================
// these are available when player is in game
playerKeymap.Bind(keyboard, w, GoAhead);
playerKeymap.Bind(keyboard, s, BackUp);
playerKeymap.Bind(keyboard, a, GoLeft);
playerKeymap.Bind(keyboard, d, GoRight);
playerKeymap.Bind( keyboard, space, DoJump );
playerKeymap.Bind( mouse, xaxis, DoYaw );
playerKeymap.Bind( mouse, yaxis, DoPitch );

// these ones are always available
GlobalActionMap.BindCmd(keyboard, escape, "", "quit();");
GlobalActionMap.Bind(keyboard, tilde, ToggleConsole);


//========================================================================
// The following functions are called from the client common code modules.
// These stubs are added here to prevent warning messages from cluttering
// up the log file.
//========================================================================
function onServerMessage()
{
}
```

```
function onMissionDownloadPhase1()
{
}
function onPhase1Progress()
{
}
function onPhase1Complete()
{
}
function onMissionDownloadPhase2()
{
}
function onPhase2Progress()
{
}
function onPhase2Complete()
{
}
function onPhase3Complete()
{
}
function onMissionDownloadComplete()
{
}
```

Right off the bat, a new ActionMap called playerKeymap is created. This is a structure that holds the mapping of key commands to functions that will be performed—a mechanism often called *key binding*, or *key mapping*. We create the new ActionMap with the intent to populate it later in the module.

Then we define the 3D control (TS, or *ThreeSpace*) we call PlayerInterface (because that's what it is), which will contain our view into the 3D world. It's not a complex definition. It basically uses a profile defined in the common code—something we'll explore in a later chapter. If we want to use our mouse to provide view manipulation, we must set the noCursor property of the control to 1, or true.

Then we define a method for the PlayerInterface control that describes what to do when the control becomes active ("wakes up"). It's not much, but what it does is activate DirectInput in order to grab any user inputs at the keyboard or mouse and then make the playerKeymap bindings active.

Next, we define a callback method for the GameConnection object (you know, the one we created back there in control/main.cs). The engine invokes this method internally when the server has established the connection and is ready to hand control over to us. In this method we assign our player interface control to the Canvas we created earlier in the InitializeClient function in the control/ initialize.cs module.

After that, we define a whole raft of motion functions to which we will later bind keys. Notice that they employ global variables, such as $mvLeftAction. This variable and others like it, each of which starts with $mv, are seen and used internally by the engine.

Then there is a list of key bindings. Notice that there are several variations of the Bind calls. First, there are binds to our playerKeymap, which makes sense. Then there are binds to the GlobalActionMap; these bindings are available at all times when the program is running, not just when an actual game simulation is under way, which is the case with a normal action map.

Finally, there is a list of stub routines. All of these routines are called from within the common code package. We don't need them to do anything yet, but as before, in order to minimize log file warnings, we create stub routines for the functions.

Server

The control/server.cs module is where game-specific server code is located. Most of the functionality that is carried in this module is found in the form of methods for the GameConnection class. Here is the control/server.cs module. Type it in, and save it as Emaga4\control\server.cs.

```
//===========================================================================
// control/server.cs
//
//  server-side game specific module for 3D2E emaga4 tutorial game
//  provides client connection management and player/avatar spawning
//
//  Copyright (c) 2003, 2006 by Kenneth C. Finney.
//===========================================================================
function OnServerCreated()
//---------------------------------------------------------------------------
// Once the engine has fired up the server, this function is called
//---------------------------------------------------------------------------
{
    Exec("./player.cs"); // Load the player datablocks and methods
}
```

```
//======================================================================
// GameConnection Methods
// Extensions to the GameConnection class. Here we add some methods
// to handle player spawning and creation.
//======================================================================

function GameConnection::OnClientEnterGame(%this)
//----------------------------------------------------------------------
// Called when the client has been accepted into the game by the server.
//----------------------------------------------------------------------
{
  // Create a player object.
  %this.spawnPlayer();
}


function GameConnection::SpawnPlayer(%this)
//----------------------------------------------------------------------
// This is where we place the player spawn decision code.
// It might also call a function that would figure out the spawn
// point transforms by looking up spawn markers.
// Once we know where the player will spawn, then we create the avatar.
//----------------------------------------------------------------------
{

   %this.createPlayer("0 0 220 1 0 0 0");
}
function GameConnection::CreatePlayer(%this, %spawnPoint)
//----------------------------------------------------------------------
// Create the player's avatar object, set it up, and give the player control
// of it.
//----------------------------------------------------------------------
{
  if (%this.player > 0)//The player should NOT already have an avatar object.
  {                    // If he does, that's a Bad Thing.
    Error( "Attempting to create an angus ghost!" );
  }

  // Create the player object
  %player = new Player() {
    dataBlock = MaleAvatar;  // defined in player.cs
    client = %this;          // the avatar will have a pointer to its
  };                         // owner's connection
```

```
    // Player setup...
    %player.setTransform(%spawnPoint); // where to put it

    // Give the client control of the player
    %this.player = %player;
    %this.setControlObject(%player);
}
//========================================================================
// The following functions are called from the server common code modules.
// These stubs are added here to prevent warning messages from cluttering
// up the log file.
//========================================================================
function ClearCenterPrintAll()
{
}
function ClearBottomPrintAll()
{
}
```

The first function, OnServerCreated, manages what happens immediately after the server is up and running. In our case we need the player-avatar datablocks and methods to be loaded up so they can be transmitted to the client.

Then we define some GameConnection methods. The first one, OnClientEnter-Game, simply calls the SpawnPlayer method, which then calls the CreatePlayer method using the hard-coded transform provided.

CreatePlayer then creates a new player object using the player datablock defined in control/player.cs (which we will review shortly). It then applies the transform (which we created manually earlier) to the player's avatar and then transfers control to the player.

Finally, there are a couple more stub routines. That's the end of them—for now—I promise!

Player

The control/player.cs module defines the player datablock and methods for use by this datablock for various things. The datablock will use the standard male model, which in this case has been named player.dts. Figure 4.3 shows the standard male avatar in the Emaga4 game world.

Figure 4.3
Player avatar in Emaga4.

Here is the control/player.cs module. Type it in, and save it as Emaga4\control\
player.cs.

```
//-------------------------------------------------------------------------
// control/player.cs
//
//  player definition module for 3D2E emaga4 tutorial game
//
// Copyright (c) 2003, 2006 by Kenneth C. Finney.
//-------------------------------------------------------------------------
datablock PlayerData(MaleAvatar)
{
   className = Avatar;
   shapeFile = "~/player.dts";
   emap = true;
   renderFirstPerson = false;
   cameraMaxDist = 4;
   mass = 100;
   density = 10;
   drag = 0.1;
   maxdrag = 0.5;
   maxEnergy = 100;
   maxDamage = 100;
   maxForwardSpeed = 15;
```

```
    maxBackwardSpeed = 10;
    maxSideSpeed = 12;
    minJumpSpeed = 20;
    maxJumpSpeed = 30;
    runForce = 4000;
    jumpForce = 1000;
    runSurfaceAngle = 70;
    jumpSurfaceAngle = 80;
};


//---------------------------------------------------------------------------
// Avatar Datablock methods
//---------------------------------------------------------------------------

//---------------------------------------------------------------------------

function Avatar::onAdd(%this,%obj)
{
}

function Avatar::onRemove(%this, %obj)
{
   if (%obj.client.player == %obj)
      %obj.client.player = 0;
}
```

The datablock used is the PlayerData class. It is piled to the gunwales with useful stuff. Table 4.2 provides a summary description of each of the properties.

There are many more properties, which we aren't using right now, available for the avatar. We can also define our own properties for the datablock and access them, through an instance object of this datablock, from anywhere in the scripts.

Last but not least, there are two methods defined for the datablock. The two basically define what happens when we add a datablock and when we remove it. We will encounter many others in later chapters.

Running Emaga4

Once you've typed in all the modules, you should be in a good position to test Emaga4. Emaga4 is a fairly minimalist program. When you launch tge.exe, you will be deposited directly into the game. Once you have been deposited in the

Table 4.2 Emaga4 Avatar Properties

Property	Description
className	Defines an arbitrary class that the avatar can belong to.
shapeFile	Specifies the file that contains the 3D model of the avatar.
emap	Enables environment mapping on the avatar model.
renderFirstPerson	When true, causes the avatar model to be visible when in first-person point-of-view mode.
cameraMaxDist	Maximum distance from the avatar to the camera in third-person point-of-view mode.
mass	The mass of the avatar in terms of the game world.
density	Arbitrarily defined density.
drag	Slows down the avatar through simulated friction.
maxdrag	Maximum allowable drag.
maxEnergy	Maximum energy allowed.
maxDamage	Maximum damage points that can be sustained before the avatar is killed.
maxForwardSpeed	Maximum speed allowable when moving forward.
maxBackwardSpeed	Maximum speed allowable when moving backward.
maxSideSpeed	Maximum speed allowable when moving sideways (strafing).
minJumpSpeed	Below this speed, you can't make the avatar jump.
maxJumpSpeed	Above this speed, you can't make the avatar jump.
runForce	The force, and therefore the acceleration, when starting to run.
jumpForce	The force, and therefore the acceleration, when jumping.
runSurfaceAngle	Maximum slope (in degrees) that the avatar can run on.
jumpSurfaceAngle	Maximum slope (in degrees) that the avatar can jump on, usually somewhat less than RunSurfaceAngle.

game, you have a small set of keyboard commands available to control your avatar, as shown in Table 4.3.

After you have created all of the modules, you can run Emaga4 simply by double-clicking Emaga4\tge.exe. You will "spawn" into the game world above the ground and then drop down. When you hit the ground, your view will shake from the impact. If you turn your player around, using the mouse, you will see the view shown in Figure 4.4.

After spawning, you can run around the countryside, admire the countryside, and jump.

Table 4.3 Emaga4 Navigation Keys

Key	Description
w	Run forward.
s	Run backward.
a	Run (strafe) left.
d	Run (strafe) right.
spacebar	Jump.
Escape	Quit game.
Tilde	Open console.

Figure 4.4
Looking around the Emaga4 game world.

Note

If you are examining the output in the console, or in console.log, you might find a line saying that the file default.cs is missing—don't worry, that file isn't used in Emaga4 (or any of the other example programs you will encounter). It is called from the common code base, which I will not be modifying, because I want to keep it "pristine"—exactly the same as it appears in the demo provided by GarageGames.

You should feel free to dive into the common code base, find the offending line that is trying to load the nonexistent file, and remove it, change it, or whatever. There are enough clues in the console log to guide you. It's good practice!

Moving Right Along

You should have a fairly simple game now. I'll be the first to admit that there is not much to do within the game, but then that wasn't the point, really. By stripping down to a bare-bones code set, we get a clearer picture of what takes place in our script modules.

By typing in the code presented in this chapter, you should have added the following files in your EMAGA4 folder:

\EMAGA4\main.cs

\EMAGA4\control\main.cs

\EMAGA4\control\client.cs

\EMAGA4\control\server.cs

\EMAGA4\control\initialize.cs

\EMAGA4\control\player.cs

The program you have will serve as a fine skeleton program upon which you can build *your* game in the manner that *you* want.

By creating it, you've seen how the responsibilities of the client and server portions of the game are divvied out.

You've also learned that your player's avatar needs to have a programmatic representation in the game that describes the characteristics of the avatar and how it does things.

In the next chapter we will expand the game by adding game play code on both the client and the server sides.

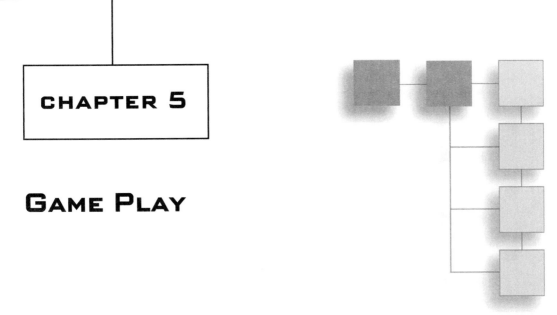

CHAPTER 5

GAME PLAY

In Chapter 4 we created a small game, Emaga4. Well, not really a game—more of a really simple virtual reality simulation. We created a few important modules to get the ball rolling.

In this chapter we'll build on that humble beginning and grow toward something with some game play challenge in it, called Emaga5. There will be some tasks to perform (*goals*) and some things to make those tasks just that much harder (*dramatic tension*).

To make this happen we'll have to add a fair number of new control modules, modify some of the existing ones, and reorganize the folder tree somewhat. We'll do that in reverse order, starting with the reorganization.

The Changes

You will recall that there are two key branches in the folder tree: common and control. As before, we won't worry about the common branch.

Folders

The control branch contained all of our code in the Chapter 4 version. For this chapter we'll use a more sophisticated structure. It's important for you to become familiar with the Emaga5 folder structure, so study Figure 5.1 for a few minutes.

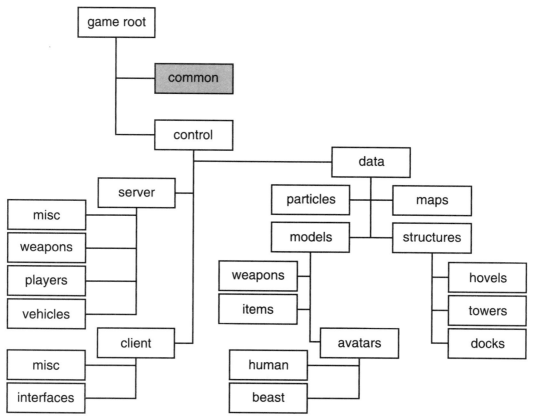

Figure 5.1
Emaga5 folder structure.

Modules

You will not need to type in the root main module again, because it won't be any different this time around. You can use the one you created for Emaga4.

In the control branch, the first major difference is that the initialize.cs module has been split in two, with a client version and a server version. Each of the new modules is now located in its respective branch: control/server/ and control/client/. They still perform the same tasks as before, but splitting the initialize functions and putting them in their permanent homes prepares us for all our later organizational needs.

There were also the two modules: control/server.cs and control/client.cs. We will now expand these and relocate them as control/server/server.cs and control/client/client.cs, respectively.

The final module from Chapter 4 is player.cs. We will be expanding it greatly and relocating it to control/server/players/player.cs.

Furthermore, we will add several new modules to handle various functional features of the game. We'll address each file as we encounter it in the chapter.

Make sure you have copied the EMAGA5 folder from the RESOURCES\CH5 folder up to your hard drive's root folder before proceeding, because that will create our folder tree for us.

Control Modules

As before, the control modules are where we focus our game-specific energies. In the root control folder is the control main module. The rest of the code modules are divided between the client and server branches. The data branch is where our art and other data definition resources reside.

control/main.cs

Type in the following code, and save it as the control main module at \EMAGA5\ control\main.cs. In order to save on space, there are fewer source code comments than in the last chapter.

```
//---------------------------------------------------------------
// control/main.cs
// Copyright (c) 2003, 2006 Kenneth C. Finney
//---------------------------------------------------------------
Exec("./client/presets.cs");
Exec("./server/presets.cs");

package control {
function OnStart()
{
    Parent::OnStart();
    Echo("\n+++++++++++++ Initializing control module +++++++++++++");
    Exec("./client/initialize.cs");
    Exec("./server/initialize.cs");
    InitializeServer(); // Prepare the server-specific aspects
    InitializeClient(); // Prepare the client-specific aspects
}
function OnExit()
```

```
{
    Parent::onExit();
}
}; // Client package
ActivatePackage(control); // Tell TGE to make the client package active
```

Right off the bat, we can see some new additions. The two Exec statements at the beginning load two files that contain *presets*. These are script variable assignment statements. We make these assignments here to specify standard or default settings. Some of the variables in those files pertain to graphics settings, others specify input modes, and things like that.

Next we have the control package, which has a few minor changes in its OnStart function. This is where we load the two new initialization modules and then call the initialization functions for the server and then the client.

Client Control Modules

Modules that affect only the client side of the game are contained in the control/ client folder tree. The client-specific activities deal with functions like the interface screens and displays, user input, and coordinating game start-up with the server side of the game.

control/client/client.cs

Many features that were in client.cs in the last chapter are now found in other modules. The key mapping and interface screen code that were located in this module, client.cs, have been given homes of their own, as you'll see later. Type in the following code, and save it as \EMAGA5\control\client\client.cs.

```
//=====================================================================
// control/client/client.cs
//   Copyright (c) 2003, 2006 by Kenneth C. Finney.
//=====================================================================
function LaunchGame()
{
    createServer("SinglePlayer", "control/data/maps/book_ch5.mis");
    %conn = new GameConnection(ServerConnection);
    %conn.setConnectArgs("Reader");
    %conn.connectLocal();
}
```

```
function ShowMenuScreen()
{
   // Start up the client with the menu...
   Canvas.setContent( MenuScreen );
   Canvas.setCursor("DefaultCursor");
}
function SplashScreenInputCtrl::onInputEvent(%this, %dev, %evt, %make)
{
   if(%make)
   {
     ShowMenuScreen();
   }
}
//==============================================================
// stubs
//==============================================================
function onServerMessage()
{
}
function onMissionDownloadPhase1()
{
}
function onPhase1Progress()
{
}
function onPhase1Complete()
{
}
function onMissionDownloadPhase2()
{
}
function onPhase2Progress()
{
}
function onPhase2Complete()
{
}
function onPhase3Complete()
{
}
function onMissionDownloadComplete()
{
}
```

Figure 5.2
The Emaga5 splash screen.

We've added three new functions, the first of which is LaunchGame. The code contained should be familiar from Emaga4. This function is executed when the user clicks the Start Game button on the front menu screen of the game. (The other options available on the front screen are Setup and Quit.)

Next is ShowMenuScreen, which is invoked when the user clicks the mouse or presses a key when viewing the splash screen. The code it invokes is also familiar from Emaga4.

The third function, SplashScreenInputCtrl::onInputEvent, is a callback method used by a GuiInputControl (in this case the SplashScreenInputCtrl). Splash ScreenInputCtrl::onInputEvent is attached to the splash screen for the narrow purpose of simply waiting for user input; when that happens, it closes the splash screen. We get the user input value in the %make parameter. Figure 5.2 shows what the splash screen looks like.

The rest of the functions are the by-now-famous stub routines. These are mostly client/server mission (map) loading and coordination functions. These will get more attention in later chapters. You are free to leave out the stub routines, but if you do, you will end up with a ton of warning messages in the log file.

control/client/interfaces/menuscreen.gui

All the user interface and display screens now have modules of their own, and they reside in the interfaces branch of the client tree. Note that the extension of these modules is .gui. Functionally, a .gui is the same as a .cs source module. They both can contain any kind of valid script code, and both compile to the .dso binary format. Type in the following code, and save it as \EMAGA5\control\ client\interfaces\menuscreen.gui.

```
new GuiChunkedBitmapCtrl(MenuScreen) {
    profile = "GuiContentProfile";
    horizSizing = "width";
    vertSizing = "height";
    position = "0 0";
    extent = "640 480";
    minExtent = "8 8";
    visible = "1";
    helpTag = "0";
    bitmap = "./interfaces/emaga_background";
    useVariable = "0";
    tile = "0";
    new GuiButtonCtrl() {
        profile = "GuiButtonProfile";
        horizSizing = "right";
        vertSizing = "top";
        position = "29 300";
        extent = "110 20";
        minExtent = "8 8";
        visible = "1";
        command = "LaunchGame();";
        helpTag = "0";
        text = "Start Game";
        groupNum = "-1";
        buttonType = "PushButton";
    };
    new GuiButtonCtrl() {
        profile = "GuiButtonProfile";
        horizSizing = "right";
        vertSizing = "top";
        position = "29 400";
        extent = "110 20";
        minExtent = "8 8";
        visible = "1";
        command = "Quit();";
        helpTag = "0";
        text = "Quit";
```

```
        groupNum = "-1";
        buttonType = "PushButton";
    };
};
```

What we have here is a hierarchical definition of nested objects. The object that contains the others is the MenuScreen itself, defined as a GuiChunkedBitmapCtrl. Many video cards have texture size limits; for some nothing larger than 512 pixels by 512 pixels can be used. The ChunkedBitmap splits large textures into sections to avoid these limitations. This is usually used for large 640 by 480 or 800 by 600 background artwork.

MenuScreen has a profile property of GuiContentProfile, which is a standard Torque profile for large controls that will contain other controls. *Profiles* are collections of properties that can be applied in bulk to interface (or *gui*) objects. Profiles are much like style sheets (which you will be familiar with if you do any HTML programming), except that they use TorqueScript syntax.

The definition of GuiContentProfile is pretty simple:

```
if(!IsObject(GuiContentProfile)) new GuiControlProfile (GuiContentProfile)
{
    opaque = true;
    fillColor = "255 255 255";
};
```

Basically, the object is opaque (no transparency allowed, even if an alpha channel exists in the object's source bitmap image). If the object doesn't fill the screen, then the unused screen space is filled with black (RGB = 255 255 255).

After the profile, the sizing and position information properties are set. See the sidebar titled "Profile Sizing Settings: horizSizing and vertSizing" for more information.

The extent property defines the horizontal and vertical dimensions of MenuScreen. The minExtent property specifies the smallest size that the object can have.

The visible property indicates whether the object can be seen on the screen. Using a "1" will make the object visible; a "0" will make it invisible.

The last significant property is the bitmap property. This specifies what bitmap image will be used for the background image of the object.

There are two GuiButtonCtrl objects contained in the MenuScreen. Most of the properties are the same as found in the GuiChunkedBitmapCtrl. But there are a few that are different and important.

The first is the command property. When the user clicks this button control, the function specified in the command property is executed.

The helpTag property is used to keep track of whether a user has encountered this object previously or not. Set to zero, it means that no help has been displayed for this object. If you decide to display help, then set the helpTag to a non-zero value so you can choose not to display help.

Next, the text property is where you can enter the text label that will appear on the button.

The groupNum property is used to indicate which group a button belongs to. Use mostly with Radio button.

Finally, the buttonType property is how you specify the particular visual style of the button.

Figure 5.3 shows the MenuScreen in all its glory.

Figure 5.3
The Emaga5 MenuScreen.

Profile Sizing Settings: horizSizing and vertSizing

These settings are used to define how to resize or reposition an object when the object's container is resized. The outermost container is the Canvas; it will have a starting size of 640 pixels by 480 pixels. The Canvas and all the objects within it will be resized or repositioned from this initial size.

When you resize a container, all of its child objects are resized and repositioned according to their horizSizing and vertSizing properties. The resizing action will be applied in a cascading manner to all subobjects in the object hierarchy.

The following property values are available:

Center	The object is positioned in the center of its container.
Relative	The object is resized and repositioned to maintain the same size and position relative to its container. If the parent size doubles, the object's size doubles as well.
Left	When the container is resized or moved, the change is applied to the distance between the object and the left edge of the screen.
Right	When the container is resized or moved, the change is applied to the distance between the object and the right edge of the screen.
Top	When the container is resized or moved, the change is applied to the distance between the object and the top edge of the screen.
Bottom	When the container is resized or moved, the change is applied to the distance between the object and the bottom edge of the screen.
Width	When the container is resized or moved horizontally, the change is applied to the width extents of the object.
Height	When the container is resized or moved vertically, the change is applied to the height extents of the object.

control/client/interfaces/playerinterface.gui

The PlayerInterface control is the interface that is used during the game to display information in real time. The Canvas is the container for PlayerInterface. Type in the following code, and save it as \Emaga5\control\client\interfaces\playerinterface.gui.

```
new GameTSCtrl(PlayerInterface) {
   profile = "GuiContentProfile";
   horizSizing = "right";
   vertSizing = "bottom";
   position = "0 0";
   extent = "640 480";
   minExtent = "8 8";
   visible = "1";
   helpTag = "0";
      noCursor = "1";
```

```
new GuiCrossHairHud() {
    profile = "GuiDefaultProfile";
    horizSizing = "center";
    vertSizing = "center";
    position = "304 224";
    extent = "32 32";
    minExtent = "8 8";
    visible = "1";
    helpTag = "0";
    bitmap = "./interfaces/emaga_gunsight";
    wrap = "0";
    damageFillColor = "0.000000 1.000000 0.000000 1.000000";
    damageFrameColor = "1.000000 0.600000 0.000000 1.000000";
    damageRect = "50 4";
    damageOffset = "0 10";
};
new GuiHealthBarHud() {
    profile = "GuiDefaultProfile";
    horizSizing = "right";
    vertSizing = "top";
    position = "14 315";
    extent = "26 138";
    minExtent = "8 8";
    visible = "1";
    helpTag = "0";
    showFill = "1";
    displayEnergy = "0";
    showFrame = "1";
    fillColor = "0.000000 0.000000 0.000000 0.500000";
    frameColor = "0.000000 1.000000 0.000000 0.000000";
    damageFillColor = "0.800000 0.000000 0.000000 1.000000";
    pulseRate = "1000";
    pulseThreshold = "0.5";
       value = "1";
};
new GuiBitmapCtrl() {
    profile = "GuiDefaultProfile";
    horizSizing = "right";
    vertSizing = "top";
    position = "11 299";
    extent = "32 172";
    minExtent = "8 8";
    visible = "1";
```

```
    helpTag = "0";
    bitmap = "./interfaces/emaga_healthwidget";
    wrap = "0";
};
new GuiHealthBarHud() {
    profile = "GuiDefaultProfile";
    horizSizing = "right";
    vertSizing = "top";
    position = "53 315";
    extent = "26 138";
    minExtent = "8 8";
    visible = "1";
    helpTag = "0";
    showFill = "1";
    displayEnergy = "1";
    showFrame = "1";
    fillColor = "0.000000 0.000000 0.000000 0.500000";
    frameColor = "0.000000 1.000000 0.000000 0.000000";
    damageFillColor = "0.000000 0.000000 0.800000 1.000000";
    pulseRate = "1000";
    pulseThreshold = "0.5";
        value = "1";
};
new GuiBitmapCtrl() {
    profile = "GuiDefaultProfile";
    horizSizing = "right";
    vertSizing = "top";
    position = "50 299";
    extent = "32 172";
    minExtent = "8 8";
    visible = "1";
    helpTag = "0";
    bitmap = "./interfaces/emaga_healthwidget";
    wrap = "0";
};
new GuiTextCtrl(scorelabel) {
    profile = "ScoreTextProfile";
    horizSizing = "right";
    vertSizing = "bottom";
    position = "10 3";
    extent = "50 20";
    minExtent = "8 8";
```

```
        visible = "1";
        helpTag = "0";
        text = "Score";
        maxLength = "255";
    };
    new GuiTextCtrl(Scorebox) {
        profile = "ScoreTextProfile";
        horizSizing = "right";
        vertSizing = "bottom";
        position = "50 3";
        extent = "100 20";
        minExtent = "8 8";
        visible = "1";
        helpTag = "0";
        text = "0";
        maxLength = "255";
    };
};
```

PlayerInterface is the main TSControl through which the game is viewed; it also contains the HUD controls.

The object GuiCrossHairHud is the targeting crosshair. Use this to aim your weapons.

There are two GuiHealthBarHud controls, one for health and one for energy. It is essentially a vertical bar that indicates the state of health or energy of the player. Each GuiHealthBarHud is paired with a GuiBitmapCtrl, which is a bitmap that can be used to modify the appearance of the health and energy displays by overlaying on the GuiHealthBarHud.

Note

HUD is a TLA (*Three-Letter Acronym*) that means *Heads Up Display.* The expression is adopted from the world of high-tech military aircraft. The HUD comprises information and graphics that are projected onto the canopy or a small screen at eye level in front of the pilot. This allows the pilot to continue to look outside for threats, while still having instant visual access to flight- or mission-critical information. In game graphics the term *HUD* is used for visual displays that appear in-game, in a fashion that mirrors the real-world application.

There are two GuiTextCtrl objects, one for holding the accumulated score (scorebox) and one to provide a simple label for the scores box (scorelabel). We will be modifying the value of the text property from within the control source code in another module.

control/client/interfaces/splashscreen.gui

The SplashScreen control displays an informational screen (you saw it in Figure 5.2 when the game is started from Windows. A mouse click or key press makes this screen go away. Type in the following code, and save it as \Emaga5\control\client\interfaces\splashscreen.gui.

```
new GuiChunkedBitmapCtrl(SplashScreen) {
   profile = "GuiDefaultProfile";
   horizSizing = "width";
   vertSizing = "height";
   position = "0 0";
   extent = "640 480";
   minExtent = "8 8";
   visible = "1";
   helpTag = "0";
   bitmap = "./interfaces/emaga_splash";
   useVariable = "0";
   tile = "0";
   noCursor=1;
   new GuiInputCtrl(SplashScreenInputCtrl) {
      profile = "GuiInputCtrlProfile";
      position = "0 0";
      extent = "10 10";
   };
};
```

The only thing special about this module is the new control, GuiInputCtrl. This control is used to accept input from the user: mouse clicks, key presses, and so on. With this control defined we can then define our own handler methods for the control's object and therefore act upon the inputs. In our case here SplashScreenInputCtrl::onInputEvent is the handler method we've defined; it's contained in the client module we talked about earlier.

control/client/misc/screens.cs

The screen.cs module is where our programmed control and management activity is located. Type in the following code, and save it as \Emaga5\control\client\misc\screens.cs.

```
//============================================================
// control/client/misc/screens.cs
//
// Copyright (c) 2003, 2006 by Kenneth C. Finney
//============================================================
function PlayerInterface::onWake(%this)
{
    $enableDirectInput = "1";
    activateDirectInput();
    // just update the key map here
    playerKeymap.push();
}
function PlayerInterface::onSleep(%this)
{
    playerKeymap.pop();
}
function refreshBottomTextCtrl()
{
    BottomPrintText.position = "0 0";
}
function refreshCenterTextCtrl()
{
    CenterPrintText.position = "0 0";
}
function LoadScreen::onAdd(%this)
{
    %this.qLineCount = 0;
}
function LoadScreen::onWake(%this)
{
    CloseMessagePopup();
}
function LoadScreen::onSleep(%this)
{
    // Clear the load info:
    if ( %this.qLineCount !$= "" )
    {
        for ( %line = 0; %line < %this.qLineCount; %line++ )
            %this.qLine[%line] = "";
    }
    %this.qLineCount = 0;
    LOAD_MapName.setText( "" );
```

```
        LOAD_MapDescription.setText( "" );
        LoadingProgress.setValue( 0 );
        LoadingProgressTxt.setValue( "WAITING FOR SERVER" );
}
```

The methods in this module are representative of the sort of methods you can use for interface controls. You will probably use `OnWake` and `OnSleep` quite a bit in your interface scripts.

`OnWake` methods are called when an interface object is told to display itself, either by the `Canvas`'s `SetContent` or `PushDialog` methods.

`OnSleep` methods are called whenever an interface object is removed from display via the `PopDialog` method or when the `SetContent` call specifies a different object.

When `PushDialog` is used the interface that is shown operates like a modal dialog control—all input events are relayed through the dialog.

There is another pair of interface display methods for other objects, called just `Push` and `Pop`. These will display the interface in a modeless manner, so that other controls or objects on the screen will still receive input events they are interested in.

`PlayerInterface::onWake` enables capturing mouse and keyboard inputs using `DirectInput`. It then makes the `PlayerKeymap` key bindings active using the `Push` method. When the `PlayerInterface` is removed from display, its `OnSleep` method removes the `PlayerKeymap` key bindings from consideration. You will need to ensure that you have defined global bindings for the user to employ; these will take over when the `PlayerKeymap` isn't in use anymore.

`RefreshBottomTextCtrl` and `RefreshCenterTextCtrl` just reposition these output controls to their default locations on the screen, in case you have moved them somewhere else during the festivities.

There is also a method called `LoadScreen::OnAdd`. `OnAdd` methods are called when an object is added to a scene or another object. They are usually used to initialize properties of the object that might differ from the default property values.

`LoadScreen::OnWake` is called when we want to display the mission loading progress. It closes the message interface, if it happens to be open. The `LoadScreen` contents are modified elsewhere for us in the mission loading process, which is covered in Chapter 6.

When `LoadScreen::OnSleep` is called, it clears all of its text buffers and then outputs a message to indicate that all we need now is for the server to chime in.

control/client/misc/presetkeys.cs

Key bindings are the mapping of keyboard keys and mouse buttons to specific functions and commands. In a fully featured game we would provide the user with the ability to modify the key bindings using a graphical interface. Right now we will satisfy ourselves with creating a set of key bindings for the user, which we can keep around to be used as the initial defaults as we later expand our program.

Type in the following code, and save it as \Emaga5\control\client\misc\presetkeys.cs.

```
//===========================================================
// control/client/misc/presetkeys.cs
// Copyright (c) 2003, 2006 by Kenneth C. Finney
//===========================================================
if ( IsObject(PlayerKeymap) ) // If we already have a player key map,
   PlayerKeymap.delete();        // delete it so that we can make a new one
new ActionMap(PlayerKeymap);

function DoExitGame()
{
   MessageBoxYesNo( "Quit Mission", "Exit from this Mission?", "Quit();", "");
}
//===========================================================
// Motion Functions
//===========================================================
function GoLeft(%val)
{
   $mvLeftAction = %val;
}
function GoRight(%val)
{
   $mvRightAction = %val;
}
function GoAhead(%val)
{
   $mvForwardAction = %val;
}
function BackUp(%val)
```

```
{
   $mvBackwardAction = %val;
}
function DoYaw(%val)
{
   $mvYaw += %val * ($cameraFov / 90) * 0.02;
}
function DoPitch(%val)
{
   $mvPitch += %val * ($cameraFov / 90) * 0.02;
}
function DoJump(%val)
{
   $mvTriggerCount2++;
}
//=============================================================================
// View Functions
//=============================================================================
function Toggle3rdPPOVLook( %val )
{
   if ( %val )            $mvFreeLook = true;
   else                   $mvFreeLook = false;
}
function MouseAction(%val)
{
   $mvTriggerCount0++;
}
$firstPerson = true;
function Toggle1stPPOV(%val)
//-----------------------------------------------------------------------------
// switch between 1st and 3rd person point-of-view.
//-----------------------------------------------------------------------------
{
   if (%val)
   {
      $firstPerson = !$firstPerson;
      ServerConnection.setFirstPerson($firstPerson);
   }
}function dropCameraAtPlayer(%val)
{
   if (%val)
      commandToServer('dropCameraAtPlayer');
}
```

```
function dropPlayerAtCamera(%val)
{
   if (%val)
     commandToServer('DropPlayerAtCamera');
}
function toggleCamera(%val)
{
   if (%val)
     commandToServer('ToggleCamera');
}
//===========================================================================
// keyboard control mappings
//===========================================================================
// available when player is in game
PlayerKeymap.Bind( mouse, button0, MouseAction ); // left mouse button
PlayerKeymap.Bind(keyboard, w, GoAhead);
PlayerKeymap.Bind(keyboard, s, BackUp);
PlayerKeymap.Bind(keyboard, a, GoLeft);
PlayerKeymap.Bind(keyboard, d, GoRight);
PlayerKeymap.Bind(keyboard, space, DoJump );
PlayerKeymap.Bind(keyboard, z, Toggle3rdPPOVLook );
PlayerKeymap.Bind(keyboard, tab, Toggle1stPPOV );
PlayerKeymap.Bind(mouse, xaxis, DoYaw );
PlayerKeymap.Bind(mouse, yaxis, DoPitch );// always available
GlobalActionMap.Bind(keyboard, escape, DoExitGame);
GlobalActionMap.Bind(keyboard, tilde, ToggleConsole);
```

The first three statements in this module prepare the ActionMap object, which we call PlayerKeymap. This is the set of key bindings that will prevail while we are actually in the game. Because this module is used in the initial setup, we assume that there should not already be a PlayerKeymapActionMap, so we check to see if PlayerKeymap is an existing object, and if it is we delete it and create a new version.

We define a function to be called when we exit the game. It throws a Message-BoxYesNo dialog up on the screen, with the dialog box's title set to the contents of the first parameter string. The second parameter string sets the contents of the dialog's prompt. The third parameter specifies the function to execute when the user clicks the Yes button. The fourth parameter indicates what action to perform if the user clicks No—in this case nothing.

Table 5.1 Basic Movement Functions

Command	Description
GoLeft and GoRight	Strafing to the left or the right.
GoAhead and BackUp	Running forward and backward.
DoYaw	Spinning or aiming horizontally by mouse or joystick control.
DoPitch	Looking vertically by mouse or joystick control.
DoJump	Momentary upward movement, with character animation.
Toggle3rdPPOVLook	Enables the "free look" feature. As long as the mapped key is pressed while the player is in third-person point of view, the player can view his avatar by moving the mouse around.

There are two other canned MessageDialog objects defined in the common code base: MessageBoxOk, which has no fourth parameter, and MessageBoxOkCancel, which accepts essentially the same parameter set as MessageBoxYesNo.

Next we have a series of motion function definitions. Table 5.1 provides a description of the basic motion functions. These functions employ player event control triggers to do their dirty work. These triggers are described in detail in Chapter 6.

Of particular note in these functions is that they all have a single parameter, usually called %val. When functions are bound to keys or mouse buttons via a Bind method, the parameter is set to a nonzero value when the key or button is pressed and to 0 when the button is released. This allows us to create toggling functions, such as with Toggle1stPPOV, which will switch between first-person perspective and third-person perspective each time the bound key is pressed.

After all the function definitions, we have the actual key bindings. With the Bind method, the first parameter is the input type, the second is the key or button identifier, and the third is the name of the function to be called.

After all the PlayerKeymap bindings, there are a few for GlobalActionMap, which is a globally predefined action map that is always available but can be overridden by other action maps. In this case we use GlobalActionMap for those bindings we want to be universally available.

Server Control Modules

Any game play features you want to implement should probably be done as a server control module, or part of one. If you are going to make a multiplayer online game, that *should probably* back there in the last sentence will change to a *must*. The only way we can ensure a level playing field and game play code security is to run the code on the server, and not on the client.

control/server/server.cs

On the server side, the server module is probably the single most influential module. It carries the server control–oriented GameConnection methods for handling players and other game objects, as well as straightforward server control routines.

Type in the following code, and save it as \Emaga5\control\server\server.cs.

```
//===========================================================================
// control/server/server.cs
//   Copyright (c) 2003, 2006 by Kenneth C. Finney.
//===========================================================================
function OnServerCreated()
//---------------------------------------------------------------------------
// Once the engine has fired up the server, this function is called
//---------------------------------------------------------------------------
{
   Exec("./misc/camera.cs");
   Exec("./misc/shapeBase.cs");
   Exec("./misc/item.cs");
   Exec("./players/player.cs");
   Exec("./players/beast.cs");
   Exec("./players/ai.cs");
   Exec("./weapons/weapon.cs");
   Exec("./weapons/crossbow.cs");
}
function StartGame()
{
  if ($Game::Duration) // Start the game timer
    $Game::Schedule = Schedule($Game::Duration * 1000, 0, "onGameDurationEnd");
  $Game::Running = true;
  schedule( 2000, 0, "CreateBots");
}
function OnMissionLoaded()
{
   StartGame();
}
function OnMissionEnded()
```

```
  {
     Cancel($Game::Schedule);
     $Game::Running = false;
  }
  function GameConnection::OnClientEnterGame(%this)
  {
     // Create a new camera object.
     %this.camera = new Camera() {
        dataBlock = Observer;
     };
     MissionCleanup.Add( %this.camera );
     %this.camera.ScopeToClient(%this);
     %this.SpawnPlayer();
  }
  function GameConnection::SpawnPlayer(%this)
  {

     %this.CreatePlayer("0 0 201 1 0 0 0");
  }
  function GameConnection::CreatePlayer(%this, %spawnPoint)
  {
     if (%this.player > 0)//The player should NOT already have an avatar object.
     {                    // If he does, that's a Bad Thing.
        Error( "Attempting to create an angus ghost!" );
     }
     // Create the player object
     %player = new Player() {
        dataBlock = MaleAvatar;   // defined in players/player.cs
        client = %this;           // the avatar will have a pointer to its
     };                           // owner's GameConnection object
     %player.SetTransform(%spawnPoint); // where to put it
     // Update the camera to start with the player
     %this.camera.SetTransform(%player.GetEyeTransform());
     %player.SetEnergyLevel(100);
     // Give the client control of the player
     %this.player = %player;
     %this.setControlObject(%player);
  }
  function GameConnection::OnDeath(%this, %sourceObject, %sourceClient,
  %damageType, %damLoc)
  {
     // Switch the client over to the death cam and unhook the player object.
     if (IsObject(%this.camera) && IsObject(%this.player))
```

```
    {
      %this.camera.SetMode("Death",%this.player);
      %this.setControlObject(%this.camera);
    }
    %this.player = 0;
    if (%damageType $= "Suicide" || %sourceClient == %this)
    {
    }
    else
    {
      // good hit
    }
}
//================================================================
// Server commands
//================================================================
function ServerCmdToggleCamera(%client)
{
    %co = %client.getControlObject();
    if (%co == %client.player)
    {
      %co = %client.camera;
      %co.mode = toggleCameraFly;
    }
    else
    {
      %co = %client.player;
      %co.mode = observerFly;
    }
    %client.SetControlObject(%co);
}
function ServerCmdDropPlayerAtCamera(%client)
{
    if ($Server::DevMode || IsObject(EditorGui))
    {
      %client.player.SetTransform(%client.camera.GetTransform());
      %client.player.SetVelocity("0 0 0");
      %client.SetControlObject(%client.player);
    }
}
function ServerCmdDropCameraAtPlayer(%client)
{
    %client.camera.SetTransform(%client.player.GetEyeTransform());
```

```
    %client.camera.SetVelocity("0 0 0");
    %client.SetControlObject(%client.camera);
}
function ServerCmdUse(%client,%data)
{
    %client.GetControlObject().use(%data);
}
// stubs
function ClearCenterPrintAll()
{
}
function ClearBottomPrintAll()
{
}
function onNeedRelight()
{
}
```

The first function in this module, OnServerCreated, is pretty straightforward. When called, it loads all the specific game play modules we need.

After that comes StartGame, which is where we put stuff that is needed every time a new game starts. In this case if we have prescribed game duration, then we start the game timer using the Schedule function.

Schedule is an extremely important function, so we'll spend a little bit of time on it here. The usage syntax is

```
%event = Schedule(time, reference, command, <param1...paramN>)
```

The function will schedule an event that will trigger in time milliseconds and execute command with parameters. If reference is not 0, then you need to make sure that reference is set to be a valid object handle. When the reference object is deleted, the scheduled event is discarded if it hasn't already fired. The Schedule function returns an event ID number that can be used to track the scheduled event or cancel it later before it takes place.

In the case of our game timer, there is no game duration defined, so the game is open-ended, and the Schedule call will not take place. If, for example, $Game::Duration had been set to 1,800 (for 30 minutes times 60 seconds per minute), then the call to Schedule would have had the first parameter set to 1,800 times 1,000, or 1,800,000, which is the number of milliseconds in 30 minutes.

OnMissionLoaded is called by LoadMission once the mission is finished loading. All it really does is start up the game play, but this is an ideal location to insert code that needs to adjust its capabilities based upon whatever mission was loaded.

The next function, OnMissionEnded, is called at the conclusion of the running of a mission, usually in the DestroyServer function. Here it cancels the end-of-game event that has been scheduled; if no game duration was scheduled—as is our case at the moment—then nothing happens, quietly.

After that is the GameConnection::OnClientEnterGame method. This method is called when the client has been accepted into the game by the server—the client has not actually entered the game yet though. The server creates a new observer mode camera and adds it to the MissionCleanup group. This group is used to contain objects that will need to be removed from memory when a mission is finished. Next, it *scopes* the camera to the client. This process is similar to key binding, except that it "connects" a network object (in this case, through a GameConnection object, via %this) to a game object. This way Torque knows where to send network events and messages. Then we initiate the spawning of the player's avatar into the game world.

The GameConnection::SpawnPlayer is a "glue" method, which will have more functionality in the future. Right now we use it to call the CreatePlayer method with a fixed transform to tell it where to place the newly created player-avatar. Normally this is where we would place the player spawn decision code. It might also call a function that would figure out the spawn point transforms by looking up spawn markers. Once we know where the player will spawn, then we would create the avatar by calling CreatePlayer.

GameConnection::CreatePlayer is the method that creates the player's avatar object, sets it up, and then passes control of the avatar to the player. The first thing to watch out for is that we must ensure that the GameConnection does not already, or still, have an avatar assigned to it. If it does, then we risk creating what the GarageGames guys call an *Angus Ghost*. This is a ghosted object, on all the clients, that has no controlling client scoped to it. We don't want that! Once that is sorted out, we create the new avatar, give it some energy, and pass control to the player, the same way we did previously in Chapter 4.

GameConnection::onDeath is called from a player's Damage handler method if the player's damage exceeds a certain amount. What we do is switch the client over to the death cam and unhook the player object. This allows the player to swivel his view in orbit around the "corpse" of his avatar until he decides to respawn. There is a code block containing the comment "good hit" where we would add code to provide points scoring and other game play functionality if we want it. We can also penalize a player for committing suicide, by either evaluating the damage type or the ID of the owner of the weapon that killed the player.

There then is a series of ServerCmd message handlers that change whether the player controls the camera or the avatar based on the message received.

ServerCmdToggleCamera alternates between attaching the player to the camera or to his avatar as the control object. Each time the function is called, it checks to see which object is the control object—camera or avatar—and then selects the other one to be the new control object.

ServerCmdDropPlayerAtCamera will move the player's avatar to wherever the camera object is currently located and sets the player-avatar's velocity to 0. The control object is always set to be the player's avatar when the function exits.

ServerCmdDropCameraAtPlayer does just the opposite. It sets the camera's transform to match the player-avatar's and then sets the velocity to 0. The control object is always set to be the camera when the function exits.

The next function, ServerCmdUse, is an important game play message handler. We call this function whenever we want to activate or otherwise use an object that the player controls, "has mounted," or holds in inventory. When called, this function figures out the handle of the client's control object and then passes the data it has received to that object's use method. The data can be anything but is often the activation mode or sometimes a quantity (like a powerup or health value). You'll see how the back end of this works later in the item module.

Finally, there are a few stub routines. As you will recall, these functions are called from within the common code script modules. We don't need their functionality for what we are doing here, so they are empty. They are included in order to minimize error messages in the console.

control/server/players/player.cs

This is "the biggie." You will probably spend more time working with, tweaking, adjusting, and yes, possibly even cursing this module—or your own variations of this module—than any other.

Type in the following code, and save it as \EMAGA5\control\server\players\ player.cs.

```
//================================================================
// control/server/players/player.cs
//  Copyright (c) 2003, 2006 by Kenneth C. Finney.
//================================================================
exec("~/data/models/avatars/orc/player.cs");

datablock PlayerData(MaleAvatar)
{
    className = OrcClass;
    shapeFile = "~/data/models/avatars/orc/player.dts";
    emap = true;
    renderFirstPerson = false;
    cameraMaxDist = 3;
    mass = 100;
    density = 10;
    drag = 0.1;
    maxdrag = 0.5;
    maxDamage = 100;
    maxEnergy = 100;
    maxForwardSpeed = 15;
    maxBackwardSpeed = 10;
    maxSideSpeed = 12;
    minJumpSpeed = 20;
    maxJumpSpeed = 30;
    runForce = 1000;
    jumpForce = 1000;
    runSurfaceAngle = 40;
    jumpSurfaceAngle = 30;
    runEnergyDrain = 0.05;
    minRunEnergy = 1;
    jumpEnergyDrain = 20;
    minJumpEnergy = 20;
    recoverDelay = 30;
    recoverRunForceScale = 1.2;
    minImpactSpeed = 10;
    speedDamageScale = 3.0;
    repairRate = 0.03;
    maxInv[Copper] = 9999;
    maxInv[Silver] = 99;
    maxInv[Gold] = 9;
```

```
        maxInv[Crossbow] = 1;
        maxInv[CrossbowAmmo] = 20;
};
//=================================================================
// Avatar Datablock methods
//=================================================================
function OrcClass::onAdd(%this,%obj)
{
    %obj.mountVehicle = false;

    // Default dynamic Avatar stats
    %obj.setRechargeRate(0.01);
    %obj.setRepairRate(%this.repairRate);
}
function OrcClass::onRemove(%this, %obj)
{
    %client = %obj.client;
    if (%client.player == %obj)
    {
        %client.player = 0;
    }
}
function OrcClass::onCollision(%this,%obj,%col,%vec,%speed)
{
    %obj_state = %obj.getState();
    %col_className = %col.getClassName();
    %col_dblock_className = %col.getDataBlock().className;
    %colName = %col.getDataBlock().getName();
    if ( %obj_state $= "Dead")
        return;
    if (%col_className $= "Item" || %col_className $= "Weapon" )
    {
        %obj.pickup(%col);
    }
}
//=================================================================
// MaleAvatar (ShapeBase) class methods
//=================================================================
function MaleAvatar::onImpact(%this,%obj,%collidedObject,%vec,%vecLen)
{
    %obj.Damage(0, VectorAdd(%obj.getPosition(),%vec),
        %vecLen * %this.speedDamageScale, "Impact");
}
```

```
function MaleAvatar::Damage(%this, %obj, %sourceObject, %position, %damage,
%damageType)
{
   if (%obj.getState() $= "Dead")
      return;
   %obj.applyDamage(%damage);
   %location = "Body";
   %client = %obj.client;
   %sourceClient = %sourceObject ? %sourceObject.client : 0;
   if (%obj.getState() $= "Dead")
   {
      %client.onDeath(%sourceObject, %sourceClient, %damageType, %location);
   }
}
function MaleAvatar::onDamage(%this, %obj, %delta)
{
   if (%delta > 0 && %obj.getState() !$= "Dead")
   {
      // Increment the flash based on the amount.
      %flash = %obj.getDamageFlash() + ((%delta / %this.maxDamage) * 2);
      if (%flash > 0.75)
         %flash = 0.75;

      if (%flash > 0.001)
      {
         %obj.setDamageFlash(%flash);
      }
      %obj.setRechargeRate(0.01);
      %obj.setRepairRate(0.01);
   }
}
function MaleAvatar::onDisabled(%this,%obj,%state)
{
   %obj.clearDamageDt();
   %obj.setRechargeRate(0);
   %obj.setRepairRate(0);
   %obj.setImageTrigger(0,false);
   %obj.schedule(5000, "startFade", 5000, 0, true);
   %obj.schedule(10000, "delete");
}
```

The first line of code loads and executes a "glue module" called player.cs. This module provides a mapping between animation sequence names and animation sequence files. How this works is covered later in Chapter 14 when we actually get around to creating an animated model for use with the Torque Engine. For now, the important thing to understand is that if we use animation sequence files (of the type .dsq), then we need to relate those files to the sequence names that Torque uses to trigger the animations, and also that we describe that relationship with an animation sequence glue module like the one being exec'd in this line.

Next is a datablock definition for a datablock called MaleAvatar of the PlayerData datablock class. Table 5.2 provides a quick reference description of the items in this datablock.

A brief word about the classname property. It's a GameBase classname property for this datablock, which in this case is MaleAvatar. We use this class name to provide a place to hang various methods, which are defined later in the module.

In Chapter 3 we encountered *environment mapping*, which is a rendering technique that provides a method of taking the game world appearance and surroundings into account when rendering an object. You can enable environment mapping when rendering the avatar model by setting the emap property to true.

If we set the property renderFirstPerson to true, then when we are playing in first-person point-of-view mode, we will be able to see our avatar, our "body," as we look around. With it set to false, then we won't see it, no matter which way we look.

To control your avatar's energy depletion, you will want to adjust the following properties: maxEnergy, runEnergyDrain, minRunEnergy, jumpEnergyDrain, and minJumpEnergy. Generally, the minimum jump energy should be set higher than the minimum run energy. Also, jump energy drain should be faster, thus a higher number, than the run energy drain value.

Next is a series of methods that are used when dealing with the avatar as a GameBase class.

The first, the MaleAvatar::onAdd, is the method called whenever a new instance of an avatar is added to the game. In this case we initialize a few variables and then transfer the value of the datablock's repairRate property (remember that a datablock is static and unchangeable once transferred to the client) to Player object in order to have it available for later use. The %obj parameter refers to the Player object handle.

Table 5.2 Emaga5 Avatar Properties

Property	Description
className	Defines an arbitrary class that the avatar can belong to.
shapeFile	Specifies the file that contains the 3D model of the avatar.
emap	Enables environment mapping on the avatar model.
renderFirstPerson	When true, causes the avatar model to be visible when in first-person point-of-view mode.
cameraMaxDist	Maximum distance from the avatar to the camera in third-person point-of-view mode.
mass	The mass of the avatar in terms of the game world.
density	Arbitrarily defined density. Low-density players will float in water.
drag	Slows down the avatar through simulated friction.
maxdrag	Maximum allowable drag.
maxDamage	Maximum damage points that can be sustained before avatar is killed.
maxEnergy	Maximum energy allowed.
maxForwardSpeed	Maximum speed allowable when moving forward.
maxBackwardSpeed	Maximum speed allowable when moving backward.
maxSideSpeed	Maximum speed allowable when moving sideways (strafing).
minJumpSpeed	Below this speed, you can't make the avatar jump.
maxJumpSpeed	Above this speed, you can't make the avatar jump.
runForce	The force, and therefore the acceleration, when starting to run.
jumpForce	The force, and therefore the acceleration, when jumping.
runSurfaceAngle	Maximum slope (in degrees) that the avatar can run on.
jumpSurfaceAngle	Maximum slope (in degrees) that the avatar can jump on, usually somewhat less than runSurfaceAngle.
runEnergyDrain	How quickly energy is lost when the player is running.
minRunEnergy	Below this, the player will not move.
jumpEnergyDrain	How quickly energy is lost when the player jumps.
minJumpEnergy	Below this, the player can't jump anymore.
recoverDelay	How long it takes to recover after a landing from a fall or jump, measured in ticks, where 1 tick = 32 milliseconds.
recoverRunForceScale	How much to scale the run force by while in the postlanding recovery state.
minImpactSpeed	Above this speed, an impact will cause damage.
speedDamageScale	Used to impart speed-scaled damage.
repairRate	How quickly damage is repaired when first aid or health is applied.
maxInv[Copper]	Maximum number of copper coins that the player can carry.
maxInv[Silver]	Maximum number of silver coins that the player can carry.
maxInv[Gold]	Maximum number of gold coins that the player can carry.
maxInv[Crossbow]	Maximum number of crossbows that the player can carry.
maxInv[CrossbowAmmo]	Maximum amount of crossbow ammunition that the player can carry.

Of course, we also need to know what to do when it's time to remove the avatar, which is what MaleAvatar::onRemove does. It's nothing spectacular—it just sets the handle properties to 0 and moves on.

One of the methods that gets the most exercise from a healthy and active avatar is the MaleAvatar::onCollision method. This method is called by the engine whenever it establishes that the avatar has collided with some other collision-enabled object. Five parameters are provided. The first is the handle of this datablock, the second is the handle of the player object, the third is the handle of the object that hit us (or that we hit), the fourth is the relative velocity vector between us and the object we hit, and the fifth is the scalar speed of the object we hit. Using these inputs, we can do some pretty fancy collision calculations.

What we do, though, is just find out what the state of our avatar is (alive or dead) and what kind of object we hit. If we are dead (our avatar's body could be sliding down a hill, for example), we bail out of this method; otherwise, we try to pick up the item we hit, providing it is an item or a weapon.

The engine calls MaleAvatar::onImpact when our avatar hits something. Unlike onCollision, this method detects *any* sort of impact, not just a collision with an item in the world. Collisions occur between ShapeBase class things, like items, player-avatars, vehicles, and weapons. Impacts occur with those things, as well as terrain and interiors. So, onImpact provides essentially the same five parameters. We use that data to calculate how much damage the player should incur, and we apply that damage to the avatar's object using its Damage method.

The MaleAvatar::Damage is where we try to ascertain what effect the damage will have on the avatar. If we want to implement hit boxes, or damage calculations based on object components, we would do that here. In this case if the player is dead, we again bail. If not, we apply the damage (which increases the accumulated damage value) and then obtain the object's current state. If the object is now dead, we call the OnDeath handler and exit the function.

Next is the MaleAvatar::onDamage method, which is activated by the engine whenever the object's damage value changes. This is the method we want to use when applying some sort of special effect to the player when damage occurs—like making the screen flash or using some audio. In this case we do flash the screen, and we also start a slow energy drain caused by the damage. At the same time, we start a slow damage repair, which means that after some period of time, we will have regained some of our health (negative health equals positive damage).

When the player's damage exceeds the maxDamage value, the player object is set to the *disabled* state. When that happens, the function MaleAvatar::onDisabled is called. This is where we deal with the final stages of the death of a player's avatar. What we are doing is resetting all the various repair values, disabling any mounted weapons, and then beginning the process of disposing of the corpse. We keep it around for a few seconds before letting it slowly fade away.

control/server/weapons/weapon.cs

This Weapon module contains *namespace* helper methods for Weapon and Ammo classes that define a set of methods that are part of dynamic namespaces class. All ShapeBase class images are mounted into one of eight slots on a shape.

There are also hooks into the inventory system specifically for use with weapons and ammo. Go ahead and type in the following module, and save it as \EMAGA5\ control\server\weapons\weapon.cs.

```
//===================================================================
// control/server/weapons/weapon.cs
// Copyright (c) 2003, 2006 Kenneth C. Finney 2003, 2006 by Kenneth
// Portions Copyright (c) 2001 GarageGames.com
// Portions Copyright (c) 2001 by Sierra Online, Inc.
//===================================================================
$WeaponSlot = 0;
function Weapon::OnUse(%data,%obj)
{
   if (%obj.GetMountedImage($WeaponSlot) != %data.image.GetId())
   {
     %obj.mountImage(%data.image, $WeaponSlot);
     if (%obj.client)
       MessageClient(%obj.client, 'MsgWeaponUsed', '\c0Weapon selected');
   }
}
function Weapon::OnPickup(%this, %obj, %shape, %amount)
{
   if (Parent::OnPickup(%this, %obj, %shape, %amount))
   {
     if ( (%shape.GetClassName() $= "Player" ||
         %shape.GetClassName() $= "AIPlayer" ) &&
         %shape.GetMountedImage($WeaponSlot) == 0)
     {
       %shape.Use(%this);
```

```
        }
    }
}
function Weapon::OnInventory(%this,%obj,%amount)
{
    if (!%amount && (%slot = %obj.GetMountSlot(%this.image)) != -1)
        %obj.UnmountImage(%slot);
}
function WeaponImage::OnMount(%this,%obj,%slot)
{
    if (%obj.GetInventory(%this.ammo))
        %obj.SetImageAmmo(%slot,true);
}
function Ammo::OnPickup(%this, %obj, %shape, %amount)
{
    if (Parent::OnPickup(%this, %obj, %shape, %amount))
    {

    }
}
function Ammo::OnInventory(%this,%obj,%amount)
{
    for (%i = 0; %i < 8; %i++)
    {
        if ((%image = %obj.GetMountedImage(%i)) > 0)
            if (IsObject(%image.ammo) && %image.ammo.GetId() == %this.GetId())
                %obj.SetImageAmmo(%i,%amount != 0);
    }
}
function RadiusDamage(%sourceObject, %position, %radius, %damage,
%damageType, %impulse)
{
    InitContainerRadiusSearch(%position, %radius,
$TypeMasks::ShapeBaseObjectType);

    %halfRadius = %radius / 2;
    while ((%targetObject = ContainerSearchNext()) != 0) {
        %coverage = CalcExplosionCoverage(%position, %targetObject,
            $TypeMasks::InteriorObjectType | $TypeMasks::TerrainObjectType |
            $TypeMasks::ForceFieldObjectType | $TypeMasks::VehicleObjectType);
        if (%coverage == 0)
            continue;
        %dist = ContainerSearchCurrRadiusDist();
```

```
%distScale = (%dist < %halfRadius)? 1.0:
   1.0 - ((%dist - %halfRadius) / %halfRadius);
%targetObject.Damage(%sourceObject, %position,
   %damage * %coverage * %distScale, %damageType);
if (%impulse) {
   %impulseVec = VectorSub(%targetObject.GetWorldBoxCenter(), %position);
   %impulseVec = VectorNormalize(%impulseVec);
   %impulseVec = VectorScale(%impulseVec, %impulse * %distScale);
   %targetObject.ApplyImpulse(%position, %impulseVec);
   }
  }
}
```

The weapon management system contained in this module assumes all primary weapons are mounted into the slot specified by the $WeaponSlot variable.

The first method defined, Weapon::onUse, describes the default behavior for all weapons when used. Mount it into the object's $WeaponSlot weapon slot, which is currently set to slot 0. A message is sent to the client indicating that the mounting action was successful. Picture this: you are carrying a holstered pistol. When the Use command is sent to the server after being initiated by some key binding, the pistol is removed from the holster, figuratively speaking, and placed in image slot 0, where it becomes visible in the player's hand. That's what takes place when you "use" a weapon.

The next method, Weapon::onPickup, is the weapon's version of what happens when you collide with a weapon, and the onCollision method of the MaleAvatar decides you need to pick this weapon up. First, the parent Item method performs the actual pickup, which involves the act of including the weapon in our inventory. (The Item method is discussed later in this chapter.) After that has been handled, we get control of the process here. What we do is automatically use the weapon if the player does not already have one in hand.

When the Item inventory code detects a change in the inventory status, the Weapon::onInventory method is called in order to check if we are holding an instance of the weapon in a mount slot, in case there are none showing in inventory. When the weapon inventory has changed, make sure there are no weapons of this type mounted if there are none left in inventory.

The method WeaponImage::onMount is called when a weapon is mounted (used). We use this method to set the state according to the current inventory.

If there are any special effects we want to invoke when we pick up a weapon, we would put them in the `Ammo::onPickup` method. The parent `Item` method performs the actual pickup, and then we take a crack at it. If we had booby-trapped weapons, this would be a good place to put the code.

Generally, ammunition is treated as an item in its own right. The `Ammo::onInventory` method is called when ammo inventory levels change. Then we can update any mounted images using this ammo to reflect the new state. In the method we cycle through all the mounted weapons to examine each mounted weapon's ammo status.

`RadiusDamage` is a pretty nifty function that we use to apply explosion effects to objects within a certain distance from where the explosion occurred and to impart an impulse force on each object to move it if called for.

The first statement in the function uses `InitContainerRadiusSearch` to prepare the container system for use. It basically indicates that the engine is going to search for all objects of the type `$TypeMasks::ShapeBaseObjectType` located within `%radius` distance from the location specified by `%position`. See Table A.1 in Appendix A for a list of available type masks. Once the container radius search has been set up, we then will make successive calls to `ContainerSearchNext`. Each call will return the handle of the objects found that match the mask we supplied. If the handle is returned as 0, then the search has finished.

So we enter a nicely sized `while` loop that will continue as long as `Container SearchNext` returns a valid object handle (nonzero) in `%targetObject`. With each object found, we calculate how much of the object is affected by the explosion but only apply this calculation based on how much of the explosion is blocked by certain types of objects. If an object of one of these types has completely blocked the explosion, then the explosion coverage will be 0.

Then we use the `ContainerSearchCurrRadiusDist` to find the approximate radius of the affected object and subtract that value from the center-of-explosion to center-of-object distance to get the distance to the nearest surface of the object. Next, damage is applied that is proportional to this distance. If the nearest surface of the object is less than half the radius of the explosion away, then full damage is applied.

Finally, a proportional impulse force vector, if appropriate, is applied using modified distance scale. This has the effect of pushing the object away from the center of the blast.

control/server/weapons/crossbow.cs

For each weapon in our game, we need a definition module that contains the specifics for that weapon—its datablocks, methods, particle definitions (if they are going to be unique to the weapon), and other useful stuff.

There is a lot of material here, so if you want to exclude some stuff to cut back on typing, then leave out all the particle and explosion datablocks. You won't get any cool-looking explosions or smoke trails, and you will get some error warnings in your console log file, but the weapon will still work.

The crossbow is a somewhat stylized and fantasy-based crossbow—rather medieval in flavor. It fires a burning bolt projectile that explodes like a grenade on impact. It's cool.

Type in the following code, and save it as \EMAGA5\control\server\weapons\ crossbow.cs.

```
//============================================================
// control/server/weapons/crossbow.cs
// Copyright (c) 2003, 2006 by Kenneth C. Finney
// Portions Copyright (c) 2001 GarageGames.com
// Portions Copyright (c) 2001 by Sierra Online, Inc.
//============================================================
datablock ParticleData(CrossbowBoltParticle)
{
    textureName          = "~/data/particles/smoke";
    dragCoefficient      = 0.0;
    gravityCoefficient   = -0.2;  // rises slowly
    inheritedVelFactor   = 0.00;
    lifetimeMS           = 500; // lasts 0.7 second
    lifetimeVarianceMS   = 150;  // ...more or less
    useInvAlpha = false;
    spinRandomMin = -30.0;
    spinRandomMax = 30.0;
    colors[0]      = "0.56 0.36 0.26 1.0";
    colors[1]      = "0.56 0.36 0.26 1.0";
    colors[2]      = "0 0 0 0";
    sizes[0]       = 0.25;
    sizes[1]       = 0.5;
    sizes[2]       = 1.0;
    times[0]       = 0.0;
    times[1]       = 0.3;
    times[2]       = 1.0;
};
```

```
datablock ParticleEmitterData(CrossbowBoltEmitter)
{
   ejectionPeriodMS = 10;
   periodVarianceMS = 5;
   ejectionVelocity = 0.25;
   velocityVariance = 0.10;
   thetaMin        = 0.0;
   thetaMax        = 90.0;
   particles = CrossbowBoltParticle;
};
datablock ParticleData(CrossbowExplosionParticle)
{
   textureName         = "~/data/particles/smoke";
   dragCoefficient     = 2;
   gravityCoefficient  = 0.2;
   inheritedVelFactor  = 0.2;
   constantAcceleration = 0.0;
   lifetimeMS          = 1000;
   lifetimeVarianceMS  = 150;
   colors[0]    = "0.56 0.36 0.26 1.0";
   colors[1]    = "0.56 0.36 0.26 0.0";
   sizes[0]     = 0.5;
   sizes[1]     = 1.0;
};
datablock ParticleEmitterData(CrossbowExplosionEmitter)
{
   ejectionPeriodMS = 7;
   periodVarianceMS = 0;
   ejectionVelocity = 2;
   velocityVariance = 1.0;
   ejectionOffset   = 0.0;
   thetaMin         = 0;
   thetaMax         = 60;
   phiReferenceVel  = 0;
   phiVariance      = 360;
   particles = "CrossbowExplosionParticle";
};
datablock ParticleData(CrossbowExplosionSmoke)
{
   textureName         = "~/data/particles/smoke";
   dragCoefficient     = 100.0;
   gravityCoefficient  = 0;
   inheritedVelFactor  = 0.25;
```

```
   constantAcceleration = -0.80;
   lifetimeMS           = 1200;
   lifetimeVarianceMS   = 300;
   useInvAlpha = true;
   spinRandomMin = -80.0;
   spinRandomMax =  80.0;

   colors[0]   = "0.56 0.36 0.26 1.0";
   colors[1]   = "0.2 0.2 0.2 1.0";
   colors[2]   = "0.0 0.0 0.0 0.0";

   sizes[0]    = 1.0;
   sizes[1]    = 1.5;
   sizes[2]    = 2.0;

   times[0]    = 0.0;
   times[1]    = 0.5;
   times[2]    = 1.0;

};
datablock ParticleEmitterData(CrossbowExplosionSmokeEmitter)
{
   ejectionPeriodMS = 10;
   periodVarianceMS = 0;
   ejectionVelocity = 4;
   velocityVariance = 0.5;
   thetaMin         = 0.0;
   thetaMax         = 180.0;
   lifetimeMS       = 250;
   particles = "CrossbowExplosionSmoke";
};
datablock ParticleData(CrossbowExplosionSparks)
{
   textureName          = "~/data/particles/spark";
   dragCoefficient      = 1;
   gravityCoefficient   = 0.0;
   inheritedVelFactor   = 0.2;
   constantAcceleration = 0.0;
   lifetimeMS           = 500;
   lifetimeVarianceMS   = 350;
   colors[0]   = "0.60 0.40 0.30 1.0";
   colors[1]   = "0.60 0.40 0.30 1.0";
   colors[2]   = "1.0 0.40 0.30 0.0";
```

```
    sizes[0]     = 0.5;
    sizes[1]     = 0.25;
    sizes[2]     = 0.25;

    times[0]     = 0.0;
    times[1]     = 0.5;
    times[2]     = 1.0;
};
datablock ParticleEmitterData(CrossbowExplosionSparkEmitter)
{
    ejectionPeriodMS = 3;
    periodVarianceMS = 0;
    ejectionVelocity = 13;
    velocityVariance = 6.75;
    ejectionOffset   = 0.0;
    thetaMin         = 0;
    thetaMax         = 180;
    phiReferenceVel  = 0;
    phiVariance      = 360;
    overrideAdvances = false;
    orientParticles  = true;
    lifetimeMS       = 100;
    particles = "CrossbowExplosionSparks";
};
datablock ExplosionData(CrossbowSubExplosion1)
{
    offset = 1.0;
    emitter[0] = CrossbowExplosionSmokeEmitter;
    emitter[1] = CrossbowExplosionSparkEmitter;
};
datablock ExplosionData(CrossbowSubExplosion2)
{
    offset = 1.0;
    emitter[0] = CrossbowExplosionSmokeEmitter;
    emitter[1] = CrossbowExplosionSparkEmitter;
};
datablock ExplosionData(CrossbowExplosion)
{
    lifeTimeMS = 1200;
    particleEmitter = CrossbowExplosionEmitter; // Volume particles
    particleDensity = 80;
    particleRadius = 1;
    emitter[0] = CrossbowExplosionSmokeEmitter;   // Point emission
```

```
    emitter[1] = CrossbowExplosionSparkEmitter;
    subExplosion[0] = CrossbowSubExplosion1;  // Sub explosion objects
    subExplosion[1] = CrossbowSubExplosion2;
    shakeCamera = true;              // Camera Shaking
    camShakeFreq = "10.0 11.0 10.0";
    camShakeAmp = "1.0 1.0 1.0";
    camShakeDuration = 0.5;
    camShakeRadius = 10.0;
    lightStartRadius = 6;            // Dynamic light
    lightEndRadius = 3;
    lightStartColor = "0.5 0.5 0";
    lightEndColor = "0 0 0";
};
datablock ProjectileData(CrossbowProjectile)
{
    projectileShapeName = "~/data/models/weapons/bolt.dts";
    directDamage        = 20;
    radiusDamage        = 20;
    damageRadius        = 1.5;
    explosion           = CrossbowExplosion;
    particleEmitter     = CrossbowBoltEmitter;
    muzzleVelocity      = 100;
    velInheritFactor    = 0.3;
    armingDelay         = 0;
    lifetime            = 5000;
    fadeDelay           = 5000;
    bounceElasticity    = 0;
    bounceFriction      = 0;
    isBallistic         = true;
    gravityMod  = 0.80;
    hasLight    = true;
    lightRadius = 4.0;
    lightColor  = "0.5 0.5 0";
};
function CrossbowProjectile::OnCollision(%this,%obj,%col,%fade,%pos,
  %normal)
{
    if (%col.getType() & $TypeMasks::ShapeBaseObjectType)
        %col.damage(%obj,%pos,%this.directDamage,"CrossbowBolt");
RadiusDamage(%obj,%pos,%this.damageRadius,%this.radiusDamage,
  "CrossbowBolt",0);
}
datablock ItemData(CrossbowAmmo)
```

```
{
    category = "Ammo";
    className = "Ammo";
    shapeFile = "~/data/models/weapons/boltclip.dts";
    mass = 1;
    elasticity = 0.2;
    friction = 0.6;

        // Dynamic properties defined by the scripts
        pickUpName = "crossbow bolts";
    maxInventory = 20;
};
datablock ItemData(Crossbow)
{
    category = "Weapon";
    className = "Weapon";
    shapeFile = "~/data/models/weapons/crossbow.dts";
    mass = 1;
    elasticity = 0.2;
    friction = 0.6;
    emap = true;
    pickUpName = "a crossbow";
    image = CrossbowImage;
};
datablock ShapeBaseImageData(CrossbowImage)
{
    shapeFile = "~/data/models/weapons/crossbow.dts";
    emap = true;
    mountPoint = 0;
    eyeOffset = "0.1 0.4 -0.6";
    correctMuzzleVector = false;
    className = "WeaponImage";
    item = Crossbow;
    ammo = CrossbowAmmo;
    projectile = CrossbowProjectile;
    projectileType = Projectile;

    stateName[0]                    = "Preactivate";
    stateTransitionOnLoaded[0]      = "Activate";
    stateTransitionOnNoAmmo[0]      = "NoAmmo";
    stateName[1]                    = "Activate";
    stateTransitionOnTimeout[1]     = "Ready";
    stateTimeoutValue[1]            = 0.6;
```

```
    stateSequence[1]                = "Activate";
    stateName[2]                    = "Ready";
    stateTransitionOnNoAmmo[2]      = "NoAmmo";
    stateTransitionOnTriggerDown[2] = "Fire";
    stateName[3]                    = "Fire";
    stateTransitionOnTimeout[3]     = "Reload";
    stateTimeoutValue[3]            = 0.2;
    stateFire[3]                    = true;
    stateRecoil[3]                  = LightRecoil;
    stateAllowImageChange[3]        = false;
    stateSequence[3]                = "Fire";
    stateScript[3]                  = "onFire";
    stateName[4]                    = "Reload";
    stateTransitionOnNoAmmo[4]      = "NoAmmo";
    stateTransitionOnTimeout[4]     = "Ready";
    stateTimeoutValue[4]            = 0.8;
    stateAllowImageChange[4]        = false;
    stateSequence[4]                = "Reload";
    stateEjectShell[4]              = true;
    stateName[5]                    = "NoAmmo";
    stateTransitionOnAmmo[5]        = "Reload";
    stateSequence[5]                = "NoAmmo";
    stateTransitionOnTriggerDown[5] = "DryFire";
    stateName[6]                    = "DryFire";
    stateTimeoutValue[6]            = 1.0;
    stateTransitionOnTimeout[6]     = "NoAmmo";
};
function CrossbowImage::onFire(%this, %obj, %slot)
{
    %projectile = %this.projectile;
    %obj.decInventory(%this.ammo,1);
    %muzzleVector     = %obj.getMuzzleVector(%slot);
    %objectVelocity   = %obj.getVelocity();
    %muzzleVelocity   = VectorAdd(
       VectorScale(%muzzleVector, %projectile.muzzleVelocity),
       VectorScale(%objectVelocity, %projectile.velInheritFactor));
    %p = new (%this.projectileType)() {
      dataBlock        = %projectile;
      initialVelocity  = %muzzleVelocity;
      initialPosition  = %obj.getMuzzlePoint(%slot);
      sourceObject     = %obj;
      sourceSlot       = %slot;
      client           = %obj.client;
```

```
   };
   MissionCleanup.add(%p);
   return %p;
}
```

We will cover the contents of the particle, explosion, and weapon datablocks in detail in later chapters when we start creating our own weapons. Therefore we will skip discussion of these elements for now and focus on the datablock's methods.

The first method, and one of the most critical, is the CrossbowProjectile:: OnCollision method. When called, it looks first to see if the projectile has collided with the right kind of object. If so, then the projectile's damage value is applied directly to the struck object. The method then calls the RadiusDamage function to apply damage to surrounding objects, if applicable.

When shooting the crossbow, the CrossbowImage::onFire method is used to handle the aspects of firing the weapon that cause the projectile to be created and launched. First, the projectile is removed from inventory, and then a vector is calculated based upon which way the muzzle is facing. This vector is scaled by the specified muzzle velocity of the projectile and the velocity inherited from the movement of the crossbow (which gets that velocity from the movement of the player).

Finally, a new projectile object is spawned into the game world at the location of the weapon's muzzle—the projectile possesses all the velocity information at the time of spawning, so when added, it immediately begins coursing toward its target.

The projectile is added to the MissionCleanup group before the method exits.

control/server/misc/item.cs

This module contains the code needed to pick up and create items, as well as definitions of specific items and their methods. Type in the following code, and save it as \EMAGA5\control\server\misc\item.cs.

```
//===========================================================
// control/server/misc/item.cs
// Copyright (c) 2003, 2005 by Kenneth C. Finney.
//===========================================================
```

```
$RespawnDelay = 20000;
$LoiterDelay = 10000;
function Item::Respawn(%this)
{
  %this.StartFade(0, 0, true);
  %this.setHidden(true);
  // Schedule a resurrection
  %this.Schedule($RespawnDelay, "Hide", false);
  %this.Schedule($RespawnDelay + 10, "StartFade", 3000, 0, false);
}
function Item::SchedulePop(%this)
{
  %this.Schedule($LoiterDelay - 1000, "StartFade", 3000, 0, true);
  %this.Schedule($LoiterDelay, "Delete");
}
function ItemData::OnThrow(%this,%user,%amount)
{
  // Remove the object from the inventory
  if (%amount $= "")
    %amount = 1;
  if (%this.maxInventory !$= "")
    if (%amount > %this.maxInventory)
      %amount = %this.maxInventory;
  if (!%amount)
    return 0;
  %user.DecInventory(%this,%amount);
  %obj = new Item() {
    datablock = %this;
    rotation = "0 0 1 " @ (GetRandom() * 360);
    count = %amount;
  };
  MissionGroup.Add(%obj);
  %obj.SchedulePop();
  return %obj;
}
function ItemData::OnPickup(%this,%obj,%user,%amount)
{
  %count = %obj.count;
  if (%count $= "")
    if (%this.maxInventory !$= "") {
      if (!(%count = %this.maxInventory))
        return;
    }
```

```
      else
          %count = 1;
    %user.IncInventory(%this,%count);
    if (%user.client)
       MessageClient(%user.client, 'MsgItemPickup', '\c0You picked up %1',
%this.pickupName);
    if (%obj.IsStatic())
       %obj.Respawn();
    else
       %obj.Delete();
    return true;
}
function ItemData::Create(%data)
{
    %obj = new Item() {
        dataBlock = %data;
        static = true;
        rotate = true;
    };
    return %obj;
}
datablock ItemData(Copper)
{
   category = "Coins";
   // Basic Item properties
   shapeFile = "~/data/models/items/kash1.dts";
   mass = 0.7;
   friction = 0.8;
   elasticity = 0.3;
   respawnTime = 30 * 60000;
   salvageTime = 15 * 60000;
   // Dynamic properties defined by the scripts
   pickupName = "a copper coin";
   value = 1;
};
datablock ItemData(Silver)
{
   category = "Coins";
   // Basic Item properties
   shapeFile = "~/data/models/items/kash100.dts";
   mass = 0.7;
   friction = 0.8;
   elasticity = 0.3;
```

```
    respawnTime = 30 * 60000;
    salvageTime = 15 * 60000;
    // Dynamic properties defined by the scripts
    pickupName = "a silver coin";
    value = 100;
};
datablock ItemData(Gold)
{
    category = "Coins";

    // Basic Item properties
    shapeFile = "~/data/models/items/kash1000.dts";
    mass = 0.7;
    friction = 0.8;
    elasticity = 0.3;
    respawnTime = 30 * 60000;
    salvageTime = 15 * 60000;
    // Dynamic properties defined by the scripts
    pickupName = "a gold coin";
    value = 1000;
};
datablock ItemData(FirstAidKit)
{
    category = "Health";
    // Basic Item properties
    shapeFile = "~/data/models/items/healthPatch.dts";
    mass = 1;
    friction = 1;
    elasticity = 0.3;
    respawnTime = 600000;
    // Dynamic properties defined by the scripts
    repairAmount = 200;
    maxInventory = 0; // No pickup or throw
};
function FirstAidKit::onCollision(%this,%obj,%col)
{
    if (%col.getDamageLevel() != 0 && %col.getState() !$= "Dead" )
    {
        %col.applyRepair(%this.repairAmount);
        %obj.respawn();
        if (%col.client)
        {
            messageClient
```

```
            (%col.client,'MSG_Treatment','\c2Medical treatment applied');
      }
   }
}
```

$RespawnDelay and $LoiterDelay are variables used to manage how long it takes to regenerate static items or how long they take to disappear when dropped.

After an item has been picked, if it is a static item, a new copy of that item will eventually be added to the game world using the Item::Respawn method. The first statement in this method fades the object away, smoothly and quickly. Then the object is hidden, just to be sure. Finally, we schedule a time in the future to bring the object back into existence—the first event removes the object from hiding, and the second event fades the object in smoothly and slowly over a period of three seconds.

If we drop an item, we may want to have it removed from the game world to avoid object clutter (and concomitant bandwidth loss). We can use the Item::SchedulePop method to make the dropped object remove itself from the world after a brief period of loitering. The first event scheduled is the start of a fade-out action, and after one second the object is deleted.

We can get rid of held items by throwing them using the ItemData::OnThrow method. It removes the object from inventory, decrements the inventory count, creates a new instance of the object for inclusion in the game world, and adds it. It then calls the SchedulePop method just described to look after removing the object from the game world.

The ItemData::OnPickup method is the one used by all items. It adds the item to the inventory and then sends a message to the client to indicate that the object has been picked up. If the object picked was a static one, it then schedules an event to add a replacement item into the world. If not, then the instance picked is deleted, and we see it no more.

The ItemData::Create method is the catchall object-creation method for items. It creates a new datablock based upon the passed parameter and sets the static and rotate properties to true before returning.

Next comes a collection of datablocks defining our coin and first-aid items. We will cover first-aid items in more detail later, in Chapter 16.

The last method of interest is FirstAidKit::onCollision. This method will restore some health, by applying a repair value, to colliding objects if it needs it. Once the treatment has been applied, a message is sent to the client for display.

Running EMAGA5

Once you've typed in all the modules, you should be in a good position to test EMAGA5. Table 5.3 shows the game action bindings that apply to in-game navigation.

Figure 5.4 shows your player-avatar shortly after spawning in Emaga5.

To test the game, travel around the world collecting gold, silver, and copper coins, and watch the total increase. You will have to watch out, though. The AI beasts will track you and then shoot you if they spot you. Like the saying goes, you can run, but you'll only die tired! You *can* grab a crossbow and shoot back. In some of the huts you will find first-aid kits that will patch you up. One more thing—don't fall off cliffs. Not healthy.

As an exercise, investigate how you would enable a game timer to limit how much time you have to gather up the coins. Also, display a message if your score exceeds a certain value.

Have fun!

Table 5.3 EMAGA5 Game Action Bindings

Key	Description
w	run forward
s	run backward
a	run (strafe) left
d	run (strafe) right
spacebar	jump and respawn
z	free look (hold key and move mouse)
tab	toggle player point of view
escape	quit game
tilde	open console
left mouse button	fire weapon

Figure 5.4
The Avatar in EMAGA5.

Moving Right Along

So, in this chapter you were exposed to more game-structuring shenanigans—though nothing too serious. It's always a good idea to keep your software organized in ways that make sense according to the current state of the project. It just makes it that much easier to keep track of what goes where and why.

Then we looked at how we can add more features: splash screens, interfaces, and so on. You should be able to extrapolate from the small amount of game play stuff we added, like crossbows and pickable items, that the world really can be your oyster. What your game will do is limited only by your imagination.

In the next chapter we'll poke a little deeper under the hood at one of the more hidden, yet very powerful capabilities that any decent game will need—messaging.

We'll also add more enhancements to our game to allow us to connect to a master server.

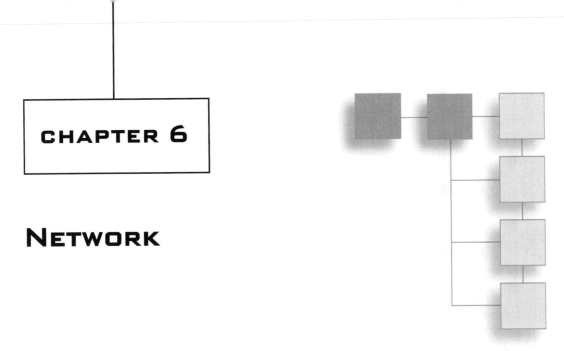

CHAPTER 6

NETWORK

Although little emphasis was given to the subject in recent chapters, a key feature of working with Torque is the fact that it was built around a client/server networking architecture.

Torque creates a GameConnection object, which is the primary mechanism that links the client (and the player) to the server. The GameConnection object is built from a NetworkConnection object. When the server needs to update clients, or when it receives updates from clients, the work is done through the good auspices of the NetworkConnection, and it is normally quite transparent at the game level.

What this means in practical terms is that the engine automatically handles things like movement and state changes or property changes of objects that populate a game world. Game programmers (like you and me) can then poke their grubby little fingers into this system to make it do their bidding without needing to worry about all the rest of the stuff, which Torque will manage— unless we decide to mess around with that too!

I know this seems a bit vague, so in this chapter we will attack the nitty-gritty so that you can really see how to use Torque's built-in networking to the best advantage.

First, we will discuss the features, and look at examples of how they can be implemented, and then later in the chapter, after you update your Emaga sample program, you can try them out.

Direct Messaging

The quickest way to get down and dirty with the client/server networking in Torque is to use the `CommandToServer` and `CommandToClient` direct messaging functions. These extremely useful "ad hoc" messaging functions are used for a wide variety of purposes in a Torque game, like in-game chat, system messages, and client/server synchronization.

CommandToServer

The `CommandToServer` function is used to send a message from a client to a server. Of course, the server needs to know that the message is coming and how to parse it to extract the data. The syntax is as follows:

CommandToServer(function [,arg1,...argn])		
Parameters:	*function*	Message handler function on the server to be executed.
	arg1,...argn	Arguments for the function.
Return:	*nothing*	

An example of how to use this function would be a simple global chat macro capability where a player would press a key, and then a specific message would be broadcast to all other players. Here is how that would work. First, we would bind a key combination to a specific function—say, bind Ctrl+H to the function we'll call `SendMacro()`. In the key binding statement, we'll make sure to pass the value 1 as a parameter to `SendMacro()`.

`SendMacro()` could be defined on the client as this:

```
function SendMacro(%value)
{
  switch$ (%value)
  {
    case 1:
      %msg = "Hello World!";
    case 2:
      %msg = "Hello? Is this thing on?";
    default:
      %msg = "Nevermind!";
  }
  CommandToServer('TellEveryone', %msg);
}
```

So now, when the player presses Ctrl+H, the SendMacro() function is called, with its %value parameter set to 1. In SendMacro(), the %value parameter is examined by the switch$ statement and sent to case 1:, where the variable %msg is stuffed with the string "Hello World!". Then CommandToServer is called with the first parameter set to the tagged string "TellEveryone" and the second parameter set to our message.

Now here is where some of the Torque client/server magic elbows its way onto the stage. The client will already have a GameConnection to the server and so will already know where to send the message. In order to act on our message, the server side needs us to define the TellEveryone message handler, which is really just a special purpose function, something like this:

```
function ServerCmdTellEveryone(%client,%msg)
{
    TellAll(%client,%msg);
}
```

Notice the prefix ServerCmd. When the server receives a message from the client via the CommandToServer() function, it will look in its message handle list, which is a list of functions that have the ServerCmd prefix, and find the one that matches ServerCmdTellEveryone. It then calls that function, setting the first parameter to the GameConnection handle of the client that sent the message. It then sets the rest of the parameters to be the parameters passed in the message from the client, which in this case is %msg stuffed with the string "Hello World!".

Then we can do what we want with the incoming message. In this case we want to send the message to all the other clients that are connected to the server, and we'll do that by calling the TellAll() function. Now we *could* put the code right here in our ServerCmdTellEveryone message handler, but it is a better design approach to break the code out into its own independent function. We'll cover how to do this in the next section.

CommandToClient

Okay, here we are—we're the server, and we've received a message from a client. We've figured out that the message is the TellEveryone message, we know which client sent it, and we have a string that came along with the message. What we need to do now is define the TellAll() function, so here is what it could look like:

```
function TellAll( %sender, %msg)
{
    %count = ClientGroup.getCount();
```

```
for ( %i = 0; %i < %count; %i++ )
{
  %client = ClientGroup.getObject(%i);
  CommandToClient(%client,'TellMessage', %sender, %msg);
}
}
```

Our intention here is to forward the message to all the clients. Whenever a client connects to the server, its GameConnection handle is added to the ClientGroup's internal list. We can use the ClientGroup's method getCount to tell us how many clients are connected. ClientGroup also has other useful methods, and one of them—the getObject method—will give us the GameConnection handle of a client, if we tell it the index number we are interested in.

If you want to test these example functions, I'll show you how to do that toward the end of the chapter. If you feel like giving it a go by yourself, here's a small hint: the commandToClient function is called from the *server* side, and the commandToServer functions belong on the *client* side.

As you can see, commandToClient is basically the server-side analogue to commandToServer. The syntax is as follows:

CommandToClient(client, function [,arg1,...argn])

Parameters:	client	Handle of the target client.
	function	Message handler function on the server to be executed.
	arg1,...argn	Arguments for the function.
Return:	nothing	

The primary difference is that although the client already knew how to contact the server when using CommandToServer, the same is not true for the server when using CommandToClient. It needs to know *which* client to send the message to each time it sends the message. So the simple approach is to iterate through the ClientGroup using the for loop, getting the handle for each client, and then sending each client a message using the CommandToClient() function, by specifying the client handle as the first parameter. The second parameter is the name of the message handler on the *client* side this time. Yup—works the same going that way as it did coming this way! Of course, the third parameter is the actual message to be passed.

So we need that message handler to be defined back over on the client. You can do it like this:

```
function clientCmdTellMessage(%sender, %msgString)
{
// blah blah blah
}
```

Notice that when we called this function there were four parameters, but our definition only has two in the parameter list. Well, the first parameter was the client handle, and because we are on the client, Torque strips that out for us. The second parameter was the message handler identifier, which was stripped out after Torque located the handler function and sent the program execution here. So the next parameter is the sender, which is the client that started this whole snowball rolling, way back when. The last parameter is, finally, the actual message.

I'll leave it up to you to decide what to do with the message. The point here was to show this powerful messaging system in operation. You can use it for almost anything you want.

Direct Messaging Wrap-up

CommandToServer and CommandToClient are two sides of the same direct messaging coin and give us, as game programmers, a tremendous ability to send messages back and forth between the game client and the game server.

Direct messaging can also be an important tool in the fight against online cheating in your game. You can, in theory and in practice, require all user inputs to go to the server for approval before executing any code on the client. Even things like changing setup options on the client—which are not normally the sort of thing that servers would control—can be easily programmed to require server control using the technique we just looked at.

The actual amount of server-side control you employ will be dictated by both available bandwidth and server-side processing power. There is a lot that can be done, but it is a never-ending series of tradeoffs to find the right balance.

Triggers

Right off the bat, there is potential for confusion when discussing the term *trigger* in Torque, so let's get that out of the way. There are four kinds of triggers that people talk about when programming with Torque:

- area triggers

- animation triggers

- weapon state triggers

- player event control triggers

I'll introduce you to all four here, but we'll talk about three of them—area triggers, animation triggers, and weapon state triggers—in more detail in future chapters.

Area Triggers

Area triggers are special in-game constructs. An area in the 3D world of a game is defined as a *trigger object*. When a player's avatar enters the bounds of the trigger area, an event message is posted on the server. We can write handlers to be activated by these messages. We will be covering area triggers in more depth in Chapter 22.

Animation Triggers

Animation triggers are used to synchronize footstep sounds with walking animations in player models. Modeling tools that support animation triggers have ways of tagging frames of animation sequences. The tags tell the game engine that certain things should happen when this frame of an animation is being displayed. We'll discuss these later, in Chapter 14.

Weapon State Triggers

Torque uses *weapon state triggers* for managing and manipulating weapon states. These triggers dictate what to do when a weapon is firing, reloading, recoiling, and so on. We'll look at this in more detail later, in Chapter 20 in the section "Weapon Sounds."

Player Event Control Triggers

Finally, there are *player event control triggers,* which are a form of indirect messaging of interest to us in this chapter. These mechanisms are used to process certain player inputs on the client in real time. You can have up to six of these triggers, each held by a variable with the prefix `$mvTriggerCountn` (where *n* is an index number from 0 to 5).

Table 6.1 Default Player Event Control Triggers

Trigger	%triggerNum	Default Action
`$mvTriggerCount0`	0	Shoots or activates the mounted weapon in image slot 0 of the player's avatar. (The "fire" button, so to speak.)
`$mvTriggerCount1`	1	Shoots or activates the mounted weapon in image slot 1 of the player's avatar. (The "alt fire.")
`$mvTriggerCount2`	2	Initiates the "jump" action and animation for the player's avatar.
`$mvTriggerCount3`	3	Initiates the "jetting" (extra boost) action and animation for the vehicle on which a player's avatar is mounted.
`$mvTriggerCount4`	4	Unassigned.
`$mvTriggerCount5`	5	Unassigned.

When we use a trigger move event, we increment the appropriate `$mvTriggerCountn` variable on the client side. This change in value causes an update message to be sent back to the server. The server will process these changes in the context of our control object, which is usually our player's avatar. After the server acts on the trigger, it decrements its count. If the count is nonzero, it acts again when it gets the next change in its internal scheduling algorithm. In this way we can initiate these trigger events by incrementing the variable as much as we want (up to a maximum of 255 times), without having to wait and see if the server has acted on the events. They are just automatically queued up for us via the `$mvTriggerCountn` variable mechanism.

Torque has default support for the first four control triggers built into its player and vehicle classes (see Table 6.1).

In the server control code, we can put a trigger handler in our player's avatar for any of these triggers that override the default action. We define a trigger handler like this:

```
function MyAvatarClass::onTrigger(%this, %obj, %triggerNum, %val)
{
  // trigger activity here
  $switch(%triggerNum)
  {
  case 0:
    //replacement for the "fire" action.
  case 1:
    //replacement for the "alt fire" action.
```

```
    case 2:
      //replacement for the "jump" action.
    case 3:
      //replacement for the "jetting" action.
    case 4:
      //whatever you like
    case 5:
      //whatever you like
  }
}
```

The MyAvatarClass class is whatever you have defined in your player avatar's datablock using the following statement:

```
className = MyAvatarClass;
```

To use a trigger handler, you merely have to increment a player event control trigger on the client, something like this:

```
function mouseFire(%val)
{
  $mvTriggerCount0++;
}
```

or this:

```
function altFire(%val)
{
  $mvTriggerCount1++;
}
```

GameConnection Messages

Most of the other kinds of messages used when making a game with Torque are handled automatically. However, in addition to the direct messaging techniques we just looked at, there are other more indirect messaging capabilities available to the Torque game developer. These are messages related to the GameConnection object.

I call these methods *indirect* because we, as programmers, don't get to use them in any old way of our choosing. But we *can,* nonetheless, use these methods, in the form of message handlers, when the Torque Engine decides it needs to send the messages.

What GameConnection Messages Do

`GameConnection` messages are of great importance to us during the negotiation process that takes place between the client and server when a client joins a game. They are network messages with game-specific uses, as opposed to being potentially more general-purpose network messages.

Torque calls a number of `GameConnection` message handlers at different times during the process of establishing, maintaining, and dropping game-related connections. In the Torque demo software, many of these handlers are defined in the common code base, whereas others aren't used at all. You are encouraged to override the common code message handlers with your own `GameConnection` message handlers or use the unused handlers, if you need to.

Specifics

During program execution, the client will at some point try to connect to the server using a set of function calls like this:

```
%conn = new GameConnection(ServerConnection);
%conn.SetConnectArgs(%username);
%conn.Connect();
```

In this example the `%conn` variable holds the handle to the `GameConnection`. The `Connect()` function call initiates a series of network transactions that culminate at the server with a call to the `GameConnection::OnConnect` handler.

The following descriptions are listed roughly in the order that the functions are used in the Emaga6 program.

onConnectionRequest()		
Parameters:	none	
Return: ""	*(null string)*	Indicates that the connection is accepted.
	none	Indicates rejection for some reason.
Description:		Called when a client attempts a connection, before the connection is accepted.
Usage:		Common—Server

This handler is used to check if the server-player capacity has been exceeded. If not exceeded, then `""` is returned, which allows the connection process to continue. If the server is full, then `CR_SERVERFULL` is sent back. Returning any value other than `""` will cause an error condition to be propagated back through the engine and sent to the client as a call to the handler GameConnection::onConnectRequestRejected. Any arguments that were passed to GameConnection::Connect are also passed to this handler by the engine.

onConnectionAccepted(handle)

Parameters:	handle	GameConnection handle.
Return:	nothing	
Description:		Called when a Connect call succeeds.
Usage:		Client

This handler is a good place to make last-minute preparations for a connected session.

onConnect(client, name)

Parameters:	client	A client's GameConnection handle.
	name	Name of a client's account or username.
Return:	nothing	
Description:		Called when a client has successfully connected.
Usage:		Server

In this case the second parameter (%name) is the value the client has used, while establishing the connection, as the parameter to the %(GameConnection). Set ConnectArgs(%username) call.

onConnectRequestTimedOut(handle)

Parameters:	handle	GameConnection handle.
Return:	nothing	
Description:		Called when establishing a connection takes too long.
Usage:		Client

When this gets called you probably want to display, or at least log, some message indicating that the connection has been lost because of a timeout.

onConnectionTimedOut(handle)

Parameters:	*handle*	GameConnection handle.
Return:	*nothing*	
Description:		Called when a connection ping (heartbeat) has not been received.
Usage:		Server, Client

When this gets called you probably want to display, or at least log, some message indicating that the connection has been lost because of a timeout.

onConnectionDropped(handle, reason)

Parameters:	*handle*	GameConnection handle.
	reason	String indicating why the server dropped the connection.
Return:	*nothing*	
Description:		Called when the server initiates the disconnection of a client.
Usage:		Client

When this gets called you probably want to display, or at least log, some message indicating that the connection has been lost because of a timeout.

onConnectRequestRejected(handle, reason)

Parameters:	*handle*	GameConnection handle.
	reason	See Table 6.2 for a list of conventional reason codes defined by GarageGames in script.
Return:	*nothing*	
Description:		Called when a client's connection request has been turned down by the server.
Usage:		Client

When this gets called you probably want to display, or at least log, some message indicating that the connection has been lost.

Table 6.2 Connection Request Rejection Codes

Reason Code	Meaning
CR_INVALID_PROTOCOL_VERSION	The wrong version of the client was detected.
CR_INVALID_CONNECT_PACKET	There is something wrong with the connection packet.
CR_YOUAREBANNED	Your game username has been banned.
CR_SERVERFULL	The server has reached the maximum number of players.
CHR_PASSWORD	The password is incorrect.
CHR_PROTOCOL	The game protocol version is not compatible.
CHR_CLASSCRC	The game class version is not compatible.
CHR_INVALID_CHALLENGE_PACKET	The client detected an invalid server response packet.

onConnectionError(handle, errorString)

Parameters:	handle	GameConnection handle.
	errorString	String indicating the error encountered.
Return:	nothing	
Description:		General connection error, usually raised by ghosted object initialization problems, such as missing files. The errorString is the server's connection error message.
Usage:		Client

onDrop(handle, reason)

Parameters:	handle	GameConnection handle.
	reason	Reason for the connection being dropped, passed from the server.
Return:	nothing	
Description:		Called when a connection to a server is arbitrarily dropped.
Usage:		Client

initialControlSet(handle)

Parameters:	handle	GameConnection handle.
Return:	nothing	
Description:		Called when the server has set up a control object for the GameConnection. For example, this could be an avatar model or a camera.
Usage:		Client

setLagIcon(handle, state)

Parameters:	*handle*	`GameConnection` handle.
	state	Boolean that indicates whether to display or hide the icon.
Return:	*nothing*	
Description:		Called when the connection state has changed, based upon the lag setting. *state* is set to `true` when the connection is considered temporarily broken or set to `false` when there is no loss of connection.
Usage:		Client

onDataBlocksDone(handle, sequence)

Parameters:	*handle*	`GameConnection` handle.
	sequence	Value that indicates which set of datablocks has been transmitted.
Return:	*nothing*	
Description:		Called when the server has received confirmation that all datablocks have been received.
Usage:		Server

Use this handler to manage the mission loading process and any other activity that transfers datablocks.

onDataBlockObjectReceived(index, total)

Parameters:	*index*	Index number of datablock objects.
	total	Count of datablock objects sent so far.
Return:	*nothing*	
Description:		Called when the server is ready for datablocks to be sent.
Usage:		Client

onFileChunkReceived(file, ofs, size)

Parameters:	*file*	The name of the file being sent.
	ofs	Offset of data received.
	size	File size.
Return:	*nothing*	
Description:		Called when a chunk of file data from the server has arrived.
Usage:		Client

onGhostAlwaysObjectReceived()

Parameters:	none	
Return:	nothing	
Description:		Called when a ghosted object's data has been sent across from the server to the client.
Usage:		Client

onGhostAlwaysStarted(count)

Parameters:	count	The number of ghosted objects dealt with so far.
Return:	nothing	
Description:		Called when a ghosted object has been sent to the client.
Usage:		Client

Finding Servers

When you offer a game with networked client/server capabilities, there needs to be some means for players to find servers to which to connect. On the Internet, a fairly widely implemented technique is to employ a *master server*. The master server's job is generally straightforward and simple. It keeps a list of active game servers and provides a client with the necessary information to connect to any one of the servers if desired.

To see the utility of such a simple system, just take a look at NovaLogic, makers of the successful *Delta Force* series of first-person shooters. NovaLogic still hosts master servers for customers who bought the original *Delta Force* games from the late 1990s! The overhead of such a simple system is minimal, and the benefit in customer goodwill is tremendous.

The *Tribes* series of games, upon which Torque is based, also offers such master servers, as do many other games out there.

On a small- to medium-sized local area network, this is not too onerous a task. An extremely simple method is to have the client merely examine a specified port on all visible nodes to see if a server is present, and that's what we're going to be doing in this chapter.

Code Changes

We are going to implement "find a server" support in our version of Emaga for this chapter. We will create Emaga6 by modifying Emaga5, the game from the last chapter.

First, copy your entire \EMAGA5 folder to a new folder, called \EMAGA6. Then, for the sake of clarity, rename the UltraEdit project file to chapter6.prj. Now open your new Chapter 6 UltraEdit project. All changes will be made in the control code. In addition to changes to the actual program code, you might want to also change any Chapter 5 comment references so they refer to Chapter 6—it's your call.

Client—Initialize Module

We'll make our first change in control/client/initialize.cs. Open that module and locate the function `InitializeClient`. Add the following statements to the very beginning of the function (after the opening brace):

```
$Client::GameTypeQuery = "3D2E";
$Client::MissionTypeQuery = "Any";
```

When one of our servers contacts the master server, it uses the variable `$Client::GameTypeQuery` to filter out game types that we aren't interested in. For your game, you can set any game type you like. Here we are going to go with 3D2E because there will be at least one 3D2E server listed on the master server, and for the purpose of illustration it is better to see one or two 3D2E servers listed than nothing at all. You can change this later at your leisure.

The variable `$Client::MissionTypeQuery` is used to filter whatever specific game play styles are available. By specifying any, we will see any types that are available. This is also something we can define in whatever way we want for our game.

Farther down will be a call to `InitCanvas`. Although it is not really important to make the master server stuff work, change that statement to this:

```
InitCanvas("Emaga6 - 3D2E Sample Game");
```

Doing so reflects the fact that we are now in Chapter 6 and not in Chapter 5 anymore.

Next, there are a series of calls to `Exec`. Find the one that loads playerinterface.gui, and put the following line after that one:

```
Exec("./interfaces/serverscreen.gui");
```

Then find the call to Exec that loads screens.cs, and add the following statement after it:

```
Exec("./misc/serverscreen.cs");
```

Finally, toward the end of the function, find the Exec call that loads connections.cs. After that statement, and before the call to Canvas.SetContent, add the following statement:

```
SetNetPort(0);
```

This statement is critical. Although we will never use port 0, it is necessary to make this call to ensure that the TCP/IP code in Torque works correctly. Later on in other modules the appropriate port will be set, depending on what we are doing.

Now we need to add a button to the main screen. Open \EMAGA6\control\client\interfaces\menuscreen.gui and at the end of the file find the last line that has a single brace/semi-colon pair }; and insert the following code just above it:

```
new GuiButtonCtrl() {
  command = "Canvas.setContent(ServerScreen);";
  text = "Connect To Server";
};
```

New Modules

More typing! But not as much as in previous chapters, so don't fret. We have to add a new interface module and a module to contain the code that manages its behavior.

Client—ServerScreen Interface Module

Now we have to add the ServerScreen *interface* module. This module defines buttons, text labels, and a scroll control that will appear on the screen; we can use it to query the master server and view the results. Type in the following code, and save it as control\client\interfaces\serverscreen.gui.

```
//==========================================================================
// control/client/interfaces/serverscreen.gui
//
// Server query interface module for 3D2E emaga6 sample game
//
// Copyright (c) 2003, 2006 by Kenneth C. Finney.
//==========================================================================

new GuiChunkedBitmapCtrl(ServerScreen) {
  profile = "GuiContentProfile";
```

```
horizSizing = "width";
vertSizing = "height";
position = "0 0";
extent = "640 480";
minExtent = "8 8";
visible = "1";
bitmap = "./emaga_background";
useVariable = "0";
tile = "0";
helpTag = "0";

new GuiControl() {
  profile = "GuiWindowProfile";
  horizSizing = "center";
  vertSizing = "center";
  position = "20 90";
  extent = "600 300";
  minExtent = "8 8";
  visible = "1";
  helpTag = "0";

  new GuiTextCtrl() {
    profile = "GuiTextProfile";
    horizSizing = "right";
    vertSizing = "bottom";
    position = "183 5";
    extent = "63 18";
    minExtent = "8 8";
    visible = "1";
    text = "Player Name:";
    maxLength = "255";
    helpTag = "0";
  };

  new GuiTextEditCtrl() {
    profile = "GuiTextEditProfile";
    horizSizing = "right";
    vertSizing = "bottom";
    position = "250 5";
    extent = "134 18";
    minExtent = "8 8";
    visible = "1";
    variable = "Pref::Player::Name";
    maxLength = "255";
```

```
      historySize = "5";
      password = "0";
      tabComplete = "0";
      sinkAllKeyEvents = "0";
         helpTag = "0";
   };

   new GuiTextCtrl() {
      profile = "GuiTextProfile";
      horizSizing = "right";
      vertSizing = "bottom";
      position = "13 30";
      extent = "24 18";
      minExtent = "8 8";
      visible = "1";
      text = "Private ?";
      maxLength = "255";
      helpTag = "0";
   };
   new GuiTextCtrl() {
      profile = "GuiTextProfile";
      horizSizing = "right";
      vertSizing = "bottom";
      position = "76 30";
      extent = "63 18";
      minExtent = "8 8";
      visible = "1";
      text = "Server Name";
      maxLength = "255";
      helpTag = "0";
   };
   new GuiTextCtrl() {
      profile = "GuiTextProfile";
      horizSizing = "right";
      vertSizing = "bottom";
      position = "216 30";
      extent = "20 18";
      minExtent = "8 8";
      visible = "1";
      text = "Ping";
      maxLength = "255";
      helpTag = "0";
   };
```

```
new GuiTextCtrl() {
  profile = "GuiTextProfile";
  horizSizing = "right";
  vertSizing = "bottom";
  position = "251 30";
  extent = "36 18";
  minExtent = "8 8";
  visible = "1";
  text = "Players";
  maxLength = "255";
  helpTag = "0";
};
new GuiTextCtrl() {
  profile = "GuiTextProfile";
  horizSizing = "right";
  vertSizing = "bottom";
  position = "295 30";
  extent = "38 18";
  minExtent = "8 8";
  visible = "1";
  text = "Version";
  maxLength = "255";
  helpTag = "0";
};
new GuiTextCtrl() {
  profile = "GuiTextProfile";
  horizSizing = "right";
  vertSizing = "bottom";
  position = "433 30";
  extent = "28 18";
  minExtent = "8 8";
  visible = "1";
  text = "Game Description";
  maxLength = "255";
  helpTag = "0";
};

new GuiScrollCtrl() {
  profile = "GuiScrollProfile";
  horizSizing = "right";
  vertSizing = "bottom";
  position = "14 55";
  extent = "580 190";
```

```
        minExtent = "8 8";
        visible = "1";
        willFirstRespond = "1";
        hScrollBar = "dynamic";
        vScrollBar = "alwaysOn";
        constantThumbHeight = "0";
        childMargin = "0 0";
        helpTag = "0";
        defaultLineHeight = "15";


        new GuiTextListCtrl(ServerList) {
            profile = "GuiTextArrayProfile";
            horizSizing = "right";
            vertSizing = "bottom";
            position = "2 2";
            extent = "558 48";
            minExtent = "8 8";
            visible = "1";
            enumerate = "0";
            resizeCell = "1";
            columns = "0 30 200 240 280 400";
            fitParentWidth = "1";
            clipColumnText = "0";
            noDuplicates = "false";
            helpTag = "0";
        };
    };


    new GuiButtonCtrl() {
        profile = "GuiButtonProfile";
        horizSizing = "right";
        vertSizing = "top";
        position = "16 253";
        extent = "127 23";
        minExtent = "8 8";
        visible = "1";
        command = "Canvas.getContent().Close();";
        text = "Close";
        groupNum = "-1";
        buttonType = "PushButton";
        helpTag = "0";
    };
```

```
new GuiButtonCtrl(JoinServer) {
  profile = "GuiButtonProfile";
  horizSizing = "right";
  vertSizing = "bottom";
  position = "455 253";
  extent = "130 25";
  minExtent = "8 8";
  visible = "1";
  command = "Canvas.getContent().Join();";
  text = "Connect";
  groupNum = "-1";
  buttonType = "PushButton";
  active = "0";
  helpTag = "0";
};

new GuiControl(QueryStatus) {
  profile = "GuiWindowProfile";
  horizSizing = "center";
  vertSizing = "center";
  position = "149 100";
  extent = "310 50";
  minExtent = "8 8";
  visible = "0";
  helpTag = "0";

  new GuiButtonCtrl(CancelQuery) {
    profile = "GuiButtonProfile";
    horizSizing = "right";
    vertSizing = "bottom";
    position = "9 15";
    extent = "64 20";
    minExtent = "8 8";
    visible = "1";
    command = "Canvas.getContent().Cancel();";
    text = "Cancel";
    groupNum = "-1";
    buttonType = "PushButton";
    helpTag = "0";
  };
  new GuiProgressCtrl(StatusBar) {
    profile = "GuiProgressProfile";
    horizSizing = "right";
```

```
      vertSizing = "bottom";
      position = "84 15";
      extent = "207 20";
      minExtent = "8 8";
      visible = "1";
      helpTag = "0";
    };
    new GuiTextCtrl(StatusText) {
      profile = "GuiProgressTextProfile";
      horizSizing = "right";
      vertSizing = "bottom";
      position = "85 14";
      extent = "205 20";
      minExtent = "8 8";
      visible = "1";
      maxLength = "255";
      helpTag = "0";
    };
  };
};
};
```

The first half of the module is an interface definition, defining a number of buttons, text labels, and a scroll control that will appear on the screen. Most of the properties and control types have been covered in previous chapters; however, some of them are of particular note here.

The first item of interest is the GuiScrollCtrl. This control provides a scrollable vertical list of records; in this case it will be a list of servers that satisfy the filters used in subsequent Query calls that we will look at a bit later.

Some of the GuiScrollCtrl properties of interest are explained in Table 6.3.

The next significant control to examine is the GuiTextEditCtrl. It has an interesting property, shown by this statement:

```
variable = "Pref::Player::Name";
```

What this does is display the contents of the variable Pref::Player::Name in the control's content. If we change that content by placing our edit cursor in the control's field while it is being displayed and typing in new text, then the contents of the variable Pref::Player::Name are also changed.

Table 6.3 Selected GuiScrollCtrl Properties

Property	Description
willFirstRespond	If set to true or 1, indicates that this control will respond to user inputs first, before passing them on to other controls.
hScrollBar	Indicates how to decide whether to display the horizontal scroll bar. The choices are alwaysOn: The scroll bar is always visible. alwaysOff: The scroll bar is never visible. dynamic The scroll bar is not visible until the number of records in the list exceeds the number of lines available to display them. If this happens the scroll bar is turned on and made visible.
vScrollBar	The same as hScrollBar but applies to the vertical scroll bar.
constantThumbHeight	Indicates whether the *thumb*, the small rectangular widget in the scroll bar that moves as you scroll, will have a size that is proportional to the number of entries in the list (the longer the list, the smaller the thumb) or will have a constant size. Setting this property to 1 ensures a constant size; 0 ensures proportional sizing.

Also in this GuiTextEditCtrl control is the following statement:

```
historySize = "0";
```

This control has the ability to store a history of previous values that were held in the control's edit box. We can scroll through the list's previous values by pressing the Up Arrow and Down Arrow keys. This property sets the maximum number of values that can be saved in the control's history. A setting of 0 means that no history will be saved.

Now go take a look at the control of type GuiControl with the name QueryStatus. This is the definition of a subscreen that will display the progress of the query. It contains a couple of other controls that we've seen before, but I just want you to note how they are nested within this control, which is nested within the larger ServerScreen.

Client—ServerScreen Code Module

Next, we will add the ServerScreen *code* module. This module defines how the ServerScreen interface module will behave. Type in the following code, and save it as control\client\misc\serverscreen.cs.

```
//=====================================================================
// control/client/misc/serverscreen.cs
//
// Server query code module for 3DGPAI1 Emaga6 sample game
//
// Copyright (c) 2003, 2006 by Kenneth C. Finney.
//=====================================================================
function ServerScreen::onWake()
{
  JoinServer.SetActive(ServerList.rowCount() > 0);
  ServerScreen.queryLan();
}


function ServerScreen::QueryLan(%this)
{
  QueryLANServers(
     28000,         // lanPort for local queries
     0,             // Query flags
     $Client::GameTypeQuery,      // gameTypes
     $Client::MissionTypeQuery,   // missionType
     0,             // minPlayers
     100,           // maxPlayers
     0,             // maxBots
     2,             // regionMask
     0,             // maxPing
     100,           // minCPU
     0              // filterFlags
     );
}


function ServerScreen::Cancel(%this)
{
  CancelServerQuery();
}


function ServerScreen::Close(%this)
{
  CancelServerQuery();
  Canvas.SetContent(MenuScreen);
}
```

```
function ServerScreen::Update(%this)
{
  QueryStatus.SetVisible(false);
  ServerList.Clear();
  %sc = GetServerCount();
  for (%i = 0; %i < %sc; %i++)
  {
    SetServerInfo(%i);
    ServerList.AddRow(%i,
      ($ServerInfo::Password? "Yes": "No") TAB
      $ServerInfo::Name TAB
      $ServerInfo::Ping TAB
      $ServerInfo::PlayerCount @ "/" @ $ServerInfo::MaxPlayers TAB
      $ServerInfo::Version TAB
      $ServerInfo::GameType TAB
      %i);
  }
  ServerList.Sort(0);
  ServerList.SetSelectedRow(0);
  ServerList.ScrollVisible(0);
  JoinServer.SetActive(ServerList.RowCount() > 0);
}

function ServerScreen::Join(%this)
{
  CancelServerQuery();
  %id = ServerList.GetSelectedId();
  %index = GetField(ServerList.GetRowTextById(%id),6);
  if (SetServerInfo(%index)) {
    %conn = new GameConnection(ServerConnection);
    %conn.SetConnectArgs($pref::Player::Name);
    %conn.SetJoinPassword($Client::Password);
    %conn.Connect($ServerInfo::Address);
  }
}

function onServerQueryStatus(%status, %msg, %value)
{
  if (!QueryStatus.IsVisible())
    QueryStatus.SetVisible(true);

  switch$ (%status) {
    case "start":
```

```
    case "ping":
      StatusText.SetText("Ping Servers");
      StatusBar.SetValue(%value);

    case "query":

    case "done":
      QueryStatus.SetVisible(false);
      ServerScreen.Update();
  }
}
```

This module is where we've put the code that controls how the Master Server screen behaves.

The first function, ServerScreen::onWake, defines what to do when the screen is displayed. In this case we first set the Join button to be active if there are any servers in the server list at the moment we display the screen. Then ServerScreen::QueryLAN is called. It executes a call to QueryLANServers, which reaches out across the local area network and talks to each computer on port 28000 (you can use any available port). If it manages to contact a computer with a game server running on that port, it establishes contact with the game server, obtains some information from it, and adds that server to a list. There are quite a few parameters to the call to QueryLANServers. The following syntax definition shows them in more detail:

QueryLANServers (port, flags, gtype, mtype, minplayers, maxplayers, maxbots, region, ping, cpu, filters, buddycount, buddylist)

Parameters:	port	The TCP/IP port where game servers are expected to be found.
	flags	Query flags. Choices:
		0×00 = online query
		0×01 = offline query
		0×02 = no string compression
	gtype	Game type string.
	mtype	Mission type string.
	minplayers	Minimum number of players for a viable game.
	maxplayers	Maximum allowable players.
	maxbots	Maximum allowable connected AI bots.
	region	Numeric discriminating mask.
	ping	Maximum ping for connecting clients; 0 means no maximum.

	mincpu	Minimum specified CPU capability.
	filterflags	Server filters. Choices:
		0×00 = dedicated
		0×01 = not password protected
		0×02 = Linux
		0×80 = current version
	buddycount	Number of buddy servers in the buddy list.
	buddylist	List of server names that are buddies to this server.
Return:	nothing	

The response to the QueryLANServers function is accessible from the ServerList array.

The next function, ServerScreen::Cancel, is called when the Cancel button is clicked while the query is under way.

After that is the ServerScreen::Close function, which is called when the user clicks the Close button. It cancels any pending query and then returns to the MenuScreen.

ServerScreen::Update is the function that inserts the obtained information in the ServerList after it is obtained from the master server. The information is found in the $ServerInfo array. To update the scrolling display, we find the number of servers that pass the filters on the master by calling GetServerCount. Then we iterate through our displayable list, extracting the fields from each $ServerInfo record. Take note of the call to SetServerInfo. Passing an index number to this function sets the $ServerInfo array to point to a specific record in the MasterServerList. Then we access the individual fields in the $ServerInfo array by referencing them with the colon operator: $ServerInfo::Name or $ServerInfo::Name, to demonstrate with two examples.

The next function, ServerScreen::Join, defines how we go about joining a server that has been selected from the list. First, we cancel any outstanding queries, get the handle of the server record that is highlighted in the interface, and then use that to obtain the index number of the server record. We use the SetServerInfo to set the $ServerInfo array to point to the right server record, and then we can access the values. After setting some network parameters, we finally use $ServerInfo::Address to make the network connection.

The last function in the module is the message handler callback that makes the whole shebang go: onServerQueryStatus. It gets called repeatedly as the server query process unfolds. We use the %status variable to determine what response we are receiving from the master server, and then we use either the %msg or %value variable, set by the master server to update various fields in the displayed server list. The start and query cases aren't needed in our example.

Dedicated Server

Sometimes we will want to host a game as a server without having to bother with a graphical user interface. One reason we might want to do this is because we want to run the server on a computer that doesn't have a 3D accelerated graphics adapter. Another reason is because we might want to test our client/server connectivity and master server query capabilities. This need arises because we can't run two instances of the Torque graphical client at the same time. However, if we have the ability to run as a dedicated server, we can run multiple dedicated servers, while running one instance of the graphical client, all on the same computer. And if we have set up the dedicated servers appropriately, other players out on the network can connect to our servers.

There are a few more modules you will have to change to implement the dedicated server capabilities.

Root Main Module

In this module we'll need to add some command line switches in case we want to use the command line interface of Windows, or we'll need to decide to embed the switches in a Windows shortcut. Either of these methods is how we can tell the game to run the server in dedicated mode. In the module main.cs located in the *root game folder* (which is the folder where the tge.exe executable is located for your Chapter 6 version of Emaga), locate the ParseArgs function, and scroll down until you find the statement containing $switch($currentarg). Type the following code in directly after the $switch statement (after the opening brace):

```
case "-dedicated":
  $Server::Dedicated = true;
  EnableWinConsole(true);
  $argumentFlag[%i]++;

case "-map":
  $argumentFlag[%i]++;
  if (%nextArgExists)
```

```
  {
     $mapArgument = %nextArgument;
     $argumentFlag[%i+1]++;
     %i++;
  }
  else
     Error("Error: Missing argument. Usage: -map <filename>");
```

Both of these switches are needed to run a dedicated server. The -dedicated switch puts us into the right mode, and then the -map switch tells us which mission map to load when the server first starts running.

The result of these changes is that we can now invoke the dedicated server mode by launching the game with the following syntax from the command line (don't try it yet): tge.exe -dedicated -map control/data/maps/book_ch6.mis.

The game will launch, and all you will see will be a console window. You will be able to type in console script statements, just as you can when you use the Tilde ("~") key in the graphical client interface. However, don't try this just yet, because we still need to add the actual dedicated server code!

You can also create a shortcut to the tge.exe executable and modify the Target box in the shortcut properties to match the command line syntax above. Then you can launch the server merely by double-clicking on the shortcut icon.

Control—Main Module

Next, we have a quick modification to make to control/main.cs. In the OnStart function, locate the line that contains InitializeClient. Replace that one line with these four lines:

```
if ($Server::Dedicated)
   InitializeDedicatedServer();
else
   InitializeClient();
```

Now, when the program detects that the -dedicated switch was used, as described in the previous section, it will fire up in dedicated mode, not in client mode.

Control—Initialize Module

Okay, the meat of the dedicated server code is contained in this module. Open up the module control/server/initialize.cs, and type in the following lines just before the `InitializeServer` function.

```
$pref::Net::DisplayOnMaster = "Never";
$pref::Master0 = "2:master.garagegames.com:28002";

$Pref::Server::ConnectionError = "You do not have the correct version of 3D2E
client or the related art needed to play on this server. This is the server for
Chapter 6. Please check that chapter for directions.";

$Pref::Server::FloodProtectionEnabled = 1;
$Pref::Server::Info = "3D Game Programming All-In-One by Kenneth C. Finney.";
$Pref::Server::MaxPlayers = 64;
$Pref::Server::Name = "3D2E Book - Chapter 6 Server";
$Pref::Server::Password = "";
$Pref::Server::Port = 28000;
$Pref::Server::RegionMask = 2;
$Pref::Server::TimeLimit = 20;
$Pref::Net::LagThreshold = "400";
$pref::Net::PacketRateToClient = "10";
$pref::Net::PacketRateToServer = "32";
$pref::Net::PacketSize = "200";
$pref::Net::Port = 28000;
```

You can change the string values to be anything you like as long as it suits your purposes. You should leave the `RegionMask` as is for now.

Next, locate the function `InitializeServer` again, and insert the following lines at the very beginning of the function:

```
$Server::GameType = "3D2E";
$Server::MissionType = "Emaga6";
$Server::Status = "Unknown";
```

The value of `$Server::Status` will be updated when the server makes contact with the master server.

Finally, you will need to add this entire function to the end of the module:

```
function InitializeDedicatedServer()
{
  EnableWinConsole(true);
  Echo("\n--------- Starting Dedicated Server ---------");

  $Server::Dedicated = true;
```

```
  if ($mapArgument !$= "") {
     CreateServer("MultiPlayer", $mapArgument);
  }
  else
     Echo("No map specified (use -map <filename>)");
}
```

This function enables the Windows console, sets the dedicated flag, and then calls `CreateServer` with the appropriate values. Now it may not do very much and therefore seem to be not too necessary, but the significance with the `InitializeDedicatedServer` function is in what it *doesn't* do compared with the `InitializeClient` function, which would have otherwise been called. So that's the reason why it exists.

Emaga6 Map Files

There is a special map (mission) file with accompanying terrain file for use with this chapter. Locate these files at RESOURCES\CH6\EMAGA6\control\data\maps\book_ch6.mis and RESOURCES\CH6\EMAGA6\control\data\maps\book_ ch6.ter, respectively, and copy them to \EMAGA6\control\data\maps\.

Testing Emaga6

With all the changes we've made here, we're going to want to see Emaga6 run. It's really fairly easy. Open a command shell in Windows, and change to the folder where you've built the code for this chapter's program (\EMAGA6). Then run the dedicated server by typing in this command: **tge.exe -dedicated -map control/ data/maps/book_ch6.mis**.

Note

When you are testing, if you should happen to peek into the console while the game is running or into the console log file afterward, you might notice a whole bunch of lines like this:

```
No such file 'control/data/models/avatars/orc/player.jpg'.
```

Don't worry—that's not even an error. When loading shapes, Torque has an automatic system that looks for texture files associated with those shapes. Torque supports both JPG and PNG image file types for use with shapes, and depending on how the textures are defined in the shape files themselves, Torque may not find the specified file immediately. When that is the case, it goes through its seek routine and spews out a message every time one of its attempts doesn't succeed. Once the correct file is located, Torque moves on to the next instruction without any further fuss over that particular shape.

After it displays lots of start-up information, it will eventually settle down and tell you in the console window that it has successfully loaded a mission. When you see these things, your dedicated server is running fine.

Tip

You may be wondering how to do this over the Internet. I've written a different version of this chapter that is available on the Internet as a supplement on a page called "Internet Game Hosting." Browse your way to http://www.tubettiworld.com/book/ALT_CH6.php and click on the ALTERNATE CHAPTER 6 PDF FORMAT link.

That supplement is provided on an as-is basis.

Next, double-click your tge.exe icon as you've done in the past to run the Emaga client. When the Menus screen appears, click the Connect To Server button. Look for the 3DGPAI1 server name (or whatever value you assigned to `$Pref:: Server::Name` in the Control—Initialize module). Select that server entry, and then click Join. Watch the progress bars, and eventually you will find yourself deposited in the game. Send copies of this to your friends, and get them to join in for some freewheeling havoc or reckless mayhem—whichever you prefer!

Testing Direct Messaging

If you will recall, back at the beginning of the chapter, in the "Direct Messaging" section, we discussed the functions `CommandToServer` and `CommandToClient`. You might want to take this opportunity to test the code shown in that section.

Put the `ServerCmdTellEveryone` and `TellAll` functions to the end of your \EMAGA6\control\server\server.cs module, and then add the `SendMacro` function to the end of your \EMAGA6\control\client\misc\presetkeys.cs module. Also in the presetkeys.cs module, add the following after the `SendMacro` function that you just added:

```
function clientCmdTellMessage(%sender, %msgString)
{
  MessagePopup( "HELLO EVERYBODY", %msgString, 1000);
}
PlayerKeymap.bindCmd(keyboard, "1", "SendMacro(1);", "");
PlayerKeymap.bindCmd(keyboard, "2", "SendMacro(2);", "");
PlayerKeymap.bindCmd(keyboard, "3", "SendMacro(3);", "");
```

You can go ahead and test it when you've completed those additions, if you like. You can test it both in stand-alone (player-hosted) form or using a dedicated server with a client on the same or different machine on a LAN.

Moving Right Along

Now you have some understanding of how to pass messages back and forth between the client and the server. Keep in mind when you contemplate these things that there can be many clients—hockey socks full of clients, even. There will probably only be one server, but you are in no way restricted to only one server. It's all a matter of programming.

You've also seen how you can track specific clients on the server via their GameConnections. As long as you know the handle of the client, you can access any of that client's data.

In the next chapter we'll poke our noses into the common code that we have been shying away from. We want to do this so that we can get a better big-picture understanding of how our game can operate.

CHAPTER 7

COMMON SCRIPTS

For the last several chapters I have been keeping the contents of the common code folder tree out of the limelight. I hope you haven't started thinking that it is some deep, dark keep-it-in-the-family-only secret, because it isn't. The reason for maintaining the obscurity is because we've been looking at the areas of scripting that you will most likely want to change to suit your game development needs, and that means stuff *not* in the common code.

Having said that, there may be areas in the common code that you will want to customize or adjust in one way or another. To that end we are going to spend this chapter patrolling the common code to get the lay of the land.

You can gain access to this code for yourself in the common folder tree of any of the Emaga versions you installed in the previous chapters.

Game Initialization

As you may recall from earlier chapters, the common code base is treated as if it were just another add-on or Mod. It is implemented as a package in the common/main.cs module. For your game you will need to use this package or make your own like it. This is in order to gain access to many of the more mundane features of Torque, especially the "administrivia"-like functions that help make your game a finished product but that are not especially exciting in terms of game play features.

Here are the contents of the common/main.cs module.

```
//-----------------------------------------------------------------------------
// Torque Game Engine
// Copyright (C) GarageGames.com, Inc.
//-----------------------------------------------------------------------------

//-----------------------------------------------------------------------------
// Load up defaults console values.

exec("./defaults.cs");

//-----------------------------------------------------------------------------

function initCommon()
{
  // All mods need the random seed set
  setRandomSeed();

  // Very basic functions used by everyone
  exec("./client/canvas.cs");
  exec("./client/audio.cs");
}

function initBaseClient()
{
  // Base client functionality
  exec("./client/message.cs");
  exec("./client/mission.cs");
  exec("./client/missionDownload.cs");
  exec("./client/actionMap.cs");

  // There are also a number of support scripts loaded by the canvas
  // when it's first initialized. Check out client/canvas.cs
}

function initBaseServer()
{
  // Base server functionality
  exec("./server/audio.cs");
  exec("./server/server.cs");
  exec("./server/message.cs");
  exec("./server/commands.cs");
```

```
    exec("./server/missionInfo.cs");
    exec("./server/missionLoad.cs");
    exec("./server/missionDownload.cs");
    exec("./server/clientConnection.cs");
    exec("./server/kickban.cs");
    exec("./server/game.cs");
}

//------------------------------------------------------------------------
package Common {

function displayHelp() {
    Parent::displayHelp();
    error(
        "Common Mod options:\n"@
        " -fullscreen          Starts game in full screen mode\n"@
        " -windowed            Starts game in windowed mode\n"@
        " -autoVideo           Auto detect video, but prefers OpenGL\n"@
        " -openGL              Force OpenGL acceleration\n"@
        " -directX             Force DirectX acceleration\n"@
        " -voodoo2             Force Voodoo2 acceleration\n"@
        " -noSound             Starts game without sound\n"@
        " -prefs <configFile>  Exec the config file\n"
    );
}

function parseArgs()
{
    Parent::parseArgs();

    // Arguments override defaults...
    for (%i = 1; %i < $Game::argc ; %i++)
    {
        %arg = $Game::argv[%i];
        %nextArg = $Game::argv[%i+1];
        %hasNextArg = $Game::argc - %i > 1;

        switch$ (%arg)
        {
            //-------------------
            case "-fullscreen":
                $pref::Video::fullScreen = 1;
                $argUsed[%i]++;
```

```
    //-------------------
    case "-windowed":
      $pref::Video::fullScreen = 0;
      $argUsed[%i]++;

    //-------------------
    case "-noSound":
      error("no support yet");
      $argUsed[%i]++;

    //-------------------
    case "-openGL":
      $pref::Video::displayDevice = "OpenGL";
      $argUsed[%i]++;

    //-------------------
    case "-directX":
      $pref::Video::displayDevice = "D3D";
      $argUsed[%i]++;

    //-------------------
    case "-voodoo2":
      $pref::Video::displayDevice = "Voodoo2";
      $argUsed[%i]++;

    //-------------------
    case "-autoVideo":
      $pref::Video::displayDevice = "";
      $argUsed[%i]++;

    //-------------------
    case "-prefs":
      $argUsed[%i]++;
      if (%hasNextArg) {
        exec(%nextArg, true, true);
        $argUsed[%i+1]++;
        %i++;
      }
      else
        error("Error: Missing Command Line argument. Usage: -prefs
<path/script.cs>");
    }
  }
}
```

```
function onStart()
{
  Parent::onStart();
  echo("\n--------- Initializing MOD: Common ---------");
  initCommon();
}

function onExit()
{
  echo("Exporting client prefs");
  export("$pref::*", "./client/prefs.cs", False);

  echo("Exporting server prefs");
  export("$Pref::Server::*", "./server/prefs.cs", False);
  BanList::Export("./server/banlist.cs");

  OpenALShutdown();
  Parent::onExit();
}

}; // Common package
activatePackage(Common);
```

Two key things that happen during game initialization are calls to InitBaseClient and InitBaseServer, both of which are defined in common/main.cs. These are critical functions, and yet their actual activities are not that exciting to behold.

```
function initBaseClient()
{
  // Base client functionality
  exec("./client/message.cs");
  exec("./client/mission.cs");
  exec("./client/missionDownload.cs");
  exec("./client/actionMap.cs");

  // There are also a number of support scripts loaded by the canvas
  // when it's first initialized.  Check out client/canvas.cs
}
function initBaseServer()
{
  exec("./server/audio.cs");
  exec("./server/server.cs");
```

```
    exec("./server/message.cs");
    exec("./server/commands.cs");
    exec("./server/missionInfo.cs");
    exec("./server/missionLoad.cs");
    exec("./server/missionDownload.cs");
    exec("./server/clientConnection.cs");
    exec("./server/kickban.cs");
    exec("./server/game.cs");
}
```

As you can see, both are nothing more than a set of script loading calls. All of the scripts loaded are part of the common code base. We will look at selected key modules from these calls in the rest of this section.

Selected Common Server Modules

Next, we will take a close look at some of the common code server modules. The modules selected are the ones that will best help illuminate how Torque operates.

The Server Module

InitBaseServer loads the common server module, server.cs. When we examine this module we see the following functions:

PortInit

CreateServer

DestroyServer

ResetServerDefaults

AddToServerGuidList

RemoveFromServerGuidList

OnServerInfoQuery

It's not hard to get the sense from that list that this is a pretty critical module!

PortInit tries to seize control of the assigned TCP/IP port, and if it can't it starts incrementing the port number until it finds an open one it can use.

CreateServer does the obvious, but it also does some interesting things along the way. First, it makes a call to DestroyServer! This is not as wacky as it might seem; while DestroyServer does release and disable resources, it does so only after making sure the resources exist. So there's no danger of referencing something that doesn't exist, which would thus cause a crash. You need to specify the server type (single- [default] or multiplayer) and the mission name. The PortInit function is called from here, if the server will be a multiplayer server. The last, but certainly not the least, thing that CreateServer does is call LoadMission. This call kicks off a long and somewhat involved chain of events that we will cover in a later section.

DestroyServer releases and disables resources, as mentioned, and also game mechanisms. It stops further connections from happening and deletes any existing ones; turns off the heartbeat processing; deletes all the server objects in MissionGroup, MissionCleanup, and ServerGroup; and finally, purges all data-blocks from memory.

ResetServerDefaults is merely a convenient mechanism for reloading the files in which the server default variable initializations are stored.

AddToServerGuidList and RemoveFromServerGuidList are two functions for managing the list of clients that are connected to the server.

OnServerInfoQuery is a message handler for handling queries from a master server. It merely returns the string ''Doing OK''. The master server, if there is one, will see this and know that the server is alive. It could say anything—there could even be just a single-space character in the string. The important point is that if the server is *not* doing okay, then the function will not even be called, so the master server would never see the message, would time out, and then would take appropriate action (such as panicking or something useful like that).

The Message Module

InitBaseServer loads the common server-side message module, message.cs. Most of this module is dedicated to providing in-game chat capabilities for players.

    MessageClient

    MessageTeam

    MessageTeamExcept

    MessageAll

    MessageAllExcept

    SpamAlert

    GameConnection::SpamMessageTimeout

    GameConnection::SpamReset

The first five functions in the preceding list are for sending server-type messages to individual clients, all clients on a team, and all clients in a game. There are also exception messages, where everyone is sent the message *except* a specified client.

Next are the three chat message functions. These are linked to the chat interfaces that players will use to communicate with each other.

These functions all use the CommandToServer function (see Chapter 6) internally. It is important to note that there will need to be message handlers for these functions on the client side.

The three spam control functions are used in conjunction with the chat message functions. SpamAlert is called just before each outgoing chat message is processed for sending. Its purpose is to detect if a player is swamping the chat window with messages, an action called *spamming the chat window*. If there are too many messages in a short time frame as determined by the SpamMessageTimeout method, then the offending message is suppressed, and an alert message is sent to the client saying something like this: "Enough already! Take a break." Well, you could say it more diplomatically than that, but you get the idea. SpamReset merely sets the client's spam state back to normal after an appropriately silent interval.

The MissionLoad Module

Torque has a concept of *mission* that corresponds to what many other games, especially those of the first-person shooter genre, call *maps*. A mission is defined in a mission file that has the extension of .mis. Mission files contain the information that specifies objects in the game world, as well as their placement in the world. Everything that appears in the game world is defined there: items, players, spawn points, triggers, water definitions, sky definitions, and so on.

Missions are downloaded from the server to the client at mission start time or when a client joins a mission already in progress. In this way the server has total control over what the client sees and experiences in the mission.

Here are the contents of the common/server/missionLoad.cs module.

```
//------------------------------------------------------------------
// Torque Game Engine
//
// Copyright (C) GarageGames.com, Inc.
//------------------------------------------------------------------


//------------------------------------------------------------------
// Server mission loading
//------------------------------------------------------------------

// On every mission load except the first, there is a pause after
// the initial mission info is downloaded to the client.
$MissionLoadPause = 5000;

function LoadMission( %missionName, %isFirstMission )
{
  EndMission();
  Echo("*** LOADING MISSION: " @ %missionName);
  Echo("*** Stage 1 load");

  // Reset all of these
  ClearCenterPrintAll();
  ClearBottomPrintAll();

  // increment the mission sequence (used for ghost sequencing)
  $missionSequence++;
  $missionRunning = false;
  $Server::MissionFile = %missionName;

  // Extract mission info from the mission file,
  // including the display name and stuff to send
  // to the client.
  BuildLoadInfo( %missionName );

  // Download mission info to the clients
  %count = ClientGroup.GetCount();
  for( %cl = 0; %cl < %count; %cl++ ) {
    %client = ClientGroup.GetObject( %cl );
    if (!%client.IsAIControlled())
      SendLoadInfoToClient(%client);
  }
```

```
  // if this isn't the first mission, allow some time for the server
  // to transmit information to the clients:
  if( %isFirstMission || $Server::ServerType $= "SinglePlayer" )
    LoadMissionStage2();
  else
    schedule( $MissionLoadPause, ServerGroup, LoadMissionStage2 );
}

function LoadMissionStage2()
{
  // Create the mission group off the ServerGroup
  Echo("*** Stage 2 load");
  $instantGroup = ServerGroup;

  // Make sure the mission exists
  %file = $Server::MissionFile;

  if( !IsFile( %file ) ) {
    Error( "Could not find mission " @ %file );
    return;
  }

  // Calculate the mission CRC.  The CRC is used by the clients
  // to cache mission lighting.
  $missionCRC = GetFileCRC( %file );

  // Exec the mission, objects are added to the ServerGroup
  Exec(%file);

  // If there was a problem with the load, let's try another mission
  if( !IsObject(MissionGroup) ) {
    Error( "No 'MissionGroup' found in mission \"" @ $missionName @ "\"." );
    schedule( 3000, ServerGroup, CycleMissions );
    return;
  }

  // Mission cleanup group
  new SimGroup( MissionCleanup );
  $instantGroup = MissionCleanup;

  // Construct MOD paths
  PathOnMissionLoadDone();

  // Mission loading done...
  Echo("*** Mission loaded");
```

```
  // Start all the clients in the mission
  $missionRunning = true;
  for( %clientIndex = 0; %clientIndex < ClientGroup.GetCount();
%clientIndex++)
    ClientGroup.GetObject(%clientIndex).LoadMission();

  // Go ahead and launch the game
  OnMissionLoaded();
  PurgeResources();
}

function EndMission()
{
  if (!IsObject( MissionGroup ))
    return;

  Echo("*** ENDING MISSION");

  // Inform the game code we're done.
  OnMissionEnded();

  // Inform the clients
  for( %clientIndex = 0; %clientIndex < ClientGroup.GetCount();
%clientIndex++) {
    // clear ghosts and paths from all clients
    %cl = ClientGroup.GetObject( %clientIndex );
    %cl.EndMission();
    %cl.ResetGhosting();
    %cl.ClearPaths();
  }

  // Delete everything
  MissionGroup.Delete();
  MissionCleanup.Delete();

  $ServerGroup.Delete();
  $ServerGroup = new SimGroup(ServerGroup);
}

function ResetMission()
{
  Echo("*** MISSION RESET");
```

```
// Remove any temporary mission objects
MissionCleanup.Delete();
$instantGroup = ServerGroup;
new SimGroup( MissionCleanup );
$instantGroup = MissionCleanup;

//
OnMissionReset();
}
```

Here are the mission loading–oriented functions on the server contained in this module:

```
LoadMission
```

```
LoadMissionStage2
```

```
EndMission
```

```
ResetMission
```

LoadMission, as we saw in an earlier section, is called in the CreateServer function. It kicks off the process of loading a mission onto the server. Mission information is assembled from the mission file and sent to all the clients for display to their users.

After the mission file loads, LoadMissionStage2 is called. In this function the server calculates the CRC value for the mission and saves it for later use.

What's a CRC Value, and Why Should I Care?

We use a *Cyclic Redundancy Check* (CRC) when transmitting data over potentially error-prone media. Networking protocols use CRCs at a low level to verify that the sent data is the same data that was received.

A CRC is a mathematical computation performed on data that arrives at a number that represents both the content of the data and how it's arranged. The point is that the number, called a *checksum*, uniquely identifies the set of data, like a fingerprint.

By comparing the checksum of a set of data to another data set's checksum, you can decide if the two data sets are identical.

Why should you care? Well, in addition to the simple goal of maintaining data integrity, CRCs are another arrow in your anticheat quiver. You can use CRCs to ensure that files stored on the clients are the same as the files on the server and, in this regard, that all the clients have the same files— the result is that the playing field is level.

Once the mission is successfully loaded onto the server, each client is sent the mission via a call to its GameConnection object's LoadMission method.

EndMission releases resources and disables other mission-related mechanisms, clearing the server to load a new mission when tasked to do so.

ResetMission can be called from the EndGame function in the control/server/misc/ game.cs module to prepare the server for a new mission if you are using mission cycling techniques.

The MissionDownload Module

Here are the contents of the common/server/missionDownload.cs module.

```
//-------------------------------------------------------------------
// Torque Game Engine
//
// Copyright (C) GarageGames.com, Inc.
//-------------------------------------------------------------------


//-------------------------------------------------------------------
// Mission Loading
// The server portion of the client/server mission loading process
//-------------------------------------------------------------------

function GameConnection::LoadMission(%this)
{
  // Send over the information that will display the server info.
  // when we learn it got there, we'll send the datablocks.
  %this.currentPhase = 0;
  if (%this.IsAIControlled())
  {
    // Cut to the chase...
    %this.OnClientEnterGame();
  }
  else
  {
    CommandToClient(%this, 'MissionStartPhase1', $missionSequence,
      $Server::MissionFile, MissionGroup.musicTrack);
    Echo("*** Sending mission load to client: " @ $Server::MissionFile);
  }
}
```

```
function ServerCmdMissionStartPhase1Ack(%client, %seq)
{
  // Make sure to ignore calls from a previous mission load
  if (%seq != $missionSequence || !$MissionRunning)
    return;
  if (%client.currentPhase != 0)
    return;
  %client.currentPhase = 1;

  // Start with the CRC
  %client.SetMissionCRC( $missionCRC );

  // Send over the datablocks...
  // OnDataBlocksDone will get called when have confirmation
  // that they've all been received.
  %client.TransmitDataBlocks($missionSequence);
}

function GameConnection::OnDataBlocksDone( %this, %missionSequence )
{
  // Make sure to ignore calls from a previous mission load
  if (%missionSequence != $missionSequence)
    return;
  if (%this.currentPhase != 1)
    return;
  %this.currentPhase = 1.5;

  // On to the next phase
  CommandToClient(%this, 'MissionStartPhase2', $missionSequence,
$Server::MissionFile);
}

function ServerCmdMissionStartPhase2Ack(%client, %seq)
{
  // Make sure to ignore calls from a previous mission load
  if (%seq != $missionSequence || !$MissionRunning)
    return;
  if (%client.currentPhase != 1.5)
    return;
  %client.currentPhase = 2;

  // Update mod paths, this needs to get there before the objects.
  %client.TransmitPaths();
```

```
  // Start ghosting objects to the client
  %client.ActivateGhosting();

}

function GameConnection::ClientWantsGhostAlwaysRetry(%client)
{
  if($MissionRunning)
    %client.ActivateGhosting();
}

function GameConnection::OnGhostAlwaysFailed(%client)
{

}

function GameConnection::OnGhostAlwaysObjectsReceived(%client)
{
  // Ready for next phase.
  CommandToClient(%client, 'MissionStartPhase3', $missionSequence,
$Server::MissionFile);
}

function ServerCmdMissionStartPhase3Ack(%client, %seq)
{
  // Make sure to ignore calls from a previous mission load
  if(%seq != $missionSequence || !$MissionRunning)
    return;
  if(%client.currentPhase != 2)
    return;
  %client.currentPhase = 3;

  // Server is ready to drop into the game
  %client.StartMission();
  %client.OnClientEnterGame();
}
```

The following functions and GameConnection methods are defined in the MissionDownload module:

```
    GameConnection::LoadMission

    GameConnection::OnDataBlocksDone
```

```
GameConnection::ClientWantsGhostAlwaysRetry

GameConnection::OnGhostAlwaysFailed

GameConnection::OnGhostAlwaysObjectsReceived

ServerCmdMissionStartPhase1Ack

ServerCmdMissionStartPhase2Ack

ServerCmdMissionStartPhase3Ack
```

This module handles the server-side activities in the mission download process (see Figure 7.1). There are three phases: Transmit Datablocks, Ghost Objects, and Scene Lighting.

This module contains the mission download methods for each client's Game-Connection object.

The download process for the client object starts when its LoadMission method in this module is called at the end of the server's LoadMissionStage2 function in the server's MissionLoad module described in the previous section. It then embarks on a phased series of activities coordinated between the client and the server (see Figure 7.2). The messaging system for this process is the CommandToServer and CommandToClient pair of direct messaging functions.

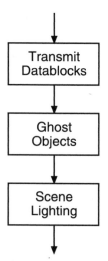

Figure 7.1
Mission download phases.

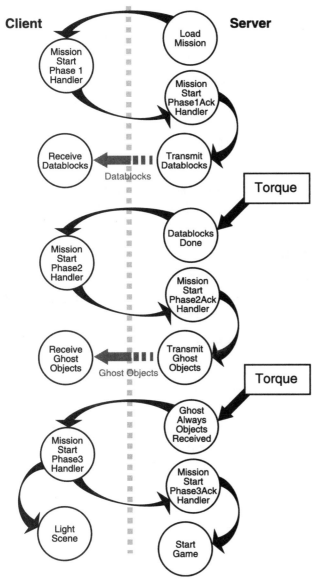

Figure 7.2
Mission download process.

The server invokes the client MissionStartPhase*n* (where *n* is 1, 2, or 3) function to request permission to start each phase. This is done using our old friend CommandToServer. When a client is ready for a phase, it responds with a MissionStartPhase*n*Ack message, for which there is a handler on the server contained in this module.

The handler `GameConnection::onDataBlocksDone` is invoked when phase 1 has finished. This handler then initiates phase 2 by sending the `MissionStartPhase2` message to the client.

The `GameConnection::onGhostAlwaysObjectsReceived` handler is invoked when phase 2 is completed. At the end of this phase, the client has all the data needed to replicate the server's version of any dynamic objects in the game that are ghosted to the clients. This handler then sends the `MissionStartPhase3` message to the client.

When the server receives the `MissionStartPhase3Ack` message, it then starts the mission for each client, inserting the client into the game.

The ClientConnection Module

The ClientConnection module is where most of the server-side code for dealing with clients is located. Here are the contents of the common/server/ clientConnection.cs module.

```
//-------------------------------------------------------------------
// Torque Game Engine
//
// Copyright (C) GarageGames.com, Inc.
//-------------------------------------------------------------------

function GameConnection::OnConnectRequest( %client, %netAddress, %name )
{
  Echo("Connect request from: " @ %netAddress);
  if($Server::PlayerCount >= $pref::Server::MaxPlayers)
    return "CR_SERVERFULL";
  return "";
}

function GameConnection::OnConnect( %client, %name )
{
MessageClient(%client,'MsgConnectionError',"",$Pref::Server::
  ConnectionError);

  SendLoadInfoToClient( %client );

  if (%client.getAddress() $= "local") {
    %client.isAdmin = true;
    %client.isSuperAdmin = true;
```

```
      }
      else {
        %client.isAdmin = false;
        %client.isSuperAdmin = false;
      }
      // Save client preferences on the Connection object for later use.
      %client.gender = "Male";
      %client.armor = "Light";
      %client.race = "Human";
      %client.skin = AddTaggedString( "base" );
      %client.SetPlayerName(%name);
      %client.score = 0;

  $instantGroup = ServerGroup;
  $instantGroup = MissionCleanup;
  Echo("CADD: " @ %client @ " " @ %client.GetAddress());

      // Inform the client of all the other clients
      %count = ClientGroup.GetCount();
      for (%cl = 0; %cl < %count; %cl + +) {
        %other = ClientGroup.GetObject(%cl);
        if ((%other != %client)) {

          MessageClient(%client, 'MsgClientJoin', "",
              %other.name,
              %other,
              %other.sendGuid,
              %other.score,
              %other.IsAIControlled(),
              %other.isAdmin,
              %other.isSuperAdmin);
        }
      }

      // Inform the client we've joined up
      MessageClient(%client,
        'MsgClientJoin', '\c2Welcome to the Torque demo app %1.',
        %client.name,
        %client,
        %client.sendGuid,
        %client.score,
        %client.IsAiControlled(),
        %client.isAdmin,
        %client.isSuperAdmin);
```

```
  // Inform all the other clients of the new guy
  MessageAllExcept(%client, -1, 'MsgClientJoin', '\c1%1 joined the game.',
    %client.name,
    %client,
    %client.sendGuid,
    %client.score,
    %client.IsAiControlled(),
    %client.isAdmin,
    %client.isSuperAdmin);

  // If the mission is running, go ahead and download it to the client
  if ($missionRunning)
    %client.LoadMission();
  $Server::PlayerCount++;
}

function GameConnection::SetPlayerName(%client,%name)
{
  %client.SendGuid = 0;

  // Minimum length requirements
  %name = StripTrailingSpaces( StrToPlayerName( %name ) );
  if ( Strlen( %name ) < 3 )
    %name = "Poser";

  // Make sure the alias is unique, we'll hit something eventually
  if (!IsNameUnique(%name))
  {
    %isUnique = false;
    for (%suffix = 1; !%isUnique; %suffix++) {
      %nameTry = %name @ "." @ %suffix;
      %isUnique = IsNameUnique(%nameTry);
    }
    %name = %nameTry;
  }
  // Tag the name with the "smurf" color:
  %client.nameBase = %name;
  %client.name = AddTaggedString("\cp\c8" @ %name @ "\co");
}

function IsNameUnique(%name)
{
```

```
  %count = ClientGroup.GetCount();
  for ( %i = 0; %i < %count; %i++ )
  {
    %test = ClientGroup.GetObject( %i );
    %rawName = StripChars( detag( GetTaggedString( %test.name ) ),
"\cp\co\c6\c7\c8\c9" );
      if ( Strcmp( %name, %rawName ) == 0 )
         return false;
  }
  return true;
}

function GameConnection::OnDrop(%client, %reason)
{
  %client.OnClientLeaveGame();

  RemoveFromServerGuidList( %client.guid );
  MessageAllExcept(%client, -1, 'MsgClientDrop', '\c1%1 has left the game.',
%client.name, %client);

  RemoveTaggedString(%client.name);
  Echo("CDROP: " @ %client @ " " @ %client.GetAddress());
  $Server::PlayerCount--;

  if( $Server::PlayerCount == 0 && $Server::Dedicated)
    Schedule(0, 0, "ResetServerDefaults");
}

function GameConnection::StartMission(%this)
{
  CommandToClient(%this, 'MissionStart', $missionSequence);
}

function GameConnection::EndMission(%this)
{
  CommandToClient(%this, 'MissionEnd', $missionSequence);
}

function GameConnection::SyncClock(%client, %time)
{
  CommandToClient(%client, 'syncClock', %time);
}
```

```
function GameConnection::IncScore(%this,%delta)
{
  %this.score += %delta;
  MessageAll('MsgClientScoreChanged', "", %this.score, %this);
}
```

The following functions and GameConnection methods are defined in the Client Connection module:

GameConnection::OnConnectRequest

GameConnection::OnConnect

GameConnection::SetPlayerName

IsNameUnique

GameConnection::OnDrop

GameConnection::StartMission

GameConnection::EndMission

GameConnection::SyncClock

GameConnection::IncScore

The method GameConnection::OnConnectRequest is the server-side destination of the client-side GameConnection::Connect method. We use this method to vet the request—for example, to examine the IP address to compare to a ban list, to make sure that the server is not full, and stuff like that. We have to make sure that if we want to allow the request, we must return a null string (" ").

The next method, GameConnection::OnConnect, is called after the server has approved the connection request. We get a client handle and a name string passed in as parameters. The first thing we do is ship down to the client a tagged string to indicate that a connection error has happened. We do not tell the client to use this string. It's just a form of preloading the client.

Then we send the load information to the client. This is the mission information that the client can display to the user while the mission loading process takes place. After that, if the client also happens to be the host (entirely possible), we set the client to be a superAdmin.

Then we add the client to the user ID list that the server maintains. After that there are a slew of game play client settings we can initialize.

Next, we start a series of notifications. First, we tell all clients that the player has joined the server. Then we tell the joining player that he is indeed welcome here, despite possible rumors to the contrary. Finally, we tell all the client-players that there is a new kid on the block, so go kill him. Or some such—whatever you feel like!

After all the glad-handing is done, we start downloading the mission data to the client starting the chain of events depicted back there in Figure 7.2.

GameConnection::SetPlayerName does some interesting name manipulation. First, it tidies up any messy names that have leading or trailing spaces. We don't like names that are too short (trying to hide something?), so we don't allow those names. Then we make sure that the name is not already in use. If it is, then an instance number is added to the end of the name. The name is converted to a tagged string so that the full name only gets transmitted once to each client; then the tag number is used after that, if necessary.

The function IsNameUnique searches through the server's name list looking for a match. If it finds the name, then it isn't unique; otherwise, it is.

The method GameConnection::OnDrop is called when the decision is made to drop a client. First, the method makes a call to the client so that it knows how to act during the drop. Then it removes the client from its internal list. All clients (except the one dropped) are sent a server text message notifying them of the drop, which they can display. After the last player leaves the game, this method restarts the server. For a persistent game, this statement should probably be removed.

The next method, GameConnection::StartMission, simply notifies clients whenever the server receives a command to start another server session in order to give the clients time to prepare for the near-future availability of the server. The $missionSequence is used to manage mission ordering, if needed.

Next, GameConnection::EndMission is used to notify clients that a mission is ended, and hey! Stop playing already!

The method GameConnection::SyncClock is used to make sure that all clients' timers are synchronized with the server. You can call this function for a client anytime after the mission is loaded but before the client's player has spawned.

Finally, the method `GameConnection::IncScore` is called whenever you want to reward a player for doing well. By default, this method is called when a player gets a kill on another player. When the player's score is incremented, all other players are notified, via their clients, of the score.

The Game Module

The server-side Game module is the logical place to put server-specific game play features. Here are the contents of the common/server/game.cs module.

```
//--------------------------------------------------------------------
// Torque Game Engine

// Copyright (C) 2001 GarageGames.com, Inc.
//--------------------------------------------------------------------
function OnServerCreated()
{
  $Server::GameType = "Test App";
  $Server::MissionType = "Deathmatch";
  createGame();
}

function OnServerDestroyed()
{
  DestroyGame();
}

function OnMissionLoaded()
{
  StartGame();
}

function OnMissionEnded()
{
  EndGame();
}

function OnMissionReset()
{
  // stub
}
```

```
function GameConnection::OnClientEnterGame(%this)
{
//stub
}

function GameConnection::OnClientLeaveGame(%this)
{
//stub
}


//--------------------------------------------------------------------
// Functions that implement game-play
//--------------------------------------------------------------------
function CreateGame()
{
  //
}

function DestroyGame()
{
  //
}
function StartGame()
{
//stub
}

function EndGame()
{
//stub
}
```

The following functions and `GameConnection` methods are defined in the Game
module:

　　　`OnServerCreated`

　　　`OnServerDestroyed`

　　　`OnMissionLoaded`

　　　`OnMissionEnded`

OnMissionReset

CreateGame

Destroy Game

StartGame

EndGame

GameConnection::OnClientEnterGame

GameConnection::OnClientLeaveGame

The first function defined, OnServerCreated, is called from CreateServer when a server is constructed. It is a useful place to load server-specific datablocks.

The variable $Server::GameType is sent to the master, if one is used. Its purpose is to uniquely identify the game and distinguish it from other games handled by the master server. The variable $Server::MissionType is also sent to the server—clients can use its value to filter servers based on mission type.

The next function, OnServerDestroyed, is the antithesis of OnServerCreated—anything you do there should be undone in this function.

The function OnMissionLoaded is called by LoadMission once a mission has finished loading. This is a great location to initialize mission-based game play features, like perhaps calculating weather effects based on a rotating mission scheme.

OnMissionEnded is called by EndMission just before it is destroyed; this is where you should undo anything you did in OnMissionLoaded.

OnMissionReset is called by ResetMission, after all the temporary mission objects have been deleted.

CreateGame, Destroy Game, StartGame, and EndGame are all stub routines. The demo expects you to override these functions with your own code game's control scripts.

The function GameConnection::OnClientEnterGame is called for each client after it has finished downloading the mission and is ready to start playing. This would be a good place to load client-specific persistent data from a database back end, for example.

`GameConnection::OnClientLeaveGame` is called for each client that is dropped. This would be a good place to do a final update of back-end database information for the client.

Although we don't use too many of the functions in this module, it is a great location for a lot of game play features to reside.

Selected Common Code Client Modules

Next, we will take a close look at some of the common code client modules. The modules selected are the ones that will best help illuminate how Torque operates.

Keep in mind that all of these modules are designed to affect things that concern the local client, even though they might require contacting the server from time to time.

This point is important: when you add features or capabilities, you must always keep in mind whether you want the feature to affect only the local client (such as some user preference change) or you want the feature to affect all clients. In the latter case it would be best to use modules that are server-resident when they run.

The Canvas Module

The Canvas module is another one of those simple, small, but critical modules. One of the key features of this module is that the primary function contained in here, `InitCanvas`, loads a number of general graphical user interface support modules. This module is loaded from the `InitCommon` function rather than from the `InitBaseClient` function, which is where the rest of the key common modules get loaded. Here are the contents of the common/client/canvas.cs module.

```
//-------------------------------------------------------------------------
// Torque Game Engine
// Copyright (C) GarageGames.com, Inc.
//-------------------------------------------------------------------------


//-------------------------------------------------------------------------
// Function to construct and initialize the default canvas window
// used by the games
```

```
function InitCanvas(%windowName, %effectCanvas)
{
  VideoSetGammaCorrection($pref::OpenGL::gammaCorrection);
   if(%effectCanvas)
    %CanvasCreate = CreateEffectCanvas ( %windowName);
   else
    %CanvasCreate = CreateCanvas ($windowName):
   if (!CreateCanvas(%windowName)) {
    quitWithErrorMessage("Copy of Torque is already running; existing.");
    return;
  }

  SetOpenGLTextureCompressionHint( $pref::OpenGL::compressionHint );
  SetOpenGLAnisotropy( $pref::OpenGL::textureAnisotropy );
  SetOpenGLMipReduction( $pref::OpenGL::mipReduction );
  SetOpenGLInteriorMipReduction( $pref::OpenGL::interiorMipReduction );
  SetOpenGLSkyMipReduction( $pref::OpenGL::skyMipReduction );

  // Declare default GUI Profiles.
  Exec("~/ui/defaultProfiles.cs");

  // Common GUI's
  Exec("~/ui/ConsoleDlg.gui");
  Exec("~/ui/LoadFileDlg.gui");
  Exec("~/ui/ColorPickerDlg.gui");
  Exec("~/ui/SaveFileDlg.gui");
  Exec("~/ui/MessageBoxOkDlg.gui");
  Exec("~/ui/MessageBoxYesNoDlg.gui");
  Exec("~/ui/MessageBoxOKCancelDlg.gui");
  Exec("~/ui/MessagePopupDlg.gui");
  Exec("~/ui/HelpDlg.gui");
  Exec("~/ui/RecordingsDlg.gui");
  Exec("~/ui/NetGraphGui.gui");
  // Commonly used helper scripts
  Exec("./metrics.cs");
  Exec("./messageBox.cs");
  Exec("./screenshot.cs");
  Exec("./cursor.cs");
  Exec("./help.cs");
  Exec("./recordings.cs");

  // Init the audio system
  OpenALInit():
}
```

```
function ResetCanvas()
{
  if (IsObject(Canvas))
  {
    Canvas.Repaint();
  }
}
```

InitCanvas is obviously the main function in this module. When it is called, it first calls VideoSetGammaCorrection using a global preferences variable. If the value passed is 0 or undefined, then there is no change in the gamma correction (see Table 7.1).

Then we attempt to create the canvas, which is an abstracted call to the Windows API to create a window. The %windowName variable is passed in as a string that sets the window's title. If we can't create the window, we quit because there is no point continuing without any means to display our game. CreateEffectCanvas is a special version of CreateCanvas that gives us some extra methods and properties for doing special effects. CreateCanvas is mostly just an abstracted way to create a window with a graphics context. It's abstracted due to the need to

Table 7.1 OpenGL Settings

Module	Function
GammaCorrection	Gamma correction modifies the overall brightness of an image. Images that are not corrected can look either overbleached or too dark.
TextureCompressionHint	The choice of how much texture compression (to reduce memory and graphics transfer bandwidth) to employ is left up to the drivers and hardware, but we can hint at how we would like the compression to work, if feasible. Valid hints are GL_DONT_CARE GL_FASTEST GL_NICEST
Anisotropy	Anisotropic filtering is used to address a specific kind of texture artifact that occurs when a 3D surface is sloped relative to the view camera. The higher the value set for this (between 0 and 1, exclusive), the more filtering is performed by the hardware. Too high a setting might cause too much fuzziness in an image.
MipReduction	See Chapter 3 for a discussion of mipmapping. This value can be from 0 to 5. The higher the number, the more mipmapping levels supported. Image textures must be created to support these levels in order to achieve the best effect.
InteriorMipReduction	The same as MipReduction, but for use in interiors (.dif file format models).
SkyMipReduction	The same as MipReduction, but for use in skybox images.

support similar capabilities on three very different platforms (Windows, Linux, and Macintosh).

Following that, there is a series of OpenGL settings, again using global preference variables. See Table 7.1 for an explanation of these settings.

Next, the function loads a bunch of support files that establish user interface mechanisms, dialogs, and profiles for describing them.

Then there is a series of calls to load modules that provide access to some common utility functions that can be used for measuring performance, taking screen shots, displaying Help information, and so on.

The ResetCanvas function checks to see if a canvas object exists, and if so, ResetCanvas then forces it to be repainted (re-rendered).

The Mission Module

The Mission module doesn't really do much. Its existence is no doubt because some forethought had been given to future expansion directions for the common code scripts. Here are the contents of the common/client/mission.cs module.

```
//---------------------------------------------------------------
// Torque Game Engine
// Copyright () GarageGames.com, Inc.
//---------------------------------------------------------------

//---------------------------------------------------------------
// Mission start / end events sent from the server
//---------------------------------------------------------------

function ClientCmdMissionStart(%seq)
{
  // The client receives a mission start right before
  // being dropped into the game.
}

function ClientCmdMissionEnd(%seq)
{
  // Received when the current mission is ended.
  alxStopAll();
  // Disable mission lighting if it's going; this is here
  // in case the mission ends while we are in the process
```

```
    // of loading it.
    $lightingMission = false;
    $sceneLighting::terminateLighting = true;
}
```

ClientCmdMissionStart is a stub routine. Not much to say here other than this routine gets called immediately before the client-player finds himself in the game. This is a handy place for last-minute client-side code; the mission is known and loaded, and all objects (including any remote clients) are ghosted. This might be a good place to build and display a map or to possibly fire up an Internet Relay Chat session, if you have written one for yourself in TorqueScript (it *is* possible—a member of the GarageGames community has done just that).

ClientCmdMissionEnd resets some lighting variables after calling alxStopAll, which halts any audio tracks that might be playing. This would be the place to undo anything you started in the ClientCmdMissionStart function.

The thing that makes this module, and therefore its functions, key is its existence. You should consider utilizing these functions in your game and expanding their functionality.

The MissionDownload Module

Just as the server side has a module called MissionDownload, so has the client code. It certainly can be confusing, so you have to stay on your toes when dealing with these modules, always being aware of whether you are dealing with the client or the server version. The choice of names is understandable though, when you realize that they are functionally complementary—the mission download activity requires synchronized and coordinated actions from both the client and the server. Two peas in a pod.

Here are the contents of the common/client/missiondownload.cs module.

```
//---------------------------------------------------------------
// Torque Game Engine
// Copyright (C) GarageGames.com, Inc.
//---------------------------------------------------------------


//---------------------------------------------------------------
// Phase 1
//---------------------------------------------------------------
```

```
function ClientCmdMissionStartPhase1(%seq, %missionName, %musicTrack)
{
  // These need to come after the cls.
  Echo ("*** New Mission: " @ %missionName);
  Echo ("*** Phase 1: Download Datablocks & Targets");
  OnMissionDownloadPhase1(%missionName, %musicTrack);
  CommandToServer('MissionStartPhase1Ack', %seq);
}

function OnDataBlockObjectReceived(%index, %total)
{
  OnPhase1Progress(%index / %total);
}


//------------------------------------------------------------------------
// Phase 2
//------------------------------------------------------------------------

function ClientCmdMissionStartPhase2(%seq,%missionName)
{
  onPhase1Complete();
  Echo ("*** Phase 2: Download Ghost Objects");
  purgeResources();
  onMissionDownloadPhase2(%missionName);
  commandToServer('MissionStartPhase2Ack', %seq);
}

function OnGhostAlwaysStarted(%ghostCount)
{
  $ghostCount = %ghostCount;
  $ghostsRecvd = 0;
}

function OnGhostAlwaysObjectReceived()
{
  $ghostsRecvd + + ;
  OnPhase2Progress($ghostsRecvd / $ghostCount);
}


//------------------------------------------------------------------------
// Phase 3
//------------------------------------------------------------------------
```

```
function ClientCmdMissionStartPhase3(%seq,%missionName)
{
  OnPhase2Complete();
  StartClientReplication();
  StartFoliageReplication();
  Echo ("*** Phase 3: Mission Lighting");
  $MSeq = %seq;
  $Client::MissionFile = %missionName;

  // Need to light the mission before we are ready.
  // The sceneLightingComplete function will complete the handshake
  // once the scene lighting is done.
  if (LightScene("SceneLightingComplete", ""))
  {
    Error("Lighting mission....");
    schedule(1, 0, "UpdateLightingProgress");
    OnMissionDownloadPhase3(%missionName);
    $lightingMission = true;
  }
}

function UpdateLightingProgress()
{
  OnPhase3Progress($SceneLighting::lightingProgress);
  if ($lightingMission)
    $lightingProgressThread = schedule(1, 0, "UpdateLightingProgress");
}

function SceneLightingComplete()
{
  Echo("Mission lighting done");
  OnPhase3Complete();

  // The is also the end of the mission load cycle.
  OnMissionDownloadComplete();
  CommandToServer('MissionStartPhase3Ack', $MSeq);
}
//-----------------------------------------------------------------
// Helper functions
//-----------------------------------------------------------------

function connect(%server)
{
```

```
  %conn = new GameConnection();
  %conn.connect(%server);
}
```

When reviewing this module, you should refer back to the server-side MissionDownload module descriptions and Figures 7.1 and 7.2.

The first function for phase 1, ClientCmdMissionStartPhase1, calls the function OnMissionDownloadPhase1, which is something you want to define in your control code. Its basic purpose is to set up for a progress display as the datablocks are loaded. As soon as this call returns, an acknowledgment is sent back to the server using CommandToServer to send the MissionStartPhase1Ack message back. At this time it also reflects the sequence number (%seq) back to the server, to ensure that the client and server remain synchronized.

The next function, OnDataBlockObjectReceived, is an important one. This message handler gets called every time the Torque Engine client-side code detects that it has finished receiving a datablock. When invoked, it then calls onPhase1Progress, which needs to be defined in our control client code.

The next function, ClientCmdMissionStartPhase2, is part of the phase 2 activities. Its duties are much the same as for ClientCmdMissionStartPhase1, but this time using OnMissionDownloadPhase2 and MissionStartPhase2Ack.

The next function, OnGhostAlwaysStarted, is called by the engine after it processes the MissionStartPhase2Ack message. It is used to track ghosted object counts.

When an object has been successfully ghosted, onGhostAlwaysObjectReceived is called from the engine. We use this to call onPhase2Progress in order to update our progress display.

The ClientCmdMissionStartPhase3 function is the last in the series. When it is called we update our progress display and then turn on two client-side replication functions. These functions provide special objects (such as grass and trees) that will be computed and rendered only by the client. For example, the server sends a seed for the location of a tuft of grass. The client-side replication code calculates the locations of hundreds or even thousands of copies of this tuft of grass and distributes them appropriately.

Because these objects are deemed not to be critical for game play, we can take the risk of client-side computation without risking someone modifying the code to cheat. Someone could modify the code, but it wouldn't gain him any online advantage.

Next we call the function LightScene to perform the scene's terrain and interior lighting passes. We pass the completion callback function SceneLightingComplete, which will be called when the lighting calculations are finished.

We also schedule a function (UpdateLightingProgress) to be repeatedly called while the lighting is under way, as follows:

```
schedule(1, 0, "updateLightingProgress");
```

In this case the function is called after one millisecond.

UpdateLightingProgress is a short function. It makes a call to update the progress display and then schedules itself to be called again in another millisecond if the lighting is not finished. It can tell if the lighting is finished by checking the variable $lightingMission. If it is true, then lighting is still under way.

SceneLightingComplete is the completion callback passed to LightScene. When SceneLightingComplete is called, lighting has completed, so it sets the variable $lightingMission to false, which will, within a millisecond or so, be detected by UpdateLightingProgress. It then notifies the server that lighting is complete by sending the MissionStartPhase3Ack message. And away we go!

The insignificant little connect function, marked as a "Helper" function by the GG code comments, is nothing more than *the most important function in the client/server code!* Heh. Take *that* somebody! You can see that it creates a new GameConnection object, and then establishes the connection. Without that call, there is no way for the client to talk to the server. Trouble is, small functions just don't get no respect!

The Messages Module

The Messages module provides front-end generic message handlers for two defined message types, as well as a tool for installing handlers at run time. You may or may not find this useful, but a look at how these functions work will help when it comes to creating your own sophisticated messaging system. Here are the contents of the common/client/message.cs module.

```
//---------------------------------------------------------------
// Torque Game Engine
// Copyright (C) GarageGames.com, Inc.
//---------------------------------------------------------------
```

```
function ClientCmdChatMessage(%sender, %voice, %pitch, %msgString, %a1, %a2,
%a3, %a4, %a5, %a6, %a7, %a8, %a9, %a10)
{
  OnChatMessage(detag(%msgString), %voice, %pitch);
}

function ClientCmdServerMessage(%msgType, %msgString, %a1, %a2, %a3, %a4, %a5,
%a6, %a7, %a8, %a9, %a10)
{
  // Get the message type; terminates at any whitespace.
  %tag = GetWord(%msgType, 0);

  // First see if there is a callback installed that doesn't have a type;
  // if so, that callback is always executed when a message arrives.
  for (%i = 0; (%func = $MSGCB["", %i]) !$= ""; %i++) {
    call(%func, %msgType, %msgString, %a1, %a2, %a3, %a4, %a5, %a6, %a7, %a8,
%a9, %a10);
  }

  // Next look for a callback for this particular type of ServerMessage.
  if (%tag !$= "") {
    for (%i = 0; (%func = $MSGCB[%tag, %i]) !$= ""; %i++) {
      call(%func, %msgType, %msgString, %a1, %a2, %a3, %a4, %a5, %a6, %a7,
%a8, %a9, %a10);
    }
  }
}

function AddMessageCallback(%msgType, %func)
{
  for (%i = 0; (%afunc = $MSGCB[%msgType, %i]) !$= ""; %i++) {
    // If it already exists as a callback for this type,
    // nothing to do.
    if (%afunc $= %func) {
      return;
    }
  }
  // Set it up.
  $MSGCB[%msgType, %i] = %func;
}

function DefaultMessageCallback(%msgType, %msgString, %a1, %a2, %a3, %a4, %a5,
%a6, %a7, %a8, %a9, %a10)
```

```
{
  OnServerMessage(detag(%msgString));
}

AddMessageCallback("", DefaultMessageCallback);
```

The first function, ClientCmdChatMessage, is for chat messages only and is invoked on the client when the server uses the CommandToClient function with the message type ChatMessage. Refer back to the server-side message module if you need to. The first parameter (%sender) is the GameConnection object handle of the player that sent the chat message. The second parameter (%voice) is an Audio Voice identifier string. Parameter three (%pitch) is rarely used, but is offered as a means for providing pitch control for an audio message. Finally, the fourth parameter (%msgString) contains the actual chat message in a tagged string. The rest of the parameters are not actually acted on so can be safely ignored for now. The parameters are passed on to the pseudo-handler OnChatMessage. It's called a *pseudo-handler* because the function that calls OnChatMessage is not really calling out from the engine. However, it is useful to treat this operation as if a callback message and handler were involved for conceptual reasons.

The next function, ClientCmdServerMessage, is used to deal with game event descriptions, which may or may not include text messages. These can be sent using the message functions in the server-side Message module. Those functions use CommandToClient with the type ServerMessage, which invokes the function described next.

For ServerMessage messages, the client can install callbacks that will be run according to the type of the message.

Obviously, ClientCmdServerMessage is more involved. After it uses the GetWord function to extract the message type as first text word from the string %msgType, it iterates through the message callback array ($MSGCB) looking for any untyped callback functions and executes them all. It then goes through the array again, looking for registered callback functions with the same message type as the incoming message, executing any that it finds.

The next function, addMessageCallback, is used to register callback functions in the $MSGCB message callback array. This is not complex; addMessageCallback merely steps through the array looking for the function to be registered. If it isn't there, addMessageCallback stores a handle to the function in the next available slot.

The last function, DefaultMessageCallback, is supplied in order to provide an untyped message to be registered. The registration takes place with the line after the function definition.

A Final Word

The common code base includes a ton of functions and methods. We have only touched on about half of them here. I aimed to show you the most important modules and their contents, and I think that's been accomplished nicely. For your browsing pleasure, Table 7.2 contains a reference to find all the functions in all common code modules.

Table 7.2 Common Code Functions

Module	Function
common/main.cs	InitCommon
	InitBaseClient
	InitBaseServer
	DisplayHelp
	ParseArgs
	OnStart
	OnExit
common/client/actionMap.cs	ActionMap::copyBind
	ActionMap::blockBind
common/client/audio.cs	OpenALInit
	OpenALShutdown
common/client/canvas.cs	InitCanvas
	ResetCanvas
common/client/cursor.cs	CursorOff
	CursorOn
	GuiCanvas::checkCursor
	GuiCanvas::setContent
	GuiCanvas::pushDialog
	GuiCanvas::popDialog
	GuiCanvas::popLayer
common/client/help.cs	HelpDlg::onWake
	HelpFileList::onSelect
	GetHelp
	ContextHelp
	GuiControl::getHelpPage
	GuiMLTextCtrl::onURL

Table 7.2   continued

Module	Function
common/client/message.cs	`ClientCmdChatMessage`
	`ClientCmdServerMessage`
	`AddMessageCallback`
	`DefaultMessageCallback`
common/client/messageBox.cs	`MessageCallback`
	`MBSetText`
	`MessageBoxOK`
	`MessageBoxOKDlg::onSleep`
	`MessageBoxOKCancel`
	`MessageBoxOKCancelDlg::onSleep`
	`MessageBoxYesNo`
	`MessageBoxYesNoDlg::onSleep`
	`MessagePopup`
	`CloseMessagePopup`
common/client/metrics.cs	`FpsMetricsCallback`
	`TerrainMetricsCallback`
	`VideoMetricsCallback`
	`InteriorMetricsCallback`
	`TextureMetricsCallback`
	`WaterMetricsCallback`
	`TimeMetricsCallback`
	`VehicleMetricsCallback`
	`AudioMetricsCallback`
	`DebugMetricsCallback`
	`Metrics`
common/client/mission.cs	`ClientCmdMissionStart`
	`ClientCmdMissionEnd`
common/client/missionDownload.cs	`ClientCmdMissionStartPhase1`
	`OnDataBlockObjectReceived`
	`ClientCmdMissionStartPhase2`
	`OnGhostAlwaysStarted`
	`OnGhostAlwaysObjectReceived`
	`ClientCmdMissionStartPhase3`
	`UpdateLightingProgress`
	`SceneLightingComplete`
	`Connect`

continued

Table 7.2 continued

Module	Function
common/client/recordings.cs	RecordingsDlg::onWake
	StartSelectedDemo
	StartDemoRecord
	StopDemoRecord
	DemoPlaybackComplete
common/client/screenshot.cs	FormatImageNumber
	FormatSessionNumber
	RecordMovie
	MovieGrabScreen
	StopMovie
	DoScreenShot
common/server/audio.cs	ServerPlay2D
	ServerPlay3D
common/server/clientConnection.cs	GameConnection::onConnectRequest
	GameConnection::onConnect
	GameConnection::setPlayerName
	IsNameUnique
	GameConnection::onDrop
	GameConnection::startMission
	GameConnection::endMission
	GameConnection::syncClock
	GameConnection::incScore
common/server/commands.cs	ServerCmdSAD
	ServerCmdSADSetPassword
	ServerCmdTeamMessageSent
	ServerCmdMessageSent
common/server/game.cs	OnServerCreated
	OnServerDestroyed
	OnMissionLoaded
	OnMissionEnded
	OnMissionReset
	GameConnection::onClientEnterGame
	GameConnection::onClientLeaveGame
	CreateGame
	DestroyGame
	StartGame
	EndGame
common/server/kickban.cs	Kick
	Ban

Table 7.2 continued

Module	Function
common/server/message.cs	MessageClient
	MessageTeam
	MessageTeamExcept
	MessageAll
	MessageAllExcept
	GameConnection::spamMessageTimeout
	GameConnection::spamReset
	SpamAlert
	ChatMessageClient
	ChatMessageTeam
	ChatMessageAll
common/server/missionDownload.cs	GameConnection::loadMission
	ServerCmdMissionStartPhase1Ack
	GameConnection::onDataBlocksDone
	serverCmdMissionStartPhase2Ack
	GameConnection::clientWantsGhostAlwaysRetry
	GameConnection::onGhostAlwaysFailed
	GameConnection::onGhostAlwaysObjectsReceived
	ServerCmdMissionStartPhase3Ack
common/server/missionInfo.cs	ClearLoadInfo
	BuildLoadInfo
	DumpLoadInfo
	SendLoadInfoToClient
common/server/missionLoad.cs	LoadMission
	LoadMissionStage2
	EndMission
	ResetMission
common/server/server.cs	PortInit
	CreateServer
	DestroyServer
	ResetServerDefaults
	AddToServerGuidList
	RemoveFromServerGuidList
	OnServerInfoQuery
common/ui/ConsoleDlg.gui	ConsoleDlg::onWake
	ConsoleDlg::onSleep
	ConsoleEntry::eval
	ToggleConsole
	UpdateConsoleErrorWindow

continued

Table 7.2 concluded

Module	Function
common/ui/LoadFileDlg.gui	GetLoadFilename
	DoOpenFileExCallback
	LoadDirTreeEx::onSelectPath
	LoadFileListEx::onDoubleClick
common/ui/SaveFileDlg.gui	GetSaveFilename
	DoSaveCallback
	SaveDirTreeEx::onSelectPath
	SaveFileListEx::onSelect

One last thing to remember about the common code: as chock-full of useful and important functionality as it is, you don't *need* to use it to create a game with Torque. You'd be nuts to throw it away, in my humble opinion. Nonetheless, you *could* create your own script code base from the bottom up. One thing I hope this chapter has shown you is that a huge pile of work has already been done for you. You just need to build on it.

Moving Right Along

In this chapter we took a look at the capabilities available in the common code base so that you will gain familiarity with how Torque scripts generally work. For the most part it is probably best to leave the common code alone. There may be times, however, when you will want to tweak or adjust something in the common code or to add your own set of features, and that's certainly reasonable. You will find that the features you want to reuse are best added to the common code.

As you saw, much of the critical server-side common code is related to issues that deal with loading mission files, datablocks, and other resources from the server to each client as it connects.

In a complementary fashion, the client-side common code accepts the resources being sent by the server and uses those resources to prepare to display the new game environment to the user.

So, that's enough programming and code for a while. In the next few chapters, we'll get more artistic, dealing with visual things. In the next chapter, we'll take a look at textures, how to make them and how to use them. We'll also learn a new tool we can use to create them.

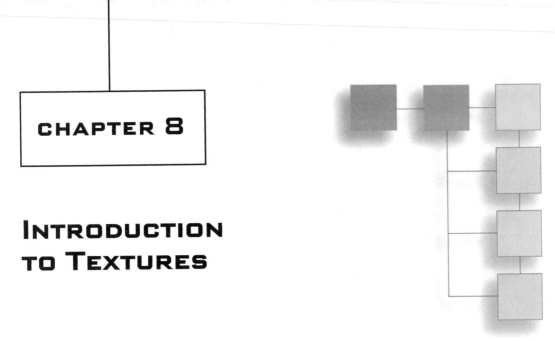

CHAPTER 8

INTRODUCTION TO TEXTURES

3D computer games are *intensely* visual. In this chapter we begin to explore the creative process behind the textures that give 3D objects their pizzazz.

Using Textures

Textures are probably the unsung heroes of 3D gaming. It is difficult to overstate the importance of textures. One of the most important uses of textures in a game is in creating and sustaining the ambience, or the look and feel, of a game.

Textures also can be used to create apparent properties of objects, properties that the object shape doesn't have—it just looks like it does. For example, blocky shapes with jutting corners can appear to be smoothed by the careful application of an appropriate texture using a process called *texture mapping*.

Another way textures can be used is to create the illusion of substructure and detail. Figure 8.1 shows a castle with towers and walls that appear to be made of blocks of stone. The stone blocks are merely components of the textures applied to the tower and wall objects. There are no stone blocks actually modeled in that scene. The same goes for the appearance of the wooden boards in the steps and other structures. The texture gives not only the appearance of wood but also the structure of individually nailed planks and boards. This is a powerful tool, using textures to define substructures and detail.

Figure 8.1
Structure definition through using textures.

Figure 8.2
Rock and icefalls appearance on a mountainside.

This ability to create the illusion of structure can be refined and used in other ways. Figure 8.2 shows a mountainside scene with bare granite rock and icefalls. Again, textures were created and applied with this appearance in mind. This technique greatly reduces the need to create 3D models for the myriad of tiny objects, nooks, and crannies you're going to encounter on an isolated and barren mountain crag.

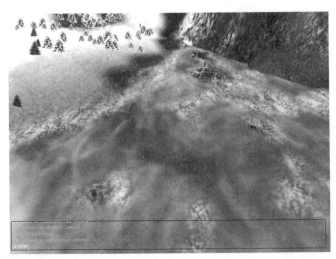

Figure 8.3
Shoreline foam and deep-water textures.

Textures appear in many guises in a game. In Figure 8.3 two different textures are used to define the water near the shoreline. A foamy texture is used for the areas that splash against rock and sand, and a more wavelike texture is used for the deep water. In this application the water block is a dynamic object that has moving waves. It ebbs and flows and splashes against the shore. The water textures are distorted and twisted in real time to match the motion of the waves.

Another area where textures are used to enhance the ambience of a game is to define the appearance of the sky. Figure 8.4 shows cloud textures being used in a skybox. The *skybox* is basically the inside of a big six-sided box that surrounds your scene. By applying specially distorted and treated textures to the skybox, we can create the appearance of an all-enveloping 360-degree sky above the horizon.

We can use textures to enhance the appearance of other objects in a scene. For example, in Figure 8.5 we see a number of coniferous trees on a hillside. By designing the ground texture that occupies the terrain location of the trees appropriately, we can achieve the forest look we want without needing to completely cover every inch of ground with the tree objects. This is helpful because the fewer objects we need to use for such a purpose—basically decoration—the more objects that will be available for us to use in other ways.

One of the most amazing uses of textures is when defining technological items. Take the tommy gun in Figure 8.6, for instance. There are only about a dozen objects in that model, and most of them are cubes, with a couple of cylinders

Figure 8.4
Clouds in a skybox using textures.

Figure 8.5
Terrain accents.

tossed in, as well as two or three irregular shapes. Yet by using an appropriately designed texture, we can convey much greater detail. The weapon is easily identifiable as a Thompson Submachine Gun, circa 1944.

Following the theme of technological detail, Figure 8.7 is another example. This model of a Bell 47 Helicopter (think *M*A*S*H*) shows two trick uses of textures in one model. The engine detail and the instrument panel dials were created

Figure 8.6
Weapon detail using textures.

Figure 8.7
Vehicle detail and structure.

using textures we've already seen. Now take a look at the tail boom and the cockpit canopy. The tail boom looks like it is made of several dozen intersecting and overlapping metal bars; after all, you can see right through it to the buildings and ground in the background. But it is actually a single elongated and pinched box or cube with a single texture applied! The texture utilizes the alpha channel to convey the transparency information to the Torque renderer. Cool, huh? Then

Figure 8.8
Player clothing, skin, and other details.

there is the canopy. It is semitransparent or mildly translucent. You can obviously see right through it, as you should when looking through Perspex, but you can still make out the sense of a solid glasslike surface.

Of course, technological features are not the only things that can be enhanced through textures. In Figure 8.8 the brawler about to enter the tavern is attired in the latest stylish leather brawling jacket. He is obviously somewhere around 40 years of age, judging by his classic male-pattern baldness, and the bat is a Tubettiville slugger. Okay, okay, the bat is a stretch, but if it were turned over 180 degrees, you would be able to see the Tubettiville logo, and then you could tell! Also note the use of the texture specifying the tavern name, named in honor of a famous *Delta Force 2* player, Insomniac.

Look at the moon in Figure 8.9. Look again, closer. Does it look familiar? It should, because the moon texture in that picture is an actual photograph of the full moon, taken outside my house with a digital camera and then used to generate the moon texture. The rest of the scene is generated using the Torque Engine with appropriate nighttime lighting parameters set.

I think by now you have a pretty good idea why I say that textures are the unsung heroes of 3D gaming. They really make a huge difference by conveying not only the obvious visual information but also the subtle clues and feelings that can turn a good game into a great experience.

Figure 8.9
Distant objects.

The Gimp 2

You are going to be creating your own textures as you travel through this book, and to do that you'll need a good tool for texture and image manipulation. Well, I've included a *great* image processing tool, the Gimp 2, on the companion CD for you to use. *The Gimp* is an unusual name, I'll grant you that, especially with *the* tacked on like that in the front and a version number dangling off the back. At various times throughout this book you might see me refer to it as "the Gimp" or even just plain "Gimp." Yeah, I'm lazy.

The Gimp is a fully featured image processing and image generation tool, created by Spencer Kimball and Peter Mattis, with scanner support, special effects and filters, image analysis statistics, and the whole nine yards.

The Gimp is free for you to use, with no limitations, other than those described in the GNU *General Public License* (GPL), which is included in Appendix E for your perusal. There's nothing startling in the license. Just don't take the source code and create your own program and try to sell it. Oh, did I forget to mention that the source code is included on the CD as well? Well, it is. In fact, that is one of the requirements of the GPL license. Now if you are a crackerjack C/C++ programmer and have an idea about how to improve the Gimp, you can actually go ahead and make the changes and submit them to the Gimp Project. Go to http://developer.gimp.org for more information. At the time of this writing, at least

162 people have provided patches, fixes, plug-ins, extensions, scripts, translations, documentation, and more.

Another nice thing about the Gimp is that it is available for Windows, Macintosh OSX, and various flavors of UNIX and Linux! I don't need to tell you how cool that is, do I?

Okay, so what next?

Well, first, you'll need to install the Gimp.

Installing the Gimp 2

To install the Gimp, we must first install the GTK graphics toolkit and then install the Gimp itself. Follow this procedure:

1. Browse to your CD in the \3D2E\TOOLS\GIMP2 folder.

2. Locate the gtk+-2.8.9-setup-1.exe file, and double-click it to open it.

3. Click the Next button until you get to the Select Components screen. Make sure you have all three of the components—Base, MS-Windows Engine, and Translations—selected. Click Next again, and then click Install. This will install GTK to its default locations. After the installation is complete, click Finish.

4. Locate the gimp-2.2.12-i586-setup.exe file, and double-click it to open it.

5. Click the Next buttons until you get to the Select Components screen. Make sure you have all three of the components—Base, Translations, and Gimp FreeType plug-in—selected.

6. Click Next again, and this time select all the graphics file types you want to be able to double-click and have the Gimp open automatically. If you have no other image processing tools, then select all the file types. Click Next.

7. Click Next two more times, and then click Install. This will install the Gimp to its default locations.

8. After the installation is complete, make sure the Launch the Gimp check box is checked, and then click Finish. The Gimp will open up in due course.

Note

The version of the Gimp used in this edition is 2.2.12. You can check to see if there are more recent versions available by browsing to http://www.gimp.org. You can also go there to look for the Mac and Linux versions as well.

Tip

You can install a Help file that includes context help by opening the file gimp-help-2-0.9-setup.exe in the \3D2E\TOOLS\GIMP2 folder and running its installer, *after* you've installed the Gimp. Just take all the defaults—except don't install all the languages offered. When you get to the Language dialog box in the installation procedure, uncheck any of the languages that you won't use, keeping any you might need checked.

Getting Started

To get this party rolling, we're going to just blast through and create a couple of textures that you can use later for whatever grabs your fancy. We'll cover just the tools and steps we need to get the job done. In a later section we'll cover the most common tools in more detail.

Creating a Texture

So, let's get down to brass tacks and create a texture from scratch. We'll create a wood texture using the built-in capabilities of the Gimp.

1. Launch the Gimp, and select File, New from the menu at the top of the main Gimp window (the one titled "The Gimp").

2. A New Image dialog box opens up. Set the width and height dimensions to 128 pixels (see Figure 8.10), and click OK.

3. We now have a blank image to work with. Over in the main Gimp window, locate the Fill tool, and select it, as shown in Figure 8.11.

   Tip

   The upper part of the Gimp's main window is called the *Toolbox*. The lower part is called the *Tool Options* area, sometimes called the *Context Options*, because the options change according to which tool (the context) is selected.

4. After selecting the Fill tool's bucket icon, look down in the context menu at the bottom of the main window, find the Fill Type section, and select the Pattern fill radio button. Ensure that the Pine pattern is selected in the text

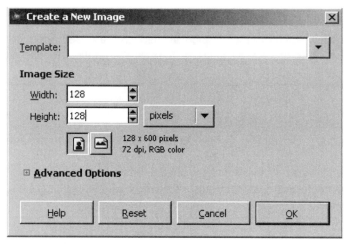

Figure 8.10
Creating a new blank image.

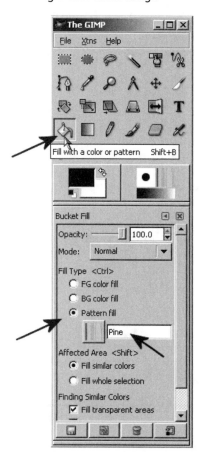

Figure 8.11
Selecting the Fill tool in the Gimp's main window.

box below and to the right of the radio button and a color image of the Pine texture is in the texture button to the left of the text box.

Tip

If Pine is not already selected for you in the Pattern fill radio button, then click the button just *below* and to the *right* of the Pattern radio button. A pop-up menu of images will appear. Scroll through until you find the Pine pattern. The patterns are ordered alphabetically.

5. Move your cursor over into the new image you created earlier, and click the mouse button. The image should fill with the Pine texture.

   Now you should have a bona fide woodgrain texture, like the one shown in Figure 8.12. You can use this texture for things like walls, planks, ladders, the wooden stock on a weapon, barrels, and whatever else you can come up with.

6. To make the image larger and easier to see, look down at the bottom of the image window (which is probably called Untitled-1.0), where there will be two downward-pointing triangular arrows. Click the rightmost one, and the

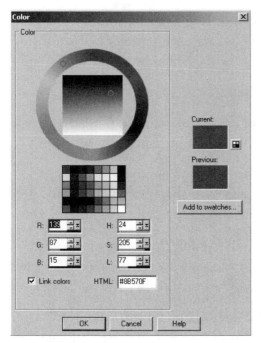

Figure 8.12
Pine texture.

selection menu containing zoom factors will appear. Select 200% (or whatever twists your crank) with a single mouse click. Your image will double in size (unless you didn't start out at 100%—and you should have; if yours is different, then it was sabotage, I tell you!).

You can use this texture to experiment with different image processing effects and touchup tools in the Gimp. Go ahead and give it a try. Leave the Gimp open when you are done.

Okay, that was so much fun, let's do another. This time we are going to tweak an image a bit searching for a specific look. The next texture will be a sort of rough-wall look that you might find on a painted cement block, or maybe a freshly poured sidewalk, or something like that. We'll call it the *sidewalk texture*, for convenience.

1. The Gimp should still be running.

2. Select File, New.

3. Set the width and height dimensions to 128 pixels, and click OK. (Take another look at Figure 8.10 if you need to refresh your memory.)

4. Select the Fill bucket, and then go back to the Fill Type section in the context pane (see Figure 8.11 for a refresher), but this time select 3D Green for the pattern.

5. Fill your new image with the 3D Green pattern.

6. Choose Select, All from the image windows menu—check to make sure you have the crawling ants around the perimeter of the image.

7. From the image window's menu, choose Tools, Color Tools, Hue-Saturation. The Hue-Saturation is one way to change the overall color values of an image, all at once. Figure 8.13 shows the Hue-Saturation dialog box.

8. Move the three sliders back and forth, and watch the image appearance change. You will need to make sure that the Preview check box at the lower left is checked in order to view the changes in real time.

9. Use the sliders to set the following values: Hue, 24; Lightness, 80; Saturation, −94. You can also directly type the values into the edit boxes for each setting.

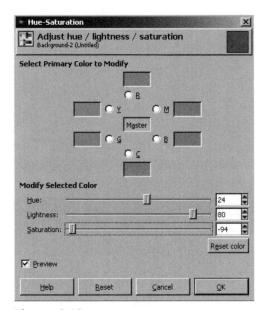

Figure 8.13
Hue-Saturation dialog box.

10. Notice the change in the texture? It should look something like Figure 8.14.

11. Click OK to close the Hue-Saturation dialog box.
Now this texture is quite a bit darker than I want it to be. I'm looking for a light gray with a hint of beige or tan color, so what we'll do is touch it up a bit using some different tools. I could probably narrow in on the desired result quite a bit more using the Hue-Saturation dialog box, but that wouldn't be any fun, now would it?

Tip

Due to the vagaries of grayscale reproductions of color images, don't expend too much energy trying to match your work with the images here in the book. Follow the values I give you in the procedures, and note the changes that occur with your work—they should at least roughly mirror the changes in the book images in a very general sense, and not much more than that.

First, we want to brighten the image and, at the same time, emphasize the bumpiness a bit. To do this, we'll use the Brightness-Contrast tool.

12. Still with the crawling ants, choose Tools, Color Tools, Brightness-Contrast. Your screen will be graced with the presence of the Brightness-Contrast dialog box, as shown in Figure 8.15.

Figure 8.14
Initial sidewalk texture.

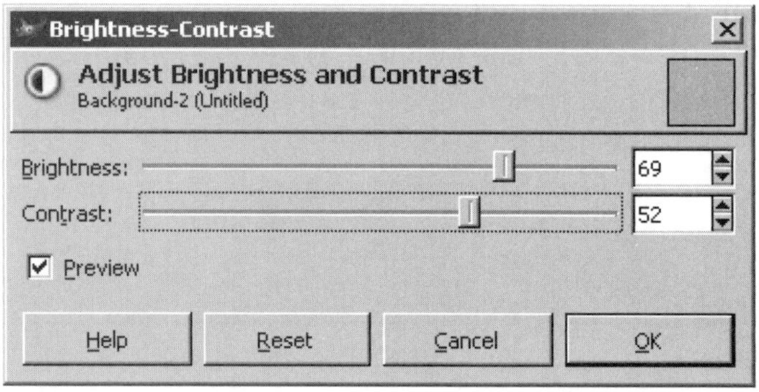

Figure 8.15
Brightness-Contrast dialog box.

13. Set Brightness to 69 and Contrast to 52. Then click OK.
    As you can see with Figure 8.16, the texture details now stand out in relief quite a bit more. This is goodness. However, the color still needs to be more tanlike.

14. Choose Tools, Color Tools, Color Balance to get the Color Balance dialog box, as shown in Figure 8.17.

Figure 8.16
Enhanced sidewalk texture.

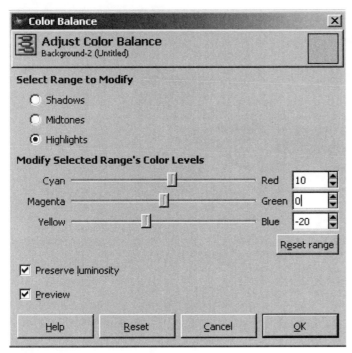

Figure 8.17
Color Balance dialog box.

There are three radio buttons in the Select Range to Modify section: Shadows, Midtones, and Highlights. Select any one of them for use in the next step.

15. Move the sliders (or type the values in directly) to set them as shown in Table 8.1.

16. Repeat setting those values for the remaining two radio button settings in the Select Range to Modify section. You should end up with a sidewalk texture that is a light gray-tan, as shown in Figure 8.18.

Table 8.1 Color Balance Settings

Slider	Value
Cyan—Red	10
Magenta—Green	0
Yellow—Blue	−20

Figure 8.18
Gray-tan sidewalk texture.

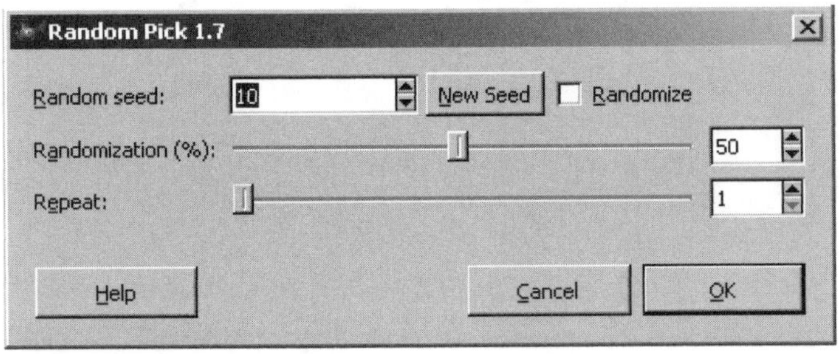

Figure 8.19
Random Pick dialog box.

Now that the color is where we want it, let's roughen it up a bit. The texture is a bit too smooth, sort of like taffy. A sidewalk usually looks grainier. To get that kind of look, we'll add *noise*.

17. Choose Filters, Noise, Pick. You'll get the Random Pick dialog box, as shown in Figure 8.19.

18. We'll stick with the default values. Note that if you intend to repeatedly use this tool when processing textures, you should probably check the Randomize check box to ensure that you get a different random seed each time. This will ensure that you won't get the same pseudo-random changes applied every time you use the tool.

The texture should now look something like the one shown in Figure 8.20. Notice that some of the visible features in the texture have been scrambled somewhat by adding the noise.

You should now have two images open in your Gimp window: the first one being the woodgrain texture and the other being the sidewalk texture. In the next section you'll learn how to save those images for later use.

Working with Files

We want to get those images saved without any further ado, but first I want to show you something. You're going to launch the Torque demo and have a peek at something.

Getting a Before View

1. Leave the Gimp running, and task switch (Alt + Tab) to the Windows desktop.

Figure 8.20
Final sidewalk texture.

Figure 8.21
View of an Orc hovel.

2. Launch the Torque FPS demo, and start a server up, just as you did back in Chapter 3.

3. After you spawn in, go run up to one of the hovels, as shown in Figure 8.21.

4. Take note of the texture used for the stone steps in the front of the Orc's hovel. Also take note of the texture used for the doorframe.

5. Resist the natural impulse to run around and blow things up. (Well, *try* to resist the natural impulse to run around and blow things up, anyway.) Instead, exit the game.

Saving Texture Files

Okay, now that you have the "before" view recorded in your mind, we'll finally get to saving those images. Switch back to the Gimp now, and follow this procedure to save your files:

1. Browse your way to the folder \3D2E\demo\data\interiors, locate the files oak2.jpg and WalNoGroove.jpg, and rename both of them by adding the word *original* to the front of their names. This way you can restore those files for use later, if needed.

2. Click the pine woodgrain image to bring it to the front (making it active).

3. Select File, Save As, and then click the Browse for other folders button just below the Save in folder part. You will get the Save Image dialog box, as shown in Figure 8.22.

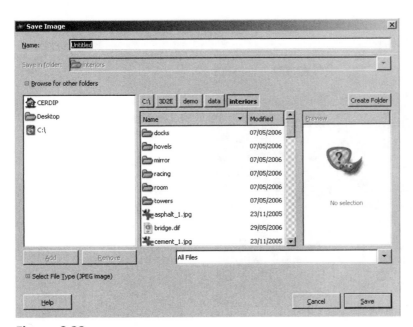

Figure 8.22
Save Image dialog box.

4. In the Save Image dialog box, make the type be JPG by clicking Select File Type, scrolling through the File Type list that appears, and selecting JPG image–JIFF Compliant.

5. In the volume pane (on the left), select the volume or drive on which you installed the Torque demo (probably C:), and then in the folder pane (in the middle), browse your way to \3D2E\demo\data\interiors.

6. Name your file oak2.jpg—the name must be exact. Click Save.

7. You will get a dialog box asking you to set the quality. Just click OK (we will *always* use the defaults in this particular dialog box).

Repeat steps 1 to 6 for the sidewalk image, using the name WalNoGroove.jpg.

Now, task switch back to the desktop, and run the Torque demo game again, just as you did before. When you spawn in the game, you will now see the floor rendered with your new texture and the overhead beams rendered with the woodgrain texture you created (see Figure 8.23). If either the floor or the beams look like they did in your "before" view, then you've probably made an error in the file name or perhaps saved them in the wrong folder. Double-check your work, and everything should turn out fine.

Figure 8.23
The modified hovel.

Congratulations! You are now an artist.

Tip

> You can restore the original textures in place of your own textures by going back to \3D2E\ demo\data\interiors with the Explorer and removing the word *original* that you placed at the front of the file name. You will need to rename or delete your custom-made version of those files first, though.

PNG Versus JPG

The Gimp supports many, many file types. If you select File, Save As, you'll get the Save Image dialog box. If you click Select File Type (By Extension), you'll get a whopping great hockey sock full of available file types. There are two of particular interest to us: JPEG (*Joint Photographic Experts Group*) and PNG (*Portable Network Graphics*). In Windows, the JPEG format file extension is .jpg; this is more commonly used than .jpeg, so *JPG* is the term I will use.

When you save files in the JPG format, the images are compressed. The type of compression used is called a *lossy* compression. This means that the technique used to squeeze the image information into less space throws away some of the information. This is not necessarily a Bad Thing. The people who devised the JPG format were pretty clever and were able to specify rules that guide the software in what to keep, what to throw away, and how to modify the information. So although there is loss of information, the effect on the image is fairly negligible in most cases, but there *is* an effect.

On top of all that, if you repeatedly open and save JPG files, the distortion will get worse each time you do it, as data is lost in the compression each time. You'll see it as a sort of smearing of colors around edges, especially in areas of high color contrast. It's similar to the messiness resulting from photocopying photocopies of photocopies.

So, if JPG has these artifacts, why use it? Because with more complex images, like photographs or similar artwork, JPG files are usually smaller than PNG files. Go ahead and try for yourself. Maybe use the one in your texture example from earlier, like the sidewalk texture. When I save the final texture as JPG, I get a file size of 3,101 bytes. As PNG, I get 17,372 bytes!

The smaller the texture files are, the more of them we can fit in a given amount of memory, and the more textures we can fit in memory, the richer the visual experience for our game.

Okay, so now you are wondering, why bother with the PNG file type, right? Well, there is a good reason for using PNG files, of course. The PNG format supports a concept called *alpha channels*, and we will need to use alpha channels for some of our game images. Not all of them, but a few. So the rule of thumb will be to use JPG for all images except when we need to specify an alpha channel—then we use PNG.

Finally, here is an important workflow tip. Save all of your original image creations in the Gimp native format: XCF. When you create and save your images in XCF format, it's a lot like having the original source code for a program. You can save all of your layers in XCF format, for example. Some other formats support layers, like PNG with its single alpha layer, but most don't. Anyway, you can save your image files in the format suitable for your game needs, PNG or JPG, when you need to.

Bitmap Versus Vector Images

Image graphics are presented in two different ways: bitmap graphics and vector graphics formats. Sometimes both methods are used together.

Bitmap images, as supported by the Gimp, are also called *raster images*. *Raster*, the older term, is the pattern of lines traced by rectilinear scanning in display systems. Although it is not exactly the same as a bitmap image, it's the term that the Gimp uses to describe such images. In this book I will use the term *bitmap* for such images, except when quoting tools or commands that use the word *raster*. Just remember that they essentially mean the same thing in this context.

A bitmap image is composed of pixels laid out on a grid. Each pixel represents a color value, one each for red, green, and blue. The weighting of each of these values determines the color of each pixel. In most image processing tools, if you increase the magnification of a bitmap image, you can see these pixels. They look like squares on the screen. A bitmap object is a collection of these pixels. An object is stored as a group of pixels with the color information about each pixel color. Pixels can be blended to create soft edges and smooth transitions between objects. Photographic images are always rendered as bitmap images because the pixel format matches well to the way that photographs are made.

You should note that an image in bitmap format is resolution-dependent. You specify the resolution and pixel dimensions when you create the image. If you later decide to increase its size, you enlarge each pixel, which lowers the image quality.

A vector image is composed of procedural and mathematical instructions for drawing the image. The Gimp doesn't work with vector graphics. As you encountered in Chapter 3, a vector is basically a line that has definite magnitude and direction. Vector objects in graphics are defined in a similar fashion. Each object in a vector image is stored as a separate item with information about its relative position in the image, its starting and ending points, and width, color, and curve information. This makes the vector format useful for things like logos, text fonts, and line drawings.

An image in vector format does not depend on the resolution. It can be resized without losing detail because it is stored as a set of instructions, not as a collection of pixels. Each time you display an image, you re-create it.

We will be doing all of our work with bitmap images. Some of the tools we'll use actually operate as vector tools until the object is committed to an image document, at which point they are converted to raster graphics.

Transparency and Translucency

Okay, so you are now able to perform the most important texture imaging operations, creating one and saving it. The next most important operation is the creation of alpha channel transparent sections of an image. Remember the helicopter tail boom?

There are other uses for alpha transparency, of course. Bitmapped GUI buttons are candidates. You may want a button that does not have straight sides and square corners. You can create irregular button shapes using transparent sections of your button image.

Another use for a bitmap with alpha transparency would be overlays on the GUI, such as health bars, status displays, and weapons crosshairs.

Let's take a look at an example of a bitmap with transparency. With Torque, there are two ways to go about it. The simplest way is to simply save your image as a PNG file, with the transparent portion assigned to the alpha channel. This keeps things in a nice, tidy single-file package. Torque will automatically employ the transparency information deployed in the alpha channel and render the image accordingly.

The second way is to use an *alpha mask* JPG image, alongside an original JPG image. For example, say you have a doughnut texture, and you want the area inside the hole, as well as the area outside the doughnut proper, to be transparent.

The image with the actual doughnut texture is the *base* image—let's call it doughnut.jpg.

Using Alpha Masks   We then create the alpha mask file by filling all those portions of the base image that would be transparent with black and all those portions that would be actual texture with white. We then name the alpha mask file with the same first part and extension as the base image file, but with *alpha* shoehorned in between a pair of periods, like this—doughnut.alpha.jpg. The *alpha* tells Torque that this is an alpha mask image for the file called doughnut.jpg.

Figure 8.24 shows the base image for the GarageGames logo.

Figure 8.25 shows the alpha mask for the GarageGames logo.

Figure 8.24
The GarageGames logo base image.

Figure 8.25
The GarageGames logo alpha mask image.

Due to the way the alpha mask in Figure 8.25 is arranged, the dark area around the circle in which the stylistic g in Figure 8.24 is encased will be completely transparent when rendered. In the alpha mask, you can also present translucency by using shades of gray rather than simple black or white. The lighter the shade of gray, the more opaque the image will be in those areas.

Another way to think about the effect is to think in terms of background image and foreground image. When you want to render an image in a scene, or in a dialog box, there will normally be some sort of background texture present. The image you want to render therefore becomes the foreground image. The white areas of the alpha mask allow the foreground image and suppress the background image. The whiter the mask area, the more foreground is admitted. As the white area gets darker, less and less foreground image is rendered and more and more background image starts to come into view. At 50 percent gray (halfway between white and black), both foreground and background images are blended together in equal amounts. When the gray is more on the black side than the white, then the background image starts to dominate the resulting blended image.

Let's make our own example. Launch Torque, and stop at the main menu. Check out the orc in the right corner. We're going to replace that image with our own.

1. Using Explorer, browse your way to \3D2E\demo\client\ui, and locate the files orc.jpg and orc.alpha.jpg. Rename them by adding *Original* to the beginning of their file names. Don't just make copies—we are going to replace orc.jpg and orc.alpha.jpg with our own files.

2. Using the Gimp, create a new 256 by 256 pixel image.

3. Using the Fill Pattern tool (the paint bucket icon), select your own favorite pattern and fill the entire blank image with it. I used the recessed pattern.

4. Save your work as \3D2E\demo\client\ui\orc.jpg.

5. Create another new 256 by 256 pixel image. This time, in the Create a New Image dialog box, click the Advanced Options button, and in the Colorspace combo box, select Grayscale.

Tip

If you forget to set the colorspace (RGB or Grayscale) of a new image when you create it, you can convert any image to the needed setting by choosing Image, Mode and then selecting which mode to convert to: RGB, Grayscale, or Indexed.

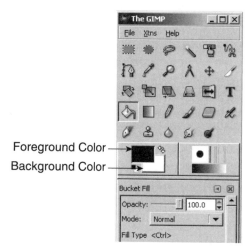

Figure 8.26
The Color area.

6. Set the background color to white by clicking the background color button in the Color area (see Figure 8.26). You will get the Change Background Color dialog box, in which you can pick the white color from the array at the lower right, so that it shows in the Current box. Click OK.

7. Set the foreground color to black by clicking the foreground color button in the Color area (again, see Figure 8.26). Go about it the same way you did for white, or you can manually set the RGB (red, green, blue) parameters in the edit boxes at the right. For black, set R, G, and B to 0; for white, set all three to 255; for 50 percent gray, set all three to 127.

8. Select the Pencil tool, and in the Options area, select a Brush of Circle 11.

9. Draw some pattern in your blank image. Figure 8.27 shows the pattern I made.

10. Save your work as \3D2E\demo\client\ui\orc.alpha.jpg.

11. Launch the Torque demo, and examine the main menu at the lower right for evidence of your handiwork.

Figure 8.28 shows my results. Hopefully yours will be similar, or even better!

Using Alpha Channels   As mentioned earlier, another, arguably simpler, way to introduce transparency into bitmap images is to use *alpha channels*. If your

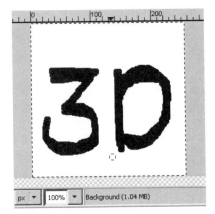

Figure 8.27
The custom alpha mask.

Figure 8.28
The alpha mask result.

imaging tool supports PNG format with alpha channels—and the Gimp does—then you can combine your texture data and transparency data in one file. This helps ease the assets management load when developing a game. Having fewer files to track means less work.

Let's get on our hands and knees and rummage around the Gimp's capabilities a bit. Don't forget to do your warm-up stretches. You don't want to sprain your mousing hand.

1. Using Explorer, browse your way to \3D2E\demo\client\ui, and locate the files orc.jpg and orc.alpha.jpg. These are the files you created in the previous

Swap Arrows

Figure 8.29
The swap arrows.

exercise. If you want to keep them around, rename them by adding *My* to the beginning of their file names. Otherwise, just delete both of them.

2. Using the Gimp, create a new 256 by 256 pixel image. In the Create a New Image dialog box, click the Advanced Options button, and in the Fill with combo box, select Transparency. Click OK. Notice that the blank image has a checkerboard pattern, signifying no color.

3. Select the Pencil tool, with its brush set to Circle (11).

4. If your foreground color is set to white, you are good to go. If not, click the swap arrows (see Figure 8.29) to move the white background to the foreground.

5. With the pencil, draw something in your blank image. I did a slightly different version of what I did in the last exercise.

6. Save your work as \3D2E\demo\client\ui\orc.png.

7. Launch the Torque demo, and once again examine the main menu at the lower right for evidence of your handiwork.

Pretty easy, huh? Now, the reason why we deleted or renamed the orc.alpha.jpg and orc.jpg files in step 1 is because when we specify image files to Torque in the scripts, we usually do *not* specify the extension in the file name. Torque then follows a plan whereby it first looks for a file with the indicated name and a .jpg extension. If it finds one, it then looks for a file with the indicated name and the extension .alpha.jpg. If it finds that, it uses it as the alpha mask and doesn't look for any more files.

If Torque *doesn't* find a file with the indicated name and a .jpg extension, then it looks for a file with the indicated name and a .png extension. Since we wanted the PNG version to be used, we had to make sure that Torque didn't find the earlier

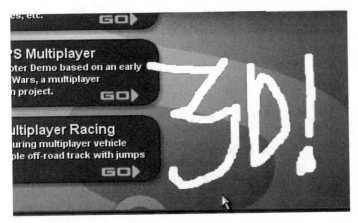

Figure 8.30
The alpha channel result.

JPG versions. Torque then used the alpha channel data for the transparency info and did its thing.

By the way, Figure 8.30 shows my results.

The Gimp Feature Highlights

I won't cover all the features that the Gimp offers—and there are a ton of them. What I'll do is cover those that I use the most when creating textures for games and present some of the most useful options and capabilities for those features.

The first thing that you can't help but notice is that the Gimp does not constrain your image documents to exist only inside the main window, like most programs do. In fact, you can't even have your documents' windows inside the main window!

It does take a little getting used to, having the floating main window reside elsewhere on your desktop. Also note that each window (main window and every document window) has its own menu bar. While all image document menus have the same sets of menu commands and submenus, the main window's menus are different. The most significant difference is that there is no Save or Save As menu command in the main window's menus. Those features exist only on the image document windows' menu bars.

Figure 8.31 shows the Gimp's main window, with the major sections marked.

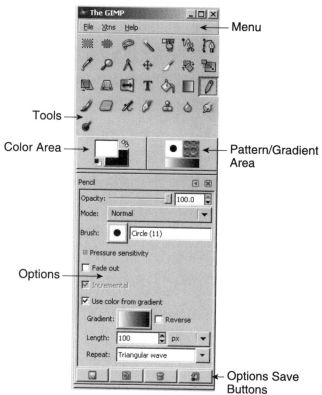

Menu

Tools

Color Area

Pattern/Gradient Area

Options

Options Save Buttons

Figure 8.31
The Gimp's main window.

Layers

A newly created Gimp image consists of one raster layer, always called the *background* layer. This is like the canvas of a painting; *every* image must have at least one layer. Additional layers float above the background like overlays.

To manipulate or manage our layers in the Gimp, we use the Layers dialog box (see Figure 8.32), which you can invoke by choosing Dialogs, Layers from an image document window or File, Dialogs, Layers from the main window or by simply pressing Ctrl + L.

When creating image resources, you should always strive to build your work up in layers. You can hide layers and rearrange them on top of or below each other as you work, helping to prevent your work from becoming visually cluttered before it is finalized.

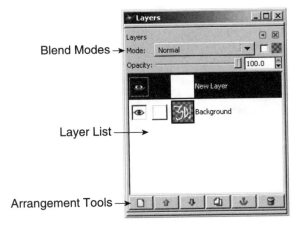

Blend Modes →

Layer List →

Arrangement Tools →

Figure 8.32
The Layers dialog box.

Creating Layers

To create a new layer, from the image window choose Layer, New Layer. You will see that creating a layer is very much like creating a new image. You can set the layer's image size as well as choose what the layer fill type will be. Usually I use the Transparency fill type, because I will be viewing several layers at once, and they normally will be merged together (the image is "flattened") later. Layers that aren't the background layer don't normally have a...um...background of their own. Typically, we are interested in only a relatively small image on a portion of a nonbackground layer.

The Layers Dialog Box

To manage your layers, you can use the arrangement tools in the Layers dialog box to move the layers up or down in the layer list. The layer that is on the top of the list is the topmost layer and will obscure any layers lower down in the list (except for where the layer is transparent, of course).

In addition to transparent areas on a layer with transparency set to the fill type (such as you would get if you erased part of the layer with the Eraser tool), you can also set the overall transparency of the layer using the Opacity slider in the Layers dialog box, as long as you have the appropriate layer selected.

You can adjust the way any selected layer interacts with other layers by opening the Mode combo box and selecting one of the many blend options listed there. See Table 8.2 for more details on the layer modes.

Table 8.2 Layer Modes

Mode	Description
Normal	The layer is viewed normally (default).
Dissolve	Dissolves the current layer into the layer below it using pixel dispersion. This means that a given pixel on the current layer is transferred to the layer below but is moved to an offset location near its original location.
Multiply	The pixel values of the current layer are arithmetically multiplied by the values of the pixels beneath it, and we see the result—the product.
Divide	Same as Multiply except using the arithmetic division operation and resulting in the quotient.
Screen	Used to enhance the brightness of an image. The values of the image pixels in the current layer and the one beneath are inverted, the values are arithmetically multiplied with each other, and then the product is inverted.
Overlay	Using this mode, a screen blend is performed and then a multiply blend is performed, after which the results of both operations are combined and displayed.
Dodge	This is very similar to Screen, except that after the first inversion, the current layer pixel values are divided by those of the layer beneath, and the second inversion operates on the quotient. A brightening effect is seen on the upper (current) layer, but there is less contrast preservation than with Screen.
Burn	This is the opposite of Dodge. The pixel values of the layers are inverted and then multiplied together, after which the product values are inverted. A darkening effect is seen on the current layer.
Hard Light	Screen and Multiplication modes combined. Color saturation is reduced as a side effect.
Soft Light	Screen and Overlay modes combined to yield a softening effect on the sharper edges of the image. Also lightens the colors as a side effect.
Grain Extract	Used to extract the grain from a scanned photograph that exhibits film grain. The grain is deposited in a new layer.
Grain Merge	Use this to merge a grain layer such as one created from a scanned photograph using the Grain Extract mode. Leaves a grainy version of the original layer.
Difference	Calculates the difference between the layers by subtracting the lower pixel values from the higher pixel values for corresponding pixels in each layer, irrespective of which layer is above or below the other.
Addition	Adds the pixel values for each pixel in both layers.
Subtract	Subtracts the pixel values of the lower layer from those of the upper layer.
Darken Only	Selects the darker pixel of the corresponding pixels in each layer, and deposits the darker value in the current layer.
Lighten Only	Selects the lighter pixel of the corresponding pixels in each layer, and deposits the lighter value in the current layer.
Hue	Averages the Hue values of the current and lower layers.
Saturation	Averages the Saturation values of the current and lower layers.
Color	Averages the Color values of the current and lower layer.
Value	Displays the current layer's brightness value only—has the effect of creating a grayscale image.

Saving Layers

If you want to retain your layers, you need to save your image document in a file in XCF format. If you need to save only one layer and the transparency information in the alpha channel (which will be a separate layer), then you can save your image in a file in PNG format. You will need to merge your layers using Image, Merge Visible Layers so that you have only one layer left *and* the alpha channel (transparency) data is preserved. Just make sure that all the layers you want to be merged are actually visible; it's a good idea to open the Layers dialog box and check to ensure that all the layers you are merging have the eye icon to the left of their entry in the list.

You could also choose Image, Flatten Image to do the same thing, except that the alpha channel is not preserved. Instead, the current background color as indicated in the Toolbox Color Area will be used to fill in the background of any unpainted areas.

The Toolbox

The Gimp has quite a selection of image processing tools. Not all of them are actually shown in the Toolbox in the main window. If you have an image document open (create a new blank one if you like), you can choose Dialogs, Tools and get the Tools dialog box. You can use this dialog box to make tools available in the Toolbox by clicking to the left of each tool to make the visibility icon appear (a little eye). Click on the eye to make it go away, which removes the tool from the Toolbox.

Figure 8.33 shows the most useful tools to keep available in the Toolbox, matching the icons to their functionality. After you develop some expertise, your selections might be different.

Brush-like Tools

The Brush-like tools (see Figure 8.33) are a gaggle of tools that operate much like their real-life analogs, and all have similar options. All the Brush tools operate by pressing and dragging the left mouse button. Note that the right mouse button will bring up a context-sensitive menu.

The Pencil tool and the Paintbrush tool are almost identical, except that the Paintbrush tool gives a soft-edge mark, while the Pencil tool lays down a sharp, hard edge with the line it creates.

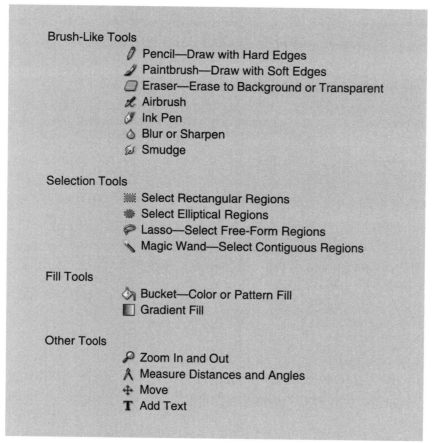

Figure 8.33
Tool icons and their functions.

The Ink Pen tool, while it might seem to be very similar to the Pencil tool, operates completely differently. The difference is very obvious when you examine the options. Essentially, the Ink Pen has variable nib shapes like a nib-pen would have. You can vary the pressure, ink flow, application angle, and so on.

The Air Brush tool simulates an airbrush, allowing you to adjust the pressure and paint flow rate, yielding a soft, blended edge. Just like the real thing. But unlike the real thing, you can use a fill gradient on the paint.

The Eraser tool obviously removes the paint from an image. You can adjust the pressure and the size and twiddle with a few other variables, like setting a hard edge to the Eraser.

The Blur or Sharpen (sometimes called Convolve) tool is used to adjust the clearness of various portions of an image. It can be used to enhance lines in a muddy image or to blend sharp edges together. When blurring, it functions very much like a drop of water on a water-based ink would work.

The Smudge tool is another way to blend or blur an image, except that it operates the same way a thumb or finger would do, as it is pushed across a page of ink, pencil, or paint.

Selection Tools

In general, the Selection tools are used to specify which pixels in an image are to be used for a given operation—deletion, movement (translation), cutting to the Clipboard, or what have you. In most cases you can add to a selection collection by holding down the Shift key and selecting more pixels, and you can remove from a selection by holding down the Control key and selecting the pixels you want to remove from an existing selection collection.

To use the Magic Wand, you just select that tool, and then click in the area of interest. All adjoining pixels that match the original pixel (within tolerance) will then be selected.

Fill Tools

The Fill tools operate by starting at a point in an image and spreading out from there. You indicate where the fill start point is by clicking once in the image at the spot you desire. From the Options pane you can select a pattern or a solid color for use with the standard Bucket Fill tool (the bucket o' paint tool) or select a gradient for use with the Blend tool.

In a slight departure from the Bucket Fill tool, the Blend tool requires you to click and drag the mouse in order to indicate the direction of the gradient as well as the size of the area over which the gradient will be created.

Other Tools

The other tools in Figure 8.33 have a variety of operation modes.

The Zoom tool zooms you in closer to the image with each click of the mouse button. To zoom out (farther away), you merely hold down the Control key while clicking the mouse button.

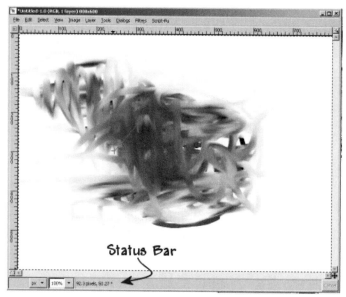

Figure 8.34
The status bar.

The Angle and Measurement tool is really quite a handy tool. If you click the tool down at the vertex of an angle to be measured, you can drag the cursor around in an arc and see the angle displayed in the status bar (see Figure 8.34). You can also draw a line between two points and see the measurement in the status bar as well.

The Move tool gives you the ability to "grab" a layer, path, or selection and drag it around the image to reposition it.

Add Text lets you add text to an image. You can edit the text up until the text is committed to the image, after which the text cannot be edited as text—you will have to move the pixels around instead or redo the text.

Tool Options

Every drawing tool has different adjustable settings that can be accessed via the main window's Tool Options pane. The contents of this palette change according to which tool is being used.

Check back to Figure 8.31 to see the location of the Tool Options in the main window. Figure 8.35 shows the Paintbrush Options, with the Brush Selection dialog box open. Unseen in the figure is the fact that the Paintbrush tool has been selected in the Toolbox, so the Paintbrush Options are being shown.

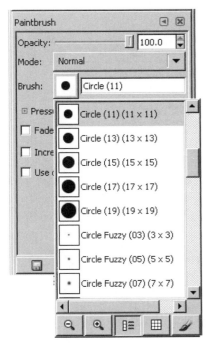

Figure 8.35
The Tool Options palette for the Paintbrush tool.

Brush-like Tools

The Tool Options palette for the various Brush-like tools will appear in the lower panes when you select one of the Brush-like tools. Some of the options are the same between all the tools; indeed, the Pencil tool and the Paintbrush tool have exactly the same options. Other Brush-like tools have their own specific options.

Table 8.3 shows the most commonly used options.

Selection Tool

The principal options available for selection tools are Antialiasing, Feather Edges, and Mode. Antialiasing applies anti-aliasing techniques to the edges of the selection where they form corners. Certain corner pixels will be selected in a semitransparent fashion so that the selection does not have "jaggie" edges. This leads to a smoother-appearing selection.

Feather Edges is similar to Antialiasing, except that the smoothing is accomplished with a border that is added around the entire selection where the pixels are selected in a semitransparent fashion.

Table 8.3 Brush-like Tool Options

Option	Description
Opacity	Opacity controls how completely the color covers the image surface. Lowering the opacity is like diluting paint. At 100 percent opacity, the color covers everything; at 1 percent, the color is almost transparent.
Mode	Sets the blend mode of the tool's colors. See Table 8.2 for more details.
Brush	Controls the size and shape of the brush. The square button contains a representation of the size and shape of the tool. Clicking the button invokes a pop-up dialog box of selectable sizes. At the bottom of the pop-up dialog box is a collection of buttons that are used to adjust the pop-up dialog box's visual settings, like zooming in or out and viewing as a list or a grid. The button at the far right (the one that looks like a paintbrush) is used to call up another dialog box, in which you can select a brush shape.
Pressure Sensitivity	Sets the relationship to a drawing palette's pressure values.
Fadeout	This check box controls whether a brush's ink fades away as the tool is used. Enabled when checked.
Incremental	When checked, each pass of a brush over other brush pixels will add to the image, up to a maximum of the opacity setting.
Use Color from Gradient	Uses color as calculated in the currently selected color gradient.

Table 8.4 Selection Modes

Option	Description
Replace	New selection replaces current selection (default).
Add	Adds each new selection to the selection collection.
Subtract	Removes the selection from a selection collection.
Intersection	The intersection of the new selection with the current selection becomes the current selection.

There are four selection modes, as shown in Table 8.4. Setting a mode in the options creates a default selection mode that can be overridden by using the Control or Shift keys.

Tip

To confine the brush painting to a specific area, use the Selection tool or the Freehand Selection tool to make a selection before painting. Then the brushwork will only be applied within the selected area. This is a handy technique to avoid "overspray" with the Air Brush.

Fill Tools

The Fill tools are used to create large area fill effects, using solid patterns, gradients, or patterns.

Both the Bucket Fill tool and the Blend tool have the ubiquitous Opacity option, which works with them the way it works with all the other tools. They also share the Mode option (refer back to Table 8.2 for more detail).

Bucket Fill Tool

The Bucket Fill tool has the following custom options: *Fill Type*, *Affected Area*, and *Finding Similar Colors*.

Fill Type   There are three Fill Types: *FG* (foreground) color fill, *BG* (background) color fill, and *Pattern* fill. The effects of FG and BG color fill are pretty obvious. Pattern fill requires you to select a pattern that will be painted into the fill area. There are a number of prepackaged patterns, and you can also create your own patterns.

Tip

> To create a custom pattern, make your pattern and save it in one of the image file formats that the Gimp supports. You need to save the pattern file somewhere inside the Gimp's pattern search path. To find the pattern search path, choose File, Preferences, Folders, Patterns. You need to ensure that your pattern is *tileable* so that as the pattern repeats, there will not be any seams between each repetition. A later chapter covers how to make tileable textures (basically the same as patterns).

Affected Area   There are two options for Affected Area: *Fill similar colors* and *Fill whole selection.*

Fill similar colors will apply the fill pattern to adjacent, contiguous (connected to the original) pixels that are sufficiently similar to the original pixel where the tool was clicked.

Fill whole selection fills the entire selected area with the fill color or pattern.

Finding Similar Colors   The options *Fill transparent areas, Sample merged,* and *Threshold* are only available when the Fill similar colors option is used.

Fill transparent areas allows the fill operation to continue into transparent pixels.

Sample merged allows layers other than the upper layers to be included in the fill merge.

The Threshold setting is how the Gimp determines the degree of similarity that will be considered when considering similar colors.

Blend Tool

The Blend tool has a different set of options, in addition to the standard mode and opacity settings: *Gradient*, *Offset*, and *Shape*.

Gradient The Gradient option provides a dialog box that allows you to specify how a color gradient works. Basically, you indicate a starting color and ending color, with possible in-between color values, As the gradient filling happens, the color being applied gradually changes from one color to another according to the specification. There are a large number of prepackaged gradients that you can choose from, or you can create your own. A check box called *Reverse* is available to cause the gradient to work in the opposite direction.

Offset Offset indicates the steepness of the gradient or how quickly the change in color takes place.

Shape Shape indicates the overall topology that the gradient filling will follow: Linear, Sawtooth Wave, and Triangular Wave. Figure 8.36 shows the relationship between a few sample shapes and their resulting gradients.

Other Tools

The **Magnify** tool has a few interesting options.

- **Auto-resize window.** If you select the Auto-resize window option, then the window will grow to accommodate a zoomed-in view as long as the window can fit on the screen.

- **Tool Toggle.** By default, clicking the Magnify tool in an image window will zoom in (the default), and holding down the Control key while clicking will zoom out. The Tool Toggle option allows you to change this behavior around, so that the default behavior is to zoom out, and holding down the Control key will zoom in.

- **Threshold.** You can also click and drag the Magnify tool so that you create a zoom rectangle; the zoom function then zooms the image to fill that window. By setting the Threshold option to a high value, you must create a fairly large zoom window before the zoom function kicks in. If you use a threshold that is too small for the current state of zoom, you will zoom in by one zoom level.

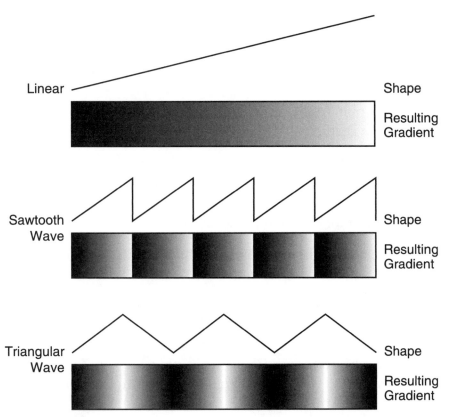

Linear   Shape

Resulting
Gradient

Sawtooth
Wave   Shape

Resulting
Gradient

Triangular
Wave   Shape

Resulting
Gradient

Figure 8.36
The Gradient Shapes.

Measure has only one option:

- **Use info window.** This handy option puts the measurement information in an external window as well as in the status bar.

The **Move** tool has two option sets:

- **Affect.** The first option set, Affect, lets you specify which of the movable entities you want to be able to transform or move. These are *layers, selections,* and *paths.*

- **Tool Toggle.** The other option set, Tool Toggle, indicates how the Move tool decides what to move. *Pick a path* allows that clicking the tool on the screen in the image document will select a layer or a guide. *Move the current path* will not attempt any layer or guide selection but will simply start moving the current layer.

The **Text** tool lets you type in text to be added to an image. There are several options:

- **Font.** The Font option lets you select a font from the pop-up list. You use the *Size* option to set the font's size, in one of several selectable metrics: *px* (pixel), *in* (inches), *mm* (millimeters), *pt* (points), or *pc* (picas). There are more size metrics available as well, via the size list's *More* option.

- **Hinting.** Hinting tells the program to use the adjustment settings to fiddle with the fonts in order to make them clearer with really small font sizes. *Force auto-hinter*, when chosen, tells the program to always try to calculate the settings needed to make suitable characters.

- **Antialiasing.** When enabled, Antialiasing will help to create smoother edges for characters, giving a more readable result.

- **Color.** You can use the Color option to set the color of the characters the next time text is committed to the image.

There are a few formatting options available, like *Justify*, which has four settings: *Left*, *Right*, *Centered*, and *Filled* (the same as Full, as it is known by many people). *Indent* allows you to set indentation values. *Line spacing* allows you to set the distance between lines of text.

Create path from text lets you create a selection path using the selected text.

Moving Right Along

In this chapter we had our first peek at the world of textures. As the book unfolds, we will examine the uses for textures in more detail.

Then we took a look at a powerful imaging tool, the Gimp, which we can use to create and edit textures. As you have seen, the Gimp has a very complete feature set.

In the next chapter we will expand our understanding of using textures in game development by learning how to skin objects, such as player models and vehicles.

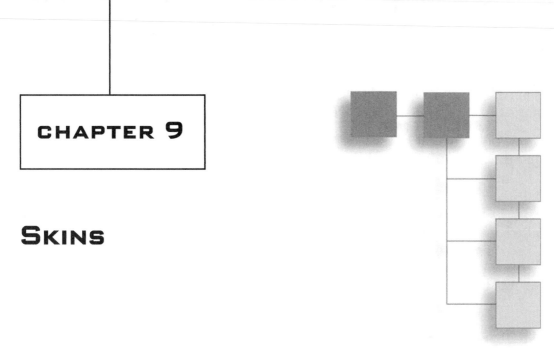

CHAPTER 9

SKINS

Skins are special textures used in games. The quality that separates skins from regular textures is that they typically wrap around the shape of a 3D model. It is fairly obvious that 3D monsters and player-characters would have texture skins, but the term can also apply to automobiles, wheelbarrows, mailboxes, rowboats, weapons, and other objects that appear in a 3D game.

Typically, skins are created after a model has been unwrapped, so that the skin artist knows how to lay the skins out in the UV template. We're going to do the process a bit backward, simply because we should stay on topic with the Gimp and textures until we've covered the topic sufficiently.

In our case here, it isn't a big issue anyway, because I'm providing you with UV templates from previously UV unwrapped models to work with.

UV Unwrapping

UV unwrapping is a necessary function to be performed prior to skinning a model. Consider it part of the *modeling* process in the context of this book. However, in this chapter we'll deal with the *texture* processing part of skinning a model and use models I've provided on the CD. Later you'll create and skin your own models and do the unwrapping and other things. We'll cover how the unwrapping works in more detail then.

When we want to apply textures to 3D objects, we need a system that specifies where each part of a texture will appear on which parts of a model. The system is called *U-V Coordinate Mapping*. The U-coordinate and the V-coordinate are analogous to the X- and Y-coordinates of a 2D coordinate system, though they're obviously not exactly the same.

Imagine (or you can actually try this at home yourself) taking a closed cardboard box and slicing it open along the edges. Then lay the whole thing out flat on the kitchen table, with no overlapping parts. There, you've unwrapped your box. Now get out your crayons and draw some nifty pictures on it. Then glue it all back together again to make a box. I think you get the idea.

With UV unwrapping we apply the technique to some complex and irregular shapes, like monsters and ice cream cones.

The Skin Creation Process

When we begin the skinning process, we will have a bare, unadorned 3D model of some kind. For this little demonstration, we'll use a simple soup can (see Figure 9.1). It's a 12-sided cylinder with a closed top and bottom (end caps). Each side face is made up of two triangles, and the end caps are made of 12 triangles each, for a total of 48 triangles. Nothing too special here.

Using the UV Unwrapping tool, we have to basically spread all our faces out over a nominally flat surface (see Figure 9.2).

We save the image of the UV template, plus we save the original model file, because the UV Unwrapping tool will have modified the UV coordinates for the

Figure 9.1
The victim—a simple can of soup.

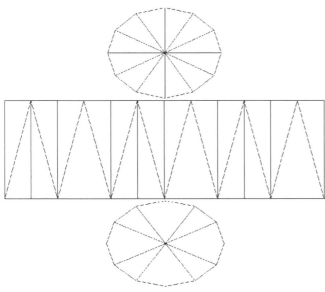

Figure 9.2
Laying it all out—the unwrapped can.

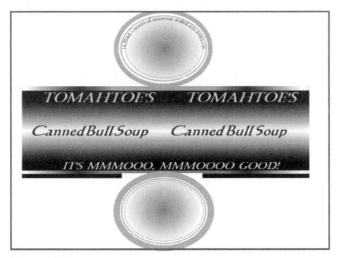

Figure 9.3
After applying textures.

objects in the model, and we can save those changes to the file so that the modeling tool can read them back in again.

Then we import the unwrapped image with the lines indicating the face edges into an image processing tool like the Gimp and apply whatever textures, colors, or symbols we need, such as shown in Figure 9.3.

Figure 9.4
Aha! Not such a simple can anymore. Nutritious, too!

Notice that for textures I simply created markings and re-created a simple label. For the top of the can I made some circular text, and for both end caps I made a circular pattern that represents the ridges you often find in those places on tin cans. The image file has now officially become a skin for the can!

The final step is to import the new skin into the modeling program (or the game) and view the results, as in Figure 9.4.

The part of the process we will focus on in this chapter is the activity shown in Figure 9.3, the actual creation of the textures on the UV template, so that it can be later used as a skin for models.

Making a Soup Can Skin

So let's dive right in and create a skin. We can use the bare model of the soup can I showed you in the last section. The procedure has quite a few steps—more than 30—so we'd better roll up our sleeves and get to it.

The Soup Can Skinning Procedure

This is how you skin a soup can:

1. Open \3D2E\RESOURCES\CH9\can.bmp in the Gimp. This file contains the UV mapping template.

Tip

Remember in the last chapter when I said that the only file types we would need to use are JPG and PNG? Well, that was sort of a lie, though not quite—you see, the only file types we will be using for *game resources* will be those two types. However, the UVMapper program outputs its UV mapping templates as one of two types: BMP (Windows bitmap) or TGA (Targa) format. So I've picked BMP to be our standard UV mapping template format. We won't be creating any game files in this format, however.

2. Choose Image, Mode, RGB. You need to do this to get access to the full range of colors.

3. Save the file as \3D2E\RESOURCES\CH9\mycan.xcf. This way you can reuse the layers over and over at later times if necessary. Make sure you save your work often as you follow the steps, in case you royally mess up, like I frequently do.

4. Choose Layer, New Layer, and you will get the New Layer dialog box (see Figure 9.5).

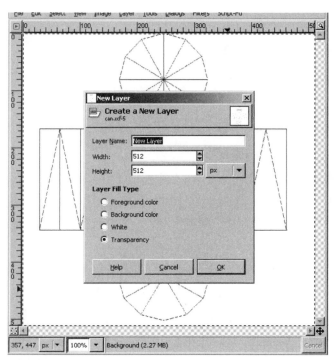

Figure 9.5
New Layer dialog box.

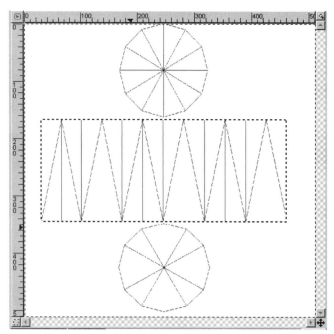

Figure 9.6
Rectangular selection.

5. Accept the default settings, and click OK.

6. Choose Dialogs, Layers, and then click the New Layer entry to highlight it and make that layer active.

7. With the Rect Select tool, make a box of crawling ants that matches the perimeter of the rectangle in the mycan image (see Figure 9.6).

8. Select the Bucket Fill tool, and then set its Affected Area option to be Fill whole selection. Ensure that the opacity setting is 100.0, the mode setting is Normal, and the fill type setting is FG color fill.

9. Change the foreground color in the color area to bright red (RGB=255,0,0), and then click in the rectangular selection. The rectangle should fill with the bright red color, obscuring the lines of the background image, as shown in Figure 9.7.

10. Next, using the same technique described in steps 7 to 9, make a long thin rectangle in the middle of the image, as shown in Figure 9.8. You might need to change either your foreground or background color to white. However, if you already have white as your background color, great! Then you can

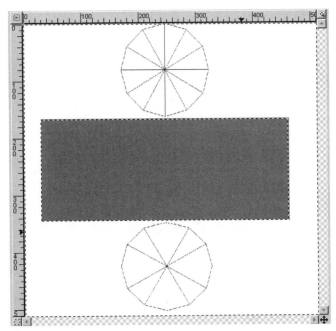

Figure 9.7
Filled rectangle.

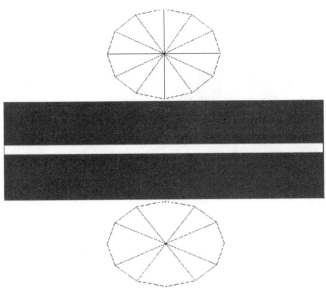

Figure 9.8
The white rectangle.

simply change the Fill Type for the Bucket Fill tool to BG color fill, and you're in business.

So now you have your basic red-and-white pattern on the sides of the can. If you look at Figure 9.1 again, you'll notice that the red area gradually blends into the white area. There are several ways to do this. For example, you could have used a gradient fill in the rectangles you created. But you're going to use another method, one that is more of a touch-up technique.

11. Use the Rect Select tool to make a selection that starts about halfway down the upper red rectangle, all the way over on the left side of the red area; then drag the selection tool down and to the right all the way to the right side and about halfway down the lower red area. You need to ensure that the left and right edges do *not* enclose the thin red line that you should have on both ends of the white bar. You may need to try this a couple of times until you get it right. Use Figure 9.9 as a guide.

12. Next, soften the transition between the red and the white. Choose Filters, Blur, Gaussian Blur. You will get the Gaussian Blur dialog box, as shown in Figure 9.10.

Figure 9.9
Selecting the mapped sides of the can.

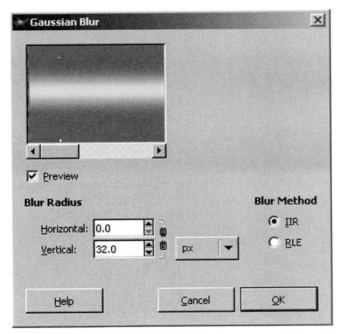

Figure 9.10
Gaussian Blur dialog box.

13. There are two Blur Radius options: Horizontal and Vertical. To the right of these options is a small icon of a chain. This links the two options together. Click the chain to break the link.

14. Next, set the Horizontal setting for Blur Radius to 0 and the Vertical setting to about 32.0. Fiddle with the values while watching the preview window until you get a satisfactorily fuzzy edge between the red and white areas. The exact amount will vary depending on the size of the white area and the relationship of the selection rectangle to the white bar. When you are happy, click OK to close the dialog box. You'll see the edges between the red and the white go blurry.

15. You'll want to add metal lips to the top and bottom of the can sides. Do this by creating a thin light gray rectangle all the way across the top and another at the bottom, as shown in Figure 9.11. The black arrows indicate the location of the lip line. Use the same technique you've learned for making the red and white rectangles.

16. Now you'll want to create the surface texture for the ends, or lids, of the can. This time, select the Ellipse Select tool.

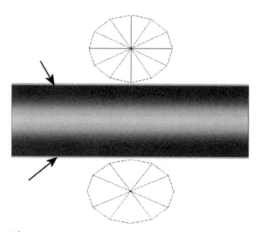

Figure 9.11
Adding the metal lips.

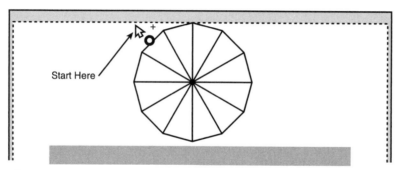

Figure 9.12
Placing the Ellipse Select tool.

17. Place the tool's cursor at the top left of the upper circle in the image, as shown in Figure 9.12.

18. Drag the tool down and to the right until the selection circle is at least as big as the circle that represents the top of the can. A smidgeon larger is okay, but try to keep it close. Don't worry about getting it exactly centered over the lid. We're going to fix that up in the next few steps.

19. Grab the Move tool from the Toolbox, and in its Affect setting in the options, choose the Transform selection.

20. In the image document, click and drag the selection circle until it's centered over the upper lid, as shown in Figure 9.13.

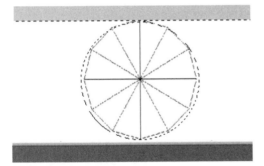

Figure 9.13
Properly positioned selection circle.

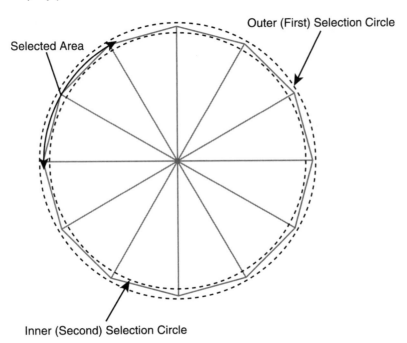

Figure 9.14
Concentric crawling ants.

Tip
_____

You can shrink or grow a selection that's already been made by choosing Select, Shrink or Select, Grow. In either case, you can set how many pixels more you want the selection to grow or shrink by.
_____

21. Next, place the Ellipse Select tool over the very center of the lid. Hold down the Control key, and drag down and to the right. You should see a circle "sprout" and grow out from the center. This is a subtraction selection. Grow this inner selection circle until it is about 90 percent of the diameter of the outer selection, as shown in Figure 9.14.

Tip

You see, the idea here is that first we select an elliptical area that's pretty much a circle that encompasses the lid, so everything inside the selection outline, is, well, selected. Next, we deselect an area inside that, so we are left with what amounts to a skinny doughnut of selected area.

22. If you haven't done it recently, save your work as mycan.xcf at this time. The selection circles will be saved along with layer data and everything else.

23. Okay, now we're going to do another gradient fill, but a slightly different one than before. First, go to the color area and set the foreground color to be a dark gray with RGB=73,73,73.

24. Next, choose the Blend tool, and make sure the Gradient is set to FG to BG in the tool options. Set the Shape to be Conical(sym).

25. Click the Blend tool down at the center of the rim, and drag it down and to the right until you get to the outer selection circle. Then release the mouse button. You should end up with a gradient-filled ring like that shown in Figure 9.15.

26. Next, choose Select, None from the image document window to discard the old selection circles so you can make a new one.

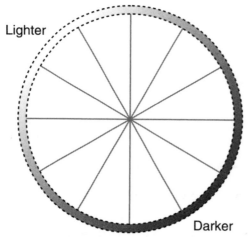

Figure 9.15
Gradient-filled ring.

27. Choose the Ellipse Select tool, and create a selection circle that goes all the way around the inner edge of the rim you just made. It's okay if the selection is just a wee bit on the large side. Remember that you can move the selection circle using the Move tool, if the circle ends up offset from center—see steps 19 and 20 if you need a refresher.

28. Grab the Blend tool again. In its Tool Options, change the Shape setting to Radial, and change the Repeat setting to Triangular wave.

29. Set the background color to a medium-light gray. Try with RGB = (150,150,150).

30. Start at the center of the lid, and drag out to the edge with the Blend tool. Figure 9.16 shows the sort of result you should see.

31. Now to make yet another selection circle. Choose the Ellipse Select tool, and make another concentric selection circle about 80 percent out from the center of the lid, as shown in Figure 9.17.

32. Set the foreground color to a medium-dark gray, somewhere around RGB=100,100,100.

33. Next, choose Dialogs, Selection Editor. The Selection Editor dialog box will appear. At the lower-right corner is a button called Stroke selection. Click this button.

Figure 9.16
Radial gradient.

Figure 9.17
80 percent selection circle.

Figure 9.18
The lid after the last concentric ring.

34. When the Stroke Selection dialog box appears, click Stroke line to choose it. Set the line width to 3.0. Make sure that Line style is set to Solid. Click the Stroke button to commit the change.

35. Choose Select, Shrink. Set the shrink value to 8 pixels. Click OK.

36. Stroke this selection circle just like you did the last one in steps 33 and 34, except this time set the line width to 1.0. Figure 9.18 shows what you should now have for your lid. This is the last of the concentric rings.

37. Choose Select, None to get rid of the crawling ants, and then choose Image, Flatten Image to squish all the layers into one layer.

38. Use your newly hard-earned selection skills to select the textured lid, and make a copy that you then paste over the bottom lid.

39. Save your work, but leave the document open.

Adding Text

And now, for our final performance, we will add some text to the lid. The text will curve to conform to the circular lid.

1. Choose the Text tool, and set the size setting in options to 10. Turn on Anti-aliasing.

2. Click in your image document somewhere near the center of the top lid. Type in some text, something like **16 fluid ounces**.

3. Choose Filters, Distorts, Curve Bend. Click the Open button.

4. In the open dialog box, browse your way to \3D2E\RESOURCES\CH9, and select the file curve_bend.points. Click Open. This is a bend file I made for use with this exercise.

5. Make sure that Smoothing, Antialiasing, and Work on copy are all enabled (checked).

6. Click OK.

7. Choose Dialogs, Layers.

8. Click the eye to the left of the 16 Fluid Ounces text layer, to hide this layer.

9. Click the empty location to the far left of the entry called curve_bend_dummylayer_b. This layer will now be visible. Use the Move tool to adjust the position of the text if needed. Figure 9.19 shows what you should have, or something like it.

10. Voilà! You will have text that follows the curve of the ellipse around in an arc.

11. Now add your main label text using the Text tool. You can type whatever you want and position it wherever you want.

Figure 9.19
The lid with curved text.

12. When you are finished, save your file one final time as \3D2E\
    RESOURCES\CH9\mycan.xcf. This is your source file.

13. Now choose Image, Flatten Image.

14. Next, save your work as \3D2E\RESOURCES\CH9\mycan.jpg. Make
    sure you've selected the JPEG type in the Save As dialog box when you
    do this.

15. If the file already exists, go ahead and overwrite it.

Testing the Soup Can Skin

Congratulations! You've made your first skin! I suppose now you want to
see what it looks like all wrapped around a tin can and everything. Okay, so
do this:

1. Read the sidebar called "Torque Show Tool Pro (TSTP) Quick Start".
   Run TSTP and create a Project Directory in TSTP that points to
   \3D2E\RESOURCES.

2. Click on the Load DTS button at upper-left in the TSTP window, and then
   locate mycan.dts in the CH9 folder.

Table 9.1 Torque Show Tool Pro Mouse Actions

Action	Description
Left-click-drag mouse	Make camera orbit object horizontally and vertically.
Right-click-drag mouse	Make camera slide horizontally and vertically.
Mouse Wheel	Zoom in and out.
Ctrl + Left-click-drag mouse	Make camera orbit object horizontally and vertically (for one button mice).
Alt + Left-click-drag mouse	Zoom in and out (for one button mice).

3. Presto! That's your skin on that there soup can. Good job!

4. You can admire your creation in all its splendor by using the mouse to move the can back and forth and rotate it about the various axes. See Table 9.1 for the Show Tool mouse actions.

5. You can view my original soup can skin by loading the soupcan.dts model.

Torque Show Tool Pro (TSTP) Quick Start

Torque Show Tool Pro (TSTP) is an advanced version of the Show Tool that comes with the Torque Demo. Dave Wyand, the gnome from Ajax, created TSTP in order to provide artists a more detailed look at their models without the need to actually run their games (which can be a cumbersome process at times). TSTP was created entirely using small engine changes and plenty of TorqueScript code. TSTP is available for Windows and OSX, but only the Windows version will be discussed here.

Installation

To install TSTP, browse your way to \3D2E\TOOLS\SHOWTOOLPRO and run the installer located there, TorqueShowToolPro.exe. Once installed, you will have a 30-day fully functional trial license. If you want to buy TSTP (and you should), you can find it on the GarageGames Web site in the products area at http://www.garagegames.com/products/browse/development/.

Setup

TSTP allows you to set up multiple project directories and switch between them at any time. This allows you to load in shapes from different games or to organize your shapes within the same game in a logical manner.

For example, the standard Torque demo as used in this book has a file pathway of \3D2E\demo. Using this for your project directory would provide access to all shapes for the demo game directory and all of its sub-directories.

When TSTP is started for the first time, no project directories are defined. Before you can load any files, you'll need to create at least one project directory. To do this, click on the Project Directory menu at the top left of the main window, and then click on [modify].

Choosing the [modify] option will open the MODIFY PROJECT DIRECTORIES window.

Click on the Add Directory button and a new project directory will be created. You can then either type a directory path into the Path to Project Directory text box or you can click on the big black arrow button. The arrow button will open a directory selection dialog from which you can select the directory you want to use for your project.

You can type a name in the Name (Optional) text box that will be used in the Project Directory pop-up menu instead of the file path.

Click on OK when you are done. The entry you just created will now appear in the Project Directory menu, and all of the settings will be saved when you exit TSTP.

Loading a Model

Ensure that you have chosen a model using the Project Directory menu. Then click on the Load DTS button. You will see a Load File window open up that lists all of the DTS models contained in your project directory and its subdirectories. Double-click on a model entry to load that model.

To load animation sequences, you first need to have a model loaded. Then you can click on the Load DSQ button to locate an appropriate sequence file to load. Once a sequence has been loaded, you need to select it from the Sequences pop-up located near the bottom of the window, to the left of the animation timeline.

To make a sequence animate, click on the Play button (the right-pointing arrow) in the animation control area to the bottom right of the window.

If you have predefined animation sequences linked to your model via a sequence linking file (located in the same folder as your DTS model, and normally called player.cs, if your model is player.dts, or bozo.cs if your model is called bozo.dts), then you can load both the model and its sequence mapping file at the same time by clicking on Load DTS & CS. In this case, providing everything went well, you should have all of the linked sequences listed in the Sequences menu.

You can have multiple models (also known as shapes) loaded. The Currently Loaded Shape pop-up in the upper-right corner lists all of the shapes you have loaded. You can choose which one you are looking at by selecting it from this pop-up.

There is a manual in a file called TorqueShowToolProManual.pdf that you can use to learn TSTP in greater detail.

In the \3D2E folder there are two shortcuts: Show Book Models and Show Demo Models. These are shortcuts that fire up the original Torque Show Tool, which has been vastly superseded in all ways and manners by Torque Show Tool Pro. You will never need to use them, but they are there, just in case. Table 9.2 shows the original Show Tool key commands if you ever need to use the Show Book Models or Show Demo Models shortcuts.

Table 9.2 Original Torque Show Tool Key Commands

Key	Description
A	rotate left
D	rotate right
W	bring closer
S	move farther away
C	rotate top backward
E	rotate top forward

Making a Vehicle Skin

Okay, soup cans are cool and soup hits the spot, too. But now that lunch break is over, let's move on to something a bit more serious. Many people are going to have vehicles in their games, and the Torque Engine does quite a nice job of supporting vehicles. We'll be making our own vehicles later, but because this chapter is all about creating skins, let's make a skin for some kind of vehicle.

For a bit of a tease, let's take a look at a vehicle that is already included in the Torque demo using Torque Show Tool Pro (TSTP).

1. Run TSTP and create a new Project Directory in TSTP that points to \3D2E\demo\data.

2. Click on the Load DTS button at upper-left in the TSTP window, and then locate buggy.dts in the demo\data\shapes\buggy folder.

3. Double-click on the buggy.dts entry.

4. Marvel at the sublime coolness of a dune buggy without wheels.

The Dune Buggy Diversion

Okay, okay. I knew you would want to do this, so I'll show you how to test-drive the dune buggy *in-game*, as long as you promise to come back here after you've tired out your driving fingers. People tend not to learn quite as well when they are pouting.

1. Browse to C:\3D2E, and click the tge.exe.

Table 9.3 Torque Racing Demo Controls

Key	Description
mouse	steer left or right
W	accelerate
S	brake
Tab	toggle from first- to third-person viewpoint
Escape	exit the game

2. When the main menu appears, click the Example: Multiplayer Racing button at the bottom of the menu screen.

3. In the Play Demo Game screen, make sure that the Create Server check box is checked.

4. Click the right arrow at the bottom to launch the demo.

5. After the game loads, you should switch to Chase view by pressing the Tab key—there's more to see. See Table 9.3 for the keyboard controls.

The Runabout Skinning Procedure

Okay, now that the old adrenaline is pumping, let's get back to making skins. We're going to create a skin for a less ambitious, but still pretty cool, vehicle—the runabout. It's a fictional creation of mine that's a convergence of memories of summers spent during childhood reading Doc Savage pulp stories and of a classic 1936 Auburn Boattail Speedster that I saw at a car show once as a teenager.

1. Open \3D2E\RESOURCES\CH9\runabout.bmp in the Gimp. This file contains the UV mapping template.
   This time I've unwrapped the object differently. If you recall, the soup can was completely unwrapped so that each individual face was lying flat. This time I unwrapped the runabout by showing only the separate objects (except the cab) from one particular view, the side or the top.
   By doing this, I can treat each of these objects as symmetrical, with the hidden side being simply a mirror image of the visible side. This is another valid technique, but it does have some pitfalls, which we will encounter. The advantage of using this approach is that it saves on image editing time, because only half of the objects' surfaces need to be given textures.

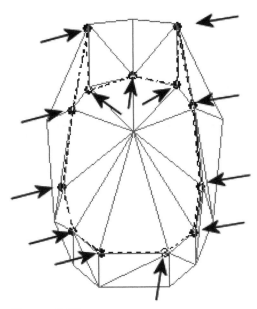

Figure 9.22
Arrows indicate the editable anchors.

you are given the finger, click the mouse, and the path will appear, with its anchors (see Figure 9.22).

11. Edit the path as you see fit by moving the anchors around. When you are again satisfied with your new path, click the Create selection from path button in the Paths tool options. The previous selection will be replaced by the new selection.

12. Once you've finished, set the foreground color to a color of your choice (bright blue would be nice), select the Bucket Fill tool, and make sure the Fill Type is set to FG Color fill.

13. Set the Fill Bucket option Affected Area to Fill whole selection, and then fill your boots . . . I mean, fill your selection!

14. After you've finished with the cabin roof, choose Select, None to deselect the area you just painted.

15. Create another new layer the same way you did in steps 3 and 4.

16. Next, choose the Path tool, and draw an outline around the entire cabin template, following the outside edges. This path will be drawn on the new layer. When you're finished, click the Create selection from path button in

the Paths tool options. Note: you'll need to restore your Edit Mode to Design, and check Polygonal, if it is still unchecked.

Tip

When you've finished using a path, you might want to make it invisible so that it won't clutter up the image. Just click the eye icon on the left side of the path's entry in the Paths dialog box.

17. Choose the Fill Bucket again, and set the foreground fill to a darker color than the one you chose for the cabin roof (dark green-gray would be helpful). The newly filled area should now obscure both the earlier roof area plus the rest of the cabin template. You can verify that you've drawn the path and selection on the proper layer by just making the top layer invisible temporarily (click its eye). The filled area should disappear, and the roof fill should appear. Click the top layer's eye to bring it back again.

18. Now we want to rearrange the layers. In the Layer dialog box, make sure the bottom layer is highlighted. Then locate the down-arrow button at the bottom of the dialog box, and click it. The layer will be pushed below the other layer. Now the roof is visible on top of the rest of the cabin (see Figure 9.23).

19. Alrighty then! Create another new layer.

20. Now choose the Paintbrush tool, making sure that the Use color from gradient Option setting is *not* checked.

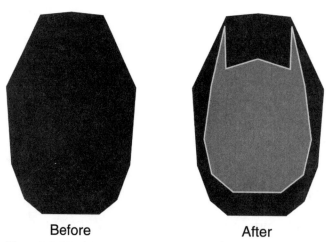

Before   After

Figure 9.23
Before using the down-arrow button and after using it.

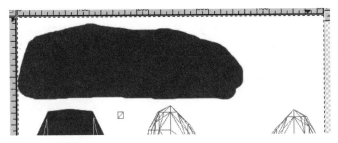

Figure 9.24
Spray-painting the body base color.

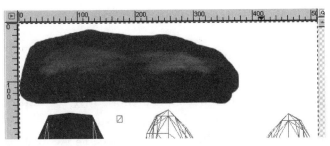

Figure 9.25
Spray-painting the accent color.

21. Set your foreground color to be the same blue (or whatever) color you used for the cabin roof.

22. Use the Paintbrush tool to cover over the outline of the car's body, as shown in Figure 9.24. You probably want a brush size of 19 or so. Remember to make sure that the new layer you created is selected in the Layers dialog box; otherwise, your painting will be applied to the wrong layer.

23. Next, select the Air Brush tool, setting the brush size to 11 and the opacity to 50 percent and checking the Fade-out check box.

24. Now change to a light blue foreground color.

25. Spray on the accent color, as shown in Figure 9.25. You can use the Smudge tool to smear the brushstrokes more and to generally touch up and tweak the accents.

26. Next, we'll apply a fancy racing stripe. First, select the Ink tool, set its size to 4.0, and select the diamond shape for the Type setting. We aren't going to draw with the pen directly, but we need it to be set correctly for a later step.

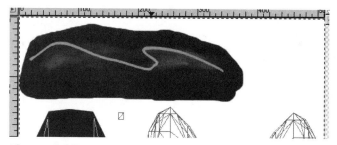

Figure 9.26
Adding the racing stripe.

27. Choose the Paths tool, and draw a path similar to the one I made in Figure 9.26.

    This can be a bit tricky. Instead of clicking each point of the line, click and *drag* at each point. When you drag the cursor after clicking, you will see a pair of handles sprout from the anchor where you clicked. These handles are used to adjust the curviness of the line. When you drag, try moving the cursor around the anchor, and notice how the line already has drawn changes. When you want to make a hard left turn at a spot, click and drag the cursor straight ahead from the anchor for just a bit, and then move the drag leftward into the direction you want the line to go. It takes a bit of practice to get the feel for this method, but it's quite intuitive once you get the hang of it. Note: if the Polygonal checkbox in the Edit Mode is checked, you won't be able to get the handles to appear, so make sure it is unchecked when you start grabbing at handles.

28. When you have your racing stripe drawn, click the Stroke path button in the Paths tool options. You will get the Stroke Path dialog box.

29. Click the Stroke with paint tool radio button.

30. Open the pop-up list by clicking the triangular button to the right of the Paint tool field. Scroll through the list until you find the Ink tool, and then select it.

31. Click the Stroke button. You will end up with a line drawn along your path, according to the Ink tool settings.

    So, there you have it—the car's body paint job is done. Notice that we used a different approach than when we did with the cab. It just goes to show that there's more than one way to skin a cat. . .er, *car*! I meant *car*! Honest.

Well, I guess it's time to get back to work. The last bits left are the four wheel-well, fender thingies. We'll do these in a fashion similar to the way we did the cab.

32. Create another new layer. Use this layer for all four fender thingies.

Tip

You might notice that after creating and stroking a path, you will have to click another tool to deselect the path. Otherwise, when you try creating a new path, the first point becomes connected to the last point of the previous path. You won't see this problem when you create a new path in a new layer. You may also choose to Select, None but you will notice that after stroking a path, Select, None is not available.

33. Using the Path tool (and Figure 9.27 as a reference), draw an outline of the upper part of the upper-left fender thingy, and fill it with the favorite color you've been using (or bright blue, nudge, nudge), employing the technique you used for the cabin in steps 5 to 14. Make a different path for the lower fender skirts, and paint them with the same color you used for the racing stripe. Again, look at Figure 9.27 to see where the fender skirts would be.

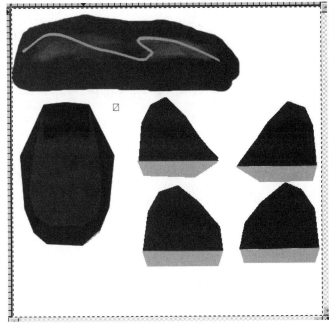

Figure 9.27
The fender thingies.

34. Repeat step 25 for the other three fender thingies.

35. When you are finished, save your file one final time as \3D2E\ RESOURCES\CH9\myauto.xcf. This is your source file.

36. Now flatten the image, and then save your skin as \3D2E\ RESOURCES\CH9\myauto.jpg.

    Once again, if you get an alert saying that the software will have to save the file as a merged image and asking if you want to continue, choose Yes.

Testing the Runabout Skin

Now it's time to take our little creation out for a spin around the block, so to speak. We'll use TSTP just like we did with the soup can.

1. Run TSTP and choose the Project Directory you created earlier in TSTP that points to \3D2E\RESOURCES.

2. Click on the Load DTS button at upper-left in the TSTP window, and then locate mycan.dts in the CH9 folder.

3. Use the mouse to move the car back and forth and to rotate it about the various axes. Refer back to Table 9.1 for the Show Tool mouse actions.

4. You can view my original runabout skin by loading the runabout.dts model.

Unfortunately, we'll have to wait until the later modeling chapters before we can take the runabout out for a real test drive. That's okay, though—we've got plenty to do in the meantime!

Making a Player Skin

Now for the Big One—the player skin, or more accurately, the *character* skin, because the following section could apply equally as well to computer-controlled characters sometimes called AI (*Artificial Intelligence*) players or NPCs (*Non-player Characters*).

The character we'll use as the basis for this section is one affectionately called the *Standard Male Character*. He was created to be the base model for derivatives to be used in the *Return to Tubettiworld (RTTW)* game that is currently in development at Tubetti Enterprises.

Figure 9.28
The *RTTW* Standard Male Character model rendered by the Torque Engine.

Figure 9.29
Concept artwork for the Standard Male Character.

Figure 9.28 shows an early prototype of the Standard Male Character striking a heroic pose in the wilderness, confronting his, um, well…some trial or tribulation, I guess. This character began life as a concept sketch I did while nestled in front of a roaring fire on vacation in the Laurentians. My wife told me what the character should look like, and I sketched him about a hundred times until she was happy with it (see Figure 9.29). My wife says he looks kinda like me, on a good day—bald spot, blond mustache, and all!

I sent the concept artwork to a talented young man who goes by the name Psionic (http://www.psionic3d.co.uk) on the Internet, and he created the original model prototypes for me. The model came out pretty well, but as I said, the character in Figure 9.28 was an early prototype. The main issue was the skin color—it was too pasty. But that was soon fixed. We have since used that model to generate variations in gender, build, ethnicity, and animation sets, mostly by modifying skins, but with some model changes as well—especially for the female versions.

The point here is that for all of your serious artwork, models, skins, and so on, it's a good idea to create concepts beforehand—on paper or digitally, it doesn't matter. This way you have a tool to communicate the idea that you have in your head. It may take weeks or months to get a model completed, and it can happen that you stray unacceptably far from your original concept. It's especially important to have concept artwork if you want to sell a game idea to build a team and recruit talent to help you. If they can go away with a few pictures in their minds of what your dream is, it will help you a great deal.

The Head and Neck

Now on with the show. Take a look at Figure 9.30. This is the unwrapped UV template for the Standard Male. I've labeled the various parts in the picture to help identify what goes where. The file \3D2E\RESOURCES\CH9\player.bmp has the proper template in it (though without the labels) for you to work with. Let's get started.

1. Open the template file (\3D2E\RESOURCES\CH9\player.bmp), save it somewhere as an XCF file with a different name, and work with that.

2. Create a new layer, and name it "Skin". You are going to create a lot of layers in this procedure—make sure you label each one as I indicate.

3. Using whichever technique you like best, cover the entire face and neck part of the template with a flesh color, as in Figure 9.31. (I use the RGB values shown in Table 9.4 for a basic flesh color. Of course, you are free to twiddle the numbers to get something you like.) Make sure you apply your color to the skin layer and *not* to the background layer that holds your template.

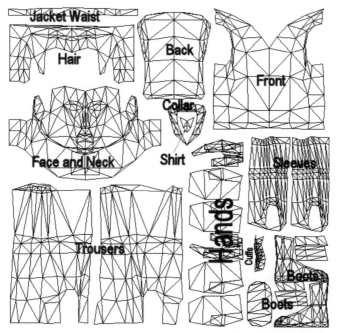

Figure 9.30
UV template for the Standard Male.

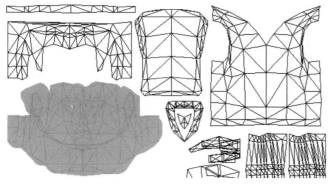

Figure 9.31
Basic flesh tone applied to the skin layer.

Tip

In Figure 9.31 you can see the lines of the UV template through the skin layer's flesh color. Do this by reducing the opacity of the skin layer to about 95 percent or so, just enough for the lines to barely show. In the Layers dialog box, slide the Opacity slider left until it gets to the value you want. The lower you set the opacity, the more you can see of the layer beneath it—however, the less your skin layer's colors will look like their actual settings.

Table 9.4 Flesh-Tone RGB Settings

	Color Component	Value
basic	red	251
	green	178
	blue	129
shadow	red	183
	green	133
	blue	83
highlight	red	247
	green	187
	blue	107

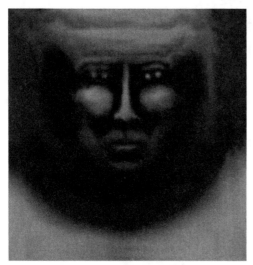

Figure 9.32
Hilite template.

4. Now comes a bit of magic. You need to get some basic skin shading done next. There is a highlight and shadow image template that I like to use to get the basic head shades in place. Figure 9.32 shows the template, and you have a copy of it (\3D2E\RESOURCES\CH9\hilite.png) that you can use for your own purposes. We're going to open it and add it as a layer to our image document in one swell foop. Choose File, Open as Layer. Browse your way to \3D2E\RESOURCES\CH9\hilite.png, and click the Open button.

5. Lower the opacity of the new layer to about 80 percent.

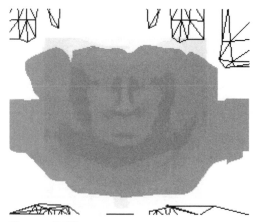

Figure 9.33
Hilite template applied over the head and neck UV template.

6. Make the skin layer invisible.

7. Drag the image around until you get the best fit over the UV template of the head and neck.
You should get an image that looks like Figure 9.33.

Being the astute observer that I know you are, you've no doubt noticed that although the hilite template fits fairly well, it's not exactly right. For one thing, the eyes are wrong—the hilite of the eye area needs to be slanted to match the contours of the UV triangles. We're going to fix that right now.

8. Make sure that the new layer with the hilites on it is active by making sure that its entry in the Layers dialog box is highlighted. Then choose the Lasso Selection tool.

9. You should probably zoom in on the area in question to 200 percent or better. Select an area around the right that encompasses the eye, the brow above, and a small amount of the upper cheek below, but no part of the bridge of the nose.

10. Choose Tools, Transform Tools, Rotate, and the Rotate dialog box will appear. Click the cursor in the selection area, and nudge it in the direction you want to rotate it to match the template.

Tip

The hilite.png template was created by taking several full-face photos and drawings and then stretching the contrast of each quite a bit in grayscale. The images were then all overlain and averaged to give a resulting template. That result was then tested in a few models and manually tweaked a few times. The originals were chosen to be all of roughly the same face shape and type. Different templates for different ethnicities and face shapes can be made this way.

11. Choose Select, None.

Tip

If you have trouble choosing Select, None because it doesn't appear in the menu, then try making sure that the Rotate dialog box is visible. Then try choosing Select, None again.

12. Repeat this process for the other eye.

13. Lower the opacity for the hilite layer to about 20 percent, and raise the opacity of the skin layer to 100 percent.

14. Save your document (just because).

Now you have something like Figure 9.34, with the rough shading and coloring of flesh tones showing the major features of the face. At this point it becomes a case of filling in the details. You can go ahead and do it however you like. Zoom in close, and use the Air Brush and Paintbrush tools. Add lip color, eyebrows, eye

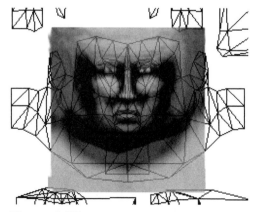

Figure 9.34
Hilite template applied over the skin layer.

details, and ears. You might find it hard to put actual iris eye color in, but give it a try.

You can add eye detail by creating ellipse selections on a scratch layer, sizing and rotating them correctly, and placing them over the eye areas. When you create eyes, remember that the colored area in the center, the combined pupil and iris regions, usually has a white or otherwise light spot offset a bit to one side and a bit above center, as shown in Figure 9.35.

Also remember that certain areas of the face are usually lighter in tone than others, like the upper part of the lower lip, the upper eyelid, the nostrils, and so on.

You can make a good five-day stubble by using the Paintbrush with the Brush setting at Galaxy (AP). You need to scroll pretty far down in the list of brushes to find it. Dab the brush in the areas where it is needed. Make a moustache by applying the stubble brush over and over to the upper lip. Encourage yourself to experiment!

Eventually you will end up with something like Figure 9.36.

Figure 9.35
An eye.

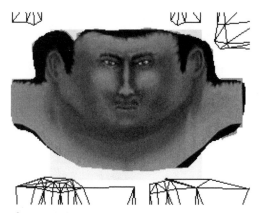

Figure 9.36
Finished face and neck.

Hair and Hands

Next we'll tackle the hair and hands of the Standard Male. We'll do these two together because they both use skin (flesh) tones (the guy is going to have a bald spot). Once these are done, we are finished with the skin part of the skin. Or something like that.

Both of the next subsections will be using the skin layer in addition to other layers.

Hair Textures

Hair has a pattern, though not a specific pattern. There is often quite a bit of randomness, but nonetheless there is a grain, if you will, like the grain in a wooden plank or the lay of a lawn. There's a clue there!

Try this:

1. Create a new layer, and call it Hair1.

2. Locate the hair portion of the UV template in your working file, player.xcf.

3. Draw a pathed selection that tightly encompasses the hair, and set the fill to match the color of the hair you used in the bits that show in the head area as in Figure 9.37. Use the hair RGB color values listed in Table 9.5.

4. Create another layer, and call it Hair2.

5. Select the path that you used on the Hair1 layer, use it now to create a new selection on the Hair2 layer, and then hide the Hair1 layer.

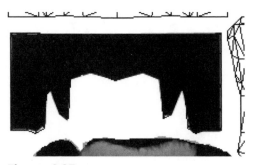

Figure 9.37
Filled hair template area.

Table 9.5 Hair Color RGB Settings

Color Component	Value
red	102
green	65
blue	13

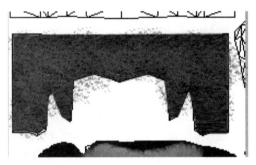

Figure 9.38
Textured hair.

6. Fill the new selection with a wood pattern (Wood#2 is good) using the Bucket Fill tool.

7. Set the Hair2 Opacity slider to about 30 percent.

8. Choose the Brush Tool, and use the Galaxy (AP) brush setting.

9. Apply the brush to the Hair2 layer until you get something that resembles Figure 9.38. You can also use the Smudge tool with the brush size set to 1 to enhance the strand-like nature of hair.

10. Make the Hair1 layer visible again.

11. Now for the bald spot. If you look at how the triangles in the UV template are arranged, you can see that the upper-left corner of the hair area and the upper-right corner of the hair area meet when they are wrapped back onto the model. The place where they meet is the crown of the head, which just so happens to be one of the two places where classic male pattern baldness begins!

    Choose the Air Brush tool, and set its size to about 19 and the foreground color to the highlight flesh tone found in Table 9.4.

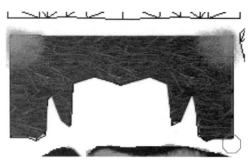

Figure 9.39
The font of wisdom under construction—the bald spot.

12. In each of the corners, spray on some bald skin, sparser toward the inner areas and denser as you move toward the corners, until you have a substantial patch of bare skin and a surrounding area of varying thinness (see Figure 9.39). Don't worry about overspraying the edges, those areas outside are not going to be rendered.

The Hands

The hands need to be skinned on three sides. You should use the basic flesh tone, with some shadow color for areas between the fingers.

1. Once again using the Paths tool draw a path that surrounds the area that constitutes the hand UV template (see Figure 9.40).

2. Set the fill color of the object you just made to the basic flesh tone.

3. Start a new layer.

4. Set the Ink tool to Adjustment Size setting of 2.0, and set the foreground color to black.

5. With the Paths tool draw the lines that separate the fingers. Use Figure 9.41 as a guide.

6. Using the Paintbrush tool, make a fingernail. Make sure the line color is black, and use a fairly bright pink for the actual nail color.

7. Place your lines and fingernails appropriately (as in Figure 9.41), and fiddle with the shapes until you are happy.

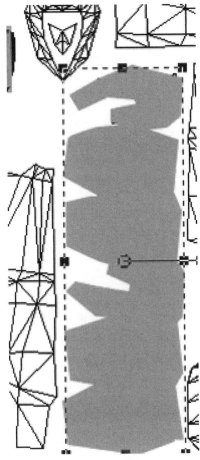

Figure 9.40
Hand area.

8. Set the opacity of the layer to about 10 percent or so. That bright pink fingernail color is not so bright anymore.

9. Merge the two layers you just created into the skin layer.

10. Using the Dodge/Burn tool, add shading and irregularity to the lines as in Figure 9.42. Make sure to use a really small brush setting, like 1 or 2.

11. Weaken some of the darker lines. Add lighter highlights around the main knuckles and darker wrinkles around the other knuckles.

12. Eventually you will arrive at something that works for you, similar to Figure 9.43.

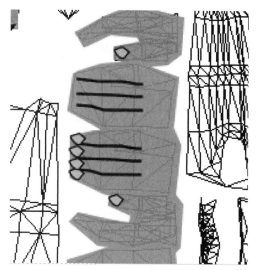

Figure 9.41
Finger lines and fingernails.

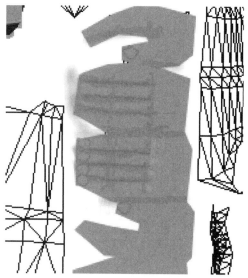

Figure 9.42
Adding hand details.

The Clothes

We'll spend most of our remaining time in this chapter working on the jacket. You've already learned and applied almost all the new skills required to do the clothing.

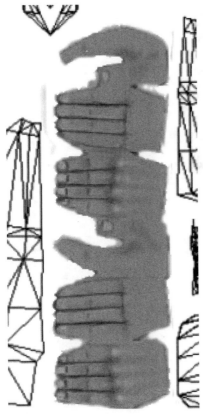

Figure 9.43
The finished hands.

The Jacket

It's a leather jacket. Quite a nice one, too. Wouldn't mind one like that myself!
The color is a basic brown, with the usual darker shadows and lighter highlights,
just like with the flesh tones. Things to note are that the jacket "blouses" at the
waist and at the cuffs. This is a wrinkling effect that occurs as the material is
gathered in for the seam work in those areas.

1. Start off by drawing pathed selections around the back, the front, the waist,
   the cuffs, the collar, and the sleeves in a fashion similar to what we've done
   in the past (see Figure 9.44). Make sure you do this on a new layer named
   "Jacket".

2. Set the fill color to the basic brown, using the values shown in Table 9.6.

3. Use the Bucket Fill tool to fill the selection with the basic brown.

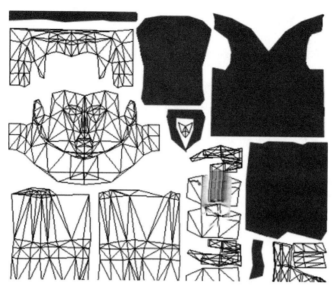

Figure 9.44
The jacket pieces.

Table 9.6 Jacket Color RGB Settings

Color Component	Value
red	140
green	68
blue	62

4. Choose the Paintbrush tool, and select animated Confetti for the Brush type.

5. Set a light brown color for the foreground.

6. Paint the leather areas of the jacket with short sharp strokes—just enough to get the stippled look to appear. Do this for all the leather areas: back, front, collar, and sleeves. Figure 9.45 gives an idea of what I've done: the back (on the left) has the stippled look, while the visible part of the front (on the right) does not.

7. Use the Dodge/Burn brush to highlight the contours of the gathers at the bottom of the front of the jacket.

8. Use the Smudge tool and the other touch-up brushes to tweak the contours to your liking (for example, as in Figure 9.46).

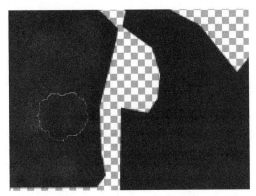

Figure 9.45
That leathery look.

Figure 9.46
Starting the gathers.

9. You can create the zipper and the zipper flap by using the Ink tool to draw a line from the neck to the bottom. Make one line with a width of about 1.0 and the rest at a size of 3.0.

10. Touch up the zipper area with stippling, and make other tweaks to get it to coordinate with the other areas of the jacket.

11. You can do all the other areas of the jacket in the same way as shown in steps 4 to 10.

The Trousers

The trousers can be done using exactly the same techniques as used for the jacket. You just need to use different colors and perhaps a different texture, airbrush density, or step value. By now, you should be pretty handy with the Toolbox in the Gimp, so I'll leave you to do the trousers on your own. Don't forget to make a belt—it goes at the bottom of the trouser area in the UV template.

The Boots

The final area where you'll want to apply texture is the boot area. Again, you've practiced all the techniques required to make the boots as well. There is one thing I want to show you, though, that will help, and that is the built-in textures in some of the tools.

Select the Bucket Fill, and then click the Pattern fill radio button. In the Pattern fill list there is a Leather pattern that would be suitable for the leather portions of a boot; there are many other textures that would be suitable for different parts of the boot.

When you have finished with the boots, make sure you save your work as player.xcf.

Then flatten your image and save another version as \3D2E\RESOURCES\CH9\ player.jpg.

Figure 9.47 shows the complete skin for the Standard Male.

Figure 9.47
Standard Male skin.

Trying It on for Size

As you learned earlier in the chapter, you can use the Torque Show Tool Pro program and load the player.dts model. You will be able to view the Standard Male Character with your new skin on it. You'll probably see areas that need fixing up, so go ahead and do just that.

Moving Right Along

In this chapter you learned how UV unwrapping relates to the texture files known as *skins*. And you learned how to apply that understanding to images for game objects ranging from the simple (a soup can) to the complex (a human character).

I hope you also take away from the chapter the idea that hand-drawn concept artwork is a useful tool. Draw everything in sketch form before you start working on your models. It's a great help.

Finally, you can see that a fully featured image processing tool like the Gimp has quite a few features to ease the effort of creating images for skins. We've only scratched the surface of what the program can do. Don't be shy about installing and using the Gimp's built-in Help utility; it's included in the TOOLS folder on your CD. It's well done and chockablock-full of information.

You also learned how to use Torque Show Tool Pro to load and examine your models without needing to run your game.

If you want to make great skins, you are going to need to practice, practice, and practice some more. Here are some of the many ways to do this:

- Create your own models and make the skins.

- Make skins for other people's models.

- Make skins for other people for popular games like *Half-Life* and *Tribes*.

- Make monster skins, policeman skins, airplane skins, and light pole skins.

- Make a set of stock skins.

- Make skin templates that you can use to make the skinning task easier.

- Make reusable, tileable patterns that you can install as custom patterns.

But most of all, get down and do it!

In the next chapter we will continue with the visual aspects of developing our game, but this time we will be looking at how to create GUI elements by using TorqueScript to insert images and controls.

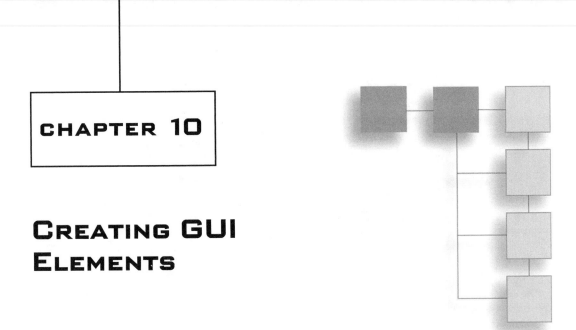

CHAPTER 10

CREATING GUI ELEMENTS

As you've seen by now, there is more to a 3D game than just the imaginary world into which the player plunks his avatar. There is the real need to provide the player with some method to make selections and otherwise control the game activities. Generally, we provide a *Graphical User Interface* (GUI) to the player to interact with the program. The menu we employed at the start-up of the program, where the player clicks buttons to launch the game, change the setup, or quit; the dialog box that shows the client's loading progress; the dialog box that asks if the player really wants to quit—these screens are all examples of GUIs.

If you take a look at Figure 10.1, you can see a sample of the variety of elements found within these interface screens. This example shows the various controls of the three tab panes of the Options dialog box in the Torque demo.

Some of the elements are things we can interact with:

- push buttons

- radio buttons

- edit boxes

- check boxes

- menus

- sliders

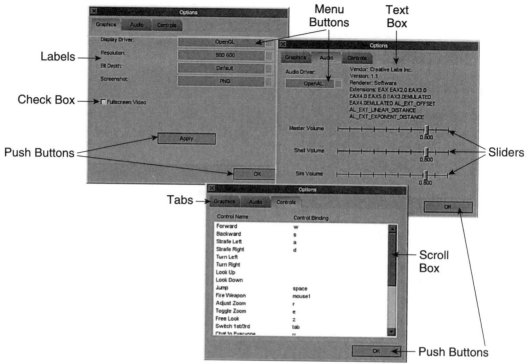

Figure 10.1
Common graphical user interface elements.

Some of the elements are things we can just look at:

■ frames

■ labels

■ backgrounds

■ text boxes

Also, during the course of discussions about graphical user interfaces, you may find the terms *GUI, window, interface,* and *screen* used interchangeably. I'll stick to the words *interface* and *screen* as much as possible, although contextually it might make more sense to use *GUI* or *window* from time to time. *GUI* is best used to describe the entire game interface with the player as a whole. *Window* is a term that most people tend to associate with the operating system of their computer.

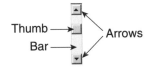

Figure 10.2
Scroll bar widgets.

The names of GUI items that are available by default with Torque don't differentiate between whether they are interactive or noninteractive GUI elements.

If you are familiar with X-Windows or Motif, you will probably have encountered the term *widgets*. If so, your definition of widgets may be a fair bit broader than the one I am about to use here. In our situation, widgets are simply visual portions of a displayed GUI control. They convey information or provide an aesthetic appearance and offer access to defined subcontrol elements.

For example, Figure 10.2 portrays a scroll bar. Within the scroll bar are the *thumb*, *arrow*, and *bar* widgets. These aren't controls in their own right but rather are necessary, specialized components of the control to which they belong.

It is possible for a control to use another control as a widget. In fact, every control in a screen can be considered a widget within the control that defines the screen. This will become clearer later on. I will only use the term *widget* to refer to a specialized component of a control that is not itself a control.

Worth noting is the fact that you can create your own GUI elements using TorqueScript if the ones that are available by default don't suit your needs.

Controls

The name says it all—*controls* are graphical items provided to the program user to control what the program will do. In Torque *interactive controls* are used by clicking them or click-dragging the mouse across them. Some controls, like edit boxes, also require you to type in some text from the keyboard. Some of the controls have built-in labels that identify their purpose, and some will require you to create an accompanying noninteractive control to provide a label. *Noninteractive controls*, as the name implies, are used only to display information and not to capture user input.

Torque provides a number of default controls right out of the box; the most commonly used ones are listed next. You will have encountered a few of these controls in earlier chapters, and we will discuss several more of them in this chapter. You can use them as is, you can modify them by adjusting the control's profile, or you can use them as the basis for defining new controls.

GuiArrayCtrl	GuiControl	GuiPlayerView
GuiAviBitmapCtrl	GuiControlListPopUp	GuiPopUpBackgroundCtrl
GuiBackgroundCtrl	GuiCrossHairHud	GuiPopUpMenuCtrl
GuiBitmapBorderCtrl	GuiEditCtrl	GuiPopUpTextListCtrl
GuiBitmapButtonCtrl	GuiFadeinBitmapCtrl	GuiProgressCtrl
GuiBitmapButtonTextCtrl	GuiFilterCtrl	GuiRadioCtrl
GuiBitmapCtrl	GuiFrameSetCtrl	GuiScrollCtrl
GuiBorderButtonCtrl	GuiHealthBarHud	GuiShapeNameHud
GuiBubbleTextCtrl	GuiInputCtrl	GuiSliderCtrl
GuiButtonBaseCtrl	GuiInspector	GuiSpeedometerHud
GuiButtonCtrl	GuiMenuBackgroundCtrl	GuiTerrPreviewCtrl
GuiCanvas	GuiMenuBar	GuiTextCtrl
GuiCheckBoxCtrl	GuiMenuTextListCtrl	GuiTextEditCtrl
GuiChunkedBitmapCtrl	GuiMessageVectorCtrl	GuiTextEditSliderCtrl
GuiClockHud	GuiMLTextCtrl	GuiTextListCtrl
GuiConsole	GuiMLTextEditCtrl	GuiTreeViewCtrl
GuiConsoleEditCtrl	GuiMouseEventCtrl	GuiWindowCtrl
GuiConsoleTextCtrl	GuiNoMouseCtrl	

Figure 10.3 shows a screen used to select missions to play. There is a list of available missions on the client, some buttons to run the mission or go back to the main menu, and a check box to indicate whether you want to host this mission for other players. Note, too, that there is a background, which is the same as the background used for our Emaga game program's start-up menu.

What we'll do next is examine each of the screen's GUI elements in detail.

GuiChunkedBitmapCtrl

The GuiChunkedBitmapCtrl class is usually used for the large backgrounds of interfaces, like menu screens. Figure 10.4 shows such a background. The name derives from the concept of breaking up an image into a collection of smaller ones (chunked bitmaps) in order to improve display performance.

Here is an example of a GuiChunkedBitmapCtrl definition:

```
new GuiChunkedBitmapCtrl(MenuScreen) {
  profile = "GuiContentProfile";
  horizSizing = "width";
  vertSizing = "height";
  position = "0 0";
```

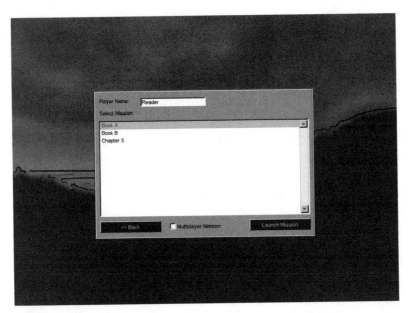

Figure 10.3
Start mission interface screen.

Figure 10.4
`GuiChunkedBitmapCtrl` background sample.

```
    extent = "640 480";
    minExtent = "8 8";
    visible = "1";
    bitmap = "./interfaces/emaga_background";
    // insert other controls here
};
```

The first thing to note about this definition is the line `// insert other controls here`. Typically, a GuiChunkedBitmapCtrl control would contain other controls, functioning as a sort of supercontainer. All other controls in a given screen using this control would be children, or subelements, of this control. This line is a comment, so in and of itself, it has no effect on the control's definition. I include it here to indicate where you would start nesting other controls.

Note the `extent` property, which specifies a width of 640 and a height of 480. These are "virtual pixels" in a way. Any subelements you insert in this control will have a maximum area of 640×480 to work with for positioning and sizing. These virtual pixels are scaled in size according to the actual canvas size, which you can change by setting the value of the global variable `$pref::Video::windowedRes` and then calling `CreateCanvas` or, if you already have a canvas, by calling `Canvas.Repaint;`—we used `CreateCanvas` in Chapter 7.

The `minExtent` property specifies the smallest size that you will allow this control to be shrunk down to when using the Torque built-in GUI Editor. We will use that editor later in this chapter.

GuiControl

The GuiControl class, as shown in Figure 10.5, is a sort of generic control container. It's often used as a tablike container, or as what other systems often

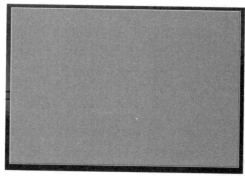

Figure 10.5
GuiControl sample.

call a *frame*. With it, you can gather together a collection of other controls and then manipulate them as a group.

Here is an example of a GuiControl definition:

```
new GuiControl(InfoTab) {
  profile = "GuiDefaultProfile";
  horizSizing = "width";
  vertSizing = "height";
  position = "0 0";
  extent = "640 480";
  minExtent = "8 8";
  visible = "1";
};
```

Probably the property you will be most interested in is the visible property. You will probably want to programmatically make the control visible or invisible based on the contents (the other controls) you place within the control. You can do that by adding either of the following statements to your scripts in a place suitable to your game design:

```
InfoTab.visible = true;
InfoTab.visible = false;
```

Note that true is the same as 1 or "1" and false is the same as 0 or "0".

GuiTextCtrl

The GuiTextCtrl, as shown in Figure 10.6, is a straightforward, commonly used control. You can use it to display any text you want. You can put it on an interface with no text and then fill in the text as the game progresses.

Here is an example of a GuiTextCtrl definition:

```
new GuiTextCtrl(PlayerNameLabel) {
  profile = "GuiTextProfile";
  horizSizing = "right";
  vertSizing = "bottom";
```

Player Name:

Figure 10.6
GuiTextCtrl sample.

```
   position = "183 5";
   extent = "63 18";
   minExtent = "8 8";
   visible = "1";
   text = "Player Name:";
   maxLength = "255";
};
```

You would specify the text font and other characteristics with your choice of profile. You can change the contents quite easily in this example by adding the following to your script in an appropriate location, dictated by your design:

```
PlayerNameLabel.text = "Some Other Text";
```

Tip

The maxLength property allows you to limit the number of characters that will be stored with the control. Specifying fewer characters saves memory.

GuiButtonCtrl

The GuiButtonCtrl, as shown in Figure 10.7, is another clickable control class. Unlike GuiCheckBoxCtrl or GuiRadioCtrl, this class does not retain any state. Its use is normally as a *command interface control*, where the user clicks it with the expectation that some action will be immediately invoked.

Here is an example of a GuiButtonCtrl definition:

```
new GuiButtonCtrl() {
   profile = "GuiButtonProfile";
   horizSizing = "right";
   vertSizing = "top";
   position = "16 253";
   extent = "127 23";
   minExtent = "8 8";
   visible = "1";
   command = "Canvas.getContent().Close();";
   text = "Close";
```

Figure 10.7
GuiButtonCtrl sample.

```
    groupNum = "-1";
    buttonType = "PushButton";
};
```

The most significant property is the command property. It contains a script statement to be executed when the button is pressed. This example will close the interface screen being shown in the canvas.

Another feature is the buttonType property. This can be one of the following:

- PushButton

- ToggleButton

- RadioButton

The property groupNum is used when the buttonType is specified to be Radio-Button. Radio buttons in an interface screen that have the same groupNum value are used in an exclusive manner. Only the most recently pressed radio button will be set to the checked value (true); all others in the group will be unchecked. Otherwise, the radio button type works the same as the GuiCheckBoxCtrl class, described in the next section.

This control is also used as a base for deriving the three button classes shown previously. You would probably be better off to use the specialized classes GuiCheckBoxCtrl and GuiRadioCtrl for types ToggleButton and RadioButton, rather than this control, because they have additional properties.

So the upshot is, if you use this control, it will probably be as a PushButton.

GuiCheckBoxCtrl

The GuiCheckBoxCtrl, as shown in Figure 10.8, is a specialized derivation of the GuiButtonCtrl that saves its current state value. It's analogous to a light switch or, more properly, a locking push button. If the box is empty when you click the control, the box will then display a check box. If it is checked, it will clear the check mark out of the box when you click the control.

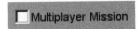

Figure 10.8
GuiCheckBoxCtrl sample.

Here is an example of a GuiCheckBoxCtrl definition:

```
new GuiCheckBoxCtrl(IsMultiplayer) {
  profile = "GuiCheckBoxProfile";
  horizSizing = "right";
  vertSizing = "bottom";
  position = "155 272";
  extent = "147 23";
  minExtent = "8 8";
  visible = "1";
  variable = "Pref::HostMultiPlayer";
  text = "Host Mission";
  maxLength = "255";
};
```

If you specify the variable property, then the value of the specified variable will be set to whatever the current state of the control is after you've clicked it. When the control is first displayed, it will set its state according to the value in the specified variable. You need to make sure that the variable you use contains appropriate data.

You can also specify the text label that will be displayed next to the check box using the text property.

Note that the GuiRadioCtrl control functions much like this control, except that it automatically enforces the principle that only one button in the same group will be checked.

GuiScrollCtrl

The GuiScrollCtrl class, as shown in Figure 10.9, is used for those famous scrolling lists that everyone likes. Okay, so not everyone may like them, but everyone *has* used them.

Figure 10.9
GuiScrollCtrl sample.

Here is an example of a GuiScrollCtrl definition:

```
new GuiScrollCtrl() {
  profile = "GuiScrollProfile";
  horizSizing = "right";
  vertSizing = "bottom";
  position = "14 55";
  extent = "580 190";
  minExtent = "8 8";
  visible = "1";
  willFirstRespond = "1";
  hScrollBar = "dynamic";
  vScrollBar = "alwaysOn";
  constantThumbHeight = "0";
  childMargin = "0 0";
  defaultLineHeight = "15";
  // insert listing control here
};
```

Normally, we would populate a scroll control with a list, usually defined by the contents of a GuiTextListCtrl control. The GuiTextListCtrl control containing the list would be added as a subelement of the GuiScrollCtrl control.

The willFirstRespond property is used to indicate whether we want this control to respond to arrow keys when they are pressed (to control scrolling) or to let other controls have access to arrow key inputs first.

Both the hScrollBar and vScrollBar properties—referring to the horizontal and vertical bars, respectively—can be set to one of these modes:

- **alwaysOn.** The scroll bar is always visible.

- **alwaysOff.** The scroll bar is never visible.

- **dynamic.** The scroll bar is visible only when the list exceeds the display space.

The property constantThumbHeight indicates whether the *thumb*, the small rectangular widget in the scroll bar that moves as you scroll, will have a size that is proportional to the number of entries in the list (the longer the list, the smaller the thumb) or will have a constant size. Setting this property to 1 ensures a constant size; 0 will ensure proportional sizing.

The property childMargin is used to constrain the viewable space inside the parent control that would be occupied by whatever control contained the list to be scrolled. In effect, it creates a margin inside the scroll control that restricts placement of the scroll list. The first value is the horizontal margin (for both left and right), and the second is the vertical margin (both top and bottom together).

Finally, defaultLineHeight defines in virtual pixels how high each line of the control's contents would be. This value is used to determine how much to scroll when a vertical arrow is clicked, for example.

GuiTextListCtrl

The GuiTextListCtrl, as shown in Figure 10.10, is used to display 2D arrays of text values.

Here is an example of a GuiTextListCtrl definition:

```
new GuiTextListCtrl(MasterServerList) {
  profile = "GuiTextArrayProfile";
  horizSizing = "right";
  vertSizing = "bottom";
  position = "2 2";
  extent = "558 48";
  minExtent = "8 8";
  visible = "1";
  enumerate = "0";
  resizeCell = "1";
  columns = "0 30 200 240 280 400";
  fitParentWidth = "1";
  clipColumnText = "0";
  noDuplicates = "false";
};
```

The enumerate property indicates which line of text is presented as highlighted.

You can allow the cells to be resized with the GUI Editor by setting the resizeCell property to true.

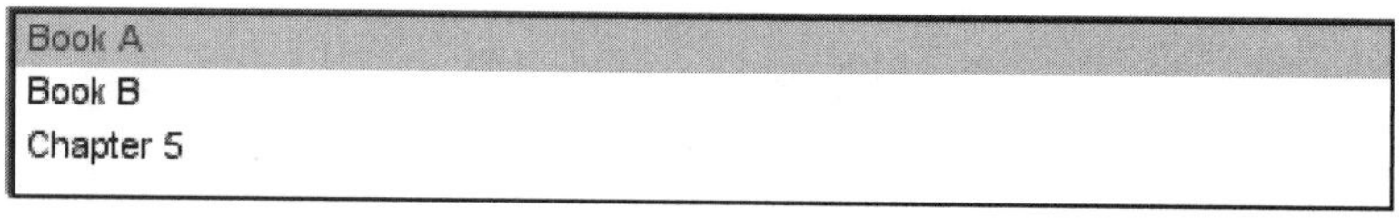

Figure 10.10
GuiTextListCtrl sample.

Each record, or line, in the array has space-delimited fields. You can format the display of these fields by using the `columns` property to indicate at which column number each field will be displayed.

The `fitParentWidth` property indicates whether the control will be enlarged in size to fill the available display space of any control that might contain this control.

We can decide whether overlong text in each column is to be clipped or will be left to overrun adjoining columns by setting the `clipColumnText` property.

We can automatically prevent the display of duplicate record entries by setting the `noDuplicates` property to `true`.

GuiTextEditCtrl

The `GuiTextEditCtrl`, as shown in Figure 10.11, provides a tool for users to manually enter text strings.

Here is an example of a `GuiTextEditCtrl` definition:

```
new GuiTextEditCtrl() {
  profile = "GuiTextEditProfile";
  horizSizing = "right";
  vertSizing = "bottom";
  position = "250 5";
  extent = "134 18";
  minExtent = "8 8";
  visible = "1";
  variable = "Pref::Player::Name";
  maxLength = "255";
  historySize = "5";
  password = "0";
  sinkAllKeyEvents = "0";
  helpTag = "0";
};
```

Figure 10.11
GuiTextEditCtrl sample.

With this control, the `variable` property is the key one. When the user types a string of text into the control's edit box, that string is entered into the variable indicated. When the control is first displayed, the contents of the indicated variable are stuffed into the edit box for display.

Text edit controls have a nifty history feature that can be quite handy. All the previous entries—up to a maximum specified by `historySize`—are saved and can be recalled using the Up Arrow key to go back in history or the Down Arrow key to go forward.

If you are using this control to accept a password, then set the `password` property to `true`. The control will substitute asterisks ("*") in place of whatever is typed by the user so that bystanders can't see what is being typed.

The `sinkAllKeyEvents` property, when set to `true`, causes the control to throw away any keystrokes that it receives but doesn't understand how to handle. When `sinkAllKeyEvents` is set to `false`, these keystrokes will be passed to the parent.

The Torque GUI Editor

Torque has an editor built in for creating and tweaking interfaces. You can invoke the GUI Editor by pressing the F10 key (this is defined in the common code base scripts, but you can change it if you want). You are perfectly free to ship your game with this editor code, or you can remove it in any shipping version to ensure that people will not fiddle with the interfaces. Or you can modify it to suit your heart's desire!

Note

If you want to edit GUIs from any of your projects (like Emaga4, 5, or 6 or, in later chapters, Koob), you'll need to do a little preparation. From your 3D2E folder locate the creator folder, and copy it to your project's folder. Next, open the root main.cs file (the one in the same folder as the tge.exe executable and the DLL files), and locate the line near the end of the file that says this:

`SetModPaths($pathList);`

And add the next line immediately after it:

`$addonList="control;creator";`

Save your revised main.cs, and then run your program. If you do this, you will get the latest Torque 1.4 editor code and interfaces. If you don't, then you may not be able to access an editor, and even if you did, it would be the older interface from version 1.2.

The Cook's Tour of the Editor

When you launch the editor by pressing the F10 key, the editor will appear and load whatever interface is current, making it ready for editing.

Visually, there are five components to the GUI Editor: the Content Editor, the Control Tree, the Control Inspector, the Tool Bar, and the Menu Bar. There is also a sixth component, in a sense: keyboard commands. Figure 10.12 shows the GUI Editor open and working with one of the earlier main menu screens from the Emaga sample game.

The Content Editor

The Content Editor is where you can place, move, and resize controls. In Figure 10.12 the Content Editor is the large rectangular area at the lower left in the GUI Editor view.

Selection   Normally, you select a control by clicking the mouse on it. Some controls can be difficult to select because of their positions. Another way to select controls is by using the Control Tree, which is covered in a later section.

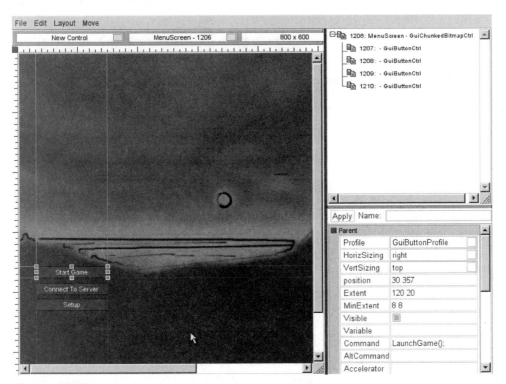

Figure 10.12
The Torque GUI Editor.

If you hold down the Shift key while clicking the mouse (*shift-clicking*) on several controls, you can select more than one control at once. Each time you shift-click you add that control to the selection. The sizing knobs turn white and can no longer be used to size the control. You can still move the controls. Only controls that share the same parent can be selected at the same time.

Movement Move a control by clicking and dragging its content area after selecting it. When you move controls, be aware of which controls they may be contained by—when you drag the control to one side or another, you may be dragging it outside the display area of its parent control, and you don't want that.

Resizing You resize a control after selection by clicking on and dragging one of the eight black sizing knobs. As with movement, you need to stay aware of how the control you are resizing is related to other controls. The sizing might be restricted by a parent control's display area. Figure 10.12 shows the sizing knobs, attached to the Start Game button.

Adding The parent control of the currently selected control is outlined with a yellow and blue band. This control is known as the *Current Add Parent*. Any new control created from the Tool Bar or pasted from the Clipboard will be added to this control. The Current Add Parent control can be set manually by either clicking one of its children or right-clicking the control's entry in the Control Tree.

The Control Tree

The Control Tree shows the current content control hierarchy. It is in the upper-right corner of the GUI Editor view.

Parent controls, also called *containers*—controls that contain other controls—have a little box to the left of their entry in the tree. If the box is a plus sign, clicking it will expand that control into the list, bringing the child controls into view. If you click it when it looks like a minus sign, it will contract the control's list back to a single entry comprising solely the parent control.

Clicking any control in the tree will cause it to be selected in the Content Editor view and cause the control's properties to be displayed in the Control Inspector view. You can see this effect by looking back at Figure 10.12.

The Control Inspector

The Control Inspector is where any currently selected control's attributes are displayed. It is located in the lower-right corner of the GUI Editor, below the Control Tree. All the properties of a control are displayed in the Control Inspector and can be changed here. After changing a value, you must click the Apply button to assert the changes.

When first displayed, all the properties are collapsed visually within categories, such as Parent, Misc, and Dynamic Fields. Parent is the only category that is present in all controls; other controls have different categories that are specific to their characteristics. To access the properties within a category, simply click the buttons in the Inspector view that have those category names, and the list expands, giving you edit boxes and buttons with which you can manipulate the properties.

The Tool Bar

The Tool Bar contains functions for creating new controls, opening existing GUIs, and setting a virtual screen size (for testing). The Tool Bar has pop-up menus for creating new controls and changing the currently edited GUI. The functions of the buttons are described in Table 10.1.

The Menu Bar

The Menu Bar contains some standard menus, like File and Edit, which have approximately the expected functionality. There are two additional specialized menus: Layout and Move. See Table 10.2.

Table 10.1 Tool Bar Button Functions

Button	Description
New Control	Displays a list of all controls from which the user can select one to add to the current content control.
Show GUI	Displays the name of the interface (GUI) currently being edited. Selecting this pop-up allows the user to choose a screen to edit from all loaded interfaces.
Virtual Screen Size	Displays the current virtual screen size of the interface (GUI) currently being edited. Selecting this pop-up allows the user to choose from one of three virtual screen sizes: 640 × 480, 800 × 600, and 1024 × 768.

Table 10.2 Menu Bar Functions

Option	Description
File, New GUI	Creates a new empty canvas on which to create a GUI.
File, Save GUI	Initiates a file-saving dialog box for saving GUIs.
File, GUI Editor Help	Opens a Help dialog box.
File, Toggle GUI Editor	Closes the GUI Editor, and returns to the previous interface, whatever that might happen to be.
Edit, Cut	Copies the current selection to the Clipboard, and removes the selection from the interface.
Edit, Copy	Copies the current selection to the Clipboard, and leaves the selection in the interface.
Edit, Paste	Pastes the contents of the Clipboard into the interface.
Edit, Select All	Selects all the controls in the interface at once.
Layout, Align Left	Aligns the left edge of all selected controls to the leftmost point of all the selected controls.
Layout, Align Right	Aligns the right edge of all selected controls to the rightmost point of all the selected controls.
Layout, Align Top	Aligns the top edge of all selected controls to the topmost point of all the selected controls.
Layout, Align Bottom	Aligns the bottom edge of all selected controls to the bottommost point of all the selected controls.
Layout, Center Horizontally	Horizontally centers all selected controls in the rectangle that bounds all the selected controls.
Layout, Space Vertically	Vertically spaces all selected controls evenly.
Layout, Space Horizontally	Horizontally spaces all selected controls evenly.
Layout, Bring Front	Arranges the selected control in front of its sibling controls.
Layout, Send Back	Arranges the selected control behind its sibling controls.
Layout, Lock Selection	Locks the selected object, preventing it from being accidentally modified.
Layout, Unlock Selection	Unlocks the selected object, allowing it to be modified.
Move, Nudge Left	Moves the selected object a small amount to the left.
Move, Nudge Right	Moves the selected object a small amount to the right.
Move, Nudge Up	Moves the selected object a small amount upward.
Move, Nudge Down	Moves the selected object a small amount downward.
Move, Big Nudge Left	Moves the selected object a large amount to the left.
Move, Big Nudge Right	Moves the selected object a large amount to the right.
Move, Big Nudge Up	Moves the selected object a large amount upward.
Move, Big Nudge Down	Moves the selected object a large amount downward.

Table 10.3 GUI Editor Keyboard Commands

Keys	Name	Description
Ctrl+A	Select All	Selects all the controls in the Current Add Parent.
Ctrl+C	Copy	Copies the currently selected control(s) to the Clipboard.
Ctrl+X	Cut	Cuts the currently selected control(s) to the Clipboard.
Ctrl+V	Paste	Pastes any control on the Clipboard into the Current Add Parent.
Arrow Keys	Movement	Moves the current control selection 1 pixel in the direction of the arrow.
Shift+Arrow Keys	Movement	Moves the current control selection 10 pixels in the direction of the arrow.
Delete/ Backspace	Delete	Deletes the current control selection.
Ctrl+L	Align Left	Aligns the left edge of all selected controls to the leftmost point of all the selected controls.
Ctrl+R	Align Right	Aligns the right edge of all selected controls to the rightmost point of all the selected controls.
Ctrl+T	Align Top	Aligns the top edge of all selected controls to the topmost point of all the selected controls.
Ctrl+B	Align Bottom	Aligns the bottom edge of all selected controls to the bottommost point of all the selected controls.

Keyboard Commands

In addition to using mouse selection and GUI button clicks, the user has a number of keyboard commands available. Table 10.3 shows these commands.

Creating an Interface

In this section you will see how easy it is to create and employ an interface using the Torque GUI Editor.

You should note that the Torque GUI Editor assumes your screen resolution is set to a minimum resolution of 800 × 600. You may find it more useful to use a higher resolution, to allow the different views more room to display their data.

1. Using Windows Explorer, browse into the \3D2E folder, and then run the Torque demo.

2. When the GarageGames/Torque main menu screen appears, press the F10 key. The various editor controls and panels will appear on the top and right side of the screen.

3. Choose File, New GUI, and enter a name for the new interface—do not use spaces in the name. Use "MyFirstInterface" for the GUI name.

4. Leave the class as GuiControl, and then click the Create button. You will now have a nice, shiny new interface to work with.

5. In the Control Tree panel, select the control named "MyFirstInterface". Its properties should appear in the Control Inspector panel.

6. Locate the profile property, and click the square button next to it on the right-hand side to get the pop-up menu.

7. Scroll through the menu until you locate the GuiContentProfile, and select that.

8. Click Apply.
   Now you have a Content Control to which you can add other controls.

9. Click the New Control button, and choose GuiButtonCtrl from the pop-up menu.

10. Select the button using one of the two techniques you've learned (via the Content Editor or the Control Tree).

11. Look in the Control Inspector view, and locate the text property for this new control. It's near the bottom in the Misc group. You will have to scroll down to find it. Put some text of your own in it.

12. Enter **quit();** in the command property. This is the ninth property from the top of the property list.

13. Click Apply.

14. Click the Save button. The Save feature will automatically use the top-level control in your interface for the file name, so leave that as is.

15. At the top of the Save dialog box is a button that you can use to select the folder in which to save the file. Choose the demo/client/ui folder. (If you are using an Emaga program, or Koob, then use the control/client/interfaces folder here and in step 2 of the next procedure.)

16. Ensure one final time that the file name to be saved is MyFirstInterface.gui, and then click Save.

There, you've created an interface using the Torque GUI Editor!

Now let's break it! No... I mean, let's test it!

1. Open the console using the Tilde ("~") key.

2. Type in the following, pressing the Enter key when you're done:

```
exec("demo/client/ui/MyFirstInterface.gui");
```

3. Now type in the following, again pressing the Enter key when you're done:

```
canvas.setContent("MyFirstInterface");
```

Your interface should pop up on the screen. Just go ahead—press that button! Now you see that the whole program quits, because that's what you programmed it to do.

Of course, this is a simple interface. They can get as complex as you need. You can see that there is a lot of power available in Torque to address your interface needs. And if Torque doesn't have it, you can create it yourself!

Moving Right Along

So now you should have a reasonable understanding of how controls are made and added to an interface. You've seen the innards of some of the more common controls that are available in Torque.

You've also learned how to use one of the valuable built-in tools that Torque supplies, the GUI Editor. It's worth your while to practice making a few interfaces—even goofy ones that have no purpose, if you like—just to reinforce the steps involved and to become comfortable using the GUI Editor.

Staying with the visual aspects of a game, we will examine structural material textures in the next chapter.

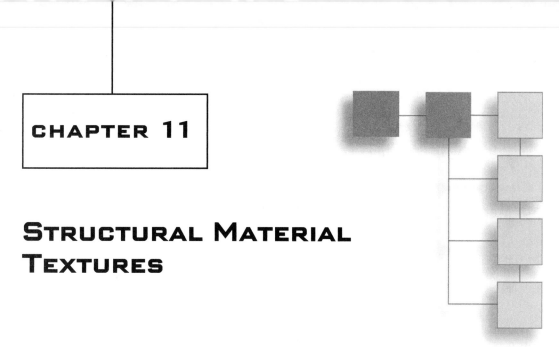

CHAPTER 11

STRUCTURAL MATERIAL TEXTURES

In earlier chapters we encountered textures used to enhance the 3D game environment in the resources included with the Emaga sample game. We only caressed the topic with the most feathery of touches. As the book progresses we'll explore the topic in depth from many different angles. In this chapter we'll look at one aspect of 3D game textures—those used to define 3D structures, like buildings, walls, sidewalks, and other virtual world artifacts.

You can judiciously and creatively use textures in several important ways. We'll use a prebuilt scene with a few basic and more complex structures to illustrate some of these principles, including the following:

- **Project information.** One of the most basic uses of textures in a 3D game is to define the object containing the textures. A simple box shape can become an electrical transformer, a house, a crate of weapons, or an air conditioner, merely by applying different textures to the shape.

- **Convey mood.** We can set a mood in a scene using different styles of textures. The amount of subtlety is up to the designers; a somewhat un-remarkable and neutral air vent high on a wall can become an ominous clue to an unseen threat by adding a graphic of slime or other unmentionable stuff oozing from its louvers.

- **Establish space and place.** A cramped machine room full of noise and whirling parts might have shapes built with textures jammed with pipes, wires, knobs, and other mechanical items. The machinery shapes would probably be busy-looking affairs, even in static form. On the other hand textures for the walls in a high-ceilinged, multistory hall might have only vertically oriented lines and long, thin curves, with high-contrast shading.

During this chapter you will be directed to use the Gimp from time to time, so it's a good idea to have it open and ready for use.

Sources

There are many ways to create textures for use in structures. Techniques can range from the obvious (photographing buildings and walls and other real-world items or drawing them with pen and pencil) to the more imaginative (making rubbings with paper and charcoal) to the more high-tech (using texture-creation software).

In this section we'll look at two of the most accessible texture-creation methods, photography and original artwork.

Photography

To use photography as a source, you'll need a camera, of course. Digital cameras with decent resolutions available can be quite inexpensive. Most digital cameras come with hardware that allows you to quickly upload the images to your computer.

Digital Versus Film

If you buy a digital camera, you should get one that will provide pictures of at least 800 pixels by 600 pixels with 32-bit color.

Your other options are to use a normal film camera and then either scan the resulting photos or send the film to a shop that will digitize the photos for you when they're developed. These shops are quite common, and the extra step of digitization of your developed film is often a no-cost "loss leader" that the shops use to attract business.

Scanners are also low-cost items. The minimum specification for a scanner that you need for use in game development would be a 600-dpi 32-bit color scanner. Flatbed scanners are best for this kind of work.

Note

If you intend to use photography as a source for textures, be aware that there are some things to watch out for. Don't use pictures of items with trademarked images or copyrighted text or graphics on them. You will probably end up in violation of trademark or copyright law if your game ends up shipping with those images in it.

If your game absolutely must include a photo of a billboard ad for a popular soft drink, for example, make sure you contact the soft drink company to obtain written permission before you ship your game. In addition to staying legal, you also might just be able to obtain sponsorship or some other support from the company for your game. Now I'll admit that this is probably not likely, but it is certainly possible.

When you have identified a candidate texture for use in your game, make sure to take several different pictures of the item from different angles, at different distances, and in different lighting, if possible. Take lots and lots of pictures, and then review them when you get back to your home or office to find what suits your needs. Keep all the originals. Sometimes, on later examination, you will discover details that you didn't notice when first taking the pictures. These details may require choosing a different shot from a different angle to ensure that they don't show. It wouldn't work to have the condensation trail of an airliner in an image used for the sky in a game that takes place in a medieval era.

Figure 11.1 shows a picture of some interlocking bricks used for a walkway. Figure 11.2 shows the same walkway with the picture taken under slightly different circumstances (for example, the area photographed for Figure 11.2 was a few feet away from the area shown in Figure 11.1). One detail I picked up on quickly when examining the photos on my computer that I didn't notice at the scene is that some of the bricks in Figure 11.2 are double bricks, lain side by side. This despite the fact that I have trodden this particular walkway literally thousands of times in the past 10 years or so!

So the lesson is this: when at the scene, don't be a censor and don't be judgmental. Just take oodles of photographs of the items in question. Then sort it all out back at the shop.

Postprocessing

After getting back to the shop, you will probably have to do a certain amount of postprocessing of the chosen photos. Even if you were creating a photorealistic game, you would still need to ensure that the lighting and palettes of the textures

Figure 11.1
Real-world candidate for sidewalk texture.

Figure 11.2
Alternate candidate for sidewalk texture.

were close enough matches to each other. This would be especially true when your texture photos were taken in different areas at different times.

It's probably best to do all of your pixel-related processing first, before you crop or extract your textures. This ensures that the changes you make are done in the proper context—the areas that you *aren't* interested in will change along with the areas you *are* interested in—thus guiding your efforts more appropriately.

All of the photo-processing capabilities of any tools you have are at your disposal. Three specific operations are generally used more than the others: color matching, lighting, and cropping.

Color Matching   The first thing you will probably need to do is match the colors of your texture to existing in-game textures and lighting conditions. Usually you will match your colors by adjusting the balance of colors. This can be done in the Gimp by choosing Tools, Color Tools, Color Balance. The dialog box that appears does a good job of guiding you in your adjustments. Note that when you reduce the red component of a color palette, you increase the cyan influence, and when you reduce the blue component, you increase the yellow. In general, cooler color temperatures are stronger in the blue/cyan influence, while warmer temperatures cavort about with more red/yellow makeup.

Unfortunately, it is extremely difficult to illustrate the differences between different temperature settings in grayscale images like the ones used in this book, so Figure 11.3 may not adequately demonstrate the subtle variations. If you installed the companion CD, you can find the full-color version of the image in the file \3D2E\RESOURCES\CH11\11-03.jpg. Of course, you can go ahead and try the various settings in the Gimp and see the differences for yourself.

In Figure 11.3, from left to right, the three settings chosen are Incandescent, Fluorescent, and Bright Sun. Compare these variations with the original shown in Figure 11.2 and found at \3D2E\RESOURCES\Ch11\11-02.jpg.

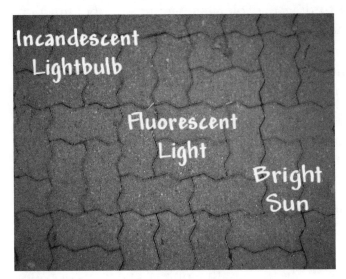

Figure 11.3
Reference image for three color temperatures.

The light of bright sunlight on a clear day contains all colors of the visible spectrum pretty well in their natural proportions, with the sole modification being some filtering by the atmosphere. This atmospheric filtering (predominantly by water molecules) scatters a certain proportion of light at the blue-violet end of the spectrum, reducing the amount of light at those wavelengths that makes it to the surface. Nonetheless, you can see that there is still a strong blue component in the bright sunlight area.

The fluorescent light area shows a somewhat more balanced spectrum, with less blue than with the bright light. The incandescent lightbulb area shows the opposite end of the spectrum from sunlight and has a much warmer feel due to the presence of more red and less blue.

So in Figure 11.3 the color temperature moves from warm on the left to cool on the right.

The original image, as shown in Figure 11.2, has a coloring somewhere between fluorescent and sunlight, leaning heavily toward the fluorescent. This is not really a surprise—I took those photos outside on a sunny clear summer day, but in the shade. The illumination is therefore provided by the light reflected from the surroundings, which in this case had the effect of moving the spectrum toward the middle.

Lighting   Lighting is closely tied to color matching. Changes in the apparent lighting of an image will tend to drag the color temperature in one direction or the other. So keep this in mind when you apply lighting changes to images.

In the context of processing 2D images for use as textures, what we are trying to achieve is imparting a sense of the light direction and light "play" upon the surface of the texture being portrayed.

For example, one feature about surface textures that we may need to enhance is the sense of depth. As shown in Figure 11.4, the texture may contain numerous small stones that protrude from a flat surface.

One simple method we can use to increase the sense of depth is to increase the contrast. The problem with adjusting the contrast is that it tends to drastically alter the color temperature—the more contrast, the warmer the overall color temperature.

The obvious way to handle this would be to boost the contrast and then tweak the color balance. Sometimes this does not work so well, especially if a wide spectrum

Figure 11.4
Pebbled surface with lighting adjustment.

of colors is represented in the image. In those cases there are other ways to deal with the issue, such as tweaking the saturation.

What you see in Figure 11.4 is the original texture on the left and the adjusted texture on the right. In this case what I did was use the Gimp to enhance the contrast by 40 percent (choose Tools, Color Tools, Brightness–Contrast) and then reduce the saturation by 41 percent (choose Tools, Color Tools, Hue–Saturation).

Note

You can't reduce the saturation on grayscale images. The Gimp won't even let you try.

Cropping   When using photographs as image sources, we rarely want to keep the entire image. Artifacts such as lighting changes at the periphery, fisheye distortion at the edges caused by extreme perspective, extraneous items in the image, and other issues typically make the outer edges of photographs unsuitable for use as textures.

The solution is to crop the image, leaving behind the portion that is useful to us. Figure 11.5 shows a piece of wood that has a texture of interest. It stretches across the entire frame from left to right but only covers somewhat less than half of the vertical area. It's also not parallel with the sides of the image. In this case we will want to crop the wood out and "de-rotate" it as well.

Figure 11.5
A photograph that needs to be cropped.

Tip

You can access the original of the photo I used here at \3D2E\RESOURCES\CH11\COLORPHOTOS\ woodencurb.jpg

---

You might be tempted to crop the wood out and then apply rotation to straighten it out, but experience shows that these operations should be done the other way around. Just as with the color and lighting operations, you should apply the geometric changes first, and then crop the texture. This allows the image processing software to make its geometry in the full context of the image parts that surround the area of interest, which can have a subtle effect on the end result.

Another reason for resolving the geometric appearance of the texture before cropping is that cropping tools tend to use rectangular shapes for selection. It is helpful to the overall process and productivity to crop images where the areas of interest are appropriately oriented horizontally and vertically.

To use the Crop tool in the Gimp, click the Crop & Resize tool icon on the Tool palette of the main window (see Figure 11.6). Click and drag the tool on the image to select the rectangular area of interest. The resulting selection rectangle will have small square handles on the sides, which you can click and drag to resize the crop area. There is also a Crop & Resize dialog box that opens up, where you

Figure 11.6
Crop tool icon.

Figure 11.7
Cropped portion of unaltered photo.

Figure 11.8
Rectangular Selection tool icon.

can manually specify crop dimensions and other parameters. When you are satisfied with your selected area, click the Crop button in the dialog box to cause the actual cropping operation to take place.

Figure 11.7 shows the result of merely cropping the image to include all portions of the wood without first altering the orientation of the wood. It still needs to be rotated. Of course, you may actually want the woodgrain to be slanted, but then you may need to remove the nonwood slivers of area above and below the woodgrain by erasing them to a fixed solid color or making those areas completely transparent.

In our case we really want the woodgrain to be parallel to the bottom and top edges of the image, so we should rotate the woodgrain portion before cropping. Use the Rectangular Selection tool (see Figure 11.8) to select the area to be rotated.

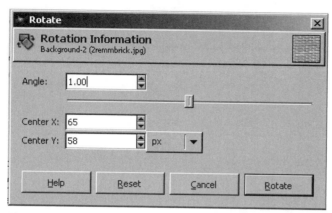

Figure 11.9
The Rotate dialog box.

Figure 11.10
The rotated woodgrain.

Then choose Tools, Transform Tools, Rotate to get the Rotate dialog box (see Figure 11.9).

In the Tools options area in the main window, ensure that Interpolation has been set to Cubic (Best) and that the Affect is set to Selection. Then, in the Rotate dialog box, type "**1.00**" in the text box labeled Angle. Click Rotate. This will rotate the selected area 1 full degree to the right (see Figure 11.10).

You should have your rotated area with the selection marquee still surrounding it. Don't touch anything yet—leave the selection as it is.

Figure 11.11
The cropped woodgrain image.

Now after having earlier explained that the Crop & Resize tool is used one way, I'll show you another way to crop the image that is sometimes more convenient. With the rotated area still selected, choose the Crop & Resize tool, and click in the selected area. Click the From selection button, and then click the Crop button. You will then end up with an image as shown in Figure 11.11, suitable for use as a texture.

Now compare Figure 11.11 with Figure 11.7, and you will see the difference.

Original Artwork

The other approach to creating textures is to use original artwork. Some people believe this is not a real option for them, because they think they can't draw or paint to save their lives. I tend to feel that everyone can learn the techniques required. My intent here, however, is not to teach you how to draw, so if you want to learn more, I encourage you to look into taking some lessons.

If you are satisfied with your artistic skills, then you have another rich avenue for texture generation available. The techniques used to convert a photograph to a texture can also be used to convert your handmade images to textures.

Another approach for creating original artwork is to create your images directly in a tool like the Gimp. You can draw freehand using the mouse or a pen tablet.

With tools like the Gimp you have a wide variety of means for creating textures, including many that can be created via the various options in the Filters and Script-Fu menus. Figure 11.12 shows examples of textures created using the built-in features of the Gimp. I encourage you to explore this tool in depth. It can really be a timesaver. And you can use it to create some knockout textures.

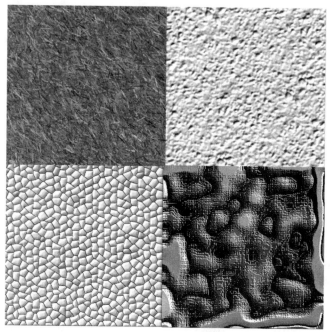

Figure 11.12
Example textures.

Scaling Issues

When creating your textures, you will need to pay attention to the issue of scale. The sizes of the things within an image that are used to make a texture have a particular relationship to other real-world objects. We are subconsciously aware of many of these relationships from our exposure to the world in general and will notice when the textures are out of proportion to the items they adorn. If it's bad enough the effect can sometimes be similar to the sound of fingernails being dragged across a chalkboard!

Figure 11.13 shows two stylized houses. The bricks in house A are far too large, while the bricks in house B are more appropriately sized yet may still be a bit too large. Yes, there are some uses for stone blocks having proportions such as those in house A, but they are rarely used in bungalow-sized or two-story homes, as depicted in the figure.

The scale issue can pop up anywhere, as you can see in Figure 11.14. The texture image in the corrugated metal bridge surface is probably about 10 times larger than is appropriate. Sometimes you might need to redo the texture to match; other times you can adjust how the texture is applied to the polygons using the

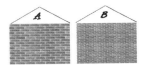

Figure 11.13
Scaling bricks.

Figure 11.14
Scaling error.

modeling tools. My rule of thumb is that if the texture image size is 64 pixels by 64 pixels or smaller and needs to be made larger, you should make a new texture at the larger size. The same goes the other way. If the image size is larger than 64 pixels by 64 pixels and needs to be made smaller, then make a new texture at the smaller size.

Tiling

Many structures have large surfaces with repeating patterns. The best way to approach making textures for these surfaces is to create one smaller texture that is replicated many times across the surface rather than simply making one large texture.

The replication will usually take place in two dimensions. It is important to make sure that the edges of the texture align properly when they meet. Figure 11.15 shows this to good effect. You can see the obvious horizontal as well as the more

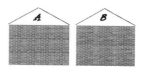

Figure 11.15
Tiled brick texture.

Figure 11.16
The brick texture with asymmetric shading.

Figure 11.17
A stone texture.

subtle artifacts in house A where the tiled brick textures don't quite line up. In house B, where care was taken to ensure that the texture edges matched up correctly, those artifacts aren't visible.

However, in house B in Figure 11.15 there is another obvious artifact of tiling, this time caused by asymmetric lighting effects in the texture shading. You can see each repeated texture tile—its position is marked by the presence of the darker shaded bricks in a repeated pattern. This effect can be quite subtle and difficult to detect in an image viewed in isolation.

Figure 11.16 shows the texture used in house B of Figure 11.15. Looking at it in isolation, you would be hard pressed to notice the subtly darker shaded bricks.

The simplest way to fix up a texture for use as a tiled texture is to copy the left edge, about 5 or 10 pixels wide, mirror the copy horizontally, and then paste the copy on the right side of the image. Do the same for the bottom edge. Of course, you can go from top to bottom or right to left as well. The important step is the mirroring.

After placing the mirrored edges, spend a little time blending their inner edges with the interior portions of the image.

Figure 11.17 shows a stone block texture that is a candidate for use in a tiling situation.

Figure 11.18 shows the texture tiled in a set of four. Again, you can see the artifacts caused by the mismatched edges.

Figure 11.19 shows the left edge being copied, mirrored, and placed on the right.

Figure 11.20 shows the same thing happening with the bottom edge.

Finally, Figure 11.21 shows the tiled result.

Figure 11.18
Poorly tiled stone texture.

Figure 11.19
Replicating the left edge.

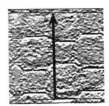

Figure 11.20
Replicating the bottom edge.

Figure 11.21
Properly tiled stone texture.

The Gimp has a helpful filter tool for use with tiling. Using a random texture of your own selection, choose Filters, Map, Make Seamless. This tool does a great job of speeding up the process of making tileable textures. Unfortunately, it doesn't give you any options to vary the effect.

Texture Types

There are far too many texture types and classes of material appearances for me to enumerate them with any sort of thoroughness. Given that, there is a much smaller set of texture types that are found over and over in nature and man-made structures.

Most of the following textures are types that are used for buildings, bridges, and other man-made items in a game world. Most of the texture types and patterns can be generated using the Gimp, by choosing Filters, Render, Pattern and using one of the many submenus that reside there.

Irregular

Irregular textures tend to have a general disorder and random appearance, like that shown in Figure 11.22. Dirt and grass are examples of irregular textures. Quite often irregular textures are combined with other, different irregular textures in order to give a weathered or damaged appearance to an area or a surface.

Figure 11.22
An irregular texture.

Figure 11.23
A rough texture.

Figure 11.24
A pebbled texture.

Rough

Rough textures, as shown in Figure 11.23, sometimes have somewhat the same sense about them as irregular textures. They are often used as tiles on a surface like a sidewalk or rough concrete walls.

Pebbled

Pebbled textures are another example of textures often used for paved surfaces and stone walls. Tarmacadam pavement is an example of a finely pebbled surface when viewed from a distance of about 5 or 6 feet. Figure 11.24 shows a more obvious pebbled texture that could be used for a wall or decorative planter.

Woodgrain

Figure 11.25 shows a woodgrain texture that has many highly variant bundles of lines ranging from fine to coarse that run roughly parallel to each other, sometimes interrupted by swirls and knots. Some kinds of stone have similar appearances.

Smooth

We all know when something is smooth—there are no discernable bumps or irregularities to the touch. Depicting smoothness in textures can be a little difficult. We usually create a rather bland surface look and then introduce a few soft and mild irregularities in order to emphasize the smoothness. Figure 11.26 shows a smooth texture.

Patterned

Patterned textures are pretty straightforward. The intent is not necessarily to convey the contour, bumpiness, or feel of a surface but rather to represent regular shapes or patterns that appear on an item. Figure 11.27 depicts a pattern that could be used to represent the louvers of an air duct in a wall.

Figure 11.25
A woodgrain texture.

Figure 11.26
A smooth texture.

Figure 11.27
A patterned texture.

Figure 11.28
A fabric texture.

Figure 11.29
A metallic texture.

Fabric

Fabric textures emulate the appearance of things like canvas or carpet. Fabrics may be woven or not, but they all tend to exhibit fine repetitive shapes. Figure 11.28 shows a woven fabric texture that could be canvas. The Gimp has a great tool available in its Script-Fu menu for simulating cloth. You can find it by choosing Script-Fu, Alchemy, Clothify and fiddling with the settings.

Metallic

Metallic textures tend to have a dominant color, with a strong dark shadow that follows the outer contours of the metallic object and a bright accent color that runs along raised surfaces. Figure 11.29 shows a texture that could be used for a metal tube.

Figure 11.30
A reflective texture.

Figure 11.31
A plastic texture.

Reflective

A reflective texture simulates the effect of a light source in the scene reflecting strongly off the surface of the textured object. Figure 11.30 is such a texture that might be depicting a bright overhead light reflecting off a window.

Plastic

Plastic textures are similar to metallic textures in their manner of shading and highlighting. Plastic tends to have more of an oily appearance to it at times, so the shading and highlights are often more sinuous. As shown in Figure 11.31, the highlights tend to be less clearly defined than with metallic textures, while the light source often appears as a distinct highlight.

Moving Right Along

In this chapter we examined how to collect images to use in applying textures to objects that represent real-world structures. We saw some of the processing techniques that we may need to use to prepare our images for use as textures, like color matching and cropping.

Some of the areas that can be more problematic when considering textures for structures are scaling the images and preparing them to be tiled if the texture will be used in a repeating fashion. A texture that can be tiled is one whose opposite edges can be mated together without producing a noticeable seam.

Finally, we explored some of the more common texture patterns and characteristics that are used in games.

In the next chapter we will look at terrains and skyboxes, two mechanisms that are often used to provide that touch of realism in our game worlds. Some of the ideas we've covered in this chapter will certainly be useful in the next chapter as well.

CHAPTER 12

TERRAINS

Many games take place exclusively inside buildings or structures, like tunnels. And many other games involve exclusive outdoor game play. Then there are some games that have a mix of each.

When your game has an outdoor component, you need to represent the *terrain,* which in game terms is the combination of the topography (hilliness, for example) and ground cover (grass, gravel, sand, and so on). The topography is modeled using a 3D model, and the ground cover is represented by textures.

In addition to representing the ground, you also need to represent the sky, if you want to have interesting outdoor game play. Typically, a construct called a *skybox* is used to represent all of the sky, from horizon to horizon.

Terrains Explained

To understand terrains in a game development context, we need to look at the characteristics of the terrain we want to model. These characteristics will drive our need for the data that defines the terrain we want to make and therefore will heavily influence how and where we obtain that data.

Terrain Characteristics

A basic unit of terrain is the *tile.* Essentially, a terrain tile is a collection of polygons that form a 3D model that represents the terrain, as depicted in Figure 12.1.

Figure 12.1
An untextured terrain tile.

When we model terrain in a game, we have to make a number of choices. We need to decide the level of terrain *fidelity* we want to achieve. Another choice is to figure out the *spread* of the terrain. Finally, we need to decide what sort of *freedom* the terrain embodies. Table 12.1 lists these characteristics and the ramifications of each choice.

There are practical considerations that direct our terrain design choices. Many game engines simply aren't capable of handling the distances involved in large-scale terrains or the number of objects required to appropriately populate them. Some game genres aren't suited to open terrains—the player needs to be confined in order to advance the game story as required.

Terrain Data

When you want to create a high-fidelity terrain model of a real place in the world, you are going to need to get the data from somewhere. If the area in question is small enough, you may be able to go out and gather the information yourself if you're handy with a theodolite (a surveyor's tool). You might be able to glean the necessary information from topographic maps. In either case there is a lot of work involved in the data-gathering phase alone. You will need accurate distance measurements and altitudes, as well as photos of the ground cover.

Table 12.1 Terrain Characteristics

Characteristic	Description
Fidelity	*Terrain fidelity* measures how accurately the terrain reflects real topography found somewhere in the world—how realistic it is. The realism can be reflected in both the modeling and the textures. Modeling fidelity can be described as any of the following: **Realistic:** Accurate at 1:1 scale in all dimensions with high-resolution textures representing the terrain cover. **Semirealistic:** Accurately scaled, usually to a smaller size. Often the vertical scale is 1:1 while the horizontal scales are around 1:2. The game *World War 2 Online* by Cornered Rat Software has all of Western Europe modeled in this fashion. The game uses medium-to-low resolution textures to represent ground cover. **Quasi-Realistic:** Not accurately scaled in any dimension, but still attempts to represent a real location in the world. Usually employs high-resolution ground cover textures. The scales and textures are chosen to give a sense of the locale that works well in the game environment. NovaLogic's *Delta Force* series takes this approach. **Unrealistic:** Everything else! Unrealistic terrain is most commonly used to specifically enhance game play or the backstory of the game.
Spread	*Terrain spread* is the degree to which areas of the terrain are unique. Terrain is created in units called *tiles*. The spread is related to these tiles in one of three ways: **Infinite:** A square terrain region is repeated, or tiled, in all cardinal directions, such that when the player leaves a region to the west, he enters a new copy of the same terrain tile from the east. This continues for as long as the player keeps moving in that one direction. **Finite:** The terrain tiles are repeated in all directions, but at some point the repetition stops. **Untiled:** Terrain tiles are not repeated.
Freedom	*Terrain freedom* is the measure of how much the player's in-game movements are restricted by the terrain. Terrain freedom is closely coupled with terrain spread. There are really only two degrees of terrain freedom: **Closed:** Closed terrain limits player movements in all cardinal directions at some point. With closed terrain, at some point after a player has been moving in a particular direction, he cannot continue that way, either because there is a virtual physical barrier or because the program prevents further movement. In any case, the terrain is usually modeled beyond the barrier only as far as the player can see. After that—nothing. **Open:** Open terrain allows player movement in any direction for as long as the player wants. Some games will warp the player to the "other side" of the world, where he will keep crossing terrain tile copies until he returns to the place he started.

But don't despair! There are sources for high-resolution terrain information available on the Internet. If you go to http://edcwww.cr.usgs.gov, the Web portal for the United States Geological Survey's research center (USGS; part of the U.S. government), you can find a wealth of terrain data.

The data is available in several forms, but the standard form is the *Digital Elevation Model* (DEM). DEM-formatted data files have the .dem file extension. Another format in use is the *Digital Terrain Model* (DTM), which uses the .dtm file extension. Finally, a powerful and complex format called *Spatial Data Transfer Standard* (SDTS) also exists but is not in wide use outside of scientific niches. SDTS files are denoted by the .ddf file extension.

In any event, the ground cover information is not included in these various model formats, so you'll need to gather that as well. Again, the USGS comes in handy with its satellite imagery—some of it taken down to a resolution of less than a meter per image pixel.

DEM files provide elevation information for specific coordinates of places on Earth. DEM files can be converted to a format used by game engines called a *height map*. We won't go into detail about how to use DEM data for your game, but you can use several of the resources listed in the appendixes to locate the data and tools needed.

Terrain Modeling

There are basically two approaches that 3D game engines use to model terrain in a 3D world. In both cases 3D polygon models represent terrains.

In the *external* method we include the terrain as just another object in the game world. This method offers much freedom of manipulation. You can rotate the terrain model, skew it, and otherwise subject it to all manner of indignities. All 3D engines support this approach. While flexible, it is usually an inefficient way to render complex large terrains.

The second approach is the *internal* method, where terrain is rendered by special code in the game engine often called a *Terrain Manager*. Using the Terrain Manager approach allows game engine programmers to apply specific memory and performance optimizations to the terrain object, because they can discard unnecessary functions that would be available to general-purpose objects. Because of this, Terrain Manager terrains can sometimes be made larger and more complex than those created using other approaches.

Most 3D engines, like Torque, that use a Terrain Manager also provide terrain generation, manipulation, and editing tools that we can use to create our own terrains. Usually importing height maps is available for terrain generation. Some engines, like Torque, have built-in Terrain Editors that allow the game developer to directly manipulate terrain polygons, within constraints, to create the desired hills, valleys, mountains, and canyons.

Height Maps

Figure 12.2 depicts a height map. As you can see, it's a grayscale image. The 2D coordinates of the height-map image map directly to surface coordinates in the game world. The brightness of each of the pixels in the image represents the altitude at that pixel's location—the brighter the pixel, the higher the elevation. Usually we use an 8-bit-per-pixel format, which means that 256 discrete elevations can be represented.

The concept is an elegant one and not difficult to grasp. If you are familiar with viewing topographic charts and maps, you'll find that height maps have a familiar flavor to them, even though the contour lines are missing. One of the deficiencies of height maps is the resolution (as you can see in Figure 12.2). To represent a geographic locale that is 1 kilometer square, a height map that represents 1 square meter as a pixel needs 1,000 pixels per side, for a total of 1 million pixels—big, but not too large. If I want to increase the terrain area to cover 16 square kilometers (4 kilometers per side), then I need to store 16 million pixels. At 8 bits (or one byte) per pixel, that equals about 16MB of data. If we want to model the terrain for an area that is 10 kilometers per side, we are looking at almost 100MB of storage!

We can, of course, reduce the terrain resolution—let's say, have a pixel equal 4 square meters in the game world. This would chop those 100MB back to 6.25MB. However, that gain is offset by the fact that our terrain will now be blockier and less realistic.

Figure 12.3 shows a terrain model generated from the height map shown in Figure 12.2. In this case MilkShape 3D was used to import the height map and create the terrain object.

Figure 12.2
A terrain height map.

Figure 12.3
A terrain created from a height map.

Terrain Cover

In the simplest sense, *terrain cover* refers to all the stuff that you find on the ground, including

- grass
- flowers
- dirt
- pebbles
- rocks
- trash
- litter
- pavement
- concrete
- moss
- sand
- stone

Obviously this is not a comprehensive list, but it does demonstrate the point.

We represent the terrain cover with textures. Our options for creating these textures are much like those we considered when we created textures for structures in Chapter 11—and the factors that dictate which way to choose are also similar. It boils down to the terrain characteristics in the game that matter to you.

We can also mix terrain cover textures in adjacent areas to portray a particular locale. It's a good idea to develop your own library of generic terrain cover for use in various situations.

Figure 12.4 illustrates some of the possible varieties of terrain cover. From left to right in the top row you can see grass, sand, and an intermixed sand and grass texture. In the bottom row from left to right is dirt, a muddy track, and eroded wet sand.

Tiling

Unless you are going to create specific terrain cover textures for every square inch of terrain, you will end up tiling your terrain cover at some point. All the issues

Figure 12.4
Some example terrain textures.

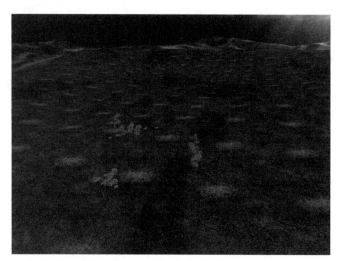

Figure 12.5
A terrain with tiling artifacts.

brought up with tiling in other contexts apply here, such as matching texture edges to get seamless transitions and ensuring lighting in the textures is both appropriate and uniform. Additionally, you should ensure that there are no patterns or marks in the texture that will stand out too much when the texture is repeated.

In Figure 12.5 you can see a repeating light pattern that tends to overpower the otherwise pleasing pastoral scene. (Okay, okay, it *would* be pastoral if a storm wasn't brewing beyond the, um . . . Mountains of Evil in the distance. But besides that . . .)

The culprit in this case is the grass texture used, which is shown in Figure 12.6.

Notice the area of lighter grass, which is quite noticeably different from the rest of the image. When repeated over and over across large swaths of terrain, that feature detracts from the intended overall effect. We can enhance the image to minimize the problem, perhaps with something like that shown in Figure 12.7.

The result is dramatic and the difference is quite obvious, as you can see in Figure 12.8. Now I confess that the texture could be better, but you have to admit that it is light-years ahead of the first version, shown in Figures 12.5 and 12.6.

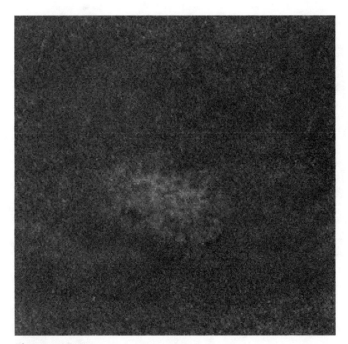

Figure 12.6
A texture with an undesirable feature.

Figure 12.7
A texture without the undesirable feature.

Figure 12.8
The terrain with improved tiled texture.

Creating Terrains

Okay, enough talk. Time for some action—let's create some terrain. We'll use the Torque Engine and its internal Terrain Manager to create the terrain, and we'll employ the height-map method using the in-game Terrain Editor. There is another method, direct manipulation using the Terrain Editor, which we'll use later in Chapter 18.

The Height-Map Method

For this section, you will need to fire up the Gimp. You should be fairly familiar with the basics by now, so I won't hold your hand too much with respect to Gimp operations.

N o t e

The default size for a terrain in Torque (when the `squareSize` property in a MIS mission file is set to 8) is 65,536 *World Units* (WU).

One WU in Torque is equal to one unit in most third-party map editors. A WU is equivalent to one scaled inch (1 WU = 1 inch).

1. Start with a drawing of the contours to create the height-map image. If you have a source for colored contour drawings for a section of land drawn at full scale (1:1), such as shown in Figure 12.9, get one that suits your needs. If not, you can use the images shown here, but in their colored

Figure 12.9
Contour map.

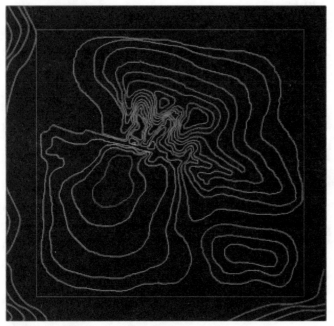

Figure 12.10
Cropped and resized contour map.

format, which you will find at \3D2E\RESOURCES\CH12. Use the files contour1.jpg and contour2.jpg as applicable.

2. Clip out the portion you want, and save it as a PNG image, as shown in Figure 12.10.

3. Now you need to do a little noodling over scale and unit numbers. In Torque each terrain square is made of two terrain triangles sized at 256 WU by 256 WU; as mentioned earlier, the default `squareSize` property in a Torque mission file equals 8 by default. The terrain has

256 of these squares per side for a total of 65,536 world units (inches) per side.

$$256 \text{ WU} \times 256 \text{ squares} = 65,536 \text{ WU(inches)}$$

If we convert the units, we get 5,461.3 feet, or 1,664.6 meters (1.034 miles, or 1.6646 kilometers).

$$65,536 \text{ inches}/12 \text{ inches} = 5,461.33 \text{ feet}$$

$$1 \text{ mile} = 5,280 \text{ feet}$$

$$5,461.33 \text{ feet}/5,280 \text{ feet per mile} = 1.034 \text{ miles}$$

$$1 \text{ mile} = 1,609 \text{ meters}$$

$$1,664.6177 \text{ meters}/1,609 \text{ meters per mile} = 1.035 \text{ miles}$$

The value 8 (for `squareSize`) and the value 65,536 (for terrain size) are not accidental; they are powers of 2. This works nicely with our images as well as the software. The size for our height-map image must be 256 pixels by 256 pixels. This means that when the image is stretched to fit our terrain of 65,536 inches by 65,536 inches, each texture pixel (*texel*) determines the horizontal distance of 256 inches (or 6.5024 meters) of terrain. Because each terrain square is 256 WU, each height-map texel is used to determine the height of one terrain square.

$$256 \text{ pixels} \times 256 \text{ WU (inches)} = 65,536 \text{ WU (inches)}$$

$$256 \text{ inches}/39.37 \text{ inches per meter} = 6.5024 \text{ meters}$$

$$6.5024 \text{ meters} \times 256 \text{ pixels} = 1,664.6144 \text{ meters} = 1.665 \text{ kilometers}$$

$$= 1.035 \text{ miles}$$

4. Based on the preceding calculations, we can get the equivalent area in the image—crop the image just inside the lines of the box I created in the Figure 12.10 drawing representing 1.035 square miles.

5. Resize the image to 256 pixels by 256 pixels.

6. Save the image as a PNG file to preserve the original colors for the contours. In a moment you will paint over this contour image using gray color values representing the heights of the contour lines. In this case the contours range from an elevation of 410 feet to 485 feet. This information is available from the source of the contour maps. The grayscale can be any sequence of gray

Table 12.2 Elevation RGB Values

Elevation	RGB	Index
485	240,240,240	1
480	224,224,224	2
475	208,208,208	3
470	192,192,192	4
465	176,176,176	5
460	160,160,160	6
455	144,144,144	7
450	128,128,128	8
445	112,112,112	9
440	96,96,96	10
435	80,80,80	11
430	64,64,64	12
425	48,48,48	13
420	32,32,32	14
415	16,16,16	15
410	0,0,0	16

RGB values within the 256 colors ranging from 0,0,0 (black) to 255,255,255 (white).

7. Establish your scale keeping in mind that it's best to have some separation between the indexed values so they can be easily seen as you paint the contours. Examination reveals that there are 16 discrete elevations in the contour range of 410 to 485. Divide the 256 colors for the grayscale range by 16, and you will get the values in Table 12.2, which starts at the color (0,0,0) and works up.

Now that we have the values, we need to create what is commonly called an indexed color palette. We need to make a different color entry for each index.

8. With your candidate contour image file open, make sure it is configured to use an indexed color palette by choosing Image, Mode, Indexed. In the dialog box that comes up, just make sure that the Generate optimum palette radio button is checked, that the maximum number of colors is set to 256, and that Color dithering is set to None.

9. Click OK to close the dialog box.

10. Choose Dialogs, Palettes to get the Palettes dialog box up.

11. In the Palettes dialog box, click the New palette button, which is the second button from the left at the bottom of the dialog box. This brings up the Palette Editor.

12. Give your new palette a name by typing it in the edit box at the top of the Palette Editor dialog box.

13. Click the Save button, the first button on the left at the bottom of the Palette Editor. It's a good idea to click this button after you create each new entry, just in case.

Now, for the next little while we will be working in the Palette Editor. To start out, we will create a new entry for our first index.

1. Open the Palette Editor Menu by clicking the menu button—that's the leftward-pointing arrow at the upper right-hand corner of the Palette Editor, to the left of the Close button (the little *x*)—and then choosing Palette Editor Menu.

2. From the Palette Editor Menu, choose New Color from FG. It doesn't matter what color is the FG (*Foreground Color*) at the moment, as long as it contrasts with your background color. We just want to create a new entry. After doing this, you will see a small box in the middle of the editor, at the left end of a long thin rectangle. This is where our colors will be displayed for each index. This smaller rectangle is your first index.

3. Click the first index, and drag and drop it immediately to the right of its position. Another copy of the color will be deposited in the new spot. Keep doing this until you have 16 copies. By happy coincidence, this is exactly how many color entries will fit in that line. If you had made more than 16 copies, then a new line of entries would have been started. But you only need 16, so if you have too many entries, select one, and then click the trash can icon at the bottom to delete it (or right-click it, and select Delete Color).

4. Click the first entry (far left), and click the Edit Color button (third from left at bottom) or right-click the entry and choose Edit Color from the pop-up menu. You will get the (by now) familiar Color dialog box, this time called the Edit Palette Color dialog box.

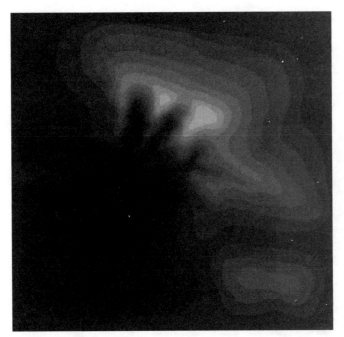

Figure 12.11
Contour map with grayscale values.

5. Enter the RGB (240,240,240) values from Table 12.2 for index 1 into the appropriate edit boxes in the dialog box, and then click OK.

6. Repeat steps 1, 2, 3, and 4 for each of the other 15 indices in the table.

7. Now fill in your image following the contour lines as shown in Figure 12.11. Use a combination of the Brush and Fill tools, at your discretion, to complete the task.

   Notice that in Figure 12.11 the grayscale value is the same at all the edges. This is because we want the edges to match when the terrain repeats itself, if it is tiled—and in this case that's what we will be dealing with. The edges could be different values; you would then just match them at the top and bottom or left and right sides.

8. When you have finished the "paint-by-number" process, convert the image to grayscale by choosing Image, Mode, Grayscale.

9. Save your image as a PNG file.

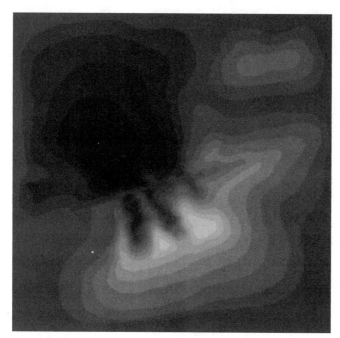

Figure 12.12
Terraced height map.

10. Flip the image around its X-axis—this flips the top with the bottom—by choosing Image, Flip. You should get an image like that in Figure 12.12. Make sure you save your work.

    Notice the terrace effect in Figure 12.12. If you import this into Torque as is, you will have a set of terraced, or stepped, surfaces. If this is what you want, then you're good to go. However, let's go a bit further.

11. Make a copy of the image you just created and continue working now with the copy.

12. Select the entire image.

13. Choose Filters, Blur, Gaussian Blur to smooth out the edges a bit. Use a radius of about 7 for both horizontal and vertical, and then save your changes to this new image as a PNG file. You should get an image much like the one shown in Figure 12.13.

14. You don't need to convert the image back to indexed mode after blurring, because Torque will do the interpolation for you when you import the image to create the terrain.

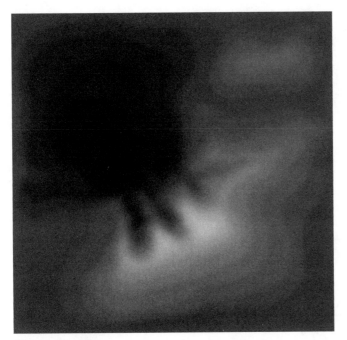

Figure 12.13
Blurred height map.

This last height-map image is the one you will work with to create the terrain. Next, we will import these images into Torque.

15. Place the images in Torque's \3D2E\creator\editor\heightscripts folder as a PNG file. If the folder does not already exist, create it.

16. Run the Torque fps demo.

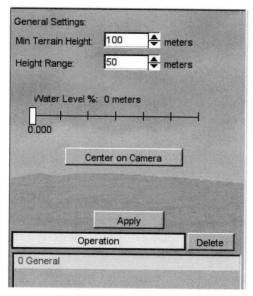

Figure 12.14
World Editor Window menu with Terrain Terraform Editor checked.

Figure 12.15
Terrain Terraform Editor.

17. Press F11 to open the Mission Editor.

18. Choose File, New Mission.

19. Choose Window, Terrain Terraform Editor (as shown in Figure 12.14) to open the Terrain Terraform Editor.

20. On the right side of the screen, in the General Settings area (see Figure 12.15), set Min Terrain Height and Height Range in meters.

Caution

The *maximum* elevation in the terrain we are modeling is to be used for Min Terrain Height. The Min Terrain Height box is mislabeled in the Editor.

You will recall that the highest elevation is 485 feet; this translates to a Min Terrain Height value of approximately 148 meters.

$$485 \text{ feet}/3.281 \text{ feet per meter} = 147.8208 \ (148) \text{ meters}$$

Height Range represents the distance from our lowest to highest elevation. The grayscale color values of our height-map image will be interpolated between these values. We need to calculate the difference and multiply that by the ratio of highest color number divided by total number of grayscale colors (256) and convert to meters. Clear as mud?

485 feet − 410 feet = 75 feet

$240/256 \times 75$ feet = 70.3 feet (240 is our highest color number in Table 12.2)

70.3 feet/3.281 feet per meter = 21.4 (21) meters

21. Now click the Operation box to roll out the Operation dialog box, as shown in Figure 12.16.

22. Select Bitmap from this dialog box—this brings up a bitmap Open File dialog box, as shown in Figure 12.17.

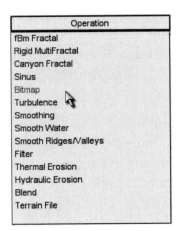

Figure 12.16
The Operation dialog box.

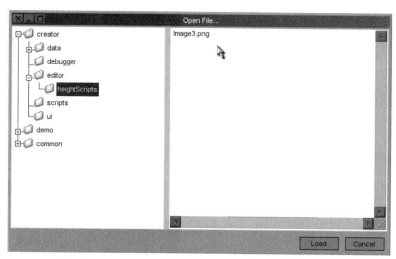

Figure 12.17
The Open File dialog box.

23. Highlight the image you want translated to a new terrain, and click the Load button. You should find the height-map image you saved earlier in \3D2E\creator\editor\heightscripts, from Gimp.

24. Click the Apply button in the panel at upper-right. You will see the terrain change. To relight the scene, choose Edit, Relight Scene. There will be a slight pause in input response while the relighting occurs. If it seems a little drab with terrain cover textures, fret not! We will add some cover later in the chapter.

25. In the lower-left of the screen the overhead map view of the terrain will change to show the contours imported from the height-map image. Notice that this image, as depicted in Figure 12.18, has the same orientation as the original one before we flipped it around the X-axis in step 10 of this list.

    The white lines in the map show the terrain boundary, representing the extents of your terrain before repeating. In the main 3D view, a green translucent box illustrates this boundary, as you can see in Figure 12.19. The terrain boundary is a fixed dimension—you can't change it.

    Figure 12.20 illustrates where to find the inner red box that represents the mission area. You can change the extents of the mission area boundary by using the Mission Editor.

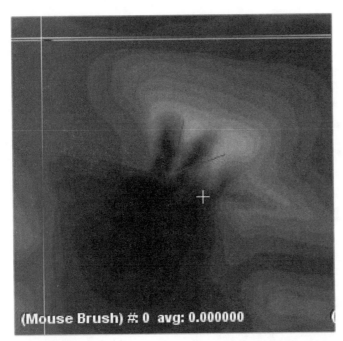

Figure 12.18
The overhead view.

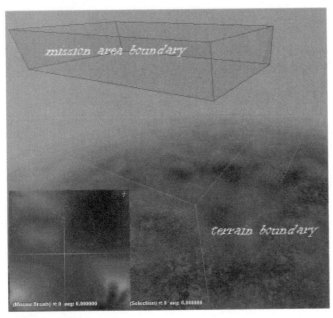

Figure 12.19
The terrain boundary.

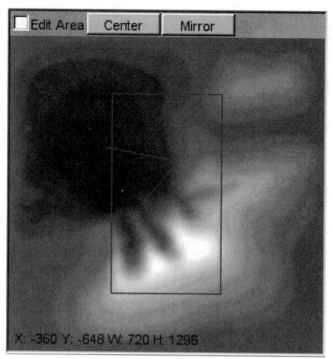

Figure 12.20
The mission area.

26. Choose File, Save As to save your mission with your own unique name. You should save your new file in the directory \3D2E\fps\data\missions.

When you save your mission, the terrain data is also saved as a TER file in the \3D2E\fps\data\missions directory. If you want, you can also import previously saved TER files rather than re-creating height maps.

Note

Reference to the newly created terrain file is stored in the mission file in a `TerrainBlock` that needs to be named "Terrain":

```
new TerrainBlock(Terrain) {
   rotation = "1 0 0 0";
   scale = "1 1 1";
   detailTexture = "~/data/terrains/details/detail1";
   terrainFile = "./myterrain.ter";
   squareSize = "8";
   locked = "true";
   position = "-1024 -1024 0";
};
```

Table 12.3 Terrain Sizes

Terrain Miles	squareSize Meters	Texels + −,total	Texels × 32 = WU		Feet
32	+ −4,096 = 8192	8,192 × 32 = 262,144	21,845.33	4.137	6,658.13
16	+ −2,048 = 4,096	4,096 × 32 = 131,072	10,922.66	2.068	3,329.06
8	+ −1,024 = 2,048	2,048 × 32 = 65,536	5,461.33	1.034	1,664.53
4	+ −512 = 1,024	1,024 × 32 = 32,768	2,730.66	0.517	832.26
2	+ −256 = 512	512 × 32 = 16,384	1,365.33	0.258	416.13

Establishing Terrain Sizes

The units displayed in the Mission Editor Map (x,y,w,h) represent the (x,y) distance of the upper-left corner of the mission area (in red) from the image center and the (w,h) width and height of the area in terrain texture units. Note that the position parameter in the mission file also uses the terrain texture units to position one terrain repetition. There are 32 repetitions of the terrain textures (don't confuse these with the height-map images), with each terrain texture image being 256 pixels by 256 pixels.

$$32 \text{ reps} \times 256 \text{ pixels} = 2,048 \text{ texture units}$$
$$65,536 \text{ WU}/2,048 \text{ texture units} = 32 \text{ WU per texel}$$

This information will be useful when you create terrain textures. Convert these values to inches by multiplying by 32. (The total area represented ranges from −1,024 to +1,024 when the terrain squareSize=8 for a total 2,048. And 2,048 × 32 = 65,536.)

If your contour area needs to be other than 1.034 miles, you can change the terrain square-Size. This will determine the area available before the terrain repeats. As you can see in Table 12.3, you must adjust the squareSize parameter in powers of 2.

Changing the terrain squareSize in the mission file also affects the control in the Terrain Editor and terrain material painter; you will have more control at smaller sizes. Be sure to change the position values of the terrain to correspond to the worldSize also. For example, if you want more control of the terrain editing, set the squareSize to 4 and the position to −512 −512 0:

```
new TerrainBlock(Terrain) {
    rotation = "1 0 0 0";
    scale = "1 1 1";
    detailTexture = "~/data/terrains/details/detail1";
    terrainFile = "./myterrain.ter";
    squareSize = "4";
    locked = "true";
    position = "-512 -512 0";
};
```

Applying Terrain Cover

Terrain textures must be PNG format images and must be 256 pixels by 256 pixels in size. These textures should be placed in a subdirectory under \3D2E\fps\data\terrains; they will also work directly in the terrains folder.

Terrain textures are stretched to 2,048 WU if the terrain squareSize is 8. This means there are 32 repetitions of a terrain texture across one terrain width or depth (1 terrain rep). This also means there are 8 WU per texture pixel (texel).

$$65,536 \text{ WU}/32 \text{ texture reps} = 2,048 \text{ WU per texture rep}$$
$$2,048 \text{ WU}/256 \text{ pixels} = 8 \text{ WU per texel}$$

If the terrain squareSize is set to 4 in the mission file, there will still be 32 terrain texture repetitions, but each repetition will only cover 1,024 WU of the terrain.

And although not a requirement, terrain cover textures will look best when they are created to be tiled, as discussed earlier; opposite edges should match so that when they are tiled you won't be able to see the edges. The images in Figures 12.21 and 12.22 are test textures that are 256 pixels by 256 pixels. The checkerboard pattern in Figure 12.21 has each white or black section sized at 128 pixels by 128 pixels.

Figure 12.21
Checkerboard texture.

Figure 12.22
Grid texture.

The grid texture in Figure 12.22 has white lines every 32 pixels and red lines at 128 pixels. You can use these images to calculate the total terrain size with respect to the dimensions of objects created in a map editor as well as to calculate the terrain square size with respect to terrain textures. In addition, you can use the image in Figure 12.22 to create sight lines when manually adjusting terrain heights.

To paint the terrain cover, follow these steps:

1. Place these images in a subdirectory under \3D2E\demo\data\terrains.

2. Use the Run fps Demo shortcut to launch Torque.

3. Select the mission you created in the previous section.

4. Press the F8 function key to switch to "fly" mode.

5. Fly up above the terrain a bit using the arrow keys to move and the mouse to aim and look down. You can use F7 to switch out of fly mode when you want.

Figure 12.23
World Editor Window menu with Terrain Texture Painter checked.

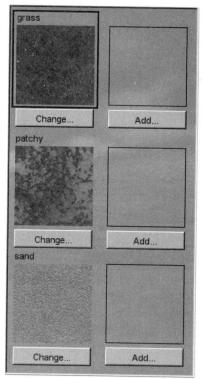

Figure 12.24
Material Selection dialog box.

6. Press F11 to open the World and Terrain Editor.

7. Choose Window, Terrain Texture Painter, as shown in Figure 12.23.

   You will now see the Material Selection dialog box (as shown in Figure 12.24) to the right. You can highlight the material you want to paint with, or you can change or add new textures here.

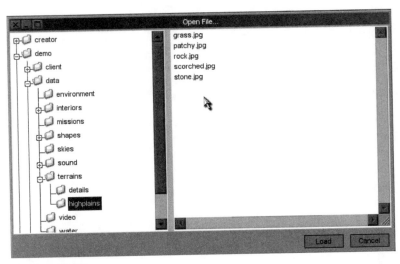

Figure 12.25
Image Open File dialog box.

8. To add a new material, click an Add or Change button, and you will get a new texture image Open File dialog box, as shown in Figure 12.25.

9. Browse your way to \3D2E\demo\data\terrains\highplains and choose a texture image file that appeals to you.

10. Highlight the file you want and click the Load button. The image in that file is now in your selection set.

11. From the Action pull-down menu, make sure Paint Material is checked as shown in Figure 12.26.

12. Now go up to the Brush pull-down menu, and select your desired brush size, as depicted in Figure 12.27.

Remember that we are using the default terrain squareSize set to 8. Table 12.4 lists the area of the terrain that is influenced based on brush size.

Figure 12.28 depicts a texture applied with the brush size set to 1, and Figure 12.29 is a depiction of the corresponding terrain grid geometry.

You can see the 32 by 32 texel influence area for one brush that corresponds to 256 WU for the terrain squares shown in the grid view.

So take your trusty Terrain Paint Brush and go nuts!

Figure 12.26
Paint Material in Action menu.

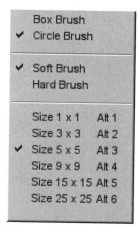

Figure 12.27
Brush options in Brush menu.

Table 12.4 Brush Sizes

Brush Size	Texels	World Units (texels × squareSize)
1	$1 \times 32 = 32$	$32 \times 8 = 256$
3	$3 \times 32 = 96$	$96 \times 8 = 768$
5	$5 \times 32 = 160$	$160 \times 8 = 1,280$
9	$9 \times 32 = 288$	$288 \times 8 = 2,304$
15	$15 \times 32 = 480$	$480 \times 8 = 3,840$
25	$25 \times 32 = 800$	$800 \times 8 = 6,400$

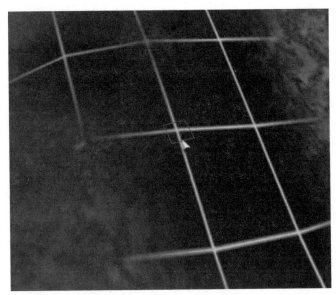

Figure 12.28
Painting terrain with a brush size set to 1.

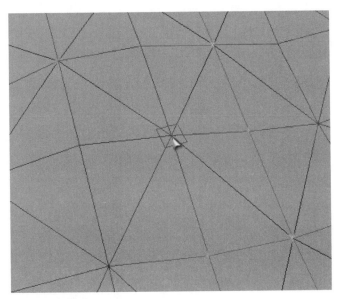

Figure 12.29
Depiction of terrain grid with a brush size set to 1.

Moving Right Along

So, now we understand why terrains need to be modeled and what our options are for obtaining real-world terrain data. If we aren't modeling a real location, we've seen how we can create our own imaginary terrain using the Gimp, so that we can satisfy the needs of our game. We also looked at terrain cover and how to create images for use as terrain cover.

Furthermore, we learned about some of the visual anomalies, like terrain tiling seams, which might make our terrains less pleasing, and how we can go about fixing those issues.

Earlier in the chapter Figure 12.8 showed an example of a finished terrain, with some hills in the distance and terrain cover applied.

In the next chapter we'll learn a pair of new tools, MilkShape and UVMapper.

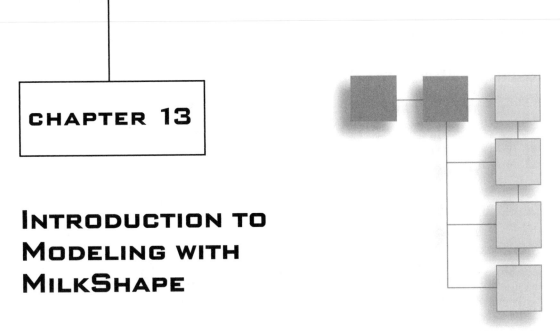

CHAPTER 13

Introduction to Modeling with MilkShape

In this and the following chapters, we will be delving into the world of low-poly modeling. We'll talk about techniques and methods that can be applied to other tools, such as the expensive 3D Max or Maya, but the practical focus will be geared toward using MilkShape, UVMapper, and other low-cost tools that are included on the accompanying CD.

MilkShape 3D

In Chapter 9 we created a skin for a simple soup can—remember that? Well, in this chapter we're going to create the model and skin it with the texture you created earlier, only this time we will go beyond just the simple soup can. But first, let's start at the beginning and learn a bit about MilkShape.

MilkShape 3D is a great low-cost low-poly 3D modeling tool created by a fellow named Mete Ciragan. Like most successful shareware applications it has evolved over the years, as Mete added features requested by his user community. He also added the capability for users to create their own plug-ins to provide additional features and import-export filters.

MilkShape is not as complex as the more expensive tools, but that does not in any way imply that it is not a capable program, especially in the low-poly world that computer games inhabit. In fact, the stripped-down nature of MilkShape certainly makes it easier to learn than most of the "big boys."

Installing MilkShape 3D

If you want to install only MilkShape 3D from the enclosed CD, do the following:

1. Browse to your CD in the \3D2E\TOOLS\MILKSHAPE 3D directory. (By the way, MS3D is the abbreviated form for MilkShape 3D. You might encounter it from time to time.)

2. Locate the ms3d179.zip file, and double-click it to unzip it. The setup program should automatically run.

3. Click the Next button for the Welcome screen.

4. Follow the various screens, and take the default options for each one, unless you know you have a specific reason to do otherwise.

The MilkShape 3D GUI

If you look at Figure 13.1, you can readily see that the MilkShape working environment, or window, is divided into three areas: the menu, the views, and the toolbox.

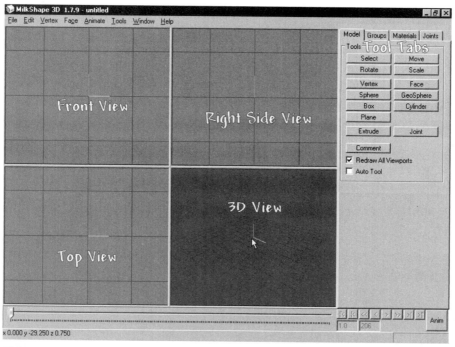

Figure 13.1
MilkShape 3D.

If you only have three views in your window when you first run MilkShape, choose Window, Viewports, 4 Window, and you should get something close to what you see in Figure 13.1.

In Figure 13.1 there are four places where the model can be seen. Each of these is what MilkShape calls a *window*. We will call them *frames* in this book, because as you probably already know, MilkShape itself is in a window.

A *view* is the angle or direction at which you look at an object. For example, if you stand in front of an object and look at it, you are seeing the *Front view*. From above, it is the *Top view*.

A *viewport* is the little frame inside the MilkShape window in which a view of a model is presented.

Thus in Figure 13.1 the 3D *view* is in the 3D *viewport*, located in the lower-right *frame* in the MilkShape *window*.

You'll notice in Figure 13.1 that I've labeled the different views. This is the way you should use your views for models that you create for Torque. Other applications and games may require your models to be oriented differently.

Three of the views are wire-frame–only views; they enable you to look at your model from directly above, directly in front, and the right-hand side. The fourth view is a 3D view in which you can rotate your model various ways and view it as a wire-frame, shaded, or fully textured model with lighting cues.

Figure 13.2 shows the tools available in the toolbox section. Although some tools for different operations are only available in the menus, most of the time you will be working with the tools in the toolbox.

Navigating in Views

In the wire-frame views, you can move the view around by holding down the Ctrl key and clicking and dragging in the window.

If you hold down the Shift key and drag the mouse while in Move mode, you can zoom in or out. Be careful though—if you are in Select mode (from the Model tab), then drag-move won't work. With practice you can master this drag-move and it will become quite useful. In all other modes the shift-drag action will always zoom the view in or out with no alternation.

If you have a wheel mouse, then the wheel can be used to zoom in or out. You will have to click in the view to get focus into the view before the zoom will work.

The 3D view allows the view movement in the same ways as the other views, except the wheel mouse zoom works backward.

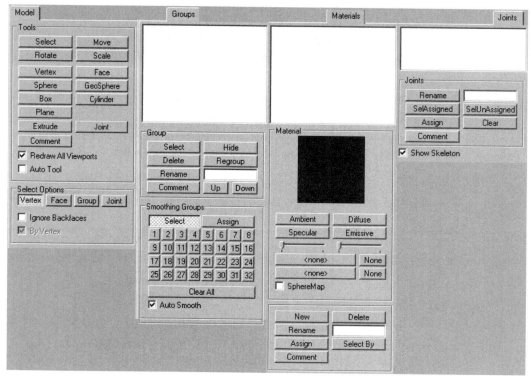

Figure 13.2
The toolbox contents.

View Scale and Orientation

When you are viewing an object from the front in MilkShape, the Y-axis is positive going up, the X-axis is positive going to the right, and the Z-axis is positive going to the front. This makes it a right-handed coordinate system.

If you look at the Right Side view (the view at the upper right of the four), you will see in the center the axis "bugs" for the Y- and Z-axes. Although it is not visible in the black-and-white pictures in this book, the Y-axis line is cyan, and the Z-axis line is magenta. The place where these two lines meet is the (0,0,0) coordinate in object space. Hold your mouse cursor over the first grid line above the (0,0,0) location, and look down to the lower-left corner of the MilkShape window while keeping your cursor over that grid line. You should see the Y-axis value at about 20.0 or so (see Figure 13.3. If you see something like 20.005 or 19.885, that's good enough. If you don't see 20.0 or so, zoom the view in or out

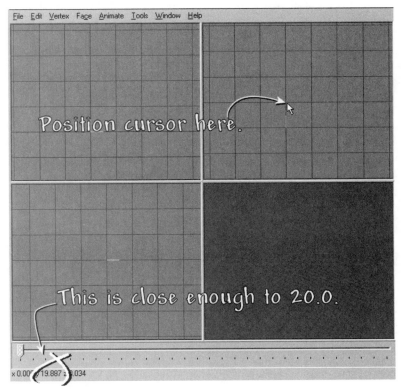

Figure 13.3
Checking the zoom in the Right Side view.

until you do. Adjust your other two wire-frame views to the same scale. If you position your cursor one grid line directly above the (0,0,0) point on the Front view (upper left), you should see the 20.0 or so also for the Y value, but for the Top view, the same relative positioning will be affected in the Z-axis.

Figure 13.4 contains various notations to help you understand the coordinate display system. In this figure I've left in MilkShape's viewport labels above each viewport's frame in order to illustrate the variation that emerges with the Torque Right Side view being seen in MilkShape's Left viewport.

The whole point of this little exercise is to expose you to the coordinate display and to ensure that your layout matches the one we'll be working with here. Of course, at times when you zoom in and out this might change, but now you have a method of recalibrating when necessary.

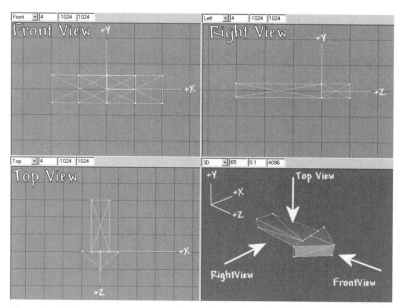

Figure 13.4
Torque-oriented object in the MilkShape viewports.

The Soup Can Revisited

Now that you have a bit of a grasp of what you are looking at in the GUI and how to move your views around to look at your model, we'll move on to actually creating a quick model to get your feet wet. There's nothing like doing for learning!

Creating the Basic Shape

A closed can is a cylinder. A cylinder is what we call a *primitive* shape, like a sphere or a cube. The primitives are added together in various ways to build up more complex shapes.

1. Choose the Model tab in the toolbox.

2. Click Cylinder.

3. Position your cursor in the Right Side view about three grid lines above (0,0,0) and one grid line to the left. Click and drag down and to the right until your object looks like Figure 13.5.

4. Choose the Groups tab. You will see a single group named cylinder01 (it may be a higher number if you made other cylinders and deleted them—MilkShape just adds 1 to the number at the end during its auto-naming).

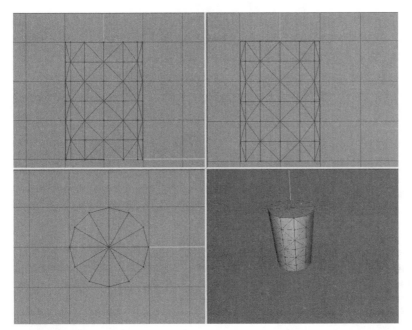

Figure 13.5
Making a cylinder.

5. Click the group name to highlight it, if it isn't already, and then type **can** in the box to the right of the Rename button where it says "Cylinder01".

6. Click Rename, and the group will now be called "can".

7. Choose the Materials tab.

8. Click New.

9. Type **label** into the Materials Rename box.

10. Click Rename.

11. In the Material frame of the Materials tab you will see two buttons labeled "<none>". These are the texture buttons. The top one assigns the standard texture, and the bottom one enables you to assign a texture whose alpha channel you want to use for this material.

12. Click the top texture button. You will get a file dialog box.

13. Browse your way to \3D2E\RESOURCES\CH9, and double-click the can.jpg file.

14. Now choose the Groups tab again, and make sure your cylinder's group is selected in the list. If your can is not already highlighted in red, click Select. You will see your can highlighted in red in the three wire-frame views.

15. While your can is still selected, switch back to the Materials tab, choose your new material in the list, and click Assign.

Tip

If your screen resolution is set to 800 × 600 or less, you will not be able to see the entire Assign or Select By buttons. The top one-quarter or so of those buttons is just visible on the lower-right corner. Assign is located below the Rename button, and Select By is located below the edit box that is to the right of the Rename button.

16. Right-click in the 3D view, and choose Textured. Your can should appear with the texture wrapped around it, like in Figure 13.6. You might have to turn off Wireframe overlay mode by right-clicking on the 3D view and choosing the Wireframe overlay item to toggle it off.

17. Save your work so far as mynewcan.ms3d somewhere, by choosing File, Save As.

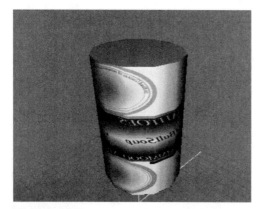

Figure 13.6
Assigned texture.

18. In preparation for UV unwrapping the can object, choose File, Export, Wavefront Obj, and export the file to \3D2E\RESOURCES\CH9 \mynewcan.obj.

Okay, so we have the soup can made, and we've assigned the texture to it. The reason the texture doesn't fit right yet is because the texture coordinates haven't been mapped to the object yet. That's our next step.

UV Unwrapping the Can

In Chapter 9 we encountered some of the theory and process behind UV unwrapping and mapping. In a later section in this chapter we'll go into more theory, as well as more detail about the UVMapper tool. For our purposes at the moment, we just want to get the texture skin mapped correctly onto the can.

Whether the skins are created before the object or the object is created first will probably change from project to project or even from phase to phase within a project. At this point in the book, we already have a skin—can.jpg—so we want to make sure the can will unwrap to match the skin. This isn't a problem in this case. It may be a problem with other projects though, so be aware of that possibility.

1. Using Windows Explorer, browse your way to \3D2E\\TOOLS\UVMAP-PER, then locate and launch UVMapper.exe.

2. Maximize the window when it opens.

3. Find the file you exported, \3D2E\RESOURCES\CH9\mynewcan.obj, and open it.

4. You will see an alert listing some statistics about the object. Click OK.

5. You will see a bunch of triangles fill your window. Ignore them for the moment.

6. Choose Edit, New UV Map, Cylindrical Cap. You will get a Cylindrical Cap Mapping dialog box.

7. Click OK. You will then get a layout of the can's triangles (like that in Figure 13.7), with a rectangular block of triangles across the middle and a circle of triangles at both top and bottom.

8. Choose File, Save Model. The OBJ Export Options dialog box then appears.

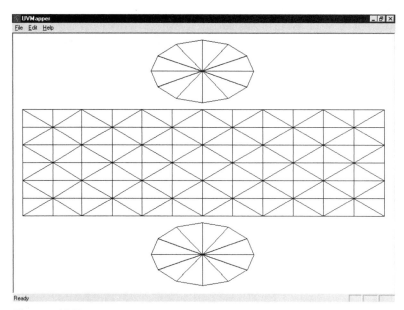

Figure 13.7
Unwrapping the can in UVMapper.

9. Set the options boxes as shown in Table 13.1, and click OK.

10. Replace the OBJ file \3D2E\RESOURCES\CH9\mynewcan.obj by saving over it.

11. Choose File, Save Texture Map. The BMP Export Options dialog box appears.

12. Set the options to the values shown in Table 13.2.

13. Save to the file name \3D2E\RESOURCES\CH9\mynewcan.bmp. This is the texture map, or UV mapping template, for your can.

14. Switch back to MilkShape.

15. Ensure that the can group is selected by choosing the Groups tab, and clicking on the can group in the list, then clicking the Select button.

16. Click the Delete button. You will replace this object with the one you exported from UVMapper.

17. Choose File, Import, Wavefront Obj, and import the mynewcan.obj file you saved from UVMapper.

Table 13.1 UVMapper OBJ Export Options Values

Value	Option
clear	Export As Single Group
set	Export Normals
set	Export UV Coordinates
clear	Flip Texture (UV) Coordinates Vertically
clear	Flip Texture (UV) Coordinates Horizontally
clear	Reverse Winding Order
clear	Invert Normals
clear	Swap Coordinates Y and Z
set	Export Materials
set	Export UVMapper Regions
clear	Export Using Rotation Settings
clear	Don't Export Linefeeds (Mac compatible)
clear	Don't Compress Texture Coordinates

Table 13.2 UVMapper BMP Export Options Values

Value	Option
512	Bitmap Size—Width
512	Bitmap Size—Height
clear	Flip Texture Map Vertically
clear	Flip Texture Map Horizontally
clear	Exclude Hidden Facets

18. On the Groups tab, click on your new object (mynewcan.obj), then click the Select button. You can also rename it if you like.

19. With the new object selected, choose the Materials tab.

Caution

After importing the .obj file from UVMapper into MilkShape, you might discover another copy of the material in the Materials list. If so, delete the second entry. This appears to be a minor bug in UVMapper. The second copy of the material doesn't have any textures assigned to it. If you only have one material, and it has the proper texture assigned to it, then leave it alone.

20. Choose the label material, and then click Assign.

21. Your texture should appear on the can in the 3D view, wrapped correctly.

22. If no texture appears, click in the 3D window to force an update.

23. If there is still no texture, make sure that you have the 3D window still set to Textured, by right-clicking in the 3D window and checking the menu. Save your work now.

Enhancing the Soup Can Model

Have a seat and stew on that for a while. When you are done, we'll carry on and start hammering at the soup can and improve the model.

How about we open the can up? The can model has a top and a bottom. We want to leave the bottom where it is and flip the top lid up.

First we need to separate the lid from the can.

1. Choose the Model tab, and click Select in the Tools area.

2. In the Select Options area, click Vertex, and select all the vertices at the bottom of the can, as shown in Figure 13.8. Use either the Side view or the Front view, and make sure that Ignore Backfaces is not checked.

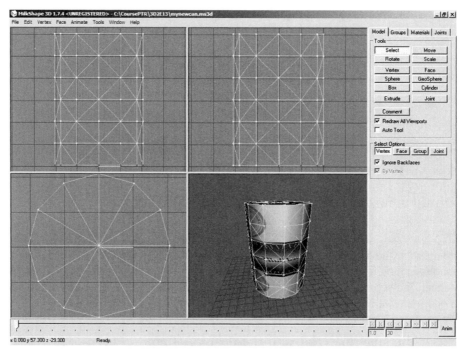

Figure 13.8
Selecting the bottom vertices.

3. From the menu bar, choose Edit, Hide Selection. The dots of the vertices will disappear. This means that none of the vertices for the bottom face are selectable.

4. Now in the Model tab, in the Select Options area, click Face. Make sure that By Vertex is checked.

5. In the Top view, select the vertex in the center of the can, as in Figure 13.9. Because you had hidden the bottom vertices, only the single center vertex for the top of the can has been selected. And because you are actually selecting faces by vertex, then all the top lid faces—and only those faces—have been selected.

6. In the Groups tab, click Regroup. This will create a new mesh with only the faces from the top of the can. The mesh will be named "Regroup01". Rename this mesh to "lid" in the same manner that you did earlier when you renamed the cylinder mesh to "can".

7. Switch back to the Model tab. Your lid mesh should still be selected.

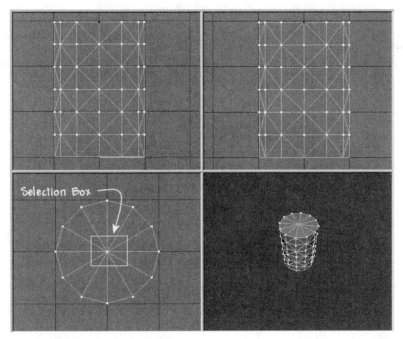

Figure 13.9
Selecting the center vertex.

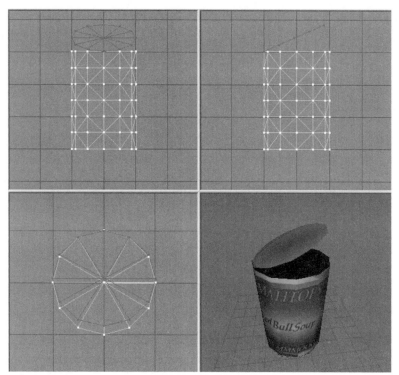

Figure 13.10
The can with lid opened.

8. Click the Move button, and then click and drag in the Side view to move the lid up and to one side from the rest of the can.

9. Click the Rotate button, and then click and drag in the Side view to rotate the lid as if you were bending the lid back (see Figure 13.10).

10. If necessary, repeat step 8 to position the lid properly. You might have to adjust it in one of the other views, depending on how you initially moved the lid.

11. Choose the Groups tab, and click Regroup. The lid faces will now be part of their own group.

12. Choose Edit, Duplicate Selection. Another copy of the lid will be made in exactly the same location as the original.

13. From the menu bar, choose Face, Reverse Vertex Order. This will invert the normals of the lid's faces, making it viewable from the other direction. You

will recall that the normal of a face is, in the simplest terms, the direction that a face is facing.

14. On the Groups tab, add the original lid to your selection by clicking on the first lid group and then clicking the Select button in the group area.

15. Select Vertex, Weld Together. The original lid is viewable from one side, and the copy is viewable from the other. They now share the exact same vertices.

    If you rotate your can in the 3D view, you'll see that your lid now has the lid part of the skin on both sides. You'll also notice that the inside of the can is black. This is because no faces are normalized to the interior, just as the lid at first did not have any faces normalized on the side.

Tip

You may be wondering why you didn't have to assign a material to the new faces you created with the Duplicate command. What happened is that when you grouped the original faces and the new faces together, the material that was assigned to the original lid faces was automatically assigned to the new group.

16. Repeat the preceding steps, but this time create, for the can body, a set of faces that are normalized to the interior instead of the exterior, and then group them together. You can use your UV mapping and the Gimp skills to create a more realistic metallic interior to the can, instead of just repeating the exterior skin on the inside.

17. Save your work—you never know when a nice can of soup may be needed for dipping your towel in!

So, here we are. You've made a model of an object, using a couple of shape primitives. And you've learned how to make double-sided textures, rotate and move meshes (or groups), and assign skins. Feel free to explore your new capabilities. Poke around and try out the other primitives.

Menus

MilkShape can perform many more features and operations than what we've just gone over. In later chapters you'll learn how to make more difficult and

Figure 13.11
The File menu.

challenging shapes, like player-characters, vehicles, and weapons. In this chapter we'll take a look at the program itself in more detail.

Most but not all the menus have shortcuts assigned to the keys. Typically, the ones that are used the most do have shortcuts. If you want to add your own shortcut, you can use a plug-in to do that. We'll cover that when we discuss the Tools menu.

File

As in most Windows programs, operations in the File menu (see Figure 13.11) relate either to the creation and saving of files or to making global alterations to the current file's properties or contents. See Table 13.3 for more detail.

Edit

The MilkShape Edit menu (see Figure 13.12) contains commands that assist the user when modifying models. It does not have Cut, Copy, or Paste but does offer commands in a similar vein for duplicating, hiding, and selecting objects. See Table 13.4 for more detail.

Vertex

You can perform a number of operations on vertices in a model. They are available through the Vertex menu (see Figure 13.13). In most cases you will need

Table 13.3 MilkShape File Menu

Command	Description
New	Creates a new blank workspace. If the current workspace is not empty, then the user is prompted to save changes or continue without saving. Only one workspace can be open at a time.
Open	Opens an existing MS3D-formatted file using the standard Open dialog box.
Save	Saves the current workspace as an MS3D file, providing that the current workspace has a name. If the workspace is unnamed, then the command will behave like Save As.
Save As	Requires the user to specify a new file name under which to save the workspace contents.
Merge	Merges together two MS3D documents: the current workspace and another workspace selected from a file.
Import	Presents a submenu of file import plug-ins. This command works like the Open command, once an import plug-in is selected, except that some plug-ins offer import options in a user dialog box.
Export	Presents a submenu of file export plug-ins. This command works like the Open command, once an import plug-in is selected, except that some plug-ins offer additional export-specific options in a user dialog box.
Preferences	Presents the Preferences dialog box. This allows the user to set definable global application attributes and behaviors.
Recent Files	Presents a list of the four most recently used files. Choosing from this list allows the user to quickly open recently used files without having to repeatedly browse around the hard drive.
Exit	Exits the MilkShape program. The user is prompted to save changes if there are any that haven't been saved.

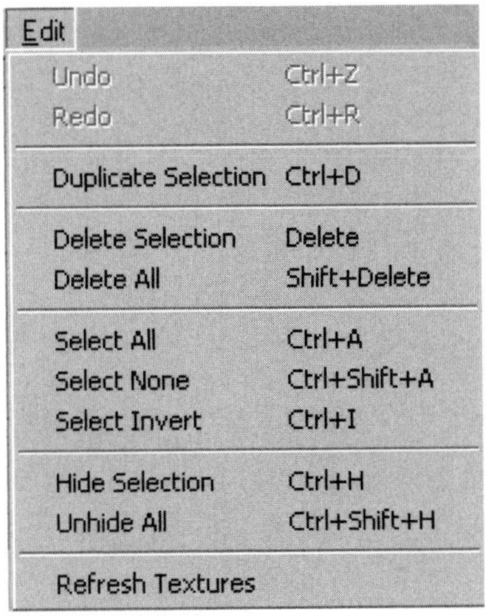

Figure 13.12
The Edit menu.

Table 13.4 MilkShape Edit Menu

Command	Description
Undo	Reverts the workspace back to the state it was in before the last user operation.
Redo	Reverts the workspace back to the state it was in before the Undo operation.
Duplicate Selection	Duplicates all selected objects in place. This command selects the new duplicates and deselects the previously selected objects.
Delete Selection	Deletes the currently selected objects.
Delete All	Deletes all objects in the workspace regardless of their selection state.
Select All	Selects al objects in the workspace.
Select None	Deselects all objects in the workspace.
Select Invert	Deselects all objects that were selected, and selects all unselected objects.
Hide Selection	Hides the selected object from view. You can also do this to groups using the Group tab in the toolbox.
Unhide All	All objects in the workspace are shown.
Refresh Textures	Reloads all textures used in materials from disk.

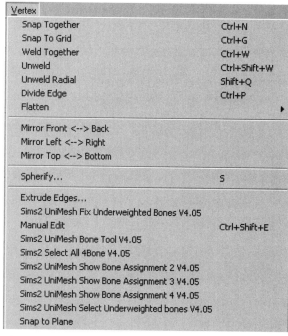

Figure 13.13
The Vertex menu.

Table 13.5 MilkShape Vertex Menu

Command	Description
Snap Together	Snaps all the selected vertices together. The middle point between all selected vertices becomes the new location for the vertices.
Snap To Grid	Moves all selected vertices to be in line with the smallest grid X, Y, and Z position (to see the smallest grid positions, zoom all the way in). The grid size can be changed using the File, Preferences menu.
Weld Together	Creates one vertex at a precise point where several vertices exist. Only selected vertices are welded together. This is the way you would join a seam of two or more abutting faces.
Unweld	Splits each selected vertex into multiple vertices. The number of vertices created depends on the number of faces the original individual vertices were bound to. For example, a vertex with three faces attached will be split into three vertices.
Unweld Radial	Is the same as Unweld but will also shift the unwelded vertices away from each other in a circular pattern. The vertices will move from the origin at which they were unwelded by half the distance from the origin to the nearest edge.
Divide Edge	Divides a face between two selected vertices into two faces. The procedure will only work with two vertices selected. This has no effect on vertices without any faces in common.
Flatten	Presents a submenu for the user to align all selected vertices to the same point on the X, Y, or Z plane. This is similar to Snap Together, but it works on only one axis instead of all three.
Mirror Front <--> Back	Mirrors, or flips, the currently selected object along the Z-axis.
Mirror Left <--> Right	Mirrors, or flips, the currently selected object along the X-axis.
Mirror Top <--> Bottom	Mirrors, or flips, the currently selected object along the Y-axis.
Spherify	Calculates a bounding sphere, and attempts to place the selected vertices on the surface of the sphere. It can be constrained in all three dimensions, and the bounds can be manually set.
Extrude Edges	Allows the extrusion of polygon edges.
Manual Edit	Allows the exact placement of one selected vertex with floating point accuracy in the X, Y, and Z planes.
Snap to Plane	Snaps all selected vertices (four or more, typically) to a common plane, which is the calculated average plane of all planes of the selected vertices.

to ensure that you've selected only vertices in a model or at least have the selection mode set to Vertex. See Table 13.5 for more detail.

Face

The Face menu (see Figure 13.14) provides commands for manipulating triangles and faces in the workspace. See Table 13.6 for more detail.

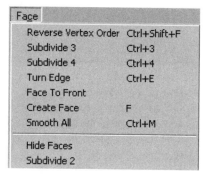

Figure 13.14
The Face menu.

Table 13.6 MilkShape Face Menu

Command	Description
Reverse Vertex Order	Changes the order of the vertex winding, which changes (negates) the normal of the face. This will turn a face inside or outside depending on its current vertex order. Counterclockwise vertex winding creates an outward face on an object.
Subdivide 3	Divides each selected face by three, creating three faces out of one.
Subdivide 4	Divides each selected face by four, creating four faces out of one.
Turn Edge	Operates on two triangles with a common edge. The common edge is removed, and a new edge is created between the two vertices (one from each triangle) that weren't previously joined by an edge.
Face To Front	Is used on selected faces to change all vertex orders to counterclockwise, outward-facing vertex ordering, or *winding*.
Create Face	Simplifies automatic creation of a face using three vertices (different from the Faces tool).
Smooth All	Corrects the normals of all faces after creation of a model, so that the normal angles change evenly from face to face.
Hide Faces	Hides faces of perspective views using a dialog box.
Subdivide 2	Divides each selected face by two, creating two faces out of one.

Animate

The Animate menu (see Figure 13.15) is used to manipulate animation frames in the model via the Keyframer. See Table 13.7 for more detail.

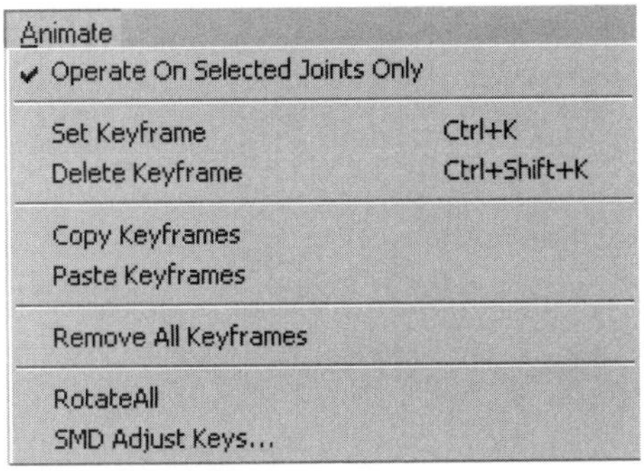

Figure 13.15
The Animate menu.

Table 13.7 MilkShape Animate Menu

Command	Description
Operate On Selected Joints Only	When this menu item is toggled on (checked), then only the joints that are currently selected will have their pose data stored for the current keyframe.
Set Keyframe	This stores the pose of the skeleton to the current keyframe (whichever keyframe that's in the keyframe number box).
Delete Keyframe	This removes the stored skeleton pose from the current keyframe.
Copy Keyframes	This copies the skeleton pose from the current keyframe. In order for the copy action to perform correctly, the user must first select the skeleton in the keyframe to be copied from.
Paste Keyframes	This pastes the copied skeleton pose to the current keyframe. After the keyframe has been pasted, you need to immediately set the keyframe in order to preserve the skeleton pose.
Remove All Keyframes	This removes all stored skeleton poses at all keyframes in the animation timeline. This is effectively the same as deleting the animation.
Rotate All	This rotates all stored skeleton poses at all keyframes in the animation timeline.
SMD Adjust Keys	This adjusts the keys in SMD type of animations.

Tools

The Tools menu (see Figure 13.16) provides access to both built-in tools and user plug-in tools. The functions available are not the same as those available in the toolbox. This is a potential source of confusion. See Table 13.8 for more detail about the Tools menu.

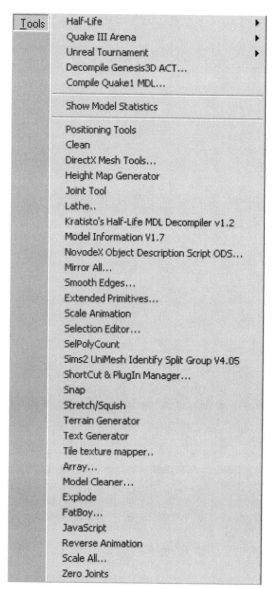

Figure 13.16
The Tools menu.

MilkShape Plug-Ins

There is quite a large list of MilkShape plug-ins that extend MilkShape's capabilities. For information about where to find them to download, tutorials about how to use them, and the names of the individual creators, see Appendix C, "Shareware and Freeware Tools." The plug-ins that were known at the time of this writing are listed; some plug-ins are import or export filters for

Table 13.8 MilkShape Tools Menu

Command	Description
Half-Life	This command contains several options used to create and save Half-Life models.
Quake III Arena	This command saves a Quake III control file to the directory you specify in the Save As dialog box.
Unreal Tournament	This command contains options for creating male and female skeletons using the default Unreal Tournament skeleton configurations.
Decompile Genesis3D ACT	This command allows you to decompile an ACT model used by the Genesis3D engine.
Compile Quake1 MDL	This command will compile a Quake 1 MDL file, used in the Quake 1 engine.
Show Model Statistics	This command brings up a statistics window showing useful statistics, such as the number of faces and vertices in the workspace.
(assorted plug-ins)	The list of plug-in tools available is user-configurable using the Shortcut and Plug-In Manager. Not all plug-ins are distributed with MilkShape. See the MilkShape sidebar for descriptions of currently available plug-ins. To get the most up-to-date information about plug-ins, visit chUmbaLum sOft's Web site: http://www.swissquake.ch/chumbalum-soft.

different file formats and aren't included here, except for the Torque DTSPlus Exporter, because we use it in this book (the standard Torque Game Engine DTS Exporter, and the Wavefront OBJ Importer and Exporter are built into MilkShape).

- **ms2dtsExporterPlus.** This plug-in exports models, animations, and materials to DTS model format for use with the Torque Engine. This plug-in appears in the File, Export menu.

- **ms2DTSExporterPlus.** This is an *advanced* plug-in for exporting models, animations, and materials to DTS model format for use with the Torque Engine. This plug-in appears in the File, Export menu. It supports sequence file exporting, texture animations, trigger frames, and more.

- **msSelectionEditor.** This plug-in edits the selection from a 3D view. There are a lot of options, and you can read some detailed information about it here.

- **msTimer.** This plug-in lets you time how long you've been working on a certain model.

- **msEdgeExtrude.** This plug-in lets you extrude edges in addition to faces.

- **msJointTool.** This plug-in allows you to add joints in the middle of the hierarchy, unlink a joint from a hierarchy, and assign vertices to the closest joint (some kind of "Assign Mesh to Skeleton" tool).

- **msSnap.** This plug-in snaps not only to 1.0, but it also snaps joints.

- **msToolArray.** This plug-in duplicates objects and then places the duplicates in 3D space according to user specifications.

- **msVertexPlane.** This plug-in is similar to the Vertex, Flatten command, except that it snaps selected vertices to a plane instead of a single point.

- **msToolFatBoy.** This plug-in will make your model fatter or thinner. This is useful for tweaking player and monster characters.

- **msOperationMirrorAll.** This plug-in will mirror everything about your model over the selected plane: bones, mesh, animation—everything.

- **msToolReverseAnimation.** This plug-in will reverse the order of the keyframes in whatever animation you have loaded.

- **msToolScaleAll.** This plug-in applies scale to all objects in the workspace at once.

- **msSelPolyCount.** This plug-in shows the selected polygon, vertex, and unique vertex counts, as well as how many polygons there are per group.

- **msBridge.** This plug-in creates a mesh connecting to previously independent meshes or groups.

- **msTerGen.** This plug-in can generate random terrains or import a bitmap file to use as a height map.

- **msTextGen.** This plug-in generates 3D objects in the form of text.

- **msModelInfo.** This plug-in provides more detailed information about a model than the Show Model Statistics command.

- **msTIleTextureMapper.** This plug-in generates texture coordinates to geometry for tile textures (also known as *seamless textures*).

- **msLathe.** This plug-in takes flat geometry and turns it around the X-axis to build a 3D model.

You can install plug-ins by simply copying them to the MilkShape directory and then launching MilkShape. They will then appear under the Tools menu beneath Show Model Statistics.

Window

The Window menu (see Figure 13.17 provides commands that determine what information is available in the MilkShape window and how it is displayed. See Table 13.9 for more detail.

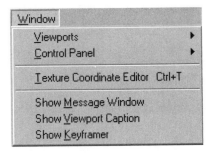

Figure 13.17
The Window menu.

Table 13.9 MilkShape Window Menu

Command	Description
Viewports	This command presents a submenu that allows you to pick an alternative viewport layout. The four-pane layout with three 2D views and one Perspective view is the default.
Control Panel	This command allows the user to set whether the toolbox frames appear on the left or right side of the main window. The right side is the default.
Texture Coordinate Editor	This is for adjusting where textures appear on the model. Although useful, it is not as powerful or flexible as using a dedicated UV Unwrapping or Mapping tool like UVMapper.
Show Message Window	This option shows a script output window that holds the results of compiling various types of models for specific games.
Show Viewport Caption	This command shows details about the viewport it appears above. From left to right, the details are the view, the field of view, the near clipping plane, and the far clipping plane.
Show Keyframer	The Keyframer is the animation box along the bottom of the main window. It is used to create keyframe positions of bones and joints in a skeleton for animation.

The Toolbox

Way back near the start of this chapter, in Figure 13.2, is a depiction of the contents of the various tabs in the toolbox. In this section here we will dig deeper into the capabilities in those tabs. Table 13.10 provides a brief summary of each toolbox tab's functions.

Table 13.10 MilkShape Toolbox Summary

Tab	Purpose
Model	This is used for the placement of vertices and shape primitives, as well as for the construction of polygons and skeletons.
Groups	This contains commands used to group vertices and polygons. Groups can also be created from existing polygons.
Materials	This deals with the creation of materials, including textures from file, ready to be assigned to groups.
Joints	This contains tools for manipulating and managing skeleton joints.

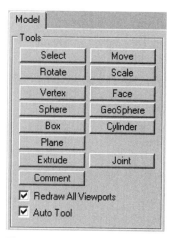

Figure 13.18
The Model tab.

You should understand that, in general, when using the functions in the toolbox, we will first have to select some object via one of the views and then operate on it using one of the toolbox commands. This sort of noun-verb operation mode requires us to make sure we have the appropriate objects selected before every action we take.

The Model Tab

The Model tab (see Figure 13.18 contains the tools necessary to create and modify the basic shape primitives: vertices, faces, cylinders, spheres, and cubes (boxes, as MilkShape calls them). Table 13.11 shows the functions of the Model tab's buttons.

Table 13.11 Model Tab Functionality

Button	Description
Select	This tool puts the program into select mode so that the user can select any object or collection of objects on one of the wire-frame views. Once you are in select mode, you can specify one of four different selection target types: vertex, face, group, or joint. You also have two optional settings: Ignore Backfaces and By Vertex (which is only available in face selection mode).
Move	This tool permits you to move any selected objects by clicking in the appropriate wire-frame view and dragging the cursor. You can also specify discrete movement by entering numbers in the Move Options boxes at the bottom.
Rotate	This tool permits you to move and rotate any selected objects around a single axis by clicking in the appropriate wire-frame view and dragging the cursor up or down. You can also specify discrete rotations and multiple axes rotations by entering numbers in the Rotate Options boxes at the bottom.
Scale	With this tool you can change the size of any selected objects along one of two available axes in each view by clicking in the appropriate wire-frame view and dragging the cursor up, down, left, or right. You can also specify discrete scaling and multiple axes scaling by entering numbers in the Scale Options boxes at the bottom.
Vertex	Use this tool to place individual vertices, one at a time, in a wire-frame view. In each different view, the vertex will be placed at the zero axis position for whichever axis is not presented in the view. This tool has no options.
Face	With this tool you can connect individual vertices to create a face, one vertex at a time, with three vertices defining a face. The Threshold option specifies how close to a vertex you need to click to add it to the current face you are building. As you build the face, select the vertices in a counterclockwise direction to create an outward normalized face.
Sphere	This tool is a shape primitive tool. To create a sphere, simply click and drag the cursor in a wire-frame view. With the Sphere options you can specify the number of slices (like the slices in a pie) or stacks (like a stack of pancakes) that make up your sphere.
GeoSphere	Use this tool to create more realistic spheres via a different program technique. You use the tool the same way as the Sphere tool, but you can only specify the complexity of the sphere with the Depth option.
Box	Use this tool to create cubes. Just click in a wire-frame view and drag until it has reached the size you want.
Cylinder	Use this tool the same way as you use the Sphere tool, even including the specification of stacks and slices. The Stacks option specifies how many layers, or stacks, to make the cylinder with. If you imagine a layer cake to be a short, squat cylinder, then each layer in the cake is the same as a stack. The Slices option is handled the same way that slices of a pizza appear. Each slice is a wedge-like shape when looking at the cylinder from the end, when the `Close with extra vertex` option is chosen.

continues

Table 13.11 continued

Button	Description
	The Close options are in the pull-down menu below the other two options, and specify if or how the cylinder will be capped at either end. If you choose Don't close, then the cylinder will appear as an open-ended pipe. The default Close option is "Close with extra vertex". There are two other Close options, which indicate alternative methods of capping the ends of the cylinder.
Plane	Use this tool to add a flat surface to a scene. This surface is square and made of a number of triangles defined by the horizontal divisions (HDivs) and the vertical divisions (VDivs) defined in the Plane Options. You can also specify different treatments of the edges of rows and columns with the Turn edge each row and Turn edge each column checkboxes.
Extrude	This tool operates only on the faces. If you have two faces aligned to create a flat surface, like a piece of cardboard, you would use this tool to extend the surface in a specific direction to create a box. Just click the mouse and drag to perform the extrusion. Using the Extrude options you can specify which directions to do the extruding in—normally you would use only one direction at a time. The Smoothing option tells the program to smooth shade the polygons as it draws the extruded shape.
Joint	This tool places special joint objects. It works the same as the Vertex tool, except that if an existing joint is already selected when you make the new joint, the new joint will be attached to the previous one by a bone. If the Show Skeleton option is turned on in the Joint tab, the bone will be visible in yellow.
Comment	This tool allows a comment to be applied to the entire model.
Redraw All Viewports	If you have this option turned on, then every time you perform one of the tool operations, the views in all the viewports will be redrawn to reflect your changes.
Auto Tool	If you have this option turned on, then the program will alternate between any tool and the Select tool each time you finish an operation. This option is handy for tweaking and repetitive adjustment techniques.

The Groups Tab

You will often want, or need, to organize your model faces into groupings that make either visual or logical sense. Whether you organize them as meshes that make visual sense or simply as logical groups, you do this with the Groups tab, shown in Figure 13.19. The Torque DTS Exporter uses special groups with the name *collision* to define collision meshes. Table 13.12 presents the functions available from the Groups tab.

The Materials Tab

With the Materials tab (see Figure 13.20), you can define the textures that will be used to skin your model, as well as what characteristics they will have when

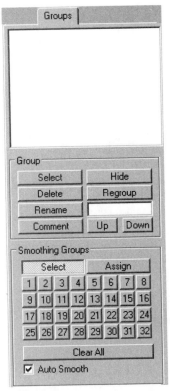

Figure 13.19
The Groups tab.

displayed. Special materials are also used to define certain model characteristics to the Torque DTS Exporter. Table 13.13 explains the functions of the Materials tab.

The Joints Tab

With the Joints tab (see Figure 13.21), you can specify the joints for skeletons, which are used in animations. Joints are also used as substitutes for the concepts of special nodes that are used by the Torque DTS Exporter. Table 13.14 describes the Joints tab functions.

The Keyframer

The Keyframer (see Figure 13.22) is a special tool used for defining animations for your model. With it, you can save skeletal positions in a model. You then produce animation by storing several keyframes to the Keyframer and playing

Table 13.12 Groups Tab Functionality

Button	Description
Group Selection Box	This is the white area at the top. It contains the names of the groups, one group per line. You always need to choose a group from this box before performing any group operations.
Select	When you use this tool, the currently chosen group in the list will become *selected* in the wire-frame views; that is, it will become drawn in red. Each time you choose a different group and click the Select tool, that group gets added to each view's selection.
Hide	With this tool you can make the chosen group's faces and vertices become invisible. This is useful for uncluttering a view or to ensure that you don't select the wrong parts for another operation.
Delete	Use this tool to permanently remove a group from the model.
Regroup	With this tool you create new groupings from whatever model elements are selected (shown in red) in the views. Any elements that already belong to other groups are removed from those groups and added to the new group.
Rename	Choose a group, type a new name in the Rename box (to the right of the button), and then click the Rename tool. Bingo! The group now has a new name.
Comment	Apply a comment to the group selected in the Group Selection Box.
Up & Down Buttons	These buttons move the highlighted group in the Group Selection Box up and down so that the user can order the groups. This has no bearing on the model information itself but instead is intended as a feature to allow the user to order the groups per their own preferences so that a particular group can be found easily.
Smoothing Groups Select	Clicking this button and then one of the Smoothing Group numbers selects the polygons assigned to that Smoothing Group. Smoothing Groups can only be selected on the numbers that have been assigned.
Smoothing Groups Assign	When you have a group of polygons selected, you can click this button and then one of the Smoothing Group numbers to assign all selected polygons to a Smoothing Group. Additional groups of polygons can be added to the same group without overwriting the previous contents of the Smoothing Group.
Smoothing Group Numbers	These numbers act as a storage bank for groups of polygons. They can have polygons assigned to them and selected from. If the Auto Smooth check box is selected, assigning groups of polygons to a Smoothing Group number will smooth shade them (Smooth Shaded shading has to be enabled to view the effect of this—right-click the 3D Perspective view and click Smooth Shaded from the pop-up menu).
Smoothing Group Clear All	This button removes the assigned Smoothing Groups from the Smoothing Group numbers. The polygons will remain smooth shaded, but they will no longer be in the same Smoothing Group.
Smoothing Group Auto Smooth	When assigning Smoothing Groups, ensure that this is checked if you wish the selected polygons to be smooth shaded.

Figure 13.20
The Materials tab.

them back. There is a set of controls for managing the playback. Typically, only frames where changes take place need to be set by the user—hence the term *keyframe*. Keyframes are key to the animation. MilkShape 3D will fill in the pose or position frames between the keyframes. You must click the Anim button at the lower right in order to work with the Keyframer.

Table 13.15 describes the primary Keyframer functions.

The Preferences Dialog Box

The Preferences dialog box (see Figure 13.23), which you reach by choosing File, Preferences, has two tabs. The Viewport tab is used to the set up the viewport's attributes, and the Misc tab offers miscellaneous settings. Table 13.16 provides details about each setting in the two tabs.

Table 13.13 Materials Tab Functionality

Item	Description
Material Selection Box	This is the white area at the top. It contains the names of the materials, one material per line. You always need to choose a material from this box before performing any material operations.
Material Preview	The currently chosen material is displayed, mapped onto a sphere. You can click and drag the sphere with the mouse to view hidden parts of the material map.
Ambient	Use this tool to get a color picker window for setting the ambient light of the environment the material is in. This attribute affects the color and the intensity of the color that the material reflects.
Diffuse	Use this tool to get a color picker window for setting the light that the material will directly reflect. This attribute has the most influence over the color of the material.
Specular Button & Specular Slider	Use this tool to set the specular highlight of the material. Basically, selecting a bright color will create a highlight on the material of the color chosen. Moving the slider below it changes the focus of the highlight. The highlight can range from appearing as a small spot to appearing as if the object is immersed in incandescent light.
Emissive	Use this tool to get a color picker window for setting the color and intensity of the light that the material emits. This attribute will appear as a glow around the material.
Transparency Slider	This slider, located beneath the Emissive button, adjusts the amount of transparency that an alphamap applies to a texture and the faces that the texture is assigned to. You must click Assign or click in the viewport to update the model to reflect your changes.
Texture Browse Button	Contains the name of the texture, or <none> if there is no texture selected. Use this tool to select a texture to apply to the material. Clicking it will yield a Windows Explorer browse box from which image files can be selected. The None button beside this button removes the texture file from the material.
Alphamap Browse Button	This button is located directly below the Texture Browse button. It contains the name of the alphamap texture, or <none> if there is no alphamap texture selected. In older versions of MilkShape 3D, prior to 1.7.0, this button allows the application of an alphamap to the material. A black-and-white image can be used to remove areas of texture where there may be holes. Black is fully occluded and white is fully visible; it is possible to use variations of gray to achieve semitransparency. The None button beside this button removes the alphamap file from the material.
	In versions of MilkShape 3D, from 1.7.0 onward, alphamaps have no effect on the material at all. Transparent areas of textures (alpha channels) are achieved by using a 32-bit texture that holds an alpha component for each pixel of the texture, like the TGA and PNG file formats.

Table 13.13 continued

Item	Description
	A texture containing an alpha channel can be handy for applying details in texture where detail would normally be applied by adding extra geometry to a model, so using transparent areas in a material allows the user to decrease geometric complexity.
SphereMap	Checking this box will turn the current material into a spheremap material. This essentially turns the surface of the model into a reflective surface with the material as the environment that is reflected on the model surface, much like an environment map.
New	The New button, when clicked, will create a new blank material with default attributes, no texture or alphamap files, and a default name.
Delete	To delete a material, choose it in the Material Selection box, and then click the Delete button. This action literally removes the material from the workspace, so use this wisely.
Rename	To rename a material, choose it in the Material Selection box, type the desired name in the box to the right of the Rename button, and then click the Rename button.
Assign	Use this tool to assign the chosen material in the Material Selection box to the selected group.
Select By	The tool selects all objects that have the currently selected material assigned to them.
Comment	This tool applies a comment to the material selected in the Material Selection box.

Figure 13.21
The Joints tab.

Table 13.14 Joints Tab Functionality

Item	Description
Joint Selection Box	This is the white area at the top. It contains the names of the joints, one joint per line. You always need to choose a joint from this box before performing any operations on joints.
Rename	This works the same as the Rename tool in the other tabs. Choose a joint, type a new name in the box to the right of the Rename button, and then click the Rename button.
SelAssigned	(Select Assigned) After you have chosen a joint, click this button to select all the vertices assigned to that particular joint.
SelUnAssigned	(Select Unassigned) Click this button to select all vertices not assigned to the chosen joint.
Assign	Use this tool to assign vertices to a joint. To do this, choose the Select-(Vertex) tool from the Model tab, highlight the joint in the Joint Selection box that you wish to assign the vertices to, and then select the vertices and click Assign.
Clear	Click this button to clear all the assigned vertices from belonging to the chosen joint in the Joint Selection box.
Comment	Applies a comment to the joint selected in the Joint Selection box.
Show Skeleton	Toggle this to show or hide the skeleton.

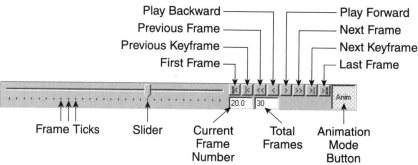

Figure 13.22
The Keyframer.

Other Features

MilkShape has a few other features that we won't cover in great depth, but two that deserve at least an honorable mention are the Texture Coordinate Editor and the Message Panel.

The Texture Coordinate Editor provides primitive texture-mapping capability. It has some rather severe limitations that prevent it from being used in even moderately complex models. The biggest limitation is that it doesn't unwrap meshes independently. For this reason we use external tools, like UVMapper. UVMapper may be a bit more awkward to use, because it isn't integrated, but it does a better job, providing more flexibility and control.

Table 13.15 Keyframer Functionality

Component	Description
Keyframe Slider	Use the slider to preview your animation before playing it. Using the slider, you can move freely backward and forward between the frames with mouse movement instead of clicking the Play Forward and Play Backward buttons to see the animation. The slider is useful for selecting animation frames in smaller animations; use the Current Frame Number Box to select frames for larger animations with many (more than a dozen or so) frames.
Playback Controls	The playback controls allow you to view your animation in MilkShape 3D in a manner similar to a VCR or DVD player. From the left, the buttons are First Frame, Previous Keyframe, Previous Frame, Play Backward, Play Forward, Next Frame, Next Keyframe, and Last Frame. All of these commands update the model to the current frame, and the slider is also moved to the appropriate frame.
Current Frame Number Box	Use this box when you have a lot of frames in your animation and the slider does not allow the accuracy you desire when selecting frames. You can type in a value here that will set the number of frames in the animation. The box will accept a whole number to indicate the frame to which you wish to go; the slider and view will change to reflect the selected frame.
Total Frames Box	In this box, enter the number of frames you want in your animation. Most modelers choose a relatively high number, depending on the number of animations the model is to perform, and key in animations between certain numbers of frames leaving a three- or four-frame gap between animations. With a Run, Walk, Jump, and Shoot animation, you would key in the Run animation first and then leave several frames, key in the Walk animation and then leave several frames, and so on.
Animation Mode Button	This button enables the Keyframer. It behaves like a toggle: when down, the Keyframer is enabled; when up, the Keyframer is disabled.

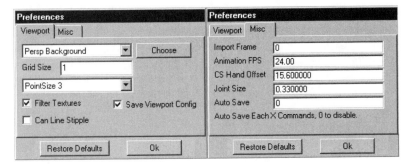

Figure 13.23
The Preferences dialog box.

Table 13.16 Preferences Choices

Component	Description
Property Selection	With MilkShape, the user can customize the colors of components used when modeling. The drop-down list contains the component names; a color for the selected component can then be chosen by clicking the Choose button next to the drop-down box. Following is the complete list of color customizable components: Persp(ective) Background (the 3D view) Ortho(graphic) Background (the 2D views) Persp(ective) Grid Ortho(graphic) Grid X-Axis Y-Axis Z-Axis Vertex Selected Vertex Face Selected Face Bone Selected Bone Selected Joint Keyed Bone
Grid Size	Use this control to set the spacing of the grid lines in the wire-frame views. The default grid size is 1×1; this gives the smallest line spacing. The grid size you use usually depends on the scale of the models you are building.
Point Size	Use this control to specify the size of the vertex points displayed in the wire-frame views. Larger point sizes are easier to see and to select individually, but they may tend to obscure model details in crowded areas at low view magnifications.

Table 13.16 continued

Component	Description
Save Viewport Config	When MilkShape 3D is opened, the orientation and position of the viewports in the world are set to default positions. Enabling this option means that when you close MilkShape 3D the viewport positions are saved so that when you next start up MilkShape 3D the viewports will maintain their positions and orientation.
Filter Textures	When set this turns on mipmapping texture filters. This will smooth the texture so that the rasterized pixels are not as noticeable.
Can Line Stipple	When moving, scaling, or extruding objects, MilkShape draws a guideline that indicates the vector of the action, denoting its direction and magnitude. This is usually a solid line, but with this option set, it is rendered as a dashed or dotted line. This also stipples the box line used for multiple selections.
Import Frame	This allows the user to specify the animation frame to be imported from MD2 or MD3 files using the Morph Target Animation mechanism.
Animation FPS	This specifies the playback speed of animations in *Frames Per Second* (FPS).
CS Hand Offset	This is used to specify the offset for either side of a decompiled CounterStrike model.
Joint Size	This allows the user to set the display size of the joints that are used in MilkShape. You should change the size to reflect the scale of the model you work with.
Auto Save	This option allows you to specify how often the program will automatically save your work. The frequency is defined by how many commands or operations you want to be able to perform before the save happens. This option can be a lifesaver but can also be a nuisance if you set the value too low—especially if you are doing a lot of experimenting and undo your previous operations frequently. A setting of about 10 seems to work well.
Restore Defaults	This will reset all of your preferences for MilkShape 3D, including all properties accessed from the Properties window as well as the viewport configurations. Hotkey assignments will not be affected.

The Message Panel displays output from executing plug-ins and modeling operations. It can be useful for providing insight into how MilkShape does its work, but its downfall is the screen space it takes up.

UVMapper

Earlier in this chapter—and even earlier than that, in Chapter 9—we used the UVMapper program created by Steve Cox to help us skin a model. As promised, here is the section with the detailed information on UVMapper. We won't cover every detail. Instead, we will concentrate on those details that we can apply to our own needs here in this book.

The first thing to know about UVMapper is that it only operates on models saved in OBJ format, as created by the Alias Wavefront program. The UV unwrapping principles involved are the same for all similar tools. The author of UVMapper has also created UVMapper Pro, a newer release with many more features and greater flexibility. The companion CD includes a demo of UVMapper Pro, a restricted version (you can't save output, which, of course, we need to do). If you want to check out the enhanced features later, go ahead and poke around.

The File Menu

As is true in most programs, UVMapper's File menu provides commands for loading, saving, importing, and exporting files. See Table 13.17 for descriptions.

The Edit Menu

The Edit menu is where the real power of UVMapper resides. Table 13.18 provides more information.

Table 13.17   UVMapper File Menu

Command	Description
Load Model	Load a Wavefront OBJ formatted model from file. After it is loaded, you will see the texture map layout in the UVMapper window. If you don't, then there are no texture coordinates included in the model. You can fix this by choosing Edit, New UV Map (see Table 13.18).
New Model	This command gives you a method for adding or creating your own models from shape primitives. The primitives are box, cone, cylinder, sphere, and torus.
Import UVs	With this command you can import UV coordinate data that has been saved separately from a model.
Save Model	Use this command to save the UV mapping data you've created along with the model you originally imported.
Save Texture Map	You can save the texture map image using this command. You can then load that image as a template into a program like the Gimp in order to apply that "artistic magic."
Export UVs	With this command you can export only the UV texture coordinates you've created using this program, without the rest of the model data.

Table 13.18 UVMapper Edit Menu

Command	Description
Settings	Here you can specify how many pixels on your screen correspond to a single measurement unit. The value you use depends on the scale of the model you are working with.
Select By	This command gives you the ability to select on-screen objects by facet (face) or by vertices. Usually you leave this set to Facet.
Color	This command will let you indicate how you want to discriminate the different parts of the display. Your choices are Black and White (no discrimination), by Group, by Material, and by Region. This capability is handy when dealing with a complex model.
Tools	This command provides three different functions: Fix Seams, Split Vertices, and Weld Vertices. MilkShape offers these same abilities, but it's nice to know we have access to them here as well.
Select	With this command you can refine your object selection ability. There are five modes: All, None, by Group, by Material, and by Region. The by Group, by Material, and by Region options each provide a Selection dialog box if these entities actually exist in the model data. Judicious naming of groups (meshes) when in MilkShape can be a great boon when working here in UVMapper.
Assign	Use this command to assign selected objects to an existing group, material, or region. Again, you would normally do this in your modeling program, but it's nice to have the ability here if you realize you've forgotten to assign some faces to a particular group.
Rotate	This command allows you to rotate a selection around any of the three axes—or all three at once, if you want.
New UV Map	This command provides several different unwrapping methods: Planar, Box, Cylindrical, Cylindrical Cap, and Spherical. The options available here are quite extensive so they warrant coverage in their own section, called "UV Mapping," later in this chapter.
Tile	This command is complementary to the Select command. Using Tile you can specify how the program displays the different parts of the model; they can be visually organized (tiled) according to group, material, or region.

The Help Menu

The Help menu provides the user some assistance when working with the program. Table 13.19 provides more detail, and Table 13.20 provides a list of UVMapper hot keys.

UV Mapping

When you choose Edit, New UV Map you will be presented with a choice of five different unwrapping methods:

- Planar

- Box

Table 13.19 UVMapper Help Menu

Command	Description
Statistics	This command will report the current status of your model. This will tell you the total vertices, textures, normals, facets, groups, and materials. Bear in mind that while you are editing a model, UVMapper will temporarily increase the number of texture coordinates allocated to the model, and so this is not a good representation of the actual number of texture coordinates the model will have upon saving. A more accurate way to obtain this information is from within the MilkShape modeling tool.
Dimensions	This command will give you the overall geometric dimensions of the model. This will report the minimum and maximum values along each of the three axes (X, Y, and Z).
Hot Keys	This command will give you a list of the available hot keys. (Table 13.20 contains a list of the UVMapper hot keys.)
About UVMapper	This command gives you information about the version, how to contact the author, and where you can obtain an updated version of the program.

Table 13.20 UVMapper Hot Keys

Key	Description
Esc	clears selection, undoes changes
Enter	clears selection, saves changes
Shift+number key	increases resize/movement amount
keypad *	quadruples size of selection
keypad /	quarters size of selection
keypad +	increases size of selection
keypad −	decreases size of selection
keypad #	moves selection
=	maximizes selection
.	snaps selection to facets
[	hides selected facets
]	shows selected facets
\	toggles facets on and off
'	hides unselected facets
uU/vV	resizes selection (fine)
x/X/y/Y	resizes selection (coarse)
Ctrl+x	inverts selection horizontally
Ctrl+y	inverts selection vertically
Ctrl+b	loads background
Ctrl+c	clears background
Ctrl+u	flips background horizontally
Ctrl+v	flips background vertically
Tab	toggles background display
t	triangulates object
Insert	checks for degenerate facets

- Cylindrical

- Cylindrical Cap

- Spherical

Each of these methods is described in more detail here. Sometimes, even when you know exactly what the unwrapping method is supposed to do, you will be surprised at the results, so don't be afraid to experiment. Once you've loaded a model, you can keep trying the different unwrapping methods with different settings. Each time you do it, the program begins from scratch, so you don't have to worry about undoing your previous efforts.

Planar

When you use the Planar method, you will be presented with the dialog box depicted in Figure 13.24. Table 13.21 provides details about using the Planar method.

Box

When you use the Box method, you will be presented with the dialog box depicted in Figure 13.25. You can get more information on using the Box method in Table 13.22.

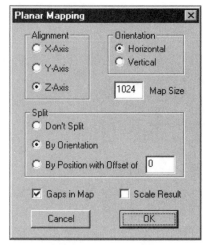

Figure 13.24
The Planar Mapping dialog box.

Table 13.21 Planar Mapping Options

Option	Description
Alignment	This allows you to specify the axis along which the model will be mapped.
Orientation	This allows you to alter the layout of the texture map template. It only has an effect when you use the Split option (described later in this table). If you select Don't Split, the Orientation option has no effect. When splitting the model into front and back sections, you can have the two halves side by side (Horizontal) or above and below each other (Vertical). Which you want to use really depends on the geometry of the model. If you don't like the layout of the texture map after using planar mapping, try changing this option.
Map Size	This will specify the maximum dimension of the texture map template. Depending on the model it may be vertical or horizontal, but the texture map is guaranteed not to exceed this value in either width or height. One side will equal this value, and the other will be scaled accordingly.
Split	This option allows you to divide the texture map into front and back sections. (To adjust the placement of these sections, see the Orientation option earlier in this table.) You have three choices: **Don't Split:** Gives you one map with the front and back facets on top of each other. **By Orientation:** Calculates the facet normals, placing all facets that face toward the eye on one side and all facets that face away on the other. **By Position with Offset of:** Allows you to divide the model based on geometry rather than facing. Using an offset of 0 will divide the model in half. You can adjust this offset to change how many facets are on each side.
Gaps in Map	This allows you to separate the sides of the box on the texture map. If the sides touch, sometimes you will see one pixel of the side on the front, for example.
Scale Result	Use this option to specify how much larger or smaller the resulting texture map should be.

Figure 13.25
The Box Mapping dialog box.

Cylindrical

When you use the Cylindrical method, you will be presented with the dialog box depicted in Figure 13.26. Table 13.23 provides details about using the Cylindrical method.

Table 13.22 Box Mapping Options

Option	Description
Map Size	This will specify the maximum dimension of the texture map template. Depending on the model it may be vertical or horizontal, but the texture map is guaranteed not to exceed this value in either width or height. One side will equal this value, and the other will be scaled accordingly.
Split front/back	Setting this option will divide the model into six sections: front, back, top, bottom, left side, and right side. Uncheck this option if you want to combine top and bottom, left and right, front and back, giving you only three sections.
Gaps in Map	This allows you to separate the sides of the box on the texture map. If the sides touch, sometimes you will see one pixel of the side on the front, for example.
Scale Result	Use this option to specify how much larger or smaller the resulting texture map should be.

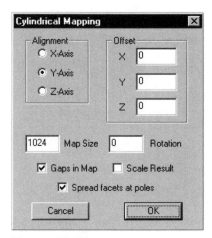

Figure 13.26
The Cylindrical Mapping dialog box.

Cylindrical Cap

When you use the Cylindrical Cap method, you will be presented with the dialog box depicted in Figure 13.27. Table 13.24 provides details about using the Cylindrical Cap method. This method is similar to the Cylindrical method, except that it assumes you are unwrapping a cylinder with end caps, as if there were closed lids on both ends of a can. The caps are mapped separately from the tubing of the cylinder.

Table 13.23 Cylindrical Mapping Options

Option	Description
Alignment	This allows you to specify the axis around which the model will be mapped.
Offset	When mapping a model with one of these methods (Cylindrical, Cylindrical Cap, or Spherical) the model is mapped around a center point. This center is calculated using the maximum and minimum geometry values along each axis. This works quite well for mapping a true sphere or cylinder, but if you have a model that is, say, a sphere with a spike on the side of it, the calculated center may not be what you want. To adjust the center of the model from what's been calculated, use this option.
Map Size	This will specify the maximum dimension of the texture map template. Depending on the model it may be vertical or horizontal, but the texture map is guaranteed not to exceed this value in either width or height. One side will equal this value, and the other will be scaled accordingly.
Rotation	Use this to specify how much, if any, rotation will be applied to the resulting texture map image template.
Gaps in Map	This allows you to separate the sides of the cylinder on the texture map. If the sides touch, sometimes you will see one pixel of the side on the front, for example.
Scale Result	Use this option to specify how much larger or smaller the resulting texture map should be.
Spread facets at poles	Oftentimes facets are squeezed together when the mapping occurs, especially at places like the "poles" (the tops and bottoms of the map, just like on maps of the Earth). With this option set, the resulting map will spread the facets at the poles to alleviate the pinching effect.

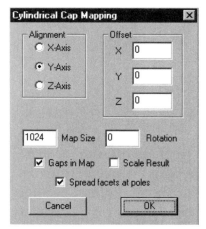

Figure 13.27
The Cylindrical Cap Mapping dialog box.

Table 13.24 Cylindrical Cap Mapping Options

Option	Description
Alignment	This allows you to specify the axis around which the model will be mapped.
Offset	When mapping a model with one of these methods (Cylindrical, Cylindrical Cap, or Spherical) the model is mapped around a center point. This center is calculated using the maximum and minimum geometry values along each axis. This works quite well for mapping a true sphere or cylinder, but if you have a model that is, say, a sphere with a spike on the side of it, the calculated center may not be what you want. To adjust the center of the model from what's been calculated, use this option.
Map Size	This will specify the maximum dimension of the texture map template. Depending on the model it may be vertical or horizontal, but the texture map is guaranteed not to exceed this value in either width or height. One side will equal this value, and the other will be scaled accordingly.
Rotation	Use this to specify how much, if any, rotation will be applied to the resulting texture map image template.
Gaps in Map	This allows you to separate the sides of the cylinder on the texture map. If the sides touch, sometimes you will see one pixel of the side on the front, for example.
Scale Result	Use this option to specify how much larger or smaller the resulting texture map should be.
Spread facets at poles	Oftentimes facets are squeezed together when the mapping occurs, especially at places like the "poles" (the tops and bottoms of the map, just like on maps of the Earth). With this option set, the resulting map will spread the facets at the poles to alleviate the pinching effect.

Spherical

When you use the Spherical method, you will be presented with the dialog box depicted in Figure 13.28. You can get more information on using the Spherical method in Table 13.25.

Moving Right Along

Well, there you have two pretty comprehensive, low-cost modeling tools: MilkShape 3D by Mete Ciragan and UVMapper by Steve Cox. These guys have done an admirable job creating these programs in the shareware or freeware spirit. Not only do they deserve a round of applause and a big thank-you, but you could also perhaps send a few dollars their way by registering their shareware programs. The cost is minuscule, and the benefits are great.

By using the common Wavefront file format, we can use each tool in complementary ways to create models for our games. This is a pretty common theme;

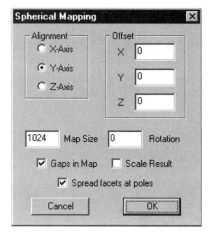

Figure 13.28
The Spherical Mapping dialog box.

Table 13.25 Spherical Mapping Options

Option	Description
Alignment	This allows you to specify the axis around which the model will be mapped.
Offset	When mapping a model with one of these methods (Cylindrical, Cylindrical Cap, or Spherical) the model is mapped around a center point. This center is calculated using the maximum and minimum geometry values along each axis. This works quite well for mapping a true sphere or cylinder, but if you have a model that is, say, a sphere with a spike on the side of it, the calculated center may not be what you want. To adjust the center of the model from what's been calculated, use this option.
Map Size	This will specify the maximum dimension of the texture map template. Depending on the model it may be vertical or horizontal, but the texture map is guaranteed not to exceed this value in either width or height. One side will equal this value, and the other will be scaled accordingly.
Rotation	Use this to specify how much, if any, rotation will be applied to the resulting texture map image template.
Gaps in Map	This allows you to separate the sides of the box on the texture map. If the sides touch, sometimes you will see one pixel of the side on the front, for example.
Scale Result	Use this option to specify how much larger or smaller the resulting texture map should be.
Spread facets at poles	Oftentimes facets are squeezed together when the mapping occurs, especially at places like the "poles" (the tops and bottoms of the map, just like on maps of the Earth). With this option set, the resulting map will spread the facets at the poles to alleviate the pinching effect.

notice also that we've used the Gimp—another low-cost tool (in fact, free!)—in the same way in conjunction with MilkShape. In the next few chapters we will tackle the Big Jobs: animated characters, vehicles, and weapons. It would not be wasted effort if you wanted to take some time out at this point to practice by designing and building some models to your own specifications.

The more you use a tool, make mistakes, and figure out what you did wrong and then make any necessary corrections on your own, the more proficient you will become.

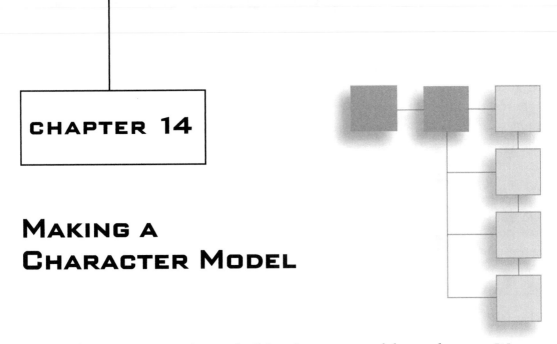

CHAPTER 14

Making a
Character Model

In this chapter we are going to build a character model, step-by-step. We are going to animate it and skin it. It's going to be a long and sometimes hectic ride, so hang on to your hat! For example, my wife took about 30 hours, spread over almost a week, to work through this chapter.

Oh yes, and remember—the more time you spend on your modeling and artwork, the better your final product will look.

Modeling Techniques

Modelers use many different approaches or techniques. The differences can be based on what tools are available to do a given job or what data is available about the item to be modeled. Other techniques are available but not described here—that's because we are modeling for games, and low-poly modeling is the philosophy we need to follow. Remember that the more polygons one model uses, the fewer polygons available for other instances of that model, or for other models, in a given rendered frame of a scene at a given frame rate. In games there is that polygon budget to consider.

Shape Primitives

In two dimensions, primitives are the simplest geometric constructions: dots or points, lines, rectangles, ovals or circles, arcs and other curves. We can assemble all other more complex shapes using these basic or "primitive" 2D shapes.

In three dimensions, the primitives are: planes or faces, boxes, cylinders, spheres, pyramids or prisms or wedges, cones, and arches. When we talk about *shapes* in three dimensions, we typically mean a fully enclosed collection of faces that simulate some real-world solid object. So, while planes and faces are certainly 3D primitives, they are not normally included in the list of 3D shape primitives.

Creating models using shape primitives can be an extremely quick way to build a low-poly model, depending on your expertise and eye for detail. The basic technique involves selecting a primitive that best matches the part of the model you are building. The primitive shape must contain enough polygons and vertices for you to adjust the shape to closely match your target.

This is the technique we are going to use to build our character model in this chapter.

Box Method

This is a variation of the Shape Primitives method, whereby we start out with a box primitive and then subdivide the faces of the box into smaller faces based on our needs for more detail in the model as the model takes shape. As we subdivide each face, we yield more polygons that can be moved around and placed. More detail means more faces, and more smoothness means more faces. When making a head, we might start with a simple box with six faces and end up with a complex shape with more than a hundred faces.

Incremental Polygon Construction

Incremental Polygon Construction is a method that fairly closely approximates modeling with clay in the real world. Sculpting with clay generally involves adding bits of clay together to create shapes that grow in size and detail. The clay can be poked and prodded, smoothed and pinched, until it accurately depicts the item being modeled.

With Incremental Polygon Construction, the process is similar. We apply vertices in 3D space that represent high points and low points of the features to be modeled, and then we build triangles or faces connecting these vertices. One point of departure from clay modeling is that we typically don't add faces on top of (such that they completely obscure) other faces, because we have no need for a solid to give us the required volume. But the principle of adding faces to the existing topology of a model as the model grows is the same, as is the useful concept that we add only what we need and no more.

The best way to get started with modeling in this way is to use photographs or sketches of the target from several directions: from directly in front, directly above, and one or both sides. From the pictures we can obtain the locations and shapes of the features and their high and low points. We mark these points in our 3D views, and then we proceed to build faces from them.

This technique can be quite slow going. It is also prone to errors that are difficult to correct, because you may have moved dozens of steps beyond where the error actually occurred before the error becomes evident.

Axial Extrusion

In the simplest sense, you start with a primitive object (usually a box, but it could be a simple facet or triangle), subdivide it, and then select specific polygons to extrude into meshes to form general shapes. When you subdivide objects, you increase the number of polygons on each side of the shape. You then adjust and refine the extruded polygons to form the details of the model. This approach is similar to making models of geographic terrain using a contour map as a guide, with cardboard or plywood sheets to build up the terrain, and then smoothing the edges with some kind of filler.

With Axial Extrusion, you limit your extrusions to one of the three axes—sometimes all three in various combinations—but individual extrusion only occurs in one axis. This technique is usually restricted to inanimate objects, but sometimes certain parts of character models are made this way.

One example of using axial intrusion in character modeling is when creating a head. A series of flat-plane profiles (called *cuts*) are made of a head, after which each profile is extruded once in each direction on the transverse axis (the axis that runs from ear to ear). Then each extruded mesh is married to the extruded meshes of the adjacent cuts by an averaging of the vertices. You'll actually get to do some of these extrusions later in this chapter and others.

Arbitrary Extrusion

Arbitrary Extrusion has much in common with Axial Extrusion, except that you extrude your base primitive shapes in whatever directions are necessary. Like Incremental Polygon Construction, this approach to modeling can be seen as similar to sculpting in clay. Machinery lends itself well to modeling with this technique.

Topographical Shape Mapping

Topographical Shape Mapping is a method usually used to model terrain, like Axial Extrusion often is, except that Topographical Shape Mapping is best suited for automated operations rather than manual modeling.

In the geographic sense, topographic data can be obtained from various government and private sources. The data consists of, at a minimum, a coordinate and an altitude for each mapped point on the real terrain's surface. Various algorithms and many programs that can read this data from a file and render a 3D view of the terrain in question are available. The data files come in various formats depending on the agency that produces them: DLG-O, DEM, SDTS, and DRG, to name just a few from that acronymic world. Normally, this approach is used in one of the many available *Geographic Information Systems* (GIS), and there are tools that can convert this data into a format you can use for modeling in games.

Hybrids

Well, the Hybrid category is the catchall category. Often it is prudent to combine techniques in a single model—use the approach that works best for the component being created. If you find yourself mixing techniques, most likely you will be doing a little bit of Incremental Polygon Construction mixed with many shape primitives or using a few primitives mixed with a great deal of Arbitrary Extrusion.

The best point to be made here is that you should use what works best for you in your current circumstances.

Modeling for Torque

When we create models that we want to export for use in Torque, there are a few (but not many) rules that must be followed. The aspect of modeling for Torque that has the most impact is supporting Torque's animation scheme. At the simplest level, Torque has built-in support for using certain animations at certain times. You merely need to create the animation sequence in one of two ways (which I'll tell you about in a minute), name the sequence appropriately, export the animation, place the model with (or without, depending on the method used) its animation in the appropriate place in the Torque folder tree, and proceed. This little process—from creating the model to using it in a game—including the tools used to execute the steps in the process, is called the *modeling tool chain.*

Torque supports animations in two ways that are covered in this book. The first way is to use *embedded* animations, where the animations are included with the model in the DTS file. The second method is the DSQ or Torque Blended Animation Sequence system, which itself has two important features: it supports *blended* animation, where two different animations are played for the same model at the same time, and it supports the separation of animation sequences from the model (DTS) using the sequence files (DSQ) format.

Using either method, you can create your own skeleton with your own bone-, joint-, or node-naming system, or you can use the Torque Blended Animation Sequence system. The caveats are (1) you need to use the Torque Blended Animation Sequence system if you want to play more than one animation sequence at a time; (2) if you want to employ the animations provided by GarageGames with the Torque demo that employ the Torque Blended Animation Sequence system, you will need to use a bone-, joint-, or node-naming convention that matches theirs; and finally, (3) you need to use DTSPlus Exporter (by Chris Robertson), which exports sequence files (DSQ). And why not use GarageGames's animation sequences? There are about three dozen animations already done for you! You would then only need to create animation sequences that fulfill your specific needs and use the stock sequences for everything else.

Anyway, even if you do not use the Torque Blended Animation Sequence system but want to use the embedded animation approach, you will still need to make sure that you name your animations properly if you want Torque to automatically invoke them for you.

Table 14.1 (found later in this chapter) has a pretty comprehensive list of animations that Torque will recognize by name, along with the contexts in which they are used. Here is a list of the most common character animations:

root	The character is standing and fidgeting.
run	The character is running forward.
walk	The character is walking forward.
back	The character is running backward.
side	The character is running sideways.
look	The character's right arm points where he is looking horizontally.
head	The character's head points where he is looking vertically.
fall	The character is falling off a cliff or building.
land	The character lands on his feet.
jump	The character jumps while running.

The Base Hero Model

But first, we need to create a character model. The technique we are going to use is basically the Shape Primitives approach. We will hand-modify various shape primitives to get the results we want.

The kind of model we are going to make is primarily a *segmented-mesh* model. An alternative would be a *continuous-mesh* model. The difference is that in the segmented-mesh model, there are different, distinct objects or meshes for different components in the model, whereas in the continuous-mesh model, the entire model has one large, convoluted surface. Our primary segments will be as follows:

- head

- torso

- right leg

- left leg

- right arm

- left arm

So that's six segments in all. (A continuous-mesh model would have one segment.) All the leg and arm segments will each have two subsegments. Each segment or subsegment can be thought of as an individual mesh, or submesh.

To get an idea of what the finished model will look like, flip ahead a bunch of pages and take a peek at Figure 14.63, "The completed Hero model". I'd insert that picture here too, but I don't want you to have too many preconceived notions about what it should look like. The point of this chapter is to learn techniques and procedures, not be a human photocopier (not that there's anything wrong with that)!

Preparation

If you haven't done it on your own already, you need to install the Torque DTSPlus Exporter by Chris Robertson. MilkShape 3D has its own built-in exporter for Torque, but it's based on an older exporter from several years ago that doesn't support many of the "gotta-have" features of Torque's DTS shape format, like blended animations and footstep triggers. So we want DTSPlus.

You will find the plug-in in \3D2E\TOOLS\MILKSHAPE 3D in the file ms2dtsExporterPlus.zip. Extract the contents to a location of your choice—you only need one file: ms2dtsExporterPlus.dll. Copy that file to your MilkShape folder (most likely at C:\Program Files\MilkShape 3D 1.7.9. If you installed a different version, then your version number will be different, but the rest of the name will be the same.

Next, you need to quit MilkShape if it is already running, and then start it up again. Check to see if the plug-in is loading by looking in the menu for File, Export, Torque DTS Plus. If it's there, you are ready to rock and roll. If not, then check to make sure you deposited the right file in the MilkShape folder, and also make sure that it didn't accidentally end up in a subfolder.

The Head

We'll use the Shape Primitives approach to build the head. The keys to successful use of this technique are (1) choosing the right primitive and (2) using a primitive with sufficient vertices to do the job.

For the head part of the model, we're going to use a cylinder with 12 faces on the tube, stacked 6 segments high. That translates to a 6-stack, 12-slice cylinder, in MilkShape terms.

Tip

Make sure to set up your views to match mine. Right-click in each view, and from the Projection submenu, choose the appropriate projection for each view:

the top-right view should be set to Projection, Left,

the top-left view to Projection, Front,

the bottom-right view to Projection, 3D and

the bottom-left view to Projection, Top.

1. Open MilkShape, create a new document, and in the Preferences dialog box, set Point Size to 3 and Grid to 1 × 1 in the Preferences dialog box. Save the new file as \3D2E\RESOURCES\CH14\myhead.ms3d.

2. Create a 6-stack, 12-slice cylinder, as depicted in Figure 14.1. Size the cylinder such that the bounds of the cylinder extend from about −20 to + 20 on all three of the axes.

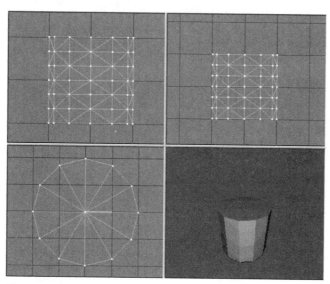

Figure 14.1
The initial cylinder.

3. Choose Select in Vertex mode, and from the side view (right pane), select the bottom layer of vertices. Ensure that both the Redraw All Viewports and Auto Tool boxes are checked.

4. Scale the selected bottom vertices to 95 percent of original (on the X and Z axes, ensure that the Y axis scale value is 1), as depicted in Figure 14.2. Make sure that the Scale Options has the Center of Mass radio button checked.

Tip

To turn off the grid display in any view, right-click in that view and choose Wireframe Overlay to uncheck that menu item.

5. Now select the top five rows of vertices, ignoring the bottom two rows, and scale them to 95 percent.

6. Next, scale the top four rows of vertices to 95 percent.

7. Repeat the scaling operation for the top three, then the top two, and finally the top row by itself. You should now have a cylinder with a bit of a bevel at the bottom that tapers gently toward the top, as shown in Figure 14.3.

8. Next, shift the top five layers of the cylinder toward the back, so that the rearmost vertices (designated A, highlighted in black, in Figure 14.4) line up,

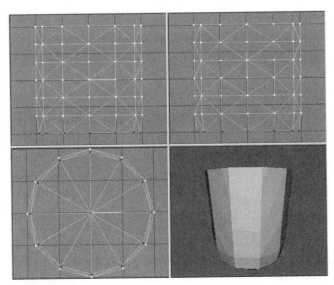

Figure 14.2
Selecting the bottom vertices.

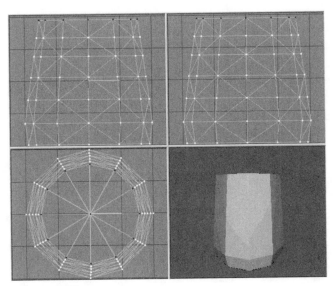

Figure 14.3
Tapering the cylinder.

at the back, with the layer of vertices that is second from the bottom (B in Figure 14.4). They don't have to be aligned precisely, but try to get them pretty close, as shown in Figure 14.4. You can cycle between Select and Move for each layer to move the layers one at a time.

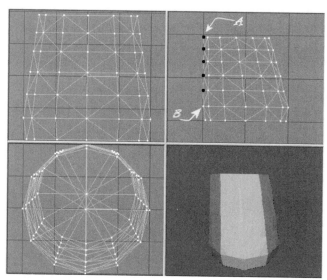

Figure 14.4
Shifting the layers.

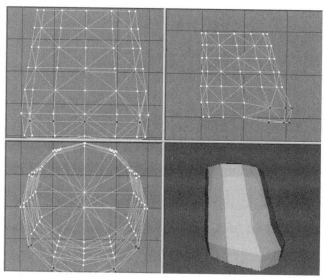

Figure 14.5
Shaping the jaw.

9. Next, working from the Right view (Top right viewport), select the bottom six vertices visible in that view (at the right side of the view), and move them down and to the right a bit. Figure 14.5 shows which vertices you want and how far to move them. These vertices make up the jaw.

10. Select all the vertices in the model, and scale to 75 percent in the Y-axis only. Do this by typing the value **0.75** into the Y scale box when you have the Scale tool selected and then clicking Scale. Set the X and Y scale values to 1. Don't forget to save!

Tip

The view in what MilkShape calls the Left viewport is for us actually the Right view (or Right Side view), located in the upper-right frame, because Torque's coordinate system is oriented differently. It's because of this that I normally use MilkShape with the Show Viewport Caption option under the Window menu turned *off*, in order to avoid confusing myself.

11. Now, using the same technique of selecting and moving (without doing any scaling) as explained in steps 4 to 9, shape the model as near as you can get to Figure 14.6. This is the Right Side view (upper-right frame). You only need to work in this view for now, and no other, and you only need to use the Select and Move tools. Now you can see the head shape taking form in profile, with the nose jutting out.

12. Okay, this next part gets a bit tricky. Using the Right Side view, select the 16 vertices in the lower-left corner (which is the lower back of the head/upper rear neck area), as shown in Figure 14.7.

13. Scale this group of vertices to 80 percent by typing **0.8** in the X-axis scale box, and then click Scale.

14. Now select just the nine vertices in the lower left, as shown in Figure 14.8, and scale these to 80 percent again.

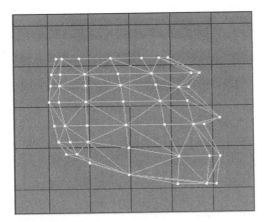

Figure 14.6
Shaping the head.

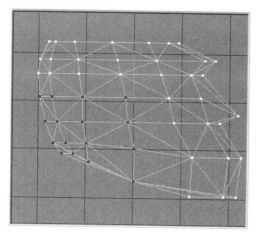

Figure 14.7
Back of the head/upper neck.

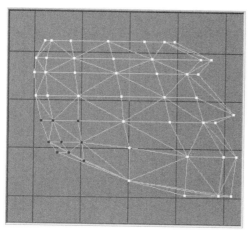

Figure 14.8
The smaller back of the head area.

What this does is make the jaw and cranium parts of the head stand out in an exaggerated fashion. By doing the scaling incrementally on the vertices in the region like that, we get a fairly smooth shape. Take a moment to swivel the model around in the 3D view, and you can now see a definite cartoonlike big-jawed, low-browed heroic figure taking shape. Okay, so not *all* heroes look like that. But we're making a game, right? So make it fun!

Now, as cute and lovable as that beetle-browed look is, it's a bit too Cro-Magnon and robotic looking, so we need to tone down the forehead and eyebrow area somewhat.

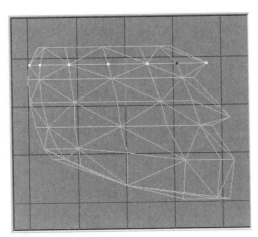

Figure 14.9
The temple vertices.

15. In the Right Side view, in the row of vertices that is second from the top (see Figure 14.9), select the vertex that is the second from the right (in the temple area) by dragging the Selection tool around it. This will have the effect of selecting that vertex and any others that are obscured behind it. There happens to be one more back there, so you will end up with two vertices selected, which you can see by examining the model in other views.

16. Drag the vertices back (to the left) a few ticks.

17. Switching now to the Front view (upper-left frame), scale those two vertices by 120 percent in the X-axis. This has the effect of widening the gap between them. (See Figure 14.10.) These steps have the effect of softening the sharp corners, just enough to make the head more organic looking.

18. Still with the Front view, select all the vertices in the top three rows, which is mostly the cranium area, and then incrementally apply 90 percent X-axis *and* Z-axis scaling to them—as you did earlier: top three, then top two, and so on. Figure 14.11 shows the results we are looking for here.

19. If you haven't saved your work recently, do it now. No particular reason, other than it's good practice to save periodically. We're getting close to being finished with the head.

20. Using Figure 14.12 as a guide, select the three ear vertices in the Right Side view.

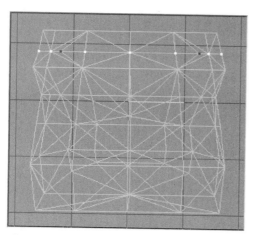

Figure 14.10
Scaling the temple vertices.

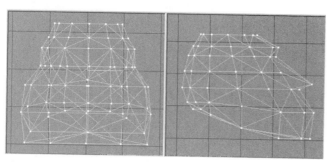

Figure 14.11
Scaling the cranium.

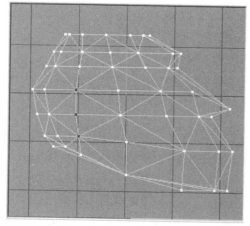

Figure 14.12
The ear vertices.

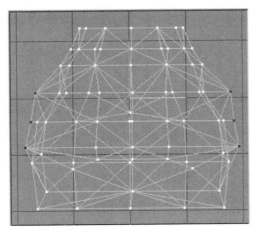

Figure 14.13
The scaled ear vertices.

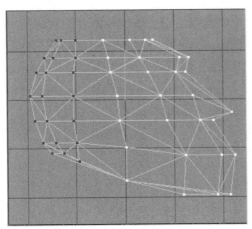

Figure 14.14
Selecting the three columns of vertices.

21. Stretch the ear vertices apart by scaling them 117 percent in the X-axis, as shown in Figure 14.13.

22. Now still in the Right Side view, guided by Figure 14.14, select the three columns of vertices at the rear of the head.

23. Drag them forward so that the rightmost column of selected vertices is just behind the unselected column (the fifth column), as shown in Figure 14.15.

24. Next, drag the two columns at the back of the head forward, so that you end up with a configuration like the one depicted in Figure 14.16.

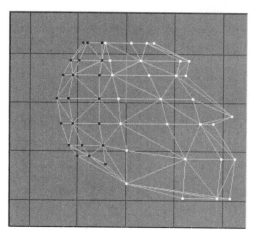

Figure 14.15
Dragging the vertices forward.

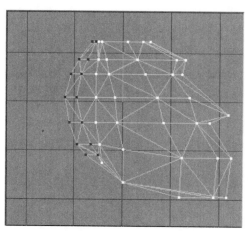

Figure 14.16
After dragging the vertices.

25. By now, you should be getting fairly adept at using the Select, Move, and Scale tools in MilkShape, so I'll give you a little assignment. Make the scalp region at the top of the head look like the scalp shown in Figure 14.17, using just these three tools and operating only on the top row of vertices. You will have to work in both the Front and Side views while monitoring your progress in the 3D view. Note that the 3D view in Figure 14.17 is smooth-shaded, not flat-shaded like most of the other figures.

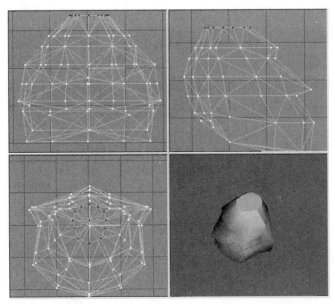

Figure 14.17
Shaping the scalp.

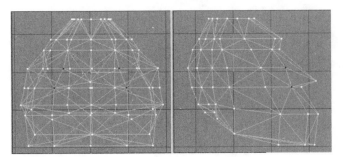

Figure 14.18
The nose vertices before scaling.

26. Next, use the same techniques to shape the nose and eyes. Figure 14.18 shows which vertices to use to shape the nose. Scale the vertices by 50 percent in the X-axis.

27. Shape the eye-socket vertices, as shown in Figure 14.19, by scaling to 30 percent in the X-axis.

28. Now this entire work should exist as one group. Rename that group as "head" in the Groups tab in the toolbox.

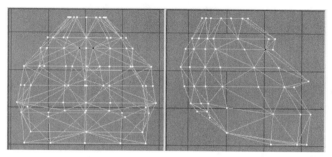

Figure 14.19
The eye-socket vertices after scaling.

Figure 14.20
The finished hero head.

29. Save your work as \3D2E\RESOURCES\CH14\myhead.ms3d. By saving the head in its own file, you can keep it safely out of the way while you work on the other parts.

30. Save your work one more time, but this time as \3D2E\RESOURCES\CH14\ myhero.ms3d. This is the hero model that we will build up as we go along.

And there you have it—as you can see in Figure 14.20, steely-eyed, big-jawed, beetle-browed genuine dyed-in-the-wool hero material!

The Torso

Like the head, the torso will be based on the cylinder shape, but this time we will use two of them and weld them together.

1. If you have the head file still open, leave it open. If you don't have it open, then open it, or you can open myhero.ms3d. Either one will do, because they both contain only the head so far.

2. Save the file as \3D2E\RESOURCES\CH14\mytorso.ms3d. We want to have the head around to use as a sizing guide when we start the torso model, and then we will delete it.

3. Drag the head mesh up until it is three or four grid lines above the model origin (the 0,0,0 coordinate), as suggested in Figure 14.21.

4. Use the Cylinder shape, and make one that has 6 segments, or stacks, and 12 slices, or faces. Give the name "chest" to the group it creates.

5. Rotate the cylinder by 90 degrees in both the X- and Y-axes.

6. Move and scale the cylinder until it has the same relationship to the head, as shown in Figure 14.22.

7. If the Auto Tool option is on, then turn it off.

8. In the Front view, select all the vertices from one end of the cylinder, then hold down the Shift key, and drag over the vertices at the other end of the

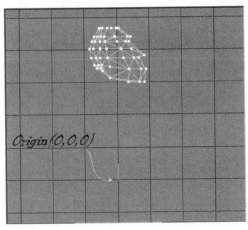

Figure 14.21
Positioning the head mesh.

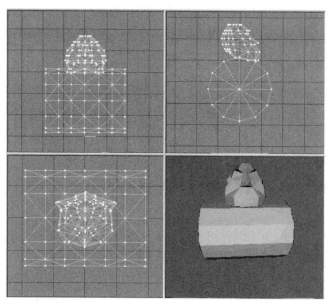

Figure 14.22
The relationship of the chest cylinder to the head.

cylinder to select them as well. These vertices form the cylinder caps for either end.

Tip

When trying to use the Shift key to add to a collection of selected objects, you might need to press the Shift key a couple of times. That's because when you are in certain modes, like Move mode, holding the Shift key toggles between zooming the view using a mouse drag and adding to the collection.

9. Scale the vertices to 50 percent in the Y- and Z-axes.

10. Drag the vertices up until the top ones are in line with the top of the cylinder. Figure 14.23 shows what the result should look like, with the head hidden. We'll keep the head object hidden for the next little while.

Tip

To hide the head, just make sure that it is the only object selected, then choose Edit, Hide Selection. You need to make sure that all the faces (triangles) in the head object are selected, not just the vertices. The best way to ensure that you select the head the right way is to open the Groups tab, highlight the head object in the list, and click the Hide button.

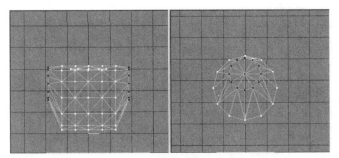

Figure 14.23
The cylinder caps after scaling and moving.

11. If you like to use the Auto Tool option, turn it back on now.

12. In the Front view, select the right-hand end cap, and rotate it by −20 degrees in the Z-axis.

13. Now rotate the left-hand end cap by +20 degrees in the Z-axis.

14. Next we will delete the head and we will need to manage our files during the process. So pay close attention here.

    First, save your current work as myhero.ms3d. That should have saved the torso and head together in the myhero.ms3d model. Then in the Groups tab in the toolbox, choose the head group and delete it. Then save again, this time saving as mytorso.ms3d. This gets the head out of the way so it won't clutter our model. We have the head already saved separately, so no worries here. We've also saved our torso in its own file for possible future use as a component in some other model. Now we can get back to working on building up myhero.ms3d some more.

15. In the Top view, select the two vertices in the middle at the bottom, in the area of the sternum, as shown in Figure 14.24, and move them toward the inside of the chest a bit.

16. Now you'll do the same for the back as for the front, but just slightly differently, for a different effect. In the Front view, select all the vertices in the top three rows, including the ones that are in the end caps.

17. Hide these vertices, using Edit, Hide Selection.

18. Now in the Top view, select the middle three vertices at the top of the view, as shown in Figure 14.25. These are the middle back vertices.

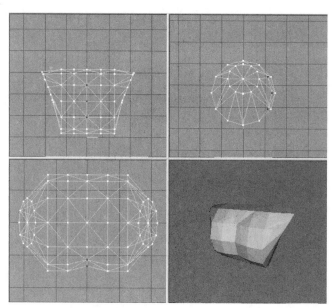

Figure 14.24
The sternum vertices after moving.

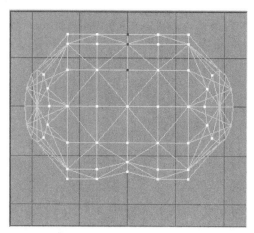

Figure 14.25
The middle back vertices.

19. Move the middle back vertices toward the inside of the chest a bit, just as you did with the sternum, but perhaps not quite as much.

20. Create another new cylinder (to be named "ab"), and give it the same 90-degree rotation in the X- and Y-axes.

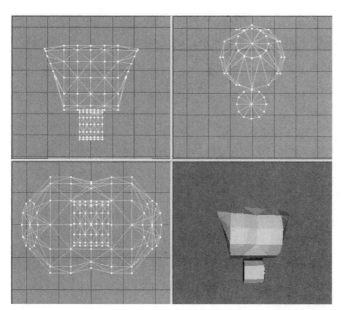

Figure 14.26
The ab cylinder relative to the chest.

21. Move and scale the ab cylinder until it has the same relationship with the chest, as shown in Figure 14.26.

    Now we have our primitive abdomen inserted. We're going to have to splice that mesh onto the chest mesh in order to complete the torso. It's actually not terribly hard to do, and after you've done it once, it will seem intuitively easy. But there are quite a few fiddly little steps involved to get there from here. So please be patient.

22. Using the Groups tab, hide the ab mesh.

23. In the Right Side view, select the bottom vertices, as shown in Figure 14.27, and then hide them using Edit, Hide Selections.

24. Back to the Groups tab, unhide the ab mesh by clicking the Hide button (which toggles between hiding and unhiding each time you click it). Don't use the general Unhide All command, because we want the chest vertices that we just hid to stay hidden.

25. In the Right Side view again, select the vertices shown in Figure 14.28, and drag them up so they are directly over the location where the hidden vertices for the chest are. Study Figure 14.28, which shows the vertices selected and

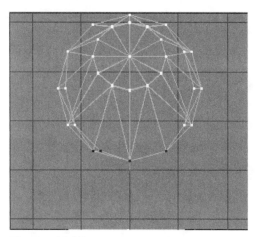

Figure 14.27
Hiding the lower chest vertices.

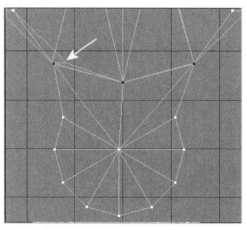

Figure 14.28
The ab vertices dragged over on top of the chest vertices.

dragged into position. Compare it with Figure 14.27 to get a sense of the right place to put the vertices. The intersection of lines shown by the white arrow in Figure 14.28 does not get a vertex at this time—we will deal with that shortly.

26. In the Front view, locate the end cap vertices, as shown in Figure 14.29, and drag them out to the position indicated in that figure.

27. Next, do the same for the vertices to the left of the previous set. Drag them to exactly the same place as the previous set, as shown in Figure 14.30.

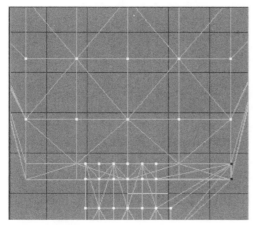

Figure 14.29
Dragging some end cap vertices over on top of chest vertices.

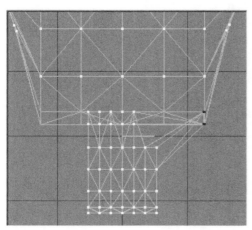

Figure 14.30
Dragging the end cap neighbor vertices over on top of the chest vertices.

28. Repeat steps 26 and 27 for the other end of the ab mesh.

29. Drag the next set of vertices over to the chest positions, as shown in Figure 14.31.

30. Repeat the drag operation for the other end. You should now have something that closely resembles the layout in Figure 14.32.

31. Zoom in on all the places that you dragged vertices to, and make sure that they are exactly over the line intersections of the chest triangles.

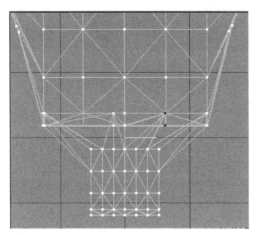

Figure 14.31
Dragging the next set of vertices into position.

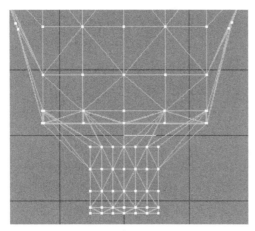

Figure 14.32
The final Front view layout.

32. In the Right Side view, select and hide all vertices on a line from the center of the cylinder forward (with forward being toward the right of the view). Figure 14.33 shows the vertices we're interested in.

33. Back in the Front view, select the center vertex at the top of the ab cylinder, as depicted in Figure 14.34. If you've done step 32 correctly, then as you scan around the other views, you will see that only one vertex has been selected.

34. Switch to the Right Side view, and drag that lone vertex up to the spot that I pointed out with the white arrow back in Figure 14.28.

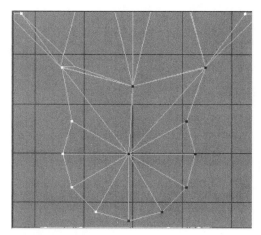

Figure 14.33
Select and hide these vertices.

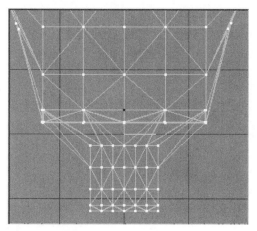

Figure 14.34
The top center cylinder vertex.

You should now have a configuration that looks like the one shown in Figure 14.35. Again, take the time to zoom in and ensure that all the dragged vertices are exactly over the line intersections of the chest triangles.

35. Unhide all the hidden vertices using the Edit, Unhide All command.

36. Select all the vertices from both meshes located at the places where you placed the dragged vertices. It's probably best to do this with the Right Side view, as I did in Figure 14.35. These are the vertices of each mesh, chest, and ab, that share the same locations.

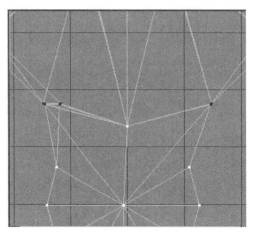

Figure 14.35
Selecting the common chest and ab vertices.

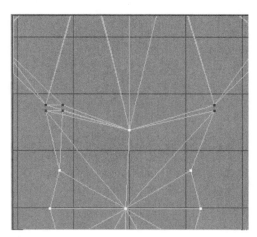

Figure 14.36
After snapping to grid . . . oops!

37. Choose Vertex, Snap To Grid. This should have the effect of forcing the closely adjacent vertices of each mesh to exactly align on the grid locations. However, if your vertices weren't aligned closely enough earlier, then they might diverge, as you can see happened to me in Figure 14.36. That's be-cause I didn't take my own advice to zoom in and tweak each moved vertex position to be exactly right.

It should be pretty obvious where the misaligned vertices have to go. If you have any that wandered off like I did, go back to the Right Side view and the

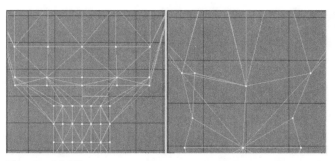

Figure 14.37
The well-aligned vertices.

Front view, and move the wayward vertices into position. Then repeat the Snap To Grid operation.

38. Compare your results with the images in Figure 14.37, making sure you have the same thing as shown there.

39. If they aren't already selected, reselect the vertices shown back there in Figure 14.35.

40. And now for the moment we've all been waiting for: choose Vertex, Weld Vertices.

All vertices that share identical common coordinates will be "welded" together. This basically means that superfluous copies of vertices will be deleted, and the polygons that we're defining will be reattached to the remaining single copy of each vertex.

41. In the Groups tab in the toolbox, choose both meshes, the chest and ab, so that they are both selected and highlighted in the wire-frame views.

42. Click Regroup, and then rename the newly consolidated group as "torso". You can now consider the torso to be finished. However, you can probably see areas where you can make obvious tweaks and adjustments. I did a few, just to make the integration of the back and the behind, as well as of the chest and the front abdomen, a bit more natural looking. I also added a wee bit of anatomical correctness, so to speak. Figure 14.38 shows the results of my tweaks. It should be fairly painless for you to duplicate these adjustments. The only operations I performed were Select (Vertex) and Move.

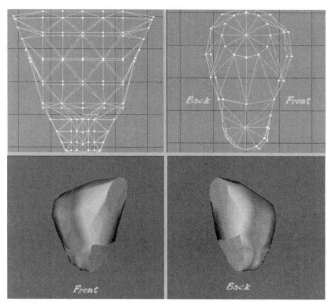

Figure 14.38
The final torso.

43. Save your mytorso.ms3d file so you don't lose all your work.

44. Open your myhero.ms3d file, and delete the older version of the torso group that is in this model.

45. Then merge the mytorso.ms3d file that you saved in step 43 into this model and save the whole shebang again as myhero.ms3d.

    This updates myhero.ms3d with the latest and greatest version of your torso. The myhero.ms3d file should now contain the finished head and the finished torso.

As we create the remaining parts of the model, we'll add them to the myhero.ms3d model by merging as we go along.

Matching the Head to the Torso

Now we should make sure that the torso and the head match correctly.

1. If the head and torso are nicely aligned, close to what you see in Figure 14.39, then you are done with this section, and you can skip to The Legs section, which comes up next. Otherwise, continue on to step 2.

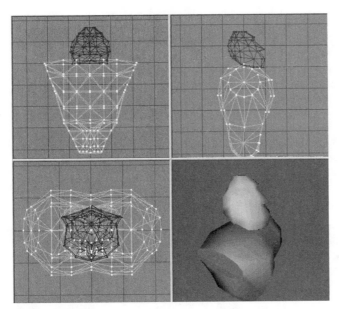

Figure 14.39
Positioning the head.

2. On the Groups tab in the toolbox, choose the head object (your torso mesh will be called "torso", so the head mesh will be the other one). Rename it as "head" if it isn't already called that.

3. Deselect the torso, and then click the Select button so that the head mesh is highlighted (and the torso mesh isn't), drag the head around in either the Front or the Side view, and position it as shown in Figure 14.39.

   I see two things I don't like right away. The head is bigger than it should be, and its shape seems to be a little too...ummm...*blah*. This isn't hard to fix, however.

4. Scale the head to 75 percent in the Y-axis only.

5. Move the head down until it just touches the top of the torso.

6. Rotate the head by 5 degrees around the X-axis so that the face is pointing a little bit down, as shown in Figure 14.40.

   There, that's more like it! Now to fiddle with the torso some more. If you liked the head better when it was bigger, simply choose Edit, Undo until you get the larger head back.

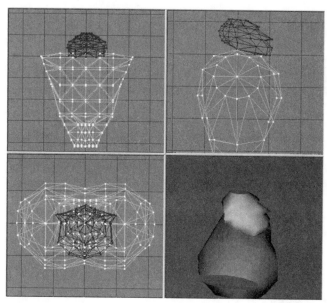

Figure 14.40
The reshaped head.

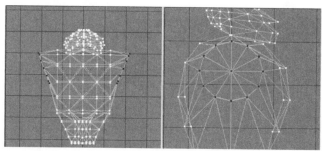

Figure 14.41
The shoulder socket vertices.

7. Select the vertices that form the shoulder sockets on both sides of the torso, using Figure 14.41 as a guide.

8. Scale the vertices to 60 percent in the Y- and Z-axes.

9. Save your work as \3D2E\RESOURCES\CH14\myhero.ms3d.

10. If you changed the head, you need to delete the torso, then save the file as myhead.ms3d to preserve your changes to the head. Then choose Edit, Undo until you get the head back.

11. Delete the head, and then save the file as mytorso.ms3d.

Now the head, torso, and overall hero files have been created, aligned, and their corresponding files are up-to-date.

The Legs

When we start the legs, we'll want to keep the torso mesh around to use as a sizing reference, at least for the first little while. However, we won't need to have the head mesh in there, cluttering things up, so we'll get rid of that.

1. If you haven't done it already, open your torso file, found at \3D2E\ RESOURCES\CH14\mytorso.ms3d.

2. Now save the same file as \3D2E\RESOURCES\CH14\mylegs.ms3d, and continue working with this version.

3. Hide the head mesh using the Groups tab in the toolbox and the Hide button found there.

4. Select the torso mesh, and drag it up about one torso's length above the origin.

5. Create a cylinder with 3 stacks (segments) and 12 slices (faces), and position and shape it as shown in Figure 14.42. This is the foot.

6. Create another cylinder, and rotate it 90 degrees in the Z-axis, making sure that it is oriented so it runs left to right where the knee would be.

7. Using Figure 14.43 as a guide, move the vertices of the top of the foot up to meet the knee cylinder.

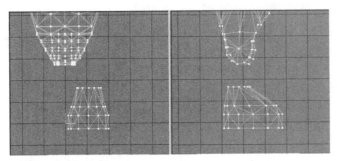

Figure 14.42
Shape and placement of the foot.

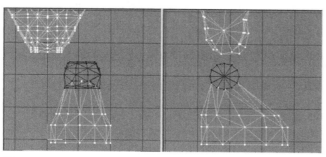

Figure 14.43
The knee.

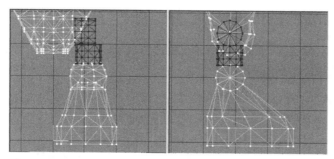

Figure 14.44
The left thigh.

By now you've probably realized that almost everything from here on is more a matter of style and taste and less of technique. So you should feel free to go ahead and deviate from the specific construction details if you think of something you might like better.

8. Reshape the knee cylinder as shown in Figure 14.44.

9. Select the foot cylinder, and rename it as "LeftFoot".

10. Create two more cylinders, and orient them as shown in Figure 14.44 to make the upper leg and hip.

11. Select the two new cylinders, plus the knee cylinder, and use the Regroup tool in the Groups tab of the toolbox. Name the resulting mesh "LeftThigh".

12. Shape the left thigh to match that shown in Figure 14.45—or to suit your own evil purposes.

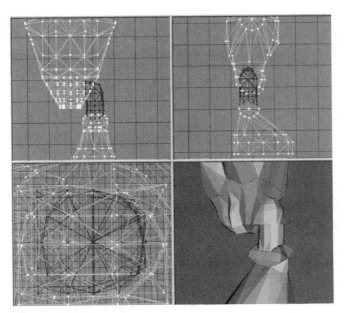

Figure 14.45
The finished left leg.

13. With the left foot mesh selected, choose Edit, Duplicate. A duplicate of the leg is created in exactly the same location as the original, so you can't see it yet.

14. Choose Vertex, Mirror Left<--> Right. The duplicate leg mesh now appears on the other side, and in the right place, or pretty darn close.

15. Rename the new leg mesh as "RightFoot".

16. Now duplicate and mirror the left thigh in the same way, renaming the new thigh mesh as "RightThigh". You should now have two legs, each made up of a thigh mesh and a foot mesh and named appropriately.

17. Next, delete the torso and head meshes from the model.

18. Save your work! You should be saving this as \3D2E\ RESOURCES\CH14\mylegs.ms3d.

Integrating the Legs to the Torso

Just as we did with the head, we now have to integrate the legs with the rest of our model.

1. Open the file \3D2E\RESOURCES\CH14\mytorso.ms3d.

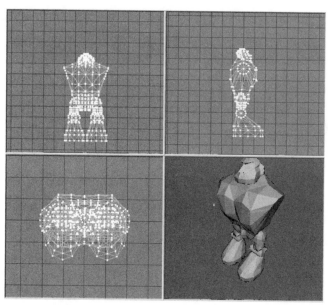

Figure 14.46
The Hero model with head, torso, and legs.

2. Select File, Merge, and choose the legs file you just created, which should be called \3D2E\RESOURCES\CH14\mylegs.ms3d.

3. Choose the right foot, right thigh, left foot, and left thigh meshes, and move them into position. You should now have a model pretty close to the one shown in Figure 14.46.

The Arms

Finally, the last set of meshes in the model. We can create the arms in exactly the same way we created the legs—building up from shape primitives, splicing them together until we have the desired mesh topology.

With arms comes the perennial question, what to do about the fingers? In some models we can make detailed meshes for each finger, with cylinders segmented at the knuckles, and so on. However, we must keep in mind that our goal here is to create a low-poly model, and that typically means fewer than about 1,500 polygons in the model. If we go over that count by a small amount, no big whoop, but we must remain mindful of it.

So, let's get to work! We'll start with the left hand.

1. Open your saved mytorso.ms3d file, and resave it as myarms.ms3d in the same location as your other work files.

2. Create a box offset to the left side (on the right in the Front view) of the torso, situated low, near the bottom of the torso.

3. Duplicate this box, and move the copy to abut the bottom of the original box.

4. Scale the second box to 80 percent.

5. Duplicate the second box, and move the new box below the second.

6. Scale the third box to 80 percent of the second box.

7. Align the boxes as shown in Figure 14.47.

8. Hide the torso mesh to keep it out of the way for the moment.

9. Using Vertex Selection, the Move tool, and the Snap To Grid and Weld tools as you did with earlier parts of the Hero model, align the vertices of the three boxes as shown in Figure 14.48, and weld the vertices together.

10. Rotate the two bottom rows of vertices by −30 degrees in the Z-axis, as shown in Figure 14.49.

11. Move the two bottom rows in the Front view to align them as shown in Figure 14.50.

12. Rotate and move the bottom row of vertices to match what is shown in Figure 14.51.

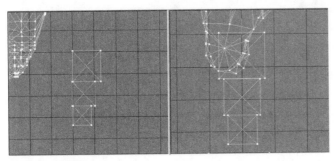

Figure 14.47
Alignment of the three boxes.

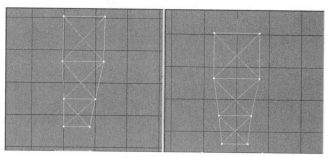

Figure 14.48
Welding the hand vertices.

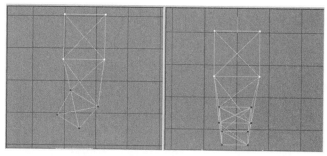

Figure 14.49
Rotating the two bottom rows.

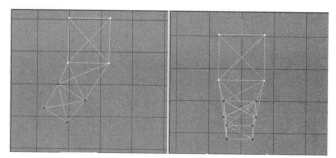

Figure 14.50
Moving the two bottom rows.

13. Now, setting the Select mode to Groups, select all the groups of boxes, duplicate them, and move them forward to abut the front of the original boxes, using Figure 14.52 as a guide.

14. Repeat the process in step 13, putting the new copies at the rear of the originals, using Figure 14.53 as a guide.

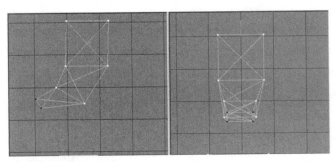

Figure 14.51
The bottom row of vertices.

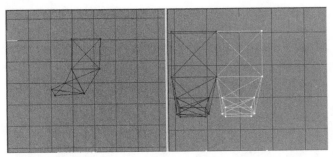

Figure 14.52
Two sets of shaped boxes abutting each other.

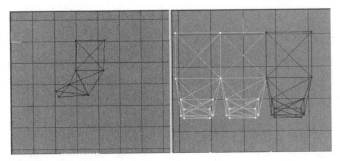

Figure 14.53
Three sets of shaped boxes.

15. Repeat the duplicating process *one more time*, but this time move the new boxes to the left side of the Front view. This is the thumb.

16. Choose Vertex, Mirror Left <--> Right to reverse the orientation of the thumb boxes (see Figure 14.54), and then scale the thumb to 50 percent.

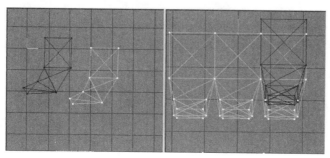

Figure 14.54
The start of the thumb.

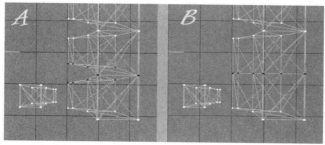

Figure 14.55
Welding the hand vertices.

17. Now we'll switch back to the hand part. In the Top view, select the vertices that are adjacent in the two forward parts of the hand boxes, as shown in Figure 14.55, panel A. Then choose Vertex, Flatten, Z, and the vertices will be brought together onto a common plane, as shown in panel B of Figure 14.55.

18. Double-check the other views, and if all vertices look to be coincident, then choose Vertex, Weld Together to weld them.

19. Repeat step 18 for the rear part of the hand, welding the result. Compare with Figure 14.56 to make sure it is correct.

20. Select the rearmost vertices, in the baby finger area, and scale them to 50 percent in the X- and Y-axes, as shown in Figure 14.57.

21. Move the scaled vertices forward until they are close to the middle hand boxes, using the Top view in Figure 14.58 as a guide.

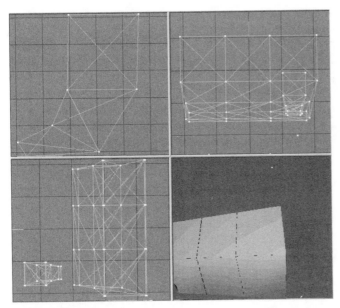

Figure 14.56
After the hand welding.

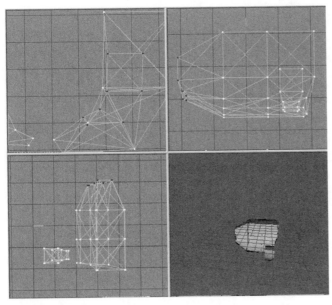

Figure 14.57
The scaled baby finger area.

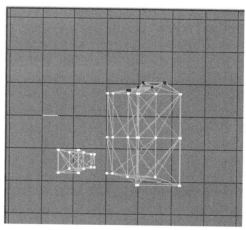

Figure 14.58
Placing the scaled baby finger vertices.

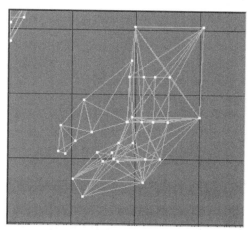

Figure 14.59
The thumb positioning.

22. Repeat steps 20 and 21 for the front index finger area.

23. In the Front view, rotate and shape the thumb to approximate what's shown in Figure 14.59.

24. Unhide the torso, and compare the size and positioning of your hand with the views shown in Figure 14.60. Rotate the hand to match, if required.

    Now you might be thinking that the hand looks awfully blocky compared to other parts of the model. You are right, but take heart. We can compensate

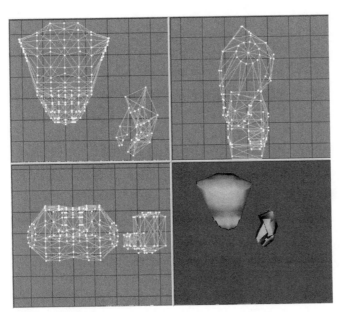

Figure 14.60
Comparison of torso with hand.

for this with our skins. Remember, we want to keep our polygon count as low as we can.

25. Using the Groups tab in the toolbox, select all the hand groups, regroup them to form a new mesh, and rename it as "LeftHand".

26. In the Front view, use the Sphere tool set to four stacks and eight slices, and create a sphere that completely fills the left shoulder socket of the torso. Check all your views to make sure that you have it pretty close.

27. Make another sphere with the same settings that fills the top of the hand, and place it there.

28. Make a one-stack, eight-slice cylinder that you can rotate, and move it into a position that connects the two spheres. Use Figure 14.61 as a guide for sphere and cylinder sizing and placement.

29. Select all the upper arm components, regroup them, and name the new mesh "LeftArm".

30. Select the new left arm mesh, duplicate it, and then choose Vertex, Mirror Right <--> Left.

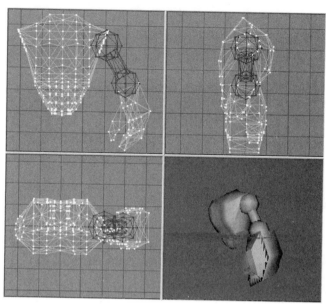

Figure 14.61
The left arm.

31. Adjust the new mesh if necessary, and rename it as "RightArm".

32. Repeat the duplicating and renaming operations for the left hand mesh, calling the newly duplicated copy "RightHand".

33. Delete the torso mesh.

34. Save your work! You should now have a pair of hefty arms that closely resemble those shown in Figure 14.62.

Integrating the Arms to the Torso

Once again, it's integration time. If you are inclined to wonder about doing the model this way rather than all at once in one file, I want to point out that now you have a different source model file for each major component of your model. This allows you to make different mix-and-match models using the same components over and over. Just make three sets of arms, four sets of legs, five heads, two torsos, or something like that. Mix 'n' match 'em, and you'll have all sorts of different model configurations!

1. Open the file \3D2E\RESOURCES\CH14\myhero.ms3d.

2. Select File, Merge, and choose the arms file you just created, which should be called \3D2E\RESOURCES\CH14\myarms.ms3d.

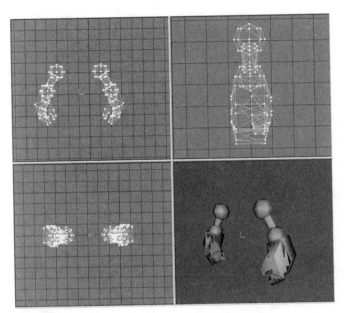

Figure 14.62
The completed arms.

3. Choose both the right arm and the left arm meshes, and move them into position. You should now have a model pretty closely resembling the one shown in Figure 14.63.

Finally, we need to scale our mesh to the correct size. We want our guy to be around 2 meters tall. We are going to export at a 1:1 scale, so we need to set the top of the head to be close to 2.0 units high in the Y-axis as measured from the scene's origin (the 0,0,0 center of the scene, where the three colored lines of the axis bug intersect). Use the Scale tool and one of two methods: (1) eyeball the height of the character as he exists now (move your cursor to the top of his head in the Side or Front views, and get the Y-axis value in the status bar of the window at the bottom left), calculate the scale in your head (or with a calculator), and enter the appropriate scale value in all three scale fields of the Scale tool (the same value for all three), or (2) click-drag the mouse in each of the views until you shrink or grow the model to where you want it. I personally prefer method 1—I get more consistent results, and it only takes two or three scale adjustments at the most.

Select the entire model and move it so that the feet straddle the axis bug, while resting squarely on the x-axis line in the front view. The x-axis line in the bug is colored yellow.

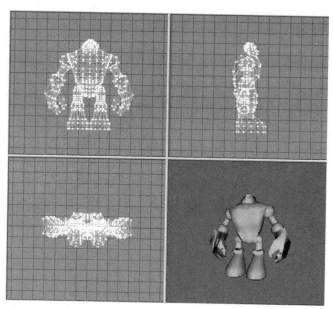

Figure 14.63
The completed Hero model.

Testing the Tool Chain

As you may have noticed by now, when we create art for games, we use an assortment of third-party tools to generate our various kinds of artwork.

Party On, Garth!

A third party is some entity that provides tools and resources used in a particular system context but that is (1) not the user of the system and (2) not the creator of the system.

An example in the context of computer systems: when you are using a computer system made by Dell, Dell does not make the operating system—Microsoft does. So in this context, you are the first party, Dell is the second party, and Microsoft is the third party.

In the context of operating systems: when you are using Windows to create flyers for your bowling league, you are the first party, Microsoft (who makes Microsoft Windows) is the second party, and your drawing software is made by a third party—unless you use Microsoft Paint, in which case there is no third party. I hope. Okay, let's not get too deep into this . . .

Anyway, in the context of game engines, Torque is the product of GarageGames, the second party. MilkShape, the Gimp, UVMapper, and so on, are all third parties.

Oh yeah, and whatever happened to Garth, anyway?

At the start of any project, or whenever any new tools are brought to bear on the project workload, there is an activity that should be performed called *testing the tool chain*, or sometimes *proving the tool chain*.

The idea is to create some art resource, at a minimal effort, perform all the steps required to get that resource into the game engine, and then use the game engine to actually view the art resource. Each time a new "layer" of resource complexity is added, the first step should be to test the tool chain with a minimal example of the new complexity. Thus, we build up our model in an incremental, step-wise fashion.

If you are familiar with the "cyclone," "tornado," or "spiral" development methodologies (essentially that's just three names for the same thing), you will find that the incremental approach is an ideal fit. If you aren't familiar with development methodologies, don't sweat it. Just understand that building up your model in a step-wise fashion is both intuitive and easy on the brain, not to mention that it fits well with current project management and development pipeline best practices. The primary advantage (and it's a huge advantage) is that most design or implementation errors are detected very early on and fixed right away, so that they don't fester and end up infecting an entire project.

Here, look at this:

Modeling Work Flow

1. **Create character model.**

2. Export model to game engine format.

3. Insert mesh into game environment.

4. Run game and view model in game environment.

5. **Add UV-mapped skin texture.**

6. Export model to game engine format.

7. Insert mesh into game environment.

8. Run game and view model in game environment.

9. **Add rigged skeleton with no animations.**

10. Export model to game engine format.

11. Insert mesh into game environment.

12. Run game and view model in game environment.

13. **Add one animation, usually idle or root.**

14. Export model to game engine format.

15. Insert mesh into game environment.

16. Run game and view model in game environment.

17. **Add another animation.**

18. Export model to game engine format.

19. Insert mesh into game environment.

20. Run game and view model in game environment.

21. **Rinse and repeat steps 17 to 20.**

Notice how we add complexity to the model a little bit at a time, and each time we add to it, we test the model in its final context. Traditionally, that first export in step 2 is the "testing the tool chain" part. The rest is just sensible work flow. Note that the UV-mapped skin texture series of steps *don't* need to happen before the rigging and animation steps, and therefore we don't need to wait until the guy doing our textures and UV mapping is done before we create and test animations.

You should be aware that the previous section of this chapter, "The Base Hero Model," was the equivalent of step 1 in the modeling work flow procedure.

So let's try it testing the tool chain right now.

Make sure you have MilkShape 3D running and you've got your freshly completed Hero model open and on full display.

1. In MilkShape, choose File, Export, Torque DTS Plus. You will see the Torque DTSPlus Exporter dialog box appear.

Caution

Do *not* use the Torque Game Engine DTS Exporter. In fact, don't use it at all in this chapter.

2. We're going to take the defaults, but we should make sure they are correct. You want to have the following check boxes enabled:

   ■ Output dump file
   ■ Copy Textures

   You should probably always have Output dump file enabled. The file that is created is called dump.dmp, and it will be in the same folder that you exported your model to. You can look in it for errors if things don't work right. You should delete all dump files before shipping your game.

   Copy Textures is a nifty and very handy feature that allows you to keep your source model and its texture files in a location far removed from the game folders. When you export to the appropriate location in the game folders, any textures that your model uses will be copied to the same folder as the exported DTS version of your model. Muy cool.

   Make sure you have the Scale field in the Options pane set to 1.

   Click Apply to save your settings, and then click Export DTS when you are ready to close the dialog box and perform the export.

3. When prompted, save your DTS output file as \3D2E\RESOURCES\CH14\ myhero.dts for now.

That was pretty painless. That's step 2 of the work flow done. We'll dust off the Torque Show Tool Pro (TSTP) program we used in Chapter 9 and check out the model.

1. Launch TSTP.

2. Ensure that you have your RESOURCES folder selected in the Project Directory pop-up.

3. Find RESOURCES/CH14/myhero.dts, and double-click on it.

4. The model should appear in the center of the screen.

5. Use the mouse actions (described in Chapter 9 in Table 9.1) to rotate the model and bring it closer to you or move it farther away. Left-click and drag will make the camera orbit the model, while right-click and drag will slide the camera around. The mouse wheel will let you zoom in and out.

6. If necessary, go back to your model in MilkShape and make adjustments to your model, and then come back here to check them out.

TSTP actually uses Torque itself to display the model (in fact, TSTP actually really is Torque, except that it is running without any mission, or networking, or the player GUI, or any other stuff like that), so we know that if the model works in the Show Tool context, then it will work in a game context in Torque.

The Hero Skin

Now it's time to skin the model. In Chapter 9 you learned how to create the textures for skins, and in Chapter 13 you learned how to do simple UV mapping for skins. Next, we have to do the UV mapping for the player-character, which is somewhat more complex. We are not going to go over the creation of the texture for Hero character skin. The Resources folder includes a mapped Hero skin texture for you to use, but I encourage you to make your own in the same fashion as the one for the Standard Male.

1. If MilkShape is not already running, launch it and open your Hero model, located at \3D2E\RESOURCES\CH14\myhero.ms3d.

2. Choose File, Export, Wavefront Obj, and export your Hero model as \3D2E\RESOURCES\CH14\myhero.obj.

3. Launch UVMapper (found at \3D2E\ TOOLS\UVMAPPER), and maximize the window.

4. Load the \3D2E\RESOURCES\CH14\myhero.obj. You will see a crazy quilt of lines. This is the "default" mapping created by MilkShape. Let's forget about that, because we are going to create our own mapping.

5. Choose Edit, New UV Map, Planar, and then use the settings shown in Figure 14.64. Click OK when finished adjusting these settings.

6. Choose Edit, Color by Group, and then click OK. Your screen should now look like Figure 14.65. Of course, your version will be in color, and so the light yellow will actually be more visible to you. In the figure, which has been converted to grayscale, the yellow has become a very light gray.

7. First, choose Edit, Select, All, and press the forward slash ("/") key on the numeric keypad to shrink the selection to 25 percent, half-sized in the x dimension and half-sized in the y dimension (the asterisk ["*"] on the numeric keypad will do the opposite). Press Enter to save your adjustment.

Figure 14.64
Planar mapping settings for Hero model.

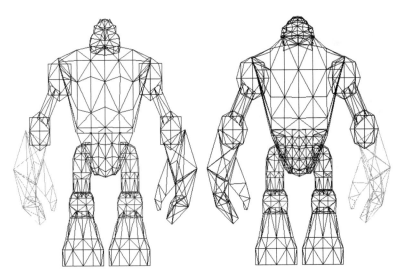

Figure 14.65
The unwrapped Hero model.

If you don't like the adjustments you just made, press Esc to undo your changes since making your last selection or remapping.

8. Choose Edit, Select by Group, choose the group "head", and then click OK.

9. Choose Edit, New UV Map, Spherical. Use the settings shown in Figure 14.66.

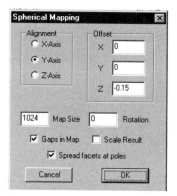

Figure 14.66
Settings for the spherical mapping of the head.

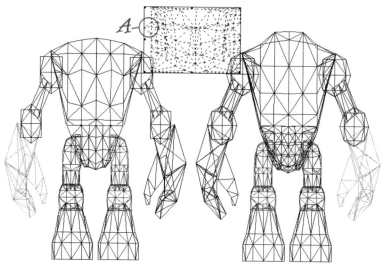

Figure 14.67
The unwrapped head.

10. Press the equal sign ("=") to expand the head selection to fill the window, and then press the forward slash on the numeric keypad a few times to shrink the selection. Use your mouse to drag the head to the upper center of the window, as shown in Figure 14.67.

Now you might notice that there appear to be two triangles out of place in the head unwrapping. Look inside circle A in Figure 14.67 and see if you can spot them. In your model this may not be the case, but the more closely your model matches the one I've done here, the more likely this is to happen. This little oddity is easily fixed. You should be able to do the

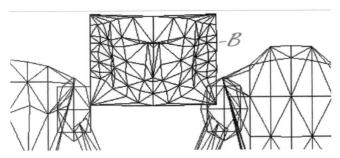

Figure 14.68
The adjusted triangles.

mapping without that happening—it's all a matter of which settings you use. You can try to get the right settings by trial and error. However, the simplest fix is to just move the miscreants to their lawful location. So that's what we'll do.

11. Drag your cursor over the middle of the two wayward triangles. Don't touch any parts of any other triangles in any other part of the model. The triangles will now appear surrounded by a selection box.

12. Click and drag them over to the right-hand side where there is that suspicious-looking gap, and place them as well as you can. Location B in Figure 14.68 shows where the triangles end up.

13. Use the arrow keys to adjust the position of the triangles. There you go! Now you need to do a bit of housekeeping-like fiddling.

14. Choose Edit, Select, All. You will get everything on the screen selected in a selection box with the little black sizing handles at the corners and midway along each side.

15. Grab the sizing handle on the right side. Your cursor should change to the left-right sizing cursor (this is an arrow pointing left and right).

16. Drag the sizing handle toward the left until you get a blank space on the right a little wider than the width of the head.

17. Choose Edit, Select, Group, and choose the head. Drag it over to the upper right, in the blank space you just created. You should now have a layout like Figure 14.69.

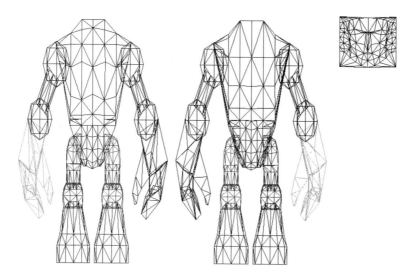

Figure 14.69
The reorganized map.

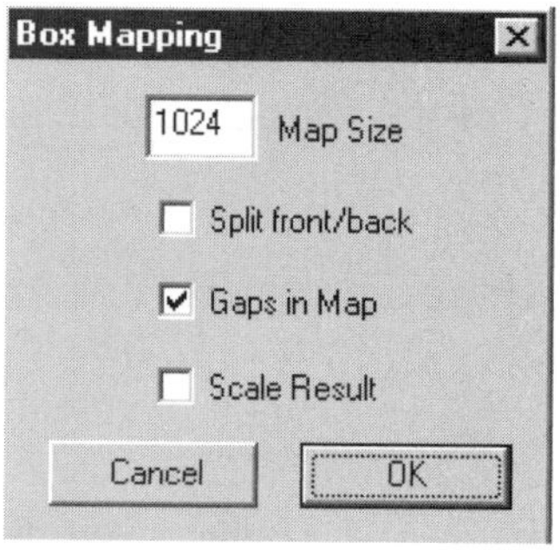

Figure 14.70
The Box Mapping settings.

As you work you will probably reorganize your layout a few times—that's perfectly normal. You want to keep it clean and make sure your items are easily selectable.

18. Now choose Edit, Select, By Group, and choose the LeftHand group.

19. Choose Edit, New UV Map, Box. You will get the Box Mapping dialog box, as shown in Figure 14.70. Make sure you have Split front/back turned off, and Gaps in Map turned on. Click OK.

The unwrapped left hand will appear in the window, surrounded by the selection box.

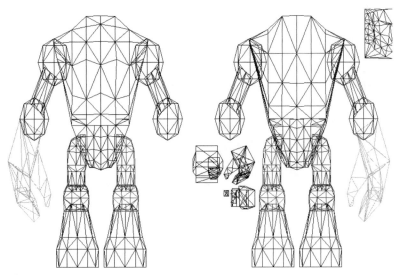

Figure 14.71
The UV-mapped hands.

20. Move and size the hand mapping, just as we did with the head, placing it in the center of the window in the blank area. Make sure it is small enough to allow the mapped right hand in here as well (see Figure 14.71).

21. Perform the same UV-mapping operation and placement operation on the RightHand group, putting them in the center space.

22. Next, map the left and right feet the same way. For each group as you unwrap it, size the sole (oval shape) so that it is longer than it is wide. Place the feet underneath the main model, as shown in Figure 14.72.

23. Next, map all the arms and legs. Use Planar mapping for these.

24. Shrink and move the mapped objects, ensuring that no mapped objects overlap any others.

25. Once all the objects are mapped, overlap similar items (with the exception of the torso front and back), and enlarge the torso, hand, and head objects as much as possible. The larger the mapping, the more detail can be applied in the texture.

26. Finally, move and arrange the objects to match the layout in Figure 14.73. This is the final texture-mapping layout that we'll use for the template.

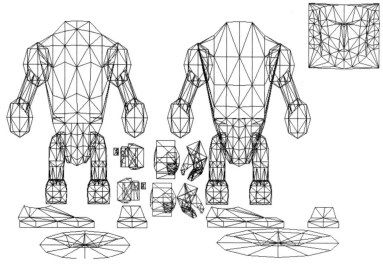

Figure 14.72
The UV-mapped feet.

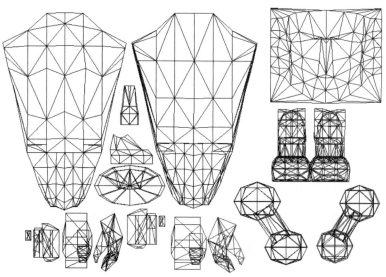

Figure 14.73
The final UV-mapping layout.

27. Choose File, Save Model, and save it as \3D2E\RESOURCES\CH14\ myhero.obj (thereby obliterating the one you created from MilkShape; don't worry though—you can always export another from MilkShape if needed).

In the Save Model dialog box, the following options should be checked: Export Normals, Export UV Coordinates, Export Materials, and Export UVMapper Regions. The rest of the options should be unchecked.

28. Choose File, Save Texture Map, and save the map as \3D2E\RESOURCES\ CH14\myhero.bmp. Make sure the texture size is set to 512 by 512.

29. Launch MilkShape, and create a new file.

30. Choose File, Import, Wavefront Obj, and import the \3D2E\RESOURCES\ CH14\myhero.obj file.

31. In the Materials tab of the toolbox, click New.

32. Click the top Texture button, and locate the \3D2E\RESOURCES\CH14\ myhero.bmp texture map template file you created in UVMapper.

33. Rename the material as "heroskin".

34. Using the Groups tab, select all the meshes, and then switch back to the Materials tab and click Assign. You should now have a 3D view that resembles Figure 14.74.

Of course, your version is in color. The lines of the triangles in the color groupings assigned in UVMapper are clearly visible. You are now in a position to go ahead and use the Gimp to create your skin for the Hero model. Refer back to

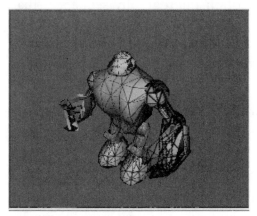

Figure 14.74
The 3D view showing the UV template texture.

Chapter 9 if you need a refresher. Make sure to save your skin as a JPG file type in order to use it in Torque. This means that you will also have to go back into MilkShape and redefine your material to point at the JPG version and not the BMP version.

If you are wondering why the exercise in Chapter 9 didn't make a skin for use on this model . . . I mean, well come on! Do you want me to do *everything* for you? Ya lazy bums! Make your own danged skins. They're likely to be 10 times better than mine anyway.

Now, if you are finished with your griping, you need to test your UV mapping. Use the Torque Show Tool Pro to view your model the same way you did back in the "Testing the Tool Chain" section.

If everything looks good with the UV mapping, we'll continue into the animation section using the UV template Hero skin that I've included in the \3D2E\ RESOURCES\CH14\hero.jpg file.

Character Animation

Well, a static model—no matter how cool looking when it's standing there—is not terribly interesting in a first-person shooter. We're going to have to animate that sucker!

If we were a big-name, big-money shop, we might go out and hire a motion capture studio to make our animations. But we're not—we're indie developers! So we will have to explore other options, and there are some.

On the Internet you can find some stop-motion photography sequences that might help you develop your character animations. There are also freely downloadable files with character animations in them; they will probably have a different skeleton structure than the one we use here, but a certain amount of tweaking can go a long way.

I know someone who manually creates animations using action figures that he poses, changing the poses step-by-step as he works through the animation, converting what his eye sees into the appropriate frame in his animation program. This is certainly a good low-budget option.

In this book we are going to hand-build our animations, because the point is to learn how to do it. They may not be the best animations in the world (or maybe they will be!), but they will be your very own if you make them yourself. If you need a model, ask a friend or family member to step slowly through whatever it is you are trying to animate, if it's humanly possible. You'd be surprised how helpful that can be. Bribe them with their favorite dessert or something.

Animating Characters in Torque

The general method for making animated characters for use in Torque is to construct a skeleton that corresponds to components of the model and then attach that skeleton to the corresponding components in a process called *rigging*. We then create a sequence of *keyframes*—essentially a series of skeleton poses. When the Torque Engine wants to animate the model, it calculates the positions of the meshes in the model by the position and rotation of the nodes (the joints where the "bones" of the skeleton connect to each other) based on where the keyframes appear in the animation timeline.

We are going to create six different basic animations:

- root (same as idle in some non-Torque systems)

- run

- look

- head

- headside

- death

Table 14.1 shows a complete list of Torque-supported animations. This is *not* the list of Torque animation sequence files that come with the demo (although all the animations that are supported are indeed included as animation sequences). It's just that many of the animation sequence files are not automatically invoked by Torque from within the engine or from anywhere in the scripts. Anyway, the ones in Table 14.1 *are* invoked by the engine or by the demo scripts, as described in the table.

These animations correspond to character animation support built into Torque. The names must match the names used by Torque; however, we can add our own arbitrary animations and activate them from within the script programs if we want. There are also other animations that Torque supports that we won't cover here.

Table 14.1 Torque-Supported Animation Sequences

Sequence Name	Description
root	This is the basic "not doing anything" animation—usually the character is standing and fidgeting.
run	This is the animation used when the character is running forward.
walk	When the character's speed is less than running speed, he walks, using this animation.
back	This is the animation used when the character is running backward.
side	This is the animation used when the character is running sideways, sometimes called *strafing*.
look	This is a simple animation where the character's right arm points where the character is looking, such as when holding a weapon.
head	The head looks up or down depending on where the character is looking.
fall	This is the pose of a character, or his animations, when the character is falling off a cliff or building.
land	This is the sudden stop at the end of a fall!
jump	This is a jump made while running.
death1	Like it says. This is one of 11 possibilities. You don't need them all, but like the old adage, "Variety is the spice of life, er, death, or something."
death2-death11	Ditto, ten more times.
looksn	This is the same as "look," but with weapon held close.
lookms	This is the same as "look," but with arms loose.
scoutroot	This is the animation used when the character is astride something like a motorbike.
headside	This is the animation used when the character is turning his head from side to side.
light_recoil	This is the weapon recoil, used to show the character's reaction to firing a weapon.
sitting	This is the animation used when the character is seated, like sitting in a car.
celsalute	This is an animation (an in-game salute or taunt animation), activated by Ctrl+S as default. You can use it for whatever you want.
celwave	Activated by Ctrl+W as default, this is another in-game salute or taunt animation.
standjump	This is another jump animation, but this time the character jumps from a standing pose, like root.
looknw	This is another weapon "look" with a variation of the loose arms pose.

In Figure 14.75 the spheres are joints, or nodes. The spike between two of the spheres is a "bone." The direction the spike is pointing indicates the relationship between the nodes. The node at the big end is the parent, while the other end is the child node. Notice that in Figure 14.75 the parent node in frame B is rotated 60 degrees in its orientation from frame A, and the child node follows the

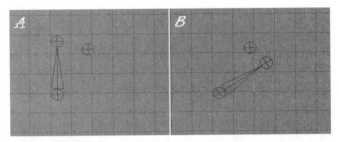

Figure 14.75
Bone movement during joint rotation.

rotation. The unattached node doesn't move. Note that the horizontal and vertical lines inside the nodes are angled in the rotated nodes but not in the unattached node.

Open your myhero.ms3d file, if it isn't already open. Set Joint Size to .05 in the File Preferences dialog box on the Misc tab. We need to use such a small joint size because the scale of the Hero model is quite a bit smaller than the Standard Male Character model from Chapter 9.

Building the Skeleton

Before we can create the animations, we need to construct the character's skeleton. We build the skeleton from the bottom-up, so to speak, beginning with the base node and working toward the outer extremities.

1. We will start with the unlink node (or joint), which we place at the origin: (0,0,0). Make sure that you click the Joint tool (lower-right corner of the Model panel, on the right side of the main window), before trying to place the joints.

Tip

To select a joint, click the Joint button in the Select Options frame in the Model tab. You can only do this when the Select tool is active (its button is pressed in the Tools frame).

2. Now make sure that the unlink node is still selected, and then place another node up in front of the head, roughly off the end of the nose, and name this one cam. Figure 14.76 shows the relative appearance of these two nodes in the Side view. This arrangement is independent of the rest of the skeleton. (See the sidebar discussion "Torque's Biped Skeleton" for an explanation of the unlink and cam nodes.)

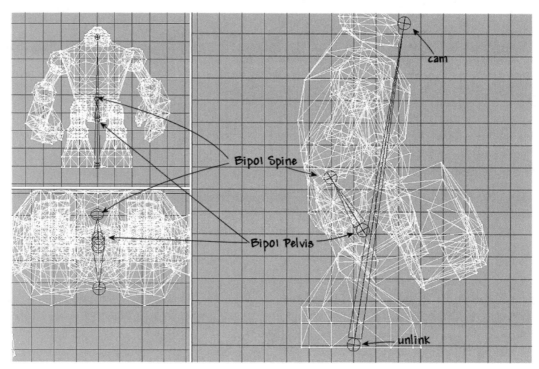

Figure 14.76
Location of Bip01 Pelvis and Bip01 Spine nodes.

Tip

If the unlink node is not selected, you need to select it before creating the cam joint. Do this by clicking the Select tool in the Model panel and then clicking the Joint button in the Select Options frame at the bottom of the Model tab's panel. Then just click the unlink joint, or click-drag a box around it.

Whenever you create a child node (in this case, the cam joint), you need to have the parent node selected before placing the child. This will make the bone connector appear, thus showing the relationship between the nodes.

3. Now we'll start on the skeleton itself. This time, make sure that you *don't* have any joints selected, while the Joint tool is selected.

4. Place a joint node directly above the unlink node, but up around where the Y value is about 0.7 or so. Name this joint Bip01 Pelvis.

5. Next, while making sure that the Bip01 Pelvis node is still selected, place another joint a little bit above and behind Bip01 Pelvis. Name this node Bip01 Spine. Figure 14.76 shows the relative appearance of these two nodes. Make

sure that the big end of the bone that joins these two joints is at the end where the `Bip01 Pelvis` node is. The big end of the bone is the *parent* end.

6. Add all the new nodes, and label them appropriately. Figure 14.77 provides a guide to the node placement and their names.

Tip

The order in which nodes are added obviously matters. Here is the sequence for the hero's skeleton:

Unlink (start)	Bip01 Spine (restart)
cam (end)	Bip01 L Thigh
Bip01 Pelvis (start)	Bip01 L Calf
Bip01 Spine	Bip01 L Foot (end)
Bip01 Spine1	Bip01 Neck (restart)
Bip01 Spine2	Bip01 R Clavicle
Bip01 Neck	Bip01 R UpperArm
Bip01 Head	Bip01 R ForeArm
eye (end)	Bip01 R Hand
Bip01 Head (restart)	mount0 (end)
Mount1 (end)	Bip01 Neck (restart)
Bip01 Spine (restart)	Bip01 L Clavicle
Bip01 R Thigh	Bip01 L UpperArm
Bip01 R Calf	Bip01 L ForeArm
Bip01 R Foot (end)	Bip01 L Hand (end)

Read the sequence from the top of the left column to the bottom. Then resume at the top of the right column, and work down to the bottom. Nodes that are tagged with (start) are parents only, not children of any other nodes. Nodes that are tagged (end) are children only, and not the parent of any other nodes. Nodes that are tagged (restart) are nodes that already exist, and are listed again in order to show where a particular child attaches. You do not have to make another copy of a (restart) tagged node, just select the one that is already there, and start adding a node to it.

7. Starting with the `Bip01 Pelvis` and moving on to the spine, hips, and shoulders (in that order), adjust the joints of the skeleton to match the skeleton pose in Figure 14.78.

Remember to rotate hip, knee, elbow, and shoulder joints to move the joints at the extremities. You want the character slightly bent at the knee joints, with his left arm bones slightly bent beside him and the right arm bent up at 90 degrees.

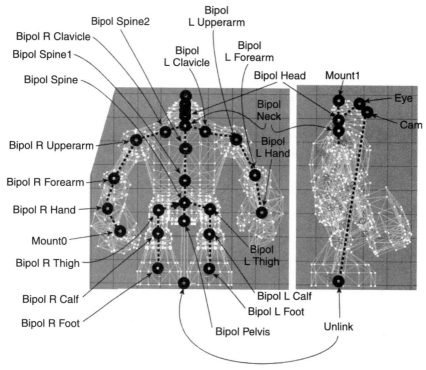

Figure 14.77
The Hero skeleton with labeled nodes.

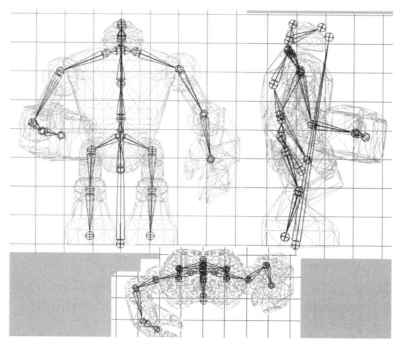

Figure 14.78
The pose-adjusted skeleton.

Pay particular attention to the placement of the Bip01 Spine and Bip01_x_Thigh nodes. The Bip01 Pelvis should be well below the level of the Bip01 Thigh nodes, and they should be just a tad higher than the lower spine.

8. Adjust the *mesh* rotations, and fine-tune the mesh group placements to match the pose of the skeleton. You might need to fiddle back and forth between the mesh groups and the joint nodes until you are satisfied with the result.

Torque's Biped Skeleton

The node names and bones you see in Figure 14.77 are somewhat of a standard for Torque. They don't have to be used, though. There are standard skeletons for other games whose nomenclature you could use instead. Torque uses a standard biped skeleton that is the same as the one used for *CounterStrike* and other games. As mentioned earlier, if we don't use the Torque skeleton, with the node names that exactly match, then we can't use the stock Torque animations.

There are some details about the skeleton and its parts that are really important, and we need to get them exactly right.

The first, and most important, is the node names. Most of the nodes—those that are joints in the "bone structure" of the skeleton—have names that start with *Bip01*. Any nodes that have this in their names *always* have a space immediately after the Bip01 string in the name. Additionally, some of the names have an *R* or *L* in them to specify right or left side, respectively. These names *always* have a space after the *R* or *L* in addition to the space in front of the *R* or *L*. (The space in front is the same space that always follows the Bip01 string.)

So, for example, with the name Bip01 L Clavicle, there is one space between *Bip01* and the *L* and one space between the *L* and the *Clavicle*. Got that? Good.

Now, notice in the Side view in Figure 14.77 the node called unlink. This node is not really a required node for our purposes. It comes from a usage requirement when exporting from programs like 3D Studio Max. I've included it here anyway, because I wanted a place to attach the cam node to and something that wasn't part of the main skeleton. With the unlink node, we just need to ensure that any animations that move the entire body forward or back also move the unlink node as well. This will have the effect of seamlessly dragging the cam node along with it. The cam node is a "child" node of the unlink node, but it has no child nodes itself. The unlink node is *not* a child of any other node, and neither does it have any children other than the cam node.

Now, you *could* attach the cam node to the head node, for example. The problem with this approach is that the cam node will then move and swivel according to how the head moves in its animations and not simply along with the body in general (the desired effect).

Finally, note that the naming convention used by Torque reflects the fact that the first tool used to make Torque (and Tribes) models was 3D Studio Max. Hence, the node names for the skeleton are names of *bones*. MilkShape 3D doesn't model its skeletons with bones for the nodes; instead, MilkShape 3D's nodes are *joints*. This is why we have a node called `Bip01 R Forearm` when the node itself is obviously the elbow (a joint) and not a forearm bone.

Here is a list of Torque's special nodes and the purposes they serve:

cam	This node establishes the third-person camera's "orbit" center.
eye	This node establishes the location of the first-person "eye view" camera.
unlink	This node is used to align `cam` node with the main body of the model.
mount0	This node is commonly used for attaching a weapon to the right hand.
mount1	This node is commonly used for attaching a hat or other headgear. It is sometimes located in the left hand for two-fisted weapon usage.
mount2	This node (not used in this skeleton) is commonly used for attaching a backpack (as a child of `Bip01 Spine1` or `Bip01 Spine2`).
ski0, ski1	These nodes (not used in this skeleton) are commonly used for a ski effect in Torque or for dust emitters.

Note that you are not obligated to use the nodes as described above. Different modelers have taken great liberties with the `mount`*n* and `ski`*n* nodes, though the `eye` and `cam` nodes tend to be used for the same purposes by everyone. You can also create your own special nodes for your own uses, like finger and thumb joints for detailed hand movement or jaw, cheek, and lip nodes for facial animations.

Rigging: Attaching the Skeleton

So far we have built the skeleton, named the nodes, and aligned the bones into a pose we like. Next we are going to attach our model to the skeleton. That way, when the skeleton is manipulated, the mesh of the model will follow suit. It is during this step that you might be inclined to thank me for insisting that you retain mesh groups for the different model components like arms and feet and so on!

Rigging the Head

We'll begin with the head, just to get a feel for the rigging operation.

1. In the Joints tab in the toolbox, choose the joint (or node) named `Bip01 Head`. Make sure it appears highlighted in red in the wire-frame views.

2. Switch to the Groups tab, and choose the head mesh. It should appear highlighted in red, as you already know.

3. Switch *back* to the Joints tab, and click Assign. Now the head mesh is assigned to the head node. To double-check, just click anywhere in a blank space in a wire-frame view to make sure that no objects are selected, choose the head joint to ensure it is selected, and then click the SelAssigned (Select Assigned) button. The head mesh should appear highlighted. If not, go back and repeat these three steps.

Aw shucks, there it is—the head is now rigged! Of course, that's not the end of the story. There is still the rest of the model.

There's also the issue of what to do when a bone is rigged wrong. Sometimes it's a trivial fix, and other times you might have to rerig the whole model. Or you might have to rig a model by attaching a node to just a few vertices rather than a whole mesh or submesh. That can get very, um, *fiddly*—I guess that would be a reasonable description.

Part of the simplicity in rigging this model comes from the technique we used; building from primitives allows us to easily define meshes and submeshes. We'll use a "one node per mesh" rule of thumb. It can get trickier using other techniques, such as assigning individual vertices to joints, but sometimes those other techniques might be more appropriate for the model you want to build. It's a judgment call, as everything important tends to be. In fact, we are going to employ a trickier technique—assigning a set of individual vertices to a joint—as the one exception (as there always is) to the "one node per mesh" rule next.

Rigging the Torso

Okay, so the head was a cakewalk. It wasn't even necessary to show any pictures for you to be able to follow along. How about the torso then—duck soup again, no?

Well, yes . . . I mean *no*, actually. No duck soup for this one!

The entire head mesh is attached to the head node, and that is fine. Tilting or rotating the head node will indeed move the head in the manner we want. There really isn't a whole lot to choose from. The neck is more a part of the spine than the head. The cam and mount1 nodes aren't even really related to the skeleton. They are *special nodes* that will have a different role to play in Torque, which we'll cover later. So that leaves the head node to control the head mesh.

The torso, though, has at least five nodes that it might be attached to. But which should it be? Let's eliminate the neck node for now. That leaves the three spine nodes and the Bip01 Pelvis node. Actually, we *can* use more than one node for a mesh, giving different parts of the mesh to different nodes. When we built the torso mesh, we actually combined two primitives together, remember that? One was the chest cylinder, and the other was the abdomen cylinder. We could have left them as two separate submeshes, but I wanted to show you how to join them together. We can still use them as if they were two separate meshes, by assigning their respective vertices to different nodes.

If you look at the nodes, you'll see that the Bip01 Spine node is pretty well the obvious candidate to control the abdomen part of the mesh. The Bip01 Spine2 node, although probably not as obvious, is likely the best candidate for the other node, for our torso, even though it exists in circumstances dissimilar to the Bip01 Spine. (Bip01 Spine2 doesn't have limbs attached.) But we'll go with these two anyway and see how that works out.

What this will mean in terms of animation is that we can have the vertices that are attached to one node move in one way, while the vertices attached to the other node move differently. Or not. It all depends on how you rig it.

None of this worrying about which node to use is strictly necessary. The animations we are going to create don't actually *require* the torso mesh to be given more than one node, but it's a good thing to learn, so we'll do it.

1. To get started with rigging the torso, let's tidy up the ol' drawing board a bit by hiding all the meshes except the torso mesh. If you've forgotten how, just go to the Groups tab of the toolbox, choose each mesh, and click Hide. Unfortunately, we can't selectively hide parts of the skeleton. It's either all or nothing when it comes to the bones.

Tip

It isn't always necessary to hide all the meshes that you aren't working with. You just need to ensure that you can easily select the individual vertices that you want in the mesh of interest. In the case of the torso mesh, in the top view, you can see pretty well every other mesh overlaps the torso.

2. Choose the Bip01 Spine node in the Joints tab.

3. Switch to the Model tab, and set the Select tool to Vertex mode. Then select the vertices that are the abdomen. You can use either the Front view or the Side view. Figure 14.79 shows the vertices to select.

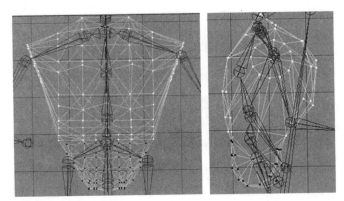

Figure 14.79
The abdomen vertices.

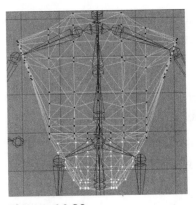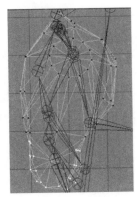

Figure 14.80
The chest vertices.

4. Back in the Joints tab, click Assign. Now the vertices are attached to the Bip01 Spine node.

5. Now choose the Bip01 Spine2 node, and then select the vertices for it, using Figure 14.80 as a guide.

6. Click Assign in the Joints tab. That should do it.

7. Double-check to make sure you didn't overlook any of the vertices by choosing each node in turn, clicking the SelAssigned button, and looking to see which vertices for that node might have been missed. If you did miss any, you can simply select the node, select the vertices, and then click Assign to add them to the nodes list.

There, that's the torso. It might not have seemed so difficult a task to you, but to me it was a nightmare! Well, maybe not that bad, but it shows you the kinds of decisions you will have to make when rigging your models. What goes where and how will it work best?

Now that we have a few nodes rigged, let's take a look and see what they actually do.

1. If you don't have an Anim button at the lower right, then choose Window, Show Keyframer, and make sure there is a check mark there.

2. Click Anim to activate the Keyframer.

3. Using the Select tool in the Joint mode, select the pelvis joint (or you can use the Joints tab to make the selection).

4. Use the Rotate tool in freeform mode in the Right Side view. You will recall that freeform rotation is a simple matter of selecting the Rotate tool, clicking in the wire-frame view, and dragging the cursor left and right.

Now what you should be seeing is the entire torso, plus the head, rotate around the Bip01 Spine node. You should also see some strange things as well. The arm, leg, foot, and hand meshes don't move. That's because they aren't rigged yet.

But notice that the leg bones are rotating when you rotate Bip01 Spine. Aha! I don't know about you, but when I bend over, my legs don't move back. Well, not unless I'm floating in water, of course. So the pelvis node, while it seems to be an obvious candidate for bending your character at the waist, looks to not be the right one.

So go back, right now, and change it. It's simply the same procedure I showed you for the pelvis, except you do it for the Bip01 Spine1 node instead. Make sure to click the Anim button to take it out of the Keyframer first, or you won't be able to make the changes. I'll wait.

Musical Interlude...

There you are. Now that that's done, go back into the Keyframer as I showed you before, and check the rotation of the Bip01 Spine1 node.

Another Musical Interlude...

Good! So everything should be working as expected now. The torso and the head meshes bend over in unison, and all the bones attached above Bip01 Spine1 bend in unison, as shown in Figure 14.81. As you've probably deduced, it is now a

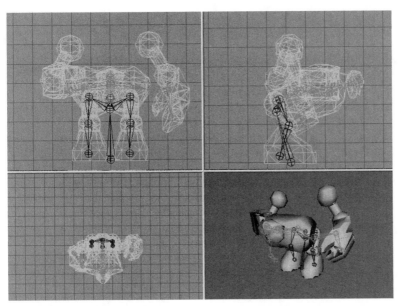

Figure 14.81
Bending at the lower spine.

Table 14.2 Hero Rigging

Node	Mesh to Be Rigged
Bip01 Head	Head
Bip01 Spine2	Torso—chest-area vertices
Bip01 Spine	Torso—abdomen-area vertices
Bip01 L Upperarm	LArm
Bip01 R Upperarm	RArm
Bip01 L Forearm	LHand
Bip01 R Forearm	RHand
Bip01 L Thigh	LThigh
Bip01 R Thigh	RThigh
Bip01 L Calf	LFoot
Bip01 R Calf	RFoot

reasonably minor matter to rig the rest of the nodes. Use Table 14.2 to guide you in your rigging.

Feel free to improve on my rigging choices. Some of the joint nodes have no vertices attached, so you can use them to get finer control of the shape's movements, if you like.

Tip

The hand meshes should attach to the forearm joints. And the foot meshes to the calf joints. Carry on.

You just need to match a mesh to a node, attach it, and move on. I'm enjoying the music here, so you go ahead and do the rest of the rigging, and I'll sit back and relax.

Yet Another Musical Interlude . . .

Great! With that done, let's move on.

Embedded Animations

Embedded animations are animations that are included with the model in the DTS file. We often use embedded animations for one-off purposes like small peculiar objects with few animations. At one time, the only kind of animation that you could export from MilkShape was embedded ones. Some modelers prefer to use them because they keep the resource's management headaches to a minimum, because there are no separate sequence files running around the hallways making nuisances of themselves, banging the doors and getting lost in closets.

Idle Animation

The idle animation is the one used by games when the character is just standing there, doing nothing in particular. In some games you will see some pretty complex idle animation where the character scratches himself in rather inconvenient locations, looks around, scuffs his feet, and so on. We're just going to do a basic breathing sequence so that you'll know that the character is alive. The name for the idle animation in Torque is *root,* so we'll be naming our idle animation that when we export the model.

Even with a basic animation, the watchword is *subtlety.* Don't overdo it.

1. Make sure the Keyframer is enabled by clicking the Anim button in the lower-right corner.

Caution

Make sure that you always leave animation mode by toggling the Anim button so that it is *not* depressed, before saving or exporting *any* aspect of your model, even sequence files. The Anim button should *only* be depressed when you are actually doing animation work. Leave animation mode as soon as your animation work is finished.

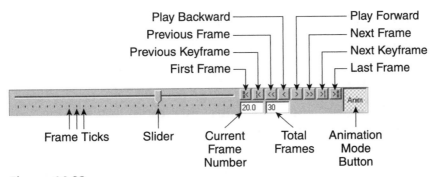

Play Backward — Play Forward
Previous Frame — Next Frame
Previous Keyframe — Next Keyframe
First Frame — Last Frame

Frame Ticks   Slider   Current   Total   Animation
                          Frame   Frames   Mode
                          Number   Button

Figure 14.82
The Keyframer control panel.

2. Set the Total Frames in the Keyframer to 30. Do this in the right-hand edit box in the lower-right corner of the Keyframer (see Figure 14.82).

3. Move the slider to the first frame.

4. Choose Animate, Set Keyframe. This indicates that this particular frame is a keyframe.

5. Move the slider to the 15th frame.

6. Take note of the angle of the elbows and hands.

7. Select the Bip01 Spine1 node, and rotate it 5 degrees around the X-axis.

8. Rotate Bip01 R Upperarm and Bip01 L Upperarm in the opposite direction to the Bip01 Spine1 node rotation by about 5 degrees to place them back where they were before.

Tip

Whenever you change the position or rotation of a joint, you might notice that you only see the update of the animation happen in the view in which you are working. To update the other views, just click in each view once.

9. Choose Animate, Set Keyframe to set the keyframe attribute for this frame.

10. Move the slider back to the second frame.

11. Turn off the Operate On Selected Joints Only feature by choosing Animate, Operate On Selected Joints Only if there is a check mark there in the menu.

12. Choose Animate, Copy Keyframes.

13. Move the slider to the 30th frame.

14. Choose Animate, Paste Keyframes.

15. Turn *on* the Operate On Selected Joints Only feature by choosing Animate, Operate On Selected Joints Only again.

Tip

From this point on, I'll be referring to Operate On Selected Joints Only as Selected Joints, to save my lazy fingers all that cutting and pasting and also to make following along go a little smoother for you.

16. Choose Animate, Set Keyframe.

17. Save your model file!

Note

Copying and pasting keyframes can seem like an activity fraught with peril, after you've done it a few times and not received the results you expected.

The key is to remember to turn *off* the Selected Joints feature *before* copying the keyframe and then turn it back *on* again *after* pasting the keyframe.

Figure 14.83 shows the subtle pose difference between the 1st and the 15th frames. Use the unlink and cam nodes as your stable points of reference—they will never be moved. Now you can test your animation by clicking the Play button on the Keyframer controls. The Play button is the one that looks like a single arrow pointing to the right.

As long as the Play button is down, the animation will loop by running to frame 30 and then back to frame 1 again. If you find it runs too fast, you can change the FPS number in the Preferences dialog box to a lower value to slow the animation.

Notice that when the animation is actually running, that subtle pose change becomes quite noticeable.

Tip

An excellent tool called characterFX is useful for creating animations, and it works well with MilkShape. Unfortunately, for logistical reasons it could not be included with the tools on the companion CD. However, it does a great job of streamlining the process and is quite flexible, so a quick Google search for it on the Internet might be worth your while!

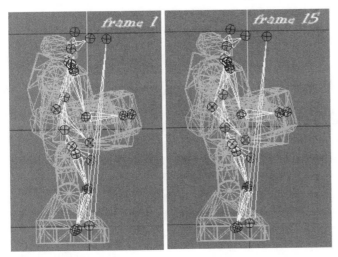

Figure 14.83
The difference in poses.

The idle animation is an example of a *cyclic* animation—one that repeats over and over, barring something more interesting to do. To this end, we make sure that the tail end of the animation blends nicely with the start by making the start and end frames of the animation exactly the same. That's why we copied the keyframe from frame 1 and pasted it at frame 30.

Run Animation

The run animation is the staple of first-person shooters. Run and shoot, run and shoot. Our Hero character has a somewhat awkward lower body, which will tend to make any animation of him running look a bit goofy. Well, we'll turn that into a feature and capitalize on that goofiness. By the way, this is another cyclic animation, so we need to make sure that the start and end frames are the same.

1. In the Keyframer, set the Total Frames to 96. Additional frames will be added after the 30 you started with for the idle animation, so that we end up with a total of 96 tick marks above the slider.

2. Move the slider to frame 31.

3. Make sure that Operate on Selected Joints Only mode in the Animate menu is *not* enabled.

What we are going to do next is make the start and end frames into keyframes first, before doing anything else. This ensures that they are "frozen" as they appear before any animation is done. That way MilkShape can't interpolate the positions behind our backs.

Note

At this time, it's a good idea to think ahead. There are a number of other later animation sequences that will require keyframes set to be identical to frame 1. These keyframes will be used as *reference* frames by Torque for those other animations. The reference frames need to be identical to the base pose, which is frame 1. At the moment, there are no other poses and no keyframes at frames higher than 30, so all the frames up to 96 should look like frame 30, which you will recall is a copy of frame 1. And frame 1 is our base pose.

Given that, it behooves us to make those reference frames now, because it helps to "pin" the MilkShape animations in place. So once you've finished step 5, where you set the keyframe for frame 67, repeat that process for frames 68, 71, 74, and 77. This sets all the reference frames we will need.

4. Choose Animate, Set Keyframe. You should have a pose in frame 31 much like that shown in Figure 14.84.

5. Move the slider to frame 67. This will be the last frame in the run cycle. Now make it a keyframe by choosing Animate, Set Keyframe. You should again have the same pose as in Figure 14.84.

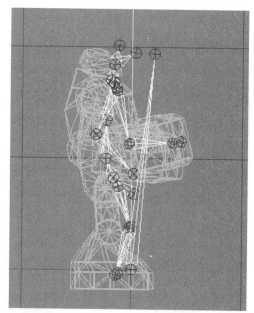

Figure 14.84
Frame 31.

6. Now make sure that Selected Joints mode is enabled again in the Animate menu. Move the slider to frame 40.

7. In the Right Side view, select the Bip01 Pelvis joint (it acts as our *base* node), and move it up about three-quarters of a grid square, as shown for frame 40 in Figure 14.85. The movement of this base node moves the entire model—it's a transformation operation.

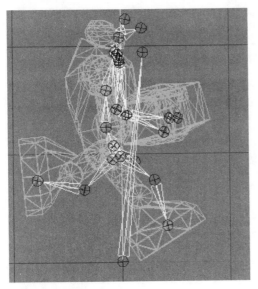

Figure 14.85
Frame 40.

8. Select the `Bip01 R Thigh` node, and then in the Side view rotate it so that the leg moves forward.

9. Rotate the `Bip01 R Calf` node forward a wee bit as well, until the leg matches the configuration in Figure 14.85.

10. Repeat the rotations for the left leg, and move its nodes backward. In order to get things looking right, you might have to adjust the joint positions slightly by moving them, but not by much. Really try hard not to do that though. You get the best and more natural looking animation results by only rotating joints.

11. Rotate the left arm using the `Bip01 L Upperarm` node and the `Bip01 L Forearm` node, swinging them forward until the hand is approximately opposite the right leg, as shown in Figure 14.85.

12. Set frame 40 to be a keyframe.

13. Move the slider to frame 49. Use Figure 14.86 as the guide for this frame.

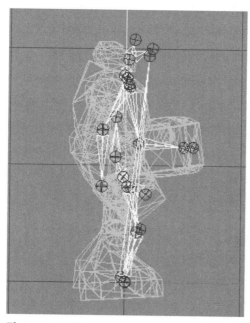

Figure 14.86
Frame 49.

14. Move the Bip01 Pelvis node back down vertically to the height where it was in frame 31.

15. Move all of your legs and joints back to approximately the same configuration as in frame 31. You want the feet to be planted properly at ground level. You might need to fiddle with Bip01 Pelvis a little until you get the foot positioning on the ground right.

16. Swing the left arm down to the side of the model.

17. Set this frame (49) to be a keyframe.

18. Move to frame 58. Use Figure 14.87 as the guide for this frame.

19. Pose frame 58 the same as frame 40, except swing the legs in the opposite directions. Don't forget to move the Bip01 Pelvis node again.

20. Swing the left arm back, and rotate the elbow so that the left hand comes up parallel to the ground.

21. Set this frame to be a keyframe.

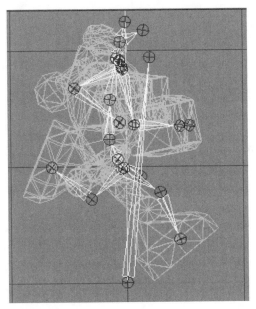

Figure 14.87
Frame 58.

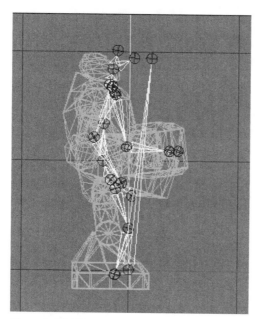

Figure 14.88
Frame 67.

22. Move to frame 67. Use Figure 14.88 as the guide for this frame.

23. Swing the arms and legs back to roughly the pose they had in frame 31.

24. Set this frame to be a keyframe. Use the Play Forward button to watch the animation. If the animation seems to be too fast or too slow, change the FPS setting in the Preferences dialog box until it seems right, and take note of the value you use.

Now you have probably noticed that although we set the pose in only five frames, the program automatically *interpolated,* or figured out, what the in-between frames should look like. Torque does the same thing for us when we use the model in game. This is goodness. That's as much of the run animation as we're going to do here, but you should practice working with this for a while. The first place you should start is to set the keyframe in the middle of the ones we've already set—at frames 35, 45, 54, and 63—and adjust the leg positions to get a better animation from the legs.

Don't try too hard to make the animation look natural though. He's a goofy character and *should* have that sort of goofy, cartoonlike appearance when running.

Head Animation

This is the animation that Torque automatically invokes when it needs to know how far to move your character's head when it is looking up or down. So basically this animation's purpose is to define limits or a boundary and not so much the movement. However, if your character's facial or head shape would change when looking up or down, then you would create a more complex head animation.

That being said, it is really quite quickly dealt with. The animation will consist of a *reference* frame, an "up" frame, and a "down" frame.

1. Frame 68 is the reference frame for this sequence, and you've already made it so, according to the note I gave you back when we were starting out with the run animation. I hope.

2. Move to frame 69.

3. In the Right Side view, rotate the `Bip01 Head` joint until the head is looking up at the maximum angle you want to allow. You may also need to move the head back a bit.

4. Make sure that Operate On Selected Joints Only mode is enabled, and make this a keyframe.

5. Move to frame 70.

6. Rotate the `Bip01 Head` joint until the head is pointed down at the maximum angle you want to allow. You may also need to move the head forward a bit.

7. Make this a Selected Joints keyframe also.

8. Save your work! There, you are done. That's the entire animation sequence! Check your frames against Figure 14.89 to make sure you got it all right.

Headside Animation

In the same way that the head animation defines the limits for the up and down motion performed by Torque, the headside animation provides the limits for the left and right motion. This is most visible from the third-person perspective when in the game.

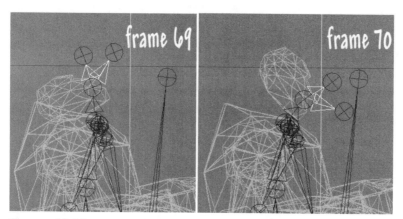

Figure 14.89
Head sequence frames.

Do the same thing you did for the head animation, but use frame 71 as the reference frame, frame 72 for the left turn, and frame 73 for the right turn. Make each of these frames a keyframe, and save your work when you finish.

Look Animation

The look animation is basically another movement-limiting animation that defines how the character's arms will be posed when he is looking up or down. Again, it is a simple two-frame animation that doesn't require us to get into in detail now. Frame 74 will be your reference frame. Use frame 75 for the down "look," or aim. Make sure you have both arms positioned sensibly. Use frame 76 for the up aim. Set both as keyframes, and save your work again.

Death Animation

As you saw earlier, there are many possible ways to die. The Torque demo supports 11 "standard" death animations, but you can easily add more by writing a minor code change into the server script for each player.

We'll cover only one death animation here. We'll have the character collapse backward and fall to the ground on his back, with his feet tossing into the air and back down again.

1. Move to frame 77, and set the pose back to resemble the resting pose as closely as you can, without spending too much time on it.

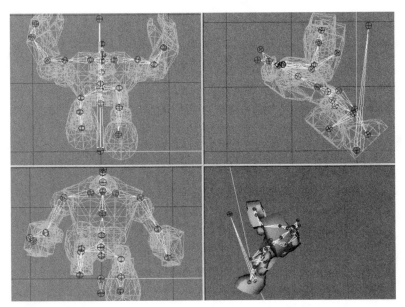

Figure 14.90
Frame 82.

2. Set this frame to be a keyframe.

3. Move to frame 82, and rotate the arms and hands to match. You can leave the character's head on but thrown back like I did or have it pop off temporarily. It's your model! Let Figure 14.90 guide you.

4. Set frame 82 to be a keyframe.

5. Move to frame 86.

6. In the Side view, drag the base node backward several grid squares.

7. Continue to rotate and move the arms and legs, and rotate the body around the Bip01 Pelvis node to make the body tip past horizontal with the bottom of the torso higher than the top, as shown in Figure 14.91.

8. If you haven't guessed it by now, make this frame a keyframe!

9. Move to frame 91.

10. The body is hitting the ground, with some momentum still in the legs. Align the bottom of the torso (which is actually the character's back) even with the ground. Rotate the legs and knees to fling the feet up over the body, and

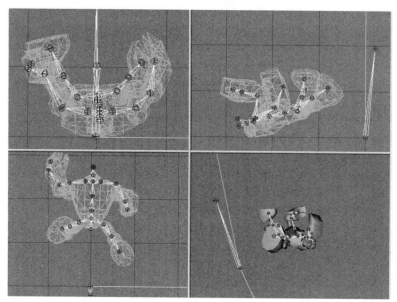

Figure 14.91
Frame 86.

rotate the arms to fling them beyond the head and away from the body, as shown in Figure 14.92. By now the Bip01 Pelvis node should be 10 or 11 grid squares or so behind the origin along the Z-axis, as seen in the Side view.

11. Yup, this is another keyframe. Go ahead, make its day.

12. Now for the final resting position. Move to frame 96.

13. Lay the body out, flat against the ground. Also, move the base node one or two more grid squares farther back, to cause the body to slide along the ground. Lay the arms flat to the sides, the feet and legs down on the ground and spread somewhat. Tilt the head back. As you can see in Figure 14.93, he's dead, Jim.

14. Keyframe him, Dano! (Okay, that's a mighty obscure reference, I'll admit. Indulge me!)

15. Save your work.

Well, that's the lot of them. Enough animations to give you what you really need to know to get moving on animating for Torque in MilkShape. There's still more to cover—we're not quite out of the woods yet. Now we have to tell Torque how to find the animations.

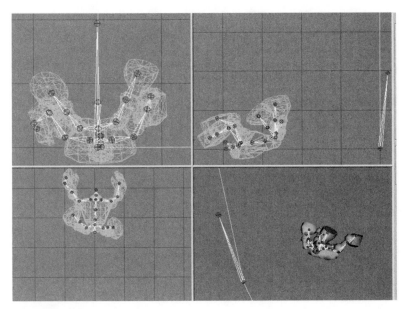

Figure 14.92
Frame 91.

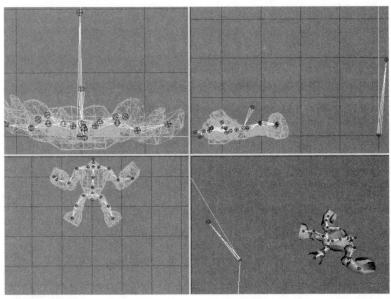

Figure 14.93
Frame 96.

Before proceeding, you need to know that we are going to go down two different paths: once using the standard DTS Exporter and once using the enhanced exporter. So, at this stage, you should save a copy of your model as myhero-Standard.ms3d and another, identical (for the moment) copy as myhero-Enhanced.ms3d. Whenever you work with the standard exporter, use myheroStandard.ms3d and only myheroStandard.ms3d. Whenever you work with the enhanced exporter (DTSPlus), use myheroEnhanced.ms3d.

Special Materials

MilkShape doesn't have built-in support for some of the information about the models that Torque's DTS format demands. That means that there needs to be some way for the artist to specify this information and save it with the source file of the model. Animation sequence information and model scale settings are two examples of this information.

The standard exporter for DTS models utilize the concept of *special materials* as a means to specify and save this information. The information about the built-in "standard" Torque DTS Exporter is included here for completeness, but I highly recommend you just read it for understanding and then move on and use the Torque DTSPlus Exporter plug-in from Chris Robertson. If you do use the standard exporter, you will need to delete the special materials you made before using the DTSPlus Exporter so that you can start with a clean slate.

Full details about each exporter are included in the last section of this chapter.

Sequences with the "Standard" Torque DTS Exporter   The Torque Engine needs to know where the various animations can be found, how long they run, what type they are, and how fast they should be run. We do this using a technique called the Animation Sequence Materials.

The general approach is that we create a special material, and embedded in the name of that material are the Torque name for the animation sequence, its desired playback frame rate, which frames belong to which sequences (inclusive from start to end), and whether the sequence cycles (loops) or plays once per invocation, as well as other characteristics.

Make sure you have myheroStandard.ms3d open, and then go to the Materials tab of the toolbox and create three new materials—one for each non-blended animation sequence. Table 14.3 lists the material names you need to use. The text

Table 14.3 Animation Sequence Material Names

Torque Sequence Name	Sequence Material Name
root	seq:root=1-30,fps=10,cyclic
run	seq:run=31-66,fps=15,cyclic
die1	seq:die1=78-96

in the "Sequence Material Name" column must *all* be included in the name, exactly as shown. These special materials tell the exporters what special operations to perform on the model as it creates the DTS-formatted file for use in Torque.

Note that some of the Sequence Material Names don't include some of the option settings. If you leave them out, the defaults are used. A little later in this chapter you'll find more detail about each exporter.

Cyclic Animations

There is something about two of the sequences that you should pay special attention to. When we created the *run* sequence, we set it up to span from frame 31 to 67, with each end frame set to be copies of the reference pose. And yet the sequence is defined in the special material to span from frame 31 to 66. This is because the animation is *cyclic*—when the last frame is reached, the animation jumps back to the first frame of the sequence.

Because frames 31 and 67 are both reference frames, they are identical. If the sequence ran to 67 and then jumped to 31, you would see a slight pause in the animation while the two identical frames are displayed.

To prevent this little hiccup, we loop the sequence at frame 66 instead of 67.

So then, you ask, why bother with the reference frame at 67? Simple—it's so that when we are viewing the animations in MilkShape, with MilkShape's interpolated frames (the ones that *aren't* keyframes), they will look right.

The same principle applies for the death animation, but in a slightly different way. We can't really know what the player will be doing when he gets killed, so we don't want his death to begin with him assuming the reference pose in frame 77 and then getting knocked onto his keister. So we start the animation on the frame *after* the reference frame. This way Torque can itself interpolate between whatever frame was last displayed (could have been running, walking, looking around, jumping, or whatever) and the *next* keyframe in the death animation, which happens to be at frame 82, so that 5 frames of the sequence can be interpolated by the engine before hitting a keyframe and being forced into a particular pose.

The head, headside, and look sequences are not created, because embedded animation sequences can't be used to create blended animations. In fact, neither can the standard exporter, so the point is doubly moot.

Finally, there is one more special material we need to make, in order to set the global scale. We built this model on a large scale so we could use the Snap To Grid function without seeing our vertices snapped way out of line. Now, when we export the model, we will need to have it scaled down. Add a material, and name it "opt:scale=1.0". This will shrink the model to one-twentieth its created size, which is about right for our needs.

Sequences with the DTSPlus Exporter   Before starting this section, make sure you have myheroEnhanced.ms3d open in MilkShape 3D. One of the nifty things about the Torque DTSPlus Exporter (golly gee willikers, did I just say "nifty"?) is that you don't have to create, type, or even remember the special materials stuff. The DTSPlus Exporter's interface does it for you (see Figure 14.94). You just need to press some buttons, check some check boxes, and fill in some fields. The exporter takes care of the rest.

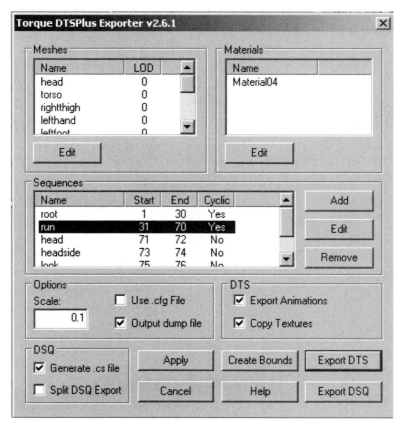

Figure 14.94
Torque DTSPlus Exporter dialog box.

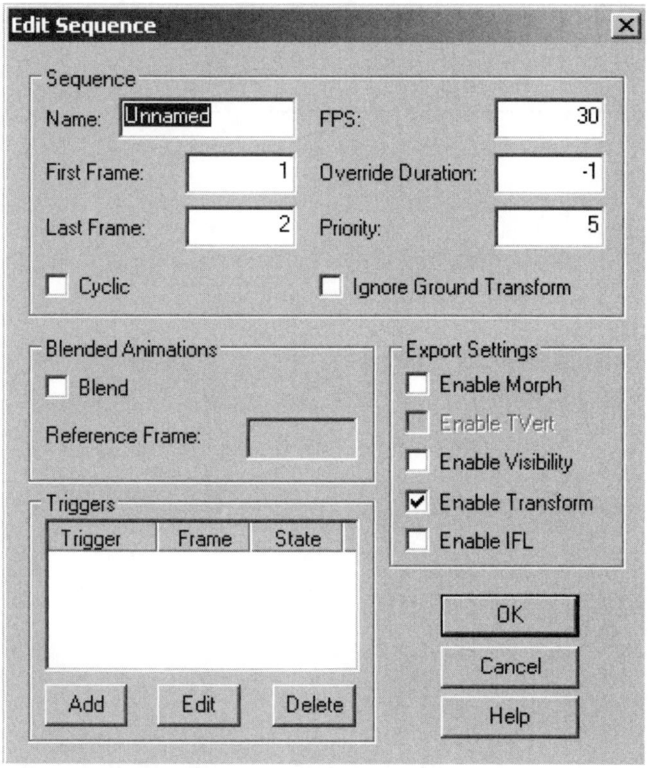

Figure 14.95
Edit Sequence dialog box.

Let's add the root animation sequence using the DTSPlus Exporter.

1. After saving your work, choose File, Export, Torque DTSPlus Exporter. You will see the Torque DTSPlus Exporter dialog box appear. Ensure that the check box called Export Animations is checked.

2. Click the Add button in the Sequences frame. You will get the Edit Sequence frame, as shown in Figure 14.95.

3. Fill in the fields, and set the check boxes with the values shown in Table 14.4.

4. Click the OK button.

Right, then—that was pretty slick, huh? You'll note that despite my earlier sidebar about leaving off the start or end frame of a cyclic animation when the keyframes at both ends are reference frames, I didn't follow my own advice here.

Table 14.4 Root Animation Settings

Option	Value
Name	root
FPS	10
First Frame	1
Override Duration	−1
Last Frame	30
Priority	5
Cyclic	*set*
Ignore Ground Transform	*clear*
Blend	*clear*
Enable Morph	*clear*
Enable TVert	*clear*
Enable Visibility	*clear*
Enable Transform	*set*
Enable IFL	*clear*
Triggers	*none*

That is because with this animation, the motion is subtle enough and slow enough that it doesn't matter. You could leave the end keyframe in the sequence or take it out. It makes no real difference.

You will also notice how many more settings there are for the sequences using the DTSPlus Exporter than with the standard exporter, due to the much greater capability of the DTSPlus Exporter.

Now, with that done, go ahead and create the sequences for the running and death animations, using Tables 14.5 and 14.6 as guides.

When you are done adding all three of the sequences, click the Apply button to commit these settings to the model, followed by Cancel to make the dialog box go away. Then save your work.

Testing the Model

Whew! That's a lot of grunt, right there. Let's see . . . we've created a 3D model, UV mapped a texture to it, created a skeleton and rigged the vertices of the model's mesh to the skeleton, then created a bunch of animations, and organized them into sequences.

Table 14.5 Run Animation Settings

Option	Value		
Name	run		
FPS	40		
First Frame	31		
Override Duration	−1		
Last Frame	66		
Priority	5		
Cyclic	*set*		
Ignore Ground Transform	*clear*		
Blend	*clear*		
Enable Morph	*clear*		
Enable TVert	*clear*		
Enable Visibility	*clear*		
Enable Transform	*set*		
Enable IFL	*clear*		
	Trigger	**Frame**	**State (Value)**
Triggers	0	31	2
	1	49	1

Table 14.6 Death Animation Settings

Option	Value
Name	death1
FPS	15
First Frame	78
Override Duration	−1
Last Frame	96
Priority	5
Cyclic	*clear*
Ignore Ground Transform	*clear*
Blend	*clear*
Enable Morph	*clear*
Enable TVert	*clear*
Enable Visibility	*clear*
Enable Transform	*set*
Enable IFL	*clear*
Triggers	*none*

Time for a short break maybe? Okay. Time's up—back to work!

Let's test these things out.

Using the "Standard" Torque DTS Exporter

A little later in this chapter, we will look in detail at the two DTS exporters for MilkShape. But for now we'll just use the standard exporter in a fundamental way to get our model to work in Torque.

1. After making sure you have myheroStandard.ms3d open, choose File, Export, Torque Game Engine DTS. You will see the Torque Game Engine (DTS) Exporter dialog box appear.

2. We're going to take the defaults, but we should make sure they are correct. You want to have Export animation and Export material information selected, and Collision Mesh should be set to None (Torque handles player collision internally). Click OK when ready.

3. Save your DTS file as \3D2E\RESOURCES\CH14\myhero.dts.

That was pretty painless. Now let's make sure the model works! We'll fire up the Torque Show Tool Pro (TSTP) we used earlier in this chapter and check out the model.

1. Launch TSTP.

2. Ensure that you have your RESOURCES folder selected in the Project Directory pop-up.

3. Find RESOURCES/CH14/myhero.dts, and double-click on it.

4. The model should appear in the center of the screen.

5. Use the mouse actions (described in Chapter 9 in Table 9.1) to rotate the model and bring it closer to you or move it farther away. Left-click and drag will make the camera orbit the model, while right-click and drag will slide the camera around. The mouse wheel will let you zoom in and out.

6. Choose an animation from the Sequences pop-up.

7. Click the Play button in the controls at the lower-right corner of the screen.

8. Check out the other sequences, but remember, the ones that don't cycle are going to run just once and will stay at the last frame.

9. If necessary, go back to your model in MilkShape 3D and make adjustments to your animations, and then come back here to check them out.

10. TSTP is a great tool, but nothing beats the real McCoy. So now jump back into MilkShape and export your model once again, changing nothing, but this time direct the exporter to create the DTS file in \3D2E\demo\data\ shapes\player\player.dts, replacing the one player.dts file that is already there. You can always restore the original later from the CD if necessary.

11. Using Windows Explorer, locate your skin texture file for the model in RESOURCES\CH14 and copy it to \3D2E\demo\data\shapes\player.

12. Run the FPS demo.

13. Once you have spawned in, press the Tab key to switch to third-person view so you can admire your character's animations.

14. Hold down the z key, and move the mouse to swing the camera around the model to view it from different angles.

After you've reviewed the root and run animations in game, you will want to see the death animation in action. In order to do this, you need to make a teensy little change to the FPS demo code. First, exit the Torque demo, right back out to the desktop.

Using UltraEdit-32, open the file \3D2E\demo\server\scripts\fps.cs, and locate the function called serverCmdSuicide. We don't want to use any of the code that is there, so you can delete everything between the braces ("{" and "}") that defines the function code block, or you can comment it out with double slashes ("//"). But don't do either of those. Instead, insert the following code in the function *after* the opening brace and *before* the line that says if (isObject(%client.player)).

```
if (isObject(%client.player))
  %client.player.kill("Suicide");
return;
```

The return statement will make Torque leave the function early and not execute the code that was already there. You might want to put a little comment there indicating that this is a change you made. Use your name or initials, plus the date, in the comment.

Now run the Torque demo again, and this time press Ctrl+K. Ugggghh. Your guy just up and dies. The view switches to an external camera, and you see the death animation.

Note

Make sure that you run around inside some of the buildings, on the hard floors. Notice something missing? No footsteps. The standard exporter doesn't support triggers.

Good job! The rule of thumb is, if it works in the Show Tool, it will work in the game, because the Torque Engine is behind both.

Using the DTSPlus Exporter

Now, load up your myheroEnhanced.ms3d model, and open the Torque DTSPlus Exporter. Click the Export DTS button, and put your DTS model in as \3D2E\demo\data\shapes\player\player.dts, replacing the file that is already there. Make sure that the Export Animations check box is checked.

Run the Torque FPS demo. Try out all three of the supported embedded animations. Watch them in action.

Note

Make sure that you run around inside some of the buildings, on the hard floors. Notice something that's *not* missing? Heh…Thwap! Thwap! Thwap! Thwap! Gotta love them footsteps. The enhanced exporter *does* support triggers. Thanks, Chris!

You now have an animated Hero character to use in your game. And it really isn't that difficult to get to this point. If you are even a halfway decent artist and have a good eye, I'm sure your model and animations are much better than mine.

A later section provides some detail into the workings of the DTS Exporter for the Torque Engine. With its help, you should take some time to fiddle with settings and different animations and add your own animation sequences.

Animation Sequence Files

So far, we've only been able to see three of our animations in action. What about those head movement thingies? Well, in order to see them working properly as blended animations, we need to create our own sequence files.

Using Your Own Sequences

Only the enhanced exporter, Torque DTSPlus Exporter, knows how to handle this, and it's really quite easy. Make sure you have your myheroEnhanced.ms3d file open.

Once you have your animations made and sequenced, deactivate the Anim button.

Select all of your mesh groups using the Groups tab, and regroup them as one mesh. Rename the mesh so that it ends with a zero so that the exporter won't get confused.

Now, run the DTSPlus Exporter and make sure that both the Generate cs File and Split DSQ Export check boxes are checked. Then click the Export DSQ button. When the Save As dialog box appears, browse to \3D2E\demo\data\shapes\player, and then type **player** into the text box. No extensions or anything, just **player**. The exporter will append an underscore to this name and then export each sequence as its own DSQ file, with the file name being made up of "player_" at the front, followed by the sequence's name, which is then followed by ".dsq". It will also create a CS script file that creates a mapping of the sequence name to the newly created sequence file for the player.dts model.

After that you will then need to re-export your model using the Export DTS button, but this time with the Export Animations check box cleared, so that only the rigged model is exported. And of course you will export it to the same place you put the sequence files, replacing the player.dts that is already there.

Now you can pop into the FPS demo, and the blended head motions will be there. You should be able to see the running, root, and death animations. A word of caution, though. You might have difficulty spotting the actual movements, because as you move the mouse in third-person mode to move the head or the whatever, your view changes at the same time. But give it a go. Under normal circumstances it would be the other players in a multiplayer game, and not yourself, that would see the animations.

Using GarageGames' Sequences

Finally, you can use the sequences that came with the Torque demo as the animations for your own model. There are some caveats, however. Your skeleton has to exactly match the GarageGames skeleton in all ways, shapes, and forms.

The nodes have to be correctly named, and the joints need to be rotated and placed close enough to the GarageGames skeleton placements.

There is one other little wrinkle, and that is how MilkShape 3D normalizes its joints every time you place a new one. This is bad for our purposes, because it means that it is next to impossible to match the rotations of the GarageGames joints.

But all is not lost! I just so happen to have the GarageGames skeleton used for the Orc monster, and have included it in the RESOURCES folder for Chapter 14. All you need to do is remove your own skeleton and replace it with the GarageGames skeleton.

1. Open your myheroEnhanced.ms3d model, and save it as myHeroGG.ms3d. From here on, work with myHeroGG.ms3d.

2. Go to the Joints tab, and delete all the joints, select Pelvis and press the Delete key and then do the same thing with the unlink node.

3. Open the DTSPlus Exporter, and remove all the sequences.

4. Click Apply and then Cancel. Save your work.

5. Choose File, Merge, and then browse to RESOURCES\CH14 and locate and select skeleton.ms3d. Click the Open button. The skeleton will be merged with your model.

6. Next, you must modify your mesh to match the skeleton, and not the other way around. Do *not* touch the skeleton; don't move its joints or rotate them or anything. Don't add or delete anything. Just keep your hands off it! However, you *will* have to move, rotate, and scale the body parts to fit them to the new skeleton.

7. Now rig the mesh to the skeleton, just like you did earlier with your own skeleton.

8. Collapse your mesh groups into one group, just like we did with the embedded animations, and make sure that the single mesh name ends with a zero.

9. Save your work in a file with "onemesh" added to the file name, so that you don't overwrite your original "final" model.

10. Using Torque DTS Plus, export your model to \3D2E\demo\data\shapes\ player\player.dts. Make sure that Export Animations is *not* checked.

11. Restore the file \3D2E\demo\data\shapes\player\player.cs from your CD if you have previously been testing your own sequence exporting in this folder.

Either use the Show Book Models shortcut for the Show Tool or run the FPS demo to view your model running using the GarageGames skeleton. In the demo, try Ctrl + S or Ctrl + W to get the hero to salute or wave.

Here's something: make sure your player is not standing at a spawn location or very close to another object. If you step into camera mode with F8, fly a little bit away from your character, and look back at it, you can see some cool things. Open the Mission Editor with F11, find the ID number of your character and record it. There will be a red dot located in the center of the player's body—the ID number 1751 will appear just above, below, or directly on the dot. Let's pretend the number was 0001. This is your character's avatar object ID or handle. Press F11 to leave the Mission Editor, keeping your camera pointed at your character. Then open the console using the Tilde ("~") key and type in the following:

```
0001.setActionThread("dance");
```

Of course, you substitute the *actual* ID of your player object for the fictitious 0001 in my example. Don't forget that semicolon at the end, and don't forget to press Enter after you type the semicolon.

Now quickly press the Tilde key again to make the console go away, and enjoy watching your player doing the funky chicken (well, it certainly isn't the macarena!). Another sequence you can try is range, which shows the range of motion of the animated character.

You can open the file \3D2E\demo\data\shapes\player\player.cs and see what the names of the sequences are on the right-hand side. For example, the line

```
sequence1 = "./player_forward.dsq run";
```

tells us that the sequence name is run and the sequence file used is ./player_ forward.dsq.

Have fun!

MilkShape 3D's DTS Exporters

As mentioned several times, there are two exporters available for getting models into Torque from MilkShape 3D: the "standard" Torque Game Engine (DTS) Exporter and the "enhanced" Torque DTSPlus Exporter. The standard version comes built into MilkShape 3D these days, while the enhanced version—the exporter of choice, by far—comes from a chap named Chris Robertson. If you find the enhanced version too intimidating, you can use the standard version until you feel ready to spread your wings!

The Standard Torque Game Engine (DTS) Exporter

The Torque Game Engine (DTS) Exporter dialog box (see Figure 14.96) has three groups of options, none of which normally need to be set. Option settings are not saved, so you rarely use this dialog box for more than just a means to double-check your option values. The recommended approach is to set options using special materials.

Collision Mesh

The exporter allows you to create as many collision meshes as you want. Each collision mesh must be named "Collision"; if you have three collision meshes, they

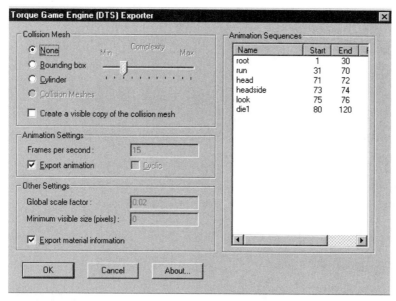

Figure 14.96
Torque Game Engine (DTS) Exporter dialog box.

will all be named "Collision". If you do not have a collision mesh defined, you may have the exporter create one for you as either a box or a cylinder. You can also manually select an existing mesh. Player-characters don't need a collision mesh at all.

Select the Create a visible copy of the collision mesh check box to make the mesh visible as well as collidable.

Animation Settings

The Animation Settings group displays the global values for the animations.

- **Frames per second.** This field indicates at what speed the Torque Engine should play the animations. This field can be set using an Export Options material and applies globally to all animation sequences (Export Options is explained in a later section). This does not affect the number of keyframes; it simply sets the rate at which they will be played.

- **Export animation.** If the model contains embedded animations that you want to export, then this box should be checked. No animations are exported if it is cleared.

Other Settings

The Other Settings group contains miscellaneous settings values.

- **Global scale factor.** The global scale factor is the amount by which the shape is scaled when it is exported. The default scale factor is 0.1, but this field can be changed to any value set using an Export Options material.

- **Minimum visible size (pixels).** If the projected screen size of the bounding radius of the shape drops to the minimum visible size, the shape will no longer render. This is normally used to switch between different detail levels, and it's recommended that you leave this at the default value: 0.

- **Export material information.** You may disable the exporting of material information (not recommended) by clearing the Export Options material information check box.

Export Options

Materials with special names can be used to set several export options. These materials are ignored during export and are solely used to set options.

Table 14.7 Export Options

Option	Description
scale=n	The global shape scale factor, where n is a floating point value. The default scale value is 0.1.
size=n	The global minimum visible pixel size. The default is 0.
fps=n	The global default frames per second value for animations. Each animation sequence may set this value, but if it's not defined by the sequence, the default value is used.
Cyclic	The global default animation looping flag. Each animation sequence may set this value, but if it's not defined by the sequence, the default value is used.

Option materials are named as follows:

```
opt: option, option,...
```

All other properties of the material are ignored. Table 14.7 lists the available options.

There may be more than one option material. If the same options are set on multiple materials, then the last one in the material list is the value used. Here are a couple examples of valid material names:

```
opt: fps=10, cyclic
opt: scale=0.1
```

Material Option Flags

Material attributes that can be set by using the MilkShape Shininess and Translucency sliders can also be set by embedding additional flags in the material name.

Environment mapping can be controlled for the model by use of the Shininess slider—it's the one on the left-hand side. Setting the slider to any value but 0.0 will enable environment mapping for the texture. Note that the texture you are using must have an alpha channel, which will be used to control the per-pixel shininess of the texture. Any value of the slider other than 1.0 or 0.0 will be ignored.

You can enable translucency by setting the MilkShape Translucency slider—this is the slider on the right-hand side. Setting the slider to any value other than 1.0, which is to the far right, will enable translucency for the texture. The texture you are using must have an alpha channel, which will be used by the Torque Engine to control the per-pixel translucency of the texture. Any value of the slider other than 1.0 or 0.0 will be ignored.

Table 14.8 Material Option Flags

Flag	Description
Add	Enables additive transparency.
Sub	Enables subtractive transparency.
Illum	Enables self-illumination (lighting doesn't affect it).
NoMip	Disables mipmapping.
MipZero	Sets the "MipMapZeroBorder" flag.

Table 14.9 Mesh Option Flags

Flag	Description
Billboard	The mesh always faces the viewer.
BillboardZ	The mesh faces the viewer but is only rotated around the mesh's Z-axis.
ENormals	This flag encodes vertex normals. It is deprecated and should not be used unless you know what you're doing.

Options that are embedded in the material name follow this format:

```
name: flag, flag, ...
```

where the : and flags are optional. Table 14.8 shows which flags are available.

A self-illuminating additive material could be called as follows:

```
Flare: Add, Illum
```

Mesh Option Flags

Meshes can have additional flags embedded in the mesh (or group) name. The mesh name follows this format:

```
name: flag, flag,...
```

where the : and flags are optional. Table 14.9 shows which flags are available.

Here are some legal mesh or group names:

- leaf

- leaf: Billboard

- leaf: BillboardZ

By default, meshes do not have any flags set.

Animation Sequences

MilkShape only provides a single animation timeline, but the Torque Engine supports multiple animation sequences, each of which can be named and have different properties. Multiple sequences in MilkShape are animated on the main timeline and are split into separate sequences by the exporter. For this to happen animation sequences must be declared, indicating where each sequence starts and ends on the master timeline. This is done through materials with special names. These materials are ignored during export and are solely used to declare animation sequences. The "Special Materials" section earlier in the chapter provides more details.

Sequence materials are named as follows:

```
seq: option, option, ...
```

All other properties of the material are ignored. Table 14.10 describes the sequence material options.

Here are some valid sequence declarations:

```
seq: fire=1-4
seq: rotate=5-8, cyclic, fps=2
seq: reload=9-12, fps=5
```

The Enhanced Torque DTSPlus Exporter

The DTSPlus Exporter does not use special materials to store its extra information in. It used to, until MilkShape 3D introduced the feature of comments for objects and other aspects of a model. Now the DTSPlus Exporter maintains its settings in comment fields in the scene.

Table 14.10 Sequence Material Options

Option	Description
name=start-end	This declares the name of the sequence followed by the starting and ending keyframes. This option must exist for the sequence declaration to be valid.
fps=n	This is the number of frames per second. This value affects the duration and playback speed of the sequence.
Cyclic	Sequences are noncyclic by default. Cyclic animations automatically loop back to the start and never end.

Notwithstanding that little tidbit of technical trivia, we never need to concern ourselves with the contents of the comment fields. DTSPlus provides a GUI interface in its dialog box that gives us all the access we need to the settings.

Main Dialog Box

Figure 14.94 a few pages back shows the main dialog box. Meshes and materials are added to the scene via MilkShape, and their special properties can be edited here by selecting them in their respective lists and clicking the Edit button adjoining the list.

Sequences are created, edited, and deleted via the Sequences list in this main dialog box. Again, select the sequence, and click the appropriate action button adjoining the list.

Other general settings and actions are shown in Table 14.11.

Table 14.11 General Settings and Actions

Setting or Action	Description
Scale	A global scale factor that is applied to the model when it is exported.
Use .cfg File	If set, the exporter will search for a config file with the same name as the exported shape (e.g., shape.cfg for the exported shape.dts). If cleared, the default configuration will be used.
Output dump file	If set, a file called dump.dmp will be created in the same directory as the exported shape.
Export Animations	If set, animation information will be written to the DTS shape. This flag is ignored when exporting DSQ files.
Copy Textures	If set, all textures used in the exported shape will be copied to the export directory. This flag is ignored when exporting DSQ files.
Generate .cs file	If set, a TorqueScript .cs file will be created that can be used to load the shape (with DSQ animations) in TGE. This flag is ignored when exporting DTS files.
Split DSQ Export	If set, each animation will be stored in a separate DSQ file. The name of each file is base_animname.dsq, where base is the name chosen in the Save As dialog box and animname is the name of the animation. If this flag is cleared, all animations will be stored in the same DSQ file. This flag is ignored when exporting DTS files.
Apply	Applies changes to the MilkShape model. The exporter dialog box will remain open.
Cancel	Closes the exporter dialog box without applying any changes.
Help	Displays the built-in Help file.
Create Bounds Mesh	Creates the bounding box mesh and Root bone if they do not already exist. The bounding box is a cube 1 MilkShape unit larger than the extents.

Configuration Files

Configuration files can be used to control the export process. To use a configuration file, it must be named the same as the exported model name, except with the extension as cfg instead of dts. It must be in the same folder that the model file will be exported to.

Default Configuration

The exporter supports configuration files. If a configuration file is not found, the following default configuration is used:

```
+Error::AllowUnusedMeshes
-Materials::NoMipMap
-Materials::NoMipMapTranslucent
+Materials::ZapBorder
+Param::SequenceExport
-Param::CollapseTransforms
=Params::AnimationDelta 0.0001
=Params::SkinWeightThreshhold 0.001
=Params::SameVertTOL 0.00005
=Params::SameTVertTOL 0.00005
=Params::weightsPerVertex 1
+Dump::NodeCollection
+Dump::ShapeConstruction
+Dump::NodeCulling
+Dump::NodeStates
+Dump::NodeStateDetails
+Dump::ObjectStates
+Dump::ObjectStateDetails
+Dump::ObjectOffsets
+Dump::SequenceDetails
+Dump::ShapeHierarchy
NeverExport
__mainTree
__meshes
```

A "+" sets the setting to true, "-" sets it to false, and "=" is used to set the value of a setting.

Nodes in the NeverExport list are not written to the DTS file.

The NeverExport list is mostly used for DSQ Export to exclude non-animating nodes. Names in the NeverExport list can include wildcards (*). For example, leg* will include both leg1 and leg2.

Settings

Here are the available settings:

Error::AllowUnusedMeshes	If true, unused meshes will not cause an exporter error.
Materials::NoMipMap	Disable mip-mapping on all textures.
Materials::NoMipMapTranslucent	Disable mip-mapping on translucent textures only.
Materials::ZapBorder	If set, translucent, non-tiling materials will automatically have the MipMapZeroBorder flag set. See Overview.
Param::SequenceExport	Allow animation sequences to be exported.
Param::CollapseTransforms	If set, nodes that do not contain any objects are remoded.
Params::AnimationDelta	Minimum change in position or scale required for a node transform to be recognized as different to the previous transform.
Params::SkinWeightThreshhold	Minimum bone weighting for a vertex to be affected by that bone. *Note: Because MilkShape only supports a single bone per vertex, bones attached to a vertex have weight 1, and bones not attached have weight 0.*
Params::SameVertTOL	Minimum distance between vertices for them to be considered unique. Vertices closer together than this distance will be welded.
Params::SameTVertTOL	Minimum distance between texture coordinates for them to be considered unique. Coordinates closer together than this distance will be welded.
Params::weightsPerVertex	Maximum number of bone weights per vertex. Note that MilkShape only supports a single bone per vertex.
Dump::NodeCollection	Output details of the node collection process to the dump file.
Dump::ShapeConstruction	Output details of the shape construction process to the dump file.
Dump::NodeCulling	Output details of which nodes have been culled to the dump file.
Dump::NodeStates	Output node states to the dump file.
Dump::NodeStateDetails	Output node state information to the dump file.
Dump::ObjectStates	Output object states to the dump file.
Dump::ObjectStateDetails	Output object state information to the dump file.
Dump::ObjectOffsets	Output object offset information to the dump file.
Dump::SequenceDetails	Output sequence details to the dump file.
Dump::ShapeHierarchy	Output the shape hierarchy to the dump file.

Table 14.12 Mesh Properties

Property	Description
Name	Name of the mesh, not including the LOD number, which is automatically appended to the end of the name.
LOD	Detail level for this mesh. The detail level indicates to the exporter what mesh is to be drawn at a given distance. The number corresponds to the pixel size in the game engine at which the shape will draw with these meshes. Meshes with negative detail levels will be exported but not drawn. If your mesh has only one detail level, use 0.
Billboard	Set if this mesh is a billboard.
Z Billboard	Set if this mesh is a Z billboard.
Sort	Set if this mesh should be sorted.
Visibility Channel	This list box defines keyframes for the meshes' visibility channel.

Mesh Properties

There are many extra properties that can be assigned to meshes (or groups, in MilkShape 3D parlance) that affect things like level of detail, billboard behavior, and visibility. To view the Edit Mesh dialog box, click the Edit button adjoining the Meshes list. Table 14.12 shows these properties and their purposes.

Collision Meshes

Any mesh whose name begins with the text string "Collision" will be used in game as a collision mesh. Collision meshes are normally given a negative detail level from −1 to −8 so that they are not drawn. You can view the collision mesh in game if you need to for debugging purposes by giving it a positive detail level.

Collision meshes should use as few polygons as possible and must be convex. Try to keep the polygon count below 50 for any given model, if at all possible, as a rule of thumb.

LOS Collision Meshes

DTSPlus supports the use of special collision meshes used to do line-of-sight collision calculations. These meshes are often used for optimized operations such as checking if a bullet will hit the model. Any mesh whose name begins with the text string "LOSCol" will be used as a line-of-sight collision mesh. Normally these meshes are given a negative detail level from −9 to −16 to ensure that they aren't rendered.

Like regular collision meshes, LOS meshes should use as few polygons as possible and must be convex.

Materials

Figure 14.97 shows DTSPlus's Edit Material dialog box, and Table 14.13 lists its features.

Animation Sequences

You've already seen a sterile view of the animation sequence editor elsewhere in this chapter. Figure 14.98 shows a view of the run sequence through the eyes of the Edit Sequence dialog box.

As you have seen in this chapter, MilkShape 3D provides only one animation timeline. Yet the Torque Engine supports multiple animation sequences, each of which can be named and have different properties. You can create multiple sequences in MilkShape 3D on the main timeline, which are differentiated into separate sequences by DTSPlus. For this to happen, animation sequences must be declared indicating where each sequence starts and ends on the master timeline using the DTSPlus Sequence Editor.

Table 14.14 shows the features of the Edit Sequence dialog box and their uses.

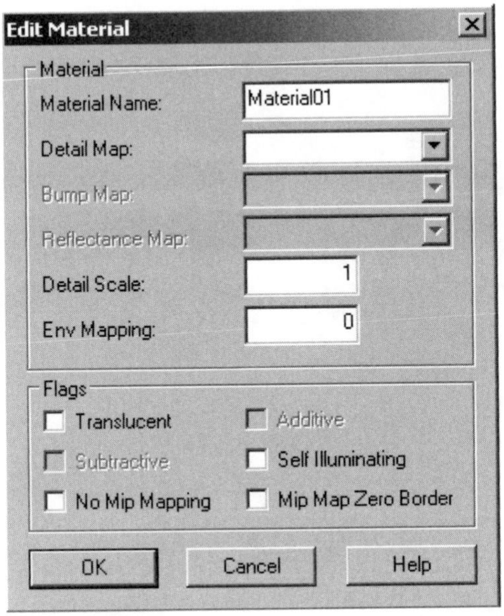

Figure 14.97
Edit Material dialog box.

Table 14.13 Edit Material Features

Property	Description
Material Name	Name of the material. This is used internally by the DTS shape and does not affect the actual texture used.
Detail Map	Name of the MilkShape material to use as a detail map.
Bump Map	Name of the MilkShape material to use as a bump map. Note that TGE does not yet support bumpmapped DTS shapes.
Reflectance Map	Name of the MilkShape material to use as a reflectance map. Not yet implemented.
Detail Scale	Scale of the detail map. See Detail Map.
Env Mapping	Amount of environment mapping to apply. 0 for none. This value is a scalar (range 0–1), which is applied to the alpha channel of the texture to determine the level of environment mapping at each point.
Translucent	Enables transparency.
Additive	Enables additive transparency (only valid if translucent flag is set).
Subtractive	Enables subtractive transparency (only valid if translucent flag is set).
Self Illuminating	Enables self-illumination (lighting doesn't affect it).
No Mip Mapping	Disables mipmapping for this material.
Mip Map Zero Border	Not implemented yet.

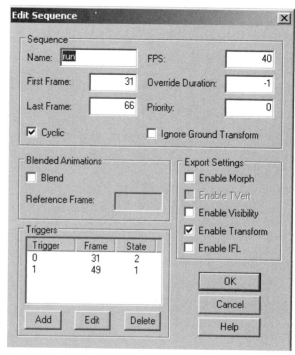

Figure 14.98
Edit Sequence dialog box.

Table 14.14 Sequence Editor Features

Property	Description
Name	Name of the sequence.
First Frame	First frame (inclusive) in the sequence. This number should match the frame number in the MilkShape animation timeline.
Last Frame	Last frame (inclusive) in the sequence. This number should match the frame number in the MilkShape animation timeline.
Cyclic	If turned on, the sequence will loop (e.g., walk and run animations). If turned off, the sequence will play once and then stop (e.g., death animations).
FPS	Frames per second for this animation. This does not affect the number of keyframes—only how fast they will be played back.
Override Duration	If you override the sequence duration, it will change the duration of the sequence when it plays in the game at time scale 1, but it won't otherwise change the animation data (same keyframes will be used, they'll just play at different times). This is useful for altering the speed of the ground transform of an object without scaling the animation. Most of the time, this is not used and should be set to −1.
Priority	Controls what sequence will affect a node when two sequences want to control the same node. The sequence with higher priority will control the node.
Ignore Ground Transform	Don't export a ground transform for this sequence. This should usually be false.
Blend	Makes the sequence a blend animation.
Reference Frame	The reference frame number for the blend animation. This is only valid if the blend flag is set.
Triggers	Set of trigger keyframes and states.
Enable Morph	This will force the exporter to export all mesh animations as a series of mesh snapshots. This is useful for certain types of animations (e.g., flags), but it will produce large files and does not contain animated nodes.
Enable TVert	Enables animated texture coordinates.
Enable Visibility	Enables use of the visibility channel.
Enable Transform	Enables transform (e.g., translation and rotation) animation. Normally this setting is enabled.
Enable IFL	Enables IFL animation.

Moving Right Along

This was a pretty busy chapter, huh? We created a character model and a texture skin for it, created a skeleton and rigged the model's meshes to the skeleton, and then proceeded to animate the skeleton. We then learned how to use two different exporters to get the animations into Torque. In fact, as you've seen, there are many different combinations of ways to get animated characters into Torque, using embedded animations and sequence file animations and even reusing animation sequences created by other people.

If it isn't obvious by now, there is very little need to use the built-in DTS Exporter in MilkShape 3D if you have Chris Robertson's DTSPlus Exporter. However, if you are already familiar with the standard exporter and have no demanding animation or special properties for your models requiring DTSPlus, then the standard exporter, which is less intimidating, will fill the bill nicely.

It's a lot of work, and that's why even the smallest game development team usually has at least one modeler on board to handle that workload.

So now that you can create your own player-character, it's time to create some sort of transportation so he can get around in the game world. That's the subject of the next chapter, "Making a Vehicle Model."

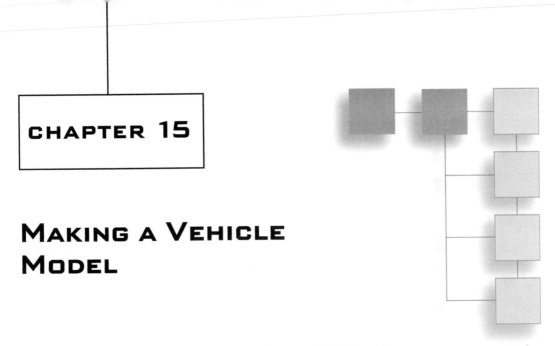

CHAPTER 15

MAKING A VEHICLE MODEL

In Chapter 9 we looked at creating skins, and during that process we created a skin for a cool runabout-type vehicle. In this chapter we'll create the model itself.

Of course, there is a whole host of different vehicle types, such as those for the open road or off road, aircraft, hovercraft, ships, and so on. In most cases the methods used to create the vehicles can be used with any type of object. But different vehicle types have different capabilities and therefore may require some specialized accommodation for those capabilities in the models.

For example, if you want your vehicles to be drivable by a player-avatar that gets into the vehicle when you want to drive, then your vehicle will need *mount points*, which are special nodes or subobjects within the model that indicate where your player-avatar gets attached to the vehicle. Different vehicle types, makes, and models will have different needs in this area.

Then there are those special nodes that indicate where other game functions will happen. Wheeled vehicles need to know where the wheels are located, as well as information about how the springs and steering mechanisms are oriented.

Some vehicles might need nodes in their models to indicate to the engine where to generate engine exhaust smoke using particles. Flying vehicles may require nodes to help the engine generate contrails (condensation trails). The list goes on.

The Vehicle Model

In this chapter we are going to build a complete wheeled vehicle, the runabout, which will wear the skin you created in Chapter 9. Then we will insert it into a little test game so that we can carom about and drive our insurance rates through the roof!

The Sketch

I find the best way to start a new model is with a sketch. Doodle out some ideas, and keep working them up on paper until you get something that suits your needs. Then choose a view (Left or Right, Top or Bottom, Front or Back) that presents you with the highest number of intersections of lines to use as points.

Figure 15.1 shows a sketch of the runabout from the right-hand side. Notice that it is really a sketch and not a drawing. As long as the general proportions and coarse features are present, it's satisfactory. Now if you were going to model a real car, you might need to use a more detailed sketch or perhaps something that would qualify more as a drawing than a sketch. Then again you may not—it all depends on how much detail is necessary to suit your needs.

The Side view is the main sketch we will use to make our model. When modeling most vehicles, you will *usually* use a Side view as your primary source for extrusion modeling. The reason for this is pretty obvious. Most vehicles are longer than they are tall or wide. The symmetries of vehicles (how one side mirrors the other) tend to reflect around the longitudinal axis, the one that runs from the rear to the front of the vehicle up the middle.

The Top view of the runabout is shown in Figure 15.2. The purpose for sketching this view is to provide a guide for your modeling efforts as they proceed. You will find yourself checking back against this drawing quite often.

One more useful thing is to make a copy of the Side view and, using the Gimp, adjust the brightness of the image. This is because when we import the sketch

Figure 15.1
Side view sketch of the runabout.

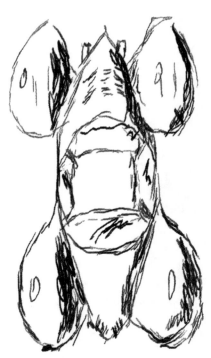

Figure 15.2
Top view sketch of the runabout.

Figure 15.3
Side view sketch adjusted for use in MilkShape.

into MilkShape, we don't want the image to overpower any of the on-screen modeling marks we make. I find the best approach is to darken the whole image by around 40 to 50 percent and reduce the contrast by about 50 to 60 percent or so. Figure 15.3 shows the adjusted Side view. I keep the original sketches as they were so that I can print them out for reference purposes (and also just to pin up on the wall because it's a cool artsy thing to do).

The Model

So pour some jet fuel in the ol' computer, grab the propeller, give it a whirl, and fire up MilkShape 3D again if it isn't already running. If you need a quick

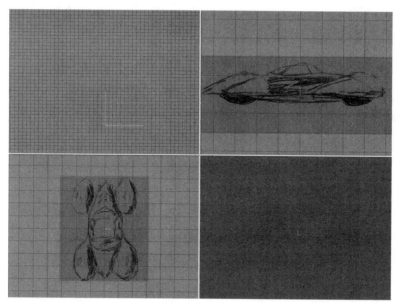

Figure 15.4
MilkShape windows with reference sketches.

refresher, you can jump back to Chapters 13 and 14. Set your MilkShape 3D GUI display to the four-view mode by choosing Window, Viewports, 4 Window.

Create a fresh new MilkShape document. It's a good idea to save the empty file right now, just to get the path set up and establish the file name.

Then you want to import the side sketch as the background in the Side view (upper right view). Right-click in the Side view, and choose Choose Background Image from the pop-up menu. Select your sketch, and click OK. You can use my sketches if you want—they are located at C:\3D2E\RESOURCES\CH15\ref_sketch.bmp.

Do the same thing for the Top view (bottom left view), using your own sketch or mine, found at \3D2E\RESOURCES\CH15\ref_top_sketch.bmp. Usually, only two views are needed, but you could also sketch in the third view if you want to.

You should end up with something like Figure 15.4.

So now we start.

Building the Body

First, we'll build the body:

1. From the Model tab, select the Vertex tool, making sure that the Auto Tool check box is cleared.

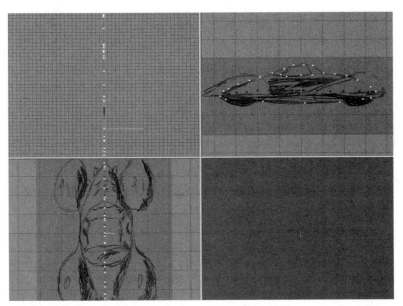

Figure 15.5
Placing vertices over the reference sketch.

Tip

Placing vertices may be the easiest and most fun job in the world. With the Vertex tool active, go to the view that you are going to use as your guide, and find a spot on a contour or line in the reference image that signifies a contour feature. This could be a turn, a point on a curve, a sharp corner, or anything else that forms the character of the contour. Click on that spot. Blam! You've stuck a vertex there. Now find another target. Blam! Keep on going. Blam! Blam! Blam! Don't get all blam-happy though—too many vertices will yield too many polygons in the long run, as well as make it hard to create the polygons in the first place. It can be difficult to continue to see the shapes when a swarm of pixels is obscuring them.

2. In the Side view, start placing vertices at all the major corners and points around the edge of the car's body—don't do the fenders yet. Just click on the appropriate location to place the vertex. See Figure 15.5 for reference.

Note

There is also a string of vertices across the "waist" of the body—in Figure 15.5 they are highlighted as black squares (they show red in MilkShape). These extra vertices are added for two reasons. First, they act as useful anchors for creating the faces that we'll make later. And second, they help add more malleability to the model for shaping the sides of the car.

After we have the vertices placed, we move on to creating the faces joined by the vertices.

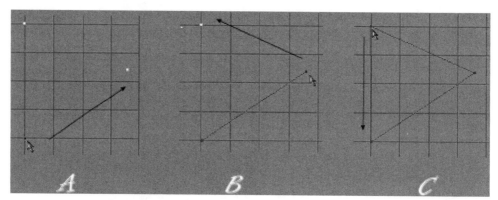

Figure 15.6
Vertex order for creating faces.

Tip

It's important to remember that when we create faces using the Face tool that is found in the Model tab, we click three vertices in sequence to create one face. The order we click the vertices is important. To create a face or polygon that is oriented toward us, we need to select the vertices in a counterclockwise order, as shown in Figure 15.6. For most cases this is not hard to do, but it's possible to get confused and lose track of the sequence. In this case you can use the Edit, Undo menu item to back up until the sequence is clear. You can also abort any three-vertex sequence by just clicking the Selection tool (or any other tool) and then clicking the Face tool again. Then you can start with a fresh trio of vertices.

The direction that a polygon faces is indicated by a mathematical construct called the *normal*, which is defined as being a line perpendicular to the plane of the face. The side of the face on which the normal is positive is the side that is facing the viewer, and this side is created when its vertices are used in a counterclockwise order.

There is another Face tool, available as a menu option in the Face menu. This tool differs from the Model tab's Face tool in one important way. The Face menu Face tool doesn't care in which order you select the vertices; instead, the manner in which the vertices were *created* dictates the vertex ordering and, thus, which way the face's normal points. You can use whichever Face tool suits your needs. In this chapter we will only use the Model tab's Face tool.

3. Starting at the right side (the front of the car), begin creating faces, moving to the left along the top as you proceed, including the window area, as shown in Figure 15.7.

   When you reach the left side, you should have something resembling Figure 15.8.

4. After completing the top row of faces, start making faces along the bottom, from the left back over to the right (see Figure 15.9).

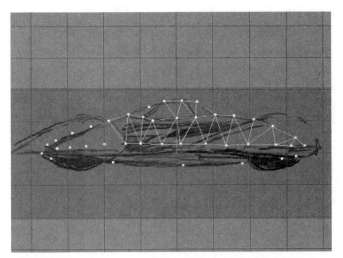

Figure 15.7
Creating faces starting from the right.

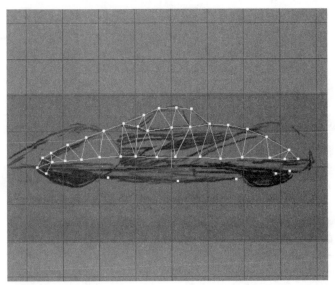

Figure 15.8
Finishing the top row of faces.

5. Finish up the faces for the side of the body. You should end up with something like Figure 15.10.

Okay, so now we have a plane of body faces. We want to make sure they are all oriented correctly. The quickest way to do this is to look at the output in the 3D Perspective view. Make sure the view (it should be the Bottom

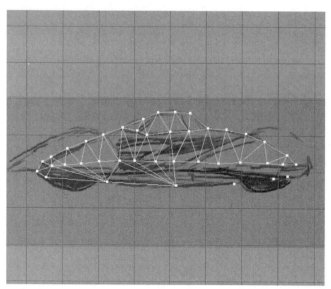

Figure 15.9
Working the bottom row of faces.

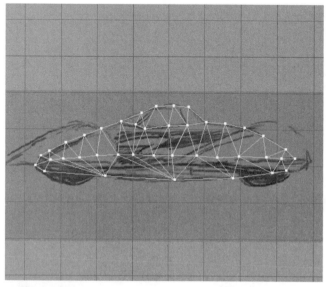

Figure 15.10
Completed plane of body faces.

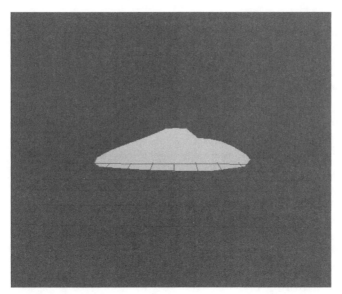

Figure 15.11
The 3D view of the initial body faces.

Right view) is set to either Flat Shaded or Smooth Shaded by right-clicking
the view and then choosing either Flat Shaded or Smooth Shaded in the
pop-up menu. What you should see is the outline of the body rendered in
white or light gray, just as in Figure 15.11.

Tip

This is a long one, so make sure you've got some popcorn handy!

Sometimes you end up with two overlapping faces: one oriented correctly and the other reversed.
These are hard to catch until they start showing strange results when rendering, as the model
grows more complex. There is another way to check for misoriented faces that is a little more
involved:

1. Pick the Selection tool, and set it to Face mode. Make sure that the Ignore Backfaces check
   box is *selected.*

2. Now use the Selection tool to select all the faces by dragging the selection rectangle around
   all of them. This will highlight all the faces.

3. Now choose Edit, Hide Selection. All the correctly oriented faces will vanish, leaving behind
   only the ones facing the wrong way.

4. To fix the problem, unhide all the hidden faces, *clear* the Ignore Backfaces check box, and
   select all the faces again. This will select all correct and incorrect faces.

5. Then choose Face, Reverse Vertex Order. This will make the good ones bad and the bad ones
   good. Still with me?

continues

6. Okay, now deselect everything by clicking the Select tool in an open area, and *select* the Ignore Backfaces check box again.

7. Drag-select over all the faces one more time. Now only the faces that were originally incorrect will be selected.

8. Choose Face, Reverse Vertex Order with those faces selected.

9. Then for one final time, *clear* the Ignore Backfaces check box, select all the faces, and choose Reverse Vertex Order. This should flip all faces back to the correct orientation. If this reminds you of manipulating a Rubik's Cube, then you think a lot like I do!

So now we'll move on to adding some width to the body.

6. Choose the Selection tool, and set it to Face mode.

7. Select all the faces.

8. Click the Extrude tool, and fill in the X entry of the XYZ boxes with the value −10.0 (that's minus ten point zero). Leave Y and Z at 0.0.

9. Click the Extrude button to the right of the XYZ boxes. You should get a new set of polygons negatively offset in the X-axis by 10 units, as shown in Figure 15.12.

Notice the way that the image in the 3D view looks. Now the body has some depth to it. It's not just a plane of faces anymore.

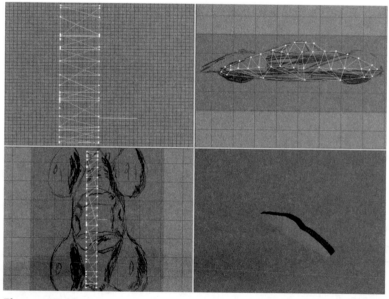

Figure 15.12
First extrusion.

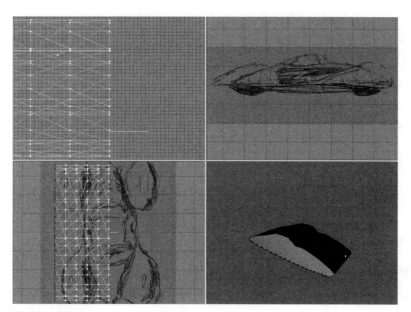

Figure 15.13
After extruding the body faces five times.

10. Repeat step 9 four more times, until you get five segments, as shown in Figure 15.13. Warning: do not click on any other tool or in the edit windows. After the fifth extrusion you want to end up with the body faces still selected.

11. The body faces should still be selected if you got my warning in time. Choose Edit, Duplicate Selection.

12. Click the Move tool, then go to the Top view at the lower left, and drag the highlighted faces (these will now be the copies, not the originals) to the right, clear of the extrusion segments, so that you get something like that shown in Figure 15.14.

13. Choose Face, Reverse Vertex Order.

14. Using the Side views and Top views, align the vertices of the copy of the body faces with their counterparts in the main body.

15. In the Top view drag the body face copy over to the right edge of the rest of the body polygons. Align the vertices as best you can by eye.

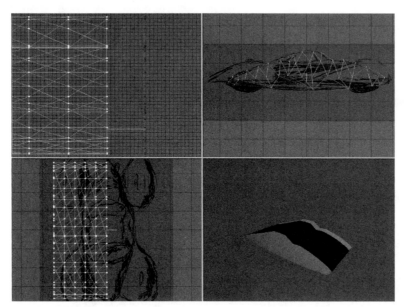

Figure 15.14
After duplicating and moving the copies.

Tip

We want to make sure that the vertices in step 15 are perfectly aligned. To do this, we'll scale our entire model up. Making our model larger in relation to the grid allows us more precision with the grid. This will help ensure good results when we snap our vertices to the grid, which is going to happen shortly.

16. Select the entire set of polygons in all the faces, and then use the Scale tool to make the entire model four times larger.

17. Select the entire model in Vertex Selection mode, and choose Vertex, Snap To Grid.

18. Choose Vertex, Weld Vertices.

19. Scale the model by 0.25. This will restore the model back to its original size.

20. In the Top view make sure the entire model is selected, and then use the Move tool to drag the model over the sketch so that it is aligned around the longitudinal center of the car in the sketch. You should now have a model that looks like that shown in Figure 15.15.

21. In the Top view select the bottom nine rows (or forwardmost nine rows) of vertices. This means that you need to ensure that the Select tool is in Face

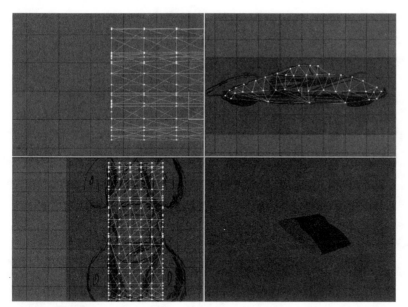

Figure 15.15
Scaling the nose of the runabout.

mode. If you haven't placed your vertices exactly as I did, don't sweat it. Just make sure that you select all of the vertices from those at the front of the car, back to the top of the windshield. Look ahead to Figure 15.16 to see what I mean, if it still isn't clear.

22. Use the Scale tool to scale the selection to 0.9 in the X-axis only; leave the other values at 1.0. Figure 15.16 shows the result of this operation.

23. Change your selection to be the bottom eight rows, and scale to 0.9.

24. Repeat the decrementing and scaling of the selection, reducing your selection vertices one row at a time until you run out of victims . . . ummm . . . I mean vertices. You should now have something that resembles that shown in Figure 15.17.

25. Repeat this iterative scaling process for the rows of vertices as seen in the Top view at the other end of the car body, until it, too, tapers, as shown in Figure 15.18. You may find it necessary to manually move a few vertices at either end to achieve the appropriate amount of taper.

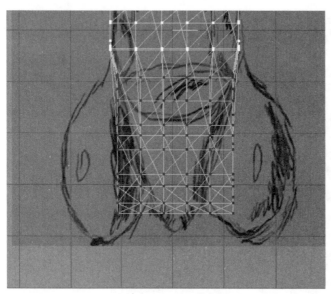

Figure 15.16
After scaling the bottom nine rows.

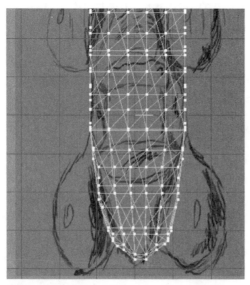

Figure 15.17
After scaling the nose.

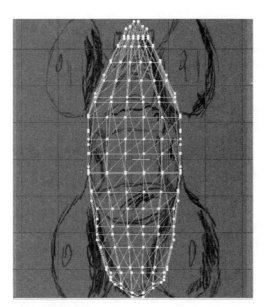

Figure 15.18
After scaling the tail.

26. Now perform the same sort of iterative scaling operations on the Front view of the car, getting it to look something like the view shown in Figure 15.19.

27. Next, use the Selection and Move tools to place the car so that it is centered around the origin (0,0,0), as shown in Figure 15.20. The axis "bug" at the origin has been enhanced as thick black lines to emphasize its location.

28. Finally, select all the polygons and use the Groups tools to regroup all polygons into a single group—name it "body".

Building the Fenders

Next, we will tackle the wheel well and fender assemblies.

1. Hide the body group.

2. On the Model tab, select the Sphere tool, and create a sphere that matches the forward curves of the forward fender, as shown in Figure 15.21.

3. Select the bottom two rows of faces, and delete them. Then move the bottom row of vertices up a bit, to get something that looks like Figure 15.22.

4. Select the leftmost three rows of vertices, and move them farther left, as shown in Figure 15.23.

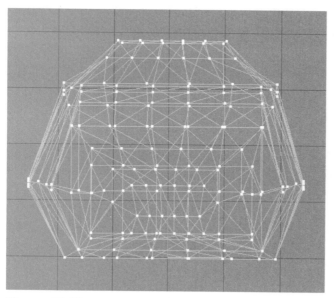

Figure 15.19
Shaping the Front view.

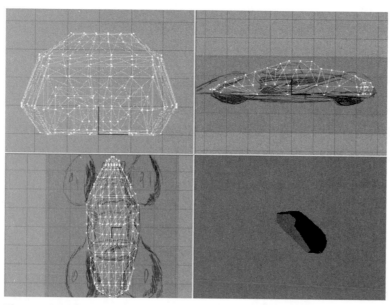

Figure 15.20
Centering the Front view.

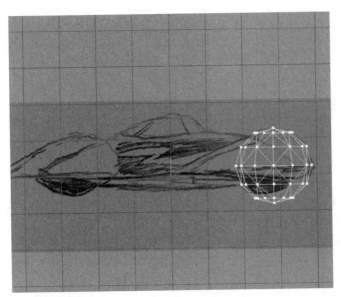

Figure 15.21
Fender sphere.

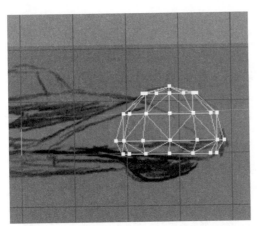

Figure 15.22
Lopping off the bottom of the fender sphere.

5. Continue to reshape the fender to match the sketch as shown in Figure 15.24, until you are happy.

The next bit is a little tricky, so move slowly. We want to drag certain of the vertices from the fender over to the exact position of vertices on the body. The vertex rows we want from the fender are the two bottom ones, and we are interested in the vertices on the body side. By dragging them over to the body, we create a fairing-cum-running board sort of affair.

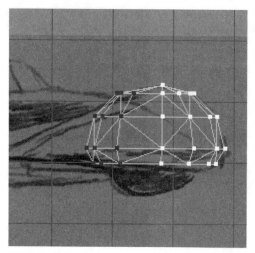

Figure 15.23
Stretching the fender.

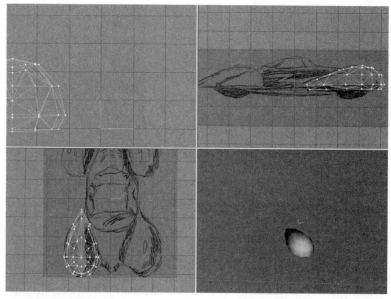

Figure 15.24
Shaping the fender.

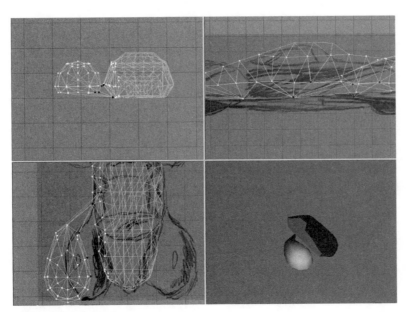

Figure 15.25
The fender vertices.

6. Unhide the body.

7. Drag the fender away from the body so that it is in the clear in the Top and Front views.

8. Select the vertices and drag them, one at a time, as shown in Figure 15.25. The vertices are on the two bottom rows and are the ones that face the body.

   Make sure to place the vertices exactly where they mate with a corresponding vertex. A close-up view is shown in Figure 15.26.

9. After each vertex is placed with a mate, use Snap To Grid to make sure they are exactly coincident, and use Weld Vertices to convert each pair of vertices into one vertex. Once you have done this for all the appropriate vertices along the fender bottom, you will get something like Figure 15.27.

10. Finally, move the fender back to a position that matches the sketched fender in the Top view, as shown in Figure 15.28.

11. Repeat steps 2 through 10 for each of the other fenders. Remember to hide the body and the other fenders when necessary to remove clutter from the screen. You should end up with the finished car, as shown in Figure 15.29. But we aren't done yet!

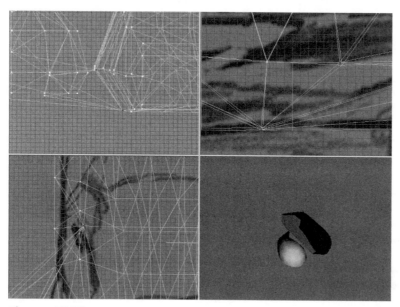

Figure 15.26
Close-up of moved vertices.

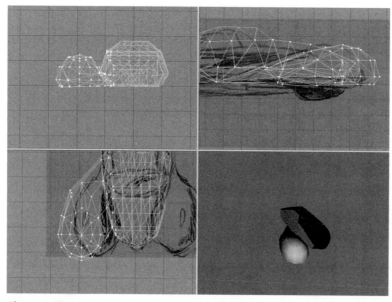

Figure 15.27
All vertices moved.

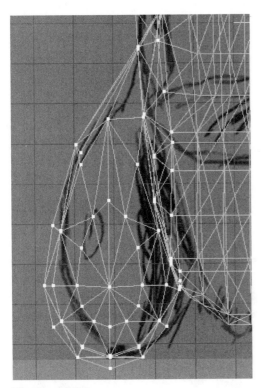

Figure 15.28
Finished fender.

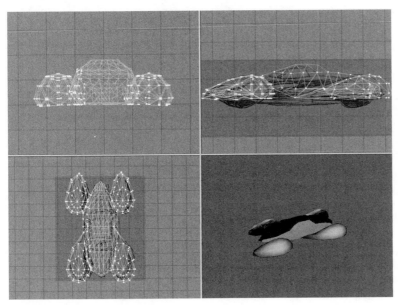

Figure 15.29
All fenders and body completed.

We need to rescale the car. I like to size my models so that the exporter doesn't need to scale them. Select your entire model (all vertices, or all faces, or all groups—it doesn't really matter—and move it so that it is centered over the axis bug, with the bottom sitting about 0.3 units above the X-Z plane (as seen from the Side view). The X-Z plane serves as the ground for us at the moment.

Now scale the car in the Y-axis so that the roof of the car is about 2 units above the ground, while the bottom is still about 0.3 units above the ground. After that, scale the car in the X-axis so that the front bumper is about 3 units in front of the axis bug, and the rear bumper is about 3 units behind the axis bug.

Save your work.

The Mount Nodes

In Chapter 14 you learned how to make a skeleton for an animated character in MilkShape using joints. In this section we are going to use the same feature, the joint, to create *nodes* that tell Torque where to mount certain things on models.

1. As shown in Figure 15.30, create four *unconnected* joints, or mounts, on the four corners of the car where the wheel hubs would be. To ensure that the joints are unconnected, you need to use the Select tool to deselect each node after it's been created.

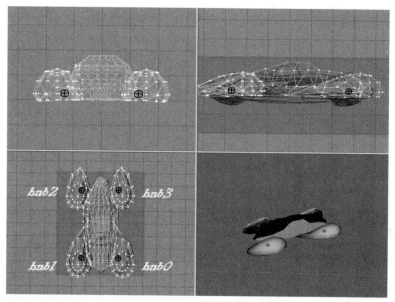

Figure 15.30
Mounts on all four corners.

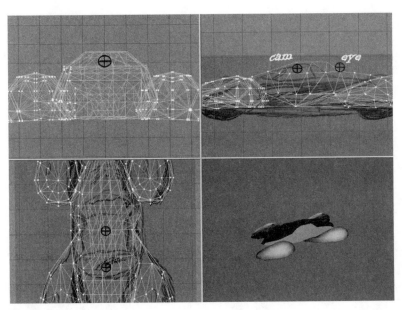

Figure 15.31
Eye and camera mounts.

2. Name each of the joints with the names shown in Figure 15.30, with hub0 being the left front joint.

3. Add two more unconnected joints to the locations shown in Figure 15.31. Name the front one "eye" and the rear one "cam".

4. Finally, add two unconnected joints to the locations shown in Figure 15.32. Name the one on the right (the left-hand seat position) "mount0" and the other one "mount1".

Now, the last two pairs of mounts are used for different, and mutually exclusive, purposes. The eye and cam mounts are used for games where the car becomes the player's avatar. The sample racing game that comes with Torque works like that. The eye node located at the point of the eye mount is the normal first-person point-of-view location for the view's eye. The cam node is for the third-person point of view; the actual camera is offset from the location of this node and so is usually actually behind and above the vehicle.

The mount0 and mount1 mounts are used for games where the player's character actually gets "in" the vehicle; they specify where the player's avatar will be mounted. The game continues to use the player's avatar's camera and eye nodes. You saw those in use back in Chapter 14.

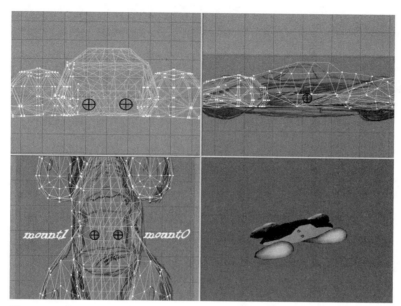

Figure 15.32
Seat mounts.

Skins

Chapter 9 covered the subject of skins and UV mapping, so I refer you back there to map the textures for your new car. You can find a copy of the skin to use at C:\3D2E\RESOURCES\CH15\runabout.jpg. Create a new folder called "runabout" in the folder C:\3D2E\demo\data\shapes, and put the skin file you created, or the premade one, in this new folder.

Collision Mesh

For all objects except player models, we need to create at least one collision mesh if we want the game engine to detect when it collides with another object, so use the Box tool in the Model tab to create a box that surrounds the vehicle, as shown in Figure 15.33.

The new box will have a name like Box01 in the Groups tab, and will be selected by default immediately after you create it. Name the collision mesh "Collision-1". Collision meshes need to be named "Collision-n", where n is a non-zero integer. You can have more than one collision mesh if you like, so number them as you create them, starting at 1, and incrementing by one each time you add one.

You should also hide the collision mesh and then save the model before exporting the model.

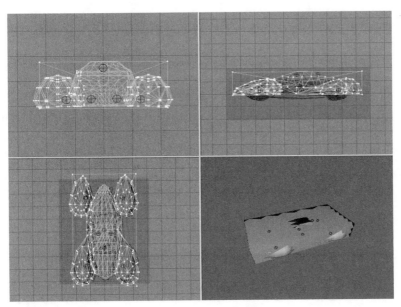

Figure 15.33
Collision mesh.

Collision Meshes

Collision meshes need to be *convex hulls* if they are to work correctly in Torque. A hull in this context is identical to a mesh. A convex hull is a mesh that has no "dent" in it—no areas where the mesh surface seems to go inwards into the mesh,

The following illustration should help in understanding.

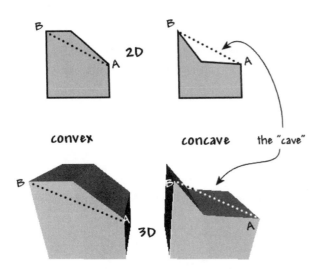

In the illustration, there are two 2D shapes at the top. The one on the left is convex, and the one on the right is concave.

Notice how a line drawn between A and B in the convex shape travels completely through the interior of the shape? With a convex shape, any line drawn between *any* two vertices will always pass entirely inside the shape. Always.

Now look at the concave 2D shape in the upper-right portion of the illustration. Line A-B in this case travels outside the boundaries of the shape. In fact the line segments of the shape running from A to the vertex between A and B and then on to B form a little indentation—something like a cave.

In fact, that is an easy way to remember which is which: Con*cave* shapes have caves. Con*vex* shapes don't.

The bottom two shapes are 3D versions of the top shapes. You will probably find it harder to spot a concave 3D shape. But just remember the "cave" and you will do fine.

The bottom-left 3D shape would work fine as a collision mesh in all ways. The bottom-right one would not. It might work in certain special cases, such as for collisions with player characters, but projectiles would not detect the mesh, and hence not collide with it.

The Wheels

Of course, a cool car needs cool wheels. There's not much to them, so I invite you to model your own wheel for use on the car. You, of course, may decide to make a complex model, but there is really no need—a lot can be done with a decent skin. A collision mesh is not needed, but do make sure that the wheel is oriented so that in the front wheel, you see the roundness of the wheel, hubcap and all. In the side view (upper right view) you should be looking at the tread of the tire on the wheel, and the inside of the wheel (the hub) should be on the left. This is not the same as they would be oriented if you modeled the wheels directly on to the car. Also ensure that the axle of the wheel and the midline of the tire are aligned with the origin bug, unless you include a hub assembly for the wheel. If you do include a hub, align the hub with the axis bug instead of the wheel.

Make sure that the wheel is about 1.5 units in diameter, and about 0.4 units wide (or thick).

Testing Your Runabout

In order to test the runabout, we first need to export it from MilkShape. We will use the built-in exporter for this task, since it is more up to the job and has fewer settings and stuff for us to get wrong.

1. After saving your work, export your model from MilkShape using the DTSPlus Exporter. Choose File, Export, Torque DTS Plus.

2. Use defaults, but make sure they are correct. You want to have Output dump file and Copy textures checked, and Use .cfg File cleared. Set the Scale to 1. The other settings don't matter.

3. Click on Export DTS to export your runabout to DTS format at C:\3D2E\demo\data\shapes\runabout\runabout.dts.

4. Open your wheel model, and export it as C:\3D2E\demo\data\shapes\runabout\wheel.dts. Keep the same settings as for the car.

   If you didn't create a wheel of your own, you can copy the one at RESOURCE\CH15 into C:\3D2E\demo\data\shapes\runabout. Make sure you copy both the wheel model and its texture file.

Next, you need to edit the script that controls the vehicle so it will look for your model and not the default one.

1. Locate the file \3D2E\demo\server\scripts\car.cs, and open it with UltraEdit.

2. Find the line that says this:

   ```
   shapeFile = "~/data/shapes/buggy/buggy.dts";
   ```

   Replace it with this line:

   ```
   shapeFile = "~/data/shapes/runabout/runabout.dts";
   ```

3. Then find the line that says this:

   ```
   shapeFile = "~/data/shapes/buggy/wheel.dts";
   ```

   And replace it with this line:

   ```
   shapeFile = "~/data/shapes/runabout/wheel.dts";
   ```

4. Save the file.

Okay, now it's time to run the racing demo. The following may look familiar to you, since we did this back in Chapter 9.

1. Browse to C:\3D2E, and click the tge.exe.

2. When the main menu appears, click the Example: Multiplayer Racing button at the bottom of the menu screen.

Table 15.1 Torque Racing Demo Controls

Key	Description
mouse	steering left or right
W	accelerate
S	brake
Tab	toggle from first- to third-person viewpoint
Escape	exit the game
F8	camera fly mode
F7	move car to camera position
Alt+C	switch between camera fly mode and car

3. In the Play Demo Game screen, make sure that the Create Server check box is checked.

4. Click the right arrow at the bottom to launch the demo.

5. After the game loads, have at it! You probably should switch to Chase view by pressing the Tab key—there's more to see. See Table 15.1 for the keyboard controls.

Moving Right Along

Building the model is only half the battle—well, maybe three-quarters. There is still the matter of defining the vehicle's characteristics, like mass, drag, speeds, particle generators, collision handlers, and so on. You take care of these things in scripts that run on the server.

To do the testing you just did, you used the existing demo buggy script that comes with the Torque Engine and simply substituted our model in place of the dune buggy. It looks like a roadster but drives like a dune buggy! In fact, you will recall that you had a test-drive of a dune buggy back in Chapter 9.

Later, in Chapter 22, we will create the script that will define the behavior of the vehicle that we've modeled here and its response to user inputs and game environment stimuli.

Coming up next, in Chapter 16, we'll continue with MilkShape and make some weapons and other items.

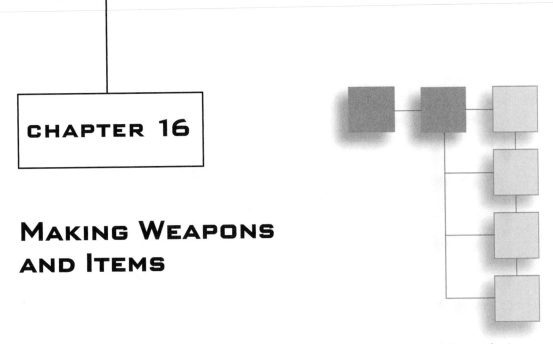

CHAPTER 16

MAKING WEAPONS AND ITEMS

In this chapter we're going to make a bunch of things. Most of the techniques used will basically be a review for you, so you can see this chapter as one big exercise in applying what you've learned to different situations.

We're going to make a few weapons, and in order to maintain balance, we'll make something that can be used in game to counteract the effects of these weapons.

We'll also make some items that one might call *decorations* for the game. The purpose of these items—some trees and a rock—is to provide some clutter. This is to help fill out otherwise sterile-looking game worlds, making them more interesting to wander around in.

The Health Kit

We'll start out with an easy one, the Health Kit. Like I said, this will be a basic review, but it's important to go over the process involved in creating an item for use in the game so that the broad steps become obvious and second nature.

The Model

The Health Kit is little more than a fancy-looking box, as you can see from Figure 16.1. So this won't take long.

1. Create a new folder: \3D2E\demo\data\shapes\items.

2. Fire up MilkShape, and create an empty document.

Figure 16.1
The Health Kit in game.

3. Use the Box tool to create a box, as shown in Figure 16.2.

4. Align the box to be centered at the origin for all three axes, as you can see in Figure 16.2.

5. On the Materials tab, create a new material, using \3D2E\RESOURCES\CH16\healthkit.png as the bitmap.

6. Name the material "healthkit".

7. Select the box, and assign the healthkit material to it.

8. Make sure that the 3D view has been set to Texture mode. You should see a nice, shiny new first-aid kit kind of item there, like that in Figure 16.3. This one always has bandages in it!

9. Scale the box to where it is about 1 unit on each side.

10. Save your work.

11. Use the DTSPlus Exporter to export your model.

12. Make sure that Copy Textures and Create dump file are checked, and that the Scale is set to 1.0.

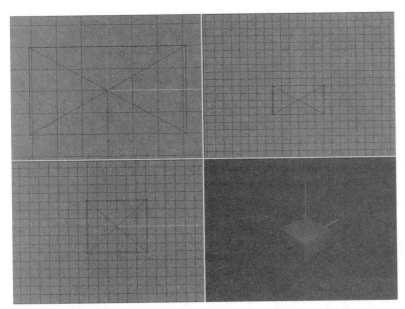

Figure 16.2
The box.

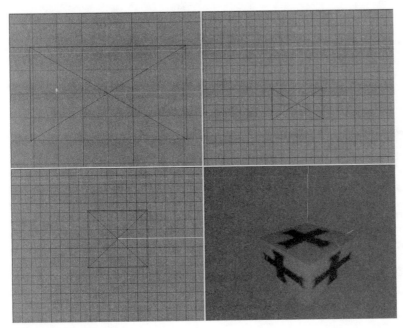

Figure 16.3
The Health Kit model.

13. Click on Export DTS to export the model to \3D2E\demo\data\shapes\ items\healthkits.dts.

Testing the Health Kit

To use the Health Kit in game, you merely have to run over it to pick it up. Then you activate it by pressing the "h" key to restore your health whenever it gets too low. You may remember using a kind of first-aid kit in one of your sample games from an earlier chapter—Emaga5—where you got health back just by running over the first-aid kit, or Health Kit. This one you have to pick up and activate; we'll test that functionality later when we get back into server scripts. Right now we just want to see our fine creation in the game world.

Once you have spawned into the FPS demo, you are going to use the World Editor to insert the Health Kit in the game world. We'll be using this procedure often, so pay attention! I'll repeat the procedure once or twice in later chapters to make sure you don't have to flail around too much. But right now, go ahead and launch the FPS demo, and then follow this procedure:

1. Press F8. This will set your player into camera fly mode.

2. Press F11. This will open up the World Editor, as shown in Figure 16.4.

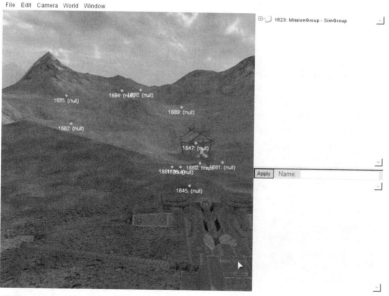

Figure 16.4
World Editor.

Figure 16.5
World Editor Creator.

3. Press F4. This will open up the World Editor Creator, as shown in Figure 16.5. The Creator pane is circled at the lower-right corner of the window.

4. In the Creator pane, click the plus sign next to Static Shapes. This will expand the listing. Now you need to drill down through the demo, data, and shapes folders.

5. Inside the shapes folder locate the items folder, and click the plus sign to open it as well. You should now have a Tree view similar to Figure 16.6.

6. Make sure that the center of the view is located in an open terrain area about 10 virtual feet in front of you. To move the view in the World Editor, hold down the right mouse button, and move the mouse.

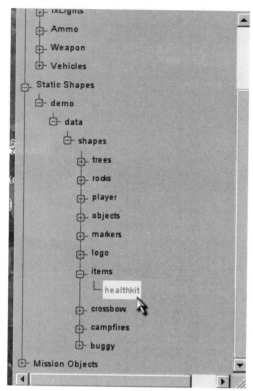

Figure 16.6
The Creator Tree view.

Figure 16.7
Health Kit model.

7. Click healthkit in the Tree view. The Health Kit model will appear; it will probably be somewhat embedded in the ground, as shown in Figure 16.7.

8. Move the cursor over on top of the vertical axis line (labeled Z) that sprouts from the top of the Health Kit model. The Z-axis label will become highlighted, as shown in Figure 16.8.

9. Click the vertical Z-axis line, and drag it up just a few pixels, until the box is completely out of the ground, as depicted in Figure 16.9.

Figure 16.8
The Z-axis label.

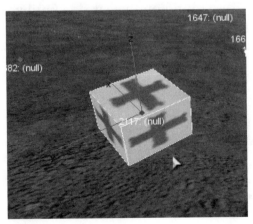

Figure 16.9
Repositioned Health Kit.

Note that this is the reason why you needed to switch to camera fly mode before entering the World Editor. If you had stayed in normal FPS view mode, you would not have been able to grab the Z-axis line and move it so easily.

10. Now press F11 to toggle out of the World Editor.

A Rock

Oh, big deal, a rock—what's up with that, you ask? Well, it *is* going to be your own handmade rock! That should be worth something.

The point here is that, even though the rock is not much more complex than the Health Kit, it *is* somewhat more complex nonetheless as you can in see Figure 16.10. It does less for us in the game, but it is one of those decoration-type items I mentioned—and stuff like this, while unglamorous, can greatly contribute to the ambience of your game.

1. Fire up MilkShape, and create an empty document.

2. Use the Sphere tool to create a sphere, as shown in Figure 16.11.

3. In the Side view, select the bottom three rows of vertices.

4. Choose Vertex, Flatten, Y. The bottom three rows should be squished together in a horizontal flat plane, as shown in Figure 16.12. Already it's starting to look like a rock.

5. Still in the Side view, drag the vertices around on the left side until you get something resembling Figure 16.13.

Figure 16.10
The rock in game.

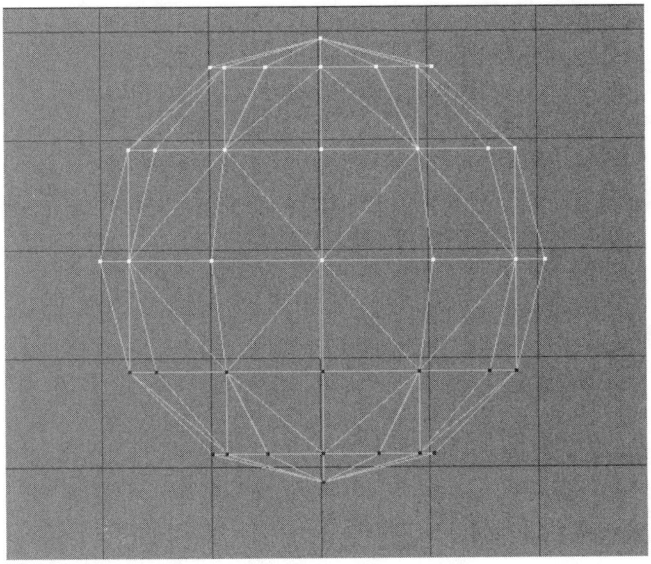

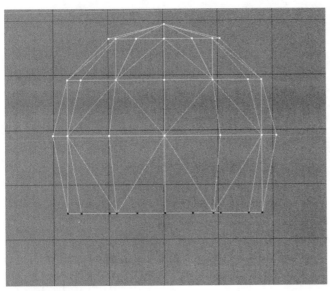

Figure 16.11
The sphere.

Figure 16.12
The truncated sphere.

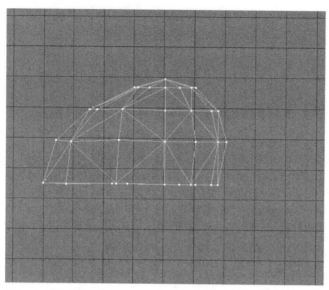

Figure 16.13
The stretched rock-sphere.

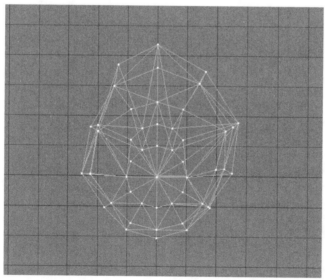

Figure 16.14
The almost rock.

6. Now in the Top view, drag some more vertices around until you get something resembling Figure 16.14. It's almost a rock now!

7. On the Materials tab, create a new material, using \3D2E\RESOURCES\ CH16\rock.png as the bitmap.

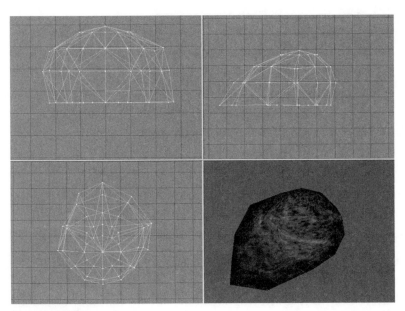

Figure 16.15
The rock model.

8. Name the material "rock".

9. Select the entire rock model, and assign the rock material to it.

10. Make sure that the 3D view has been set to Texture mode. You should see a nice lumpy and ancient-looking rock there, like that in Figure 16.15.

11. Save your work.

12. After saving your work, export your rock using the DTSPlus Exporter.

Use the same settings and procedure that you used for the Health Kit.

Testing the Rock

The rock has a bounding box set for collision because it is, after all, a rock—you can't go through it.

1. Run the FPS demo.

2. After the game loads, insert your rock in the same way you did with the Health Kit. The rock should be in the items folder along with the Health Kit.

3. Run over to the rock. Abuse it.

4. If you get blood from the rock, pat yourself on the back, and apply for a job at a collections agency. You're a natural.

Trees

If Joyce Kilmer had been a game developer, he might have written, "I think that I shall never see a model so annoying as a tree." Or something like that. But he didn't, so that's too bad. Really talented game developer–poets are rare.

Nonetheless, computer model trees really *are* annoying. There is this conundrum. If you can interact reasonably well with a model tree, then it looks awful. If the tree looks really good, then interacting with it is awful.

The problem is twofold. We see them everywhere, in most parts of the world, so they provide a great deal of the background to our daily lives. This means that in virtual worlds, if there are no trees in the background, we just *know* something's wrong even if we can't quite put our finger on the problem. They are ubiquitous. And that means we also have a highly developed subconscious sense of what they should look like, when we aren't . . . ummm . . . actually looking at them. With me so far? Okay, that's problem number one.

The other problem is that they are so dad-blamed complex! Even a sapling has lots of little branches and twigs and leaves and buds and stuff. If you have a polygon budget (and if you are making games, *you have a polygon budget!*), then these suckers will dry up that account faster than a barking moonbat can change its mind.

So, on the one hand, to have convincing trees that satiate the subconscious gamer's mind, we need to be attentive to details. And on the other hand, those very details can drag our frame rates lower than a snake's belly in a wheel rut.

To interact well with a tree means several things. When you approach it, circle it, look up into its branches and leaves, you see things properly in three-dimensional perspective. You can collide with the thicker parts like the trunk and the big lower branches, but if you fell onto a tree from above, you would likely fall a long way down through the airy upper structures before you stopped.

But unless you want to put 30,000 polygon trees into your game world, you'll have to compromise on all those fiddly details. There are ways to strip off a few thousand polygons here and there, but long before you get anywhere reasonable, your compromises start making the tree much less treelike. So then you have to pass a few edicts like this:

> From this point hence, this tree, and all other trees like this tree that grace our fair land, may only be viewed from certain angles—all of the afore-mentioned angles being from a level on the ground to a level not exceed-ing the height that one man can jump.

But then you start to drain the flexibility out of your game world. What if you are standing on the back of a truck? Or on a nearby hill? Or flying overhead in an ornithopter? Well, you can't do any of those things if you really want to save the trees!

And don't even talk to me about having forests of these things in a game, though there *are* ways to make trees look absolutely stunning from a distance and only take one or two polygons to accomplish the task! Using a technique called *billboarding* we can create trees that look great from any angle as long as we are at least moderately far from the tree—say, a couple dozen meters or more. But up close they are nothing but flat planes that turn to always face you. You can't look up into them from below and search for robins' nests. You can't climb them. And you certainly can't fall into them from above! I mean, what fun is that?

So why all the blather, you ask? Well, I'll tell you. We're going to look at modeling some game-friendly trees in this section, and I want you to enter into this prepared, understanding why I'm going to show you two different ways to model a tree. There are other ways, but these two ways represent the opposite extremes. First, we'll create a "normal" low-polygon *solid tree* with a collision mesh. One that you could potentially climb using appropriate program code. One that you could actually get beneath and peer up into. It won't look all that great, but it will look like a tree. After that, we'll create a *billboard tree*, which can be used to make vast forests of trees that will actually look like forests.

The Solid Tree

The solid tree is constructed of 3D object primitives, mostly cylinders that join end to end and taper. The one we'll make won't have any leaves—it's a generic big backyard tree in the winter.

I should warn you now that we aren't going to build a megapolygon old oak tree or anything like that here. Instead, we're going to do just enough so you'll have a

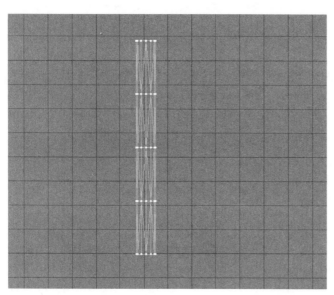

Figure 16.16
Four-stack cylinder.

good idea where you can go with the model and what's involved with this approach.

Having said all that, go ahead and create a new empty document in MilkShape, and let's get crackin'.

1. Select the Cylinder tool, and set it to 4 stacks and 12 slices in the parameter boxes.

2. Click your cursor in the Side view, and drag down and to the right to create a cylinder like the one shown in Figure 16.16.

3. Still in the Side view, select the vertices in the second row from the bottom, and then use the Move tool to shift them to one side.

4. Switch to the Top view, and do the same thing, moving the vertices slightly away from being aligned with the center of the cylinder.

5. Repeat steps 3 and 4 with the next two rows of vertices going up, one row at a time, using Figure 16.17 as a guide.

6. Do an incremental scaling, working from the second row of vertices going up, so that you get a tapered trunk, like that shown in Figure 16.18.

7. Use the Duplicate function to make a copy of the trunk.

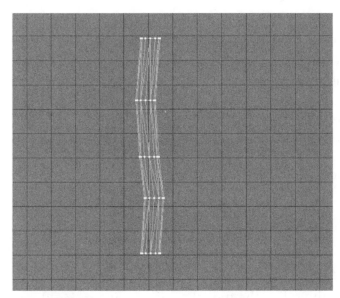

Figure 16.17
Crooked cylinder.

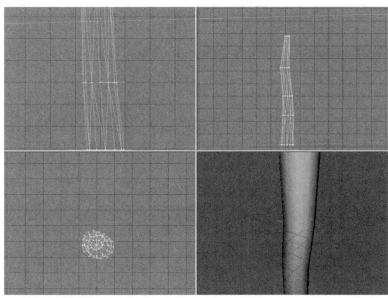

Figure 16.18
Crooked cylinder becomes a tree trunk.

T i p

If you've forgotten how to duplicate an object, I'll go over it quickly here.

First, make sure that the object to be copied has been selected in Face mode. Then choose Edit, Duplicate Selection. Make sure you only do that once, and don't click your mouse in the window.

It will look like nothing happened, but a copy was made in place. Select the Move tool, and then drag the selected object to a clear area. There you go—you will have the copy, and the original object will have been left behind.

8. Move the copy to one side. Then scale it and rotate it so that you get something that looks like Figure 16.19.

9. Drag the branch over to the trunk, and place it with the larger end inside the bounds of the trunk.

10. Make more copies of the branch, scaling, rotating, and tweaking them as desired, until you get something like the model shown in Figure 16.20.

11. On the Materials tab, create a new material, using \3D2E\RESOURCES\ CH16\bark.png as the bitmap.

12. Name the material "bark".

13. Select the trunk using the Groups tab, and assign the bark material to it.

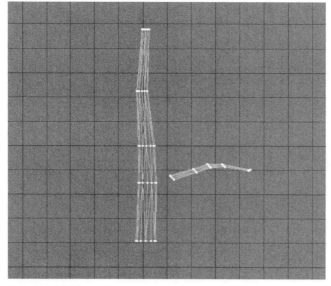

Figure 16.19
Branching out.

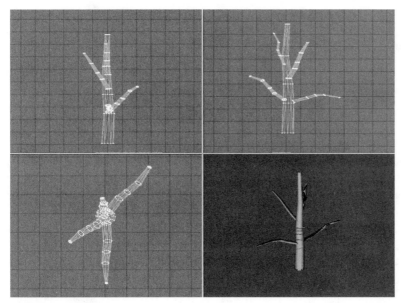

Figure 16.20
Adding more branches.

14. Assign the bark material to each of the branches. Do not select them all at once and assign the material; instead, do them one at a time.

15. Make sure that the 3D view has been set to Texture mode. You should see the textured tree there, like that in Figure 16.21.

    Okay, we'll stop there. Of course, we could go on and on, making it more detailed, and that's certainly something I encourage you to do later. It's just pointlessly repetitive to do it right now. Let's move along and add a collision mesh.

16. Create a box, and position it as shown in Figure 16.22.

17. Rename the box, calling it "Collision".

18. Save your work.

19. After saving your work, choose File, Export, Torque Game Engine DTS.

20. You want to take all the defaults (Collision Mesh should set to Bounding Box).

21. Export the box to \3D2E\demo\data\shapes\trees\solidtree.dts.

Figure 16.21
The textured tree.

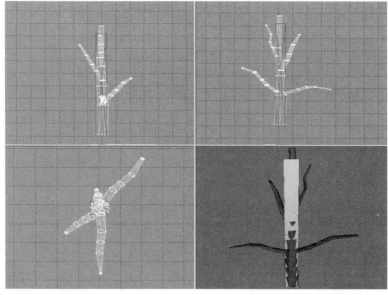

Figure 16.22
The tree collision mesh.

Testing the Solid Tree

The solid tree has a collision mesh—you can't go through it. You also can't climb it as is (you could if you wrote the appropriate script code). Anyway, to test out our solid tree, do the following:

1. Run the FPS demo.

2. Using camera fly mode, whip on over to the little clear area in the village, between the hovels.

3. Open the Mission Editor with F11, then call up the Creator with F4.

4. Drill down through Static Shapes, demo, data, shapes, and trees, locate the solid tree object, and place it.

5. Exit the Mission Editor with F11, press F7 to spawn your character where the camera is, and then run over to the tree and admire your handiwork.

6. Try to run through the tree. If you hurt your head, you know where the first-aid kit is!

The Billboard Tree

The billboard tree is the Ferrari of game trees. It looks good and is so low on polygons that if you remove one polygon, it vanishes! But it is specialized, and you can't do much with it on its own. And Torque has something to say about this. Torque has a special object type called fxFoliageReplicator, designed to use things like billboard trees (and grass, bushes, and so on) in a very useful way. You see, with fxFoliageReplicator, all we need to do is create our tree textures (the primary texture and the alphamap texture) add them to a Foliage Replicator, and pow! Instant forest—just add water. Ahem.

I'm not going to make you create a texture for your tree, although you can certainly do so if you like. You will need two textures. Let's say your tree texture was going to be named flattree.jpg. You'll need to create your tree image in that texture file. Then you need to create the alpha mask. This is a grayscale (256 color) image of exactly the same size as your primary image. The alpha mask image will have pure black everywhere that will be transparent (no tree parts). And it will be pure white everywhere that there will be tree parts. You can use varying shades of gray to indicate translucent areas. If your primary tree image file is named flattree.jpg, then the alpha mask image file needs to be named flattree.alpha.jpg. To get a better idea, take a look in the \3D2E\demo\data\ shapes\trees folder at the files named foliage.jpg, foliage2.jpg, and shrub.jpg, as well as their alpha mask sidekicks: foliage.alpha.jpg, foliage2.alpha.jpg, and shrub.alpha.jpg.

On with the show!

1. Run the FPS demo.

2. While pointing the center of your player's view at an appropriate area that looks like it could use a forest, open the Mission Editor in Creator mode (see Figure 16.23), then choose Mission Objects, Environment, fxFoliageReplicator. Give the new object a name in the dialog box that appears. You will end up with an object-encompassing box placed in the world, with the name you gave it as a label.

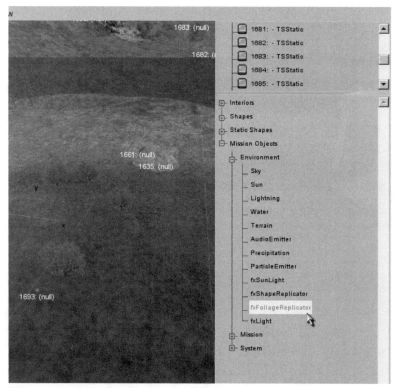

Figure 16.23
Insert the fxFoliageReplicator object.

3. Change to the Inspector (F3), and scroll to the bottom of the list, where you will find an entry for the fxFoliageReplicator you just inserted. Select the object.

Tip

Sometimes when you open the Mission Editor, and try to open up the Inspector, the function key (F3) doesn't work. I'm not sure why this is. It's easy to deal with, though. Simply choose Word Editor Inspector from the Window menu. An even more convenient way is to open the Creator first (F4) and then open the Inspector (F3).

4. In the lower-right panel, scroll through until you locate the property for this object, called FoliageFile (see Figure 16.24). On the right-hand side of the edit box is a button with three dots (ellipsis). Click this button, and a file dialog box will appear.

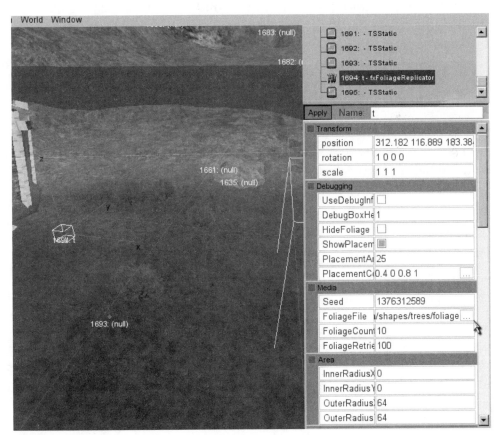

Figure 16.24
Locating the FoliageFile property.

5. Browse your way to demo/data/trees, and click the file foliage.jpg. Click the Load button. The path and file name will be inserted in the edit box for you. But there's a teensy problem. The file name was entered with the .jpg extension included. We don't want that. So delete the extension part of the name (including the dot).

6. Click the Apply button. Assuming you changed no other properties for the fxFoliageReplicator object that you made, then 10 copies of the tree image will appear scattered about the terrain.

7. Go romp around amongst the trees. Experiment with different settings. When you are done, exit to the desktop.

As you can see, the billboard tree is kind to your video card and will keep your frame rates right up there. In fact, you can build forests of these things using as many polygons as found in just one of the solid trees! To adjust the numbers and density of the trees, change the count to a higher number, or fiddle with the inner and outer radius settings. The larger the outer radius, the larger the area that is covered. To adjust visibility at a distance, play with the values in the culling section. Make the trees sway and appear to shimmer using various animation section settings. Go nuts.

Oh, and by the way. If you really, really want to have a forest of modeled tree shapes (like the solid tree we created earlier, remember?), then look in the Creator window, right above where you found fxFoliageReplicator. See that entry called fxShapeReplicator? Guess what it does, hmmmm?

The Tommy Gun

The famous Thompson submachine gun is a somewhat obsolete weapon that most people are familiar with visually, even if they don't know what it's called.

The technique we will use is the Extrusion method. When it comes to modeling weapons, Extrusion is probably the method of choice for the simple reason that it often works well when using photographs for source material. There are dozens and dozens of books and many Internet resources available that have photographs and technical drawings of weapons, but remember that much of the source material is copyrighted.

For our tommy gun, I'll work from a sketch I made, shown in Figure 16.25.

Figure 16.25
Tommy gun sketch.

Tip

To create your weapons, you can use a photograph or detailed diagram of your own if you like; however, you are perfectly free to use my sketches and artwork in any way you want to. The choice is yours.

The sketch is rough and not very detailed, but it will do just fine for our purposes. This model will have as few polygons in it as I think we can get away with. I've made two versions of it for you to use: one for the skin and one to act as the extrusion reference image.

Making the Model

Get MilkShape running and warming up in the driveway, and we'll get started in a minute. We will use \3D2E\RESOURCES\CH16\tommygun.png as the texture for the tommy gun's skin. You can find the extrusion guide sketch at \3D2E\RESOURCES\CH16\tommygun_ref.bmp. You need to set the latter as the background image for the Side view window in MilkShape; we'll use the former later in this section.

1. Select the Vertex tool, making sure that the Auto Tool check box is cleared.

2. In the Side view, start placing vertices at all the major corners and points around the components of the gun. See Figure 16.26 for reference.

3. Start making faces. No! I meant in the model, not at me! You will probably have to zoom in some to get enough separation between the vertices.

   Be careful as you move along, making sure you get all the faces. For tips and other information on faces, check back to Chapter 15. Figure 16.27 shows the finished polygon faces around the muzzle, which can be a bit fiddly. Notice how far I zoomed in.

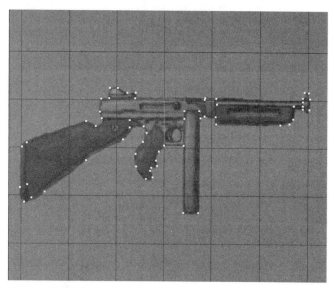

Figure 16.26
Tommy gun vertices.

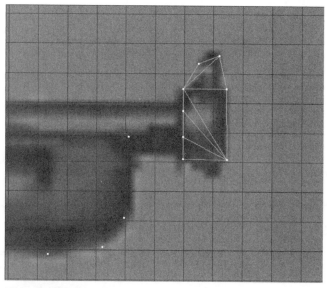

Figure 16.27
Tommy gun muzzle faces.

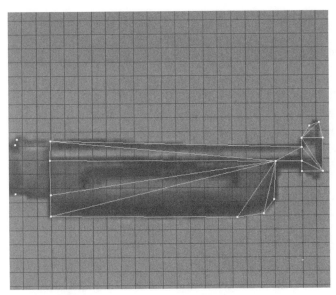

Figure 16.28
Tommy gun barrel and forestock faces.

Figure 16.28 shows the barrel and forestock faces. A warning about the barrel is in order here, I think. In this model we will stick with a straight extrusion exercise, but I highly recommend that after you complete this section you rework the model and make the barrel a cylinder object. The results will be nicer.

Figure 16.29 shows the faces completed for the grip, the receiver, the magazine, and other metal parts of the main body of the gun. Note that I haven't modeled the trigger or the trigger guard hole—leaving these out saves a ton of polygons. If you want you can add in the detail for the trigger, but you will probably take a hit on frame rate in the game.

Figure 16.30 shows the faces of the wooden shoulder stock.

Now take a look at Figure 16.31. Notice the missing polygon down there in the 3D view? It's not evident by looking at the wire-frame view that the polygon was missed, but its absence really shows in the 3D view. Don't let this happen to you! Heh.

If it does happen to you, fix up the wayward faces, and we'll move on to the extrusion.

4. Select all the faces.

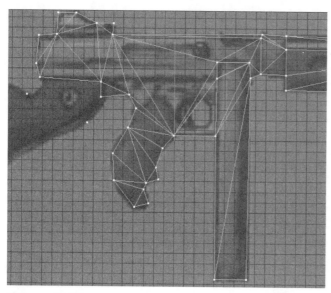

Figure 16.29
Tommy gun metal body faces.

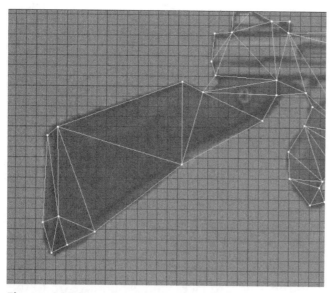

Figure 16.30
Tommy gun shoulder stock faces.

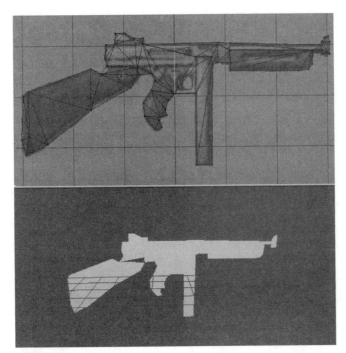

Figure 16.31
Tommy gun loses face—film at 11.

5. Use an X value of −2.0, and then click the Extrude button. Do not deselect the highlighted faces after this operation. You should get something that looks like Figure 16.32.

   Next, we will have to cap off one end of the extrusion, like we did with the car model. It's a simple operation but sometimes a bit touchy.

6. Choose Edit, Duplicate Selection and then quickly reverse the normals by choosing Face, Reverse Vertex order while the duplicate is still selected. This is so that the faces on the duplicate will be oriented 180 degrees from the original.

   You might also have to reverse the normals on some of the faces on the top or bottom of the gun. If the face shows black in the 3D view, then just select the face and choose Face, Reverse Vertex Order.

7. Use the Move tool to drag the copy of the faces back over to the side of the model, using the Front view window to monitor the activity.

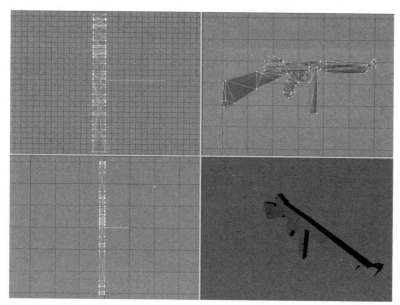

Figure 16.32
Extruded tommy gun.

8. Zoom in on a few of the vertices in the Front view, and make sure that the copy of the faces perfectly align with the edge vertices on this side of the model.

9. Select all vertices in the model, and then choose Vertex, Snap To Grid. One or two of the vertices might snap to an awkward location, so go ahead and manually fix them.

10. Choose Vertex, Weld Together.

The model as built so far is fine, except that it was created at a scale four times larger than we want for use in game. This was deliberate. A larger scale allows us to use larger reference images for the background image, which gives us access to more detail. Also, the larger the scale, the finer the granularity available when we want to snap points to the grid. So after all this work, we need to scale the model back to the correct size.

11. Select all parts of the model.

12. Use the Scale tool to set the scale to 0.25 in all three axes.

Figure 16.33
Shrunken gun.

13. Click the Scale button to the right of the axis boxes. The gun will shrink and should appear roughly as shown in Figure 16.33.

    Next, we have three nodes to add: one to indicate where the gun is held, one to indicate where the muzzle is, and one to indicate where expended shells are ejected. These nodes inform the engine where these spots are; a script that will be defined later dictates how they are used.

14. Create three unconnected joints, positioned and named as shown in Figure 16.34. The three node names are mountPoint, ejectPoint, and muzzlePoint.

    We have one more thing to do. We need the gun to have the correct posture when held by the player model.

15. In the Top view, select all faces.

16. Rotate the gun about 8 degrees to the left, as shown in Figure 16.35.

17. Move the nodes to align them with the gun, using Figure 16.35 as a guide.

Voilà! Insta-gun. Save your work.

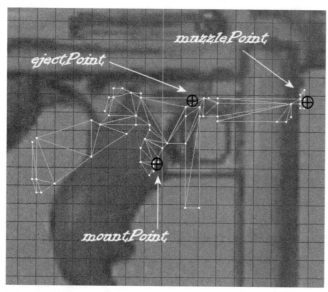

Figure 16.34
The tommy gun nodes.

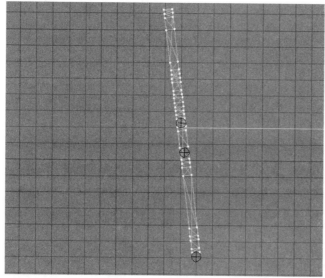

Figure 16.35
The rotated tommy gun.

Skinning the Tommy Gun

Way back in Chapter 13 you learned how to use UVMapper and the Gimp to create a skin for objects. In this chapter we'll look at using the built-in Texture Coordinate Editor in MilkShape to accomplish the same thing. It can be awkward to use but is suitable for our purpose here because we will already have a texture to use for the skin—in this case we will use a version of my original sketch.

1. Create a new material, using the file tommygun.bmp as the bitmap for the texture.

2. Assign the new material to the tommy gun object.

    If you have more than one object, select all the faces in all the objects, then regroup them. After that you can assign the new material to the single object.

3. Use the Groups tab, and select the tommy gun object.

4. Choose Window, Texture Coordinate Editor. You will get the Texture Coordinate Editor dialog box, as shown in Figure 16.36.

    When the Texture Coordinate Editor first opens, you often see just some confusing white lines over the top of the texture assigned to the object you are skinning. Not to worry.

5. Select the appropriate view from the view selection combo box at the right side of the dialog box. In the case of the tommy gun, this is the Left view.

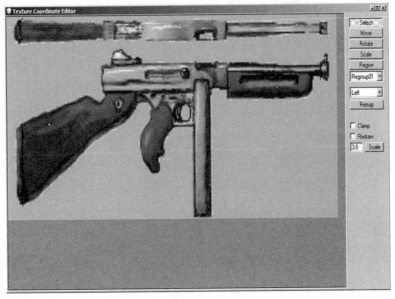

Figure 16.36
Texture Coordinate Editor dialog box.

6. Click the Remap button. You should get something like that shown in Figure 16.37. The shape of the tommy gun may not line up with the texture, so go ahead and use the Select and Move buttons inside this editor to move the vertices until they are in place. Figure 16.37 is a good guide to what the final result should look like.

7. Close the Texture Coordinate Editor dialog box, and take a look in your 3D view (make sure that it is set to Texture mode). There it is—your tommy gun! Compare your work with Figure 16.38. As you examine it closely, you will see why it might be a good idea to redo the barrel as a cylinder.

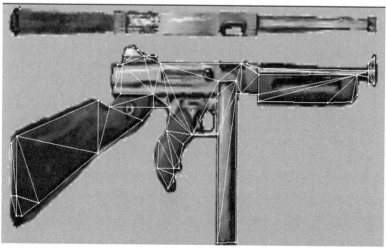

Figure 16.37
Remapped view.

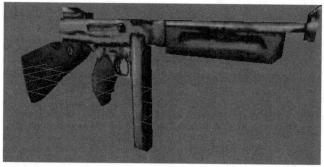

Figure 16.38
Finished tommy gun.

You might notice that the gun appears to be textured only on one side in the 3D view. This is because of the rotation. It actually is textured on both sides, but the lighting effect in the 3D view casts one side in shadow.

Testing the Tommy Gun

In order to test the tommy gun, we first need to export it from MilkShape.

1. Create a new folder, \3D2E\demo\data\shapes\Tommygun, and save your work there, too, if you like.

2. Use DTPlus to export your gun, using the same settings as used earlier in this chapter for the other exports.

3. Click DTS Export to send the gun on its merry way to its new life as \3D2E\demo\data\shapes\Tommygun\Tommygun.dts.

Okay, now it's time to see the gun in the game. I can hear you now: "woohoo! Mayhem and noise and stuff!"

1. Run the FPS demo.

2. Follow the same procedure as you did with the Health Kit and the rock, but this time insert the tommy gun into the game world instead.

3. Go over and have a look. The gun is, at the moment, a static shape—it doesn't know how to do that cool machine gun stuff yet. That will come in a later chapter.

So much for the mayhem. Patience, grasshopper!

The Tommy Gun Script

Just as we encountered with the runabout in Chapter 15, making the model for a weapon is not the whole job. We have yet to create the weapon script that defines how the weapon works. That is something we will cover later, in Chapter 22, when we look at the code that brings all of these models together in our sample game.

Moving Right Along

This chapter was a bit of a review of techniques covered in earlier chapters, but we applied these techniques to a few different kinds of items with different features: collision meshes, no collision meshes, billboard textures, and translucent textures.

This helps demonstrate the wide variety of characteristics that modeled items can have in a game world.

We also looked at the MilkShape's Texture Coordinate Editor a little bit, enough to be able to use it to tweak texture maps if the situation warrants.

In the next chapter we'll learn a new sort of 3D modeling tool and use it to make structures.

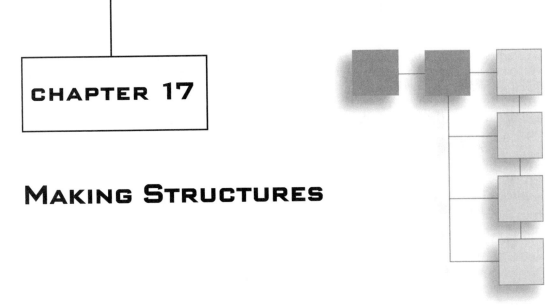

CHAPTER 17

MAKING STRUCTURES

There are quite a few different options available to the game developer when creating objects for use in a game. We've already seen how to make things like trees and weapons using MilkShape to create DTS-type objects. But what about complex structures, like buildings and bridges?

Well, you can also use DTS objects for those, making sure to create multiple collision meshes where needed. Buildings have a lot of surfaces that either you can walk on or at the very least you can't walk *through*. So you will spend a great deal of effort creating collision meshes. Also, DTS objects don't inherently understand the concept of lighting and shadows, so if you make a building as a DTS object, you will also have to light it yourself using another object—which is possible, but you'll have to do that for every building. This is a real issue for structures that are interiors. Bridges and ramps are not such a big deal when it comes to lighting, but you still have the collision mesh workload.

Fortunately, there is a solution to this problem. In Torque a different kind of object is supported—a DIF-type object, also called an *interior*. Now, using the word *interior* is a bit misleading, because you could (and probably will, at some point) use the same kind of object for complex structures that don't have interior lighting but do have many collidable surfaces. Therefore, I prefer to use the word *structure* to describe DIF objects.

There are several tools available to use for creating DIF objects. A very good open source (published under the GNU General Public License, it doesn't cost you anything to use) is QuArK (Quake Army Knife). A version of QuArK is included on the companion CD, along with an electronic copy of reference material from the first edition of this book.

Along the way, the good folks at GarageGames decided that they really needed a CSG tool that was more empathetic to the way the Torque Engine likes to do things. One of the most important of these things was cross-platform compatibility. Torque runs on PC (Windows), Macintosh, and Linux. So GarageGames, spearheaded by Matt Fairfax, teamed up with some bright and industrious fellows named Dave Wyand, Tom Brampton, John Kabus (aka Bob the C Builder), and Ron Yacketta, and scoped out a tool called *Torque Constructor*. Constructor is made with the Torque Engine, and that means—yup, you guessed it—Constructor, when in full release, will be available for Windows, Macintosh, and Linux!

CSG Modeling

In the 3D graphics world, tools like Constructor and others that I'll mention here in passing (including QuArK, Hammer, and 3D World Studio) are known as *CSG Modeling* tools. CSG stands for *Constructive Solid Geometry,* where 3D models are built out of things called *brushes* and models are built up using a collection of 3D brushes.

A brush in this sense is like a building block. You select a particular brush (also called a *polyhedron*) for a particular need and apply it to your model. There is a small set of shape primitives that serve as the basic brushes (see Figure 17.1): the cube (or box), the cylinder, the cone (or spike), and the ramp (or wedge). Some programs also include the arch and the sphere, as shown in Figure 17.2. Each of these primitives is a closed 3D solid.

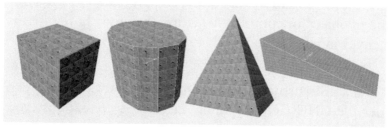

Figure 17.1
Cube, cylinder, cone, and ramp solids.

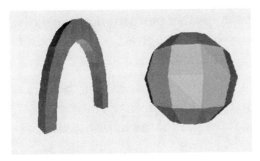

Figure 17.2
Arch and sphere solids.

N o t e

Now, when looking at the third object from the left in Figure 17.1 you might be inclined to think, "Waitaminute! That's not a cone, it's a pyramid! What's up with that?" Well, just imagine that instead of four sides meeting at the point at the top, as shown in the picture, there were actually 64 sides meeting at the top. What do you think you would see: a pyramid or a cone? Well? Of course, it would be a cone. And don't even start on me with that "but a cube is just a cylinder with four sides instead of 64 sides" business, or I'll take away your mouse. Sometimes things just are what they are. So let's get on with the program.

The primary modeling operations that you apply to CSG brushes are known as *Boolean operations*. You might remember Boolean logic from way back in Chapter 2. In this case, the Boolean operations are borrowed from mathematical *set* theory, a subvariation of *logic* theory, but in this case applied to representations of solid objects. That guy Boole sure had a lot of wacky ideas. Wacky ideas that work! There are three CSG operations: *intersection, subtraction,* and *union.*

The simplest operation to grasp is the *union.* Simply place two brushes (solids) in space such that part of one is "embedded" in the other, and treat them as one resultant solid, and you have a union. With most CSG modeling programs, you simply overlap the two brushes as appropriate and then group them together. That's the way it works with Constructor.

Difference results are the result of *subtraction* operations. What you get depends on which brush is the *Minuend* (the brush on which the subtraction will be performed, and also which will be left over afterward) and which brush is the *Subtrahend* (the brush that is subtracted from the Minuend, dictating the nature of the subtraction operation). Some people call the Subtrahend brush the *Subtraction* brush.

As performed by Constructor (and most other apps that perform Booleans), the Subtrahend is the brush that must be selected when the subtraction operation is performed.

Again, place two brushes in space such that one is "embedded" in the other. Select the Subtrahend brush, and perform the subtraction operation. Then remove the Subtrahend brush. You will see that the part of the minuend that was coincident between the two brushes has been removed.

View A in Figure 17.3 shows two brushes before and after performing a Boolean operation on them. View B shows the union of the two brushes; they haven't been actually joined but have been merely placed in coincident locations.

In Figure 17.4 we see on the left the result of a subtraction operation, where the (now removed) cylinder was the subtrahend. We are left with the Cube brush

Figure 17.3
Two brushes.

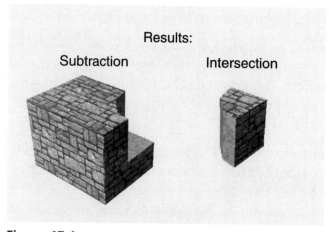

Figure 17.4
Boolean operation results.

with a "bite" taken out of it, the shape of which matches the part of the cylinder that was previously situated there.

On the right in Figure 17.4 is the result of the intersection operation. You'll note that all that remains is a brush in the shape of the cubic area that the cube and the cylinder occupied together. With an intersection operation, all solids involved must be selected when the operation is performed.

Now, with Constructor you aren't limited to only performing CSG operations. You can also shape and distort brushes in various ways by manipulating vertices and faces in ways similar to the more familiar "polysoup" programs like Milk-Shape and 3D Studio Max.

The key here, in using the CSG approach, is that there are limitations and restrictions on the topologies available to us to creating brushes. This is a *feature*, not a problem. These limitations allow the Torque Engine to employ extremely efficient collision detection and rendering operations. The limitations also mean that it is reasonably easy to create software to parse the model and generate the collision hulls (or convex shapes) automatically, eliminating the need for the modeling artist to manually create collision hulls.

Torque Constructor

The folks at GarageGames were kind enough to let me have access to a prerelease beta version of Constructor in order to present it to you, the gentle reader, in this second edition. There are likely going to be some minor differences between what I show you here and what the released demo or full versions offer. That can't be helped. Knowing those grease monkeys at the garage, the differences are sure to all be for the better.

Installing Constructor

To install Constructor, you will need to obtain it from the GarageGames Web site. The demo can be downloaded from here: http://demos.garagegames.com/ken_finney/Constructor_Demo.exe, or you can buy the full version when it becomes available, here: http://www.garagegames.com/makegames.

Note

Unfortunately, due to publishing lead times, neither a demo version nor the release version of Constructor was available when it came time to submit the CD content.

In order to make sure that you have all the tools you need to build your game, I've included QuArK, which appeared in the first edition of this book, on the CD in TOOLS\QUARK. You will also find a PDF file in there that contains the original first edition Chapter 17 combined with the first edition appendix that provided reference material for QuArK.

Constructor is a superior tool in every way, but QuArK is up to the job in its own right.

Note that there is no official Constructor installation procedure or installer at the time of this writing. If you have the full version or the demo version, please make sure you follow its installation instructions, and substitute the path where you install Constructor for the path I use here. After you finish you will have Constructor installed into a directory structure that should look something like that in Figure 17.5, notwithstanding variations between the beta and release versions.

The Cook's Tour

Let's have a very quick look at the Constructor interface—enough to be able to talk intelligently about it. Then we'll get into making something. After that we'll

Figure 17.5
Constructor directory structure.

take another look at some of the other features of the program. Launch Constructor using the shortcut you created.

Note

When you first run Constructor, you might be prompted for an ignition key. If you have purchased Constructor, then an ignition key for it will appear in your list of purchases in your account information on the GarageGames Web site. You will also probably get an automated e-mail informing you what your ignition key is. In all GG products to date, you can simply copy and paste your key into the ignition key field.

If you have a demo, then you most likely will be able to bypass the ignition key—except that your license will expire in a given period of time. Purchasing an ignition key would permanently enable your Constructor.

The Main Screen

When you fire up Constructor, you will be greeted by the pleasing view of the Constructor main screen, as shown in Figure 17.6. Now that just looks like muscle, right there.

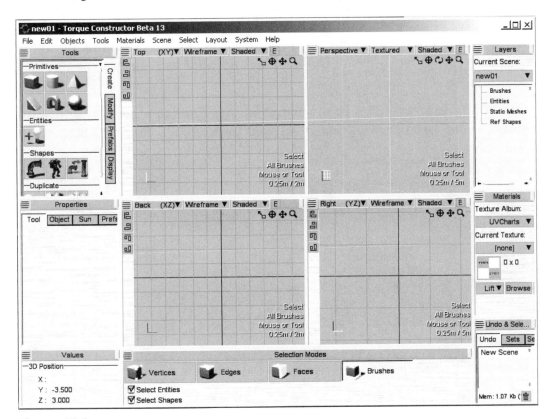

Figure 17.6
The Constructor main screen.

Your view of the main screen may vary slightly, depending on your computer's screen resolution. Figure 17.6 was snapped at 1024 pixels by 768 pixels. If you have higher resolution, you may see more things on your screen, especially in the toolbars on the sides, because Constructor automatically adjusts its contents to suit the available screen real estate.

Resizable Forms

Direct your eyes down into the upper-left corner of the screen, and you will see an area in a box with the label Tools. Oddly enough, this is where you find the tools! Okay, Dave will probably hit me upside the head with a fish for saying that, but in my own defense, I have seen some programs use some fairly strange words when what they really meant to say was "tools." Anyway, if your screen resolution is fairly low, you might find that the contents of the Tools form are not completely visible, which is the case in Figure 17.7, and as it was in Figure 17.6.

Note the two-way arrow cursor pointing left and right located over the right-side bezel that surrounds the form. Leave that alone for a minute. On the same side of the toolbar is a really teensy, tiny, skinny little twig of a scroll bar. Fortunately, there is a "scroll bar" label there in the figure, with an arrow pointing up to the actual scroll bar. There are two itsy-bitsy, teeny-weeny solid black arrows at each end of the scroll bar. See that? Cute, eh?

Move your cursor over the Tools form, and move your mouse wheel forward and backward. See the scroll bar move and the contents change? Okay, don't spend too long playing with the wheel. You can also click and drag the "thumb" (the darker part of the scroll bar—the part that slides) up and down instead of using the mouse wheel, or you can click those little arrows.

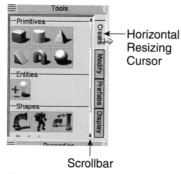

Figure 17.7
The Tools form with horizontal resizing cursor.

Forms, Palettes, Toolbars, and Tabs . . . It's Torque Terminology Time!

Different programs use different words to describe things like the little graphical containers that hold tools, menus, or other visual devices, like the container for Preferences. There is no real standardization in terminology. Some programs call them *toolbars*, or *bars*. Some call them *palettes*. Some, like Paint Shop Pro, use both *toolbar* and *palette* and have some features available in one and different features in the other. Some people use the word *tab*, although that has a more precise, and different, meaning usually. Dave Wyand calls them *forms*. And if that's what Dave wants to call them, then that's what I'm calling them!

Why so small? Real estate. The less screen space the tools take up, the more space there is for your actual model in the view windows, which we will come to later.

Now back to that two-way arrow on the left in Figure 17.7. Just move your cursor to the same location where the two-way arrow is in the figure, and you will see your cursor change to the two-way arrow. Click and drag leftward until you can see as much of the Preferences content as you need, in the horizontal aspect.

You can do the same thing by "grabbing" the bezel at the top of the toolbar to resize the form in the vertical sense, as shown in Figure 17.8.

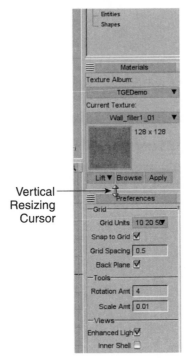

Vertical Resizing Cursor

Figure 17.8
The Preferences form with vertical resizing cursor.

And yes, in case you are wondering, you can perform all of these same operations on all the forms. That is why we went through this exercise, so that you can get your forms in your Constructor screen to conform to your personal requirements based on your computer configuration. In the next section we'll briefly go wandering amongst these forms, and while doing that you can go ahead and adjust the sizing of the various forms to suit your fancy.

The Forms

Take a look at Figure 17.9. Notice anything different compared to Figure 17.6? Okay, you Macophiles can stop jumping up and down now! In Figure 17.9 is Constructor shown using the *OSX Graphite* theme, as might appear on a Macintosh, rather than the Windows-centric *Neutral* theme that Figure 17.6 uses. I've inserted it here to make that point, but also to provide a handy reference for this next part of the tour.

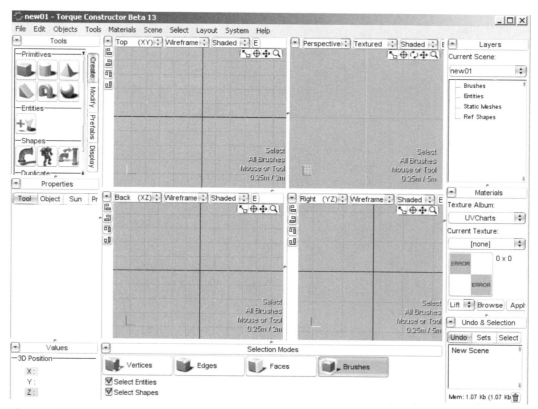

Figure 17.9
The Constructor screen with the OSX Graphite theme.

Starting at the top of the screen, you'll find the familiar *menu bar*. It contains a few of the standard menus, like File and Edit, and then a string of specialized menus, culminating with a familiar Help menu. As you click each menu, you will see the familiar drop-down menu. If you choose Layout, Themes, you will see where you can switch between the Macintosh (OSX Graphite) and Windows (Neutral) themes.

The menu bar is the only major visual feature of Constructor that does not have its label out there dangling in the electronic breeze. And I might also point out that it is most assuredly *not* a form but a menu bar, and I don't care what Dave says (*smiles and waves at Dave*)!

So, having gotten the menu bar out of the way, let's proceed on our tour in an orderly fashion. If you would, please step to the far right and upper corner of the screen where you will find the *Layers* form. In the Layers form you can switch between loaded *maps,* or between the brushes, entities, static meshes, and reference shapes (yes, *shapes!*).

Immediately below the Layers form is the *Materials* form. In this form you can select materials using a browser or a list, switch between texture albums, and perform some materials and texture operations.

In the lower-right corner is the by-now-infamous *Preferences* form. You can adjust global program settings like grid values and operations, scene lighting, and so on.

Moving to our left now, we find stretched across the bottom of the window the *Selection Modes* form. We use this mode to establish what scene objects are chosen when we perform a selection operation in one of the modeling view panes.

Moving farther to our left, arriving at the far-left and bottom of the Constructor screen, we encounter the *Values* form in all its glory. For the moment, the only values reported are the scene coordinates coinciding with the 2D position of the cursor in any one of the view panes. In the 2D views (top, back, right, and so on) only the relevant 2D coordinates are reported. If your cursor is in the Perspective view pane, then the full 3D coordinates are reported in the Values form.

Moving up the left side, we find the *Properties* form. This is where we set the parameters for the various modeling tools we can use. The contents change according to which tool is currently active.

Finally, above the Properties form, and ending our little tour, is the *Tools* form. Here we can select various kinds of tools, for creating, modifying, or displaying objects or for using prefab objects, depending on which tab we select. The tabs run down the right side of the Tools form. Within each tab, to varying degrees, is a variety of tools and operations that can be selected, depending on the context.

In the center of the screen, where they refuse to be overlooked, are the four default *View* forms. Within each of the View forms is a view pane, providing a look into the scene from various angles. At the lower-left corner of each view pane is an *axis bug* that shows you the orientation of the scene in the view. The blue axis is the Z-axis: positive going up. The red axis is the X-axis: positive going right. And the green axis is the Y-axis: positive going back, or away from the "front," and deeper into the scene. The lower-right side of each view pane contains a number, in units of meters, that indicates the distance that the view's camera is from the center of the scene. Along the top of the view pane is a series of buttons that you can use to tweak the way the view works, what view angles are used, and other options.

Now I know that was not a very detailed examination, but the goal was to drag you around the Constructor screen and set the scene, so to speak.

Quick Start

What we'll do is run Constructor and quickly create a structure that we can stick in our sample Torque game and poke around with. It won't be anything particularly useful, but the point is to establish mastery of the *tool chain*. The tool chain is in essence the collection of programs and procedures you need to follow from source creation of a piece of artwork to using a compiled version inside the game engine.

Note

More taxing terminology! In CSG development circles what you create are often called *rooms*. This hearkens back to early editors for Quake, where everything was a room. There were no outdoor areas as such—no external terrain. When we create the rooms and save them, we save them as *map* files, because Valve used the word *map* to describe their version of what id Software (the guys who made Quake) called a *room*. Clear as mud?

And of course, just to be persnickety, GarageGames calls these creations *interiors* (which fetches back to the term *rooms*, in a way) in Torque, and that derives from Torque's journeyman days as the Tribes engine. I use the word *structure*, which I think is both pithy and generic at the same time. My use of structure can encompass room, map, and interior as they are used in their respective contexts while still also applying to things like bridges and guard towers.

Oh yeah, one more thing. In Constructor the entire collection of all the objects you've created in one file is called a *scene*. A scene is a collection of 3D objects, and the word is used in the context of game engines and most 3D shape tools. Constructor uses this terminology because it has the ability to combine CSG objects created in Constructor or other CSG tools, like Hammer, with "polysoup" or mesh objects or shapes created with tools like MilkShape or 3D Studio Max all at the same time! So another word was needed to encompass all of these things. Hence, scene. When we save our scene, we save it as a map file (I tossed this in just in case you might be thinking that you finally understand everything).

So scene = room = map = interior = structure. Sort of, sometimes. In any event, the source format for the files we will be dealing with are MAP, a text file format, while the compiled version is called DIF, a binary format.

We can also save our work as Constructor scenes in CSX format. This is what would be called the *native* format for Constructor creations. See the sidebar, "CSX vs. MAP."

We save our work as .map and compile the work to .dif for use in Torque using a program called *map2dif_plus*. More about this later.

CSX vs. MAP

Using CSX format files, we can save information about scenes that MAP format files don't support and wouldn't understand, like the placement of reference shapes as static meshes and various other features, as shown here:

Constructor Feature	CSX	MAP
Detail Levels	Yes	No
Game Types	Yes	No
Brushes	Yes	Yes
Entities	Yes	Yes
Static Meshes	Yes	No
Scene Shapes	Yes	No
Groups	Yes	No
Selection Sets	Yes	No
Named Workplanes	Yes	No

So why use MAP format? Well, there are dozens of tools out there that support MAP format in addition to Constructor—Valve Hammer, 3D World Studio, Quake 3's tools and QuArK to name but a few. It's ubiquitous.

1. If Constructor is not running, launch it now.

2. Locate the Tools form in the upper-left corner and, within it, the Cube brush in the Primitives section, as shown in Figure 17.10.

3. Click the Cube brush to select it. The brush icon and the cursor will change, as shown in Figure 17.11.

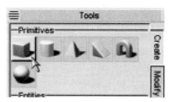

Figure 17.10
About to select the Cube brush.

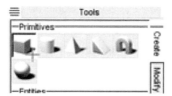

Figure 17.11
The selected Cube brush.

4. Move the cursor over to the Top view pane, positioning it four grid squares left and four grid squares up from the center (where the heavy dark grid lines meet).

5. Click the mouse button, drag down and to the right until you are positioned four grid squares below and four squares to the right of the center (as shown in Figure 17.12), and then release the mouse button.

   Note the small red object handles on the left and right sides, and the small green handles on the top and bottom sides (which, when in the Top view, are actually the front and back sides of the object, as oriented in the scene). You can grab these handles and resize the object in this view, or any of the other 2D views, without having *committed* the brush to the scene. In other words, we only have a "phantom" brush object at the moment.

6. Press the Enter key (the main one, not the keypad Enter key) to commit the brush to the scene. Note the change in appearance of the cube.

   The handles have now disappeared, and colored arrows sprout from the center of the object. Collectively these three arrows are called the *Axis Gizmo*. Each arrow points along an axis in the positive direction. The red arrow is for the X-axis, green for the Y-axis, and blue for the Z-axis. You can

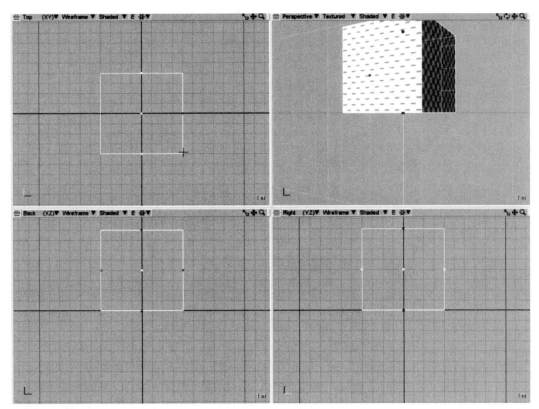

Figure 17.12
After click-dragging from upper left to lower right.

also see the little axis labels at the end of each arrow. The gizmo not only shows the axes and their orientation but also serves as the "grab handle" for different transformation operations, as we'll see shortly. Figure 17.13 shows the new appearance of the cube object.

While we're at it, we ought to do something about the awful texture we're stuck with, created for us by default.

7. Cast your eyes over to the right-hand side, into the Materials form. That *perfectly horrid* texture is there, glaring at us in yellow and blue. Just below the texture, locate the Browse button, as shown in Figure 17.14. Click it, and watch the Texture Browser dialog box appear.

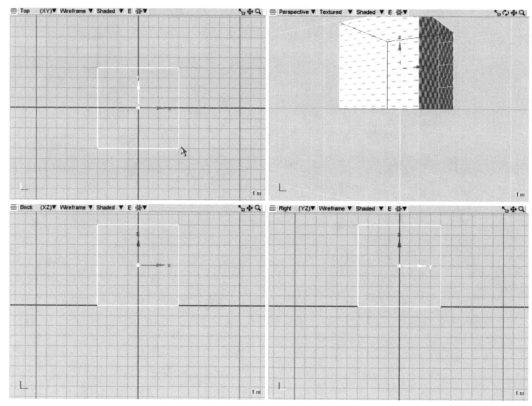

Figure 17.13
Cube after being committed to the scene.

Note

"That *perfectly horrid* texture is there. What's up with that? Is this the Texture Taste Police?"

I actually heard you say that out loud, you know (*waggles index finger*).

Yeah, that one. All yellow and blue with "Error" written all over it and stuff. Well, note that it's the *default* texture. Unless you choose a different texture (the procedure for which is covered just a little bit later in this section), then every time you create an object in the scene, it will have this texture assigned to all faces. There is a good reason for this.

The usual way most modelers create structures using CSG tools is to first create the structure and then apply the textures when the structure is finished and the artist is happy with the result. In other programs often the *null* texture is assigned as the default texture. The only problem is that the null texture *doesn't show in the game engine.* The face will be completely transparent, since there is not actually a texture present (it was null, see?). If you forget to assign a proper texture to a face, you might have a lot of difficulty detecting this visually. At various angles you might see a background texture behind the face with the null texture and not realize that the texture is missing. And yet from another angle that hole where the texture is missing might provide a view into or out of an area that would interfere with game play in a serious way.

By using such a garish default texture, if you were to miss out on texturing a face and then went into the game to visually verify your model, you would have a *much* better chance of detecting your error.

8. On the left side of the Texture Browser, select the entry (or *album*), TGEDemo, by clicking it. Figure 17.15 shows what this looks like.

9. Click the first texture in the upper-left corner of the texture array (concrete) in the Texture Browser. The contents of the browser change, focusing on the texture you chose, as shown in Figure 17.16.

10. At the lower-right corner of the Texture Browser resides the Make Active button. Click it, and then click the Close button directly below it. The Texture Browser will close.

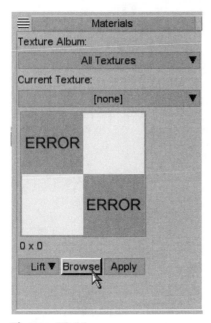

Figure 17.14
The Browse button.

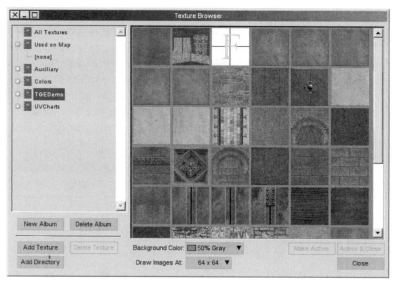

Figure 17.15
Texture Browser with TGEDemo selected.

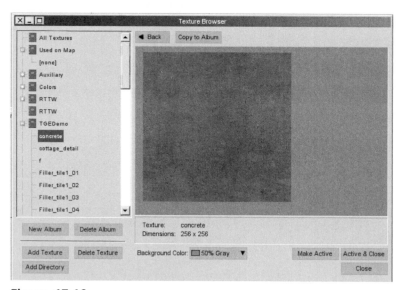

Figure 17.16
Texture Browser with the concrete texture.

11. Back over in the Materials form on the right, locate and click the Apply button, just below the little picture of the texture you just selected. Take a look in the Perspective view pane at the upper right. You will see the cube with the new texture applied to it, on all faces.

Tip

If you find yourself stuck in some mode that you don't want to be in, press the Escape key. This will allow you to go and select things again, or change your modes, or whatever. There's a reason why it's called "Escape"!

This won't work as well if you are in a dialog box, however. But then, it's hard to get stuck into an unknown mode while in a dialog box.

12. Now we have to export our scene. Go to the File menu, and choose Save As. The Save As dialog box will open.

13. Save your work as test.map in the Constructor folder.

14. Choose File, Export, Torque (map2dif_plus). You will get a dialog title Browse for Folder.

15. Do what the dialog title tells you, and browse your way to \3D2E\demo\data\ and then click on the Interiors folder to highlight it. Click on the OK button. You will get the Execute Script dialog box, telling you the progress as the MAP file is processed into a DIF file.

    You will know you have successfully exported the structure when the last line of output reads:

    `Writing Resource: persist..(C:/3D2E/demo/data/interiors/test.dif) Done.`

16. Click on the Close button to make the dialog box go wherever it is these things go when you have no further need for them. Maybe the neighborhood bar? I dunno . . .

17. Anyway, now go launch your Torque demo, as you've done in the past. After you've spawned in, switch to camera fly mode (F8), go up a little bit in altitude, and aim your cursor to a point in the game world where you want the test structure to be. A good place to go would be over next to the original great hall—that big cathedral-like building—and park yourself on the side where the water is. Then aim the center of your screen to the open area to the side of the Great Hall.

18. Open the Mission Editor by pressing F11. If you get a dialog box welcoming you to the Mission Editor, nod your head in thanks, read the helpful information it presents, then make it go away by clicking the OK button. It could probably use a drink anyway.

19. Open the World Editor Creator by pressing F4.

20. From the tree list on the lower right, open the Interiors group by clicking the little plus sign to its left. Then drill down through demo, data, and interiors, and you will see test.

21. Click once on the test entry in the Interiors group list. Your creation will be plunked down at the spot where the center of your screen intersects the terrain. A little dialog box will pop up at the bottom of your screen, telling you that the scene needs to be relit. Before doing anything else, take a gander into your scene. Notice that the cube has been placed, but it is black, not textured.

22. Click the Relight Scene button on the little dialog box. After a not too particularly long pause, you will see your cube changed to its proper textured form. Then click the Hide button on the little dialog box.

Tip

You can also relight the scene at any time while in the Mission Editor by pressing Alt + L or by choosing the Edit, Relight Scene menu. In fact, you can easily make your textures appear on your structures just by grabbing them and dragging them a bit. But the scene will still need relighting, because the shadows will need to be re-baked.

You should have ended up with something like what you see in Figure 17.17. Of course, where the cube actually is depends upon where you decided to plunk it.

Figure 17.17
Cube test object in the demo game.

That took a while, but what we've done, in addition to learning the basic steps involved in getting a structure exported in Torque, is to prove the tool chain. We now know that we have all the required bits and pieces to get this kind of artwork into the engine. The CSG tool (Constructor), the exporter (map2dif_plus), and, of course, the in-game Torque Mission Editor. In fact, future versions of Constructor will likely have map2dif_plus built right in so that we can export directly to the DIF format. This might seem trivial, but proving the tool chain is an important first step in any project involving multiple programs and processing steps.

Managing Your Textures

When you make a model with Constructor, no doubt you will be using textures on the faces. You need to ensure that you copy the textures from whatever folder they are contained in to the folder in the Torque path where they will be needed.

The textures we will be using in this chapter are in the \Constructor\textures\tgedemo folder. By happy coincidence the textures in that folder are the same ones that you'll find in \3D2E\demo\data\interiors. So we don't need to do anything special.

But even if the textures weren't already in the Interiors folder where we deposited the DIF file, Constructor automatically copies them for you. So you only need to keep the source of your textures up-to-date. The destination is synchronized seamlessly.

Building Bridges

So, you've had a taste of how you can use Constructor. Now let's dive in and muck about with it a bit and actually create something. Because this is our first real structure, we'll start out with something not too complex—a stone bridge.

1. Launch Constructor.

2. Select the Cube brush.

3. In the top view, create an Oblong brush that is 4 units (grid squares) wide in the Y-axis, and 20 units long in the X-axis.

4. In the front view use the little blue handle to move the bottom or the top edge (doesn't matter which) until the shape is only 1 unit high in the Z-axis. Then, if needed, continue to use the red, green, or blue handles to resize the brush where needed, and the little light-blue handle in the center of the brush to move it until you have something resembling Figure 17.18. This is the roadbed of the bridge.

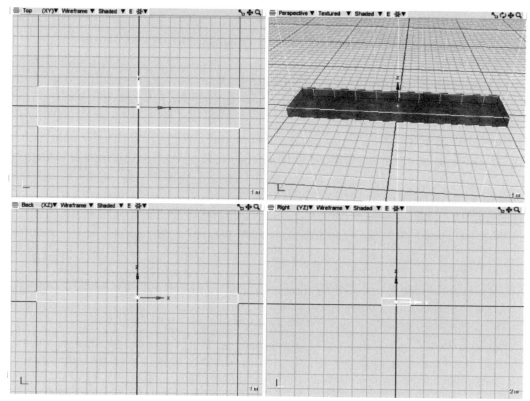

Figure 17.18
Oblong brush.

5. Press the Enter key to commit the brush when you are satisfied with your handiwork.

Tip

If you want to check the dimensions of your brushes, just position your cursor over the boundary lines at appropriate places, and look in the Values form at the lower left. Your cursor's coordinates in the window where the cursor is located will be shown. Remember that if the center of your brush is at the same location as the center of the scene, then boundary values for your brush will show as exactly half of the dimension being checked.

For example, if we want the Oblong brush to be 20 units long, then when you place your cursor over one end of the brush in the Top view pane, the X value will be 10.000.

6. Create two more Cube brushes, and place them as shown in Figure 17.19. These will be the bridge pylons.

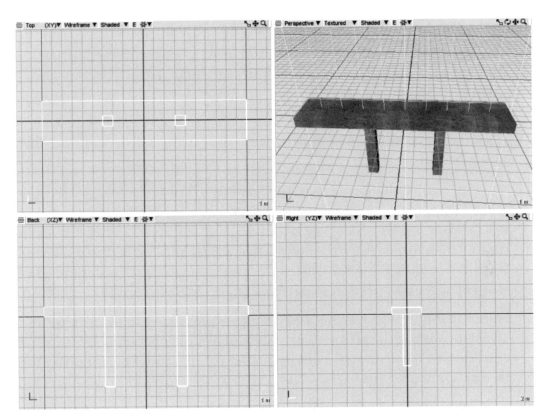

Figure 17.19
Bridge with pylons.

Tip

You can create a copy of a brush simply by selecting a brush, holding down the Shift key, clicking on one of the axis arrows for the brush, and then dragging in the direction of the axis arrow. A copy of the selected brush will be dragged away from the original.

Next, we are going to add some texture to the bridge.

Tip

If you have the texture you want selected when you create a brush, then the brush will automatically receive that texture on all of its faces when you commit the brush to the scene.

7. Ensure that the Brushes button is depressed in the Selection form at the bottom of your window, and then move your cursor to the Perspective view pane.

8. Click your cursor inside the Roadbed brush to select that brush.

9. In the Materials form at the right, click Browse to invoke the Texture Browser.

10. Click the texture album called TGEDemo to select it.

11. Locate and select the Floor_set_stone texture.

12. Click the Active & Close button, to make the texture active, and close the dialog box all at once.

13. You will see that the texture has been applied to the brush already, because we had the brush selected when we clicked the Active & Close button in the dialog box. If the brush was not selected, we would have to select it. Back in the Materials form, click the Apply button. Check the Perspective view pane for evidence of success. You will see the cube with the new texture applied to it, on all faces, as shown in Figure 17.20.

Notice that the texture seems really big and a bit blurry. Now we have to adjust the scale of the texture. This is a bit of a fiddly operation. By eyeball, I estimate that the texture is about four times too big. So we need to make the texture about 25% (or 0.25) its current size.

14. In the Selection Mode form at the bottom, click the Faces button.

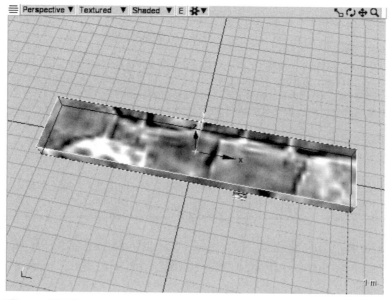

Figure 17.20
Roadbed with Floor_set_stone texture.

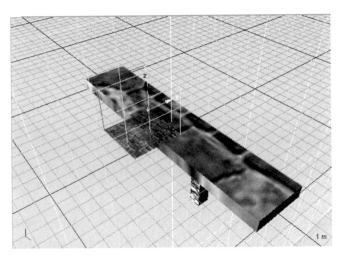

Figure 17.21
Selected brush face.

15. In the Perspective window, click one of the faces of the Roadbed brush. It will be highlighted as shown in Figure 17.21. It's pretty hard to see the color effect in that grayscale image—the highlighted face will have an aquamarine or green hue to it. Also note that a small cubelike device appears that shows the orientation of the applied texture. In Figure 17.21 the selected face is the top face.

16. Choose the Tools, Modify, Scale menu. On the left side, the Properties form will have a section in it called Transform Scale.

17. In the Transform Scale part of the Properties form, locate the Scale fields. In each field (X, Y, and Z) type in **0.25**. Be sure to include the zero in front of the decimal.

18. Click the Make button, located in the Properties form, near the top. You should now have a brush face that looks like Figure 17.22.

Tip

One way to adjust the scale of a texture is by using arbitrary values in the Properties form, as shown in the text. However, there is a quicker, but less precise, method.

When you have a face selected and have chosen the Tools, Modify, Scale menu, you can then move your cursor over one of the axis gizmos in an appropriate 2D view. Click and drag along the axis you want to scale, and watch the texture scale change accordingly. You can change the rate at which the "drag-scale" method operates when you drag the mouse. Look in the Tools section of the Preferences form at the lower right. Change the Scale Amt field to a lower number to slow the scaling rate and to a higher number to speed it up.

> You can rotate and move (offset) a texture using the same technique. Choose Tools, Modify, Translate or Tools, Modify, Rotate, and then click-drag on an axis. You can only adjust the rotation rate in the Preferences form using Rotate Amt.

19. Now go ahead and apply textures and adjust them as you want, for all the other faces.

20. Save your scene as bridge.map in the \Constructor folder, and then choose File, Export, Torque (map2dif_plus) to export your bridge to Torque, just like you did in the last section.r.

21. Now go launch your Torque demo, as you've done before. After spawning, switch to camera fly mode (F8), go up a little bit in altitude, and aim your cursor to a point in the game world where you want the bridge structure to be.

22. Open the Mission Editor by pressing F11. If you get a dialog box welcoming you to the Mission Editor, click the OK button.

23. Open the World Editor Creator by pressing F4.

24. From the tree list on the lower right, open the Interiors group by clicking the little plus sign to its left. Then drill down through demo, data, and interiors, and you will see `bridge` listed in blue.

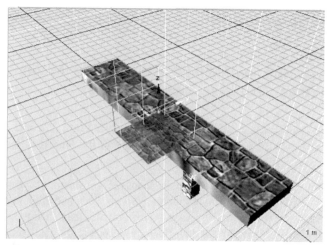

Figure 17.22
Scaled face texture.

25. Click once on the `bridge` entry in the Interiors group list to insert the bridge, click the Relight Scene button on the little dialog box, and then click the Hide button on the little dialog box.

Building a House

The bridge was nice and certainly useful albeit fairly simple. If you actually need a bridge you will probably make something more ornate. The point here is to learn the tools. Artistry is up to you.

In this section we will go a little bit further and make something a bit more complex: a hut with a door opening and a window created using CSG Boolean operations.

1. Launch Constructor.

2. Select the Cube brush, and create a cube that measures eight units in length (along the X-axis) by six units in width (along the Y-axis) by seven units in height (along the Z-axis).

   Remember that you can check the dimensions by hovering the cursor over various points on the cube and looking in the lower-left corner of the Map Editor window.

3. Position the Cube brush so that it is horizontally centered in the top and back views and vertically offset upward in the back and right views so that two units are below the centerline and five units are above it. See Figure 17.23 for guidance.

   The brush is offset vertically so that the centerline can be used to represent ground level. Because this is going to be a building that might be placed in somewhat rough terrain, we need to make sure to have a "foundation" or "basement" that extends fairly far below the ground level. Although I am not doing so here, you might consider using a separate brush for the basement, so that you could use a texture different from the aboveground textures. A nice concrete texture would be suitable.

4. Don't forget to press Enter to commit the brush to the scene.

Tip

Don't forget that there are several selection modes: Brushes, Faces, Edges, and Vertices. The buttons are at the bottom of the screen. Make sure you are in the selection mode you need for the operation you want to perform.

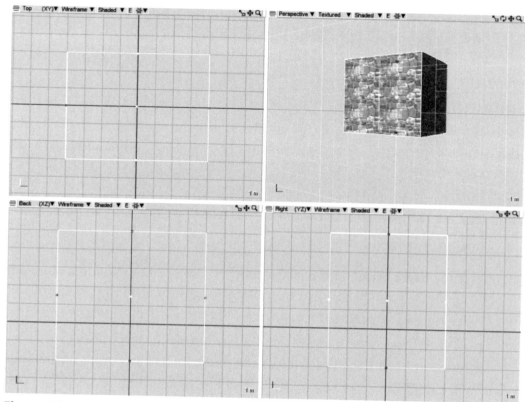

Figure 17.23
Properly sized and positioned initial brush.

5. Next, go back and select the Cube brush tool again, and make another brush inside the first one, except make this new oblong seven units in length by five units in width by four units in height.

6. Position the new brush so that it is centered horizontally inside the first brush and positioned vertically aboveground so that it is centered between the top of the first brush and the ground level. Figure 17.24 shows what this should look like.

7. Commit the brush to the scene. The new brush will remain selected, and that's what we want for the next step.

Tip

Just a quick reminder: if you find yourself stuck in some mode that you don't want to be in, press the Escape key.

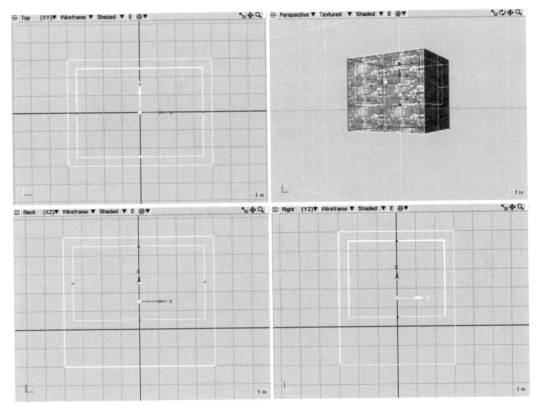

Figure 17.24
New brush inside the first brush.

8. In the Tools form on the left there are tabs whose labels are displayed sideways down the right-hand side of the Tools form. Click the Modify tab.

9. In the CSG group of iconified buttons that now appear in the Tools form, the one on the far left is the button for the Boolean Subtract operation. Click that button. This will subtract the volume of the second brush from the first brush. You will notice a subtle change in the 2D and Perspective views after you've clicked the Boolean Subtract button. There will be some extra lines. The second brush is still selected.

Tip

When you've performed a Boolean CSG operation on a brush, the brush will be transected into multiple different brushes which together make the resultant brush. You can select each of these sub-brushes and treat them like normal brushes, because in actuality, they are just normal brushes.

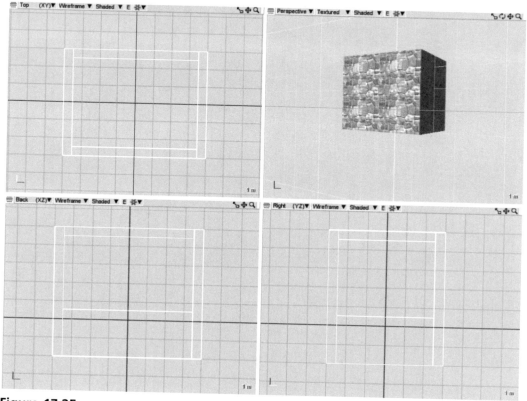

Figure 17.25
Hollow brush.

10. Press Delete. The second brush will be removed. It might not be obvious, but your first brush is now hollow, and it should look like what's shown in Figure 17.25.

11. Back in the Tools form, click the Create tab on the right-hand side of the form (with the label written sideways).

12. Select the Cube brush yet again. (Are you getting the feeling that you will become intimately familiar with the Cube brush in fairly short order?)

Tip

Don't get too focused on working in only one view. Sometimes everything needs to be done in a single view, but you should glance in the other views to monitor your progress and to ensure that you aren't doing something really dumb that isn't visible in the view you are working with.

13. Make a brush for the door that is two units long, three units deep, and three units high. Position it so that the bottom is level with the "floor" and

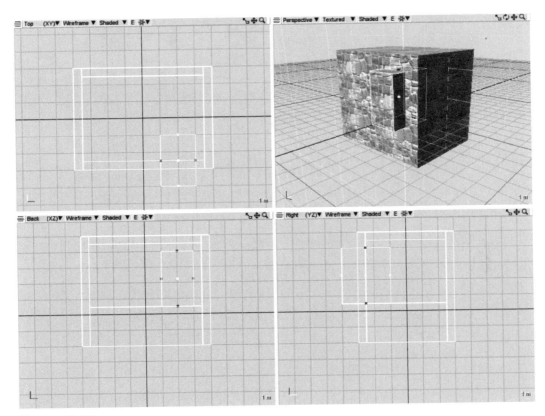

Figure 17.26
Protruding Door brush.

so that it protrudes from inside the hollow brush to the outside, as shown in Figure 17.26. Commit the brush.

14. Now click the Modify tab again, in the Forms menu, and then click the Boolean Subtract button (far left) once more. This will carve out the door.

15. This time, *don't* delete the Subtraction brush. Instead, grab that sucker by its X-axis gizmo in the Back view, drag it left, and then drag it up using the Z-axis gizmo. We can reuse this brush (it's the Earth Day thing to do!) to make a nice little window. Drag it around in the Back view until it's positioned to the left of the door and suitably up from the floor.

16. In the Tools form, in the Transform section, click the far-right button— that's the Scale button. Doing this in the Tools form is exactly the same as choosing the Tools, Modify, Scale menu.

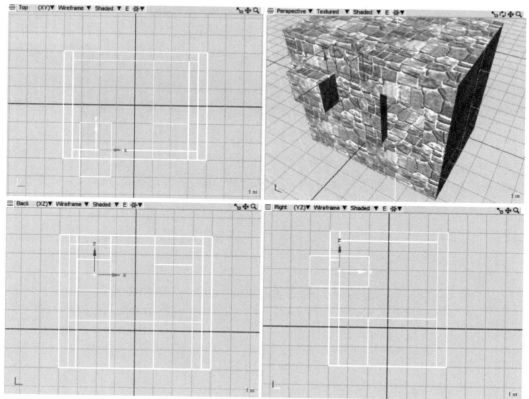

Figure 17.27
Making a window.

17. Move your cursor directly over the center of the Subtraction brush in the Back view, then click and drag your cursor to resize the window to your liking, using Figure 17.27 as a guide.

To quickly go back to the mode where you can move objects around by clicking them and dragging (translating), just press the Escape key.

18. Once you are happy with the position of the Subtraction brush, click the Boolean Subtract button again. This will carve out the window.

19. Press Delete to remove the Subtraction brush. Now you will have a handy one-room house, as shown in Figure 17.28.

Note that I've used the Floor_set_stone texture for all of these brushes. You, of course, have been empowered and are free to use whatever textures you want!

20. Save your file as \Constructor\house.map.

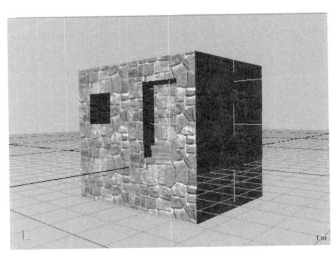

Figure 17.28
House with door and window.

Okay, compile your house, using the technique I showed you earlier. As an extra challenge, compile your house for use in the Emaga6 program. Go ahead, I dare you! Remember, you will have to change some of the path information in the build_dif.bat batch file, and you will need to ensure that you have copied the textures you used to wherever you put your house.dif file in the Emaga6 folder hierarchy. Good luck!

Moving Right Along

So, in this chapter you've learned yet another tool. Constructor is a pretty feature-complete tool for creating structures for Torque. You've built the two most common sorts of structures: an outdoor structure (the bridge) and a building using CSG operations.

Your imagination is the only real limit here. Castles, complex underground tunnel systems, factories, playgrounds, and just about anything else can be created with Constructor.

Normally, I would include a reference section for Constructor in this chapter. However, the program has so many features and options that the material is just too hefty to present in the chapter. Instead, I've included the Constructor reference in Appendix D.

In the next chapter we'll take a look at how to make things for the game world environment.

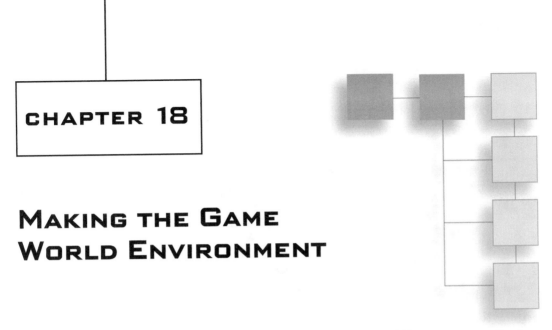

CHAPTER 18

MAKING THE GAME WORLD ENVIRONMENT

In many games having a full suite of character models, buildings, trees, and other visual clutter is still not enough to accomplish the needed sense of immersion. There are a number of other aspects to the game world that come from the world around us that we often take for granted: the background sky, the appearance of water, the appearance of clouds in motion, and the terrain. Figure 18.1 is a nice serene picture of ocean-side forested hills just after sunset. No, it's not a photograph—it's a screen shot from the game *Return to Tubettiworld* being developed using the Torque Game Engine.

Now way back in Chapter 12 we covered terrains to a certain extent, so you probably have a reasonable sense of what is involved with creating terrains using a height map. In this chapter we will revisit terrains using the more labor-intensive method of manually building up a terrain with the in-game editor. We'll get into that at the end of this chapter.

First, however, we will visit sky, clouds, and water—the environmental triad of computer game ambience.

Sky

When you are tasked to create a 3D game that offers unrestricted movement in unlimited vistas, you will need to come up with ways to provide that open, outdoors perception. A technique that works well is to provide a static

Figure 18.1
A serene scene.

background sky that contains elements of the sky that we often take for granted, like clouds, and a color gradient that changes as you move farther away from the horizon. We do this using a construct known as a *skybox*.

Skyboxes

A skybox is a cube that surrounds the game player. The player stands *inside* the box, and no matter which way he turns, he will see some part of the box as long as it isn't obscured by other in-game objects. The box never rotates, and the sides are always the same distance away from the player no matter how far or how fast he moves.

How Skyboxes Work

Because of the way the images on the faces of the skybox are created, the player does not have the feeling that he is inside a big cube. The skybox images are on the *inside* faces of this cube, as you can see in Figure 18.2. The back view has been left out to help illustrate the point.

When using skyboxes, we treat them as if they are infinitely large. Only objects that the player can never reach will look correct, like clouds in the sky or distant mountains. If you limit a player's movement to just viewing from a fixed location, you could even use a skybox for nearby scenery.

Figure 18.2
A pictorial skybox.

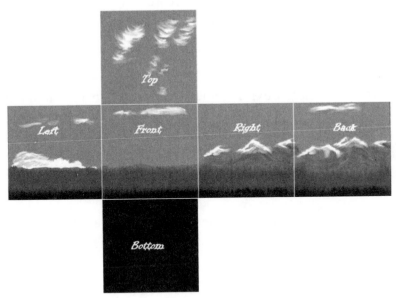

Figure 18.3
An exploded skybox.

Figure 18.3 shows an exploded view of the skybox images and how they relate to each other. Note that the image for the bottom is a black field. If you were depicting an area with a usable view in that direction, you would of course include an appropriate image.

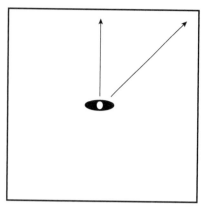

Figure 18.4
Skybox edge distances.

To create the illusion that the player is embedded in a large and seamless world, there are two things that you must get right when creating a skybox: seamless, matching adjacent edges and correct perspective.

The edge-matching issue is one we are already familiar with from previous texture endeavors.

The perspective issue is a little less obvious when you first consider making skyboxes—but take a look at Figure 18.4. Remember that the skybox is always the same distance away from the player, and the orientation is fixed. The front face, if it happens to be facing north, will always face north, no matter which way the player is facing or looking. This causes a visual problem when viewing the images on the skybox faces.

The image areas that are on the face closest to the player will appear larger than the portions of the image nearest the corners, because the corners are farther away. Figure 18.5 simulates what that would look like.

In order to remove the distortion when the image is viewed in game, we need to distort its appearance *outside* the game environment in such a way that when the perspective comes into play in game, the image looks natural. Figure 18.6 shows such a predistorted image.

Each of the six square skybox images should be created with the same resolution. The most common resolution to use is 256 by 256 pixels. The higher the resolution, the better the skybox will look in most cases, but there is a limit

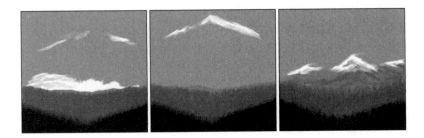

Figure 18.5
Distorted image.

Figure 18.6
Predistorted image.

beyond which higher skybox image resolution doesn't help the appearance. Because we are always worried about memory used and processing time consumed, we want to make sure we don't go higher than the maximum. If you are interested in using larger skybox images, there is a way to calculate the maximum resolution to use as your upper limit, using this mathematical formula:

```
maxSkyboxResX = maxScreenResX * 1/tan(FOV/2)
maxSkyboxResY = maxScreenResY * 1/tan(FOV/2)
```

The basic concept is that the smaller the *Field of View* (FOV), the higher the resolution you will need for the skybox. This is because as the FOV gets smaller, you are looking farther and at a smaller portion of the skybox image. This smaller portion fills the view, and therefore the pixels are larger. Typical first-person point-of-view games use a 90-degree FOV and often have a 60-degree (or even smaller) zoomed-in view for sniper scopes or binoculars.

For example, if our screen resolution is 800 by 600 pixels and our FOV is 90 degrees, then applying our formula yields this:

```
maxSkyboxResX = 800 * 1/tan(90/2)
maxSkyboxResX = 800 * 1/1
maxSkyboxResX = 800
```

It also follows that we don't need to recompute the Y resolution because it will scale proportionally. So for this 800 by 600 pixel display with a 90-degree FOV, the highest resolution we should use for the skybox images is 800 by 600 pixels, by happy coincidence!

However, if we want to know the deal for the 60-degree FOV that our player's binoculars provide, we need to recompute that value as follows:

```
maxSkyboxResX = 800 * 1/tan(60/2)
maxSkyboxResX = 800 * 1/ 0.57735
maxSkyboxResX = 800 * 1.732
maxSkyboxResX = 1386
```

For the Y resolution, the value is 1,039. So if you decide to create a high-resolution skybox, you should probably go with nothing larger than 1,280 by 1,024 pixels. (Most games, including Torque, need the image resolution values to be powers of two.)

Personally, I would go with 1,024 by 1,024 as a reasonable compromise for a maximum resolution. These dimensions would apply to all of your skybox panels in a given skybox. The size you eventually choose for your game will in the end be a judgment call, but if you use the previous calculations, it will not be just a hopeful stab in the dark.

Creating the Skybox Images

As with other texture-related issues, there is always the question of where to obtain source material. Once again, you have the option of creating your own by

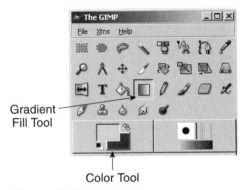

Gradient
Fill Tool

Color Tool

Figure 18.7
The Gimp pane with Gradient Fill tool and Color tool.

using a digital camera or a camera and scanner combination or by simply drawing your own images.

In this section I will walk you through drawing some clouds on the horizon for your skybox—this is a common sunny-day sort of scene. Low cumulus clouds in the distance peek just above the horizon, all around you.

1. Open the Gimp, and create a new image by selecting File, New. Fill in the dialog box with 256 for both the height and width of the blank image. Make sure that the Advanced Options, Colorspace is set to RGB Color and the resolutions are 72 dpi for both X and Y. The Fill with box should be set to Transparency. A new canvas in its own window will appear.

2. Save this blank file as \Emaga6\control\data\maps\skyfront.png.

3. Over in the Gimp's tool pane, select the Gradient Fill tool (see Figure 18.7). Below the Gimp pane, another pane appears, called Blend.

4. In the Blend pane, locate the Gradient button, and click it. A pop-up list portraying various gradient fill strategies will appear, as shown in Figure 18.8.

5. Select the third gradient, called FG to BG (RGB). This means that the fill gradient will be created using the foreground (FG) color as the start value and the background (BG) color as the end value. The gradient will be created between those two colors.

6. Fetch back to Figure 18.7, and locate the Color tool. Click the leftmost color box (the top one) to open the Change Foreground Color dialog box.

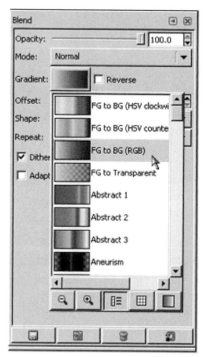

Figure 18.8
The Gradient Fill pop-up.

7. In the Change Foreground Color dialog box, enter the RGB values as 215 for R, 215 for G, and finally 255 for B.

8. Click the OK button to commit the change and dismiss the dialog box, and then use the rightmost color box (the bottom box) of the Color tool to set the background color to 0 for R, 0 for G, and 192 for B, the same way you did for the foreground.

9. Click OK to commit the change and dismiss the dialog box.

10. Now, with the Gradient tool still selected, click in the image window a little bit below the vertical halfway point (between two-fifths of the way up from the bottom and halfway up). *Don't* release the mouse button.

11. Drag the cursor up until it is about one-quarter of the way down from the top of the image window, and then release the mouse button. See Figure 18.9 for a guide to the click and release points.

After you release the mouse button, the gradient will be rendered, and you should get an image very similar to Figure 18.10.

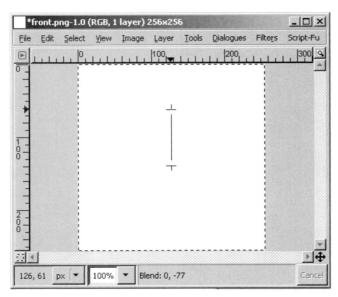

Figure 18.9
Preparing to make the gradient.

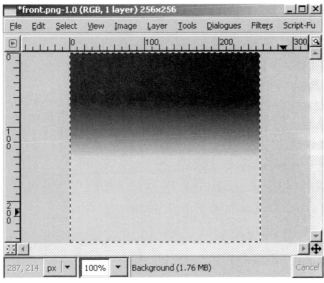

Figure 18.10
Image with gradient.

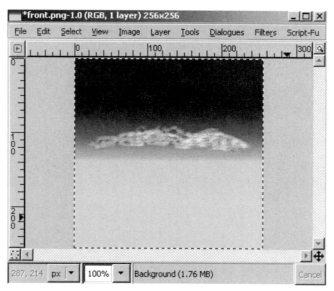

Figure 18.11
Some clouds.

12. Go back to the Color tool, and set the foreground color to pure white (RGB=255,255,255).

13. Next, select the Air Brush tool (the fourth tool over to the right of the Gradient tool), select size 13 from the Brush drop-down list in the Airbrush pane (click the button with the black circle in the middle), and set the Rate and Pressure to 11 and the Opacity to 60.

14. Now draw some cloudlike shapes between about half and two-thirds of the way from the bottom of the image so that you get something like Figure 18.11. Save your work as skyfront.png.

15. Create three more versions of this image, naming the others "skyleft.png", "skyright.png", and "skyback.png" in the same place you saved sky-front.png. Go ahead and make each one different in its own way, if you like.

16. Make a fifth image that is solid blue, with RGB values of 0,0,192. This color matches the darkest blue in the gradient we made. Name this file "skytop.png".

17. Make the sixth and final image and fill it in with black. Name this one "skybottom.png".

    Now it's time to test out your images.

18. Locate the file in your Emaga6 map folder called \Emaga6\control\data\ maps\sky_day.dml. Make a copy of this file in the same directory, and name the copy "sky_book.dml".

19. Open the sky_book.dml file with UltraEdit. Change the first six lines to read as follows:

```
skyfront
skyright
skyback
skyleft
skytop
skybottom
```

20. Save the file.

21. Open \Emaga6\control\data\maps\book_ch6.mis, and locate the line that looks like this:

```
materialList = "./sky_day.dml";
```

and replace it with this:

```
materialList = "./sky_book.dml";
```

Save the file.
Almost there!

22. You need to check to ensure that the right mission file will be used when you run your test. Open the script file Emaga6\control\client\client.cs in UltraEdit and find the line that starts with:

```
createServer("SinglePlayer",
```

The entire line should read as:

```
createServer("SinglePlayer", "control/data/maps/book_ch6.mis");
```

If it says book_ch5 instead of book_ch6, change the 5 to 6, and then save the script file.

23. Launch the Emaga6 sample program, and enter into the game. Take a look around. Notice the corners? See how your clouds become distorted?

You already know how to fix up the textures so that they join seamlessly, so I'll leave you to do that. Note that you *probably* don't have to worry about the top edges, because the top image and the top edges of the side images all have the same RGB value—0,0,192.

Also, the bottom doesn't need to be blended either, because it's not going to be visible beneath our terrain. So that just leaves the perspective distortion to fix.

Adjusting for Perspective

Although we are going to be adjusting for perspective distortion, we aren't going to use the built-in perspective tools in the Gimp. Instead, we will use the Warp tool.

1. In the Gimp, open up one of your side images, like the front one, for example.

2. Choose Dialogs, Layers to open up the Layers dialog box. Move the dialog box to a place on your screen where it doesn't obscure the image or the Gimp's main pane.

3. Choose Filters, Distorts, Curve Bend.

4. Ensure that the Automatic preview, Smoothing, Antialiasing, and (most importantly) Work on copy check boxes are selected. Also, the radio buttons Upper in the Curve for Border section and Smooth in the Curve Type section need to be selected.

5. In the Modify Curves section on the right-hand side of the Curve Bend dialog box, place your cursor in the center of the horizontal black line in the grid, and drag it up one square. Your image will be distorted as shown in Figure 18.12.

6. Take a look in your Layers dialog box, and you'll see a new layer has been added called curve_bend_dummylayer_b. This layer was created because we had the Work on copy check box selected in the Curve Bend dialog box.

7. Click on the leftmost of the two boxes to the left of the curve_bend_dummylayer_b layer image. An eye will appear, indicating that this layer has been made visible. Look at your image, and you'll see the perspective corrected result.

8. Now we have to merge our layers. The simplest way is to choose Image, Flatten Image.

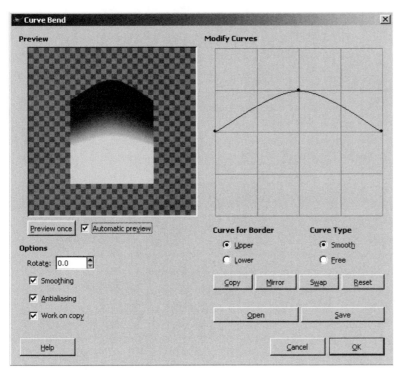

Figure 18.12
Applying perspective-correcting warp.

9. Save your work.

10. Repeat the warping for all three of the other image files so that you've corrected all the lateral view images, left, right, front, and back.

11. Run Emaga6 and check your work.

Now you might find that after you've done the distortion you now have seams again in your skybox. If so, go back and fix the edges.

There you have it! Your very own do-it-yourself skybox!

The Sky Mission Object

You may have noticed when you were editing the Emaga6 MIS file that there was an object defined in there called "Sky". There are lots of goodies in that object for us sky worshippers.

Here it is:

```
new Sky(Sky) {
    position = "-1088 -928 0";
    rotation = "1 0 0 0";
    scale = "1 1 1";
    materialList = "./sky_book.dml";
    cloudHeightPer[0] = "0.349971";
    cloudHeightPer[1] = "0.25";
    cloudHeightPer[2] = "0.199973";
    cloudSpeed1 = "0.0002";
    cloudSpeed2 = "0.0004";
    cloudSpeed3 = "0.0006";
    visibleDistance = "1100";
    fogDistance = "1000";
    fogColor = "0.820000 0.828000 0.844000 1.000000";
    fogStorm1 = "0";
    fogStorm2 = "0";
    fogStorm3 = "0";
    fogVolume1 = "500 0 100";
    fogVolume2 = "0 0 0";
    fogVolume3 = "0 0 0";
    windVelocity = "0.1 0.1 0";
    windEffectPrecipitation = "1";
    SkySolidColor = "0.547000 0.641000 0.789000 0.000000";
    useSkyTextures = "1";
    renderBottomTexture = "0";
    noRenderBans = "0";
        locked = "true";
};
```

We have already encountered the MaterialList property and have seen that it is used to point to a file that contains the names of the images that will be displayed on the interior faces of our skybox.

Not all the properties in the skybox are particularly interesting; they owe their presence to Torque's beginnings as the code that drives the *Tribes 2* game. The position, scale, and rotation properties don't accomplish much when you use them; they are there because all objects have those properties whether or not they are meaningful.

The cloudHeight properties *are* useful, and we will cover them in the next section. The same applies to the properties for fog.

One of the most useful properties is visibleDistance. This property specifies the distance, in world units, beyond which the terrain and all game objects will not be rendered. This is a useful, though rather ham-handed, method for increasing frame rates in game worlds that have many objects present. In conjunction with the fogDistance property, this *sort of* simulates the concept that all landscape artists are familiar with—that objects become hazier and harder to see at a distance. This is because there is simply more atmosphere between you and the objects you are viewing in the distance, and the greater the distance, the more the air obscures your view. This effect is a well-known one called *atmospheric perspective*. The great Leonardo da Vinci studied this effect quite a bit back in the 15th and 16th centuries; he called it *aerial perspective*.

By exaggerating this effect we have a useful mechanism to reduce the number of objects that the video card needs to render, and this improves your frame rate.

The fogDistance property specifies the distance from you that the haziness we just talked about begins. The distant fogginess starts at this point and gets thicker as the distance increases, until the visibleDistance is reached, after which nothing is rendered. By using these two properties, you can prepare a game world where there is a natural-appearing haziness that slowly obscures distant objects until they disappear completely.

Note

You should *always* make sure that visibleDistance is a bigger number than fogDistance; otherwise, you risk crashing the game engine in clients in certain situations. In fact, for the sake of safety, always make sure that visibleDistance is at least 50 units larger than fogDistance. Less than that is not really useful anyway.

If you don't want to use a skybox, there is the SkySolidColor property, which you can set. Then you will get a uniformly colored sky all around with a band of changing color near the horizon to simulate the lightening effect we see—something like the gradient we made for our skybox. In this case, to disable the skybox, set useSkyTextures to 0 or False. Set noRenderBans to 0 or False to enable the simulated horizon coloring, and set it to True to disable the coloring.

You can also just prevent the bottom image in the skybox from being rendered, or considered for rendering, by setting renderBottomTexture to 0 or False. This might eke out a frame or two of frame rate for you.

The `windVelocity` and `windEffectPrecipitation` precipitation properties have no effect on their own. They are used in conjunction with the storm effects we will cover later.

Clouds

Your game's sky doesn't start and end with the skybox. A beautiful background sky is nice, and important in some settings, but it's static. If you go outside on a nice day and look around, you will often see a sky with clouds that presents itself much like the one you can make with the skybox.

But more often, you will see that *and* you will have clouds moving across the sky above you, blowing in the wind. In fact, you will probably notice layers of clouds—often two layers and sometimes even three layers.

The lower layers of clouds can whip rapidly across the view above you, while the upper layers move at a more sedate pace, sometimes even in a different direction. There might even be in-between layers moving at various speeds, with a different visual.

In Torque we can define up to three layers of moving clouds with the Sky mission object in the MIS file that the server uses to define the game world.

Cloud Specifications

For each layer, we define its altitude as a percentage of a pseudo-altitude. Now this is tricky and might be a bit difficult to understand. The first thing to get is that your player can *never* go up—either in camera fly mode or in a flying vehicle—high enough to reach the lowest cloud layer. In this sense, cloud layers operate somewhat like a skybox. However, you *can* position the three layers relative to each other. The reason for this is so that the motions of each cloud layer can be calculated in correct proportion to each other. If you have a steady wind that is the same at all altitudes, then the lowest cloud layer will seem to move faster than the others, and the highest will seem to move slower than the others. How much faster or slower depends on the distance between the cloud layers and their distance from your player, as the observer.

And that's what the `cloudHeightPer` properties do—they define the *visual* appearance of the clouds but not their *physical location* in the game.

Now another consideration is that wind speeds are not the same at all altitudes in real life. Usually, the speeds of *winds aloft* (winds at altitudes of at least 1,000 feet above the ground) are higher the higher you go, up to about 30,000 or 40,000 feet or so. Then it starts to get really weird.

You can plug in the movement speeds for the clouds at different altitudes using the cloudSpeed*n* for each specified cloudHeightPer[*n*] and have the game engine figure out the relative motion based on pseudo-altitude and the speed at that altitude. Unfortunately, Torque doesn't handle wind direction for clouds so well—that would be the final link needed to provide really neat cloud motion. Wind direction is specified by a single windVelocity property that applies to all layers. In real life, wind directions *back* and *veer* according to altitude, but we can't do that here.

Using the windVelocity property requires a little thought. The value is expressed as an XYZ coordinate. The third value, the Z, is irrelevant, but the X and Y values are used to calculate the vector on the horizontal plane in two dimensions. The vector then points to the world origin (or center). If we look up at the sky and imagine the X- and Y-axes pasted up there, somewhat like in Figure 18.13, we can figure out the direction.

The value "1 −1 0" would describe a wind from the southeast, as illustrated in Figure 18.13, and "1 0 0" would be a wind from the east.

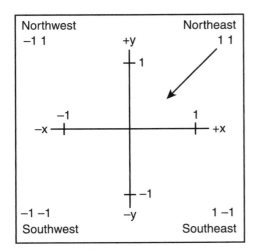

Figure 18.13
Wind velocity conversion.

Cloud Textures

Now, you need to tell the engine what all those clouds you have zipping around up there actually *look* like. You do this by specifying an image file in the same material file that you used to specify the skybox image files.

After the first six lines in that file that indicate the skybox images, the next line indicates the image that will provide the reflection map for your character if you have environment mapping enabled in your player's control script. If you look in \Emaga6\control\server\players\player.cs and locate the MaleAvatar datablock, you'll find a line like this:

```
emap=true;
```

When set to true, then the environment mapping is turned on, and your character's model will have the reflection map added to its skin. This can be a very subtle effect or very strong, depending on the interplay of the reflection map image, your character's skin, and the scene lighting. We often use a sky image for the reflection map.

The last three lines indicate the cloud image files. One line equals one cloud layer, with the first line after the reflection map line indicating layer 1, the next being layer 2, and the last being layer 3, like this:

```
skyfront
skyright
skyback
skyleft
skytop
skybottom
day_0007
no_cloud
cloud1
cloud1
```

That is the contents of sky_book.dml. Notice the use of the name "no_cloud" for the first cloud layer. In this example I didn't want to have any clouds at that first layer, so for this layer I created an image file that has no clouds in it.

So, you are asking, how do we make a cloud texture that *does* have clouds? Glad you asked! Let's make one.

1. Open the Gimp, and create a new image by selecting File, New. Fill in the dialog box with 256 for both the height and width of the blank image. Make

Figure 18.14
A simple cloud texture.

sure that the Advanced Options are set to RGB Color with 72 dpi in both X and Y resolutions. The Fill with box should be set to Transparency. A new canvas in its own window will appear.

2. Save this empty image file as \Emaga6\control\data\maps\no_cloud.png.

3. Next, select the Air Brush tool, set it to spray white, and then spray a little bit around your new image, avoiding the edges, like in Figure 18.14. Or spray the edges, but make sure you adjust the edges so that the image is suitable for tiling.

4. Save your image as \Emaga6\control\data\maps\mycloud.png.

5. Edit \Emaga6\control\data\maps\sky_book.dml so that the last three lines look like this:

```
no_cloud
mycloud
no_cloud
```

Now run your game, and check out the clouds! Of course, you can add more cloud images for the other layers, or you can use the same image for all three.

Water

Water, water, everywhere, and not a drop to drink. In addition to being completely necessary for life to flourish, water can be a complete nuisance as well. It's a nuisance that we willingly put up with, though.

In games, water is often used in several forms: as pools, rivers, lakes, and oceans that act as barriers that need to be overcome; or as weather effects, like fog, mist, rain, and snow that obscure visibility while adding ambience and moodiness to a scene.

Fog

Fog is, of course, another nifty weather feature. We've already encountered one kind of fog that is used to obscure distant objects and terrains. There is another kind of fog that operates in layers, just like the clouds—except that with fog, these are real layers in the game world that you can actually get into with your player, depending on where the layers are placed.

This layered fog is a limited form of *volumetric* fog. It is limited in the sense that although you can specify the upper and lower bounds of the fog, it will appear at those levels throughout the entire map.

You can use this layered fog to complement the moving cloud textures to create clouds (except that the fog will never be at the same altitude as the cloud textures). You can also deposit fog in low-lying river valleys.

A good use for this fog is underwater, helping to reduce visibility there. This reduced visibility results because of silt and other materials that often exist underwater, cutting down your ability to see far.

This layered volume fog is specified in the Sky mission object that we looked at earlier. An entry looks like this:

```
fogVolume1 = "500 0 100";
```

The three parameter numbers are, from left to right, distance, bottom, and top. Their meanings are shown in Table 18.1.

You already know how to edit the mission file and change the properties of the various mission objects, so go ahead and putz around with the fog values and see how they work.

Table 18.1 Volume Fog Settings

Parameter	Description
distance	View distance when in the layer. This works like fogDistance, except that a value of 0 here means there is no fog at all. If you want a really, really close view distance, use 1, not 0.
bottom	Bottom of fog layer.
top	Top of fog layer.

Storms

Torque has built-in capabilities to generate storms, using lightning, rain, and thunder. It's pretty cool how this is done. You can manually instigate a storm using script code, and there are some functions provided that will automate aspects of a storm for you.

Note

The lightning storm features require the use of sound effects files, but we don't cover those until the next chapter. So you will have to add the appropriate code to make the sound effects work. This will be done with minimal commentary here—just enough to get the thunder sounds working. See Chapters 19 and 20 for a more detailed look at sounds.

Setting Up Sound

There's some preparation we need to do at this point before proceeding with the rest of the weather features. We need to get some sound files, images, and supporting code files and put them in the right places for our game, as follows:

1. In the folder \3D2E\RESOURCES\CH18, locate the file settingsscreen.cs and copy it to the directory \Emaga6\control\client\misc\. Then copy settingsscreen.gui from RESOURCES\CH18 to \Emaga6\control\client\interfaces\.

2. If you don't have a folder called \Emaga6\control\data\sound, create it now. Copy the following files from the \3D2E\RESOURCES\CH18 folder to the \Emaga6\control\data\sound folder:

```
thunder1.wav
thunder2.wav
thunder3.wav
thunder4.wav
buttonOver.wav
rain.wav
```

3. Next—pay attention—copy the following files *from* RESOURCES\ CH18:

```
lightning.dml
lightning1frame1.png
lightning1frame2.png
lightning1frame3.png
```

```
water_splash.jpg
rain.jpg
mist.jpg
water_splash.alpha.jpg
rain.alpha.jpg
mist.alpha.jpg
```

But, this time they go *to* the folder \Emaga6\control\data\maps\.

4. Next, edit the file \Emaga6\control\client\Initialize.cs, and locate the following line:

```
Exec("./interfaces/serverscreen.gui");
```

and after it, add this line:

```
Exec("./interfaces/settingsscreen.gui");
```

5. Then locate this line:

```
Exec("./misc/serverscreen.cs");
```

and after it, add this line:

```
Exec("./misc/settingsscreen.cs");
```

6. Edit the file \Emaga6\control\client\default_profile.cs, and add the following line near the top:

```
GuiButtonProfile.soundButtonOver = "AudioButtonOver";
```

7. Copy the file RESOURCES\CH18\OpenAL32.dll to the directory \Emaga6\.

8. Locate the file \Emaga6\control\client\initialize.cs, and add these lines to the top:

```
$pref::Audio::driver = "OpenAL";
$pref::Audio::forceMaxDistanceUpdate = 0;
$pref::Audio::environmentEnabled = 0;
$pref::Audio::masterVolume   = 1.0;
$pref::Audio::channelVolume1 = 1.0;
$pref::Audio::channelVolume2 = 1.0;
$pref::Audio::channelVolume3 = 1.0;
$pref::Audio::channelVolume4 = 1.0;
$pref::Audio::channelVolume5 = 1.0;
$pref::Audio::channelVolume6 = 1.0;
$pref::Audio::channelVolume7 = 1.0;
$pref::Audio::channelVolume8 = 1.0;
```

```
$GuiAudioType     = 1;
$SimAudioType     = 2;
$MessageAudioType = 3;
new AudioDescription(AudioGui)
{
   volume    = 1.0;
   isLooping= false;
   is3D      = false;
   type      = $GuiAudioType;
};

new AudioDescription(AudioMessage)
{
   volume    = 1.0;
   isLooping= false;
   is3D      = false;
   type      = $MessageAudioType;
};

new AudioProfile(AudioButtonOver)
{
   filename = "~/data/sound/buttonOver.wav";
   description = "AudioGui";
      preload = true;
};
```

Now that we've done that, we can move on to the storm-specific stuff.

9. Type the following into a new file, and save it as \Emaga6\control\server\ misc\weather.cs.

```
datablock AudioProfile(HeavyRainSound)
{
   filename    = "~/data/sound/rain.wav";
   description = AudioLooping2d;
};
datablock AudioProfile(ThunderCrash1Sound)
{
   filename    = "~/data/sound/thunder1.wav";
   description = Audio2d;
};
datablock AudioProfile(ThunderCrash2Sound)
{
   filename    = "~/data/sound/thunder2.wav";
```

```
        description = Audio2d;
    };
    datablock AudioProfile(ThunderCrash3Sound)
    {
        filename = "~/data/sound/thunder3.wav";
        description = Audio2d;
    };
    datablock AudioProfile(ThunderCrash4Sound)
    {
        filename = "~/data/sound/thunder4.wav";
        description = Audio2d;
    };
    datablock LightningData(LightningStorm)
    {
        strikeTextures[0] = "control/data/maps/lightning1frame1.jpg";
        strikeTextures[1] = "control/data/maps/lightning1frame2.jpg";
        strikeTextures[2] = "control/data/maps/lightning1frame3.jpg";
        thunderSounds[0] = ThunderCrash1Sound;
        thunderSounds[1] = ThunderCrash2Sound;
        thunderSounds[2] = ThunderCrash3Sound;
        thunderSounds[3] = ThunderCrash4Sound;
    };
    datablock PrecipitationData(HeavyRain)
    {
        dropTexture = "~/data/maps/mist";
        splashTexture = "~/data/maps/water_splash";
        soundProfile = "HeavyRainSound";
        dropSize = 10;
        splashSize = 0.25;
        splashMS = 250;
        useTrueBillboards = true;
    };
    datablock PrecipitationData(MediumRain)
    {
        dropTexture = "~/data/maps/rain";
        splashTexture = "~/data/maps/mist";
        soundProfile = "HeavyRainSound";
        dropSize = 0.75;
        splashSize = 0.25;
        splashMS = 250;
        useTrueBillboards = true;
    };
```

10. Open the file \Emaga6\control\server\server.cs. In the function called
    OnServerCreated, locate the following line:

```
Exec("./misc/item.cs");
```

and add this line after it:

```
Exec("./misc/weather.cs");
```

11. Finally, add some objects to the mission file to cause our new storm features to load when the game launches. Locate the mission file again, \Emaga6\control\data\maps\book_ch6.mis, and find the last two lines of code, which should look like this:

```
};
//--- OBJECT WRITE END ---
```

And add the following two objects *before* those last two lines:

```
new Precipitation(RainStorm) {
        datablock = "HeavyRain";
        minSpeed = 10;
        maxSpeed = 15;
        numDrops = 800;
        boxWidth = 80;
        boxHeight = 50;
        minMass = 0.05;
        maxMass = 5;
        rotateWithCamVel = true;
        doCollision = true;
        useTurbulence = true;
        maxTurbulence = 0.1;
        turbulenceSpeed = 0.2;
};
new Lightning(ElectricalStorm) {
    position = "200 100 300";
    scale = "250 400 500";
    datablock = "LightningStorm";
    strikesPerMinute = "30";
    strikeWidth = "2.5";
    chanceToHitTarget = "100";
    strikeRadius = "250";
    boltStartRadius = "20";
    color = "1.000000 1.000000 1.000000 1.000000";
    fadeColor = "0.100000 0.100000 1.000000 1.000000";
    useFog = "1";
    locked = "true";
};
```

Figure 18.15
Raindrop images.

That should do it. Launch your game, and enjoy the storm!

Storm Materials

The visual appearance of precipitation is defined by a special image file that contains the sprites, or bitmaps, that represent the raindrops or snowflakes or what have you. These image files are referenced by a precipitation datablock that also defines other properties of the precipitation.

Figure 18.15 shows what a rain image file looks like. It has 16 images of raindrops in a 4 by 4 grid arrangement.

Now, the actual texture file has a difference—the areas shown in black in Figure 18.15 are really transparent when viewed in the file.

To create your own such file, launch the Gimp, and make a new file set to 128 pixels square. Make sure that the Advanced Options are set to RGB Color with 72 dpi in both X and Y resolutions. The Fill with box should be set to Transparency.

Next up, we need to set up a grid to guide us. First, make sure that Show Grid is enabled in the View menu. Next, choose Image, Configure Grid, and you will get the Configure Grid dialog box. Set the foreground color to a yellow shade by clicking the color bar to the right of the label Foreground colour. In the color picker dialog box that opens, you can fiddle with the color sliders until you get the perfect shade of yellow.

Then set the grid spacing width and height to 32 pixels using the Width and Height fields in the Spacing section. Finally, set the Line Style to Dashed in the Appearance section. Click OK.

A 4 by 4 grid made of dashed yellow lines will appear in your view of the new blank image. Draw your own version of each of the different 16 raindrops in each grid box on the image. Be aware that the grid is *not* actually part of the image.

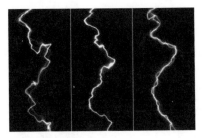

Figure 18.16
Lightning strike images.

Save the file and deposit it in the same place where you had put the rain.png file, and give it a unique name, like myrain.png or something. Then edit the PrecipitationData datablock in the Emaga6\control\server\misc\weather.cs file to point to your new myrain version instead of the original.

A slightly different process applies to making the lightning images: a lightning image doesn't contain a grid like the rain image did. Each lightning image file contains only one sprite of a lightning bolt. You've already copied three sprite image files of lightning bolts to your Emaga6 project:

```
lightning1frame1.png
lightning1frame2.png
lightning1frame3.png
```

Figure 18.16 shows each of these images in order, from left to right.

When making the lightning frame files, you need to make them 128 pixels wide by 256 pixels high. Draw your lightning bolts on a black background—all the areas you leave black will be treated as transparent. That is, they *really are black* and are not just rendered that way for purposes of the picture, as was the case back with Figure 18.15.

Lightning

Now, let's take a look at what makes lightning tick, as it were. There are two significant declarations: one is the LightningData datablock in the server code, and the other is the Lightning object definition that resides in the mission file. The datablock is transmitted to the client when the mission is loaded with the Lightning object definition getting transmitted to the client. The datablock describes what resources are used to create the lightning visuals and sound effects, as follows:

```
datablock LightningData(LightningStorm)
{
    strikeTextures[0] = "control/data/maps/lightning1frame1.jpg";
    strikeTextures[1] = "control/data/maps/lightning1frame2.jpg";
    strikeTextures[2] = "control/data/maps/lightning1frame3.jpg";
    thunderSounds[0] = ThunderCrash1Sound;
    thunderSounds[1] = ThunderCrash2Sound;
    thunderSounds[2] = ThunderCrash3Sound;
    thunderSounds[3] = ThunderCrash4Sound;
};
```

Every time Torque triggers a lightning bolt, one of the three lightning sprites is rendered. You can create even more and add them to the mix if you want to. In the same fashion, every time Torque triggers the thunder, one of the listed thunderSound*n* properties is chosen randomly. How and when the bolts and thunderclaps are triggered is defined by the properties of the Lightning object as follows:

```
new Lightning(ElectricalStorm) {
    position = "200 100 300";
    rotation = "1 0 0 0";
    scale = "250 400 500";
    datablock = "LightningStorm";
    strikesPerMinute = "30";
    strikeWidth = "2.5";
    chanceToHitTarget = "100";
    strikeRadius = "250";
    boltStartRadius = "20";
    color = "1.000000 1.000000 1.000000 1.000000";
    fadeColor = "0.100000 0.100000 1.000000 1.000000";
    useFog = "1";
    locked = "true";
};
```

Obviously, it's important to indicate which datablock to use. This is done with the datablock property. There are then a couple of self-evident properties: strikesPerMinute and chanceToHitTarget. Then strikeWidth indicates the scale factor applied to the image overlay of the lightning bolt that comes from the image files.

When a bolt is generated, a random spot within a circular area is chosen to be the place where the bolt begins, and then another random spot within a different circular area is chosen to be the spot where the bolt hits. The size of the starting area is defined by boltStartRadius, and the size of the strike area is defined by strikeRadius.

The centers of the start and strike areas are defined by the position property. The whole shebang can be made larger or smaller based on the scale property. The rotation property has no effect.

The color property defines a coloring that is applied when the bolt first appears, and the color values are changed over the life of the bolt until they reach the settings in fadeColor.

The useFog property indicates whether the fog defined by the stormFog$n$ property in the Sky mission object will be used.

In Figure 18.17 you can see a lightning bolt coming out of the sky in the game setting.

Rain

You can make it rain in much the same way as you make thunder and lightning, though there are differences in the details.

Figure 18.17
A lightning bolt.

For one thing, the `Precipitation` datablock is somewhat smaller.

```
datablock PrecipitationData(HeavyRain)
{
    dropTexture = "~/data/maps/mist";
    splashTexture = "~/data/maps/mist";
    soundProfile = "HeavyRainSound";
    dropSize = 10;
    splashSize = 0.25;
    splashMS = 250;
    useTrueBillboards = true;
};
```

The `dropTexture` property specifies the sprite image file that will be used to provide the raindrop sprites, while the `splashTexture` property specifies the file that will provide the splash sprites.

The `soundProfile` property points to an audio profile that establishes things like which sound file will be played.

The properties `dropSize` and `splashSize`, dictate the scaled size of the drops while falling, and the splash effect when the drops hit the ground.

The `splashMS` property dictates how long a splash effect lingers. The `useTrueBillboards` property is set to `true` if you want the raindrop sprites to always be facing you.

If you experiment with the datablock, realize that the rain is generated at the client. Other players don't see the exact same raindrops at the same instant that you do—it would be lunacy to try to make the server track each drop! Therefore, the rain is generated in a box that envelops the player and moves around as the player moves. The drops are initiated at the top of the box and tracked and rendered as they move down, pulled by gravity. That little bit of detail might help you with your experimentation.

The `Precipitation` object declaration looks like this:

```
new Precipitation(RainStorm) {
        datablock = "HeavyRain";
        minSpeed = 10;
        maxSpeed = 15;
        numDrops = 800;
        boxWidth = 80;
        boxHeight = 50;
```

```
        minMass = 0.05;
        maxMass = 5;
        rotateWithCamVel = true;
        doCollision = true;
        useTurbulence = true;
        maxTurbulence = 0.1;
        turbulenceSpeed = 0.2;
    };
```

The datablock property points to a datablock like the one we looked at earlier.

The minSpeed and maxSpeed properties describe the lower and upper bounds (respectively) of randomly chosen drop speeds. numDrops indicates how many rain drops will populate the area of the precipitation at any given time.

boxWidth and boxHeight establish the boundaries of the precipitation area.

minMass and maxMass dictate the lower and upper bounds of the mass of the rain drops for physics calculations related to splashing. rotateWithCamVel, when set to true, makes the rain drops rotate the camera at the same speed that the camera is turning, keeping the drops in view as they fall.

doCollision, when set to true, ensures that the drops collide with shape objects they encounter, and generate a splash. useTurbulence, when set to true, introduces a chaotic nature to the drops falling pattern, simulating wind turbulence. maxTurbulence limits the amount of turbulence effect allowed, while turbulenceSpeed dictates the speed that is imparted on the rain drops by the turbulence effect.

A Perfect Storm

Okay, so it may not be perfect, but it *is* neat. There are two useful object methods that you can use to move a storm in and out gradually without the need to manipulate the storm-related objects in detail.

The first is the stormCloud method that belongs to the Sky object. It looks like this:

```
Sky.stormCloud (flag, fade)
```

Set the flag to 1 if you want to create storm clouds and 0 if you want them to go away. To use the method, you would first call Sky.stormClouds(0, 0) as soon as your game starts to ensure that the clouds are not visible—all you would see is the skybox.

Then, at the moment you decide to call up a storm with your wand, you would call Sky.stormClouds(1, 60) somewhere in your script. This will cause the engine to gradually fade in your clouds over a 60-second time frame. When the storm clears, you make them go away gradually by calling Sky.stormClouds(0, 60). Of course, you could use a different fade value, making it as long or short as you desire.

The second method is a nice complement to the stormCloud method. It is called stormModify and belongs to the Precipitation class. The precipitation object we created is called RainStorm, so using stormModify would work like this:

```
RainStorm.stormModify(flag, fade)
```

It works the same way as stormCloud but obviously applies to the precipitation.

Use the two methods together, with appropriate fade values, to get a nice storm effect. Try them out in your sample game by entering the commands manually in the console.

Water Blocks

Water blocks are special objects that we can insert into our game world via a mission file. Following is an example of a water block. The property settings may be different from any particular water block you encounter.

```
new WaterBlock(Water) {
            position = "-1024 -1024 0";
            rotation = "1 0 0 0";
            scale = "2048 2048 125";
            UseDepthMask = "1";
            surfaceTexture = "~/data/water/water_center";
            ShoreTexture = "~/data/water/water_edge";
            envMapOverTexture = "~/data/skies/storm_env";
            specularMaskTex = "~/data/water/water_spec";
            liquidType = "OceanWater";
            density = "1";
            viscosity = "15";
            waveMagnitude = "3";
            surfaceOpacity = "0.2";
            envMapIntensity = "1";
            TessSurface = "50";
```

Table 18.2 Water Block Properties

Property	Description
surfaceTexture	Specifies the texture generally used for the surface.
ShoreTexture	Specifies the texture used in shallow areas.
envMapOverTexture	Defines the environment map texture used when looking over the fluid surface.
envMapUnderTexture	Defines the environment map texture used when looking under the fluid surface.
surfaceOpacity	Specifies the maximum opacity of the surface (0.0 —> 1.0).
envMapIntensity	Specifies the intensity of the applied environment map (0.0 —> 1.0). Setting the intensity to 0 results in the environment map pass being skipped, which increases performance slightly.
UseDepthMask	Toggles the depth map feature on and off.
ShoreDepth	Specifies the depth at which the shore texture will start being applied. Larger values result in larger shore texture areas.
DepthGradient	Specifies the gradient that the shore textures will interpolate between MinAlpha and MaxAlpha. The value of 1 equates to linear interpolation, whereas values 0 —> 1 equate to fast fade-out/slow fade-in, and the values 1 —> inf equate to slow fade-out/fast fade-in (from deep to shallow).
MinAlpha/MaxAlpha	Specifies the alpha levels used from shore to deep fluid. The MinAlpha can be used to prevent totally transparent areas. You will always be able to see underneath the fluid surface, so use the fog volumes from the Sky object to restrict visibility underwater.
TessSurface/TessShore	Specifies the number of times the textures are repeated over the water block surface for surface/shore textures.
SurfaceParallax	Renders the surface as two layers. When the surface is distorting or flowing, then this controls the ratio of one surface with respect to the other. If you set this to 0.5, then one surface will move at half the speed of the other.
FlowAngle/FlowRate	Specifies the way the fluid flows. The FlowRate controls how fast the fluid flows, and the FlowAngle is a polar angle controlling its direction. Using a FlowRate of 0 completely stops the fluid from flowing.
DistortGridScale/ DistortMag/ DistortTime	Controls the distortion effect of the fluid surface. This allows you to create many different surfaces. To control the speed, use DistortTime. Use DistortMag to control the overall magnitude of the distortion. DistortGridScale normally does not need adjusting but can be used to adjust a setting for a small water block that may not look correct on a large one.

```
TessShore = "60";
SurfaceParallax = "1";
FlowAngle = "220";
FlowRate = "0.1";
DistortGridScale = "0.1";
DistortMag = "0.1";
DistortTime = "2";
ShoreDepth = "14";
DepthGradient = "1";
MinAlpha = "0.01";
MaxAlpha = "0.4";
tile = "1";
removeWetEdges = "0";
specularColor = "1 0.8 0.46 1";
specularPower = "10";
locked = "true";
params0 = "0.32 −0.67 0.066 0.5";
textureSize = "32 32";
Extent = "100 100 10";
params3 = "1.21 −0.61 0.13 −0.33";
params2 = "0.39 0.39 0.2 0.133";
floodFill = "1";
seedPoints = "0 0 1 0 1 1 0 1";
params1 = "0.63 −2.41 0.33 0.21"; };
```

Water blocks repeat in the same way that terrain blocks repeat, and because water blocks are flat, the only positioning information of real interest is the height. Table 18.2 describes the most significant properties, and there are many.

Not all properties need to be defined. If you leave any out, Torque will simply use default values. There are also other properties that you don't see in the example.

Water block textures, as described in various places in Table 18.2, can be created in exactly the same way as cloud textures. In fact, you can even get away with using cloud textures in a pinch!

Take a look at Figure 18.18 to see a water block in action.

Terraforming

You already saw in Chapter 12 how to create a terrain using height maps. Torque also has a built-in Terrain Editor that you can use to manually modify the terrain height map and square properties.

Figure 18.18
Water in a game setting.

Figure 18.19
A Terrain brush.

Terrain editing is done using a Terrain brush. The brush is a selection of terrain points centered on the mouse cursor in either a circular or square configuration of different selectable sizes, as you can see in Figure 18.19. Notice all the tiny hollow squares drawn on the terrain; these define the areas that the brush affects.

The brush can also be either a hard brush that has a uniform effect across the surface of the brush or a soft brush whose influence on terrain diminishes toward the edges of the brush. You can adjust the soft brush falloff rate in the Terrain

Editor Settings dialog box, found under the menu Edit, Terrain Editor Settings. The Terrain Editor is not enabled yet in our Emaga6 example game, although it will be in a later chapter. So to get a feel for the Terrain Editor, we can use the Torque demo.

1. Run the Torque demo, and after you have spawned into the game, press F8 to switch to fly mode.

2. Fly up a fair bit to get a good overview of the surrounding terrain.

3. Press F11 to switch to the Editor GUI.

4. Choose Window, Terrain Editor.

5. Wave your cursor over the terrain, and notice the Terrain brush marked on the terrain.

6. Drag your mouse up and down after clicking over some area of terrain. You will see your terrain change to conform.

7. Experiment with using different actions to see how the Terrain Editor works.

Tip

Every now and then while in the Terrain Editor, press Alt + L to redo the lighting. The cursor will freeze for a few moments while the lighting is redone. This will cause the new terrain changes you've made to properly generate shadows.

Table 18.3 Terrain Editor Functions

Function	Description
Select	Selects grid points that will be painted with the brush.
Adjust Selection	Raises or lowers the currently selected grid points as a group.
Add Dirt	Adds "dirt" to the center of the brush.
Excavate	Removes "dirt" from the center of the brush.
Adjust Height	Drags the brush selection to raise or lower it.
Flatten	Sets the area bounded by the brush surface to be a flat plane.
Smooth	Smoothes, within the bounds of the brush, rough areas of varying terrain height.
Set Height	Sets the terrain within the brush to a constant height as specified in the Terrain Editor settings.
Set Empty	Converts the squares covered by the brush into holes in the terrain.
Clear Empty	Makes the squares covered by the brush solid.
Paint Material	Paints the current terrain texture material with the brush.

Table 18.4 Terrain Terraform Editor Functions

Function	Description
fBm Fractal	Creates bumpy hills.
Rigid Multifractal	Creates ridges and sweeping valleys.
Canyon Fractal	Creates vertical canyon ridges.
Sinus	Creates overlapping sine wave patterns with different frequencies, useful for making rolling hills.
Bitmap	Imports an existing 256 by 256 bitmap as a heightfield.
Turbulence	Perturbs another operation on the stack.
Smoothing	Smoothes another operation on the stack.
Smooth Water	Smoothes water.
Smooth Ridges/Valleys	Smoothes an existing operation on edge boundaries.
Filter	Filters an existing operation based on a curve.
Thermal Erosion	Erodes an existing operation using a thermal erosion algorithm.
Hydraulic Erosion	Erodes an existing operation using a hydraulic erosion algorithm.
Blend	Blends two existing operations according to a scale factor and mathematical operator.
Terrain File	Loads an existing terrain file onto the stack.

8. Every now and then remember to save your work. In the Mission Editor, choose File, Save.

Table 18.3 describes the Terrain Editor functions that are available in the Action menu.

Table 18.4 describes the functions of the Terrain Terraform Editor (see also Figure 18.20), the one we used in Chapter 12 dealing with height maps. These functions are available in the Operation pull-down menu in the Terrain Terraform Editor.

Moving Right Along

So, you've now seen how you can create and modify your game environment. The three main environmental elements are sky, clouds, and water. We looked at the different ways each of those three elements can be created using tools and techniques available in Torque.

In most cases, you will probably use some form of all of those techniques when you create your game. For example, you would judiciously mix overhead cloud layers with skybox renderings of distant clouds on the horizon.

Figure 18.20
Terrain Terraform Editor.

We've also looked at the combined weather effects involved in storms and how you can initiate an automated process to start and end storms over time using TorqueScript.

In this chapter we were introduced to sounds in the form of thunder for the lightning strikes. In the next chapter we will more thoroughly explore how to incorporate sounds in our game.

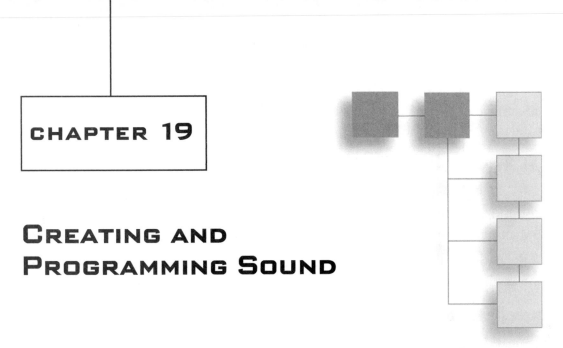

CHAPTER 19

CREATING AND
PROGRAMMING SOUND

As I mentioned in Chapter 1, audio artists compose the music and sound in a game. Good designers work with creative and inspired audio artists to create musical compositions that intensify the game experience.

It also bears repeating that audio artists work closely with the game designers, determining where the sound effects are needed and what the character of the sounds should be. They often spend quite a bit of time experimenting with sound-effect sources, looking for different ways to generate the precise sound needed. Visit an audio artist at work and you might catch him slapping rulers and dropping boxes in front of a microphone. After capturing the basic sound, an audio artist will then massage the sound with sound-editing tools, varying the pitch, speeding up the sound or slowing it down, removing unwanted noise, and so on. It's often a tightrope walk balancing realistic sounds with the need sometimes to exaggerate certain characteristics in order to make the right point in the game context.

When creating your game, you have a choice between two basic approaches: obtain a good source of sound effects and music (like an audio library) or create your own sounds. Of course, you also have the option to combine the two approaches. Audio libraries are available from a wide variety of sources; the commercial ones are quite thorough and professionally made. Some audio libraries are available free via the Internet, but the quality of these sources varies widely in breadth, depth, and recording fidelity.

In this book we are going to take the do-it-yourself approach. The main advantage of going this way is the price; a secondary advantage is that you have total control over the contents of your sound files.

Audacity

There are several tools available to use for recording and editing sound effects and music. A very good open source program—it doesn't cost you anything to use and is made available under the GNU General Public License—is Audacity.

This chapter will show you how to use Audacity (see Figure 19.1) to make sounds for use in your game.

Installing Audacity

To install Audacity, do the following:

1. Browse to your CD in the \TOOLS\AUDACITY folder.

2. Locate the audacity-win-1.2.4b.exe file, and double-click it to run it.

3. Click the Next button on the Welcome screen.

4. Follow the various screens, and take the default options for each one, unless you know you have a specific reason to do otherwise.

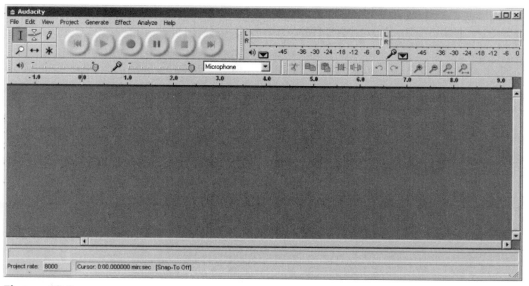

Figure 19.1
Audacity main window.

Note

You will also find a beta version of Audacity in the TOOLS\AUDACITY folder. This is the latest release, but it has not been thoroughly tested and is almost guaranteed to be incomplete or have buggy capabilities. However, it does have a bunch of new features to try out if you are feeling adventurous. Use it at your own risk!

Using Audacity

You need to ensure that your microphone is set up properly—connected to the MIC or microphone input jack on your sound card. Of course, you don't need to obtain your sounds directly from a microphone; you can record from a CD or another audio source. In any event, you need to have that source connected to the correct input and ensure that your audio mixer is set up to record from that source. You should refer to your sound card documentation if you don't know how to do this.

The basic operation of Audacity is quite straightforward for recording, simple editing, playback, and saving your data.

Tip

If, when you launch Audacity, you don't see all the toolbars that are shown in Figure 19.1, you can fix that up in a jiffy. Choose Edit, Preferences, and then click the Interface tab. If, for example, you are missing the Mixer toolbar (shown as Output Displays in Figure 19.9), then make sure that the Enable Mixer Toolbar check box is checked, and away you go.

Recording

Let's record some sound:

1. Launch Audacity by choosing Start, Programs, Audacity. You will get the main window, as you saw earlier, in Figure 19.1.

2. Click the Record button, as shown in Figure 19.2.

Figure 19.2
The Record button.

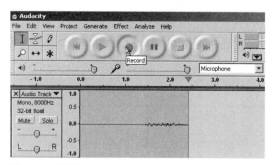

Figure 19.3
Recording in progress.

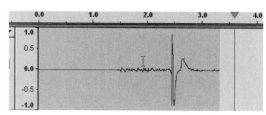

Figure 19.4
Waveform in Audacity.

The program is now recording from the microphone. You can see the progress of the recording and the waveforms of the sounds in the window as the recording proceeds, as shown in Figure 19.3.

3. Speak into the microphone, or if you don't want to hear your own voice, make a noise, like slapping a book down on the desk or something. You will see the sound you made appear in the waveform. Figure 19.4 shows the waveform created when I tapped a pen on the desk next to the microphone.

4. When you have your sound recorded, click the Stop button, as shown in Figure 19.5.

5. Now you can play back your recording, by clicking the Play button, as shown in Figure 19.6.

We'll continue working with Audacity in a moment, but first I want to point out that if you have a waveform but don't hear any sound, make sure that you have the volume turned up high enough on your speakers. Also be sure that it is turned up high enough—and is not muted—in your Windows Volume Control applet

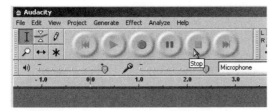

Figure 19.5
Stop recording.

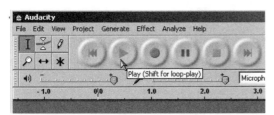

Figure 19.6
Playback.

(in the Control Panel, and usually on the Windows System Tray on the right side of the taskbar). Finally, check the microphone level in the Mixer Control in Audacity, and ensure that it isn't too low. How low is too low is hard to say, because Windows also has recording level controls in its own mixer application. Try to make sure everything is set roughly halfway between 0 and maximum, and you should be fine.

Simple Editing

Now, if you're like me you probably have a long period of dead air before the sound effect you made and another chunk afterward. That's fine, because it's easy to fix. So, picking up where we left off in the previous section:

6. Place your cursor to one side of the portion of the waveform you want to eliminate, and drag it across to the other side. This selects an area to be worked on. See Figure 19.7.

7. Choose Edit, Delete. The selected portion will be excised from the wave-form.

8. Repeat the preceding two steps for the unwanted portions of the waveform on the other side of your sound effect. Eventually you will end up with something like Figure 19.8.

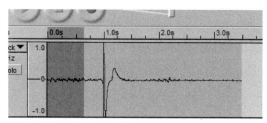

Figure 19.7
Selecting a portion of the waveform.

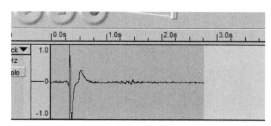

Figure 19.8
The final waveform of the sound effect.

We're not finished with our procedure yet; there's still some exporting to do. But before we cover that, I want to mention that above the waveform panel is a series of numbers on a scale. This is the elapsed time scale. The example in Figure 19.8 shows that my final waveform is just a little more than three-quarters of a second in duration.

Exporting

Now, once again picking up where we left off, you need to save the sound effect as a file before you can use it:

9. Choose File, Export as WAV. Name your file, and save it somewhere convenient for the moment, such as on your desktop.

10. Browse to your desktop (or wherever you saved your file), and double-click your newly created file. Whichever program is set up to play sounds in Windows on your computer will be launched and play your sound.

There are other export options available, but we'll stick with the WAV format for its simplicity and wide availability on Windows platforms. For other platforms, Ogg Vorbis is probably the format of choice on Linux, and AIFF for Macintosh.

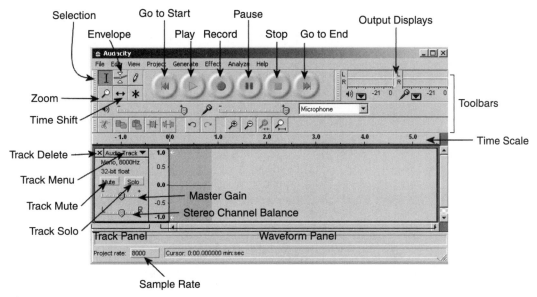

Figure 19.9
The Audacity main screen.

Audacity Reference

This section contains some useful reference details to help you use Audacity.

The Main Screen

Figure 19.9 shows the Audacity main screen, with some of the major components labeled. This section will provide some detail on these and other useful components.

The toolbar is where you will find the tools that you will probably use more than any other tools available with Audacity. Use Figure 19.9 to locate the tools in the toolbar, and refer to Table 19.1 to review their functions. To get the output displays to show, just widen the window a little bit—about ten pixels or so.

The Track Panel contains tools for managing specific tracks and groups of tracks. See Table 19.2 for details.

Audacity supports four different track types that can be viewed simultaneously when they exist in a single channel. These four track types let you view waveform (audio), time data, MIDI information, and label information for a given audio file. Table 19.3 describes each of the four types.

Table 19.1 Toolbar Tools

Tool	Description
Selection	Selects a portion of the audio track. You can set the position of the track cursor simply by clicking at the right place in the track. Select a range of audio by clicking and dragging over the desired portion. Select multiple tracks by holding down Shift and dragging across the tracks. Playback begins at the position of the track cursor and will play to the end of the track. If you have selected a range of audio, only the selected range will be played.
Time Shift	Changes the positioning of tracks relative to one another in time. Select this tool, then click in a track and drag it to the left or right.
Envelope	Provides a handy audio processing tool. Its presence directly in the main window of the program is an innovative move. You get detailed control over how tracks fade in and out, right in the main track window with this tool. When you select the Envelope tool, the amplitude envelope of each track is highlighted in a blue line; there are control points at the beginning and end of each track. To move a control point, click it and drag it to its new position. To add a new point, click anywhere in the track where a control point doesn't already exist. To remove a point, drag it outside of the track.
Zoom	Zooms in or out of a specific part of the audio. Clicking anywhere in the audio will zoom you in. Right-click or shift-click to zoom out. You can also zoom into a region by dragging the mouse to highlight the region while you have the Zoom tool selected.
Play	Enables you to listen to the audio file currently loaded or to a recording you have just created. The spacebar can be used as a stop and start toggle. Playback always begins at the current cursor position. If a region of audio is selected, only the selected region will play. To play the entire project, choose Edit, Select All, and then click the Play button. All tracks on a given channel will be mixed automatically for playback.
Stop	Halts playback.
Record	Records a new track from your microphone or another input device. You can configure recording options by choosing Edit, Preferences. Recording always happens at the project's default sample rate, which is configurable on the Quality tab.
Master Gain	Controls the volume of the audio output by Audacity to your hardware. Volume increases as you move the slider from left to right.

Table 19.2 Track Panel Tools

Tool	Description
Track Menu	Allows the user to display a track in different formats. This drop-down menu also provides the Name option, which allows the user to create a name for a given track.
Track Delete	Immediately deletes a track, without the option to undo. Use this button carefully.
Track Solo	Switches the current track to solo mode. You can change a track out of solo mode by clicking it again. When a track is in solo mode, the button for that track turns red. Only tracks that have the Solo button enabled will be played when in solo mode.
Track Mute	Switches off a track without deleting it. You can unmute a track just by clicking the Mute button again. When a track is muted, its Mute button will be blue.

Table 19.3 Track Types

Tool	Description
Audio	Audio tracks contain digitally sampled sounds. Two stereo channels are represented by two stereo tracks. Each audio track has a sample rate that is the same as the project sample rate.
Label	Label tracks can be used to mark a document with annotations. Annotations can be saved to a text file.
Time	Time tracks can be used to mark a document with time stamps for synchronization purposes.
MIDI	Note tracks display data loaded from a MIDI file. They cannot be changed or played, only viewed.

Table 19.4 Common Sample Rates

Frequency	Usage
8000 Hertz	Typical telephone
11025 Hertz	Minimum "voice quality"
16000 Hertz	Typical "voice quality"
22050 Hertz	Common digital interactive media
44100 Hertz	CD audio, DAT (digital audiotape)
48000 Hertz	Digital studio quality
96000 Hertz	Digital studio quality (newer)

Note

Common values for audio sample rates are shown in Table 19.4.

Menus

The Audacity menus provide access to functions for managing files, editing, adjusting views, managing Audacity projects, creating special effects, and other features. There is also a standard Help menu.

The File Menu

Figure 19.10 shows the File menu, and Table 19.5 contains an itemized description of the menu. Note that menu items that have names ending with an ellipsis (three dots) will bring up a dialog box where you can fill in some parameters.

File	
New	Ctrl+N
Open...	Ctrl+O
Close	Ctrl+W
Save Project	Ctrl+S
Save Project As...	
Recent Files...	▶
Export As WAV...	
Export Selection As WAV...	
Export As MP3...	
Export Selection As MP3...	
Export As Ogg Vorbis...	
Export Selection As Ogg Vorbis...	
Export Labels...	
Export Multiple...	
Page Setup...	
Print...	
Exit	

Figure 19.10
File menu.

Table 19.5 File Menu

Menu Item	Description
New	Creates a new, empty project window.
Open	Presents you with a dialog box to choose a file to open. If a project window is open and empty, the new file will appear in that window; otherwise, a new project window will open.
Close	Closes the current project window.
Save Project	Saves the current Audacity project file in AUP format. Audacity projects are not usable by other programs. Audio data for an Audacity project is not stored in the AUP file; instead, it is stored in a directory with the same name as the project.
Save Project As	Saves the current Audacity project file, with a different name or directory path.
Recent Files	Provides a submenu listing recently used files, for easy access.
Export As WAV	Exports the current Audacity project as a standard audio file format, such as WAV or AIFF. Change the format of the exported file in the Preferences dialog box.
Export Selection As WAV	The same as Export As WAV, but only exports the selected portion of the project.

Menu Item	Description
Export As MP3	Exports the current Audacity project as an MP3 file. Exporting MP3 files requires that you install a separate MP3 encoder, which is not included with Audacity.
Export Selection As MP3	The same as Export As MP3, but only exports the selected portion of the project.
Export As Ogg Vorbis	Exports the current Audacity project as an Ogg Vorbis file.
Export Selection As Ogg Vorbis	The same as Export As Ogg Vorbis, but only exports the selected portion of the project.
Export Labels	Exports label tracks to a text file.
Export Multiple	Allows you to export multiple files in a project all at once. The files can be split apart according to tracks or according to labels.
Page Setup	Allows user to configure track waveforms in Audacity for printing and to choose printer.
Print	Prints the main window, including tracks and waveforms.
Exit	Closes all project windows and exits Audacity. It will ask if you want to save changes to your project.

The Edit Menu

Figure 19.11 shows the Edit menu, and Table 19.6 contains an itemized description of the menu. Parts of this menu contain the standard Cut, Copy, and Paste functions; the rest are related functions that are specific to Audacity's capabilities.

The View Menu

The View menu provides functions that you can use to control what you see in the Audacity window and how you see it. Figure 19.12 shows the View menu, and Table 19.7 contains an itemized description of the menu.

The Project Menu

Audacity uses the concept of projects that you've encountered elsewhere, such as with UltraEdit earlier in this book. By using projects, you can organize data files as well as configuration and operational parameters in one collection that can be recalled at any time. This really helps when dealing with complex tasks. Figure 19.13 shows the Project menu, and Table 19.8 contains an itemized description of the menu.

The Effect Menu

Audacity includes many built-in effects and also lets you use plug-in effects. To apply an effect, simply select part or all of the tracks you want to modify,

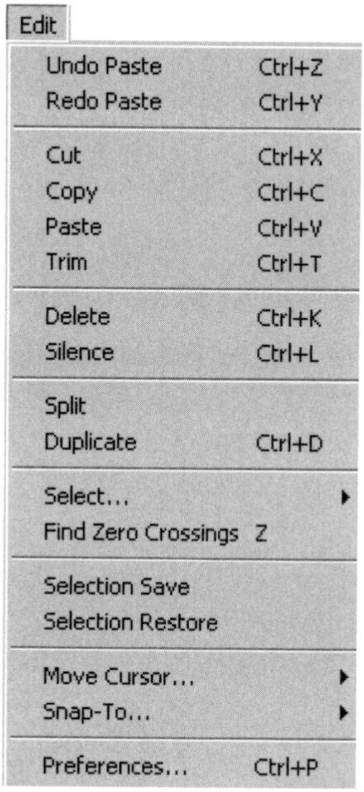

Figure 19.11
Edit menu.

Table 19.6 Edit Menu

Menu Item	Description
Undo	Undoes the last edits performed. Allows you to undo every operation going back to the last time the document was saved.
Redo	Redoes edits that were just undone. The redo history remains available until you do a fresh edit.
Cut	Removes the selected audio data and moves it to the Clipboard.
Copy	Copies the selected audio data to the Clipboard.
Paste	Inserts the Clipboard contents at the position of the selection cursor in the project, replacing any selected data.
Trim	Removes everything except the selected waveform data.
Delete	Removes selected data without copying it to the Clipboard.
Silence	Replaces selected audio data with silence.
Split	Moves the selected region into its own track or tracks, replacing the affected portion of the original track with silence.
Duplicate	Makes a copy of all or part of a track or set of tracks into new tracks.

Menu Item	Description
Select	Presents three selection modes in a submenu:
	All Selects the entire track that contains the cursor.
	Start to Cursor Selects from the beginning of the track to the cursor.
	Cursor to End Selects from the cursor to the end of the track.
Find Zero Crossings	Makes a slight modification to the selection so that the selection starts and ends at a point where the signal crosses zero, thereby eliminating clicks and pops.
Selection Save	"Remembers" the current selection, so that it can be restored later.
Selection Restore	Restores a saved selection.
Move Cursor	Presents four cursor relocation modes in a submenu:
	to Track Start Moves the cursor to the beginning of the current track.
	to Track End Moves the cursor to the end of the current track.
	to Selection Start Moves the cursor to the beginning of the current selection.
	to Selection End Moves the cursor to the end of the current selection.
Snap-To	Allows you to turn the selection snap feature on or off using the submenu. The selection snap feature, when turned on, constrains selections to one-second intervals.
Preferences	Allows adjusting many of the values, parameters, and operation modes of the program.

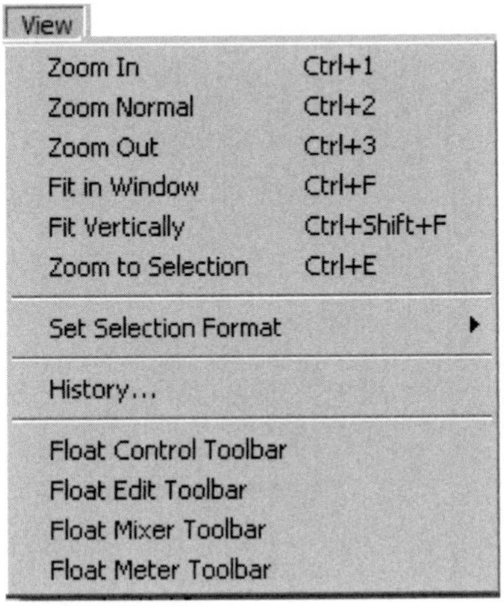

Figure 19.12
View menu.

Table 19.7 View Menu

Menu Item	Description
Zoom In	Zooms in on a portion of the audio data. Doing this allows you to view more data detail for a smaller time period.
Zoom Normal	Changes the zoom factor to one inch of data for one second of time; this is the default zoom factor.
Zoom Out	Zooms out so you can see a larger time base, at the cost of less detail.
Fit in Window	Adjusts the zoom factor so that the entire project fits exactly in the window.
Fit Vertically	Like Fit in Window, except considers only the vertical dimension.
Zoom to Selection	Similar to Fit in Window, except uses the current selection instead of the window as the zoom fitting target.
Set Selection Format	Provides a submenu with a myriad of selection time formats.
History	Provides a list of previously executed commands. You can restore a project to an earlier state by clicking on an earlier entry.
Float Control Toolbar	Detaches the Control toolbar from the window, allowing you to place it arbitrarily anywhere on the screen.
Float Edit Toolbar	Detaches the Edit toolbar from the window, allowing you to place it arbitrarily anywhere on the screen.
Float Mixer Toolbar	Detaches the Mixer toolbar from the window, allowing you to place it arbitrarily anywhere on the screen.
Float Meter Toolbar	Detaches the Meter toolbar from the window, allowing you to place it arbitrarily anywhere on the screen.

Figure 19.13
Project menu.

Table 19.8 Project Menu

Menu Item	Description
Import Audio	Imports audio into your project. Use this function to add another track to a project with at least one existing track. You can also mix the imported track with an existing track.
Import Labels	Imports a text file that contains time codes and labels, turning them collectively into a label track.
Import MIDI	Imports a MIDI file into a note track. MIDI files can be viewed but not played, edited, or saved.
Import Raw Data	Allows you to open a file in virtually any uncompressed format. Audacity will examine the file contents to determine their format. You will need to listen to the result in order to decide if the program made the right format choice. You can use the dialog box the function displays to direct the program in its attempts. Sometimes a successful operation has a bit of noise at the beginning; this is caused by the unrecognized header format. The rest of the data usually plays correctly. You can then edit out the noise.
Edit ID3 Tags	Opens a dialog box, allowing you to edit the ID3 tags associated with a project. These are used for MP3 exporting.
Quick Mix	Mixes selected tracks down to one or two tracks. Note that if you try to mix two loud tracks together, you may get clipping that sounds like pops, clicks, and noise. To avoid this, you should first adjust the gain (amplification) of the tracks to a lower level.
New Audio Track	Creates a new audio track with no data.
New Stereo Track	Creates a new stereo track with no data.
New Label Track	Creates a new label track with no data.
New Time Track	Creates a new time track with no data.
Remove Tracks	Removes the selected track or tracks from the project. You only need to select a portion of a track for it to be removed.
Align Tracks	Provides a large selection of track alignment options, which adjust the time offset of selected multiple tracks to make them start at some specified time in relation to each other.
Align and move cursor	Same as Align Tracks, except moves the cursor along with the tracks. This allows you to shift tracks without losing your relative position.
Add Label At Selection	Creates a new label at the current selection.
Add Label At Playback Position	Creates a new label at the spot where playback or recording is currently located.

and select the effect from the menu. Figure 19.14 shows the Effect menu, and Table 19.9 contains an itemized description of the menu.

Many menu items can be invoked by the use of the standard Windows accelerator key combinations, such as Ctrl + W to close a window. Table 19.10 lists the shortcut keys.

Figure 19.14
Effect menu.

Table 19.9 Effect Menu

Menu Item	Description
Repeat *(last effect)*	Repeats the last effect command. The name of the last effect command will appear after the word *Repeat*, once that effect command has been used.
Amplify	Increases or decreases the volume of a track or set of tracks. Audacity computes for you the maximum amount you could amplify the selected audio without being so loud that the signal is clipped.
Bass Boost	Amplifies the lower frequencies, yet leaves most of the other frequencies untouched. Recommended maximum boost is 12 dB.
Change Pitch	Changes the audio pitch *without* changing the tempo.

Menu Item	Description
Change Speed	Changes the speed of the audio by resampling. Higher speed yields a higher pitch and vice versa.
Change Tempo	Changes the tempo (or speed) of the audio *without* changing the pitch. The length of the selection changed will change.
Click Removal	Removes clicking, popping, and other sharp transient noises.
Compressor	Compresses the dynamic range of the selection so that the louder parts are quieter while the quiet parts are unchanged.
Echo	Repeats the audio you have selected again and again, softer each time. There is a fixed time delay between each repeat.
Equalization	Amplify or diminish specified frequencies using one of the built-in curves, or a custom curve.
Fade In	Fades in linearly to the selected audio data.
Fade Out	Fades out linearly to the selected audio data.
FFT Filter	Applies a Fast Fourier Transform according to specifications using a curve on a linear scale.
Invert	Flips the audio samples upside down.
Noise Removal	Removes constant background noise, such as fans, tape noise, or hums. This does not work well for removing background speech or music.
Normalize	Corrects for a vertical offset (DC offset) of a track's signal.
Nyquist Prompt	Uses a programming language to massage an audio track.
Phaser	Combines phase-shifted signals with the original signal.
Repeat	Repeats a selection a given number of iterations.
Reverse	Reverses the selected audio temporally (in time). After the effect has been applied, the end of the audio will be heard first and the beginning last. This is useful for trying to find satanic messages in songs—heh!
Wahwah	Give us a little wah-wah, George! Uses a moving bandpass filter to create the famous wah-wah sound. This function also adjusts the phase of the left and right channels of a stereo recording to make the effect travel between the speakers.
(others)	Any effects available in the menu beyond this point are custom plug-in effects provided by third parties; these are not really standard Audacity features.

OpenAL

Torque, along with many other game engines, uses OpenAL—an open-source audio API (*Application Programmer's Interface*). In this book we won't be directly addressing programming with OpenAL, but we do need to ensure that OpenAL is installed with the correct version. The Torque installation procedure you followed in an earlier chapter will have taken care of that for you. In your root main directory, make sure that the file OpenAL32.dll is there. If it isn't, you

Table 19.10 Shortcut Keys

Menu Item	Shortcut
File, New	Ctrl + N
File, Open	Ctrl + O
File, Close	Ctrl + W
File, Save Project	Ctrl + S
File, Preferences	Ctrl + P
Edit, Undo	Ctrl + Z
Edit, Redo	Ctrl + Y
Edit, Cut	Ctrl + X
Edit, Copy	Ctrl + C
Edit, Paste	Ctrl + V
Edit, Delete	Ctrl + K
Edit, Silence	Ctrl + L
Edit, Duplicate	Ctrl + D
Edit, Select All	Ctrl + A
Edit, Preferences	Ctrl + P
View, Zoom In	Ctrl + 1
View, Zoom Normal	Ctrl + 2
View, Zoom Out	Ctrl + 3
View, Fit in Window	Ctrl + F
View, Fit Vertically	Ctrl + Shift + F
Zoom to Selection	Ctrl + E
Project, Import Audio	Ctrl + I
Project, Add Label at Selection	Ctrl + B

can copy it from your CD in the 3D2E folder. If you use the stock Options menu in the Torque demo games, then make sure you enable the OpenAL interface there.

Audio Profiles and Datablocks

Torque uses the concept of *datablocks* and *profiles* to help define and organize resources for use in the game. We encountered this concept when building our Emag*an* sample games in earlier chapters.

There are essentially two ways to make sounds occur in a Torque game. We can *directly* activate a sound (or music, for that matter) with program code, or we can attach sounds to in-game objects and let the Torque Engine activate and control the sounds *indirectly* on our behalf.

Most of the time we will use the latter—indirect—approach because once the relationship of sound-effects file to object has been defined in the right place, we don't need to worry about it anymore. However, the first approach—direct activation—is more flexible. We'll look at both approaches in the remainder of this chapter.

Audio Descriptions

Audio datablocks are used no matter whether we directly or indirectly activate sounds. Audio datablocks are defined using the keyword `AudioDescription` when they are defined. Here is an example of an audio datablock:

```
new AudioDescription(AudioTest)
{
   volume    = 1.0;
   isLooping= false;
   is3D      = false;
   type      = 0;
};
```

In this example `AudioTest` is the handle to this description.

The `volume` property indicates the default volume for this channel. This property is itself not changeable, but when the audio channel is used, the volume can be changed via script statements.

The property `isLooping` indicates whether to repeat the sound after it has finished playing.

The `is3D` property is used to tell Torque whether this channel needs to be processed to produce positional information.

The `type` property is essentially the channel for this sound. All sounds on a given channel can be controlled via script statements that are channel specific.

With this datablock we have defined the nature of the `AudioTest` sound, so to speak—its characteristics. However, there's obviously not enough here to actually produce any sound. We need at least a sound file with a sample waveform in it, and then we need to associate that file with the appropriate `AudioDescription`. This is how we do it programmatically:

```
$Test = alxCreateSource("AudioTest",expandFilename("~/data/sound/test.wav"));
```

This statement creates an audio object. The first parameter is the datablock we saw earlier. The second parameter first invokes a call to the `expandFilename` function, which knows how to make sure it finds the correct full path of the file. The return value is a handle to the actual audio object created by Torque.

Now to activate the sound, we simply call the following:

```
alxPlay ($Test);
```

As you see, we just needed to tell `alxPlay` the name of the object, and away it goes.

We can adjust the volume for this playback, but we need to do it before we play the sound. We do that this way:

```
alxListenerf(AL_GAIN_LINEAR, %volume);
$Test = alxCreateSource("AudioTest",expandFilename("~/data/sound/test.wav"));
alxPlay ($Test);
```

The `alxListenerf` function sets the volume for the listener (the player) and does it using a linear (versus logarithmic) gain (amplification) adjustment. With a linear gain, a volume of 0.5 is half as loud as a volume of 1.0. With the nonlinear (logarithmic) gain, a volume of 0.5 is about two-thirds as loud as a volume of 1.0.

Note that this volume adjustment is performed on the value of the volume in the datablock, where the volume was set to 1.0.

So if we call `alxListenerf` with a volume of 0.75, then the actual volume would be 0.75 multiplied by 1.0, or 0.75—and all loudness calculations would follow from that. If we call `alxListenerf` with a volume of 0.75, and if the datablock's volume had been set to 0.5, then the actual volume would be 0.75 multiplied by 0.5, or 0.375.

Now using `alxPlay` this way is useful for sounds that have no positional information requirements, like GUI button beeps or the sound of a player's throbbing headache. But what if we want to place the sound in the game world?

In this case, we need to first create a profile:

```
new AudioProfile(AudioTestProfile)
{
   filename = "control/data/sound/test.wav";
   description = "AudioTest";
};
```

Notice that now the file name is contained in the profile. The second property, description, points to the datablock we defined earlier. We then activate the sound as follows:

```
alxPlay(AudioTestProfile, 100, 100, 100);
```

Notice now that the function call refers to the profile, not the description datablock. The three parameters that follow define a location in 3D coordinates in the game world. The sound, when played, will seem to come from that location. It's important to understand that when activating sounds in this manner, you must ensure that the sound file contains a monophonic sound and not stereo. Also, the is3D property in the datablock must be set to false.

Tip

Take note of whether you are creating the AudioDescription or AudioProfile on the client or the server.

On the client, you define it this way:

```
new AudioDescription(AudioTest)
{
};
```

and

```
new AudioProfile(AudioTestProfile)
{
}
```

If the code resides on the server, do it this way:

```
datablock AudioDescription(AudioTest)
{
};
```

and

```
datablock AudioProfile(AudioTestProfile)
{
}
```

In point of fact, this rule applies for all datablock types, because the server can only define `true` datablocks.

Trying It Out

Let's try it out, using your Emaga6 sample game. Open up your root main file (main.cs), and add the following lines to the very top:

```
new AudioDescription(AudioTest)
{
  volume   = 1.0;
  isLooping= false;
  is3D     = false;
  type     = 0;
};
new AudioProfile(AudioTestProfile)
{
  filename = "control/data/sound/rain.wav";
  description = "AudioTest";
      preload = true;
};

function AudioTestA(%volume)
{
  echo("AudioTest volume="@%volume);
  alxListenerf(AL_GAIN_LINEAR, %volume);
  $pref::Audio::masterVolume = %volume;

    $AudioTestHandleA = alxCreateSource("AudioTest",
expandFilename("control/data/sound/rain.wav"));

  echo("AudioTest object="@$AudioTestHandleA);
    alxPlay($AudioTestHandleA);

}

function AudioTestB(%volume)
{
  echo("AudioTest volume="@%volume);
  alxListenerf(AL_GAIN_LINEAR, %volume);
```

```
$pref::Audio::masterVolume = %volume;
alxPlay(AudioTestProfile, 100, 100, 100);
}
```

Now launch your game. After you've spawned in, open the console window (using the Tilde key), and type in the following:

```
AudioTestA(1.0);
```

You should hear the sound of rain falling. Play with the volume setting, trying different values less than 1.0.

Next, type this into the console window:

```
AudioTestB(1.0);
```

Here comes the rain again, but this time seeming to come from a specific direction.

Again, play with the volume setting, trying different values less than 1.0. You can also play with the 3D coordinate values in the call to `alxPlay()` in the `AudioTestB()` function.

Koob

In the following chapter and in later chapters, we will be using audio features a great deal more, so take the time in the balance of this chapter to add some more files to your sample program.

First, copy your Emaga6 directory, and name the copy "KOOB" or any other name—but I'll be using KOOB as the folder name, and Koob as the game name.

Now record a sound, any sound, in a WAV file (you could also save in Ogg Vorbis format as an OGG file—Torque and Audacity support both file formats). Make sure that the file is not a stereo file. Copy your new sound file into \KOOB\control\data\sound, and name it "test.wav".

Next, create a new script file: \KOOB\control\client\misc\sndprofiles.cs. Insert the following lines of code:

```
// Channel assignments (channel 0 is unused in-game).
$GuiAudioType     = 1;
$SimAudioType     = 2;
$MessageAudioType = 3;
```

```
new AudioDescription(AudioGui)
{
  volume    = 1.0;
  isLooping = false;
  is3D      = false;
  type      = $GuiAudioType;
};

new AudioDescription(AudioMessage)
{
  volume    = 1.0;
  isLooping = false;
  is3D      = false;
  type      = $MessageAudioType;
};

new AudioProfile(AudioButtonOver)
{
  filename = "~/data/sound/buttonOver.wav";
  description = "AudioGui";
  preload = true;
};
```

This sets up some datablocks and a profile for use on our client.

Next, create a new script file: \KOOB\control\server\misc\sndprofiles.cs. Note that the file name is the same as the last one you just created, but this time, there is a different path. Insert the following lines of code:

```
datablock AudioDescription(AudioDefault3d)
{
   volume    = 1.0;
   isLooping= false;
   is3D      = true;
   ReferenceDistance= 20.0;
   MaxDistance= 100.0;
   type      = $SimAudioType;
};

datablock AudioDescription(AudioClose3d)
{
   volume    = 1.0;
   isLooping= false;
```

```
   is3D     = true;
   ReferenceDistance= 10.0;
   MaxDistance= 60.0;
   type     = $SimAudioType;
};

datablock AudioDescription(AudioClosest3d)
{
   volume   = 1.0;
   isLooping= false;
   is3D     = true;
   ReferenceDistance= 5.0;
   MaxDistance= 30.0;
   type      = $SimAudioType;
};

// Looping sounds
datablock AudioDescription(AudioDefaultLooping3d)
{
   volume   = 1.0;
   isLooping= true;
   is3D     = true;
   ReferenceDistance= 20.0;
   MaxDistance= 100.0;
   type      = $SimAudioType;
};

datablock AudioDescription(AudioCloseLooping3d)
{
   volume    = 1.0;
   isLooping= true;
   is3D      = true;
   ReferenceDistance= 10.0;
   MaxDistance= 50.0;
   type      = $SimAudioType;
};

datablock AudioDescription(AudioClosestLooping3d)
{
   volume    = 1.0;
   isLooping= true;
   is3D      = true;
   ReferenceDistance= 5.0;
```

```
        MaxDistance= 30.0;
        type      = $SimAudioType;
};


// Used for non-looping environmental sounds (like power on, power off)
datablock AudioDescription(Audio2D)
{
    volume = 1.0;
    isLooping = false;
    is3D = false;
    type = $SimAudioType;
};

datablock AudioDescription(AudioLooping2D)
{
    volume = 1.0;
    isLooping = true;
    is3D = false;
    type = $SimAudioType;
};
```

All of this sets up some datablocks for the server—we will use them in the next chapter. I include them here for you to peruse within the context of what we've covered in this chapter. For practice, you can try various calls to alxPlay and create some profiles that use these descriptions.

Moving Right Along

In this chapter you've explored a new tool—this time for dealing with sound. You've learned how to create and export a WAV file for use in a game and then how to insert a sound into a Torque game. You've also seen how you can adjust a sound using TorqueScript, as well as position a sound in the 3D game world.

In the next chapter we'll look at sound effects in the game world in more detail.

CHAPTER 20

GAME SOUND
AND MUSIC

In the last chapter you saw how to create and edit sounds using Audacity. We're now going to move to the next level, using those sounds for effects initiated by the player, by weapons and ammo, by vehicles, and by places and things in the world at large.

Also, we'll touch on the issue of in-game music and how you can use it. I'm not going to even attempt to teach you how to compose music—that's far out of scope for this book. However, I will include some musical pieces on the CD that you are free to experiment with as we look at the issue. You can find them in RESOURCES\CH20\MUSIC. They are in Ogg Vorbis format (fully compatible with Torque), and by three promising game music composers: The Thevenin, Deffmute, and Black Blaze. You can find more of their work, and the work of others for free at http://www.download.com by following the links to the Music>Electronic & Dance>Electronic>Game Soundtracks section.

Player Sounds

In a first-person shooter-styled game, player sounds add to the sense of "being there," sometimes in a big way. There are two kinds of player sounds: world sounds and client-only sounds.

World sounds are effects that are generated on the server that represent sound effects emitted by your player-avatar in the game world. In this sense, they are much the analogue of the way you emit sounds in real life: walking, talking, firing

791

weapons, banging on doors, and so on. The server places a sound effect "in the world" at your location and then updates all the affected clients so that they will emit the sound (if the client's player-avatars are close enough to hear the sound) as it was made, with appropriate modifications, such as attenuation because of distance or Doppler effect due to the sound source moving toward or away from the listener.

These sorts of sounds are usually called *3D sounds*. The actual sound effects have no inherent 3D characteristics, but the game client handles them in a manner that imparts 3D positional information to each client.

Client-only sounds are those sounds that a player's avatar makes that really only matter to the player. These can be personal noises, like the sounds of heavy breathing to portray exertion, the sound of something being hit by a bullet, or the rustle of clothing. Nothing is cut-and-dried though. You might want to use the sounds in some of those examples as world sounds in order to perhaps betray the location of a player who is sneaking around in the dark. It all depends on your game play design.

Some sounds can be attached to the player, like the sounds of footsteps, triggered by a frame in the animation. The MilkShape DTS Exporter supports this capability, and we created footstep triggers with our model back in Chapter 14.

However, that being said, there is a way for us to handle attached sound effects like footsteps using program code, and that's what we'll be doing in the next section, except we will be making our clothes rustle instead.

Other sounds can be emitted in an ad hoc fashion, wherever and whenever we want. Some examples of these sorts of sounds are utterances or taunts. You press a key, and your player's avatar utters a taunt of some sort, such as "Loser!" or "Ha ha, ya missed me!" You can also use ad hoc sounds to issue prerecorded audible commands. The limits are your imagination. Heck, you could have your player carry around a boom box and play annoying music!

When you use world sounds, you also have the choice of using them in 3D mode, where the sound is played on all the clients as if they were emanating from a specific location in the game world, or in 2D mode, where the server still directs the clients to play the sounds, but they have no positional quality to them.

Before we get started, there is a small change to make to your code to fully incorporate the sound profiles we did back in Chapter 19. Open \KOOB\control\ server\server.cs, find the function OnServerCreated, and inside it, locate the line

```
Exec("./misc/camera.cs");
```

And immediately *above* it, insert the following line:

```
Exec("./misc/sndprofiles.cs");
```

That little number makes sure that the sound profiles we created at the end of Chapter 19 actually get loaded up when the server starts. If you feel the urge, save your work, and then go run Koob now. You will finally hear the rain and thunder.

Rustlers

In our first example we are going to use the serverPlay3D function to make rustling clothing for our player. Each time the player takes a step, his pants swish together and the arms of his jacket rustle against his sides. First, you should record some rustling. Just a single recording will be enough, if you like, but if you record a half dozen or so different versions that are all similar though slightly different, you can offer a more natural sound effect by randomly choosing which sound to play for a given footfall. Make sure to record the sound at 22050 Hz or maybe even 11025 Hz to keep the file size fairly small. Save the sound as \KOOB\control\data\sound\rustle1.wav.

After you have the sound effect made, you need to add the following code in \KOOB\control\server\players\player.cs at the start of the file (after the line that reads: exec("~/data/models/avatars/orc/player.cs");).

```
datablock AudioProfile(Rustle1)
{
  fileName = "~/data/sound/rustle1.wav";
  description = AudioClosest3d;
  preload = true;
};

function serverCmdStartRustle(%client)
{
 %client.player.schedule(200,playRustle);
 %client.player.rustleon= true;
}
function serverCmdStopRustle(%client)
{
 %client.player.rustleon = false;
}
```

```
function Player::playRustle( %this )
{
  if(%this.rustleon)
  {
    serverPlay3D(Rustle1,%this.getTransform());
    %this.schedule(500,playRustle);
  }
}
```

First, there is an AudioProfile datablock. This datablock tells the engine where the sound effect is and which AudioDescription to use. The particular AudioDescription in question already resides in \KOOB\control\server\misc\sndprofiles.cs and looks like the following (*do not* type this in because we already created it back in Chapter 19):

```
datablock AudioDescription(AudioClosest3d)
{
  volume  = 1.0;
  isLooping= false;

  is3D    = true;
  ReferenceDistance= 5.0;
  MaxDistance= 60.0;
  type    = $SimAudioType;
};
```

The next thing in the new code we added was a message handler for receiving a message from a client. We defined the message in this case to be StartRustle, and our only parameter is the handle to the client that sends the message. That handler makes a call to a method of the Player object called schedule. This schedules a function execution event for processing sometime later. We also set the flag %client.player.rustleon to true for future reference. The event delay is set to 200 milliseconds, or a fifth of a second, in the future. You can change this value to something else or even have it vary according to movement speed. At the appointed time, that function, playRustle, is called, and provided that the %this.rustleon property is set to true, it executes the serverPlay3D function. Note that in this case, %this is set to be the handle of the object the method is being called for. That object is the Player object, which happens to be exactly the same object as %client.player, and it's a good thing that it is, too!

The way serverPlay3D works is that it accepts an AudioProfile and 3D coordinates in the world space. Conveniently we can get those coordinates from a simple call to getTransform. The serverPlay3D function then internally tells all clients to play that sound effect at those world coordinates.

And hey, presto! You have a rustle.

Before exiting playRustle, the schedule method is called again to schedule another rustle in half a second. It will keep doing this until told to stop. You tell it to stop by using the stopRustle message, whose handler merely sets %client.player.rustleon to false, so that the next time playRustle is called, the flag is found to be false, the sound is played, and the event isn't rescheduled.

So that's the guts of getting the sounds to play, but we still need to deal with *when* to play them. We want the steps to happen when the player is running and to stop when he stops moving.

We can easily do this as part of the work-around by trapping the keyboard inputs that tell the player to move and stop. The function that does this is a client-side function located in \KOOB\control\client\misc\presetkeys.cs.

Open that file, and locate the function GoAhead, which looks like this:

```
function GoAhead(%val)
//-----------------------------------------------------------------
// running forward
//-----------------------------------------------------------------
{
   $mvForwardAction = %val;
}
```

Change it to this:

```
function GoAhead(%val)
//-----------------------------------------------------------------
// running forward
//-----------------------------------------------------------------
{
   $mvForwardAction = %val;
   if (%val)
     commandToServer('startRustle');
   else
     commandToServer('stopRustle');
}
```

In GoAhead the parameter %val is nonzero when the key that has been mapped to this function is being pressed, and it is zero when the key is released. Therefore, the simple if-else code block will send the startRustle message to the server when the GoAhead key is pressed and the stopRustle message when it is released. The GoAhead key is defined later in the same file to be the w key.

If you like, you can pop into Koob and check out the rustling clothes. I'll be here when you get back.

Now if you have been browsing around \KOOB\control\server\sndProfiles.cs looking at the datablocks in there, you might have come across another work-around you're tempted to try—the AudioClosestLooping3d datablock. You might look at that and say to yourself, "Self, that has looping *built in*. No need to fool with scheduling events on a repeating basis." And you would be right in making that deduction. However, there is a problem with that approach. Once you trigger that sound effect at a particular location, it will continue looping, all right—but *at the same location*. The rustling won't follow your player.

Like I said earlier, the absolute best way to do these kinds of repetitive player sounds is to attach them to the player's movement animations via triggers in the model. However, this approach, while inferior to triggered footsteps, is actually a pretty convenient way to add repetitive sounds like clinking armor, clattering ammo cans, jingling change, and what have you.

Footsteps

You're probably tired of having your orc fella gliding along with what seems like gossamer wings, when you know darn well that he's tromping along just in that way that orcs do. Well, let's put some code in there to hear his tromping.

First, find the file footstep1.ogg in the RESOURCES\CH20 folder, and copy it to \KOOB\control\data\sound.

Next, use UltraEdit to open \KOOB\control\server\players\player.cs. Locate the datablock definition for the MaleAvatar that starts with this line:

```
datablock PlayerData(MaleAvatar)
```

Scroll down to the end of the datablock, and just after the line that says:

```
maxInv[CrossbowAmmo] = 20;
```

Type in the following code:

```
FootSoftSound      = FootLightSoftSound;
FootHardSound      = FootLightHardSound;
```

```
FootMetalSound       = FootLightMetalSound;
FootSnowSound        = FootLightSnowSound;
FootShallowSound     = FootLightShallowSplashSound;
FootWadingSound      = FootLightWadingSound;
FootUnderwaterSound  = FootLightUnderwaterSound;
```

These are properties of the PlayerData datablock, and we are pointing them to various audioprofile datablocks for different flavors of footsteps. So now we need to put those datablocks in as well.

So, in that same file, type the following, inserting it just above the code you typed in for the rustling clothes:

```
datablock AudioProfile(FootLightSoftSound)
{
  filename   = "~/data/sound/footstep1.ogg";
  description = AudioClosest3d;
  preload = true;
};
datablock AudioProfile(FootLightHardSound)
{
  filename   = "~/data/sound/footstep1.ogg";
  description = AudioClose3d;
  preload    = true;
};
datablock AudioProfile(FootLightMetalSound)
{
  filename   = "~/data/sound/footstep1.ogg";
  description = AudioClose3d;
  preload    = true;
};
datablock AudioProfile(FootLightSnowSound)
{
  filename   = "~/data/sound/footstep1.ogg";
  description = AudioClosest3d;
  preload    = true;
};
datablock AudioProfile(FootLightShallowSplashSound)
{
  filename   = "~/data/sound/footstep1.ogg";
  description = AudioClose3d;
  preload    = true;
};
```

```
datablock AudioProfile(FootLightWadingSound)
{
  filename    = "~/data/sound/footstep1.ogg";
  description = AudioClose3d;
  preload     = true;
};
datablock AudioProfile(FootLightUnderwaterSound)
{
  filename    = "~/data/sound/footstep1.ogg";
  description = AudioClosest3d;
  preload     = true;
};
```

Save your work, and go fire up Koob. You should be able to hear the running footsteps and the rustling clothes. Notice that you will hear the footsteps no matter which way you run, but you can only hear the rustling when you run forward. The footsteps are handled by animation triggers in the sequence files for the model. You, of course, are responsible for the rustling. It shouldn't take you too long to get the rustling happening for sideways and backwards movement as well as the forward movement.

Utterances

Let's make our avatar guy say something, something that other players can hear, by pressing a key. The process is going to be similar in some ways to the rustling clothes.

First, make another recording, at the sample rate of your choosing. Holler something into the mike, like, "Your mother wears army boots!" or something equally endearing. Save it as \KOOB\control\data\sound\insult1.wav.

Then add the following code in \KOOB\control\server\players\player.cs at the end of the file.

```
datablock AudioProfile(Insult1)
{
  fileName = "~/data/sound/insult1.wav";
  description = AudioClose3d;
  preload = true;
};

function serverCmdHurlInsult(%client)
```

```
{
  serverPlay3D(Insult1,%client.player.getTransform());
}
```

In this code, serverCmdHurlInsult is the message handler on the server that receives a direct message sent from the client (which we will get to just a little further on). There is noticeably less stuff than for the rustling clothes, because we don't need to loop the sound effect. We just hurl our insult and maybe run for cover after that! Now, notice that the profile uses a different AudioDescription. This time it's AudioClose3d. (Don't type this in—it's already in \KOOB\control\ server\misc\sndProfiles.cs.)

```
datablock AudioDescription(AudioClose3d)
{
  volume    = 1.0;
  isLooping= false;

  is3D      = true;
  ReferenceDistance= 10.0;
  MaxDistance= 60.0;
  type      = $SimAudioType;
};
```

The reason for using this datablock is because it defines a sound effect that can be heard from farther away. The ReferenceDistance is 10 world units. This means that the sound effect *attenuates* (the volume decreases) over a longer distance, so it can be heard from farther away than the rustling clothes.

Next, we need to send the message from the client to the server so that the server can then notify all the other clients. We'll do that again with a client-side function that we'll call Yell.

Open \KOOB\control\client\misc\presetkeys.cs, and add the following to the end:

```
function Yell(%val)
{
  if (%val)
    commandToServer('HurlInsult');
}
PlayerKeymap.bind(keyboard, "y", Yell);
```

The function sends the HurlInsult message to the server, but only when the key is pressed (%val is nonzero), not when it's released. Then we need to bind a key to press to trigger the whole thing. We use `PlayerKeymap.bind` to do that, pointing it to the `Yell` function.

There you go—you're in business.

T i p

You might have trouble hearing your insults over the sound of the crashing lightning. If so, you can simply rename the datablocks that the `Precipitation` (`RainStorm`) and `Lightning` (`ElectricalStorm`) objects in your mission file point to. Just open \KOOB\ control\data\maps\book_ch6.mis and scroll down to the bottom where you inserted those two storm objects (in the last chapter). In each object's definition, look for a line that starts with "`datablock =`" and put a letter in front of the datablock name like this: "xLightningStorm". Any letter will do. This will cause the engine to not find the datablock, and therefore not create the storm objects. To restore your storm objects, just remove those letters you inserted.

Another way to stop the thunder from interfering is to open the console, and type (assuming you did not change the datablock pointers as described in the last paragraph):

`ElectricalStorm.strikesperminute=1;`

This will change the thunderstorm so that only one strike happens roughly every minute. Do not set the `strikeperminute` property to 0, however! This will cause an "inifinite" number of thundercrashes to happen all at once.

One more variation you should try is recording several different insults and saving them as insult1.wav, insult2.wav, insult3.wav, and so on. Let's go ahead and record five additional different insults.

Now make five more different `AudioProfiles` that have incremental names starting with `Insult2` and ending with `Insult6`. Each should uniquely point at one of the six recordings you made. Then inside the message handler use a bit of random number code to pick a number between 1 and 6.

`%n=getRandom(5) + 1;`

This will pick an integer between 0 and 5. Now increment it by 1 so that the result will be between 1 and 6.

Then rewrite the call to `serverPlay3D` to look like this:

`serverPlay3D("Insult" @ %n, %client.player.getTransform());`

This will modify the name of the `AudioProfile` by putting the random number at the end. Then every time you hurl the insult, a different epithet will be directed with withering precision on your foe. Fun for the whole family!

While we're at it, you might want to hear what utterances a dying orc makes (it's gruesome), so add the following to the top of the file \KOOB\control\server\players\player.cs, above all those AudioProfile datablocks you typed in earlier for the rustling clothes and footsteps:

```
datablock AudioProfile(DeathCrySound)
{
  fileName = "~/data/sound/orc_death.ogg";
  description = AudioClose3d;
  preload = true;
};

datablock AudioProfile(PainCrySound)
{
  fileName = "~/data/sound/orc_pain.ogg";
  description = AudioClose3d;
  preload = true;
};
```

And add the following to the very end of that same file:

```
function Player::playDeathCry( %this )
{
  %this.playAudio(0,DeathCrySound);
}

function Player::playPain( %this )
{
  %this.playAudio(0,PainCrySound);
}
```

Don't close the file just yet—one more change to go. While still in player.cs, locate the function MaleAvatar::onDisabled and type these two lines in at the start of the function, after the opening brace:

```
%obj.playDeathCry();
%obj.playDeathAnimation();
```

That's a wrap. Save your work.

Death sounds and pain sounds. Oh joy. Well, if we want to actually hear those in all their excruciating, um, excruciatingness, we'll need some sound files too. Copy orc_pain.ogg and orc_death.ogg from RESOURCES\CH20 to \KOOB\control\data\sound. Then go and find an enemy orc to kill you, or shoot exploding bolts at the ground at your feet until you die. Naturally it's a little weird getting plonked by an orc, or blowing your feet up, without any sound for the explosions. Well, that just happens to be covered next. . .

Weapon Sounds

Weapon sounds are an interesting study. Weapons have specific support in Torque, through the use of a programming construct called a *state machine*. The basic idea is that we break the operation of a weapon down into different stages, called *states*, and we define a specific set of behaviors for each state. Within each state, we are not aware of what the previous state was, only what needs to be done in this state.

Using this system, we can quite readily define some rather complex behaviors.

Before continuing, there is some preparatory work that needs to be done first.

Installing the Mission Editor

As we've grown our sample game, starting back in Chapter 4, moving through the various Emaga mutations, and on into Koob, one body of code that has been deliberately ignored is the Mission Editor code. Now is the time for us to stop ignoring it. The Mission Editor code body is quite extensive and complex. I'll not be diving into the code much, but we do need to get it running, so there are some non-trivial edits to make to get it working.

If you will recall, back in Chapter 10, I included a note in the Torque GUI Editor section that instructed you in setting up that editor for use with Emaga6 by copying the `creator` folder from \3D2E to \Emaga6 and applying some edits. If you applied those changes, then we're ready to proceed with the rest of the preparations for the Mission Editor. If you didn't, please slog on back to Chapter 10, to "The Torque GUI Editor" section, and follow the instructions in the note near the start of that section before advancing beyond this point.

Next, we have to make some changes to a few files in the creator code to integrate the various creator-based editors with our sample game.

In the file \3D2E\creator\editor\editor.cs, locate the line (near the bottom of the file):

```
Editor.close("PlayGui");
```

And change it to:

```
Editor.close("PlayerInterface");
```

Save the file.

Next, make the exact same change in a *different* file. This time make the change in the file \3D2E\creator\editor\EditorGui.cs—the line is located roughly one-quarter of the way into the file.

Then, keeping the EditorGui.cs file open, locate the line (about one-third of the way into the file) in the EditorGui::onWake function:

```
MoveMap.push();
```

And change it to:

```
PlayerKeymap.push();
```

Right after that is the EditorGui::onSleep function, and we need to make the same change. Find:

```
MoveMap.pop();
```

And change it to:

```
PlayerKeymap.pop();
```

After that, open the file \KOOB\control\client\Initialize.cs, and scroll down to the function (near the top of the file) called InitializeClient. Inside this function, locate the line that says:

```
Exec("./interfaces/serverscreen.gui");
```

And add these lines after it:

```
Exec("./interfaces/chatbox.gui");
Exec("./interfaces/messagebox.gui");
```

And our final change for this section: in the same function, scroll down a bit and locate the line that says:

```
Exec("./client.cs");
```

And add these lines after it:

```
exec("./misc/chatbox.cs");
exec("./misc/messagebox.cs");
```

There, that's that bit done.

Remapping Keys

The Settings screen (accessed by clicking on the Setup button on the main menu) works like the Options screen in the Torque Demo. All of the functionality is already there, as a result of the work you did in Chapter 18. All of the functionality, except one bit, that is—remapping the key command bindings.

The key bindings are already pre-defined (*hard coded*) in the file \KOOB\control\client\misc\presetkeys.cs (this module is functionally the same as \3D2E\demo\client\scripts\default.bind.cs in the Torque Demo). This is how we can ensure that there will always be key bindings for the commands that absolutely need them. But we also may want to allow our users to redefine the bindings, and that is what the Controls tab in the Settings screen is for.

When the changes are made, the user's key bindings are saved to \3D2E\control\client\config.cs. When the game restarts, it should load config.cs module *after* it has loaded the presetkeys.cs file, thus overriding the predefined key bindings with the user's choices. To get the game to actually do this, you need to open up \3D2E\control\client\initialize.cs and in the `InitializeClient` function, immediately below the line about loading presetkeys.cs, insert this line:

```
Exec("./config.cs");
```

You are also going to need a button on your main menu screen in order to access the Settings screen. Open \3D2E\control\client\interfaces\mainmenu.gui and locate the last line that consists of a closing brace/semicolon pair } ; and place the following code *above* that line:

```
new GuiButtonCtrl() {
   command = "Canvas.pushDialog(SetupScreen);";
   text = "Setup";
};
```

That is what I call a minimalist button control! Only the text of the button and the command it needs to execute are specified. All the other properties receive default values from Torque. This means that the button will appear at the upper-left corner of your screen, and it won't be sized to match the other buttons. Have no fear! You can use the GUI Editor (invoked by the F10 key) to move and resize your button, and so on. Or you can peruse the other button controls in mainmenu.gui and let them guide you in making the changes manually in code.

Oh, and by the way—I'm leaving the actual implementation of the key remapping as an exercise for the reader. But I'm not *that* evil. The Settings screen is already functional; there's only the actual key remapping that needs to be made to work. Here are some clues: you need to copy the file remapdialog.gui from the Chapter 20 resources folder into one of the folders in \KOOB\control. You will also need to add a line of code to ensure that the file is loaded and run during the initialization of the game. Look elsewhere in this section, in this chapter, and maybe even back to Chapter 18 for some guidance, if you need to.

Crossbow Sounds

We're going to make your tommy gun from an earlier chapter generate its sound effects, but before we do that, let's get the sound humming along for the Orc's crossbow. From your RESOURCES\CH20 folder, copy the following files to your \KOOB\control\data\sound folder:

```
ammo_pickup.wav
crossbow_explosion.ogg
crossbow_firing.ogg
crossbow_firing_empty.ogg
crossbow_reload.ogg
```

Next, copy RESOURCES\CH20\crossbow.cs to the \KOOB\control\server\ weapons folder. You should get a message box asking you if you want to replace the existing file. Click on Yes. Then run your KOOB game, go grab a crossbow and some ammo, and go make lots of explosions.

The difference between the two crossbow.cs files is that the new one contains all of the audio profile declarations that we need. Now go ahead and jump into the game and make some big booms. You know you want to.

Tommy Gun Preparation

To set up for getting the tommy gun sounds going, go find the tommy gun model you created back in Chapter 16, and copy the model (the DTS file) and the artwork (the PNG file) that goes with the model to \KOOB\control\data\ models\weapons\. Then go to the folder \3D2E\RESOURCES\CH20\ and copy the file tommygun.cs into \KOOB\control\server\weapons\.

Next, from the same resources directory, copy the following files to \KOOB\control\ data\models\weapons\:

```
ammo.jpg
bullethole.png
muzzleflash.png
tgammo.dts
tgprojectile.dts
tgshell.dts
```

Now for the sounds. I'm not going to make you record your own sounds. You can copy them from the same resources directory.

```
ammo_pickup.wav
dryfire.wav
shortreload.wav
tommygun.wav
weapon_pickup.wav
weapon_switch.wav
```

Deposit these sound files into \KOOB\control\data\sound\.

Now open the file \KOOB\control\server\server.cs, and find the function
OnServerCreated at the start of the file. Inside that function is a block of Exec()
statements. Insert the following at the bottom of that block of statements, after
the line about the crossbow:

```
Exec("./weapons/tommygun.cs");
```

This tells the engine to load our tommy gun definition file.

Next, open the file \KOOB\control\server\players\player.cs, and near the
beginning of the file, find the line that reads as follows:

```
datablock PlayerData(MaleAvatar)
```

At the end of the datablock that starts with that line, before the closing brace ("}")
that ends the datablock, insert the following lines:

```
maxInv[Tommygun] = 1;
maxInv[TommygunAmmo] = 20;
```

This indicates how many of the listed items the player can have in his possession,
or inventory, at any given time.

And finally, open the file you copied earlier, \KOOB\control\server\weapons\
tommygun.cs, and at the *very top* of the file add the following lines:

```
datablock AudioProfile(TommyGunMountSound)
{
  filename   = "~/data/sound/shortreload.wav";
  description = AudioClose3d;
  preload = true;
};

datablock AudioProfile(TommyGunReloadSound)
{
  filename   = "~/data/sound//Weapon_pickup.wav";
  description = AudioClose3d;
  preload = true;
};

datablock AudioProfile(TommyGunFireSound)
{
  filename   = "~/data/sound/tommygun.wav";
  description = AudioClose3d;
  preload = true;
};
```

```
datablock AudioProfile(TommyGunDryFireSound)
{
  filename   = "~/data/sound/dryfire.wav";
  description = AudioClose3d;
  preload = true;
};

datablock AudioProfile(WeaponSwitchSound)
{
  filename   = "~/data/sound/Weapon_switch.wav";
  description = AudioClose3d;
  preload = true;
};
```

And now, add the following rather long datablock to the *end* of \\KOOB\control\ server\weapons\tommygun.cs

```
//------------------------------------------------------------------------
// TommyGun image which does all the work.  Images do not normally exist in
// the world, they can only be mounted on ShapeBase objects.

datablock ShapeBaseImageData(TommyGunImage)
{
  shapeFile = "~/data/models/weapons/TommyGun.dts";
  offset = "0 0 0";
  mountPoint = 0;
  emap = true;

  className = "WeaponImage";

  item = TommyGun;
  ammo = TommyGunAmmo;
  projectile = TommyGunProjectile;
  projectileType = Projectile;
  casing = TommyGunShell;
  armThread = "look2";

  // State Data
  stateName[0]                  = "Preactivate";
  stateTransitionOnLoaded[0]    = "Activate";
  stateTransitionOnNoAmmo[0]    = "NoAmmo";
  stateName[1]                  = "Activate";
  stateTransitionOnTimeout[1]   = "Ready";
```

```
stateTimeoutValue[1]                  = 0.7;
stateSequence[1]                      = "Activated";
stateSound[1]                         = WeaponSwitchSound;

stateName[2]                          = "Ready";
stateTransitionOnNoAmmo[2]            = "NoAmmo";
stateTransitionOnTriggerDown[2]       = "Fire";
stateScript[2]                        = "onReady";
stateTransitionOnReload[2]            = "Reload";

stateName[3]                          = "Fire";
stateTransitionOnTimeout[3]           = "Ready";
stateTimeoutValue[3]                  = 0.096;
stateFire[3]                          = true;
stateRecoil[3]                        = LightRecoil;
stateAllowImageChange[3]              = false;
stateSequence[3]                      = "Fire";
stateScript[3]                        = "onFire";
stateSound[3]                         = TommyGunFireSound;
stateEmitter[3]                       = TommyGunFireEmitter;
stateEmitterTime[3]                   = 1.0;
stateEmitterNode[3]                   = "muzzlePoint";

stateName[4]                          = "Reload";
stateTransitionOnNoAmmo[4]            = "NoAmmo";
stateTransitionOnTimeout[4]           = "FinishedReloading";
stateTimeoutValue[4]                  = 3.5; // 0.25 load, 0.25 spinup
stateAllowImageChange[4]              = false;
stateSequence[4]                      = "Reload";
stateScript[4]                        = "onReload";
stateSound[4]                         = TommyGunReloadSound;

stateName[5]                          = "FinishedReloading";
stateTransitionOnTimeout[5]           = "Activate";
stateTimeoutValue[5]                  = 0.04;
stateScript[5]                        = "onFinishedReloading";

stateName[6]                          = "NoAmmo";
stateTransitionOnAmmo[6]              = "Reload";
stateSequence[6]                      = "NoAmmo";
stateScript[6]                        = "onNoAmmo";
stateTransitionOnTriggerDown[6]       = "DryFire";
```

```
stateName[7]                    = "DryFire";
stateSound[7]                   = TommyGunDryFireSound;
stateScript[7]                  = "onDryFire";
stateTimeoutValue[7]            = 0.5;
stateTransitionOnTimeout[7]     = "NoAmmo";

stateName[8]                    = "WaitTriggerRelease";
stateScript[8]                  = "onWaitTriggerRelease";
stateTransitionOnTimeout[8]     = "WaitTriggerRelease";
stateTimeoutValue[8]            = 0.01;
stateTransitionOnTriggerUp[8]   = "Ready";

autoFire            = true;
weaponDamage        = 60;
minSpread           = 0.01;
maxSpread           = 0.045;
spreadRate          = 0.019;   // amount spread should increase per shot
spreadRecoverRate   = 0.003;
};
```

The first thing this new code does is define a bunch of audio profiles, TommyGun
MountSound, TommyGunReloadSound, TommyGunFireSound, TommyGunDryFireSound,
and WeaponSwitchSound. These profiles are used in each of the different weapon
firing states. Those states are defined in the next part of the new code.

That next part is a datablock of the type ShapeBaseImageData. This is what defines
the gun itself and how it works.

First, there is a set of basic properties, like where to find the model that represents
the image and so on. For this example, I have used the same model as the one that
is used for the external view—the view of your player-model that everyone else
sees. You, though, only see the weapon image. This means that to do this right,
you will need to make another model of the weapon for use in this image. Later
on you will see why this matters.

Now we add the WeaponImage namespace as a parent. The WeaponImage namespace
provides some hooks into the inventory system that are necessary for picking up
the gun.

Next are a bunch of pointers that tell what various resources we will need in order
to use this gun.

Finally, we encounter the code that defines the state machine. What happens is that when you pick up the gun, the Torque Engine sets it to the first state: Preactivate.

In the Preactivate state, we have only two variables, and they tell the state machine what to do immediately next. If the gun is loaded, it should change to the Activate state; if not, it should change to the NoAmmo state. If you scroll down until you find the line that says stateName[6] = "NoAmmo"; you will find that state's definition.

In the NoAmmo state, there are several directives that the engine must follow while in this state. If we suddenly receive some ammo, then we change to the Reload state. If the gun's trigger is pressed, we enter the DryFire state. Note that there is also a pointer to a function (the onNoAmmo function) that we can execute when we find ourselves in this state. This can also be called the *state handler*.

All the rest of the states operate in a similar way, and the directives are quite easy to read and follow. The important ones for this chapter are the stateSound directives, which tell the engine what audio profiles to use when we arrive in that state.

The state machine definition in the TommyGunImage datablock you've just seen is really quite easy to follow. You can modify it in all sorts of ways to accommodate any variation you might imagine.

Now after getting \KOOB\control\server\weapons\tommygun.cs typed in and double-checking it all, you're going to want to test it out. Well in order to do that, you will need to be able to place objects in the mission. And that means having the freedom to go where you want, and that means you'll need to be able to use the camera fly mode, just like you do in the Torque demo. Well, the code for that is in the scripts, but the key bindings aren't. So that means we'll have to add the key bindings. This is a good opportunity to try out the new Setup button.

Launch Koob, and click on the Setup button in your main menu screen. Next, click on the Controls button, then scroll down to the very bottom of the list of controls.

Double-click on the "Toggle Camera" entry, then press the F6 key when the little dialog box saying REMAP "Toggle Camera" pops up. Next, in the same way, assign F8 to "Drop Camera at Player". Finally, use F7 for "Drop Player at Camera".

By the way: "Drop Camera at Player" is the same as entering camera fly mode.

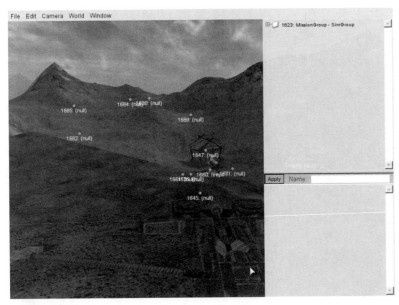

Figure 20.1
World Editor.

Launch your Koob game. Once you have spawned in, you are going to use the
World Editor to insert a tommy gun and some ammo into the game world.

1. Press F8. This will set your player into camera fly mode.

2. Press F11. This will open up the World Editor, as shown in Figure 20.1.

3. Press F4. This will open up the World Editor Creator, as shown in Figure 20.2.
   The Creator pane is circled at the lower-right corner of the window.

4. In the Creator pane, click the plus sign next to Shapes. This will expand the
   listing.

5. Locate Weapon, and click the plus sign to open it as well. You should now
   have a Tree view similar to Figure 20.3.

6. Make sure that the center of the view is located in an open area about 10
   virtual feet in front of you. To move the view in the World Editor, hold
   down the right mouse button, and move the mouse.

7. Click Tommygun in the Tree view. The tommy gun model will appear;
   it will probably be somewhat embedded in the ground, as shown in
   Figure 20.4, and it will be rotating.

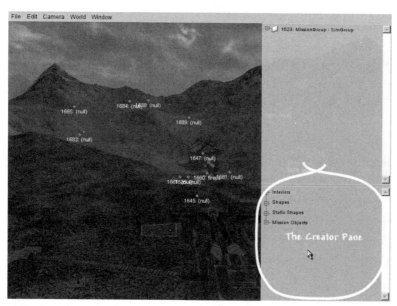

Figure 20.2
World Editor Creator.

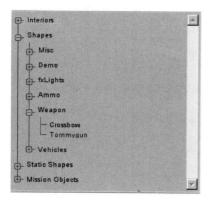

Figure 20.3
The Creator Tree view.

8. Move the cursor over on top of the vertical axis line (labeled Z) that sprouts from the top of the gun model. The Z-axis label will become highlighted, as shown in Figure 20.5.

9. Click the vertical Z-axis line, and drag it up just a few pixels, until the gun is completely out of the ground, as depicted in Figure 20.6.

Note that this is the reason why you needed to switch to camera fly mode before entering the World Editor. If you had stayed in normal

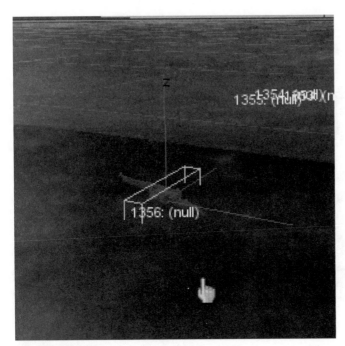

Figure 20.4
Tommy gun model.

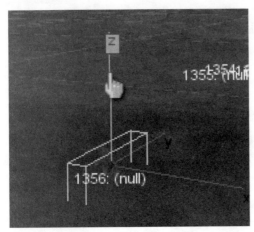

Figure 20.5
The Z-axis label.

FPS view mode, you would not have been able to grab the Z-axis line and move it.

10. Now turn your view slightly to the side, and repeat the same process by placing an ammo box, as shown in Figure 20.7. The ammo box can be found in the Tree view at Shapes, Ammo, TommygunAmmo.

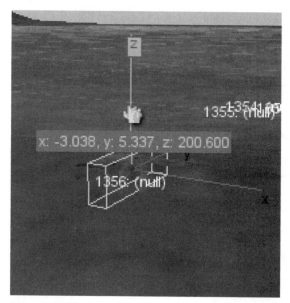

Figure 20.6
Repositioned tommy gun.

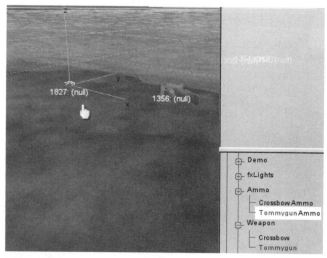

Figure 20.7
Placing ammo box.

Tip

You should consider placing lots and lots of ammo boxes. Submachine guns like the tommy gun go through ammo at a prodigious rate! If you do put lots of ammo boxes in, you might consider modifying the player datablock so that the player can have more tommy gun ammo in his inventory.

11. Now press F11 to toggle out of the World Editor. If you are in camera fly mode, press F6 to toggle yourself back into your character.

Okay, now run on over and pick up the ammo and the tommy gun by just passing right over on top of them. Take note, don't pick up the crossbow first, because you have no way of getting rid of it. Also, wait several seconds after you have picked up both the gun and the ammo before actually trying to shoot. There is a several seconds delay in the sequence to simulate the time it takes to mount the magazine in the gun, pull back the charging handle, and so on.

You will immediately notice that the gun doesn't carry properly. However, go ahead and shoot it, and listen to the firing sequence and all the sounds we've been dealing with. You can make another model to act as the mounted (carried) version of the gun. Also, you will need to adjust your model animations to ensure the model will carry the gun properly—the provided example character doesn't do that.

You can go back to your ShapeBaseImageData in the tommygun.cs file and fiddle with the state machine and other variables and see how they affect your gun's behavior.

Vehicle Sounds

Vehicles are obvious sound sources. An idling engine, squealing tires, whirring propellers—the kind of vehicle dictates the needs. Torque has several defined vehicle types, but we'll just look at the wheeled vehicle and add some sound effects to the runabout.

To start, you will need to record sound effects for the following:

- engine idle

- acceleration

- wheel impact

- wheel squeal

- soft crash

- hard crash

In lieu of creating your own, feel free to use the sounds that I have provided at \3D2E\RESOURCES\CH20\. Deposit the files into \KOOB\control\data\sound\.

Next, copy the car definition module, \3D2E\RESOURCES\CH20\car.cs, to \KOOB\control\server\vehicles. If the directory doesn't exist, create it.

Then copy your runabout model (from Chapters 9 and 15) and all its artwork into \KOOB\control\data\models\vehicles. Again, if the directory doesn't exist, create it. Make sure your runabout is named runabout.dts and the wheel model is named wheel.dts. Your texture files would be runabout.jpg and wheel.jpg, unless you used different names.

Now open the file \KOOB\control\server\server.cs, and find the function OnServerCreated at the start of the file. Inside that function is a block of Exec() statements. Insert the following at the bottom of that block of statements:

```
Exec("./vehicles/car.cs");
```

This tells the game engine to load your car definition file.

And finally, open that very same definition file, \KOOB\control\server\vehicles\car.cs, and add the following lines to the beginning, just in front of the TireParticleParticleData datablock:

```
datablock AudioProfile(CarSoftImpactSound)
{
  filename    = "~/data/sound/vcrunch.ogg";
  description = AudioClose3d;
  preload = true;
};


datablock AudioProfile(CarHardImpactSound)
{
  filename    = "~/data/sound/vcrash.ogg";
  description = AudioClose3d;
  preload = true;
};


datablock AudioProfile(CarWheelImpactSound)
{
  filename    = "~/data/sound/impact.ogg";
  description = AudioClose3d;
  preload = true;
};
```

```
datablock AudioProfile(CarThrustSound)
{
  filename    = "~/data/sound/caraccel.ogg";
  description = AudioDefaultLooping3d;
  preload = true;
};

datablock AudioProfile(CarEngineSound)
{
  filename    = "~/data/sound/caridle.ogg";
  description = AudioClose3d;
  preload = true;
};

datablock AudioProfile(CarSquealSound)
{
  filename    = "~/data/sound/squeal.ogg";
  description = AudioClose3d;
  preload = true;
};
```

Be sure to replace the Ogg Vorbis file name that I used in those audioprofiles with the ones you recorded yourself.

Now add this following block of code to the same file, car.cs, but this time put it at the very end of the file:

```
datablock WheeledVehicleData(DefaultCar)
{
  category = "Vehicles";
  className = "Car";
  shapeFile = "~/data/models/vehicles/runabout.dts";
  emap = true;

  maxDamage = 1.0;
  destroyedLevel = 0.5;

  maxSteeringAngle = 0.785;  // Maximum steering angle
  tireEmitter = TireEmitter; // All the tires use the same dust emitter

  // 3rd person camera settings
  cameraRoll = true;        // Roll the camera with the vehicle
  cameraMaxDist = 6;        // Far distance from vehicle
  cameraOffset = 1.5;        // Vertical offset from camera mount point
```

```
    cameraLag = 0.1;                    // Velocity lag of camera
    cameraDecay = 0.75;                 // Decay per sec. rate of velocity lag

    // Rigid Body
    mass = 200;
    massCenter = "0 -0.5 0";    // Center of mass for rigid body
    massBox = "0 0 0";              // Size of box used for moment of inertia,
                                       // if zero it defaults to object bounding box
    drag = 0.6;                        // Drag coefficient
    bodyFriction = 0.6;
    bodyRestitution = 0.4;
    minImpactSpeed = 5;                // Impacts over this invoke the script callback
    softImpactSpeed = 5;          // Play SoftImpact Sound
    hardImpactSpeed = 15;         // Play HardImpact Sound
    integration = 4;                // Physics integration: TickSec/Rate
    collisionTol = 0.1;          // Collision distance tolerance
    contactTol = 0.1;           // Contact velocity tolerance

    // Engine
    engineTorque = 4000;           // Engine power
    engineBrake = 600;            // Braking when throttle is 0
    brakeTorque = 8000;          // When brakes are applied
    maxWheelSpeed = 30;         // Engine scale by current speed / max speed

    // Energy
    maxEnergy = 100;
    jetForce = 3000;
    minJetEnergy = 30;
    jetEnergyDrain = 2;

    // Sounds
    engineSound = CarEngineSound;
    jetSound = CarThrustSound;
    squealSound = CarSquealSound;
    softImpactSound = CarSoftImpactSound;
    hardImpactSound = CarHardImpactSound;
    wheelImpactSound = CarWheelImpactSound;
};
```

As you've seen in earlier sections, we start out with a gaggle of AudioProfiles that define each of our sounds.

After that comes the vehicle datablock. Most of the properties are explained in the code commentary or are self-explanatory. The ones that we are most interested in are at the end.

The engineSound property is the sound the vehicle makes while idling. As long as the vehicle is running, it will make this noise.

The jetSound property is the one used when the vehicle accelerates. The name is a holdover from the *Tribes 2* game engine in the early Torque days.

The squealSound property is the sound emitted by the tires when the vehicle is manhandled around a corner, causing the tires to slip.

The two impact sound properties, softImpactSound and hardImpactSound, are used when the vehicle collides with objects at different speeds, as defined by the softImpactSpeed and hardImpactSpeed properties earlier in the datablock.

Finally, the wheelImpactSound is the sound emitted when the wheels hit something at greater than the minimum impact speed, defined by minImpactSpeed earlier in the datablock.

Now we have to make some changes to our player's behavior. What we want is to have the player get in the car when he goes up to it.

Open the file \KOOB\control\server\players\player.cs, and locate these lines:

```
{
  %obj.pickup(%col);                      // otherwise, pick the item up
}
```

and insert the following after the second brace:

```
%this = %col.getDataBlock();
if ( %this.className $= "Car" )
{
    %node = 0;   // Find next available seat
    %col.mountObject(%obj,%node);
    %obj.mVehicle = %col;
}
```

Next, add the following code to the end of the file:

```
function MaleAvatar::onMount(%this,%obj,%vehicle,%node)
{
  %obj.setTransform("0 0 0 0 1 0");
```

```
  %obj.setActionThread(%vehicle.getDatablock().mountPose[%node]);
  if (%node == 0)
  {
    %obj.setControlObject(%vehicle);
    %obj.lastWeapon = %obj.getMountedImage($WeaponSlot);
    %obj.unmountImage($WeaponSlot);
    %db = %vehicle.getDatablock();
  }
}

function MaleAvatar::onUnmount( %this, %obj, %vehicle, %node )
{
  %obj.mountImage(%obj.lastWeapon, $WeaponSlot);
}

function MaleAvatar::doDismount(%this, %obj, %forced)
{
  // This function is called by the game engine when the jump trigger
  // is true while mounted

  // Position above dismount point
  %pos    = getWords(%obj.getTransform(), 0, 2);
  %oldPos = %pos;

  %vec[0] = " 1  1   1";
  %vec[1] = " 1  1   1";
  %vec[2] = " 1  1  -1";
  %vec[3] = " 1  0   0";
  %vec[4] = "--1  0   0";

  %impulseVec  = "0 0 0";
  %vec[0] = MatrixMulVector( %obj.getTransform(), %vec[0]);

  // Make sure the point is valid
  %pos = "0 0 0";
  %numAttempts = 5;
  %success     = -1;

  for (%i = 0; %i < %numAttempts; %i++)
  {
    %pos = VectorAdd(%oldPos, VectorScale(%vec[%i], 3));
    if (%obj.checkDismountPoint(%oldPos, %pos))
    {
```

```
    %success = %i;
    %impulseVec = %vec[%i];
    break;
   }
  }
 if (%forced && %success == -1)
   %pos = %oldPos;
 %obj.unmount();
 %obj.setControlObject(%obj);
 %obj.mountVehicle = false;

 // Position above dismount point
 %obj.setTransform(%pos);
 %obj.applyImpulse(%pos, VectorScale(%impulseVec, %obj.getDataBlock().
mass));
}
```

This code allows us to get in (mount) the car and then get out (dismount). When we get out of the car, we want to get far enough away from it so that we don't automatically get back into the car—that's what all the impulse vector calculation is about. There's nothing about the sound in there, but it is convenient to have this ability to get in and out whenever we want.

Now use the same procedures with the World Editor as with the tommy gun to insert the car into the game world. You will find the car in the Tree view under Shapes, Vehicles. Remember to tug the model up out of the ground if it's embedded in the ground—but don't tug it too hard, or you might fling it into outer space!

Run up to the car, and you will automatically go inside and be seated. Use the normal forward movement key (Up Arrow) to accelerate and the mouse to steer left and right. Press the spacebar to jump out. Have at it!

Environmental Sounds

A silent world is a dreary one. You can liven up your game world by inserting sounds to give a sense of the environment using AudioEmitters.

First, copy the file \3D2E\RESOURCES\CH20\loon.wav over to \KOOB\control\ data\sound\.

Then open \KOOB\control\server\misc\sndprofiles.cs, and add the following AudioProfile to the end of the file:

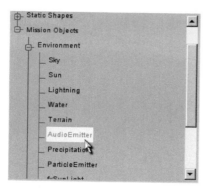

Figure 20.8
AudioEmitter in Tree view.

```
datablock AudioProfile(LoonSound)
{
  filename   = "control/data/sound/loon.wav";
  description = AudioDefaultLooping3d;
};
```

Run your game, and open the World Editor and then the World Editor Creator as before.

Next, in the Tree view, locate Mission Objects, Environment, AudioEmitter, as shown in Figure 20.8. Click AudioEmitter while facing a location where you would like to place the AudioEmitter.

In the dialog box presented (see Figure 20.9), click the Sound Profile button. From the list that opens, choose the LoonSound Profile.

Make sure the Use profile's desc?, Looping?, and Is 3D sound? check boxes are selected, and then click OK. Check Figure 20.9 to verify the settings.

An AudioEmitter marker will be placed in the game world at the center of your screen, on the ground, as shown in Figure 20.10.

Now exit the editor by toggling the F11 key, make sure you are in camera fly mode, and move up and away from where you placed the marker. Then go back in to the editor. You should see two concentric spheres, as shown in Figure 20.11. The inner sphere is very faintly defined with gray lines in the figure, while the outer sphere is defined with black lines. In the Torque Editor, the inner sphere is made with red lines, and the outer sphere is made with blue lines.

The inner sphere represents the reference (or minimum) distance, and the outer sphere represents the maximum distance. The larger the outer sphere, the more

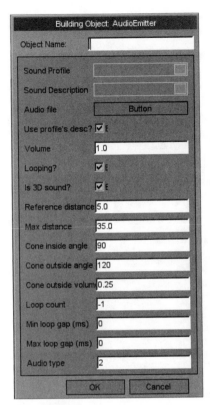

Figure 20.9
The Building Object: AudioEmitter dialog box.

gradual the drop-off in sound as you move away from the emitter. The larger the inner sphere, the farther the sound will carry.

Press F3 to switch to World Editor Inspector, and then click the hand cursor on the marker. At the lower right, the editor frame contains the properties for the object, as shown in Figure 20.12.

You can use this frame to adjust the settings for the emitter. Click the buttons in the Inspector frame to expand a selection of properties. After making changes, make sure to click the Apply button to have your changes applied to the selected object.

Interface Sounds

Torque has a mechanism built in to offer sound effects when you use buttons. Objects that use the GuiDefaultProfile profile have two sound effects available: soundButtonDown and soundButtonOver.

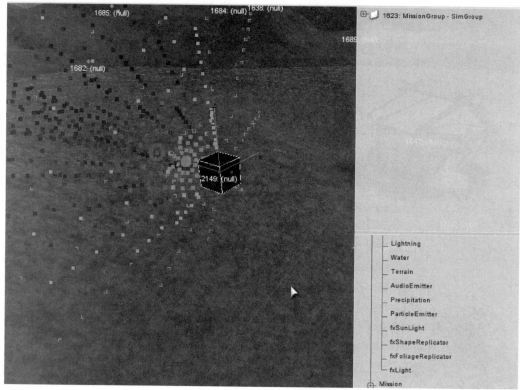

Figure 20.10
The AudioEmitter marker.

If you look in \KOOB\control\client\default_profiles, you will find a sound effect for the buttonover context that I've created. This sound occurs whenever the cursor passes over a GUI button that has been defined to use the `GuiDefaultProfile`. The line looks like this:

```
GuiButtonProfile.soundButtonOver = "AudioButtonOver";
```

It points the property to client-side `AudioProfile`. The profile is located in \KOOB\control\client\misc\sndprofiles.cs.

The `AudioButtonOver` profile looks like this:

```
new AudioProfile(AudioButtonOver)
{
  filename = "~/data/sound/buttonOver.wav";
  description = "AudioGui";
  preload = true;
};
```

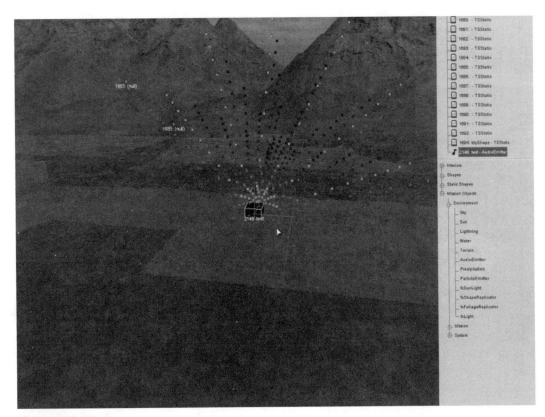

Figure 20.11
The AudioEmitter spheres.

We need the client-side profiles loaded before the main menu screen loads. In fact, we really need them to load before any client-side things get loaded, so that they are ready when needed. To do that, we will load them from \3D2E\ control\main.cs, which actually initiates both the client- and server-side script loading. So open \3D2E\control\main.cs and locate the line that says:

```
Exec("./client/initialize.cs");
```

And place the following line directly above it:

```
Exec("./client/misc/sndprofiles.cs");
```

With that done, you can pop into Koob and wave your cursor around over the various buttons and hear the beeping goodness. You can also now go into the Setup screen and move the volume sliders around, and hear the test sound volume change to match the slider settings.

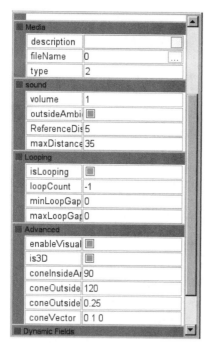

Figure 20.12
World Editor Inspector frame.

A useful exercise for you at this point would be to create a sound effect for pressing down on the button, insert the appropriate audio profile code, and then point the `soundButtonDown` property at it, just as I showed you for the `sound-ButtonOver` property.

Music

You can handle music in much the same way as the simple sound effect I showed you at the beginning of this chapter. A useful way to employ music is to provide a background for the different dialog boxes or menu screens in the GUI. Of course, you can also insert music into the game as AudioEmitters or even attach it to vehicles or players.

We'll take a slightly more conventional approach and put in some start-up music. First, locate the file \3D2E\RESOURCES\CH20\TWLOGO.WAV, and copy it over to \KOOB\control\data\sound\.

Next, open the file \KOOB\control\client\misc\sndprofiles.cs, and add the following code to the top of the file:

```
new AudioDescription(AudioMusic)
{
  volume   = 0.8;
  isLooping= false;
  is3D     = false;
  type     = $MusicAudioType;
};


new AudioProfile(AudioIntroMusicProfile)
{
  filename = "~/data/sound/twlogo.wav";
  description = "AudioMusic";
  preload = true;
};
function PlayMusic(%handle)
{
  if (!alxIsPlaying(%handle))
    alxPlay(%handle);
}

function StopMusic()
{
  alxStopAll();
}
```

Now open \KOOB\control\client\initialize.cs, and in the `InitializeClient` function you will find a line that starts with `InitCanvas`.

Add the following just below it:

```
PlayMusic(AudioIntroMusicProfile);
```

This will start the opening music playing as soon as the sound system is activated immediately after the game application has been launched.

Now open the file \KOOB\control\client\client.cs, and insert the following line as the first line in the `LaunchGame()` function:

```
StopMusic();
```

This line will ensure that if the opening music is still playing when you actually go to start the game, it will be turned off.

Now go ahead and launch the game and listen to the music.

You can use the same technique in combination with the `CommandToClient` (*XXXX*)/`clientCmd`*XXXX* system that we've used in earlier chapters to have the server trigger music cues on all or selected clients whenever you want.

Moving Right Along

There you go. Enough sound that the people around you will be pestering you to turn the blasted game down!

You've seen the ways that sounds can be added for player-avatars, vehicles, and weapons. You've seen what a state machine does and how it helps define what sounds occur, and when, when using a weapon.

Then there's the ability to hurl insults at other players—a very important feature to know how to put into a game!

You've seen how to add sounds into your game world at specific locations, so that you can bring life to a babbling brook or make the wind howl on an open plain.

Adding sounds to the user interfaces, like buttons on interface screens, is really reasonably simple, as you've seen.

Finally, adding music to your game is really no more complex than adding any other sound, and in some cases it's easier. You've seen how you can control the playing of music using TorqueScript.

In the next chapter we begin rolling together all the things covered in earlier chapters, by starting to create a game world.

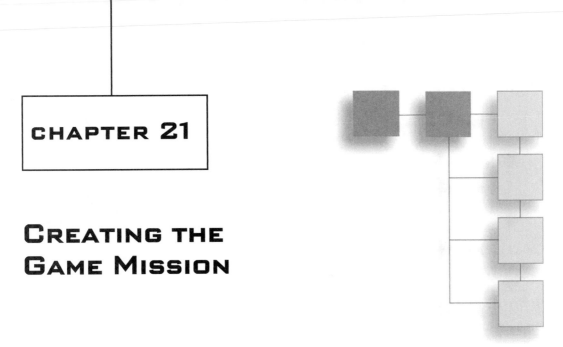

CHAPTER 21

CREATING THE
GAME MISSION

Let's take a moment to step back and see where we are.

In the first chapters of the book you learned the basics of programming and how to apply those concepts to real things that can be done with a modern game engine. In the process you learned how to use a programming editor—UltraEdit—and how to use Torque to try out our ideas. You saw that Torque has a powerful script system and the things you can do with it are almost limitless.

We then moved on to artwork, starting with textures and graphic images. You learned about a couple of new tools—the Gimp 2 and UVMapper—and how to apply them to the task of skinning 3D objects and GUI screens.

Then we got into modeling 3D objects, using a few more tools—MilkShape and QuArK—to create the models using different techniques. Animating our objects using MilkShape helped bring static models to life.

After that it was on to some nifty things like creating skyboxes and images for weather effects, such as lightning and rain.

Then it was sound effects, recording them and using them in a game in different ways.

Now you might think that all of this is leading somewhere. And you would be right!

Game Design

Okay, enough typing and programming for now. It's time to examine some higher-level issues, like game design.

Start with a vision.

You have an idea. It can be an amorphous, gee-I'm-not-really-sure-but-something-like-this idea, or it can be concrete, specific, and detailed. Using that as your reference, start asking yourself questions, write them down, and don't worry about answering them . . . yet.

Requirements

There are myriad questions you can ask yourself when considering the design of your game:

- What will the genre or play style be like?

- Will this be a single-player or multiplayer game?

- If it is to be a multiplayer game, will it be an online game or a split-screen type of multiplayer game?

- Does the game relate to real-world activities?

- Does the player play as a creature-character (human, animal, alien, and so on) or as some sort of machine?

- If the player isn't a creature or a machine, is he some sort of higher-level being that directs or controls a multitude of game entities?

- What are the player's goals?

- How do we measure player success, and what are the scoring mechanisms?

- What are the challenges that the game presents to us as players?

- Will the challenges be designed (planned by the game developers), or will they be random?

- What is the backstory (the narrative that describes the world the game takes place in), if any?

- What is it about the game that will make people want to play it?

- What is the one skill or skill set that the game requires the player to master in order to succeed?

- What other skills will contribute to player success?

- What mechanisms can the game offer that will help players develop those skills?

- How much game enhancement of skills is too much help?

Feel free to add more questions of your own.

As you can see, the list is big, and we've only scratched the surface here. By answering these questions, and any others you may want to add, you can build a list of requirements. It is important to generate at least this list—the *requirements specification*—in order to know where you are going with your design and how to measure your progress toward completion.

Software design is a big-ticket item, and hundreds of books have been written about it and the various design methodologies that have been proposed. It's an industry unto itself. There are dozens of different ideas about the best approach to take—and much disagreement. The one area *everyone* seems to agree on, however, is the need for the requirements to be determined and recorded in a meaningful way. Functional specs, test plans, schedules, and the like may or may not work for you, but you will get nowhere fast if you don't know what it is you are trying to accomplish.

Some of the questions lead to other questions. Some answers may need to be deferred until later when you have more information. Even if your list of questions exceeds your list of answers, it is still an important activity. Keep the list nearby, return to it regularly, and update the answers. See where it leads you. Perhaps you can see that you are wandering away from your original vision. The list may uncover things you'd never considered before, that *really are* important, and prevent you from wasting time on a mistaken approach.

When you work your way through creating the questions, try hard to stay general—steer away from specifics until they can't be avoided any longer.

At some point you will want to ask yourself, "What technology should I use to create this game?" Don't ask this question at the very beginning. In most cases you should wait until you know the answers to the bulk of your questions—in other words, wait until your requirements are starting to look meaty and useful—before you ask yourself technology questions.

Constraints

We usually have to accept that there are constraints that can arbitrarily force us to move in particular directions or prevent us from moving in others.

The design should drive the technology and not the other way around. However, in a low-budget development shop, this is often an unaffordable luxury. There are budgetary constraints caused by available funds that will force us in certain technological directions. In our case, because this book is about making games with minimal expenditure and using the Torque Game Engine to help us achieve that goal, we will have to accept that constraint and monitor the effect it has on our design as we build it up.

Again in our case, because we already know the technology we are going to use, we should examine it for its limitations and measure our constraints starting there.

As mentioned elsewhere Torque is designed for online, multiplayer, first-person shooter-style games. This means that whenever implementation tradeoffs had to occur when creating the game engine, the developers always tried to make their decisions in a way that favored efficient and fast networking, first-person perspective 3D rendering, and multiplayer support.

One thing that Torque, right out of the box, doesn't address in its design is massive multiplayer support. Torque can easily handle 64 players logged in to one session. It can even handle more than 100. In fact, there is no hard-coded limit to the number of players that could log in to the same server. But because of its design, Torque really starts to lose its shine when you exceed the realm of about 100 players.

Massively multiplayer games require the ability to have thousands of players playing the same game together. Torque just doesn't handle this kind of load.

So the server load is a constraint. While Torque's ability to handle 100 players at once is better than most, if not all, other FPS-style games out there, that still doesn't translate to thousands. We must keep this in mind.

The tools we have available can dictate other constraints. It's fine to decide that you will have a certain feature, but it may require an expensive 3D modeling tool to create and thus sit out of reach. So make sure you can create the things you want.

Koob

Let's go about listing some requirements for Koob, the game we are making. Feel free to add your own, but the list of 29 items here will serve as a starting place.

1. First-person and third-person perspective play.

2. Internet multiplayer game play.

3. Global in-game chat.

4. Ability to use at least one weapon.

5. Ability to get in and out of vehicles.

6. Ability to drive vehicles.

7. A road or track in the world to drive on.

8. Trees and other foliage.

9. Powerups: health, energy, ammunition, coins (for points).

10. Buildings that serve as hiding places and storage locations for powerups.

11. All other players are enemies.

12. All point values configurable from a setup file.

13. 1 point per enemy killed.

14. 3 points per vehicle destroyed.

15. Ability to race around the track and score 5 points for each lap you lead.

16. Laps can only be scored in the car.

17. A 10-lap race with no time limit.

18. A 10-point bonus for winning the race.

19. On-screen scorecard.

20. Scores retained at the end of each race restored when player resumes the game.

21. Each player gets an account at startup and must use a password to log in to the game.

22. Track must be clearly marked on the terrain.

23. Checkpoints along the way to measure progress and ensure the player stays on course.

24. Laps can only be completed when all checkpoints are completed for that lap.

25. Checkpoints must be completed in sequential order.

26. Coins of three denominations will be randomly scattered around the maps. The values will be 1 point, 10 points, and 100 points for copper, silver, and gold, respectively.

27. Some nice burning objects to admire as we play.

28. A waterfall to drive through just for the heck of it.

29. When one map is finished, cycle to the next in the list.

So as you can probably gather, Koob is a kind of death-match scavenger-hunt game. The player tries to win the race, accumulate some loot, and, at the same time, stop his enemies from winning.

As we progress from here to the end of the book, we'll check back against this list of requirements to make sure we've covered all the items.

Right off the bat, we can check off item 1. A few of the other items are definitely doable because we've chosen the Torque Engine to create the game, but we have some programming yet to do to make them happen.

Torque Mission Editor

You've already been exposed to the Mission Editor—a little bit here, a little bit there. As you've seen, the Mission Editor contains several subeditors: the World Editor, Terrain Editor, Terrain Terraform Editor, Terrain Texture Editor, and Mission Area Editor. The main point of this section is to place objects in the game world and adjust them as required. To do this we will use the World Editor, which has two components: the World Editor Creator and its partner, the World Editor Inspector.

In the Mission Editor the normal movement keys can be used to control both the player and the camera. The right mouse button is used to rotate the camera or adjust the player's view.

File Menu

Disk and file operations are carried out using the items in the File menu, as shown in Table 21.1. These include opening, saving, importing, and exporting.

Edit Menu

As is standard with windowed applications these days, there is an Edit menu that houses a variety of object and item editing commands. As you can see in Table 21.2,

Table 21.1 File Menu Commands

Command	Description
New Mission	Creates a new empty mission with a default terrain and sky.
Open Mission	Opens an existing mission for editing.
Save Mission	Saves changes to the current mission to disk.
Save Mission As	Saves the current mission under a new name.
Import Terraform Data	Imports Terraform rules from an existing terrain file.
Import Texture Data	Imports terrain texture rules from an existing terrain file.
Export Terraform Bitmap	(Only active from the Terrain Terraform Editor.) Exports the current Terraform map to a bitmap.
Toggle Map Editor	Closes the editor and return to the previous interface (usually the game HUD).
Quit	Quits the game or demo.

Table 21.2 Edit Menu

Menu Item	Description
Undo	Undoes the last action in terrain or world editing. Not all actions can be undone.
Redo	Redoes the last undone action.
Cut	Cuts the selected objects in the World Editor from the mission to the Clipboard.
Copy	Copies the selected objects in the World Editor to the Clipboard.
Paste	Pastes the current clipboard contents into the mission.
Select All	Selects all mission objects in the World Editor.
Select None	Clears the current selection in the World and Terrain Editors.
Relight Scene	Recomputes the mission's static lighting and applies it.
World Editor Settings	Accesses the settings dialog box for the World Editor.
Terrain Editor Settings	Accesses the settings dialog box for the Terrain Editor.

Table 21.3 Camera Menu

Menu Item	Description
Drop Camera At Player	Moves the camera object to the location of the player, and sets the mode to camera movement mode (*camera fly mode*).
Drop Player At Camera	Moves the player object to the location of the movable camera, and sets the mode to player movement mode (*player mode*).
Toggle Camera	Toggles between player and camera fly movement modes. Your view will also switch to the location of either the player or the camera, depending on the mode.
Slowest *to* Fastest	Adjusts the movement speed of the camera fly mode.

in addition to the ubiquitous Cut, Copy, and Paste functions, there are also commands used to access various settings for the editors.

Camera Menu

Use the Camera menu, as described in Table 21.3, to change camera modes and adjust the camera fly mode speed.

Other Menus

The World menu is available by default and contains functions related to the World Editor. Its capabilities will be described in the "World Editor" section, which is coming up next.

The Window menu is pretty straightforward, so it doesn't require a table to describe its functions. It is used to invoke each of the available subeditors.

World Editor

The World Editor provides a view of the 3D world. Objects in this view, like structures, interiors, shapes, and markers, can be manipulated with either the mouse or the keyboard.

There are three frames in the view: the World Editor Tree, the World Editor Inspector, and the World Editor Creator.

World Editor Tree

The World Editor Tree view is displayed in the frame in the upper-right screen corner in both the World Editor Inspector and the World Editor Creator. This tree displays the hierarchy of the mission data file. Objects selected in the Tree view will also be selected in the main view. Objects in the Tree view can be organized into groups.

There is a special group selection called the *Instant Group,* which is displayed with gray highlighting in the Tree view. This is the group in the Tree view where newly created or pasted objects are placed. Objects created from the World Editor Creator are also placed in the Instant Group. To change the current Instant Group, Alt + Click on a group in the Tree view.

World Editor Inspector

The World Editor Inspector lets you examine and specify properties of mission objects. When you select an object in Inspector mode, that object's properties are displayed in the frame at the lower right of the screen. After editing an object's properties, click the Apply button to commit those properties to the object. Dynamic properties can be assigned to objects with the Dynamic Fields Add button. Dynamic fields can be accessed via the scripting language and are normally used to add game-specific properties to objects.

World Editor Creator

The World Editor Creator displays an extra Tree view frame in the lower-right corner of the screen. This view contains all objects that can be created in a mission. Selecting an object from this list creates a new instance of it and drops the new object at the center of the screen (by default) or as specified by the selected Drop at command in the World menu, which is shown in Table 21.4.

You can use both the mouse and the keyboard for editing, as shown in Table 21.5.

Gizmos are the visual representation of each object's three axes. When you select an object, and if you have gizmos enabled in the World Editor Settings dialog box, accessed from the Edit menu, then they will appear centered on that object's local origin.

If gizmos are enabled, they can be clicked and dragged (as described in Table 21.6) in order to modify the object to which they are attached.

Terrain Editor

We use the Terrain Editor to manually modify the terrain height map and square properties by using a mouse-operated brush. The brush is a selection of terrain

Table 21.4 World Menu

Menu Item	Description
Lock Selection	Locks the current selection so that it cannot be manipulated from the World Editor view.
Unlock Selection	Unlocks a locked selection.
Hide Selection	Hides the current selection to help reduce visual clutter.
Show Selection	Unhides hidden objects in the selection.
Delete Selection	Deletes the currently selected objects.
Camera To Selection	Moves the camera to the selected objects.
Reset Transforms	Resets the rotation and scale on the selected objects.
Drop Selection	Drops the selected objects into the mission according to the drop rule (see Drop Selection menu items that follow). If the object is already placed, it is picked up and dropped again.
Add Selection to Instant Group	Adds whatever object is currently selected to the Sim Group, which is highlighted in light gray in the Inspector pane on the right-hand side of the Mission Editor interface.
Drop at Origin	Drops newly created objects at the origin.
Drop at Camera	Drops newly created objects at the camera's location.
Drop at Camera w/ Rot	Drops newly created objects at the camera's location with the camera's current orientation.
Drop below Camera	Drops newly created objects below the camera's current location.
Drop at Screen Center	Drops newly created objects where the view direction hits an object.
Drop at Centroid	Drops newly created objects at the center of the selection.
Drop to Ground	Drops newly created objects to the terrain ground level at their current location.

Table 21.5 Mouse and Keyboard Operations

Operation	Description
Click an Unselected Object	Deselects all the currently selected objects, and selects the clicked object.
Click in Empty Space	Click-drags a box around the objects, and selects all the objects in the box.
Shift + Click an Object	Toggles selection of the clicked object.
Mouse Drag a Selected Object	Moves the selected objects, either on a horizontal plane or sticking to the terrain, depending on the setting of the Planar Movement check box in the World Editor Settings dialog box.
Ctrl + Click and Drag	Moves the selected objects vertically.
Alt + Click and Drag	Rotates the selected objects about the vertical axis.
Alt + Ctrl + Click and Drag	Scales the selected object by a face on the bounding box.

Table 21.6 Gizmo Operations

Operation	Description
Click and Drag Gizmo Axis	Moves the selection along the selected axis.
Alt + Click and Drag Gizmo Axis	Rotates the selection on the selected axis.
Alt + Ctrl + Click and Drag Gizmo Axis	Scales along the selected axis.

Table 21.7 Terrain Editor: Brush Menu

Menu Item	Description
Box Brush	Uses a square-shaped brush.
Circle Brush	Uses a circular brush.
Soft Brush	Sets the brush so that its influence on the terrain diminishes toward the edges of the brush. The brush square colors vary from red, where the influence is greatest, to green, where the influence is least. The Terrain Editor Settings dialog box Filter view has controls that adjust the falloff.
Hard Brush	Sets the brush so that the effect on the terrain is the same across the surface of the brush. All squares in the brush are the same red color.
Size 1 × 1 *to* 25 × 25	Sets the brush sizes.

points or squares centered around the mouse cursor. Table 21.7 describes the functions available in the Brush menu.

When we use the Terrain Editor, we modify the terrain as if we are piling dirt onto it or shoveling holes into the ground. Table 21.8 shows the operations available in the Terrain Editor via the Action menu.

Terrain Terraform Editor

The Terrain Terraform Editor uses mathematical algorithms to generate terrain heightfields (height maps). Heightfield operations are arranged in a *stack,* which is an ordered list of operations. Operations in the stack depend on the results of previous operations to produce new heightfields. The results of the final operation on the stack can be applied to the terrain using the Apply button.

There are two Terrain Terraform Editor frames. The top frame displays information about the currently selected operation, and the bottom frame shows the current operation stack. Between them is a pull-down menu for the creation of new operations. The first operation in the stack is always the General operation, which can't be deleted.

Table 21.8 Terrain Editor: Action Menu

Menu Item	Description
Select	Moves the brush in a painting motion to select grid points.
Adjust Selection	Raises or lowers the terrain at the currently selected grid points as a group by dragging the mouse up or down.
Add Dirt	Adds terrain "dirt" to the terrain at the center of the brush, raising the affected terrain area.
Excavate	Removes dirt from the center of the brush.
Adjust Height	Raises or lowers the area marked by the brush by dragging the mouse.
Flatten	Sets the area marked by the brush to a flat plane height.
Smooth	Smoothes the area marked by the brush—peaks are lowered and troughs are raised.
Set Height	Sets the area marked by the brush to a constant height—the height is set using the Terrain Editor Settings.
Set Empty	Makes a hole in the terrain in the squares covered by the brush.
Clear Empty	Fills in any holes in the squares covered by the brush.
Paint Material	Paints the current terrain texture material with the brush.

Table 21.9 shows the operations available.

Click the Apply button to commit the current terrain operation list to the terrain file.

Terrain Texture Editor

The Terrain Texture Editor uses mathematical techniques to place terrain textures based on the heightfield at the bottom of the Terraformer heightfield stack. The editor has three main interface elements on the right side of the screen. From top to bottom they are the operation Inspector frame, the Material list, and the Placement Operation list.

Terrain materials are textures that are added using the Add Material button. This will look for any texture (.png or .jpg) in a subdirectory of any directory named *terrains* (in this book, this *also* applies to any directory named maps). Once a material is added to the terrain, the user can select one of several placement operations that govern where that material will be placed on the terrain. They are shown in Table 21.10.

Click the Apply button to commit the current texture operation list to the terrain file.

Table 21.9 Terraform Operations

Operation	Description
fBm Fractal	Creates bumpy hills.
Rigid Multifractal	Creates ridges and sweeping valleys.
Canyon Fractal	Creates vertical canyon ridges.
Sinus	Creates overlapping sine wave patterns with different frequencies useful for making rolling hills.
Bitmap	Imports an existing 256 by 256 bitmap as a heightfield.
Turbulence	Jumbles the effects of another operation on the stack.
Smoothing	Smoothes the effects of another operation on the stack.
Smooth Water	Smoothes water.
Smooth Ridges/Valleys	Smoothes an existing operation on edge boundaries.
Filter	Applies a filter to an existing operation based on a curve.
Thermal Erosion	Applies an erosion effect to an existing operation using a thermal erosion algorithm.
Hydraulic Erosion	Applies an erosion effect to an existing operation using a hydraulic erosion algorithm.
Blend	Blends two existing operations according to a scale factor and a mathematical operator.
Terrain File	Loads an existing terrain file onto the stack.

Table 21.10 Terrain Texture Editor Placement Operations

Operation	Description
Place by Fractal	Places the terrain texture randomly across the terrain based on a Brownian motion fractal operation.
Place by Height	Places the texture based on an elevation filter.
Place by Slope	Places the texture based on a slope filter.
Place by Water Level	Places the texture based on the water level parameter in the Terraform Editor.

Mission Area Editor

The Mission Area Editor defines regions in the game that are used to constrain player travel. If we use mission areas in a game, we normally give warnings or disqualifications if a player leaves a mission area. Of course, you can probably find other uses for such a feature.

The Mission Area Editor displays an overhead height-map view of the current mission map in the upper-right corner of the screen. There are markers for mission objects, a box for the mission area, and a pair of lines denoting the current field of view. Clicking anywhere on the display will move the current view object (either camera or player) to that location in the mission area.

To edit the mission area, select the Edit Area check box. This will display eight resizing knobs on the mission area box that can be dragged with the mouse.

Clicking the Center button will cause the terrain file data to be repositioned and centered at 0,0 in the center of the mission area box.

To mirror the terrain, click the Mirror button. This will put the Mission Area Editor in mirror mode. The Left and Right Arrow buttons adjust the mirror plane angle to one of eight different angles (two axis aligned, two 45-degree splits). Click the Apply button to commit the terrain mirroring across the mirror plane. Mirroring a mission area is a useful way to quickly create terrain for team-based games where each side would begin with identical terrain. This would stop either side from having a terrain advantage. You create the terrain for one side and then simply mirror it for the other side.

Building the World

Let's get to work building the game world, and let's start with items 27 and 28 from our requirements list. I've chosen the fire and the waterfall to start with here because we haven't really looked at particles much yet, and with particles we get to touch on various topics we've covered in this chapter, like easing into using the Mission Editor, the World Editor Creator, and the World Editor Inspector. And besides that, particles are cool.

Particles

Remember the raindrops in Chapter 18? Those were particles. *Particles* are basically single-faced polygons that are generated in bulk by a game engine to simulate a variety of somewhat related real-world phenomena, such as rain, smoke, wispy fog, splashing and spraying water or mud, fire, and flames. Particles can be used to simulate any sort of constantly changing fluid- or gaslike entity. Even a swarm of mosquitoes can be generated using particles.

What I'll do in this section is show you how to use the Torque particle system to make a campfire and a waterfall.

Particles are made of three parts:

■ **Particle.** The actual things we see.

- **Particle Emitter.** The thing that causes the particles to come into existence.

- **Particle Emitter Node.** The object that the emitter is attached to.

If you attach the word *data* to the end of each and remove the spaces, you'll have the formal names of the datablocks that define those terms of the particle system:

```
ParticleData
ParticleEmitterData
ParticleEmitterNodeData
```

Particles can live in the game world in one of two ways: as freestanding particles or as attached particles. Freestanding particles are defined using all three of the datablocks just mentioned, while attached particles only require defining the `ParticleData` and the `ParticleEmitterData`. The nodes aren't needed, because we are attaching the particle to some other object that supports particles. The object classes that support particles are players, weapons, projectiles, and all vehicle types. As noted already, `Rain` is a specialized object that has a built-in particle capability.

So in the case of freestanding particle emitters, one more definition of interest is required for placing emitters in the world:

```
ParticleEmitterNode
```

We'll look at freestanding particle emitters a bit more shortly.

Campfire

To make a campfire, we'll need two particle definitions: one for the flames and one for the smoke. The particle types used will be freestanding, so we will need to define all three particle datablocks for both the smoke and the flames.

First, copy the image file \3D2E\RESOURCES\CH21\flame.png to \KOOB\ control\data\particles.

Next, create the file \KOOB\control\server\misc\particles.cs, and add the following code to it:

```
datablock ParticleData(Campfire)
{
    textureName        = "~/data/particles/flame";
    dragCoefficient    = 0.0;
    gravityCoefficient = -0.35;
    inheritedVelFactor = 0.00;
    lifetimeMS         = 580;
```

```
        lifetimeVarianceMS  = 150;
        useInvAlpha    = false;
        spinRandomMin = -15.0;
        spinRandomMax = 15.0;

        colors[0]    = "0.8 0.6 0.0 0.1";
        colors[1]    = "0.8 0.65 0.0 0.1";
        colors[2]    = "0.0 0.0 0.0 0.0";

        sizes[0]    = 1.0;
        sizes[1]    = 2.0;
        sizes[2]    = 4.0;

        times[0]    = 0.1;
        times[1]    = 0.4;
        times[2]    = 1.0;
    };

datablock ParticleEmitterData(CampfireEmitter)
{
    ejectionPeriodMS = 15;
    periodVarianceMS = 5;

    ejectionVelocity = 0.35;
    velocityVariance = 0.20;

    thetaMin     = 0.0;
    thetaMax     = 60.0;

    particles = "Campfire" TAB "Campfire";
};

datablock ParticleEmitterNodeData(CampfireEmitterNode)
{
    timeMultiple = 1;
};
```

Now open \KOOB\control\server\server.cs, locate the function `OnServerCreated`, and add the following line to the end of the function, before the closing brace ("}"):

```
Exec("./misc/particles.cs");
```

Next, open your mission file (\KOOB\control\data\maps\koobA.mis, or whatever your mission file is called, as long as it is the same as the one used for Chapter 6

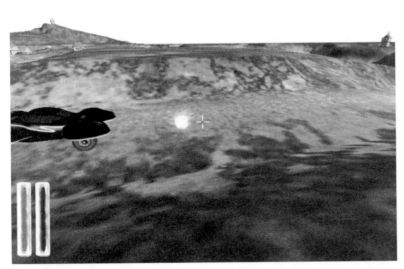

Figure 21.1
Campfire.

and uses the same terrain), and add the following before the closing brace of the file:

```
new ParticleEmitterNode() {
    position = "13.2665 -2.0218 196.6";
    rotation = "1 0 0 0";
    scale = "1 1 1";
    dataBlock = "CampfireEmitterNode";
    emitter = "CampfireEmitter";
    velocity = "1";
};
```

Okay, save your files, and then launch Koob. When your player spawns in, turn to the right—you should see a little fire burning in the gully there, as shown in Figure 21.1.

The flame is the glowing object to the left of the crosshair in the picture. Now let's add the smoke. We'll do it slightly differently. We begin by defining the particle and emitter as before, but then we'll place it in an easier way using the World Editor.

Open up the \KOOB\control\server\misc\particles.cs file you created earlier, and add the following:

```
datablock ParticleData(CampfireSmoke)
{
    textureName          = "~/data/particles/smoke";
    dragCoefficient      = 0.0;
    gravityCoefficient   = -0.15;
    inheritedVelFactor   = 0.00;
    lifetimeMS           = 4000;
    lifetimeVarianceMS   = 500;
    useInvAlpha     = false;
    spinRandomMin   = -30.0;
    spinRandomMax   = 30.0;
    colors[0]       = "0.5 0.5 0.5 0.1";
    colors[1]       = "0.6 0.6 0.6 0.1";
    colors[2]       = "0.6 0.6 0.6 0.0";
    sizes[0]        = 0.5;
    sizes[1]        = 0.75;
    sizes[2]        = 1.5;
    times[0]        = 0.0;
    times[1]        = 0.5;
    times[2]        = 1.0;
};
datablock ParticleEmitterData(CampfireSmokeEmitter)
{
    ejectionPeriodMS = 20;
    periodVarianceMS = 5;
    ejectionVelocity = 0.25;
    velocityVariance = 0.20;
    thetaMin      = 0.0;
    thetaMax      = 90.0;
    particles = CampfireSmoke;
};
datablock ParticleEmitterNodeData(CampfireSmokeEmitterNode)
{
    timeMultiple = 1;
};
```

Tip

To figure out which mission file you are loading and spawning into, open \KOOB\control\client\client.cs and look in the LaunchGame function for the CreateServer function call. The second argument to that call is the path to the mission file you are opening when you run Koob.

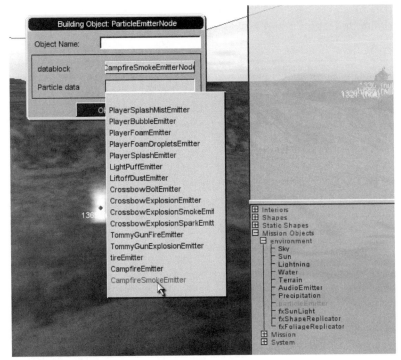

Figure 21.2
Adding smoke.

Save your work, and then launch Koob. Locate the campfire, and face it in camera fly mode (press F8). Open the World Editor (press F11), and then enter the World Editor Creator (press F4). Browse the Tree view until you locate Mission Objects, Environment, particleEmitter. Click it to place another particle emitter.

You will get the Building Object: ParticleEmitterNode dialog box. Using the illustration as a guide, choose CampfireSmokeEmitterNode from the datablock list, and then choose CampfireSmokeEmitter from the particle data list (see Figure 21.2).

After the smoke appears, move it with the cursor until it's positioned directly over the campfire. Press F11 to get out of the editor, grab some s'mores, and get cookin'!

As you can see, ParticleEmitterNodes are useful for creating nodes that are stationary but animated. Place them in your world by adding a datablock and emitter references in your mission file, either through the Torque World Creator or by directly editing the mission file.

Table 21.11 ParticleEmitterNode Properties

Property	Description
velocity	Acts as a master speed control modifying the settings for the ParticleEmitter-NodeData, ParticleData, and ParticleEmitterData datablocks.
datablock	The name of the ParticleEmitterNodeData defined elsewhere that will be used.
emitter	The name of the ParticleEmitterData defined elsewhere that will be used.

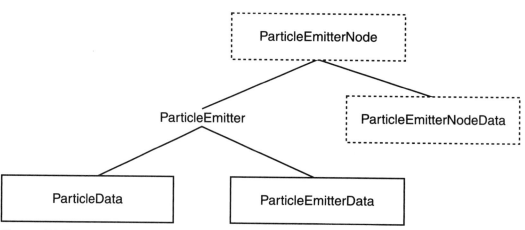

Figure 21.3
Particle system elements.

Table 21.11 describes the significant properties of the ParticleEmitterNode datablock. This describes the actual node object that is inserted in a mission file for a freestanding particle emitter.

Now, if you look at Figure 21.3, you'll see the relationship between the various datablocks involved in particles. The items in rectangles need to be defined somehow—you've seen how to do this. The one gotcha in the diagram is that the items in the dashed rectangles only need to be defined when placing freestanding particles in the game world. When you attach particles to objects like the player or vehicles, only the datablocks shown in the solid rectangles (ParticleData and ParticleEmitterData) need to be defined.

Table 21.12 describes the significant property of the ParticleEmitterNodeData datablock.

There is only one parameter in this datablock: timeMultiple. You can create any number of these datablocks with different settings and names.

Table 21.12 ParticleEmitterNodeData Property

Property	Description
timeMultiple	Ranges from 0.01 to 100.0, specifying how often the particles are emitted from the node. Smaller values are for shorter time intervals between emissions, which means there is a higher emission frequency.

Table 21.13 describes the significant properties of the ParticleEmitterData datablock, although we won't be using them all here. Those that we don't use will be assigned default values by Torque.

Table 21.14 describes the significant properties of the ParticleData datablock. Again, we don't use all of these properties in the campfire, but we do use most of them in the waterfall, which is in the next subsection.

Waterfall

As promised, we will build a waterfall. Add the following particle system datablocks to your particles.cs file:

```
datablock ParticleData(WFallAParticle)
{
textureName = "~/data/particles/splash";
dragCoefficient = 0.0;
gravityCoefficient = 0.5;
windCoefficient = 1.0;
inheritedVelFactor = 2.00;
lifetimeMS = 15000;
lifetimeVarianceMS = 2500;
useInvAlpha = false;
spinRandomMin = -30.0;
spinRandomMax = 30.0;
colors[0] = "0.6 0.6 0.6 0.1";
colors[1] = "0.6 0.6 0.6 0.1";
colors[2] = "0.6 0.6 0.6 0.0";
sizes[0]  = 5;
sizes[1]  = 10;
sizes[2]  = 15;
times[0]  = 0.0;
times[1]  = 0.5;
times[2]  = 1.0;
};
```

Table 21.13 ParticleEmitterData Properties

Property	Description
ejectionPeriodMS	Controls how often a particle is emitted in milliseconds (ms). A value of 1000 equals 1 particle per second (1 ms minimum).
periodVarianceMS	Introduces randomness to the ejection period. The variance must be less than ejectionPeriodMS and less than the lifetimeMS setting in the ParticleData section.
ejectionVelocity	Controls how fast the particle image is moved along the emission vector. Must be equal to or greater than 0, up to 3 meters per second maximum.
velocityVariance	Introduces randomness to the ejectionVelocity. The variance must be less than ejectionVelocity.
ejectionOffset	Modifies the start position of the particle ejection to occur at an offset along the ejection vector.
thetaMax, thetaMin	Sets the range (in degrees) for rotation around the X-axis of the ParticleNode object. thetaMin must be less than thetaMax, and both must be in the range of 0.0 to 180 degrees. The particle generator will randomly pick a value between those limits. Think of these properties together as "how high" the emitter's "aim" is.
phiReferenceVel, phiVariance	Sets the rotation angle around the Z-axis. Both arguments must be in the range of 0.0 to 180 degrees, with phiVariance less than phiReferenceVel. Think of these properties together as the "direction" the emitter is pointing.
overrideAdvances	Defaults to false. When set to true, this will disable updating the particle as soon as it is created. This can be used to clean up particles generated by fast-moving objects.
orientParticles	Defaults to false. When set to false, the particle image is presented as a billboard that always faces the camera. When set to true, the particle image is oriented with respect to the ejection vector.
orientOnVelocity	Defaults to false. When set to true, the particle is displayed oriented with respect to the ejection vector. At the start the particle faces the screen, because velocity at the very beginning is 0.
particles	Contains the name of the ParticleData datablock to use. Multiple ParticleData datablocks can be specified in the string, separated by tab characters. The particle engine will cycle through the list repeatedly.
lifetimeMS	Defines how long this emitter will generate particles. It cannot be a negative value. A setting of 0 specifies no time limit. If not specified, then the default is 0.
lifetimeVarianceMS	Introduces randomness to the lifetime of the emitter. This value must be less than (and not equal to nor greater than) lifetimeMS.
useEmitterSizes	Does nothing if this datablock belongs to a ParticleEmitterNode. Otherwise, when set to true, use emitter-specified sizes instead of datablock sizes.
useEmitterColors	Does the same as useEmitterSizes, but for colors.

Table 21.14 ParticleData Properties

Property	Description
textureName	Specifies path and file name of a PNG or JPG image. Particle textures use black for the image areas that will be treated as the alpha (transparency) channel. PNG images will also use black for the transparent areas but will also alternatively use the real alpha channel for transparent image regions if one is included. If a real alpha channel is specified in a PNG image, then black will not be used for transparency. Images must be sized in powers of 2, to a maximum of 512 pixels by 512 pixels.
useInvAlpha	Switches from using black to using white for transparent regions.
inheritedVelFactor	Specifies how much of a parent object's velocity should be imparted in particles emitted.
constantAcceleration	Specifies acceleration rate for each particle along the ejection vector.
dragCoefficient	Specifies deceleration rate for each particle along the ejection vector.
windCoefficient	Specifies how much the game world's wind velocity vector should be imposed on particles emitted.
gravityCoefficient	Specifies acceleration rate for each particle vertically. Positive values indicate acceleration toward the ground.
lifetimeMS	Controls how long the particle image is displayed as it follows its ejection vector. Short lifetimes have a pronounced strobe effect. Default is 1000 (1 second) with a minimum value of 100.
lifetimeVarianceMS	Introduces randomness to the lifetime of the particle. This value must be less than (and not equal to nor greater than) lifetimeMS.
spinSpeed	Dictates how fast images will be randomly rotated around the vertical axis, if particles aren't set to be billboarded using the orientParticles or orientOnVelocity properties of the ParticleEmitterData.
spinRandomMax	Specifies the maximum allowable angle that a particle image can be randomly rotated. Allowable range is −10000.0 to +10000.0. spinRandomMax must be greater than spinRandomMin.
spinRandomMin	Specifies the minimum allowable angle that a particle image can be randomly rotated. Allowable range is −10000.0 to +10000.0. spinRandomMin must be less than spinRandomMax.
animateTexture	Allows use of animated particle image textures, when set to true.
framesPerSec	Specifies the animation frame rate.
animTexName	Specifies a DML file that contains a list of texture image files. Each file is a single frame in the animation.
colors[n]	Specifies the color interpolation values for three sequences of particle emissions.
sizes[n]	Specifies the scale interpolation values for three sequences of particle emissions.
times[n]	Specifies the time stamp values that pin the moments for the three particle emission sequences.

```
datablock ParticleEmitterData(WFallAEmitter)
{
ejectionPeriodMS = 10;
periodVarianceMS = 5;
ejectionVelocity = 0.55;
velocityVariance = 0.30;
thetaMin = 0.0;
thetaMax = 90.0;
particles = WFallAParticle;
};
datablock ParticleEmitterNodeData(WFall1EmitterNode)
{
timeMultiple = 1;
};
//------------------------------
datablock ParticleData(WFallBParticle)
{
textureName = "~/data/particles/splash";
dragCoefficient = 0.0;
gravityCoefficient = -0.1; // rises slowly
inheritedVelFactor = 2.00;
lifetimeMS = 3000;
lifetimeVarianceMS = 500;
useInvAlpha = false;
spinRandomMin = -30.0;
spinRandomMax = 30.0;
colors[0] = "0.4 0.4 0.7 0.1";
colors[1] = "0.5 0.6 0.8 0.1";
colors[2] = "0.6 0.6 0.9 0.0";
sizes[0] = 10;
sizes[1] = 15;
sizes[2] = 20;
times[0] = 0.0;
times[1] = 0.5;
times[2] = 1.0;
};
datablock ParticleData(WFallCParticle)
{
textureName = "~/data/particles/splash";
dragCoefficient = 0.0;
gravityCoefficient = -0.1; // rises slowly
inheritedVelFactor = 2.00;
lifetimeMS = 3000;
```

```
lifetimeVarianceMS = 300;
useInvAlpha = false;
spinRandomMin = -30.0;
spinRandomMax = 30.0;
colors[0] = "0.4 0.4 0.5 0.1";
colors[1] = "0.5 0.5 0.6 0.1";
colors[2] = "0.0 0.0 0.7 0.0";
sizes[0]  = 5;
sizes[1]  = 5;
sizes[2]  = 5;
times[0]  = 0.0;
times[1]  = 0.5;
times[2]  = 1.0;
};
datablock ParticleEmitterData(WFallBParticleEmitter)
{
ejectionPeriodMS = 15;
periodVarianceMS = 5;
ejectionVelocity = 0.25;
velocityVariance = 0.10;
thetaMin = 0.0;
thetaMax = 90.0;
particles = "WFallBParticle" TAB "WFallCParticle";
};
datablock ParticleEmitterNodeData(WFall2ParticleEmitterNode)
{
timeMultiple = 1;
};
```

Save your work, and launch your game. The area where you want to make your waterfall is shown in Figure 21.4; the annotations show where I think is the best place for a waterfall. Anywhere along the water will do, though.

To get there, use F8 to get into camera fly mode, and fly straight up for a second (do this by looking straight down at the ground and press the w key to go backward and up). Then turn 180 degrees away from the direction you were facing when you spawned, and fly over to the area shown in the figure.

Once there, use the same methods used when you added the campfire smoke in the earlier section. For the top of the waterfall, use WFall1ParticleEmitterNode with the WFallAEmitter. Then for the splashing effect at the water surface, use WFall2ParticleEmitterNode with the WFallBEmitter. You should get something that looks like Figure 21.5.

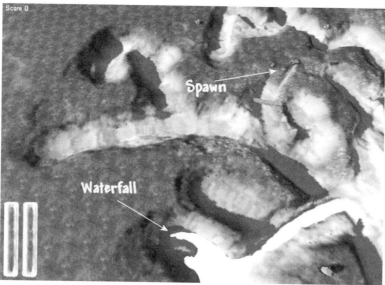

Figure 21.4
Locating the falls.

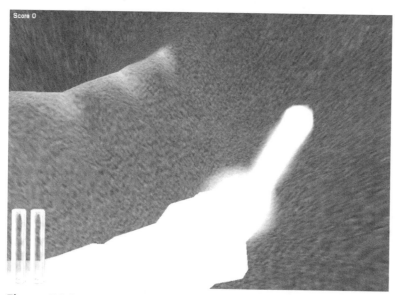

Figure 21.5
The falls.

You can refine your waterfall by using three nodes for the top—one each for the left, right, and center of the falling water—and perhaps two at the bottom. You'll notice when you look at some waterfalls that the center stream of water has a different character than the outer fringes—hence the use of three particle emitters. Also, when the water hits the pool at the bottom, there are typically two observable phenomena: splashing and spraying of fine mist. So two emitters at the bottom would go a long way as well.

The Terrain

I've prebuilt two terrains—trackA.ter and trackB.ter—for use in Koob. Of course, you are free to make your own. Each of these terrains has a different—in fact, a somewhat opposite—appearance.

trackA.ter is a bit claustrophobic in places, with much of the action happening in and around canyons and riverbeds, as you can see in Figure 21.6.

trackB.ter, in Figure 21.7, is more wide open, driving around a series of foothills and mountains.

In both cases, as I laid out the track, I wanted to make sure there was no way to grossly cheat and find a shortcut that would allow someone who knew of the shortcut to obtain a huge advantage. In fact, I designed trackB.ter to have two built-in shortcuts that may or may not be quicker than staying on the track. See if you can find them!

Also, the specification that says that checkpoints must be used will help minimize shortcut use as cheating.

Figure 21.6
trackA.ter.

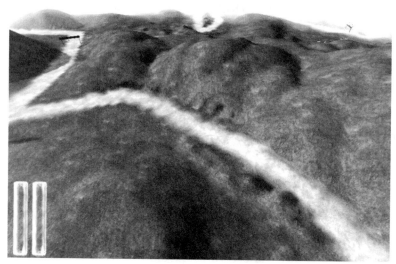

Figure 21.7
trackB.ter.

The trackA terrain is quite similar to the test terrain we've been using with Emaga6 and earlier revisions of Koob. trackB is entirely new. If you want to check them out, then copy the files trackA.mis, trackA.ter, trackB.mis, and trackB.ter from \3D2E\RESOURCES\CH21\ and deposit them in the \KOOB\ control\data\maps\ directory.

Next, you will need to edit the file \KOOB\control\client\client.cs and find this line:

```
createServer("SinglePlayer", "control/data/maps/koobA.mis");
```

You can enter the file name of whichever mission file (and thus terrain) you want to look at—trackA.mis or trackB.mis. Now I know this seems to be an awkward way to select missions. We will be addressing this issue in the next chapters.

Items and Structures

Go ahead and set up Koob to use trackB. Once that's done, copy all the files located in \3D2E\RESOURCES\CH21\STRUCTURES, and put them in \KOOB\ control\data\maps\. If you get a dialog box asking if you want to overwrite existing files, your answer is yes.

Now launch the game and go into camera fly mode after you've spawned. You should be in the middle of a big parking lot.

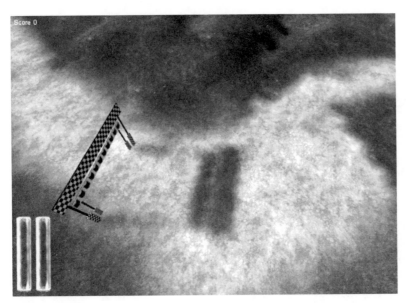

Figure 21.8
The start/finish line.

Enter the World Editor Creator (press F11 followed by F4), and browse the Tree view until you find Interiors, Control, Data, Structures. Then look for the startfinish item and the checkpoint item, placing one of each in the game world, using Figure 21.8 as a guide.

Note

> When you insert new structures, Torque helpfully provides you with a notification that the lightmap has changed with a little long message box at the bottom of your screen. If you are not busy placing dozens of objects in your scene, then go ahead and press on the Relight Scene button. If you *are* busy placing lots of things, then just press the Hide button, because relighting scenes can take quite a while, depending on how complex your scene is.

To rotate an object, select it, hold down the Alt key, and hover the cursor over one of the gizmo axes (X, Y, or Z) of the item. When the axis label appears, click and hold. Then drag your cursor left or right, up or down, to cause the item to rotate around the chosen axis.

If you need to go back and adjust an object already placed, press F4 to enter the World Editor Inspector to select and adjust the items. Switch back to the World Editor Creator to resume placing items.

To move an item, select it, hover the cursor over one of the axis gizmos, and click and drag in the direction you want to move.

Figure 21.9
Barrier.

To scale an object along an axis, select the axis as before, and then hold down both the Alt and Ctrl keys while dragging the cursor. The checkpoint object will have to be scaled a bit horizontally and vertically to fit it inside the startfinish object, as depicted earlier in Figure 21.8.

To define the track, you can use a number of other structures, like barriers (see Figure 21.9) and direction signs (see Figure 21.10).

You should place checkpoints at the locations indicated in Figure 21.11. There will be a total of five checkpoints: one at the start/finish line and four more around the track.

Place barriers strategically to prevent access to certain areas, and use the direction signs to assist players in understanding which direction the track will be heading.

You should also place a tommy gun and crossbow accompanied by an ammo box for each somewhere in the vicinity of the start/finish line.

Place a Health Kit somewhere near the start/finish line as well. Also place a HealthPatch object near each checkpoint. You can use a block structure from the Interiors list to place these items on to improve visibility. Make sure to sink the block low enough into the ground that the player can jump up on it.

Figure 21.10
Direction sign.

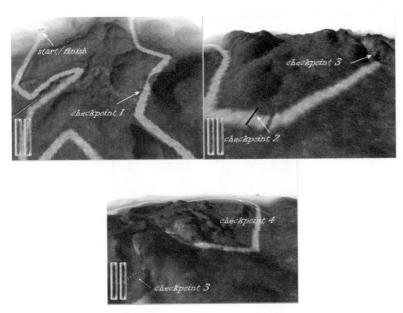

Figure 21.11
Checkpoint locations.

Also from the Interiors list, locate the hovels, and place a few around the track, near it but not too close. Make sure there is a way for a player to get to the hovels, and perhaps provide enough space to hide a vehicle behind them.

Select some trees and rocks from the Static Shapes list under Static Shapes, Control, Data, Models, Items. Place them around your map at visually appealing as well as strategic locations—you want to provide places for people to hide during an ambush. (Rocks to hide cars behind and so on.)

Go on and do the same sorts of things for trackA. There is a large flat area in a canyon near where you currently spawn (it's actually behind you), with a bridge leading across the river nearby. This is where you should put your start/finish line. The direction of travel will be to head from the start directly across the bridge and on from there. You probably won't need more than four checkpoints (other than the start/finish line) to complete the route. If you find you need to adjust the terrain to accommodate a building or something, by all means do it.

Don't worry about placing the coins. That is something we will handle with program code in the next chapter.

Moving Right Along

Well, things got a little more hectic in this chapter. As you saw, designing a game is about answering questions. Often, the answers are the easy part—coming up with the questions can be tougher at times. Creating a requirements specification for your game is not only useful, it's almost a mandatory activity.

There are things that constrain our design, and we need to keep those constraints in mind. Every project will have different limits. One example you saw was that you probably shouldn't consider using Torque to make a massively multiplayer game.

We then looked at the Mission Editor in detail. You can use it to place and align all the objects that will inhabit your game world. We used it to place some particle effects, in the form of a campfire and a waterfall, as well as some structures that will be useful for game play.

Let's examine our requirements again. We checked off item 1 right from the get-go. Now we can check off a bunch of other items: 4, 5, 6, 7, 8, 10, 22, 27, and 28. We've also done parts of 9, 23, 24, and 25, but they need some programming as well to make them reality.

In the next chapter we will delve into more server-side game play issues, like spawning the player into random locations, getting a vehicle into the world, and triggering events.

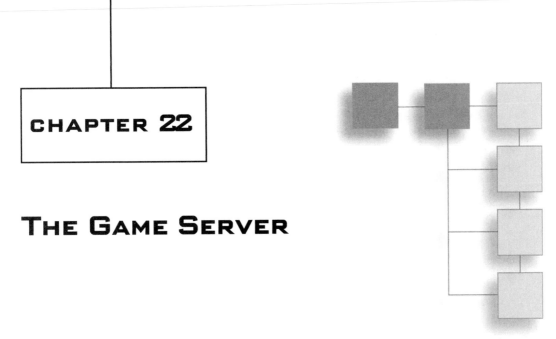

CHAPTER 22

THE GAME SERVER

Now we have some things we've either added to the game world in recent chapters or simply included in our game requirements that are not yet supported in the program code.

In this chapter we'll focus on adding the server-side code we need to support the requirements, as well as adding in some code to bring certain concepts to a more complete state.

The Player-Character

You've probably noticed a few things that are odd or incomplete in the player behavior or appearance in the code and art we've dealt with up to this point. We'll tackle those things now.

Player Spawning

For our example games, we've used a fixed spawn point. Well, there is a convenient spawn point system available that we can employ.

First thing we need for this system is what we call a *marker*. Create a new file named \koob\control\server\misc\marker.cs, and add the following to it:

```
datablock MissionMarkerData(SpawnMarker)
{
    category = "Markers";
```

```
      shapeFile = "~/data/models/markers/sphere.dts";
};

function MissionMarkerData::Create(%block)
{
   switch$(%block)
   {
      case "SpawnMarker":
        %obj = new SpawnSphere() {
            datablock = %block;
        };
        return(%obj);
   }
   return -1;
}
```

This has the by-now-familiar datablock, this one for a `MissionMarkerData`. The `Create` function tells the World Editor Creator how to make the new marker in the game world. Note the use of the `switch$` block, even though there is only one case—this is for later use for other kinds of markers. Save your work.

Now copy the directory \3D2E\RESOURCES\CH22\markers and all of its contents to \koob\control\data\models\markers, creating a new folder if you need to.

Now open the file \koob\control\server\server.cs and locate the line:

```
Exec("./misc/item.cs");
```

Add the following entry after it:

```
Exec("./misc/markers.cs");
```

Save your file.

With that done, launch Koob, go into camera fly mode, and then move to a position overseeing the start/finish line, looking down at it. Go into World Editor Creator (press F11 followed by F4), and then add a `PlayerSpawns` group by choosing Mission Objects, System, SimGroup from the Tree view at the lower right and entering `PlayerSpawns` as the object name in the dialog box. Make `PlayerSpawns` the current group by locating it in the hierarchy at the upper right and then holding down the Alt key while clicking the `PlayerSpawns` entry. The `PlayerSpawns` folder icon should now be green. Next, add a spawn marker by choosing Shapes, Markers,

SpawnMarker from the Tree view at the lower right. A gray-white sphere will be placed in the world. Position about half a dozen or so of these around the start/finish area, hiding a few of them. Make sure they were all created in the `PlayerSpawns` group.

Save your mission and exit to the desktop.

Now open the file \koob\control\server\server.cs, and locate the function `SpawnPlayer`. Change the `createPlayer` call to look like this:

```
%this.createPlayer(SelectSpawn());
```

Next, add the following method to the end of the file (or immediately after the `SpawnPlayer` function, if you like):

```
function SelectSpawn()
{
    %groupName = "MissionGroup/PlayerSpawns";
    %group = nameToID(%groupName);

    if (%group != -1) {
        %count = %group.getCount();
        if (%count != 0) {
            %index = getRandom(%count-1);
            %spawn = %group.getObject(%index);
            return %spawn.getTransform();
        }
    else
            error("No spawn points found in " @ %groupName);
    }
    else
        error("Missing spawn points group " @ %groupName);

    return "0 0 201 1 0 0 0"; // if no spawn points then center of world
}
```

This function will examine the `PlayerSpawns` group and count how many spawn markers are in it. It then randomly selects one of them and gets its transform (which contains the marker's position and rotation) and returns that value.

With this done, go ahead and try your game. Notice how each time you spawn, it's in a different place.

Vehicle Mounting

In recent chapters, when you've made your player-character get into the car, you may have noticed—especially from the third-person perspective—that the player is standing, with his head poking through the roof.

This is addressed by assigning values to a `mountPose` array. What we do is for each vehicle, we create `mountPoints` in the model (which we've done for the car). We need to specify in the car's model some nodes that will act as the mount points. We'll address the pose part of the player model in the next section, leaving the rest until a later section that covers vehicles.

The Model

In recent chapters I have been using the standard "Kork" the Torque Orc model as a filler for testing the code, maps, and other models. Now, however, it's time for you to use your own model, the Hero model we created back in Chapter 14. There are a few things we need to adjust in that model, so make a copy of your Hero model, and add him to your Koob models directory at \koob\control\ data\models\avatars\hero. Create the hero directory if you haven't already done it. Copy all of your Hero model files, including the texture files, into that directory.

You also need to change the player definition file to point to your hero model. Open \3D2E\control\server\players\player.cs and locate the `PlayerData(MaleAvatar)` datablock.

In that datablock, find the line that reads:

```
shapeFile = "~/data/models/avatars/orc/player.dts";
```

and change it to:

```
shapeFile = "~/data/models/avatars/hero/myhero.dts";
```

If you didn't name your guy "myhero" use the name you gave him.

Also, notice the top line of this same file that says:

```
exec("~/data/models/avatars/orc/player.cs");
```

Even though the file in that line has the same name, "player.cs", you will notice by the path that it's a different file. This is the animation sequence binding file. It associates sequence files with animations that Torque supports. If you have created your model to use the Torque animation sequences, then leave this line as it is.

If you created your own animation sequences, then change the path in that line to point to a sequence binding file of your own. You can use the standard one as a model, and just change the internal references to point to your own sequence files. The best place to keep your sequence binding file and the sequence files themselves is in the same folder as your model. You should also name your sequence file with the same name as your model's shape file. For example, if your model's shape file is "myhero.dts", then name your sequence binding file "myhero.cs".

So, to support your own sequences, change that line at the top of player.cs to be:

```
exec("~/data/models/avatars/hero/myhero.cs");
```

and ensure that myhero.dts, its textures and sequence files, and myhero.cs are all in the \3D2E\control\data\models\avatars\hero folder.

And while we're talking about heroes, go back into \3D2E\control\server\players\ player.cs and change all instances of OrcClass to HeroClass. There are probably four places—once in the PlayerData datablock:

```
className = OrcClass;
```

and three times in method declarations, looking like this:

```
OrcClass::onAdd
OrcClass::onRemove
OrcClass::onCollision
```

Adjusting Model Scale

You may find that your character is not the right size for your needs. If that is the case, it is easy to resolve. Make a judgment about how his size needs to change. For the moment, let's pretend he needs to be 50 percent bigger than he is now.

Fire up MilkShape and load your model. Choose File, Export, Torque DTS Plus to run the DTSPlus Exporter. If the scale value in the name Scale box is 0.2, then change it to 0.3 (that's 1.5 times larger than, or 150 percent of, 0.2).

Animations

To properly mount your character in a vehicle, you will need to create a sitting pose. In MilkShape add some more frames in the animation window—make sure to click the Anim button first!

Then select the last frame, and move the joints around until the character looks something like that shown in Figure 22.1.

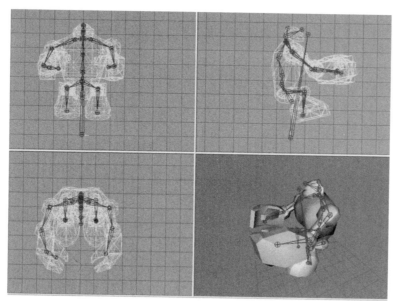

Figure 22.1
Sitting pose.

Create a special material to be the sequence entry for this—it will be a one-frame sequence. Name the material "seq:sitting=102-102", save your work, and then export the file to your \koob\control\data\models\avatars\hero\ directory. The rest of the mounting stuff will be handled shortly, in the "Vehicle" section.

Server Code

Back in Chapter 6 you saw how we can set up a Torque game to run as a dedicated server. When a server is dedicated, it doesn't need to be able to display any of the fancy editors that Torque makes available. Since wasted code is wasted memory, let's put in a simple statement that checks to see if the dedicated server is running, and if it is, then bypass the Creator functionality.

We already have the variable $Server::Dedicated that is set to true when the -dedicated command line switch is used to run a dedicated server. We can use it in our little bypass trick. Open the file \3D2E\creator\main.cs and locate the line:

```
Parent::onStart();
```

Immediately below that line, insert the following:

```
if ($Server::Dedicated)
     return;
```

That's it! If $Server::Dedicated turns out to be true, we just bail out the Creator's OnStart method, which happens to be where all the Creator capability is fired up. Now we avoid all that wasted memory. Now on to other things.

Back in Chapter 20 I provided you with some code to mount and unmount the vehicle, just so you could hop in and out and test sounds. I didn't say much about what it did or why. Let's take a look now.

Collision

The premise is that you simply run up to a car and collide with it to get in. Now you must be mindful not to hit it too hard, or you will hurt yourself when you get in. If you think that it shouldn't be so easy to hurt yourself, then you can edit your player's datablock to suit. Simply open \koob\control\server\players\ player.cs, find the line that starts with minImpactSpeed=, and increase the value— maybe to around 15 or so.

When your player collides with anything, the server makes a call, via the class name of your character's datablock to the callback method onCollision.

Tip

The class name for any datablock can be set via script like this:

```
classname = classname;
```

In the case of our player, *classname* is HeroClass, so the line is

```
classname = HeroClass;
```

Then methods are defined as

```
HeroClass::myMethod()
{ /// code in here
}
```

And they are invoked as

```
MyAvatarObjectHandle.myMethod();
```

OnCollision looks like this:

```
function HeroClass::onCollision(%this,%obj,%col,%vec,%speed)
{
   %obj_state = %obj.getState();
   %col_className = %col.getClassName();
   %col_dblock_className = %col.getDataBlock().className;
   %colName = %col.getDataBlock().getName();
```

```
if ( %obj_state $= "Dead")
  return;
if (%col_className $= "Item" || %col_className $= "Weapon" )
{
   %obj.pickup(%col);
}

%this = %col.getDataBlock();
 if ( %this.className $= "Car" )
 {
    %node = 0;   // Find next available seat
    %col.mountObject(%obj,%node);
    %obj.mVehicle = %col;
 }
}
```

In the parameters, %this refers to the datablock that this method belongs to, %obj is a handle to the instance of the avatar object that is our player in the game, %col is a handle to the object we've just hit, %vec is our velocity vector, and %speed is our speed.

The first thing we do is to check our object state, because if we are dead, we don't need to worry about anything anymore. We want to do this because dead avatars can still slide down hills and bang into things, until we decide to respawn. Therefore we need to stop dead avatars from picking up items in the world.

After that we check the class name of the object we hit, and if it is an item that can be picked up, we pick it up.

Next, if the class is a Car, then this is where the mount action starts. The variable %node refers to the mount node. If %node is 0, then we are interested in the node mount0. That node is created in the model of the car, and the next section will show how we put that in. (This is not difficult—it's just a matter of creating a joint in the right place and naming it mount0.)

Then we make the call into the engine to mountObject for the car's object instance, and the game engine handles the details for us. We then update our player's instance to save the handle to the car we've just mounted.

If the object can't be picked up and is also not mountable, then we actually hit it. The next bit of code calculates our force based on our velocity and applies an impulse to the object we hit. So if we hit a garbage can, we will send it flying.

Mounting

Now when you call the `mountObject` method, the engine calls back to a method in the `ShapeBase` from which your avatar is derived. The method is `onMount`, and it looks like this:

```
function MaleAvatar::onMount(%this,%obj,%vehicle,%node)
{
  %obj.setTransform("0 0 0 0 1 0");
  %obj.setActionThread(%vehicle.getDatablock().mountPose[%node]);
  if (%node == 0)
  {
    %obj.setControlObject(%vehicle);
    %obj.lastWeapon = %obj.getMountedImage($WeaponSlot);
    %obj.unmountImage($WeaponSlot);
  }
}
```

Now if you are wondering why the `onCollision` handler is accessed via the class name and the `onMount` handler is accessed via `ShapeBase`, I'll just have to admit that I'm not sure, and the answer isn't really that apparent. It's one of the quirks of Torque, but if you keep it in mind, you won't have any problems.

The `onMount` method is interested in the `%obj`, `%vehicle`, and `%node` parameters. Our player is `%obj`, and obviously the vehicle we are mounting is `%vehicle`. The parameter `%node` refers to the mount node, as discussed earlier.

The first thing the code does is set our player to a null transform at a standard orientation, because the rest of the player object's transform information will be handled by the game engine, with the object *slaved* to the car—wherever the car goes, our player automatically goes as well.

Next, the mount pose is invoked, with the call to `setActionThread`. The animation sequence that was defined in the datablock as referring `mount0` is set in action. The animation sequence itself is only one frame, so the player just sits there, inside the car. However, your player won't sit until a change is made to the vehicle definition, which comes later in this chapter.

Now, if we are dealing with node 0, which by convention is always the driver, then we need to do a few things: arrange things so that our control inputs are directed to the car, save the information about what weapons we were carrying, and then unmount the weapon from our player.

Dismounting

Dismounting, or *unmounting*, is accomplished using whatever key is assigned to the jump action. It's a bit more involved than the mount code. First, there is this bit:

```
function MaleAvatar::doDismount(%this, %obj, %forced)
{
    %pos    = getWords(%obj.getTransform(), 0, 2);
    %oldPos = %pos;
    %vec[0] = "1  1  1";
    %vec[1] = "1  1  1";
    %vec[2] = "1  1  -1";
    %vec[3] = "1  0  0";
    %vec[4] = "-1  0  0";
    %impulseVec = "0 0 0";
    %vec[0] = MatrixMulVector( %obj.getTransform(), %vec[0]);
    %pos = "0 0 0";
    %numAttempts = 5;
    %success     = -1;
    for (%i = 0; %i < %numAttempts; %i++)
    {
        %pos = VectorAdd(%oldPos, VectorScale(%vec[%i], 3));
        if (%obj.checkDismountPoint(%oldPos, %pos))
        {
            %success = %i;
            %impulseVec = %vec[%i];
            break;
        }
    }
    if (%forced && %success == -1)
        %pos = %oldPos;
    %obj.unmount();
    %obj.setControlObject(%obj);
    %obj.mountVehicle = false;
    %obj.setTransform(%pos);
    %obj.applyImpulse(%pos, VectorScale(%impulseVec, %obj.getDataBlock().mass));
}
```

Most of the code here is involved in deciding if the point chosen to deposit the player after removing him from the car is a safe and reasonable spot or not. We start by setting a direction vector, applying that vector to our player to figure out in advance where the proposed landing site for the freshly dismounted player will be, and then making sure it's okay using the checkDismountPoint method. If it isn't okay, the algorithm keeps moving the vector around until it finds a place that is suitable.

Once the site is determined, the unMount method is invoked, and we return control back to our player model, deposit the model at the computed location, and give our player a little nudge.

When unMount is called, the game engine does its thing, and then it summons the callback onUnmount. What we do here is restore the weapon we unmounted.

```
function MaleAvatar::onUnmount( %this, %obj, %vehicle, %node )
{
  %obj.mountImage(%obj.lastWeapon, $WeaponSlot);
}
```

Vehicle

We need to revisit the runabout to prepare it for use as a mountable vehicle. The enhancement is not complex—just some changes to its datablock.

Oh Yeah, the Model

If you recall, in Chapter 15 we created a vehicle with two mount nodes. These mount nodes are the locations in the vehicle where the player model will be mounted. I have slapped Figure 22.2 here just to give you a convenient visual reminder of what that looks like.

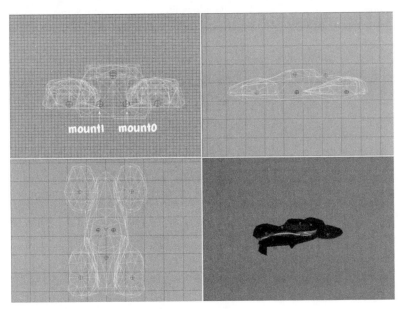

Figure 22.2
Car mount nodes.

Datablock

We need to add a few things to the datablock. Open your file \koob\control\server\vehicles\car.cs, and find the datablock. It looks like this:

```
datablock WheeledVehicleData(DefaultCar)
```

Add the following to the end of the datablock:

```
mountPose[0]        = "sitting";
mountPose[1]        = "sitting";
numMountPoints      = 2;
```

The properties are pretty straightforward—"sitting" refers to the name of sequence in the model that we created earlier with the Hero model in the sitting pose. The name was defined in a special material.

Table 22.1 contains descriptions of the most significant properties available for adjustment in the WheeledVehicleData datablock, even if we aren't using them all with the Runabout.

Table 22.1 WheeledVehicleData Properties

Property	Description
maxDamage	Specifies the maximum number of damage points a vehicle can take before it becomes disabled. Destroyed and disabled states are calculated percentages of this value.
destroyedLevel	Specifies the percentage of MaxDamage that, when reached, causes the vehicle's onDestroyed callback to be called by the engine.
disabledLevel	Specifies the percentage of MaxDamage that, when reached, causes the vehicle's onDisabled callback to be called by the engine.
maxSteeringAngle	Specifies the maximum steering angle.
tireEmitter	Specifies a dust emitter that is used by all the tires.
cameraRoll	Rolls the camera with the vehicle when it rolls.
cameraMaxDist	Specifies the farthest distance from the vehicle in third-person view.
cameraOffset	Specifies the vertical offset from the camera mount point.
cameraLag	Specifies the velocity lag of the camera in third-person view.
cameraDecay	Specifies the decay per second rate of velocity lag in third-person view.
mass	Specifies the mass of the vehicle in quasi-kilograms.
massCenter	Specifies the center of mass for rigid body expressed in object space 3D coordinates.
massBox	Specifies the size of box used for moment of inertia; if 0 it defaults to the object's bounding box.

Property	Description
drag	Specifies the drag coefficient. Used to counteract acceleration.
bodyFriction	Determines "stickiness" when the body brushes against the terrain or other objects.
bodyRestitution	Determines, by using rigid body physics, how much deformation is reversed.
minImpactSpeed	Specifies the speed at and above which the vehicle's onImpact callback will be called by the engine.
softImpactSpeed	Specifies the speed at and above which the engine will play the vehicle's SoftImpact sound.
hardImpactSpeed	Specifies the speed at and above which the engine will play the vehicle's HardImpact sound.
integration	Specifies the physics integration value: TickSec/Rate. Higher values here yield higher integration. Higher integration leads to more accurate simulation but at the potential cost of CPU performance.
collisionTol	Specifies the collision distance tolerance. A higher number means that a collision will be detected sooner (objects are farther apart) than with a lower number.
contactTol	Specifies the contact velocity tolerance. How much leeway is allowed in determining whether objects have collided or have merely contacted, or brushed, each other. A higher number means that a more forceful contact can occur without the contact being considered a collision.
engineTorque	Specifies the engine power, which causes acceleration, which leads to higher velocities.
engineBrake	Specifies the braking force caused by the engine when throttle is 0—simulates the internal "drag" of an engine that tends to slow a vehicle when it is in gear.
brakeTorque	Works as the opposite of EngineTorque, when brakes are applied.
maxWheelSpeed	Specifies the maximum rotation speed of the wheels, which directly affects the speed of the vehicle based on the wheel diameter and deformation factors. Wheel speed derives from engine speed and other factors.
maxEnergy	Specifies the maximum amount of energy available to the vehicle for conversion into motion. Energy can be seen to be the same as fuel load.
jetForce	Specifies the additional boost force—a holdover term from the *Tribes* days. Means the same as acceleration.
minJetEnergy	Specifies the smallest amount of energy needed to apply a jetting boost.
jetEnergyDrain	Specifies how quickly the energy of the vehicle is drained by use of jetting.
jetSound	Specifies the sound played when jetting or accelerating.
engineSound	Specifies the sound played when the engine is idling.
squealSound	Specifies the sound played when the tires skid.
softImpactSound	Specifies the sound played when a mild collision occurs.
hardImpactSound	Specifies the sound played when a serious collision occurs.
wheelImpactSound	Specifies the sound played when the wheels and tires hit something.

Two other datablocks have significant effect on the behavior of the car: Wheel-edVehicleTire and WheeledVehicleSpring, shown here:

```
datablock WheeledVehicleTire(DefaultCarTire)
{
  shapeFile = "~/data/models/vehicles/wheel.dts";
  staticFriction = 4;
  kineticFriction = 1.25;
  lateralForce = 18000;
  lateralDamping = 4000;
  lateralRelaxation = 1;
  longitudinalForce = 18000;
  longitudinalDamping = 4000;
  longitudinalRelaxation = 1;
};
datablock WheeledVehicleSpring(DefaultCarSpring)
{
  // Wheel suspension properties
  length = 0.85;            // Suspension travel
  force = 3000;             // Spring force
  damping = 600;            // Spring damping
  antiSwayForce = 3;        // Lateral anti-sway force
};
```

In the WheeledVehicleTire datablock you can see that tires act as springs in two ways. They generate lateral and longitudinal forces to move the vehicle. These distortion/spring forces are what convert wheel angular velocity into forces that act on the rigid body.

Triggering Events

When you need your players to interact with the game world, there is a lot that is handled by the engine through the programming of various objects in the environment, as we saw with collisions with vehicles. Most other interactions not handled by an object class can be dealt with using triggers.

A *trigger* is essentially a location in the game world, and the engine will detect when the player enters and leaves that space (*trigger events*). Based on the event detected we can define what should happen when that event is triggered using *event handlers* or *trigger callbacks*. We can organize our triggering to occur when there is an interaction with a specific object.

Creating Triggers

If you recall, some of our Koob specifications require us to count the number of laps completed. What we'll do is add a trigger to the area around the start/finish line, and every time a car with a player in it passes through this area, we'll increment the lap counter for that player.

For the trigger to know what object to call `onTrigger` for, you need to add an additional dynamic field with the name of instance of the trigger when it is created using the Mission Editor.

Open the file \koob\control\server\server.cs, and at the end of the `onServer-Created` function, add this line:

```
exec("./misc/tracktriggers.cs");
```

This will load in our definitions.

Now create the file \koob\control\server\misc\tracktriggers.cs, and put the following code in it:

```
datablock TriggerData(LapTrigger)
{
    tickPeriodMS = 100;
};

function LapTrigger::onEnterTrigger(%this,%trigger,%obj)
{
  if(%trigger.cp $= "")
    echo("Trigger checkpoint not set on " @ %trigger);
  else
    %obj.client.UpdateLap(%trigger,%obj);
}
```

The datablock declaration contains one property that specifies how often the engine will check to see if an object has entered the area of the trigger. In this case it is set to a 100-millisecond period, which means the trigger is checked 10 times per second.

There are three possible methods you can use for the trigger event handlers:

`onEnterTrigger`, `onLeaveTrigger`, and `onTickTrigger`.

The `onEnterTrigger` and `onLeaveTrigger` methods have the same argument list. The first parameter, `%this`, is the trigger datablock's handle. The second parameter, `%trigger`, is the handle for the instance of the trigger object in question.

The third parameter, %obj, is the handle for the instance of the object that entered or left the trigger.

In this onEnterTrigger the method is called as soon as (within a tenth of a second) the engine detects that an object has entered the trigger. The code checks the cp property of the trigger object to make sure that it has been set (not set to null or ""). If the cp property (which happens to be the checkpoint ID number) is set, then we call the client's UpdateLap method, with the trigger's handle and the colliding object's handle as arguments.

You can use onLeaveTrigger in exactly the same way, if you need to know when an object leaves a trigger.

The onTickTrigger method is similar but doesn't have the %obj property. This method is called every time the tick event occurs (10 times a second), as long as any object is present inside the trigger.

Tip

Since we're going to be using the Mission Editor a lot in this next section, we'll need to change the resolution so we can work with the various editors' options comfortably. Launch Koob and at the startup screen, click the Setup button. Change the Resolution to 800 × 600, or even higher if you can. Be sure to leave the program in windowed mode, in case something goes wrong and you have to force-kill the program with Alt + F4. Click OK and start the game.

Next, we need to place the triggers in our world. We are going to put five triggers in: one at the start/finish line and one at each of the checkpoints.

Go into camera fly mode, and then move to a position overseeing (looking down at) the start/finish line. Go into the World Editor Creator (press F11 followed by F4), and then add a trigger by choosing Mission Objects, Mission, Trigger from the Tree view at the lower right.

Tip

Don't forget that when you are placing a new trigger, you need to give it a relevant name. You also need to select the LapTrigger datablock from the datablock pop-up in the New Object dialog box.

Also, establish the extents of your trigger using the scale property—don't bother fiddling with the polyhedron values.

Once you have your trigger placed, rotate and position it as necessary underneath the start/finish banner, and resize it to fill the width and the height of the area

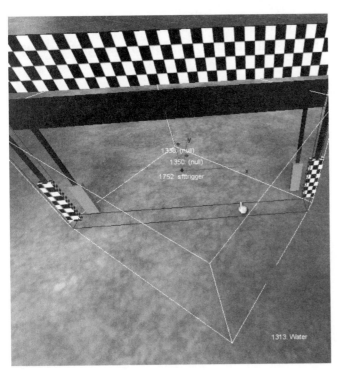

Figure 22.3
Placing a trigger.

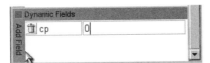

Figure 22.4
The Add dynamic field dialog box.

under the banner. Make the thickness roughly about one-tenth of the width, as shown in Figure 22.3.

Now switch to the World Editor (F3), locate your new object in the hierarchy at the upper right, and click on it to select it. In the Inspector frame, locate the Dynamic Fields section, and then click the sideways button called Add Field (the arrow cursor in Figure 22.4 points to it). You will see a new entry appear in the Dynamic Fields section that says "NewDynamicField" on the left side in the name box, and "Default Value" on the right side in the value box. Enter "cp" in the name box and "0" in the value box. Then click the Apply button to commit the changes to the object. What we've done is added a property to the object and named it "cp" with the value 0. We can access this property later from within the program code. The next checkpoint will be numbered 1, the one after that will be 2, next is 3, and finally 4, which is the fifth checkpoint. The numbering proceeds in a counterclockwise direction.

Tip

If you need to get rid of a dynamic field, just click on the little trash can icon on the left side of the field.

Go ahead and add those checkpoints now, using the same technique as just noted. You can copy and paste the first trigger object to create the rest if you like—just remember to change the cp property accordingly.

Tip

Some objects behave a little oddly when added via copy and paste. After pasting an object into the world, even though it will be visually selected in the view of the world, it still needs to be selected in the Inspector hierarchy in the upper-right frame. There are times when this may not be strictly necessary, but if you move, rotate, or resize the object by directly manipulating it via the gizmo handles, the changes will not be reflected in the Inspector frame until you reselect the object in the hierarchy.

Now we have the ability to measure progress around the track. We have to add code to use these triggers, and that will be done as part of the scoring system, which is in the next section.

Scoring

We need to keep track of our accomplishments and transmit those values to the client for display.

Laps and Checkpoints

Open the file \koob\control\server\server.cs, and put the following code at the end of the GameConnection::CreatePlayer method:

```
%client.lapsCompleted = 0;
%client.cpCompleted = 0;
%client.ResetCPs();

%client.position = 0;
%client.money = 0;
%client.deaths = 0;
%client.kills = 0;
%client.score = 0;
```

These are the variables we use to track various scores. Now add the following methods to the end of the file:

```
function GameConnection::ResetCPs(%client)
{
    for (%i = 0; %i < $Game::NumberOfCheckpoints; %i++)
      %client.cpCompleted[%i]=false;
}
function GameConnection::CheckProgress(%client, %cpnumber)
{
    for (%i = 0; %i < %cpnumber; %i++)
    {
      if (%client.cpCompleted[%i]==false)
        return false;
    }
    %client.cpCompleted = %cpnumber;
    return true;
}
function GameConnection::UpdateLap(%client,%trigger,%obj)
{
    if (%trigger.cp==0)
    {
      if (%client.CheckProgress($Game::NumberOfCheckpoints))
      {
          %client.ResetCPs();
          %client.cpCompleted[0] = true;
          %client.lapsCompleted++;
          %client.DoScore();
          if(%client.lapsCompleted >= $Game::NumberOfLaps)
            EndGame();
      }
      else
      {
        %client.cpCompleted[0] = true;
        %client.DoScore();
      }
    }
    else if (%client.CheckProgress(%trigger.cp))
    {
      %client.cpCompleted[%trigger.cp] = true;
      %client.DoScore();
    }
}
```

```
function GameConnection::DoScore(%client)
{
  %scoreString =              %client.score            @
                   " Lap: " @ %client.lapsCompleted @
                   " CP:  " @ %client.cpCompleted+1 @
                   " $:   " @ %client.money           @
                   " D:   " @ %client.deaths          @
                   " K:   " @ %client.kills;
  commandToClient(%client, 'UpdateScore', %scoreString);
}
```

Starting from the last, the DoScore method merely sends a string containing scores to the client using the messaging system. The client code to handle this string will be presented in Chapter 23.

Before that is the meat of these particular functions: UpdateLap. You will recall that this is the method that is called for the client from the onEnterTrigger method.

The first thing UpdateLap does is to check to see if this is the first checkpoint, because it has a special case. Because we will start and drive through the first checkpoint at the start/finish line, it can be legitimately triggered without any other trigger events having occurred. We want to check for this condition. We check this by calling CheckProgress to see how many triggers have been passed. If the answer is none (a false return value), then we are starting the race, so we mark this checkpoint as having been completed and update our score to reflect that fact.

If this *isn't* the first checkpoint, then we want to check if all the checkpoints up until this checkpoint have been completed for this lap. If so, then mark this one completed and update the score; otherwise, just ignore it.

Now finally, if we are back at checkpoint 0 and if when we check to see if all the other checkpoints have been passed the result is true, then we are finishing a lap. So we increment the lap, reset the checkpoint counters, mark this checkpoint completed, update the score, and then check to see if the race is over; if not, we continue.

The previous method, CheckProgress, is called from UpdateLap and receives the current checkpoint ID number as a parameter. It then loops through the checkpoint array for this client and verifies that all lower-numbered checkpoints have been set to true (they have been passed). If any one of them is false, then this checkpoint is out of sequence and not legitimate. The function then returns false; otherwise, all is in order, and it returns true.

And then first, but not least (grins), is the method ResetCPs. This simple method just riffles through the checkpoint array setting all entries to false.

Now there are a few odds and ends to deal with. Earlier in this file, server.cs, is the StartGame function. Locate it, and add these lines after the last code in there:

```
$Game::NumberOfLaps = 10;
$Game::NumberOfCheckpoints = 5;
```

Of course, you should adjust these values to suit yourself. You might want to set NumberOfLaps to a lower number, like 2, for testing purposes. Speaking of testing, if you want to test this, but before addressing the client-side code, then you can add some echo statements and view the output in the console window (invoked by pressing the Tilde key). A good place to put such a statement would be just before the CommandToClient call in DoScore. It would look like this:

```
echo( "Score " @ %scoreString );
```

Money

Another requirement is to have randomly scattered coins in the game world.

Open \koob\control\server\server.cs, locate the function StartGame, and add the following line to the end of the function:

```
PlaceCoins();
```

Then place the following function just after the StartGame function:

```
function PlaceCoins()
{
%W=GetWord(MissionArea.area,2);
%H=GetWord(MissionArea.area,3);
%west = GetWord(MissionArea.area,0);
%south = GetWord(MissionArea.area,1);
  new SimSet (CoinGroup);
  for (%i = 0; %i < 4; %i++)
  {
    %x = GetRandom(%W) + %west;
    %y = GetRandom(%H) + %south;
    %searchMasks = $TypeMasks::PlayerObjectType |
    $TypeMasks::InteriorObjectType |
    $TypeMasks::TerrainObjectType |
    $TypeMasks::ShapeBaseObjectType;
    %scanTarg = ContainerRayCast(%x SPC %y SPC "500", %x SPC %y SPC "-100",
    %searchMasks);
```

```
    if(%scanTarg && !(%scanTarg.getType() & $TypeMasks::InteriorObjectType))
    {
      %newpos = GetWord(%scanTarg,1) SPC GetWord(%scanTarg,2) SPC
GetWord (%scanTarg,3) + 1;
    }
    %coin = new Item("Gold "@%i) {
      position = %newpos;
      rotation = "1 0 0 0";
      scale = "5 5 5";
      dataBlock = "Gold";
      collideable = "0";
      static = "0";
      rotate = "1";
    };
    MissionCleanup.add(%coin);
    CoinGroup.add(%coin);
  }
  // repeat above for silver coin
  for (%i = 0; %i < 8; %i++)
  {
    %x = GetRandom(%W) + %west;
    %y = GetRandom(%H) + %south;
    %searchMasks = $TypeMasks::PlayerObjectType |
    $TypeMasks::InteriorObjectType | $TypeMasks::TerrainObjectType |
    $TypeMasks::ShapeBaseObjectType;
    %scanTarg = ContainerRayCast(%x SPC %y SPC "500", %x SPC %y SPC "-100",
    %searchMasks);
    if(%scanTarg && !(%scanTarg.getType() & $TypeMasks::InteriorObjectType))
    {
      %newpos = GetWord(%scanTarg,1) SPC GetWord(%scanTarg,2) SPC GetWord
(%scanTarg,3) + 1;
    }
    %coin = new Item("Silver "@%i) {
      position = %newpos;
      rotation = "1 0 0 0";
      scale = "5 5 5";
      dataBlock = "Silver";
      collideable = "0";
      static = "0";
      rotate = "1";
    };
    MissionCleanup.add(%coin);
    CoinGroup.add(%coin);
  }
```

```
// repeat above for copper coin
for (%i = 0; %i < 32; %i++)
{
  %x = GetRandom(%W) + %west;
  %y = GetRandom(%H) + %south;
  %searchMasks = $TypeMasks::PlayerObjectType |
  $TypeMasks::InteriorObjectType | $TypeMasks::TerrainObjectType |
  $TypeMasks::ShapeBaseObjectType;
  %scanTarg = ContainerRayCast(%x SPC %y SPC "500", %x SPC %y SPC "-100",
%searchMasks);
  if(%scanTarg && !(%scanTarg.getType() & $TypeMasks::InteriorObjectType))
  {
   %newpos = GetWord(%scanTarg,1) SPC GetWord(%scanTarg,2) SPC GetWord
(%scanTarg,3) + 1;
  }
  %coin = new Item("Copper "@%i) {
    position = %newpos;
    rotation = "1 0 0 0";
    scale = "5 5 5";
    dataBlock = "Copper";
    collideable = "0";
    static = "0";
    rotate = "1";
  };
  MissionCleanup.add(%coin);
  CoinGroup.add(%coin);
 }
}
```

The first thing this function does is to obtain the particulars of the MissionArea. For this game you should use the Mission Area Editor (press F11 followed by F5) to expand the MissionArea to fill the entire available terrain tile.

The %H and %W values are the height and width of the MissionArea box. The variables %west and %south combined make the coordinates of the southwest corner. We use these values to constrain our random number selection.

Then we set up a search mask. All objects in the Torque Engine have a mask value that helps to identify the object type. We can combine these masks using a bitwise-or operation, in order to identify a selection of different types of interest.

Then we use our random coordinates to do a search from 500 world units altitude downward until we encounter terrain, using the ContainerRayCast function.

When the ray cast finds terrain, we add one world unit to the height and then use that plus the random coordinates to build a position at which to spawn a coin. Then we spawn the coin using the appropriate datablock, which can be found in your new copy of item.cs.

Next, we add the coin to the MissionCleanup group so that Torque will automatically remove the coins when the game ends. We also add it to the CoinGroup in case we want to access it later.

After putting that code in, copy \3D2E\RESOURCES\CH22\item.cs over to \koob\control\server\misc, replacing the existing item.cs. You will find the datablocks for the coins (where the coin values are assigned) in there.

Note that when we added the coins in the preceding code, the static parameter was set to 0. This means that the game will not create a new coin at the place where the coin was picked up, if it is picked up. The weapons of the ammo do this, but we don't want our coins to do it. It's a game play design decision.

In addition to the datablocks for the coins in item.cs, you will also find this code:

```
if (%user.client)
{
    messageClient(%user.client, 'MsgItemPickup', '\c0You picked up %1',
%this.pickupName);
    %user.client.money += %this.value;
    %user.client.DoScore();
}
```

The last two statements in there allow the player to accumulate the money values, and then the server notifies the client of the new score. Note that it is similar in that small way to the checkpoint scoring.

Again, until the client code is in place, you can insert echo statements there to verify that things are working properly.

Deaths

We want to track the number of times we die to further satisfy requirements, so open \koob\control\server\server.cs, locate the method GameConnection::onDeath, and add these lines at the end:

```
%this.deaths++;
%this.DoScore();
```

By now these lines should be familiar. We can expand the player death by adding some animation. Add the following to the end of \koob\control\server\players\ player.cs:

```
function Player::playDeathAnimation(%this,%deathIdx)
{
  %this.setActionThread("Die1");
}
```

Now "Die1" should actually be the name of whatever animation you made for the character's death back in Chapter 14. If you are using Torque's sequences, then you probably want to use "Death1" instead. In fact, there are 11 Torque death sequences, so it would be good practice for you to create code in the above function to randomly pick one of the 11 animations.

We covered how to randomly pick a number and add it to a string back in Chapter 20, when we were hurling insults at each other.

Kills

The victim, who notifies the shooter's client when he dies, actually does the kill tracking. So we go back to GameConnection::onDeath and add this to the end of the function:

```
%sourceClient = %sourceObject ? %sourceObject.client : 0;
if (%obj.getState() $= "Dead")
{
    if (isObject(%sourceClient))
    {
        %sourceClient.incScore(1);
        if (isObject(%client))
          %client.onDeath(%sourceObject, %sourceClient, %damageType, %location);
    }
}
```

This bit of code figures out who shot the player and notifies the shooter's client object of this fact.

Now it is important to remember that all this takes place on the server, and when we refer to the client in this context, we are actually talking about the client's *connection object* and not about the remote client itself.

Okay, so now let's move on to the client side and finish filling the requirements!

Moving Right Along

So, now we have our player's model ready to appear in the game as our avatar, wheels for him to get around in, and a way to figure out where he's been.

We've also put some things in the game world for the player to pursue to accumulate points and a way to discourage other players from accumulating too many points for themselves (by killing them).

All of these features are created on the server. In the next chapter we will add the features that will be handled by the game client.

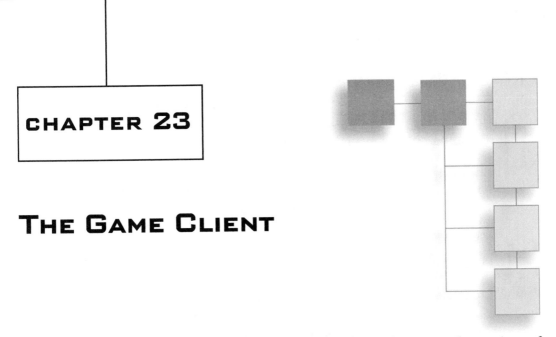

CHAPTER 23

THE GAME CLIENT

By now we've met most of our requirements, at least to the point of implementation. Testing them for correct operation and completeness I will leave as an exercise for you, gentle reader, because you may (and probably will) want to modify and enhance the requirements anyway.

According to my list, the requirements that remain outstanding are the following:

2. Networked multiplayer game play.

3. Global in-game chat.

11. All other players are enemies.

12. All point values configurable from a setup file.

14. 3 points per vehicle destroyed.

15. Ability to race around the track and score 5 points for each lap you lead. (*partial*)

16. Laps can only be scored in the car.

17. A 10-lap race with no time limit.

18. A 10-point bonus for winning the race.

29. When one map is finished, cycle to the next in the list.

Of this list, I will leave numbers 14, 16, 17, and 18 and the remaining portion of number 15 (scoring 5 points) to you to complete as exercises. They are variations of the coin scoring and the lap and checkpoint tracking we covered in Chapter 22. The functioning code is available in RESOURCES\Koob, if you need help.

Most of the remaining work requires additional client code to support the server additions we made in the last chapter—we'll add some multiplayer support, a little bit more client support, and user interfaces to access those capabilities.

Client Interfaces

We are going to add code to allow users to run a server and to allow players to connect to a server. In order to make that connection, we will want to provide the user with an interface he can use to find servers, decide which one offers an interesting game, and then connect to the server.

Another thing we need to do is make sure that when the user quits a server, he returns to his selection interface rather than simply exiting as Koob does now.

Additionally, we need to add a capability to the playing interface to provide a chat window with a text entry where players can type in messages to send to other players. Maybe they'll want to exchange recipes or something. Yeah, that's it—recipes! It's not like they're going to taunt anyone anyway, is it?

In Chapter 6 you saw the ServerScreen interface module that combined these interfaces. In this chapter we'll look at the same issue but in a slightly different way, in order to show how easy it is to make different—yet equally valid—design decisions.

Also, we'll need to modify a few of the files, like the MenuScreen interface, to more closely conform to our needs.

In a later section we'll add the code required to make these interfaces functional.

MenuScreen Interface

We will make some changes to our main menu screen so that it provides the user with the additional choices to

- view information about the games and credits
- play in single-player mode (as it already has)
- host a game
- connect to another server

Open your MenuScreen.gui file, in KOOB\control\client\interfaces and locate the following line:

```
command = "LaunchGame();";
```

This line is a property statement in a GuiButtonCtrl. Delete the entire control, from where it says

```
new GuiButtonCtrl() {
```

down to the closing brace ("}").

In the place of the deleted control, insert the following:

```
new GuiButtonCtrl() {
  profile = "GuiButtonProfile";
  horizSizing = "right";
  vertSizing = "top";
  position = "30 138";
  extent = "120 20";
  minExtent = "8 8";
  visible = "1";
  command = "Canvas.setContent(SoloScreen);";
  text = "Play Solo";
  groupNum = "-1";
  buttonType = "PushButton";
    helpTag = "0";
};
new GuiButtonCtrl() {
  profile = "GuiButtonProfile";
  horizSizing = "right";
  vertSizing = "top";
  position = "30 166";
  extent = "120 20";
  minExtent = "8 8";
  visible = "1";
  command = "Canvas.setContent(ServerScreen);";
  text = "Find a Server";
  groupNum = "-1";
  buttonType = "PushButton";
    helpTag = "0";
};
new GuiButtonCtrl() {
  profile = "GuiButtonProfile";
  horizSizing = "right";
```

```
      vertSizing = "top";
      position = "30 192";
      extent = "120 20";
      minExtent = "8 8";
      visible = "1";
      command = "Canvas.setContent(HostScreen);";
      text = "Host Game";
      groupNum = "-1";
      buttonType = "PushButton";
        helpTag = "0";
   };
   new GuiButtonCtrl() {
     profile = "GuiButtonProfile";
     horizSizing = "right";
     vertSizing = "top";
     position = "30 237";
     extent = "120 20";
     minExtent = "8 8";
     visible = "1";
     command = "getHelp();";
     helpTag = "0";
     text = "Info";
     groupNum = "-1";
     buttonType = "PushButton";
   };
```

You may, if you wish, use the built-in GUI Editor (press F10) to do this. Make sure that you set all the properties to match those just listed.

The significant thing to note about these controls is the command property. Each one replaces a displayed MenuScreen interface with a new interface, according to its function, with the exception of the Info button.

The Info button uses the getHelp feature of the common code base. It searches all the directories nested under the root main directory looking for files with the extension .hfl, and then it lists them in alphanumeric order. If you preface the file name with a number (such as 1., 2., and so on), it will sort them numerically.

This should give you a main menu that looks like Figure 23.1.

SoloScreen Interface

The SoloScreen interface, as shown in Figure 23.2, prepares a list of mission files that it finds in the maps subdirectory in the control\data directory tree. From this

Figure 23.1
MenuScreen interface.

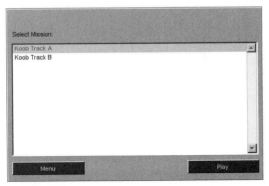

Figure 23.2
SoloScreen interface.

list, you can select the map or mission you want to play. Its code and definition can be found in the SoloScreen modules.

It's worth remembering that even when you play in solo mode, underneath the hood, the Torque Engine is still running in two parts: a client and a server. They are just closely coupled with no cross-network calls being made.

Host Interface

The Host interface is somewhat similar, as you can see in Figure 23.3, but it offers more options: the ability to set a time limit and a score limit, plus map selection modes. Its code and definition can be found in the HostScreen modules.

If both time and score limits are set, the first one reached ends the game. A setting of 0 makes that limit infinite. The sequence mode causes the server to step through the maps in order as shown in the listing, as each game finishes and the new one loads. The random mode causes the server to randomly select a map for each game. The time limit is saved by the control in the variable $Game::Duration, and the score limit is saved as $Game::MaxPoints.

FindServer Interface

The FindServer interface, shown in Figure 23.4, lets you browse for servers. Its code and definition can be found in the ServerScreen modules. It will find servers

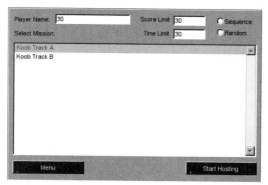

Figure 23.3
Host interface.

Figure 23.4
FindServer interface.

that are running on the local LAN you are connected to (if you are connected to one, of course), and it can attempt to reach out via the Internet to contact the master servers at GarageGames and find games for you to connect to. You are not required to use the GarageGames master servers, but then you will have to write your own master server software to connect to. This can be done using TorqueScript but is beyond the scope of this book. There are master server resources available from the GarageGames user community.

ChatBox Interface

In order to display chat messages from other players, we need to put a control in our main player interface. We also need to have a control that will allow us to type in messages to be sent to other players, as depicted in Figure 23.5.

Open the file \KOOB\control\client\Initialize.cs, and look for the following lines in the function InitializeClient:

```
Exec("./interfaces/chatbox.gui");
Exec("./interfaces/messagebox.gui");
```

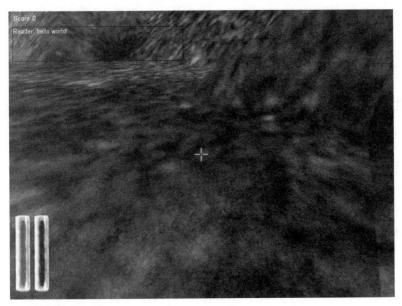

Figure 23.5
ChatBox interface.

These exec statements load the files that will provide our chat interface. These files have been sitting in the interfaces folder ever since back in Chapter 5. Time to put them to work.

Open the file \KOOB\control\client\misc\presetkeys.cs, and add the following keyboard input binding statements to the end of the file:

```
function pageMessageBoxUp( %val )
{
  if ( %val )
  PageUpMessageBox();
}
function pageMessageBoxDown( %val )
{
  if ( %val )
    PageDownMessageBox ();
}
PlayerKeymap.bind(keyboard, "t", ToggleMessageBox );
PlayerKeymap.bind(keyboard, "PageUp", PageMessageBoxUp );
PlayerKeymap.bind(keyboard, "PageDown", PageMessageBoxDown );
```

The first two functions are glue functions that are called by two of the key bindings at the bottom and then make the appropriate call to the functions that scroll the messages in the message box. We need these functions in order to filter out the key up and key down signals from the engine. We only want the action to take place when the key is pressed. We can do this by checking the value of %val when we enter the function—it will be nonzero when the key is pressed and zero when it is released.

Then there is a binding that calls ToggleMessageBox, which is defined in message-box.cs (one of the files we've copied in an earlier chapter that we will examine shortly).

In the interface files there are a couple of concepts you should note. To illustrate, look at the definition of the ChatBox interface, contained in chatbox.gui:

```
new GuiControl(MainChatBox) {
  profile = "GuiModelessDialogProfile";
  horizSizing = "width";
  vertSizing = "height";
  position = "0 0";
  extent = "640 480";
  minExtent = "8 8";
```

```
visible = "1";
modal = "1";
setFirstResponder = "0";
noCursor = true;

new GuiNoMouseCtrl() {
   profile = "GuiDefaultProfile";
   horizSizing = "relative";
   vertSizing = "bottom";
   position = "0 0";
   extent = "400 300";
   minExtent = "8 8";
   visible = "1";

   new GuiBitmapCtrl(OuterChatFrame)
   {
      profile = "GuiDefaultProfile";
      horizSizing = "width";
      vertSizing = "bottom";
      position = "8 32";
      extent = "256 72";
      minExtent = "8 8";
      visible = "1";
      setFirstResponder = "0";
      bitmap = "./hudfill.png";

      new GuiButtonCtrl(chatPageDown)
      {
         profile = "GuiButtonProfile";
         horizSizing = "right";
         vertSizing = "bottom";
         position = "217 54";
         extent = "36 14";
         minExtent = "8 8";
         visible = "0";
         text = "Dwn";
      };

      new GuiScrollCtrl(ChatScrollFrame)
      {
         profile = "ChatBoxScrollProfile";
         horizSizing = "width";
         vertSizing = "bottom";
```

```
        position = "0 0";
        extent = "256 72";
        minExtent = "8 8";
        visible = "1";
        setFirstResponder = "0";
        willFirstRespond = "1";
        hScrollBar = "alwaysOff";
        vScrollBar = "alwaysOff";
        constantThumbHeight = "0";

        new GuiMessageVectorCtrl(ChatBox)
        {
            profile = "ChatBoxMessageProfile";
            horizSizing = "width";
            vertSizing = "height";
            position = "4 4";
            extent = "252 64";
            minExtent = "8 8";
            visible = "1";
            setFirstResponder = "0";
            lineSpacing = "0";
            lineContinuedIndex = "10";
            allowedMatches[0] = "http";
            allowedMatches[1] = "tgeserver";
            matchColor = "0 0 255 255";
            maxColorIndex = 5;
        };
      };
     };
    };
};
```

You've probably noticed that there is a heck of lot of indenting. This shows that
there are many nested objects within objects. Each nesting level is there for a
reason.

The outer level, owned by MainChatBox, is a general-purpose GuiControl container that encompasses the entire screen, occupying the same extents as the
Canvas that we view the 3D world through.

Inside that is a GuiNoMouseCtrl control whose role is to shield the chat boxes
within it from being accessible by a mouse cursor, if you were to display one on
the screen.

Inside that is the `GuiBitmapCtrl` control named `OuterChatFrame`, which has two useful functions. You can use it to provide a nice bitmap background for your chat box if you want one, and it holds two subobjects.

One of those subobjects is an icon that appears to tell you when you've scrolled the chat box up far enough to hide text off the bottom of the box. That control is a `GuiButtonCtrl` named `chatPageDown`.

The other control is a `GuiScrollCtrl` named `ChatScrollFrame`, which provides scroll bars for both vertical and horizontal scrolling.

And finally, in the inner sanctum is the actual control that contains the text of the chat box when it is displayed. This `GuiMessageVectorCtrl` supports multiline buffers of text that will display new text at the bottom and scroll older text up. You can use commands (that we have bound to the PageUp and PageDown keys) to scroll up and down through the text buffer.

MessageBox Interface

The `MessageBox` interface is where we type in our messages, as shown in Figure 23.6.

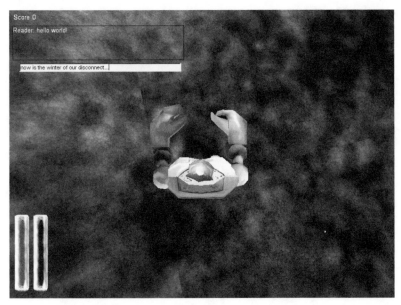

Figure 23.6
`MessageBox` interface.

It is not normally on the screen but pops up when we press the key we bound to it. This, too, has several nested levels, though not as many as the ChatBox interface.

```
new GuiControl(MessageBox)
{
    profile = "GuiDefaultProfile";
    horizSizing = "width";
    vertSizing = "height";
    position = "0 0";
    extent = "640 480";
    minExtent = "8 8";
    visible = "0";
    noCursor = true;

  new GuiControl(MessageBox_Frame)
  {
      profile = "GuiDefaultProfile";
      horizSizing = "right";
      vertSizing = "bottom";
      position = "120 375";
      extent = "400 24";
      minExtent = "8 8";
      visible = "1";

    new GuiTextCtrl(MessageBox_Text)
    {
        profile = "GuiTextProfile";
        horizSizing = "right";
        vertSizing = "bottom";
        position = "6 5";
        extent = "10 22";
        minExtent = "8 8";
        visible = "1";
    };

    new GuiTextEditCtrl(MessageBox_Edit)
    {
        profile = "GuiTextEditProfile";
        horizSizing = "right";
        vertSizing = "bottom";
        position = "0 5";
        extent = "10 22";
        minExtent = "8 8";
```

```
        visible = "1";
        altCommand = "$ThisControl.eval();";
        escapeCommand = "MessageBox_Edit.onEscape();";
        historySize = "5";
        maxLength = "120";
    };
  };
};
```

It is all familiar stuff, but take note that the outer object, MessageBox, is initially invisible. The code that pops the box up will make it visible and invisible again as needed.

There is a GuiTextCtrl named MessageBox_Text that is at the same level as the GuiTextEditCtrl named MessageBox_Edit. The MessageBox_Text can be used to put a prompt in front of the area where the message will be typed in, although it has no text here in the definition. The MessageBox_Edit control is the control that accepts our typed-in message. The altCommand property specifies what statement to execute when the Enter key is pressed, and the escapeCommand property specifies what to do when the Escape key is pressed. The handlers for these two functions will be discussed later in the code discussion in the following "Client Code" section.

Client Code

I'm not going to make you type in great reams of program code at this stage of the game, though you don't get off the hook completely. You will have to make some changes to accommodate the new stuff, and we'll also examine the contents of some of the new stuff to see what it does.

MenuScreen Interface Code

Open the file \KOOB\control\client\initialize.cs, locate the function Initialize Client, and add the following lines in the grouping with the other similar statements:

```
Exec("./misc/hostscreen.cs");
Exec("./misc/soloscreen.cs");

Exec("./interfaces/hostscreen.gui");
Exec("./interfaces/soloscreen.gui");
```

Like I promised, I won't make you type in all the files referenced in those exec statements; you can copy them from \3D2E\RESOURCES\CH23 and put them into the directories under the \KOOB\control\client\ directory in the sub-directories specified in the exec statements.

Each of these files is basically one module split into two parts. The actual interface definitions are in the files with the .gui extensions, while the code that manages the interfaces is in the files with the same prefix name but ending with the .cs extension.

If you go back to the previous code listing for menuscreen.gui, you will see where each of the interfaces is invoked. HostScreen is defined in hostscreen.gui, and SoloScreen is defined in soloscreen.gui.

Each interface has roughly the same form. There is an OnWake method for the interface object that is called by the engine when that object is displayed by the SetContent call in the related button in the MenuScreen interface. This method prepares the interface and fills the various data fields in the interfaces.

SoloScreen Interface Code

The SoloScreen interface that you saw in Figure 23.2 prepares a list of mission files that it finds so that you can select one of them to play with. The functional code for the SoloScreen interface, extracted from soloscreen.cs, is shown here for discussion:

```
function PlaySolo()
{
  %id = SoloMissionList.getSelectedId();
  %mission = getField(SoloMissionList.getRowTextById(%id), 1);
  StopMusic(AudioIntroMusicProfile);
  createServer("SinglePlayer", %mission);
  %conn = new GameConnection(ServerConnection);
  RootGroup.add(ServerConnection);
  %conn.setConnectArgs("Reader");
  %conn.connectLocal();
}

function SoloScreen::onWake()
{
  SoloMissionList.clear();
  %i = 0;
```

```
    for(%file = findFirstFile($Server::MissionFileSpec);
        %file !$= ""; %file = findNextFile($Server::MissionFileSpec))
      if (strStr(%file, "CVS/") == -1 && strStr(%file, "common/") == -1)
        SoloMissionList.addRow(%i++, getMissionDisplayName(%file) @ "\t" @
%file );
    SoloMissionList.sort(0);
    SoloMissionList.setSelectedRow(0);
    SoloMissionList.scrollVisible(0);
}
function getMissionDisplayName( %missionFile )
{
    %file = new FileObject();
    %MissionInfoObject = "";
    if ( %file.openForRead( %missionFile ) ) {
        %inInfoBlock = false;

        while ( !%file.isEOF() ) {
            %line = %file.readLine();
            %line = trim( %line );

            if( %line $= "new ScriptObject(MissionInfo) {" )
            %inInfoBlock = true;
            else if( %inInfoBlock && %line $= "};" ) {
            %inInfoBlock = false;
            %MissionInfoObject = %MissionInfoObject @ %line;
            break;
            }

            if( %inInfoBlock )
                %MissionInfoObject = %MissionInfoObject @ %line @ " ";
        }

        %file.close();
    }
    %MissionInfoObject = "%MissionInfoObject = " @ %MissionInfoObject;
    eval( %MissionInfoObject );
    %file.delete();
    if( %MissionInfoObject.name !$= "" )
      return %MissionInfoObject.name;
    else
      return fileBase(%missionFile);
}
```

The onWake method is as described in earlier chapters; in this case the onWake method makes clear the mission list and then populates it according to the matching files it finds in the path indicated by $Server::MissionFileSpec. This variable is set in the file \KOOB\control\server\initialize.cs with the following line in the InitializeServer function:

```
$Server::MissionFileSpec = "*/maps/*.mis";
```

There are a couple of things you should understand about the way the search is done in the code presented.

First, there is the matter of the syntax used here. It can be difficult to decipher C-based code because of the looseness allowed—and TorqueScript's syntax is extremely close to that of the C language and C++. You will recall that with most statements that employ a code block, such as if and for, you can use the long form or the short form, depending on your needs.

For example, the long form using braces

```
if (%a==1) { %x=5; }
```

can also be written as

```
if (%a==1) {
    %x=5;
}
```

or as

```
if (%a==1)
{
    %x=5;
}
```

There are also other minor variations, but I'm sure you get the idea. The compiler doesn't care about the lines the code appears on, and it doesn't care about the amount of *white space* (tabs, spaces, and carriage returns). It only cares that the correct tokens and keywords are in the right place and that they make sense according to the compiler's parsing rules. Of course, white space is used to separate tokens and keywords, but the amount is not important to the parser.

The short form of these kinds of statements does depend on statement context, however. First, note that the preceding code can also be written as

```
if (%a==1)% x=5;
```

This demonstrates that the braces in the earlier example are superfluous in this particular flavor of statement. However,

```
if (%a==1)
    %x=5;
```

is a valid rendition of the short form—*but the conditional code that you want executed must exist as a single statement that immediately follows the conditional test.* In this example, if the test is satisfied, %x is assigned the value 5. If the test is not satisfied, the ensuing assignment is not carried out.

However, using the same form

```
if (%a==1)
    %x=5; %b=6;
```

if the test is satisfied, %x is assigned the value 5 as before, and %b is assigned the value 6. But (and this is a big *but*) if the test is not satisfied, although the ensuing assignment statement is not carried out, the one after it *still is.* So with this last bit of code, %b always gets assigned the value 6.

By now you may be wondering why this digression. Here's why: the SoloScreen::onWake method has the following statements that search for available mission files to use to populate its list:

```
for(%file = findFirstFile($Server::MissionFileSpec);
    %file !$= ""; %file = findNextFile($Server::MissionFileSpec))
    if (strStr(%file, "CVS/") == -1 && strStr(%file, "common/") == -1)
        SoloMissionList.addRow(%i++, getMissionDisplayName(%file) @ "\t" @
%file );
```

You might be tempted to misinterpret this code, even if you thoroughly understand programming in C or TorqueScript. What we need to do is simplify the code to remove obfuscation introduced by the line context: We'll change all instances of findFirstFile($Server::MissionFileSpec) to fFF(), all instances of findNextFile($Server::MissionFileSpec)) to fNF(), and finally, all instances of getMissionDisplayName(%file) to gMDN(). Now the code will look like this (it won't compile, but we don't care about that):

```
for(%file = fFF();
    %file !$= ""; %file = fNF())
    if (strStr(%file, "CVS/") == -1 && strStr(%file, "common/") == -1)
        SoloMissionList.addRow(%i++, gMDN()@ "\t" @ %file );
```

If we tidy up the white space a bit, we get this:

```
for(%file = fFF(); %file !$= ""; %file = fNF())
        if (strStr(%file, "CVS/") == -1 && strStr(%file, "common/") == -1)
            SoloMissionList.addRow(%i++, gMDN()@ "\t" @ %file );
```

And hey, presto! The code structure reveals the algorithm quite nicely. The original line wrapping made the code hard to understand and made it look wrong when it actually wasn't. There are several lessons to be learned here:

1. Make sure your programming editor lets you display long lines of maybe 150 characters or more, just in case you have them.

2. Pay attention to your function and variable name lengths. Long descriptive names are extremely useful when you are trying to understand unfamiliar or long-forgotten code, but there are times when they can confuse more than explain.

3. Your own code may confuse you at some later point just as much as it might confuse someone else who needs to understand it (someone you've called in to fix bugs for you, for example).

What fix do I recommend for this? Shorter names? No. Instead, use braces and indenting and put the statements in the long form in order to remove any contextual ambiguity.

```
for(%file = findFirstFile($Server::MissionFileSpec);
        %file !$= ""; %file = findNextFile($Server::MissionFileSpec))
{
    if (strStr(%file, "CVS/") == -1 && strStr(%file, "common/") == -1)
    {
      SoloMissionList.addRow(%i++, getMissionDisplayName(%file) @ "\t" @
%file );
    } // end of if
  } // end of for
```

You can also add comments if they clarify what you are doing. Don't worry about insulting the intelligence of expert programmers by doing this. Any seasoned hand will greatly appreciate anything you do to make it quick and easy to understand what you are doing. *Especially* if they are doing code reviews for you!

Now, after that long-windedness, we can address the second issue about that code: what does it do?

The initial findFirstFile uses the variable to search the specified directory for the first instance of a matching file. If you actually *do* find a match, the path name is deposited in the %file variable, and you enter a loop. In each iteration of the loop, calls are made to findNextFile, which will find any new file in the sequence that matches the search criteria. If findNextFile does not find any more matching files, the %file variable is set to NULL, and the loop exits. In the loop we check the contents of the path name in %file for the existence of two potential invalid directory names: CVS (used for source code management and not part of Torque) and common. If the file we found is *not* in either of those two directories, then we consider it to be valid and add it to our mission list using the SoloMissionList.addRow method.

The findFirstFile-findNextFile construct is a powerful one. It maintains an internal list of the files that it has found on your behalf. You just need to extract the path names as they appear.

Having said all that about such a small chunk of code, I should point out that this interface is a basic one. You might consider adding a few more capabilities, such as the sequence or random map selection option you'll find next in the Host interface.

The getMissionDisplayName is a bigger and more impressive-looking bit of work, but its function is fairly straightforward, albeit with a semimagical twist to it, so to speak. It opens up a file as directed and looks through it for the line that contains the statement "%MissionInfoObject = ". It then creates an actual MissionInfoObject using that statement and uses the name property of the object to obtain the name and return the name to the calling function. This is a pretty clever way to examine a file. Pretty sensible, too, when you realize that mission files are simply TorqueScript files with a different extension.

This bit of code presents to you a lot of possibilities about how you can use TorqueScript. One that comes to mind is a reprogrammable AI robot, where you merely read in the new instructions at run time, with the instructions written in TorqueScript. No need to create your own robot control language!

Host Interface Code

The Host interface code is similar to the SoloScreen code that you just looked at. There is nothing remarkable about it that hasn't already been mentioned, except that you should add some code to provide the player the ability to choose between playing maps in sequence (as exists now) or randomly.

You will want to have the Sequence and Random buttons that I've already provided in HostScreen.gui set a variable that your `onWake` code can examine. If the variable has one value, leave things as they are. If the variable has a different value, then have the `onWake` method choose a map randomly. One simple method to introduce the randomness is to select a random value between 0 and the number of available maps and then to reject that many maps when the `findNextFile` function returns them. Then you would accept the next map returned.

Give it a try.

FindServer Interface Code

You saw the `FindServer` interface way back there in Figure 23.4. It lets you browse for servers with which you can connect. We've already looked at how this part of Torque works, back in Chapters 5, 6, and 7, so I won't go into too much detail here. The functional code for the `FindServer` interface, extracted from Server-Screen.cs, is shown here for a brief discussion:

```
function ServerScreen::onWake()
{
  MasterJoinServer.SetActive(MasterServerList.rowCount() > 0);
}
function ServerScreen::Query(%this)
{
  QueryMasterServer(
    0,                    // Query flags
    $Client::GameTypeQuery,      // gameTypes
    $Client::MissionTypeQuery,   // missionType
    0,            // minPlayers
    100,          // maxPlayers
    0,            // maxBots
    2,            // regionMask
    0,            // maxPing
    100,          // minCPU
    0             // filterFlags
    );
}
function ServerScreen::Cancel(%this)
{
  CancelServerQuery();
}
function ServerScreen::Join(%this)
```

```
  {
    CancelServerQuery();
    %id = MasterServerList.GetSelectedId();
    %index = getField(MasterServerList.GetRowTextById(%id),6);
    if (SetServerInfo(%index)) {
      %conn = new GameConnection(ServerConnection);
      %conn.SetConnectArgs($pref::Player::Name);
      %conn.SetJoinPassword($Client::Password);
      %conn.Connect($ServerInfo::Address);
    }
  }
}
function ServerScreen::Close(%this)
{
  cancelServerQuery();
  Canvas.SetContent(MenuScreen);
}
function ServerScreen::Update(%this)
{
  ServerQueryStatus.SetVisible(false);
  ServerServerList.Clear();
  %sc = getServerCount();
  for (%i = 0; %i < %sc; %i++) {
    setServerInfo(%i);
    ServerServerList.AddRow(%i,
      ($ServerInfo::Password? "Yes": "No") TAB
      $ServerInfo::Name TAB
      $ServerInfo::Ping TAB
      $ServerInfo::PlayerCount @ "/" @ $ServerInfo::MaxPlayers TAB
      $ServerInfo::Version TAB
      $ServerInfo::GameType TAB
      %i);  // ServerInfo index stored also
  }
  ServerServerList.Sort(0);
  ServerServerList.SetSelectedRow(0);
  ServerServerList.scrollVisible(0);

  ServerJoinServer.SetActive(ServerServerList.rowCount() > 0);
}
function onServerQueryStatus(%status, %msg, %value)
{
  if (!ServerQueryStatus.IsVisible())
    ServerQueryStatus.SetVisible(true);
  switch$ (%status) {
```

```
    case "start":
      ServerJoinServer.SetActive(false);
      ServerQueryServer.SetActive(false);
      ServerStatusText.SetText(%msg);
      ServerStatusBar.SetValue(0);
      ServerServerList.Clear();
    case "ping":
      ServerStatusText.SetText("Ping Servers");
      ServerStatusBar.SetValue(%value);
    case "query":
      ServerStatusText.SetText("Query Servers");
      ServerStatusBar.SetValue(%value);
    case "done":
      ServerQueryServer.SetActive(true);
      ServerQueryStatus.SetVisible(false);
      ServerScreen.update();
  }
}
```

Here the OnWake method makes the list active if there is anything already available from a previous incarnation to list. It's invoked as soon as the interface object is displayed on the screen.

When you click the Query Master button, the Query method is called, which sends a query packet to the master server, informing the master about what sort of servers are of interest. If the master server returns any information, it is deposited in the server information list, the Update method is invoked, and the list is created on the screen. This back-and-forth transaction is described in greater detail in Chapter 6.

The onServerQueryStatus method handles the various responses from the master server and deposits returned information, according to the changing states, into the various fields of the list.

ChatBox Interface Code

Open the file \KOOB\control\client\Initialize.cs, and add the following lines to the function InitializeClient:

```
Exec("./misc/chatbox.cs");
Exec("./misc/messagebox.cs");
```

Note: it's important that you place these lines *above* the line that execs pre-setkeys.cs, because there will be code in presetkeys.cs in the future that will rely on those other two files being loaded first.

These two exec statements load the files that will provide our chat interface. You can copy them from \3D2E\RESOURCES\CH23 and put them into the directories under the \KOOB\control\client\ directory in the subdirectories specified in the exec statements.

Now, let's add something to one of the files you just copied: \KOOB\control\client\chatbox.cs. Open that file, and at the very top of the file add these two lines above everything else:

```
new MessageVector(MsgBoxMessageVector);
$LastframeTarget = 0;
```

Save your work.

The first line creates a dynamic array that carries chat messages (a MessageVector) and the second line is a variable that tracks the position within that array.

The ChatBox interface receives its text via a rather convoluted route. The message text originates at one of the clients and is sent to the server. The server receives the typed message and passes it to some common code that handles chat messages between the server and the client. Once the message arrives at the client common code, it is passed to the message handler called onChatMessage, which we provide in our client control code in our ChatBox.cs module. There is a parallel handler we are expected to supply in our client control code called onServerMessage, which is essentially the same as the one for the chat messages. These two functions look like this:

```
function onChatMessage(%message, %voice, %pitch)
{
  if (GetWordCount(%message)) {
    ChatBox.AddLine(%message);
  }
}
function onServerMessage(%message)
{
  if (GetWordCount(%message)) {
    ChatBox.AddLine(%message);
  }
}
```

Not much needed here—just add the new text to the ChatBox object using its AddLine method.

The AddLine method is where all the heavy lifting is done; it looks like this:

```
function ChatBox::addLine(%this,%text)
{
  %textHeight = %this.profile.fontSize;
  if (%textHeight <= 0)
     %textHeight = 12;
  %chatScrollHeight = getWord(%this.getGroup().getGroup().extent, 1);
  %chatPosition = getWord(%this.extent, 1) - %chatScrollHeight +
       getWord(%this.position, 1);
  %linesToScroll = mFloor((%chatPosition / %textHeight) + 0.5);
  if (%linesToScroll > 0)
     %origPosition = %this.position;
  while( !chatPageDown.isVisible() && MsgBoxMessageVector.getNumLines() &&
        (MsgBoxMessageVector.getNumLines() >= $pref::frameMessageLogSize))
  {
    %tag = MsgBoxMessageVector.getLineTag(0);
    if(%tag != 0)
       %tag.delete();
    MsgBoxMessageVector.popFrontLine();
  }
  MsgBoxMessageVector.pushBackLine(%text, $LastframeTarget);
  $LastframeTarget = 0;
  if (%linesToScroll > 0)
  {
    chatPageDown.setVisible(true);
    %this.position = %origPosition;
  }
  else
    chatPageDown.setVisible(false);
}
```

We start out by getting the font size from the profile. We need this in order to determine the height and width spacing requirements for scrolling and frame sizing.

Then we use getGroup to obtain the handle for the object group this control belongs to. And we use that handle to get the parent group's handle. Then we use that handle to get the extent property, which tells us the height and width of the parent object. We take the second value in the extent—which is the height—by using `getWord` to get word number 1, which is actually the second word. (We perverted programmers usually count starting at 0 instead of 1—but not always!)

The object retains the current output position using the `position` parameter, and that is used to calculate where the next position will be and saved as `%chatPosition`. We then use the calculations to figure out `%linesToScroll`, which dictates the text scroll action and the scroll bar actions.

Next, we enter a loop that extracts text from the text buffer called `MsgBoxMessage` `Vector` line by line and inserts the lines in the `ChatBox` control.

Finally, we adjust the visibility of the scroll down prompt based on whether or not our position causes text to be out of sight at the bottom of the display.

While we're at it, let's get that chat box to appear on the player's display. Open the file KOOB\control\client\screens.cs and add the following lines to the first method in the file, `PlayerInterface::onWake`, placing the lines just below the call to `activateDirectInput`:

```
Canvas.pushDialog( MainChatBox );///***KCF CHAT
chatBox.attach(ChatMsgMessageVector);///***KCF CHAT
```

There you go. We linked the chat box to the display, and then linked the message vector to the chat box.

MessageBox Interface Code

The `MessageBox` interface accepts our input from the keyboard.

We need to add a message handler to the server to receive the typed messages when they are sent from the client. Because of the context, it makes more sense to do that here than in Chapter 22, even though we are dealing with client issues in this chapter.

Open the file \KOOB\control\server\server.cs, and add the following function to the end of the file:

```
function serverCmdTypedMessage(%client, %text)
{
  if(strlen(%text) >= $Pref::Server::MaxChatLen)
  %text = getSubStr(%text, 0, $Pref::Server::MaxChatLen);
   ChatMessageAll(%client, '\c4%1: %2', %client.name, %text);
}
```

This handler grabs the incoming typed message, makes sure that it isn't too long (we may want to restrict chat messages in order to preserve bandwidth requirements), and then sends the message to the common code server function called `ChatMessageAll`. The `ChatMessageAll` function will distribute the message to all the other clients logged in to our game.

Next, let's look at the code that manages this on behalf of the `MessageBox` interface:

```
function MessageBox::Open(%this)
{
  %offset = 6;
  if(%this.isVisible())
    return;
  %windowPos = "8 " @ ( getWord( outerChatFrame.position, 1 ) + getWord(
outer ChatFrame.extent, 1 ) + 1 );
  %windowExt = getWord( OuterChatFrame.extent, 0 ) @ " " @ getWord(
MessageBox_ Frame.extent, 1 );
  %textExtent = getWord(MessageBox_Text.extent, 0);
  %ctrlExtent = getWord(MessageBox_Frame.extent, 0);
  Canvas.pushDialog(%this);
  MessageBox_Frame.position = %windowPos;
  MessageBox_Frame.extent = %windowExt;
  MessageBox_Edit.position = setWord(MessageBox_Edit.position, 0, %textExtent
+ %offset);
  MessageBox_Edit.extent = setWord(MessageBox_Edit.extent, 0, %ctrlExtent -
%textExtent - (2 * %offset));
  %this.setVisible(true);
  deactivateKeyboard();
  MessageBox_Edit.makeFirstResponder(true);
}
function MessageBox::Close(%this)
{
  if(!%this.isVisible())
    return;
  Canvas.popDialog(%this);
  %this.setVisible(false);
  if ( $enableDirectInput )
    activateKeyboard();
  MessageBox_Edit.setValue("");
}
function MessageBox::ToggleState(%this)
{
  if(%this.isVisible())
    %this.close();
```

```
  else
    %this.open();
}
function MessageBox_Edit::OnEscape(%this)
{
  MessageBox.close();
}
function MessageBox_Edit::Eval(%this)
{
  %text = trim(%this.getValue());
  if(%text !$= "")
    commandToServer('MessageSent', %text);
  MessageBox.close();
}
function ToggleMessageBox(%make)
{
  if(%make)
    MessageBox.toggleState();
}
```

The Open method does some assignments of local variables based on the settings of properties of the MainChatBox object. This is so we can place the message box into a position relative to the chat display; in this case we are going to put it below and offset a little bit to the right.

Once we've done this, the code loads the MessageBox control into the Canvas using Canvas.pushDialog(%this), where %this is the handle of the MessageBox control object, and positions it according to the values of the earlier saved local variables.

When we've completed the positioning of the control, then the code makes it visible.

Next, the code turns off keyboard input for the Canvas object and sets the MessageBox_Edit subobject responsible for handling key inputs. From this point on, all typing goes into the MessageBox_Edit subobject, until something changes that.

The Close method removes the control from the Canvas, makes the control invisible again, and restores keyboard input handling to the Canvas.

The ToggleState method merely opens or closes the message box in a toggle fashion. If the control is open, it closes it, and vice versa.

The OnEscape method closes the control. This method is defined as the escape Command property value in the interface definition in MessageBox.gui.

The Eval method obtains the entered text, trims empty spaces from the end, and sends the text to the server as the parameter for a TypedMessage message, which the server knows how to handle.

Finally, the ToggleMessageBox method is bound to the "t" key in our presets.cs file. When it receives a non-null value in %make, it changes the current MessageBox open state using the ToggleState method.

Game Cycling

The final feature we need to implement is the ability to cycle games when they are over—that is, when a player has reached either the score limit or the time limit.

First, add the following functions to the end of \KOOB\control\server\server.cs:

```
function cycleGame()
{
  if (!$Game::Cycling) {
    $Game::Cycling = true;
    $Game::Schedule = schedule(0, 0, "onCycleExec");
  }
}
function onCycleExec()
{
  endGame();
  $Game::Schedule = schedule($Game::EndGamePause * 1000, 0, "onCyclePause
End");
}

function onCyclePauseEnd()
{
  $Game::Cycling = false;
  %search = $Server::MissionFileSpec;
  for (%file = findFirstFile(%search); %file !$= "";
       %file = findNextFile(%search)) {
    if (%file $= $Server::MissionFile) {
      %file = findNextFile(%search);
      if (%file $= "")
        %file = findFirstFile(%search);
      break;
```

```
      }
    }
    loadMission(%file);
}
```

The first function, cycleGame, schedules the actual cycling code to occur at some later point. In this case we do it right away after making sure that we aren't actually already cycling.

The function onCycleExec actually ends the game. The endGame function just stops when it finishes, not doing anything else. Further action is scheduled to be taken by the onCyclePauseEnd function. This allows us to put up a victory screen or other messages and leave them up for an appropriate viewing time before continuing on to the next game.

In order to provoke the actual cycleGame function into being, we do two things. First, when the game is launched, we schedule its demise based on $Game::Duration. Locate the function StartGame farther up in the server.cs file, and look at these lines:

```
if ($Game::Duration)
    $Game::Schedule = schedule($Game::Duration * 1000, 0, "CycleGame" );
```

This starts the game timer running. When it expires it invokes the CycleGame function.

Something we need to do is add some code that checks to see if a player has hit the $Game::MaxPoints limit.

Locate the function GameConnection::DoScore(), and add this code to the top of the function:

```
%client.score = (%client.lapsCompleted * $Game::Laps_Multiplier) +
                (%client.money * $Game::Money_Multiplier) +
                (%client.deaths * $Game::Deaths_Multiplier) +
                (%client.kills * $Game::Kills_Multiplier) ;
```

This code accumulates the various scoring values into a single overall score. Now add the following code to the end of the same DoScore function:

```
if (%client.score >= $Game::MaxPoints)
    cycleGame();
```

This causes the game cycling activity to happen if any one player hits the score limit. Game cycling entails ending the game, loading a new map, and dropping the players into the game in the new map.

Final Change

The final, very, very last piece of code we are going to change will allow us to remain in the program after we exit a game. Previously, when we exited a game using the Escape key, the program quit. This final change tidies that up for us. Open the file \KOOB\control\client\misc\presetkeys.cs, locate the function DoExitGame(), and change it to match the following:

```
function DoExitGame()
{
  if ( $Server::ServerType $= "SinglePlayer" )
    MessageBoxYesNo( "Exit Mission", "Exit?", "disconnect();", "" );
  else
    MessageBoxYesNo( "Disconnect", "Disconnect?", "disconnect();", "" );
}
```

This function now checks to see if we are in single- or multiplayer mode. It does this to provide a customized exit prompt depending on which mode it is. In any event, the disconnect function is called to break the connection with the game server.

Moving Right Along

So, there you have it. I hope your fingers aren't worn to the bone. You can see that there is a great deal of power available to those worn fingertips. I'm sure that as you've progressed through the preceding chapters, your head began to fill with all sorts of ideas about things you might want to do. In the next and final chapter of the book, I have a few things I want to say on that topic.

CHAPTER 24

THE END GAME

By now you've worn many hats, as programmer, 2D artist, 3D modeler, sound engineer, and level designer, to mention just the big ones. It should be fairly evident that each of these specialties has a great deal of depth, and it is hard to do justice to any one of them in a book like this.

However, it should also be apparent that you can make complex and feature-rich games without the need for million-dollar budgets. In this chapter we'll look at some of the things that didn't quite fit as topics in the earlier chapters.

A great deal of the work is done for us by the Torque Engine, but that's just where the process starts—the end is wherever you want it to be. There are other game engines out there, ranging from free to expensive, but the relationship between the end result and the price of the engine is not a linear one. The result is dependent on the amount of effort and inspiration *you* bring to the table. Making successful games is about transforming a great idea into a great game, and that operation can't be bought with mere money.

If you are going to put together a small team to develop a game using Torque, I would suggest you fill the artistic slots first—at least sign up a dedicated 3D modeler. You will also need one programmer to manage your script work. Finally, you need someone responsible for doing map layout, creating game rules, and managing the relationships between the models and the code. This makes a three-person team, which is probably as close to an ideal size as you're going to get for a small, low-budget development team. If you have the luxury of adding another team member, make sure you give him the sound-engineer responsibilities.

Testing

To properly test your game you are going to need to go back to your requirements and review them. For each specific requirement you have to decide what procedure *someone else* would need to perform to prove to you that *their* software fulfilled that requirement. Write the procedure down, and move on to the next requirement. Be hypercritical, a skeptic's skeptic.

Basics

There are many formalized testing methodologies, but the basic need when testing is to investigate at least these two aspects of any feature:

1. Does the program feature (operation, appearance, behavior) work the way it should, when it should?

2. Does the feature make something else *not* work the way it should, when it should?

Take your list of test procedures and run through your software answering these two questions. It is certainly a lot tougher to answer the second question—sometimes you will see something not working, only to find out later that it was some *other* feature that was causing the problem that you witnessed.

You will end up with a list of problems and probably some ideas about how to fix them. Fill your list up first before running off to repair the bugs, and then sit back and examine the list of problems to try to identify problems that may share the same root cause. You can possibly save much effort and time by fixing the root cause. Otherwise you might end up with a series of individual fixes and hacks, each of which only addresses a single issue, and each of which exposes another issue.

Regression

The phenomenon *regression* is caused by bug fixes that introduce new bugs or sometimes expose hidden bugs. Some software engineers dispute the idea of referring to exposing hidden bugs as regression, but to me it's a difference without a distinction. The result is the same.

To deal with regression, we need to run our tests after every bug-fixing session. Ask the same questions and look for the answers. If you have the time and patience (neither of which is commonly overly abundant), you should run your regression test after each bug fix. In other words, don't do your entire list of bug-fixing programming all at once and then jump back to your regression test. If new bugs have been introduced, it may be hard to find them, because the new code can be quite extensive.

Play Testing

You will also want to enlist a bevy of play testers because there can be more wrong with the game than simple (or not-so-simple) bugs. You need to ensure that the game is fun to play, and you need to ensure that the things you can do in the game have the effect you want them to have. If your game features an Easter egg hunt, you want to make sure that the players can actually *find* the hidden items. At the same time, you will probably want to make sure that the items aren't too easy to find. Achieving the balance in game play is why you want to use play testers.

When you and members of your development team are testing the software, this is usually referred to as the *alpha* test phase. Alpha testing can be considered complete when the development team's own testing is no longer finding problems. This, however, doesn't mean that testing is finished! You will eventually need to use people who have not been involved in the creation of the game for testing. Once you start letting outsiders play-test your game, you are now in the *beta* test phase. If the game is fun (and it will be, right?) then you should not have much trouble interesting people in being beta testers. And this will introduce a problem (it's a problem you want to have, but still a problem), which is that many beta testers will be playing the game and not testing it. While it is good for them to be enjoying themselves, you need them to take notes and record problems, issues, and general feelings about the way the game is played. You need these notes in order to know what to fix and what to change or add.

Test Harnesses

You should also consider creating *test harnesses* to use in your testing. These are programs that are designed to provide the inputs that will cause the various features of the game to be exercised. The testing software should log its output to a file, automatically take screens shots, or record whatever else is needed so that you can review the results.

For example, you could create a special version of the client that will automatically run and play as if it were a real player. Then you could launch dozens of these clients in order to simulate client loads on the server.

Hosted Servers

As you've seen with the example programs, with Torque there are three different execution modes:

- client only

- server only

- hosted server

Depending on your needs, you might want to create one monolithic program that will run in all three modes. This is certainly possible with Torque; in fact, the Torque demo as created by GarageGames supplies this capability by default.

However, you may want to create two or three different program distributions: one for each mode, or one for client only, the other being one or both of the server modes. There are some reasons for doing this, and probably the best is for server security. It depends on your business model (if you have one). If you are planning to provide all of the server-side hosting, then you might want a client-only version to be distributed to users. By not sending out the server code, you minimize the risk of unscrupulous players hacking the game to gain an advantage over other players in online play.

There are pitfalls to the multiple-version approach, the most noteworthy of which is the need to maintain two or more different versions of programs. That's a potential nightmare looking for a place to happen. Proceed with caution.

Having said all that, the distribution of multiplayer games that allow players to host other players while they all play in the same game is a common approach. Not only do many games offer it, but thousands of players use the capability.

Dedicated Servers

Some games, especially those that offer persistent role-playing style features, are hosted on dedicated servers only. The game's developer, or a service company that represents the developer, usually operates these servers. These games generally offer virtual environments where hundreds or thousands of players connect to the same world and interact in varying ways. This usually presents bandwidth and CPU costs well beyond the abilities of casual players and hobbyists looking for an evening's entertainment.

These sorts of "big iron" servers are often hosted on clustered servers at dedicated hosting service companies with battery-backup systems and racks and racks of computers.

This does not mean that you shouldn't offer your users the ability to run a dedicated server. There are many 16- or 32-player first-person shooter games on the market that have hordes of fans that run permanent 24/7 servers. Offering a dedicated server mode allows your users to run the servers on computers with less capability than they might otherwise use as their game-playing computer. That is to say, dedicated servers are an ideal way for users to utilize that two-year-old computer sitting in the corner gathering dust!

FPS Game Ideas

You might be tempted to think that all the great first-person shooter ideas have already been done to death. I doubt that's true. There are a few ideas that have been tried and have not been terribly successful, but that doesn't mean they can never be successful. Maybe with a bit of tweaking, you could make a successful version of a game that previously bombed. That's an important concept to keep in the back of your head.

One such example that immediately comes to mind is the Western—you know, the Wild, Wild West. Hollywood has produced a ton of successful Western movies. But there haven't been any equivalent games. That's an assignment for *someone* out there, and if it is ever going to be fulfilled, it will likely be an independent like you who does it.

One of the games I'd really like to see someone create in the FPS genre is a chess game played out with individual battles between pieces, where you can have each player able to engage in combat appropriate to the chess pieces as they are moved. There are game play issues that would need to be resolved, but that's something a clever designer could overcome. Here are some of the issues that would have to be tackled:

- Who decides the moves if the game is team based?

- Should each piece have different combat styles?

- Should the standard rules of chess play (movement rules, for example) prevail?

- Might you need to modify them slightly?

- Should you ever have an overhead board view?

If you broaden the scope a bit and don't focus on the *shooter* part of the FPS genre, the horizon starts to recede—first-person perspective play without the shooting has been barely touched.

Firefighting is one such topic that seems like it might be ripe for a game, especially team-based play. You could do forest fires, building fires, and so on. The biggest challenge would be the fire-propagation algorithms, such as the following:

- Exactly what conditions cause this item or that item to burst into flames?

- How does smoke move through a forest, a building, and so on, and how do you render that?

- How do you score the game?

- How realistic should the game be?

Other Genres

If you now shift a little to encompass third-person perspective play, the horizon opens up yet again. Almost any sport you can think of can be simulated from this point of view: bullfighting, surfing, Rugby, and sailboarding, to name a few.

One that I would like to see is a mountain-biking game. I'd especially like to see one that accepted input from a stationary bicycle! Imagine being able to ride single-track trails at Moab while buried under 3 feet of snow in Ontario! That would be cool. In fact, I think there is an untapped market here: hooking up the various machines in a gym to computers running games that people can play, using the exercise machines as the input devices. Exercise equipment manufacturers have put out some weak attempts at this, but there could be so much more—especially in the online multiplayer realm.

Instead of running on a treadmill hooked up to a computer with software that simulates running on a trail in Oregon, how about using the treadmill to provide motive input for your player as a rifleman in World War II Online? In fact, there is hardware that hasn't even been designed yet that could probably be used in this way.

Modifying and Extending Torque

If you sign up with GarageGames and buy a developer's license for their Torque Game Engine, you get all the source code. Every single bit of it.

Stop and think about that for just a minute. Not only do you get the capabilities already described in this book—features you've been learning how to use to make your game—but you also get access to the core engine code, with the right to change it as you like to make your game do *absolutely whatever you want it to do!*

Earlier I'd pointed out that Torque is not really designed for massively multiplayer games. With access to the source code, you could change that, adding the missing bits and modifying the existing bits to accommodate your needs.

How about huge, I mean gigantic, game worlds? You could do this by modifying the Terrain Manager code to accommodate *paging terrain*, where the game only loads the terrain in the immediate and viewable area of the player. You would probably need to make a special world creation tool for managing large worlds—a tool you would create with Torque. Or you might investigate the *Torque Shader Engine* (TSE). TSE is not a finished product as of this writing—it's still in *Early Adopter* (EA) stage. However, you can obtain a low-cost EA license and thus gain access to size-unlimited demand paged terrains with pixel shader 3.0 support. I'm just sayin' . . .

If you go to the GarageGames Web site (http://www.garagegames.com) and browse the various menus, you will find a user community that is large, active, and thriving. Several of the retail games made with Torque are included on the companion CD for this book. At the GarageGames forums you will see the developers of these games in continuous conversation with people designing and making their own games—every one of them an independent just like you.

As you browse around, make your way to the Resources postings, and you will find a whole slew of code modifications submitted by members of the community to enhance the core capabilities of the Torque Engine. In fact, you will find that a substantial number of the features that Torque now has that it *didn't* have when it was first released were added as submissions from the user-developer community.

In addition to extending the core capabilities, another reason for modifying the engine would be to move the more CPU-intensive parts of your game scripts into the core engine in order to improve the execution speed and sometimes even the memory footprint (how much memory your game uses). To do these things you will have to learn how to program in C/C++ or at least obtain the services of a competent C/C++ programmer.

Go for It

As an independent game developer, you owe nothing to anyone except yourself and your family. That being the case, there is an important and sometimes underrecognized imperative for every independent game developer: have fun!

Given that you've picked up this book, you probably already have some ideas rattling around inside your head, and you've been thinking about making them happen. Armed with the tools and information from this book, you can afford to try out your ideas without being afraid of wasting years of your life finding out that an idea didn't work.

Now you can "waste" a few weeks finding out that an idea doesn't work and then spend a few more weeks to refine it, several more weeks to tweak it, and a few months to build on it, finally coming up with something that might really fly.

Well, we are at the end of our journey. I hope you have enjoyed it as much as I have. I think the key thing to come away with is this: believe in yourself.

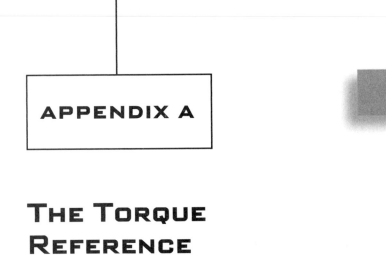

APPENDIX A

THE TORQUE REFERENCE

The following tables refer to the Torque release **version 1.4** engine build. Here are some notes about the functions:

- Some functions are available for use on the client only. For the most part, this is very obvious. For example, any hardware-related functions are client-only. However, for other functions this may not be so obvious. These functions are marked "client-only."

- Torque is not case-sensitive with respect to identifiers, like variables and function names. Internally in Torque, the commands in this list all begin with lowercase letters, even though in many programming circles it is conventional for function identifiers to begin with capitals. The TorqueScript Command Reference is written to conform to the Torque internal representation, but you may capitalize the functions if you need to to match your programming standards.

TorqueScript Command Reference

activateDirectInput()

Parameters:	*none*
Return:	*nothing*
Description:	Activates direct input device polling.
Usage:	`activateDirectInput();`

activateKeyboard()

Parameters:	none	
Return:	numeric	1 = success, 0 = fail.
Description:	Enables DirectInput polling of the keyboard.	
Usage:	`%result = activateKeyboard();`	

activatePackage(name)

Parameters:	name	String containing the name of the package.
Return:	nothing	
Description:	Tells Torque to start using the package specified by *name*.	
Usage:	`activatePackage(Show);`	

addBadWord(word)

Parameters:	word	String containing the bad word to be filtered.
Return:	nothing	
Description:	Adds a bad or obscene word to the bad word filter.	
Usage:	`addBadWord("dagnabbit");`	

addCardProfile(vendor, renderer, safeMode, lockArray, subImage, fogTexture, noEnvColor, clipHigh, deleteContext, texCompress, interiorLock, skipFirstFog, only16, noArraysAlpha, profile)

Parameters:	vendor	Name of card vendor.
	renderer	Name of renderer.
	safeMode	`true` or `false`.
	lockArray	`true` or `false`.
	subImage	`true` or `false`.
	fogTexture	`true` or `false`.
	noEnvColor	`true` or `false`.
	clipHigh	`true` or `false`.
	deleteContext	`true` or `false`.
	texCompress	`true` or `false`.
	interiorLock	`true` or `false`.
	skipFirstFog	`true` or `false`.
	only16	`true` or `false`.
	noArraysAlpha	`true` or `false`.
	profile	Name of profile.
Return:	nothing	
Description:	Creates a profile of features of a video card for later reference.	

Usage:

```
addCardProfile(%vendor, %renderer, true, true, true, true, true, false,
          false, true, true, false, false, false,"")
```

addMaterialMapping(material, sound, color)

Parameters: *material*   Name of string to identify the material.

             sound   Name of sound profile to attach to material.

             color   Color specification to attach to material.

Return: *nothing*

Description: Adds sound and dust color to specified material.

Usage:

```
addMaterialMapping("sand", "sound:0", "color:0.3 0.3 0.5 0.4 0.0");
```

addOSCardProfile(vendor,renderer,allowOpenGL,allowD3D,preferOpenGL)

Parameters: *vendor*   Name of card vendor.

             renderer   Name of renderer.

             allowOpenGL   true or false.

             allowD3D   true or false.

             preferOpenGL   true or false.

Return: *nothing*

Description: Stores certain aspects of a video card for later usage.

Usage: `addOSCardProfile(%vendor,%renderer,true,true,true);`

addTaggedString(string)

Parameters: *string*   Normal string to be added.

Return: *numeric*   The tag.

Description: Adds a string to the tagged string list (`NetStringTable`). Deprecated.

Usage: `%tagname = AddTaggedString(%name);`

aiConnect(id)

Parameters: *id*   ID reference number (0 to 20) of the AI bot.

Return: *numeric*   New object handle.

Description: Creates a new uncontrolled AI connection. The AI is treated the same as a player.

Usage: `aiConnect(1);`

alGetListener3f(ALenum)

Parameters: *ALenum*   The enum string. Choices:
"AL_VELOCITY"
"AL_POSITION"
"AL_DIRECTION"

Return: *numeric*
Description: Queries the value of the *ALenum*.
Usage: `%direction = alGetListener3f("AL_DIRECTION");`

alGetListeneri(ALenum)

Parameters: *ALenum*   The enum string. Choices:
"AL_CONE_INNER_ANGLE"
"AL_CONE_OUTER_ANGLE"
"AL_LOOPING"
"AL_STREAMING"
"AL_BUFFER"

Return: *numeric*
Description: Queries the value of the *ALenum*.
Usage: `%looping = ;alGetListeneri("AL_LOOPING");`

alGetString(ALenum)

Parameters: *string*   The enum string. Choices:
"AL_VENDOR"
"AL_VERSION"
"AL_RENDERER"
"AL_EXTENSIONS"

Return: *string*
Description: Obtains the string specified.
Usage: `%vendor = alGetString("AL_VENDOR");`

alListener3f(ALenum, ["x y z"] I [x,y,z])

Parameters: *ALenum*   The enum string. Choices:
"AL_VELOCITY"
"AL_POSITION"
"AL_DIRECTION"

            "x y z"   The string contains a tuple indicating where to place the enumed property in 3D world space.

x,y,z		(alternative) If "x y z" isn't used, then this is a tuple indicating where to place the audio object in 3D world space. *Note:* these are three numerics, not a string!

Return: *nothing*

Description: Sets the *ALenum* to *value* for the listener (the player, who "hears" a sound).

Usage: `alListener3f("AL_GAIN_LINEAR", $pref::Audio::masterVolume );`

allowConnections(switch)

Parameters: switch   1 (or `true`) = enable, 0 (or `false`) = disable.

Return: *nothing*

Description: Enables and disables connections to the game server.

Usage: `allowConnections(1);`

alxCreateSource({ profile, [x,y,z] } | { description, filename, [x,y,z] })

Parameters: profile   Descriptor string.

    x,y,z   If *profile* is used, then this is a tuple indicating where to place the audio object. *Note:* these are three numerics, not a string!

    description   (alternative) If *profile* isn't used, then this is an audio object description string.

    filename   If *description* is used, then this string specifies the audio file to use for the sound.

    x,y,z   If *description* is used, then this is a tuple indicating where to place the audio object. *Note:* these are three numerics, not a string!

Return: *numeric*   Handle to audio object.

Description: Loads an audio source file into memory, and initializes it for use.

Usage: `$handle = alxCreateSource("Audio0","~/data/sounds/test.wav");`

alxGetChannelVolume(channel)

Parameters: channel   Channel ID number.

Return: *numeric*

Description: Queries the volume of *channel*.

Usage: `%vol = alxGetChannelVolume(%channel);`

alxGetListenerf(ALenum)

Parameters: ALenum   The enum string. Choices:

                   "AL_GAIN"

                   "AL_GAIN_LINEAR"

Return: *numeric*
Description: Queries the value of the *ALenum*.
Usage: `%gain=alxGetListenerf("AL_GAIN");`

alxGetSource3f(handle, ALenum)

Parameters: *handle*   Handle to audio object.
               ALenum   The enum string. Choices:
                           "AL_VELOCITY"
                           "AL_POSITION"
                           "AL_DIRECTION"
Return: *string* "x y z".
Description: Obtains the value of *ALenum* for the specified *handle*.
Usage: `%pos = alxGetSource3f(%handle[%sender], "AL_POSITION");`

alxGetSourcef(handle, ALenum)

Parameters: *handle*   Handle to audio object.
               ALenum   The enum string. Choices:
                           "AL_PITCH"
                           "AL_REFERENCE_DISTANCE"
                           "AL_MAX_DISTANCE"
                           "AL_CONE_OUTER_GAIN"
                           "AL_GAIN"
                           "AL_GAIN_LINEAR"
Return: *numeric*
Description: Obtains the value of *ALenum* for the specified *handle*.
Usage: `%gain = alxGetSourcef(%handle[%sender], "AL_GAIN");`

alxGetSourcei(handle, ALenum)

Parameters: *handle*   Handle to audio object.
               ALenum   The enum string. Choices:
                           "AL_CONE_INNER_ANGLE"
                           "AL_CONE_OUTER_ANGLE"
                           "AL_LOOPING"
                           "AL_STREAMING"
                           "AL_BUFFER"
Return: *numeric*   The pitch value.
Description: Obtains the value of *ALenum* for the specified *handle*.

Usage: `%pitch = alxGetSourcei(%handle[%sender], "AL_PITCH");`

alxGetStreamDuration(handle)

Parameters: *handle*   Handle to the streaming data.

Return: *numeric*   Duration of streaming data, in seconds.

Description: Obtains the length, in seconds, of the streaming data specified by *handle*.

Usage: `%secs = alxGetStreamDuration(%streamDataHandle);`

alxGetStreamPosition(handle)

Parameters: *handle*   Handle to the streaming data.

Return: *numeric*   Current playback position in the streaming data, in seconds.

Description: Obtains the position, measured in seconds, of the current playback position, in the streaming data specified by *handle*.

Usage: `%posit = alxGetStreamPosition(%streamDataHandle);`

alxGetWaveLen(fileName)

Parameters: *string*   fileName.

Return: *numeric*   Length of file in bytes.

Description: Obtains the length in bytes of the .wav file specified by *fileName*.

Usage: `%len = alxGetWaveLen(%pathToWaveFile);`

alxIsPlaying(handle)

Parameters: *handle*   Handle to audio object.

Return: *numeric*   `1 = true, 0 = false`.

Description: Queries if a *handle* is currently playing.

Usage: `%isPlaying = alxIsPlaying(%handle);`

alxListenerf(ALenum,value)

Parameters: *ALenum*   The enum string. Choices:

"AL_GAIN"

"AL_GAIN_LINEAR"

value   Numeric gain value.

Return: *nothing*

Description: Sets the *ALenum* to *value* for the listener (the player, who "hears" a sound).

Usage: `alxListenerf("AL_GAIN_LINEAR", %vol );`

alxPlay([handle] | [profile [, x, y,z]])

Parameters: handle   Handle to audio object.

Profile   (alternative) Descriptor string.

x,y,z   (optional) If *profile* is used, then this is a tuple indicating where to place the audio object. *Note:* these are three numerics, not a string!

Return: *numeric*   Returns object handle if profile is used.

Description: Begins audio playback with audio object specified by *handle.* Alternatively, if *profile* is used, this function creates an object, begins playback at optional *x,y,z* coordinates, and then returns a handle to the created object.

Usage:
```
%handle0 = alxCreateSource("Audio0", "~/data/sounds/test.wav");
alxPlay(%handle0);
%handle1 = alxPlay("Audio1", "100, 100, 10");
```

alxSetChannelVolume(channel, volume)

Parameters: channel   Channel ID number.

volume   Volume value.

Return: *numeric*   1 = success, 0 = fail.

Description: Sets the *channel* to *volume.*

Usage: `%result = alxSetChannelVolume(%channel, %volume);`

alxSource3f(handle,ALenum, ["x y z"] | [x,y,z])

Parameters: handle   Handle to audio object.

ALenum   The enum string. Choices:

"AL_VELOCITY"

"AL_POSITION"

"AL_DIRECTION"

"x y z"   String containing a tuple indicating where to place the enumed property in 3D world space.

x,y,z   (alternative) If "x y z" isn't used, then this is a tuple indicating where to place the audio object in 3D world space. *Note:* these are three numerics, not a string!

Return: *nothing*

Description: Sets *ALenum* for the specified *handle* to 3D.

Usage: `alxSource3f(%handle[%sender], "AL_POSITION", "100 100 20");`

alxSourcef(handle, ALenum, value)

Parameters: *handle*   Handle to audio object.

ALenum   The enum string. Choices:

"AL_PITCH"

"AL_REFERENCE_DISTANCE"

"AL_MAX_DISTANCE"

"AL_CONE_OUTER_GAIN"

"AL_GAIN"

"AL_GAIN_LINEAR"

value   Numeric (floating point) value to set *ALenum* to.

Return: nothing

Description: Sets *ALenum* for the specified *handle* to the floating point *value*.

Usage: `alxSourcef(%handle[%sender], "AL_GAIN", %gain);`

alxSourcei(handle, ALenum, value)

Parameters: *handle*   Handle to audio object.

ALenum   The enum string. Choices:

"AL_CONE_INNER_ANGLE"

"AL_CONE_OUTER_ANGLE"

"AL_LOOPING"

"AL_STREAMING"

"AL_BUFFER"

value   Numeric value to set *ALenum* to.

Return: nothing

Description: Sets *ALenum* for the specified *handle* to the floating point *value*.

Usage: `alxSourcei(%handle[%sender], "AL_LOOPING", true);`

alxStop(handle)

Parameters: *handle*   Handle to audio object.

Return: nothing

Description: Stops the playback from *handle*.

Usage: `alxStop(%handle[%sender]);`

alxStopAll()

Parameters: none

Return: nothing

Description: Stops the playback on all registered channels.

Usage: `alxStopAll();`

backtrace()

Parameters:	*none*
Return:	*nothing*
Description:	Enables echo of script call stack to console.
Usage:	`backtrace();`

buildTaggedString(string, format)

Parameters:	*string*	Normal string to be added.
	format	Format specifying string.
Return:	*string*	
Description:	Builds and adds a tagged string using *string* with specified *format*.	
Usage:	`%tagstring = buildTaggedString(%name, %format);`	

calcExplosionCoverage(location, handle, mask)

Parameters:	*location*	Where the target object is.
	handle	Target object.
	mask	Object type mask of objects that may block the explosion.
Return:	*numeric*	1 = affected, 0 = unaffected.
Description:	Determines if an object at a location was affected by an explosion. Listed object types will be taken into consideration in the calculation, if they would block the explosion force.	

Usage:
```
%coverage = calcExplosionCoverage(%location, %targetObject,
$TypeMasks::InteriorObjectType | $TypeMasks::TerrainObjectType
| $TypeMasks::VehicleObjectType);
```

call(function [, args ...])

Parameters:	*function*	String containing the name of the function.
	args	Zero or more arguments as needed by *function*.
Return:	*string* Function's return value embedded in a string.	
Description:	Executes the function with the name *function* with supplied arguments, *args*.	
Usage:	`%result = call(%func, %arg1, %arg2);`	

cancel(id)

Parameters:	*id* ID number of supposed event.
Return:	*nothing*
Description:	Cancels the event specified by *id*.
Usage:	`cancel($eventid);`

cancelServerQuery()

Parameters: *none*

Return: *nothing*

Description: Cancels the current query and drops anything outstanding in the ping list.

Usage: `cancelServerQuery();`

clearServerPaths()

Parameters: *none*

Return: *none*

Description: Clears all stored paths held by the Path Manager and releases the memory used.

Usage: `clearServerPaths();`

clearTextureHolds()

Parameters: *none*

Return: *numeric*   Amount of memory released.

Description: Releases any textures not being used, and frees the memory.

Usage: `%clearedMem = clearTextureHolds();`

cls()

Parameters: *none*

Return: *none*

Description: Clears the console screen.

Usage: `cls();`

collapseEscape(text)

Parameters: *text*   String.

Return: *string*   The resultant string.

Description: Removes escaped characters in text. For example, \\n becomes \n.

Usage: `%coltext = collapseEscape(%text);`

commandToClient(client, function [,arg1, . . . argn])

Parameters: *client*   Handle of the target client.

function   Function on the server to be executed.

arg1, . . . argn   Arguments for the function.

Return: *nothing*

Description: Tells the client to execute the command specified by *function*, and passes it the arguments. On the client, the function is declared in the following format:

```
function clientCmdfunction( arg1, ... argn) { ... }
```

The identifier fragment `clientCmd` is prepended to the function name.

Usage: `commandToClient( %client, 'SyncClock', %time);`

commandToServer(function [, arg1, ... argn])

Parameters: function   Function on the server to be executed.

        arg1, ... argn   Arguments for the function.

Return: *nothing*

Description: Tells the server to execute the command specified by *function*, and passes it the arguments. On the server, the function is declared in the following format:

```
function serverCmdfunction(%client, arg1, ... argn) { ... }
```

The identifier `serverCmd` is prepended to the function name. The first parameter is always the handle of the client that sent the command, and the actual command arguments follow.

Usage: `commandToServer('ToggleCamera');`

compile(filename)

Parameters: filename   String containing the file name.

Return: *numeric*   1 = success, 0 = fail.

Description: Compiles the source script file *filename*.

Usage: `%result = compile("/common/default.cs");`

containerBoxEmpty(mask, loc, rad [,yrad, zrad])

Parameters: mask   Object type mask.

        loc   Coordinate tuple.

        rad   Radius distance (or X-axis distance).

        yrad   Optional distance in Y-axis.

        zrad   Optional distance in Z-axis.

Return: *numeric*

Description: Returns `true` if any objects of given types exist in a sphere of the specified extent *rad* and `false` otherwise. If *yrad* is specified, then *rad* is the X-axis extent, and *yrad* is the Y-axis extent. If *zrad* is specified, it becomes the Z-axis extent.

Usage: `%isAny=containerBoxEmpty(ItemObjectType,"10.0 10.0 100.0", 100);`

containerFindFirst(type, point, x, y, z)

Parameters: *type*   The type mask of objects to find.

point   Location of container.

x, y,z   Numeric bounds of container specified. Not a string.

Return: *numeric* Handle of the object found.

Description: Finds objects of *type* within the box specified with *x,y,z* at the given point *point.* Returns the handle of the first object found.

Usage: `%objectHandle = containerFindFirst(type, point, x, y, z);`

containerFindNext()

Parameters: *none*

Return: *numeric*   Handle of the object found.

Description: Finds the next object in the container specified immediately preceding call to `containerFindFirst`, and gets its handle.

Usage: `%objectHandle = containerFindNext();`

containerRayCast(start, end, mask, [exclude])

Parameters: *start*   Starting coordinate tuple.

end   Ending coordinate tuple.

mask   Object type mask.

exclude   List of handles.

Return: *string*   Hit list.

Description: Finds a list of objects of type *mask* between the two coords supplied. A list of object handles can be included in the *exempt* parameter that will not be returned in the hit list.

Usage: `%tgt=containerRayCast(%cameraPoint, %rangeEnd, ItemObjectType);`

containerSearchCurrDist()

Parameters: *none*

Return: *numeric*

Description: Gets the current container search distance.

Usage: `%dist=containerSearchCurrDist();`

containerSearchCurrRadiusDist()

Parameters: *none*

Return: *numeric*

Description: Gets the current container search radius distance.
Usage: `%rad = containerSearchCurrRadiusDist();`

containerSearchNext()

Parameters: *none*
Return: *numeric*
Description: Gets the next object in a container search.
Usage: `%nc = containerSearchNext();`

containsBadwords(text)

Parameters: *text*   String containing text to compare to the bad word list.
Return: *numeric*   1 = success (bad word was found), 0 = fail.
Description: Compares any arbitrary string against the bad word list, looking for bad words.
Usage: `%result = containsBadwords("well shucks, dagnabbit, that rOxxOrszzzz!");`

createCanvas(title)

Parameters: *title*   String containing the title of the window.
Return: *numeric*   1 = success, 0 = fail.
Description: Creates a graphics context called a canvas in a window. All graphics operations are performed within the bounds of the canvas.
Usage: `%result = createCanvas("My Game");`

createEffectCanvas(title)

Parameters: *title*   String containing the title of the window.
Return: *numeric*   1 = success, 0 = fail.
Description: Creates a special effects graphics context called a canvas in a window. All graphics operations are performed within the bounds of the canvas. Combined with changes to the core engine code that would need to be made, effects like in-game interactive 3D panels can be created.
Usage: `%result = createEffectCanvas("My Effects Game");`

dbgSetParameters(port, pw)

Parameters: *port*   Connection port.
               pw   Password.
Return: *nothing*
Description: Initializes telnet debug connection request parameters.
Usage: `dbgSetParameters(1130, "games");`

deactivateDirectInput()

Parameters: *none*
Return: *nothing*
Description: Disables DirectInput device polling (mouse, keyboard, joystick).
Usage: `deactivateDirectInput();`

deactivateKeyboard()

Parameters: *none*
Return: *nothing*
Description: Disables DirectInput polling of the keyboard.
Usage: `deactivateKeyboard();`

deactivatePackage(name)

Parameters: *name*   String containing the name of the package.
Return: *nothing*
Description: Tells Torque to stop using the package specified by *name*.
Usage: `deactivatePackage(Show);`

debug()

Parameters: *none*
Return: *nothing*
Description: Enables debug mode.
Usage: `debug();`

decreaseFSAA()

Parameters: *none*
Return: *nothing*
Description: Decrements `FSAA` level by 1.
Usage: `decreaseFSAA();`

deleteDataBlocks()

Parameters: *none*
Return: *nothing*
Description: Unloads and removes all registered data blocks from the game.
Usage: `deleteDataBlocks();`

deleteVariables(wildcard)

Parameters: *wildcard*   Match string to specify variables.
Return: *nothing*

Description: Deletes global variables specified by *wildcard*. The wildcard string supports "*" to match any number of any characters and "?" to match any single character.

Usage: `deleteVariables("*");`

detag(tstring)

Parameters: *tstring* Tagged string.

Return: *string* String value for the tagged string.

Description: Detags a tagged string.

Usage: `%name=detag(%test.name);`

disableJoystick()

Parameters: *none*

Return: *nothing*

Description: Disables DirectInput polling of the joystick device.

Usage: `disableJoystick();`

disableMouse()

Parameters: *none*

Return: *nothing*

Description: Disables DirectInput polling of the mouse device.

Usage: `disableMouse();`

DNetSetLogging(switch)

Parameters: *switch* 1 (or `true`) = enable, 0 (or `false`) = disable.

Return: *nothing*

Description: Enables network packet logging to the console.

Usage: `DNetSetLogging(1);`

dumpConsoleClasses()

Parameters: *none*

Return: *nothing*

Description: Dumps all registered console classes to the console.

Usage: `dumpConsoleClasses();`

dumpConsoleFunctions()

Parameters: *none*

Return: *nothing*

Description: Dumps all registered console functions to the console.

Usage: `dumpConsoleFunctions();`

dumpFontCacheStatus()

Parameters: *none*
Return: *nothing*
Description: Dumps current state of the font cache to the console.
Usage: `dumpFontCacheStatus();`

dumpMemSnapshot(filename)

Parameters: *filename*   String containing the file name.
Return: *nothing*
Description: Dumps memory statistics to the named file.
Usage: `dumpMemSnapshot("dump.txt");`

dumpNetStringTable()

Parameters: *none*
Return: *nothing*
Description: Dumps the `NetStringTable` stats to the console.
Usage: `dumpNetStringTable();`

dumpResourceStats();

Parameters: *none*
Return: *nothing*
Description: Dumps texture information to the console in the following format:
`path, resource, lockCount.`
Usage: `dumpResourceStats();`

dumpTextureStats()

Parameters: *none*
Return: *nothing*
Description: Dumps texture information to the console in the following format:
`type, refCount, holding` (yes or no), `textureSpace, texFileName.`
Usage: `dumpTextureStats();`

DumpUnflaggedAllocs(filename)

Parameters: *filename*   String containing the file name.
Return: *nothing*
Description: Dumps memory allocation information to the named file.
Usage: `dumpTextureStats("allocs.txt");`

duplicateCachedFont(oldfont, oldsize, newfont)

Parameters: *oldfont*   String containing a font name to be replaced.

oldsize   String containing the size of the font to be replaced.

newfont   String containing a new font name that will be used.

Return: *nothing*

Description: Creates a new copy of font that exists in the disk cache.

Usage: `duplicateCachedFont(oldFontName, oldFontSize, newFontName);`

echo(text)

Parameters: *text*   String.

Return: *nothing*

Description: Prints *text* to the console with the standard font. Text can be formatted according to the string rules.

Usage: `echo("Hello World");`

echoInputState()

Parameters: *none*

Return: *nothing*

Description: Displays the current state of DirectInput (mouse, keyboard, and joystick).

Usage: `echoInputState();`

enableJoystick()

Parameters: *none*

Return: *nothing*

Description: Enables DirectInput polling of the joystick device.

Usage: `enableJoystick();`

enableMouse()

Parameters: *none*

Return: *numeric*   1 = success, 0 = fail.

Description: Enables DirectInput polling of the mouse device.

Usage: `%result=enableMouse();`

enableWinConsole(switch)

Parameters: *switch*   1 enables, 0 disables.

Return: *nothing*

Description: Displays the console window.

Usage: `enableWinConsole(1);`

error(text)

Parameters:	*text*	String.
Return:	*nothing*	
Description:	Prints *text* to the console with red font. Text can be formatted according to the string rules.	
Usage:	`error("I'm sorry, Dave, I'm afraid I can't do that.");`	

eval(string)

Parameters:	*string*	String containing script code.
Return:	*string*	
Description:	Executes functions, assigns variables, and loads packages and data blocks contained within the *string* parameter.	
Usage:	`%result = eval( %MissionInfoObject);`	

exec(fileName [, nocalls [,journalScript]])

Parameters:	*filename*	String containing the file name.
	nocalls	When set to `true`, prevents functions from being called.
	journalScript	When set to `true`, indicates that *filename* is a journal script.
Return:	*string*	
Description:	Compiles, executes functions, assigns variables, and loads packages and data blocks read from contents of the file *filename*. If *nocalls* is set to `true`, functions are not executed, but the other operations still take place.	
Usage:	`%result = exec("/common/default.cs");`	

expandEscape(text)

Parameters:	*text*	String.
Return:	*string*	The resultant string.
Description:	Escapes all of the escape characters in *text*. For example, \n becomes \\n. In this case the \n would be printed to the console instead of the new line it would otherwise cause.	
Usage:	`%extext = expandEscape(%text);`	

expandFilename(filename)

Parameters:	*filename*	String containing the file name.
Return:	*string*	
Description:	Obtains the actual OS-specific absolute path of *filename*.	
Usage:	`%fullmissionpath = expandFilename("~/data/missions/test.mis");`	

export(searchString [, fileName [,append]])

Parameters:	*search*	Prefix of variables to search for.
	filename	String containing the file name.
	append	Indicates whether to append to the file or overwrite.
Return:	*nothing*	

Description: Saves the values of variables starting with *search* to the file named *filename*. When *append* is set to true, the file is appended; when set to false, the file is overwritten. The search string supports "*" to match any number of any characters and "?" to match any single character.

Usage: `%result = export("$Pref::Game::*", "./game/prefs.cs", False);`

exportCachedFont(fontname, fontsize, filename, padding, kerning)

Parameters:	*fontname*	String containing a font name to be exported.
	fontsize	String containing the size of the font to be exported.
	filename	String containing a file name used to store the font.
	padding	String specifying the size of the spacing between character images in the PNG file.
	kerning	String specifying the global kerning value used for all characters.
Return:	*nothing*	

Description: Exports the specified font to the specified file name as a PNG. The image can then be processed with image processing tools and reimported using `importCachedFont`. Characters in the font are exported as one long strip image.

Usage: `exportCachedFont("Arial", 24, "Arial24.png", 3, -1);`

fileBase(filename)

Parameters:	*filename*	String containing the fully pathed file name.
Return:	*string*	String containing the base name.

Description: Gets the base name of the file specified by the fully pathed *filename*.

Usage: `%base=fileBase("/common/server/script.cs");`

fileExt(filename)

Parameters:	*filename*	String containing fully pathed file name.
Return:	*string*	String containing the extension.

Description: Gets the extension of the file specified by the fully pathed *filename*.

Usage: `%name = fileExt("script.cs");`

fileName(filename)

Parameters: *filename*   String containing the fully pathed file name.
Return: *string*   String containing the name.
Description: Gets the file name portion of the file specified by the fully pathed *filename.*
Usage: `%name=fileName("scripts.cs");`

filePath(filename)

Parameters: *filename*   String containing the full file name.
Return: *string*   String containing the path.
Description: Gets the path portion of the file specified by the fully pathed *filename.*
Usage: `%path=filePath("/common/server/script.cs");`

filterString(baseString, replacementChars)

Parameters: *baseString*   String pattern.
        replacementChars   String containing a sequence of characters that will replace any bad words found in the `baseString`.
Return: *string*   The resulting string.
Description: Scans the baseString comparing it against the bad words list, and replaces the bad words text portions of the string with the contents of replacementChars.
Usage: `%result=filterString("Gee willikers, Mr. Froople. That sure looks yummy, dagnabbit!", "*");`

findFirstFile(pattern)

Parameters: *pattern*   String pattern.
Return: *string*   The file's name.
Description: Finds the name of the first file in the Torque Script file name buffer matching the given *pattern.* Supports "*" to match any number of any characters and "?" to match any single character.
Usage: `%result=findFirstFile("/common/*.cs");`

findNextFile(pattern)

Parameters: *pattern*   String pattern.
Return: *string*   The file's name.
Description: Finds the name of the next file in the Torque Script file name buffer matching the search by the call immediately preceding

findFirstFile. Supports "*" to match any number of any characters and "?" to match any single character.

Usage: `%result=findNextFile("/common/*.cs");`

firstWord(text)

Parameters: *text*   String with space-delimited words.
Return: *string*   The resultant string.
Description: Gets the first word-string within *text*.
Usage: `%tgt=firstWord(%text);`

flagCurrentAllocs()

Parameters: *none*
Return: *nothing*
Description: Walk through memory, flagging all memory blocks that are currently allocated.
Usage: `flagCurrentAllocs();`

flushTextureCache()

Parameters: *none*
Return: *nothing*
Description: Deletes cached textures from memory.
Usage: `flushTextureCache();`

freeMemoryDump()

Parameters: *none*
Return: *nothing*
Description: Prints free memory statistics.
Usage: `freeMemoryDump();`

getBoxCenter(box)

Parameters: *box*   String containing two 3D tuples defining the box.
Return: *string*
Description: Computes the center of a box.
Usage: `%c=getBoxCenter("10,10,10,50,50,50");`

getBuildString()

Parameters: *none*
Return: *string*
Description: Obtains the BUILD type (Release or Debug) of the current build.
Usage: `%bs=getBuildString();`

getClipboard()

Parameters: *none*
Return: *string*   Clipboard contents.
Description: Extracts the text contained in the current OS clipboard (this is the clipboard that the OS uses for copy/paste operations).
Usage: `%text=getClipboard ();`

getCompileTimeString()

Parameters: *none*
Return: *string*
Description: Obtains the compile time and date of the current build.
Usage: `%ct=getCompileTimeString();`

getControlObjectAltitude()

Parameters: *none*
Return: *numeric*
Description: (Client-only.) Obtains the altitude of the player object.
Usage: `%altitude = getControlObjectAltitude();`

getControlObjectSpeed()

Parameters: *none*
Return: *numeric*
Description: (Client-only.) Obtains the speed of the player object.
Usage: `%speed = getControlObjectSpeed();`

getCoreLangTable()

Parameters: *none*
Return: *numeric*
Description: (Client-only.) Obtains the language table ID number.
Usage: `%speed = getCoreLangTable();`

getDesktopResolution()

Parameters: *none*
Return: *string*
Description: Reports the current desktop resolution.
Usage: `%res = getDesktopResolution():`

getDisplayDeviceList()

Parameters: *none*
Return: *string*

Description: Obtains the device name for each display device.

Usage: `%name = getDisplayDeviceList();`

getEventTimeLeft(eventHandle)

Parameters: *eventHandle*   String containing the handle of the scheduled event.

Return: *numeric*

Description: Returns the amount of time, in milliseconds, before the scheduled event will trigger.

Usage: `%remaining = getEventTimeLeft(%evtHandle );`

getField(text, index)

Parameters: *text*   String with field-delimited words.

               index   Field-based offset into the text string.

Return: *string*   Contains the found field-string.

Description: Gets the field-string at *index* within *text*. In the usage example that follows, if `%text` equaled "Of Mice and Men", then `%word` would be set to "and" when the function returned.

Usage: `%field = getField(%text, 0);`

getFieldCount(text)

Parameters: *text*   String with field-delimited words.

Return: *numeric*

Description: Gets the number of field-strings within *text*.

Usage: `%count = getFieldCount( %text );`

getFields(text, first [, last])

Parameters: *text*   String with space-delimited fields.

               first   Field-based offset into the text string specifying the first field to extract.

               last   Field-based offset into the text string specifying the last field to extract.

Return: *string*   Contains the found fields.

Description: Gets one or more field-strings at *index* within *text*. If *count* is specified, gets *count* number of field-strings.

Usage: `%position = getFields(%obj.getTransform(), 0, 2);`

getFileCount(pattern)

Parameters: *pattern*   String pattern.

Return: *numeric*

Description: Gets the number of files in the Torque Script file name buffer that match *pattern*.

Usage: `%count = getFileCount("/common/server/*.cs");`

getFileCRC(filename)

Parameters:	*filename*	String containing the full file name.
Return:	*numeric*	The *Cyclic Redundancy Check* (CRC) value.

Description: Gets the CRC value of the file specified by *filename*.

Usage: `%crc = getFileCRC("/common/server/script.cs");`

getJoystickAxes(instance)

Parameters:	*instance*	The joystick object.
Return:	*string*	

Description: Obtains the current axes of the joystick pointed to by *instance*.

Usage: `%joyAxes = getJoystickAxes(3);`

getMaxFrameAllocation()

Parameters: none

Return: numeric

Description: Gets the maximum memory frame allocation unit.

Usage: `%maxFrameAlloc = getMaxFrameAllocation();`

getModPaths()

Parameters: none

Return: string

Description: Gets the current Mod path.

Usage: `$mp = getModPaths();`

getRandom([[max] | [min, max]])

Parameters:	*max*	(optional)High limit.
	min	(optional)Low limit.
Return:	*numeric*	Ranges from 0 to 1, exclusive, if no parameters given; otherwise, see description.

Description: Computes a pseudo-random number. If *min* is not included, then 0 is the minimum. If *max* is not included, then 4,294,967,295 (highest 32-bit number minus 1) is the maximum.

Usage: `%random = getRandom(1, 99);`

getRandomSeed()

Parameters: none
Return: numeric
Description: Obtains the current random seed.
Usage: `%seed = getRandomSeed();`

getRealTime()

Parameters: none
Return: numeric
Description: Gets the real time (in milliseconds) since this computer started.
Usage: `%rt = getRealTime();`

getRecord(text, index)

Parameters: text   String with new line-delimited records.
          index   Record-based offset into the text string.
Return: string   Contains the found record-string.
Description: Gets the record-string at *index* within *text*. In the usage example that follows, if `%text` equaled "Of Mice and Men\nGrapes of Wrath\nCannery Row", then `%record` would be set to "Grapes of Wrath" when the function returned.
Usage: `%record = getRecord(%text, 1);`

getRecordCount(text)

Parameters: text   String with new line-delimited records.
Return: numeric
Description: Get the number of record-strings within *text*.
Usage: `%count = getRecordCount(%text);`

getRecords(text, first [, last])

Parameters: text   String with new line-delimited records.
          first   Record-based offset into the text string specifying the first record to extract.
          last   Record-based offset into the text string specifying the last record to extract.
Return: string   Contains the found records.
Description: Gets one or more record-strings at *index* within *text*. If *count* is specified, gets *count* number of record-strings.
Usage: `%books = getRecords(%obj.getTransform(), 0, 2);`

getRes()

Parameters: none
Return: string   "w h bpp"
                    w: width
                    h: height
                    bpp: bits per pixel
Description: Gets the width, height, and bit depth of the screen.
Usage: `%res = getRes():`

getResolutionList(devicename)

Parameters: devicename   Name of the device to query.
Return: string
Description: Obtains all available resolutions for the specified device.
Usage: `%rl = getResolutionList(%device);`

getScheduleDuration(eventHandle)

Parameters: eventHandle   Handle of the scheduled event.
Return: string
Description: Returns the programmed duration of the scheduled event.
Usage: `%time = getScheduleDuration(%evtHandle);`

getServerCount()

Parameters: none
Return: numeric
Description: Gets the number of available servers from the master server.
Usage: `%sc = getServerCount();`

getSimTime()

Parameters: none
Return: numeric
Description: Gets the current game time.
Usage: `%st = GetSimTime();`

getSubStr(str, loc, count)

Parameters: str   String to be processed.
               loc   Offset into str to where the substring starts
               count   Number of characters to get.
Return: string   The processed resultant string.

Description: Gets the substring of *string* that begins at *loc,* continuing for *count* characters or to the end of the string, whichever comes first.

Usage: `%sub = getSubStr(%text, 5, 99);`

getTag(tstring)

Parameters: tstring   Tagged string.

Return: *string*

Description: Gets the tag for the tagged string *tstring.*

Usage: `%tag = getTag(%variable);`

getTaggedString(tag)

Parameters: tag   Numeric tag of string to be removed.

Return: *string*

Description: Gets the string associated with *tag.*

Usage: `%name = getTaggedString(%tagname);`

getTerrainHeight(pos)

Parameters: pos   2D coordinate.

Return: *numeric*

Description: Gets the terrain height at the specified position.

Usage: `%height = getTerrainHeight(%pos);`

getTimeSinceStart(eventHandle)

Parameters: eventHandle   Handle of the scheduled event.

Return: *string*

Description: Returns the time since the scheduled (and untriggered) event was posted.

Usage: `%time = getTimeSinceStart(%evtHandle);`

getVersionNumber()

Parameters: none

Return: *numeric*

Description: Obtains the hard-coded engine version number of the current build.

Usage: `%vn = getVersionNumber();`

getVersionString()

Parameters: none

Return: *string*

Description: Obtains the hard-coded engine version string of the current build.

Usage: %vs = getVersionString ();

getVideoDriverInfo()

Parameters: none
Return: string
Description: Gets device driver information.
Usage: %info = getVideoDriverInfo();

getWord(text, index)

Parameters: *text*   String with space-delimited words.
               index   Word-based offset into the text string.
Return: *string*   Contains the found word-string.
Description: Gets the word-string at *index* within *text*. In the usage example that
               follows, if %text equaled "Of Mice and Men", then %word would be
               set to "and" when the function returned.
Usage: %word = getWord(%text, 2);

getWordCount(text)

Parameters: *text*   String with space-delimited words.
Return: *numeric*
Description: Gets the number of word-strings within *text*.
Usage: %count = getWordCount(%text);

getWords(text, first [, last])

Parameters: *text*   String with space-delimited words.
               first   Word-based offset into the text string specifying the first
                         word to extract.
               last   Word-based offset into the text string specifying the last
                         word to extract.
Return: *string* Contains the found words.
Description: Gets one or more word-strings between the offsets *first* and *last*.
Usage: %position = getWords(%obj.getTransform(), 0, 2);

GLEnableLogging(switch)

Parameters: *switch*   1 enables, 0 disables.
Return: *nothing*
Description: Enables OpenGL logging to gl_log.txt.
Usage: GLEnableLogging(1);

GLEnableMetrics(switch)

Parameters: *switch*   1 enables, 0 disables.
Return: *nothing*
Description: Tracks metrics data for OpenGL features.
Usage: GLEnableMetrics(1);

GLEnableOutline(switch)

Parameters: *switch*   1 enables, 0 disables.
Return: *nothing*
Description: Enables OpenGL wire-frame mode.
Usage: GLEnableOutline(1);

gotoWebPage(address)

Parameters: *address*   URL of Web page.
Return: *nothing*
Description: Opens the default browser with the specified address.
Usage: gotoWebPage("http://www.tubettiworld.com/");

increaseFSAA()

Parameters: *none*
Return: *nothing*
Description: Increments FSAA level by 1.
Usage: increaseFSAA()

initContainerRadiusSearch(loc, radius, mask)

Parameters: *loc*   3D coordinate.
               radius   To be searched.
               mask   Mask of the object type to look for.
Return: *nothing*
Description: Searches for objects of type *mask* within a radius around the location.
Usage: initContainerRadiusSearch("0 450 76", %somerad, DebrisObjectType);

inputLog(filename)

Parameters: *filename*   String containing the file name.
Return: *nothing*
Description: (Windows only.) Enables or disables logging of DirectInput events
               to log file specified by string.
Usage: inputLog(DI.log);

isDebugBuild()

Parameters: none
Return: numeric   1 = true, 0 = false.
Description: Queries if this version of Torque is a special debug build or not.
Usage: `%isDebug=isDebugBuild();`

isDeviceFullScreenOnly(devicename)

Parameters: *devicename* Name of device to query.
Return: numeric   1 = yes, 0 = no.
Description: Queries if device is capable of full screen only.
Usage: `isDeviceFullScreenOnly(%devicename);`

isEventPending(%id)

Parameters: *id*   ID number to check.
Return: numeric   1 = true, 0 = false.
Description: Queries if an event is pending with an ID number of *id.*
Usage: `%status = isEventPending($eventid);`

isFile(filename)

Parameters: *filename*   String containing the full file name.
Return: numeric   1 = true, 0 = false.
Description: Queries if the file exists in the Torque Script file name buffer.
Usage: `%result = isFile("/common/server/script.cs");`

isFullScreen()

Parameters: none
Return: numeric   1 = yes, 0 = no.
Description: Queries whether the screen mode is set to full screen.
Usage: `%result = isFullScreen();`

isJoystickDetected()

Parameters: none
Return: numeric   1 = true, 0 = false.
Description: Determines if a joystick is present.
Usage: `%jd = isJoystickDetected();`

isKoreanBuild()

Parameters: none
Return: string

Description: Korean registry key checker.
Usage: `%kb = isKoreanBuild();`

isObject(handle)

Parameters: *handle*   Handle of the supposed object.
Return: *numeric*   1 = `true`, 0 = `false`.
Description: Queries if *handle* is an object.
Usage: `%status = isObject(%chopper);`

isPackage(name)

Parameters: *name*   String containing the name of the package.
Return: *numeric*   1 = `true`, 0 = `false`.
Description: Queries if *name* is a registered package.
Usage: `%status = isPackage(Show);`

isPointInside(point)

Parameters: *point*   "x y z".
Return: *numeric*   1 = `true`, 0 = `false`.
Description: Queries if *point* is coincident with the interior of any object.
Usage: `%status = isPointInside("123 345 25");`

isWriteableFileName(filename)

Parameters: *filename*   String containing the full file name.
Return: *numeric*   1 = `true`, 0 = `false`.
Description: Queries if file specified by *filename* is writeable.
Usage: `%result = isWriteableFileName("/common/server/script.cs");`

lightScene(completion)

Parameters: *completion*   Completion callback.
Return: *numeric*   Function handle.
Description: Lights the current mission using the callback function pointed to by
               completion when mission lighting is finished.
Usage: `%result = lightScene("CompletionCallback");`

loadChunkFile(filename)

Parameters: *filename*   String containing the name of the chunk file to load.
Return: *numeric*   Handle to the loaded resource.
Description: Loads a file in chunked format into memory as a resource.
Usage: `%handle = loadChunkFile(%filename);`

lockMouse(switch)

Parameters: *switch*   1 (or `true`) = lock, 0 (or `false`) = unlock.

Return: *nothing*

Description: Toggles the mouse state.

Usage: `lockMouse(true);`

ltrim(str)

Parameters: *str*   String to be processed.

Return: *string*   The processed resultant string.

Description: Strips any white space from the left side (before all other characters) of *str*. White space is defined as spaces, carriage returns, or new line characters.

Usage: `%tidystring = ltrim(%yuckystring);`

mAbs(x)

Parameters: *x*   Operand. Can be an integer or a floating point.

Return: *numeric*

Description: Computes the absolute value of *x*.

Usage: `%val = mAbs(76.3);`

mAcos(x)

Parameters: *x*   Radians. Can be an integer or a floating point.

Return: *numeric*

Description: Computes the arc cosine.

Usage: `%val = mAcos(2.0);`

makeTestTerrain(filename)

Parameters: *filename*   String containing the file name.

Return: *nothing*

Description: Makes a test terrain file.

Usage: `makeTestTerrain("testfile");`

mAsin(x)

Parameters: *x*   Radians. Can be an integer or a floating point.

Return: *numeric*

Description: Computes the arc sine.

Usage: `%val = mAsin(1.5);`

mAtan(x, y)

Parameters: *x*   Radians. Can be an integer or a floating point.

            y   Radians. Can be an integer or a floating point.

Return: *numeric*
Description: Computes the arc tangent.
Usage: `%val = mAtan(-1.667,2);`

mathInit(mode)

Parameters: *mode* The string specifier. Choices:

"DETECT" : Autodetect math lib settings.

"C" : Enable the C math routines. C routines are always enabled.

"FPU" : Enable floating point unit routines.

"MMX" : Enable MMX math routines.

"3DNOW" : 3DNOW' Enable 3dNow! math routines.

"SSE" : Enable SSE math routines.

Return: *nothing*
Description: Enables math extensions based on CPU type.
Usage: `mathInit("DETECT");`

matrixCreate(vector, angledvector)

Parameters: *vector*   "x y z".

angledvector   "x y z angle".

Return: *string*
Description: Generates a matrix from the specified values.
Usage: `%mtx = MatrixCreate("10 10 30", "30 40 50 10");`

matrixCreateFromEuler(valstring)

Parameters: *valstring* "x y z".
Return: *string*
Description: Generates a matrix from given arguments.
Usage: `%val = matrixCreateFromEuler("5.5 90 200");`

matrixMulPoint(matrix, point)

Parameters: *matrix*

point

Return: *string*
Description: Multiplies a matrix by a point.
Usage: `%mtx = matrixMulPoint(%matrix,%point);`

matrixMultiply(matrixA, matrixB)

Parameters: *matrixA*

matrixB

Return:	*string*
Description:	Multiplies two matrices.
Usage:	`%mtx = matrixMultiply(matrix1, matrix2);`

matrixMulVector(matrix, vector)

Parameters:	*matrix*
	vector
Return:	*string*
Description:	Multiplies a matrix by a vector.
Usage:	`%mtx = matrixMulVector(matrix, vector);`

matrixReloaded()

Parameters:	*none*
Return:	*none*
Description:	Hah! Got ya! No such function. Yet.
Usage:	`There` *still* `isn't any such function :-)`

mCeil(x)

Parameters:	*x* Operand. Can be an integer or a floating point.
Return:	*numeric*
Description:	Finds the smallest integral value greater than or equal to the operand.
Usage:	`%val = mCeil(%dialogHeight / %textHeight);`

mCos(x)

Parameters:	*x* Radians. Can be an integer or a floating point.
Return:	*numeric*
Description:	Computes the cosine.
Usage:	`%val = mCos(69);`

mDegToRad(degrees)

Parameters:	*degrees* Degrees to be converted. Can be an integer or a floating point.
Return:	*numeric*
Description:	Converts degrees to radians.
Usage:	`%rads = mDegToRad(90);`

mFloatLength(x, len)

Parameters:	*x* Operand. Can be an integer or a floating point.
	len Number of decimal places.
Return:	*numeric*

Description: Returns *x* as a floating point value with *len* decimal places.

Usage: `%mypi = mFloatLength((21/7),8);`

mFloor(x)

Parameters: *x* Operand. Can be an integer or a floating point.

Return: *numeric*

Description: Finds the largest integral value less than or equal to the operand.

Usage: `%val = mFloor(%dialogHeight / %textHeight);`

mLog(x)

Parameters: *x* Radians. Can be an integer or a floating point.

Return: *numeric*

Description: Computes the natural logarithm.

Usage: `%val = mLog(7654.98);`

mPow(x, y)

Parameters: *x*   Base. Can be an integer or a floating point.

               y   Exponent. Can be an integer or a floating point.

Return: *numeric*

Description: Computes *x* raised to the power of *y*

Usage: `%val = mPow(2, 4);`

mRadToDeg(radians)

Parameters: *radians* Radians to be converted. Can be integers or floating points.

Return: *numeric*

Description: Converts radians to degrees.

Usage: `%degs = mRadToDeg(1);`

msg(handle, message)

Parameters: *handle*   Handle of the object to receive the message.

               message   String containing the message.

Return: *nothing*

Description: Sends *message* to the object specified by *handle*.

Usage: `msg(%objhandle, %msg);`

mSin(x)

Parameters: *x*   Radians. Can be an integer or a floating point.

Return: *numeric*

Description: Computes the sine.

Usage: `%val=mSin(65);`

mSolveCubic(a, b, c, d)

Parameters:	*a, b, c, d*	Operands. Can be integers or floating points.
Return:	*string*	
Description:	Computes a cubic solution for *x*. $ax\text{\textasciicircum}3 + bx\text{\textasciicircum}2 + cx + d = 0$.	
Usage:	`%val = mSolveCubic(a, b, c, d);`	

mSolveQuadratic(a, b, c)

Parameters:	*a, b, c*	Operands. Can be integers or floating points.
Return:	*string*	
Description:	Computes a quadratic solution for *x*. $ax\text{\textasciicircum}2 + bx + c = 0$.	
Usage:	`%val = mSolveQuadratic(a, b, c);`	

mSolveQuartic(a, b, c, d, e)

Parameters:	*a, b, c, d, e*	Operands. Can be integers or floating points.
Return:	*string*	
Description:	Computes a quartic solution for *x*. $ax\text{\textasciicircum}4 + bx\text{\textasciicircum}3 + cx\text{\textasciicircum}2 + dx + e = 0$.	
Usage:	`%val = mSolveQuartic(a, b, c, d, e);`	

mSqrt(x)

Parameters:	*x*	Operand. Can be an integer or a floating point.
Return:	*numeric*	
Description:	Computes the square root of *x*.	
Usage:	`%val = mSqrt(81);`	

mTan(x)

Parameters:	*x*	Radians. Can be an integer or a floating point.
Return:	*numeric*	
Description:	Computes the tangent.	
Usage:	`%val = mTan(45.0);`	

nameToID(name)

Parameters:	*name*	String containing the name of the object.
Return:	*nothing*	
Description:	Gets the ID number of the named object.	
Usage:	`nameToID(%chopper);`	

nextResolution()

Parameters:	*none*	
Return:	*numeric*	1 = success, 0 = fail.

Description: Increases the next highest resolution.

Usage: `%result = nextResolution();`

nextToken(str, token, delim)

Parameters: *str*   Initializes the tokenizer when set to a valid string variable. Uses an empty string ("") to specify follow-up operation on the same string.

token   References the handle to the variable that will receive the found token. *Note:* when passing a variable by reference to a function, such as with this parameter, you do not prefix the variable name with % or $.

delim   Specifies the character that delimits the tokens.

Return: *string* Balance of the string after the found token.

Description: Sets *token* to the next substring in *str* delimited by *delim*. The initial call to this function specifies *str*; subsequent calls to this function that operate on the same string must pass the empty string ("").

Usage: `%str = NextToken("one, two, three", number, ",");`

openALInitDriver()

Parameters: *none*

Return: *numeric*

Description: Initializes the sound driver.

Usage: `openALInitDriver();`

openALRegisterExtensions()

Parameters: *none*

Return: *numeric*

Description: As of this writing, this function, although present, does nothing.

Usage: `OpenALRegisterExtensions();`

openALShutdownDriver()

Parameters: *none*

Return: *nothing*

Description: Disables the sound driver.

Usage: `openALShutdownDriver();`

panoramaScreenShot(filename)

Parameters: *filename*   String containing the file name.

Return: *nothing*

Description: Captures the panoramic screen view and saves it to the PNG file specified by *filename*. The engine will take the panoroma shot as a sequence of three screen captures, looking left, center, then right.

Usage: `panoramaScreenShot("myPanorama");`

pathOnMissionLoadDone()

Parameters: none

Return: nothing

Description: Sets the Mod path that will be active when a mission is finished loading.

Usage: `pathOnMissionLoadDone("missE/mission");`

playJournal(name, [break])

Parameters: name   String containing the file name of the journal.

break   If `true`, then this stops playback after each event.

Return: nothing

Description: Plays back the saved journal specified by *name*.

Usage: `playJournal("myjrnl.jnl");`

png2jpg(filename, quality)

Parameters: filename   String containing the file name of the PNG file to convert.

quality   Conversion quality, numeric range 0 to 100.

Return: numeric   −1 = failure, 0 = success.

Description: Converts the PNG-formatted file specified by *filename* to JPG format, and writes the resulting image file to disk with the same name and path as *filename* but with the JPG extension instead of PNG.

Usage: `png2jpg("image1.png", 100);`

populateAllFontCacheRange(start, end)

Parameters: start   Start of range.

end   End of range.

Return: none

Description: Populates the font cache for all fonts with Unicode code points in the specified range. Only BMP-0 is supported, so code points range from 0 to 65535.

Usage: **populateAllFontCacheRange**(0,100);

populateAllFontCacheString(string)

Parameters: string String of characters that does populating.

Return: none

Description: Populates the font cache for all fonts with characters from the specified string.

Usage: `populateAllFontCacheString("abcdefg");`

populateFontCacheRange(face, size, start, end)

Parameters: *face*   String containing the name of the font face.

           size   String containing the size of the font face.

           start   Start of range.

           end   End of range.

Return: *none*

Description: Populates the font cache for the specified font with Unicode code points in the specified range. Only BMP-0 is supported, so code points range from 0 to 65535.

Usage: `populateFontCacheRange("ariel",12,0,100);`

populateFontCacheString(face, size, string)

Parameters: *face*   String containing the name of the font face.

           size   String containing the size of the font face.

           string   String of characters that does populating.

Return: *none*

Description: Populates the font cache for all fonts with characters from the specified string.

Usage: `populateFontCacheString("ariel",12, "abcdefg");`

prevResolution()

Parameters: *none*

Return: *numeric*   1 = success, 0 = fail.

Description: Decreases the next highest resolution.

Usage: `%result=prevResolution();`

profilerDump()

Parameters: *none*

Return: *nothing*

Description: Dumps `NetStringTable` statistics to the console.

Usage: `profilerDump();`

profilerDumpToFile(filename)

Parameters: *filename*   String containing the file name.

Return: *nothing*

Description: Dumps `NetStringTable` statistics to the file specified by *filename.*

Usage: `profilerDumpToFile(dump.txt);`

profilerEnable(switch)

Parameters: *switch*   1 enables, 0 disables.

Return: *nothing*

Description: Enables or disables profiling.

Usage: `profilerEnable(0);`

profilerMarkerEnable(markerName, switch)

Parameters: *markerName* Name of the profile marker.

switch   1 enables, 0 disables.

Return: *nothing*

Description: Enables or disables profiling for `markerName`.

Usage: `profilerMarkerEnable("mark",1);`

profilerReset()

Parameters: *none*

Return: *nothing*

Description: Resets the profiler, clearing all of its data.

Usage: `profilerReset();`

purgeResources()

Parameters: *none*

Return: *nothing*

Description: Purges all resources used by the game through the resource manager.

Usage: `purgeResources();`

queryLANServers(port, flags, gametype, missiontype, minplayers, max-players, maxbots, regionmask, maxping, mincpu, filterflags)

Parameters: *port*   Host server port.

flags   The query flags. Choices:

0x00 = online query

0x01 = offline query

0x02 = no string compression

gametype   Game type string.

missiontype   Mission type string.

minplayers   Minimum number of players for a viable game.

maxplayers	Maximum allowable players.
maxbots	Maximum allowable connected AI bots.
regionmask	Numeric discriminating mask.
maxping	Maximum ping for connecting clients; 0 means no maximum.
mincpu	Minimum specified CPU capability.
filterflags	Server filters. Choices:

0x00 = dedicated

0x01 = not password protected

0x02 = Linux

0x80 = current version

Return: *nothing*

Description: Queries all computers found in the LAN, examining the port specified with *port*. The responses are accessible from the ServerList array.

Usage:

```
queryLANServers(
28000, 0, $Client::GameTypeQuery, Client::MissionTypeQuery,
0, 100, 0, 2, 0, 100, 0);
```

queryMasterServer
(port, flags, gametype, missiontype, minplayers, maxplayers, maxbots, regionmask, maxping, mincpu, filterflags)

Parameters:	*port*	Host server port.
	flags	The query flags. Choices:

0x00 = online query

0x01 = offline query

0x02 = no string compression

	gametype	Game type string.
	missiontype	Mission type string.
	minplayers	Minimum number of players for a viable game.
	maxplayers	Maximum allowable players.
	maxbots	Maximum allowable connected AI bots.
	regionmask	Numeric discriminating mask.
	maxping	Maximum ping for connecting clients; 0 means no maximum.
	mincpu	Minimum specified CPU capability.

filterflags	Server filters. Choices:	
	0x00 = dedicated	
	0x01 = not password protected	
	0x02 = Linux	
	0x80 = current version	

Return: *nothing*

Description: Queries a master server looking for specified information. The responses are accessible from the `ServerList` array. *Note: buddycount* and *buddylist* are obsolete arguments and no longer included or used.

Usage:

```
queryMasterServer(
28000, 0, $Client::GameTypeQuery, Client::MissionTypeQuery,
0, 100, 0, 2, 0, 100, 0);
```

querySingleServer(address, flags)

Parameters:	*address*	IP address of server.
	flags	The query flags. Choices:
		0x00 = online query
		0x01 = offline query
		0x02 = no string compression

Return: *nothing*

Description: Queries a single server looking for a game being served. The responses are accessible from the `ServerList` array.

Usage: `querySingleServer("192.168.100.1", 0);`

quit()

Parameters: *none*

Return: *nothing*

Description: Quits the game engine.

Usage: `quit();`

quitWithErrorMessage(msg)

Parameters: *msg*   String containing an error message.

Return: *nothing*

Description: Quits the game engine and displays the specified message *msg* while quitting.

Usage: `quitWithErrorMessage("Doh! You're losing, so you quit, huh?");`

redbookClose()

Parameters: *none*
Return: *numeric*   1 = success, 0 = fail.
Description: Closes the currently open redbook (CD) device.
Usage: `%result = redbookClose();`

redbookGetDeviceCount()

Parameters: *none*
Return: *numeric*
Description: Queries for the number of redbook (CD) devices.
Usage: `%count = redbookGetDeviceCount();`

redbookGetDeviceName(idx)

Parameters: *idx*   Device index.
Return: *string*
Description: Queries the device name of a redbook (CD) at the specified device index.
Usage: `%name = redbookGetDeviceName(1);`

redbookGetLastError()

Parameters: *none*
Return: *string*
Description: Queries for the last error from a redbook (CD) device.
Usage: `%error = redbookGetLastError();`

redbookGetTrackCount()

Parameters: *none*
Return: *numeric*
Description: Queries the number of redbook (CD) tracks.
Usage: `%tracks = redbookGetTrackCount();`

redbookGetVolume()

Parameters: *none*
Return: *numeric*
Description: Queries the current volume level of a redbook (CD) device.
Usage: `%volume = redbookGetVolume();`

redbookOpen([name])

Parameters: *name*   If non-null, then this specifies the device.
Return: *numeric*   1 = success, 0 = fail.

Description: Opens a redbook (CD) device.

Usage: `%result = redbookOpen();`

redbookPlay(track)

Parameters: *track*   Index of a track.

Return: *numeric*   1 = success, 0 = fail.

Description: Plays a track on a redbook (CD) device.

Usage: `%result=redbookPlay(2);`

redbookSetVolume(volume)

Parameters: *volume*   Volume setting.

Return: *numeric*   1 = success, 0 = fail.

Description: Sets the volume of a redbook (CD) device.

Usage: `%result = redbookSetVolume(%volume);`

redbookStop()

Parameters: *none*

Return: *numeric*   1 = success, 0 = fail.

Description: Stops playing on the current redbook (CD) device.

Usage: `%result = redbookStop();`

removeField(text, index)

Parameters: *text*   String with field-delimited words.

            index   Field-based offset into the text string.

Return: *string*   The resultant string.

Description: Removes the field-string at *index* from *text*.

Usage: `%result = removeField(%text, 0);`

removeRecord(text, index)

Parameters: *text*   String with new line-delimited records.

            index   Record-based offset into the text string.

Return: *string*   The resultant string.

Description: Removes the record-string at *index* from *text*.

Usage: `%str = removeRecord(%text, 0);`

removeTaggedString(tag)

Parameters: *tag*   Numeric tag of the string to be removed.

Return: *nothing*

Description: Removes a tagged string from the list.

Usage: `removeTaggedString(%tagname);`

removeWord(text, index)

Parameters: *text*   String with space-delimited words.

            index   Word-based offset into the text string.

Return: *string*   The resultant string.

Description: Removes the word-string at *index* from *text*.

Usage: `%str = removeWord(%text, 0);`

resetLighting()

Parameters: *none*

Return: *nothing*

Description: Resets the current lighting.

Usage: `resetLighting();`

restWords(text)

Parameters: *text*   String with space-delimited words.

Return: *string*   The resultant string.

Description: Returns the words remaining after the first word in *text*.

Usage: `%data = restWords(%text);`

rtrim(str)

Parameters: *str*   String to be processed.

Return: *string*   The processed resultant string.

Description: Strips any white space from the right side (after all other characters) of *str*. White space is defined as spaces, carriage returns, or new line characters.

Usage: `%tidystring=rtrim(%yuckystring);`

saveChunkFile(chunk, filename)

Parameters: *chunk*   The chunk to be written.

            filename   The name of the file that will be written.

Return: *numeric*   1 (`true`) = success, 0 (`false`) = fail.

Description: Writes a chunk hierarchy to a file. There must be a root chunk or the function will fail.

Usage: `%result = saveChunkFile(%filename);`

saveJournal(name)

Parameters: *name*   String containing the file name of the journal.

Return: *nothing*

Description: Saves a journal to the file specified by *name*.

Usage: `saveJournal("myjrnl.jnl");`

schedule(time, reference, command, <arg1 ... argN>)

Parameters: *time*   Time to wait for the trigger, in milliseconds.

reference   Handle of the object to attach the schedule to, or 0.

command   Command to execute.

arg1 ... argN (optional)Arguments to accompany the command.

Return: *numeric*   Event ID.

Description: Schedules an event that will trigger in *time* milliseconds and execute *command*, with *args*. If *reference* is not 0, then it must be a valid object handle. If the object is deleted, the scheduled event is discarded.

Usage: `$evt = schedule(5000, 0, "updateRadar");`

screenShot(filename, format)

Parameters: *filename*   String containing the file name.

format   One of JPEG or PNG.

Return: *nothing*

Description: Captures the screen view and saves it to the file specified by *filename*.

Usage: `screenShot("myScreens", PNG);`

setClipboard(string)

Parameters: *string*   String containing text.

Return: *nothing*

Description: Inserts the contents of *string* into the OS copy/paste clipboard.

Usage: `setClipboard("stuff to be pasted");`

setCoreLangTable(table)

Parameters: *table*   Index of the language table to set.

Return: *nothing*

Description: Sets *table* to be the core language table, by indexed reference.

Usage: `setCoreLangTable(%idx);`

setDefaultFov(fov)

Parameters: *fov*   Numeric in degrees.

Return: *nothing*

Description: Sets the default field of view.

Usage: `setDefaultFov( 60 );`

setDisplayDevice(deviceName[, width[, height[, bpp[, fullScreen]]]])

Parameters: *deviceName*   Name of the target device driver.

width   Screen width.

height   Screen height.

	bpp	Bits per pixel.
	fullScreen	1 enables, 0 disables.
Return:	*numeric*	1 = success, 0 = fail.

Description: Sets up the display device with specified values.

Usage: `%result = setDisplayDevice( "OpenGL", 800, 600, 32, true );`

setEchoFileLoads(switch)

Parameters: *switch*   1 (or `true`) enables, 0 (or `false`) disables.

Return: *nothing*

Description: Enables or disables File Load echo to console.

Usage: `setEchoFileLoads(1);`

setField(text, index, subst)

Parameters:	*text*	String with field-delimited words.
	index	Field-based offset into the text string.
	subst	Substitute string.
Return:	*string*	The resultant string.

Description: Substitutes the field-string *subst* for the word-string found at *index* in the string *text*.

Usage: `%rec = setField(%text, 0, "blah");`

setFov(val)

Parameters: *val*   The field of view (degrees).

Return: *nothing*

Description: Sets the current field of view.

Usage: `setFov(90);`

setFSAA(switch, level)

Parameters:	*switch*	1 enables, 0 disables.
	level	Target level.

Return: *nothing*

Description: Enables or disables `Full Screen Anti-Aliasing` at the specified *level*.

Usage: `setFSAA(%newstate,%lvl);`

setInteriorFocusedDebug(which)

Parameters: *which* Handle of interior for focus. If *which* has a value, then debugging is enabled; if *which* is empty (not passed), then debugging is disabled.

Return: *nothing*

Description: Enables the debug mode for interior focused objects.

Usage: `setInteriorFocusedDebug();`

setInteriorRenderMode(mode)

Parameters: *mode* *Interior detail render mode, one of:*

`$Interior::NormalRender`	= 0,
`$Interior::NormalRenderLines`	= 1,
`$Interior::ShowDetail`	= 2,
`$Interior::ShowAmbiguous`	= 3,
`$Interior::ShowOrphan`	= 4,
`$Interior::ShowLightmaps`	= 5,
`$Interior::ShowTexturesOnly`	= 6,
`$Interior::ShowPortalZones`	= 7,
`$Interior::ShowOutsideVisible`	= 8,
`$Interior::ShowCollisionFans`	= 9,
`$Interior::ShowStrips`	= 10,
`$Interior::ShowNullSurfaces`	= 11,
`$Interior::ShowLargeTextures`	= 12,
`$Interior::ShowHullSurfaces`	= 13,
`$Interior::ShowVehicleHullSurfaces`	= 14,
`$Interior::ShowVertexColors`	= 15,
`$Interior::ShowDetailLevel`	= 16

Return: *nothing*

Description: Sets the detail render level for interiors. Only one mode can be inoked at a time.

Usage: `setInteriorRenderMode(7);`

setLogMode(mode)

Parameters: *mode* The numeric mode value. Choices:

0 Disables logging to console.log file.

1 Enables logging to console.log in append mode. All entries are appended to the existing log file. This means that to remove the logging info from earlier sessions, you need to delete console.log manually via the operating system (using the command shell or Explorer). The log output buffer is flushed and the console.log file is closed after every logging write operation to the file. If the first time that Torque encounters `setLogMode(1)` in script, it (`setLogmode`) is setting the log mode to 1, then logging to the console.log file will begin at that first encounter, and the output begins at the point in the script where that first encounter takes place.

2 Enables logging to console.log in overwrite mode. Every time the Torque demo is launched, the old contents of console.log

are overwritten with new information. The log file remains open while the Torque demo is running. This yields higher performance, since there is only one log file open operation and one log file close operation per run session of the Torque demo. If the first time that Torque encounters setLogMode(1) in script, it (setLogmode) is setting the log mode to 2, then logging to the console.log file will begin at that first encounter, and the output begins at the point in the script where that first encounter takes place.

3　　Not used.

4　　Not used.

5　　Same as mode 1, except all of the contents of the console window created prior to the point where the setLogMode(5); statement is encountered are flushed out to the log file when this first setLogMode(5); statement is encountered in TorqueScript.

6　　Same as mode 2, except all of the contents of the console window created prior to the point where the setLogMode(6); statement is encountered are flushed out to the log file when this first setLogMode(6); statement is encountered in TorqueScript.

Return:　　*nothing*

Description:　Enables or disables error logging to disk according to the mode descriptions.

Usage:　　setLogMode(1);

setModPaths(path)

Parameters:　*path*　　String containing the path.

Return:　　*nothing*

Description:　Sets the mod path. This specifies which folders will be visible to the scripts and the resource engine.

Usage:　　setModPaths("common;game");

setNetPort(port)

Parameters:　*port*　　　Port number.

Return:　　*numeric*　　1 = success, 0 = fail.

Description:　Sets the network port.

Usage:　　%result = setNetPort(1313);

setOpenGLAnisotropy(level)

Parameters:　*level*　　0 = trilinear, 1 = bilinear.

Return:　　*nothing*

Description: Sets the level of anisotropy.

Usage: setOpenGLAnisotropy(0);

setOpenGLInteriorMipReduction(level)

Parameters: *level*   Mipmap level (0 = minimum detail, 5 = maximum detail).

Return: *nothing*

Description: Sets interior texture detail.

Usage: setOpenGLInteriorMipReduction(2);

setOpenGLMipReduction(level)

Parameters: *level*   Mipmap level (0 = minimum detail, 5 = maximum detail).

Return: *nothing*

Description: Sets shape texture detail

Usage: setOpenGLMipReduction(2);

setOpenGLSkyMipReduction(level)

Parameters: *level*   Mipmap level (0 = minimum detail, 5 = maximum detail).

Return: *nothing*

Description: Sets skybox and cloud texture detail.

Usage: setOpenGLSkyMipReduction(2);

setOpenGLTextureCompressionHint(hint)

Parameters: *hint*   The compression level hint. Choices:

GL_DONT_CARE =   0x1100

GL_FASTEST =   0x1101

GL_NICEST =   0x1102

Return: *nothing*

Description: Suggests texture compression mode.

Usage: setOpenGLTextureCompressionHint(GL_NICEST);

setPowerAudioProfiles(up, down)

Parameters: *up*   Power up profile.

down   Power down profile.

Return: *nothing*

Description: Sets the ambient audio manager's power up/down profiles.

Usage: setPowerAudioProfiles(AudioPowerUpProfile, AudioPowerDownProfile);

setRandomSeed([seed])

Parameters: *seed*   Starting point.

Return: *nothing*

Description: Sets the current starting point for generating a series of pseudo-random numbers. If no seed is provided then the current time in ms is used.

Usage: `setRandomSeed();`

setRecord(text, index, subst)

Parameters: *text*   String with new line-delimited records.

                index   Record-based offset into the text string.

                subst   Substitute string.

Return: *string*   The resultant string.

Description: Substitutes the record-string *subst* for the record-string found at *index* in the string *text*.

Usage: `%str = setRecord(%text, 0, "blah");`

setRes(width, height, bpp)

Parameters: *width*   Screen width.

                height   Screen height.

                bpp   Bits per pixel.

Return: *numeric*   1 = success, 0 = fail.

Description: Sets the screen resolution to specified values.

Usage: `%result=setRes(640, 480, 32);`

setScreenMode(width, height, bpp, fullScreen)

Parameters: *width*   Screen width.

                height   Screen height.

                bpp   Bits per pixel.

                fullScreen 1 enables, 0 disables.

Return: *numeric*   1 = success, 0 = fail.

Description: Sets up the screen with specified values.

Usage: `%result = setScreenMode( 800, 600, 32, 1 );`

setServerInfo(index)

Parameters: *index*   Row of interest in the server list.

Return: *numeric*   1 = success, 0 = fail.

Description: Changes the indexed reference into the `ServerList`.

Usage: `%result = setServerInfo(%index);`

setShadowDetailLevel(level)

Parameters: *level*   Numeric range 0.0 to 1.0.
Return: *nothing*
Description: Sets the level of detail for shadows.
Usage: `setShadowDetailLevel( 1.0 );`

setVerticalSync(switch)

Parameters: *switch*   1 enables, 0 disables.
Return: *numeric*   1 = `true`, 0 = `false`.
Description: Enables or disables the use of Vertical Sync.
Usage: `setVerticalSync(1);`

setWord(text, index, subst)

Parameters: *text*   String with space-delimited words.
    index   Word-based offset into the text string.
    subst   Substitute string.
Return: *string*   The resultant string.
Description: Substitutes the word-string *subst* for the word-string found at *index*
    in the string *text*.
Usage: `%str = setWord(%text, 0, "blah");`

setZoomSpeed(speed)

Parameters: *speed*   Transition speed. Ranges from 0 to 2,000 milliseconds.
Return: *nothing*
Description: Sets the transition speed when changing the field of view.
Usage: `setZoomSpeed(speed);`

showDeleteThread(threadID)

Parameters: *threadID*   Thread handle.
Return: *nothing*
Description: Deletes the specified animation thread in the Show tool.
Usage: `showDeleteThread( %deathAnim );`

showNewThread( )

Parameters: *none*
Return: *nothing*
Description: Starts a new animation thread in the Show tool.
Usage: `showNewThread( );`

showPlay(threadID)

Parameters: *threadID*   Thread handle.
Return: *nothing*
Description: Plays the specified animation thread in the Show tool.
Usage: showPlay(2);

showSelectSequence( )

Parameters: *none*
Return: *nothing*
Description: Starts the currently selected animation thread in the Show tool.
Usage: showSelectSequence( );

showSequenceLoad(threadID)

Parameters: *threadID*   Thread handle.
Return: *nothing*
Description: Loads the specified animation thread in the Show tool.
Usage: showSequenceLoad(%deathAnim);

showSetCamera(orbit)

Parameters: *orbit*   String specified whether to orbit or free-fly.
Return: *nothing*
Description: Sets camera motion to t or T to orbit; otherwise uses the free-fly mode in the Show tool.
Usage: showSetCamera(%orbit);

showSetDetailSlider( )

Parameters: *none*
Return: *nothing*
Description: Forms the level-of-detail slider and sets it to working in the Show tool.
Usage: showSetDetailSlider( );

showSetKeyboard(shape)

Parameters: *shape*   String containing the name of the shape to use.
Return: *nothing*
Description: Sets keyboard control for the shape in the Show tool.
Usage: showSetKeyboard(%deathAnim);

showSetLightDirection( )

Parameters: *none*
Return: *nothing*

Description: Incrementally moves the light direction in the Show tool.

Usage: `showSetLightDirection();`

showSetPos(threadID, position)

Parameters: *threadID*   Thread handle.

             position   Animation frame number in the animation thread.

Return: *nothing*

Description: Sets the thread *threadID* to the specified position in the animation thread.

Usage: `showSetPos(1,25);`

showSetScale(threadID,scale)

Parameters: *threadID*   Thread handle.

             scale   Scale value to assign to the animation thread.

Return: *nothing*

Description: Adjusts the size of *threadID* by *scale* size, where 1.0 as *scale* is 1:1, in the Show tool.

Usage: **showSetScale**(2.0);

showShapeLoad(name, faceCamera)

Parameters: *name*   String containing the name of the shape to load.

             faceCamera   `true` = shape loads facing the camera.

                                 `false` = shape loads facing as it was created.

Return: *nothing*

Description: Loads the specified shape into the Show Tool, and orients the model either facing the camera, or as model was originally created..

Usage: `showShapeLoad( %shape, true );`

showStop(threadID)

Parameters: *threadID*   Thread handle.

Return: *nothing*

Description: Stops the specified animation thread in the Show tool.

Usage: `showStop(2);`

showToggleRoot()

Parameters: *none*

Return: *nothing*

Description: Toggles the root animation sequence on or off.

Usage: `showToggleRoot();`

showToggleStick()

Parameters: none
Return: nothing
Description: Toggles whether the animated shape is kept rooted to the ground each time the function is called in the Show tool.
Usage: showToggleStick();

showTurnLeft(amount)

Parameters: amount   Rate of turn.
Return: nothing
Description: Commands the shape to start a leftward rotation at the given rate in the Show tool.
Usage: showTurnLeft(0.5);

showTurnRight(amount)

Parameters: amount   Rate of turn.
Return: nothing
Description: Commands the shape to start a rightward rotation at the given rate in the Show tool.
Usage: showTurnRight(0.5);

showUpdateThreadControl()

Parameters: none
Return: nothing
Description: Updates controls and values displayed in the Show tool.
Usage: showUpdateThreadControl();

snapToggle()

Parameters: none
Return: nothing
Description: Toggles the mouse movement handler for shapes on and off.
Usage: snapToggle();

startClientReplication()

Parameters: none
Return: nothing

Description: Starts the client-side shape replicator running. Note that you must actually have the right kind of shapes (fxShapeReplicator) applied in a mission for this function to actually do anything.

Usage:　　`startClientReplication();`

startFoliageReplication()

Parameters: none

Return:　　nothing

Description: Starts the client-side foliage replicator. This works the same way as the shape replicator described in **startClientReplication**.

Usage:　　**startClientReplication**`();`

startHeartbeat()

Parameters: none

Return:　　nothing

Description: Begins periodic messages to the master server that show that this server is still alive.

Usage:　　`schedule(0,0,startHeartbeat);`

stopHeartbeat()

Parameters: none

Return:　　nothing

Description: Stops the heartbeat messages.

Usage:　　`stopHeartbeat();`

stopServerQuery()

Parameters: none

Return:　　nothing

Description: Cancels the current query, and marks outstanding pings as finished.

Usage:　　`stopServerQuery();`

strchr(str, char)

Parameters: str　　String to be processed.

　　　　　char　　String containing the character to be found.

Return:　　string

Description: Finds the first substring in the string that begins with *char*.

Usage:　　`%file = strchr("data/file.dat", "/" );`

strcmp(str1, str2)

Parameters: *str1*   First string.

                str2   Second string.

Return: *numeric*   < 0   *str1* is less than (but not equal to) *str2*.

                                   0   *str1* is equal to *str2*.

                              > 0   *str1* is greater than (but not equal to) *str2*.

Description: Makes a case-*sensitive* comparison of two strings: *str1* and *str2*.

Usage: `if(strcmp(%weaponName,"candlestick")==0) return %weaponFound;`

stricmp(str1, str2)

Parameters: *str1*   First string.

                str2   Second string.

Return: *numeric*   < 0   *str1* is less than (but not equal to) *str2*.

                                   0   *str1* is equal to *str2*.

                              > 0   *str1* is greater than (but not equal to) *str2*.

Description: Makes a case-*insensitive* comparison of two strings: *str1* and *str2*.

Usage: `if(stricmp(%weaponName,"CandleStick")==0) return %weaponFound;`

stripChars(str, chars)

Parameters: *str*   String to be processed.

                chars   String containing characters to be stripped.

Return: *string*   The processed resultant string.

Description: Removes all characters in the string *chars* from the string *str*.

Usage: `%stripped = stripChars(%value, "~" );`

stripColorCodes(str)

Parameters: *str*   String to be processed.

Return: *string*   The processed resultant string.

Description: Removes all color code characters from the string *str*.

Usage: `%stripped = stripColorCodes("\c0Hello\c6World!\cp" );`

stripMLControlChars(string)

Parameters: *string*

Return: *string*

Description: Strips ML special control characters from a string.

Usage: `%text = stripMLControlChars(%string);`

stripTrailingSpaces(string)

Parameters: *string* Input string.

Return: *string*

Description: Strips trailing spaces and underscores from the string to be used for a player name.

Usage: `%name = stripTrailingSpaces( strToPlayerName( %name ) );`

strlen(str)

Parameters: *str* String.

Return: *numeric*

Description: Obtains the number of characters in *str*.

Usage: `%len = strlen(%weaponName);`

strlwr(str)

Parameters: *str* String to be processed.

Return: *string* The processed resultant string.

Description: Converts all characters in *str* to lowercase.

Usage: `%var = strlwr(%value);`

strpos(str, target[, offset])

Parameters: *str* String to be searched.

target String to find.

offset (optional)Search starts at offset.

Return: *numeric*

Description: Finds the first occurrence of the target string in the search string, with optional starting offset. *Note:*this function is identical to strstr when *offset* isn't used.

Usage: `%pos = strpos(%weaponName, "gun");`

strreplace(str, target, subst)

Parameters: *str* String to be processed.

target Target string to be replaced.

subst Substitute string.

Return: *string* The processed resultant string.

Description: Replaces all instances of *target* with *subst*.

Usage: `%dospath = strreplace(%path, "/", "\");`

strstr(str, target)

Parameters: *str* String to be tested.

target Target substring to find.

Return: *numeric*   Offset within *str* where *target* was found.
Description: Finds the first occurrence of *target* within *str*.
Usage: %loc = strstr(%weaponName, "stick");

strToPlayerName(string);

Parameters: string   Player name string.
Return: *string*
Description: Converts a name string to a properly formatted player name string. Proper formatting means the player name is limited to 16 characters in length. Leading and trailing spaces are trimmed; reserved characters are removed.
Usage: %newname = strToPlayerName(%name);

strupr(str)

Parameters: str   String to be processed.
Return: *string*   The processed resultant string.
Description: Converts all characters in *str* to uppercase.
Usage: %var = strupr(%value);

switchBitDepth()

Parameters: none
Return: *numeric*   1 = success, 0 = fail.
Description: Switches between 16 and 32 bits per pixel in full-screen mode.
Usage: %result = switchBitDepth();

telnetSetParameters(port, consolePW, listenPW[,remoteEcgo])

Parameters: port   Connection port.
                 consolePW   Console password.
                 listenPW   "Listener" password.
                 remoteEcho   (optional)Enable echo back to client 1 = on, 0 = off.
Return: *nothing*
Description: Initializes telnet connection request parameters. Remote echoing is off by default.
Usage: telnetSetParameters(4123, "garage", "games");

toggleFullScreen()

Parameters: none
Return: *numeric*   1 = success, 0 = fail.
Description: Switches between windowed mode and full-screen mode.
Usage: %result = toggleFullScreen();

trace(switch)

Parameters: *switch*   1 (or `true`) enables, 0 (or `false`) disables.

Return: *nothing*

Description: Turns execution trace on or off.

Usage: `Trace(1);`

trim(str)

Parameters: *str*   String to be processed.

Return: *string*   The processed resultant string.

Description: Strips any white space from the left or right side (before or after all other characters) of *str*. White space is defined as spaces, carriage returns, or new line characters.

Usage: `%tidystring=trim(%yuckystring);`

validateMemory()

Parameters: *none*

Return: *nothing*

Description: Ensures that sufficient memory is available for the program.

Usage: `validateMemory();`

vectorAdd(vector1, vector2)

Parameters: *vector1*   "x y z".

               vector2   "x y z".

Return: *string*

Description: Adds *vector2* to *vector1*.

Usage: `%result=vectorAdd("87.21 54.11 10.0", "9.99 12.6 6.00");`

vectorCross(vector1, vector2)

Parameters: *vector1*   "x y z".

               vector2   "x y z".

Return: *string*

Description: Computes the cross product between two vectors.

Usage: `%product = vectorCross("x y z","x y z");`

vectorDist(vector1, vector2)

Parameters: *vector1*   "x y z".

               vector2   "x y z".

Return: string
Description: Computes the distance between two vectors.
Usage: %delta = vectorDist(%vector1, %vector2);

vectorDot(vector1, vector2)

Parameters: *vector1*   "x y z".
                vector2   "x y z".
Return: string
Description: Computes the dot product between two vectors.
Usage: %product = vectorDot("0 0 1",%eye);

vectorLen(vector)

Parameters: *vector*   "x y z".
Return: string
Description: Computes the length of the vector.
Usage: %len = vectorLen(%vector);

vectorNormalize(vector)

Parameters: *vector*   "x y z".
Return: string
Description: Normalizes a vector.
Usage: %nvector = vectorNormalize("5 10 30");

vectorOrthoBasis(vector)

Parameters: *vector*   "x y z".
Return: string
Description: Computes the orthogonal normal for a vector.
Usage: %normal = vectorOrthoBasis("x y z angle");

vectorScale(vector, scalar)

Parameters: *vector*   "x y z".
                scalar   Can be an integer or a floating point.
Return: string
Description: Computes the result of the vector sized by the scale.
Usage: %svector = vectorScale("5 10 30", 100);

vectorSub(vector1, vector2)

Parameters: *vector1*   "x y z".
                vector2   "x y z".

Return: string
Description: Subtracts *vector2* from *vector1*.
Usage: `%result=vectorSub("34.0989 989.3249 100.00", %position);`

videoSetGammaCorrection(gamma)

Parameters: gamma   Gamma correction setting.
Return: nothing
Description: Sets the gamma correction.
Usage: `videoSetGammaCorrection(0.5);`

warn(text)

Parameters: text   String.
Return: nothing
Description: Prints *text* to the console with light gray font. Text can be formatted
             according to the string rules.
Usage: `warn("Danger, Will Robinson!!");`

writeFontCache()

Parameters: none
Return: nothing
Description: Forces all cached fonts to be written to disk.
Usage: `writeFontCache();`

Torque Reference Tables

Table A.1 TorqueScript Object Type Masks

Mask Identifier	Number	Mask Bit Position
DefaultObjectType	0	no bits set
StaticObjectType	1	1
EnvironmentObjectType	2	2
TerrainObjectType	4	3
InteriorObjectType	8	4
WaterObjectType	16	5
TriggerObjectType	32	6
MarkerObjectType	64	7
AtlasObjectType	128	8
InteriorMapObjectType	256	9
DecalManagerObjectType	512	10

continued

Table A.1 continued

Mask Identifier	Number	Mask Bit Position
GameBaseObjectType	1024	11
ShapeBaseObjectType	2048	12
CameraObjectType	4096	13
StaticShapeObjectType	8192	14
PlayerObjectType	16384	15
ItemObjectType	32768	16
VehicleObjectType	65536	17
VehicleBlockerObjectType	131072	18
ProjectileObjectType	262144	19
ExplosionObjectType	524288	20
CorpseObjectType	1048576	21
unassigned	2097152	22
DebrisObjectType	4194304	23
PhysicalZoneObjectType	8388608	24
StaticTSObjectType	16777216	25
AIObjectType	33554432	26
StaticRenderedObjectType	67108864	27
DamagableItemObjectType	268435456	28
unassigned	536870912	29
unassigned	1073741824	30
unassigned	2147483648	31

Table A.2 Torque Object Methods

Object Class	Method
ActionMap	bind(device,action,[modifier,spec,mod. . .],command)
ActionMap	bindCmd(device,action,makeCmd,breakCmd)
ActionMap	getBinding(command)
ActionMap	getCommand(device,action)
ActionMap	getDeadZone(device,action)
ActionMap	getScale(device,action)
ActionMap	isInverted(device,action)
ActionMap	pop()
ActionMap	push()
ActionMap	save([fileName],[append])
ActionMap	unbind(device,action)
AIConnection	getAddress()

Table A.2 continued

Object Class	Method
AIConnection	getFreeLook()
AIConnection	getMove(field)
AIConnection	getTrigger(trigger)
AIConnection	setFreeLook(isFreeLook)
AIConnection	setMove(field,value)
AIConnection	setTrigger(trigger,set)
AIPlayer	clearAim()
AIPlayer	getAimLocation()
AIPlayer	getAimObject()
AIPlayer	getMoveDestination()
AIPlayer	setAimLocation(target)
AIPlayer	setAimObject(obj,[offset])
AIPlayer	setMoveDestination(goal,slowDown=true)
AIPlayer	setMoveSpeed(speed)
AIPlayer	stop()
AIWheeledVehicle	getMoveDestination()
AIWheeledVehicle	setMoveDestination(goal,slowDown=true)
AIWheeledVehicle	setMoveSpeed(speed)
AIWheeledVehicle	setMoveTolerance(speed)
AIWheeledVehicle	stop()
Camera	getPosition()
Camera	setFlyMode()
Camera	setOrbitMode(orbtObj,mat,minDist,maxDist,curDist,ownClientObj)
ConsoleLogger	attach()
ConsoleLogger	detach()
CreatorTree	addGroup(group, name, value)
CreatorTree	addItem(group, name, value)
CreatorTree	clear()
CreatorTree	fileNameMatch(world,type,filename)
CreatorTree	getName(item)
CreatorTree	getParent(n)
CreatorTree	getSelected()
CreatorTree	getValue(n)
CreatorTree	isGroup(g)
DbgFileView	clearBreakPositions()
DbgFileView	findString(findThis)
DbgFileView	getCurrentLine()
DbgFileView	open(filename)

continued

Table A.2 continued

Object Class	Method
DbgFileView	removeBreak(line)
DbgFileView	setBreak(line)
DbgFileView	setBreakPosition(line)
DbgFileView	setCurrentLine(line,selected)
Debris	init(position,velocity)
DebugView	addLine(start,end,color)
DebugView	clearLines()
DebugView	clearText(line=−1)
DebugView	setText(line,text,color=NULL)
EditManager	gotoBookmark(slot)
EditManager	setBookmark(slot)
EditTSCtrl	renderCircle(pos,normal,radius,segments=NULL)
EditTSCtrl	renderLine(start,end,width)
EditTSCtrl	renderSphere(pos,radius,subdivisions=NULL)
EditTSCtrl	renderTriangle(a,b,c)
FileObject	close()
FileObject	isEOF()
FileObject	openForAppend(filename)
FileObject	openForRead(filename)
FileObject	openForWrite(filename)
FileObject	readLine()
FileObject	writeLine(text)
FlyingVehicle	useCreateHeight(enabled)
fxLight	attachToObject(obj)
fxLight	detachFromObject()
fxLight	reset()
fxLight	setEnable(enabled)
fxSunLight	reset()
fxSunLight	setAzimuthKeys(keys)
fxSunLight	setAzimuthTime(time)
fxSunLight	setBlendMode(mode)
fxSunLight	setBlueKeys(keys)
fxSunLight	setBrightnessKeys(keys)
fxSunLight	setBrightnessTime(time)
fxSunLight	setColourTime(time)
fxSunLight	setElevationKeys(keys)
fxSunLight	setElevationTime(time)
fxSunLight	setEnable(status)
fxSunLight	setFadeTime(time)

Table A.2 continued

Object Class	Method
fxSunLight	setFlareBitmaps(local,remote)
fxSunLight	setFlareBrightness(brightness)
fxSunLight	setFlareColour(r,g,b)
fxSunLight	setFlareSize(size)
fxSunLight	setFlareTP(status)
fxSunLight	setGreenKeys(keys)
fxSunLight	setLerpAzimuth(status)
fxSunLight	setLerpBrightness(status)
fxSunLight	setLerpColour(status)
fxSunLight	setLerpElevation(status)
fxSunLight	setLerpRotation(status)
fxSunLight	setLerpSize(status)
fxSunLight	setLinkFlareSize(status)
fxSunLight	setMaxAzimuth(azimuth)
fxSunLight	setMaxBrightness(brightness)
fxSunLight	setMaxColour(r,g,b)
fxSunLight	setMaxElevation(elevation)
fxSunLight	setMaxRotation(rotation)
fxSunLight	setMaxSize(size)
fxSunLight	setMinAzimuth(azimuth)
fxSunLight	setMinBrightness(brightness)
fxSunLight	setMinColour(r,g,b)
fxSunLight	setMinElevation(elevation)
fxSunLight	setMinRotation(rotation)
fxSunLight	setMinSize(size)
fxSunLight	setRedKeys(keys)
fxSunLight	setRotationKeys(keys)
fxSunLight	setRotationTime(time)
fxSunLight	setSingleColourKeys(status)
fxSunLight	setSizeKeys(keys)
fxSunLight	setSizeTime(time)
fxSunLight	setSunAzimuth(azimuth)
fxSunLight	setSunElevation(elevation)
fxSunLight	setUseAzimuth(status)
fxSunLight	setUseBrightness(status)
fxSunLight	setUseColour(status)
fxSunLight	setUseElevation(status)
fxSunLight	setUseRotation(status)

continued

Table A.2 continued

Object Class	Method
fxSunLight	setUseSize(status)
GameBase	getDataBlock()
GameBase	setDataBlock(db)
GameConnection	activateGhosting()
GameConnection	chaseCam(size)
GameConnection	clearCameraObject()
GameConnection	delete(reason=NULL)
GameConnection	getCameraObject()
GameConnection	getControlCameraFov()
GameConnection	getControlObject()
GameConnection	isAIControlled()
GameConnection	isDemoPlaying()
GameConnection	isDemoRecording()
GameConnection	isFirstPerson()
GameConnection	listClassIDs()
GameConnection	play2D(ap)
GameConnection	play3D(ap,pos)
GameConnection	playDemo(demoFileName)
GameConnection	resetGhosting()
GameConnection	setBlackOut(doFade,timeMS)
GameConnection	setCameraObject(id)
GameConnection	setConnectArgs(arg1,...)
GameConnection	setControlCameraFov(newFOV)
GameConnection	setControlObject(object)
GameConnection	setFirstPerson(firstPerson)
GameConnection	setJoinPassword(pw)
GameConnection	setMissionCRC(CRC)
GameConnection	startRecording(fileName)
GameConnection	stopRecording()
GameConnection	transmitDataBlocks(sequence)
GuiAviBitmapCtrl	play()
GuiAviBitmapCtrl	setFilename(filename)
GuiAviBitmapCtrl	stop()
GuiBitmapButtonCtrl	setBitmap(filepath)
GuiBitmapCtrl	setBitmap(filename)
GuiBitmapCtrl	setValue(xAxis,yAxis)
GuiButtonBaseCtrl	getText()
GuiButtonBaseCtrl	performClick()
GuiButtonBaseCtrl	setText(text)

Table A.2 continued

Object Class	Method
GuiButtonBaseCtrl	setTextID(id)
GuiCanvas	cursorOff()
GuiCanvas	cursorOn()
GuiCanvas	getContent()
GuiCanvas	getCursorPos()
GuiCanvas	hideCursor()
GuiCanvas	isCursorOn()
GuiCanvas	popDialog(ctrl=NULL)
GuiCanvas	popLayer(layer)
GuiCanvas	pushDialog(ctrl,layer)
GuiCanvas	renderFront(enable)
GuiCanvas	repaint()
GuiCanvas	reset()
GuiCanvas	setContent(ctrl)
GuiCanvas	setCursor(visible)
GuiCanvas	setCursorPos(pos)
GuiCanvas	showCursor()
GuiChunkedBitmapCtrl	setBitmap(filename)
GuiClockHud	getTime()
GuiClockHud	setTime(time,in,sec)
GuiColorPickerCtrl	getSelectorPos()
GuiColorPickerCtrl	setSelectorPos()
GuiColorPickerCtrl	updateColor()
GuiControl	getExtent()
GuiControl	getMinExtent()
GuiControl	getPosition()
GuiControl	getValue()
GuiControl	isActive()
GuiControl	isAwake()
GuiControl	isVisible()
GuiControl	makeFirstResponder(isFirst)
GuiControl	resize(x,y,w,h)
GuiControl	setActive(active)
GuiControl	setProfile(p)
GuiControl	setValue(value)
GuiControl	setVisible(visible)
GuiDirectoryFileListCtrl	getSelectedFile()
GuiDirectoryFileListCtrl	setPath(path,filter)

continued

Table A.2 continued

Object Class	Method
GuiDirectoryTreeCtrl	getSelectedPath()
GuiDirectoryTreeCtrl	setSelectedPath(path)
GuiEditCtrl	addNewCtrl(ctrl)
GuiEditCtrl	addSelection()
GuiEditCtrl	bringToFront()
GuiEditCtrl	clearSelection()
GuiEditCtrl	deleteSelection()
GuiEditCtrl	getSelected()
GuiEditCtrl	justify(mode)
GuiEditCtrl	loadSelection(fileName)
GuiEditCtrl	moveSelection(deltax,deltay)
GuiEditCtrl	pushToBack()
GuiEditCtrl	removeSelection()
GuiEditCtrl	saveSelection(fileName)
GuiEditCtrl	select(ctrl)
GuiEditCtrl	selectAll()
GuiEditCtrl	setCurrentAddSet(ctrl)
GuiEditCtrl	setRoot(root)
GuiEditCtrl	toggle()
GuiFilterCtrl	getValue()
GuiFilterCtrl	identity()
GuiFilterCtrl	setValue(f1,f2,...)
GuiFrameSetCtrl	addColumn()
GuiFrameSetCtrl	addRow()
GuiFrameSetCtrl	frameBorder(index,enable=true)
GuiFrameSetCtrl	frameMinExtent(index,w,h)
GuiFrameSetCtrl	frameMovable(index,enable=true)
GuiFrameSetCtrl	getColumnCount()
GuiFrameSetCtrl	getColumnOffset(index)
GuiFrameSetCtrl	getRowCount()
GuiFrameSetCtrl	getRowOffset(index)
GuiFrameSetCtrl	removeColumn()
GuiFrameSetCtrl	removeRow()
GuiFrameSetCtrl	setColumnOffset(index,offset)
GuiFrameSetCtrl	setRowOffset(index,offset)
GuiGraphCtrl	addAutoPlot(plotID,variable,update)
GuiGraphCtrl	addDatum(plotID,v)
GuiGraphCtrl	getDatum(plotID,samples)
GuiGraphCtrl	matchScale(plotID,plotID,...)

Table A.2 continued

Object Class	Method
GuiGraphCtrl	removeAutoPlot(plotID)
GuiGraphCtrl	setGraphType(plotID,graphType)
GuiInspector	inspect(Object)
GuiInspector	setName(NewObjectName)
GuiInspectorDynamicField	renameField(newDynamicFieldName)
GuiInspectorDynamicGroup	addDynamicField()
GuiInspectorField	apply(newValue))
GuiMenuBar	addMenu(menuText,menuId)
GuiMenuBar	addMenuItem(mnu,mnuItmTxt,mnuItmId,acc=NULL,chkGrp=−1)
GuiMenuBar	clearMenuItems(menu)
GuiMenuBar	clearMenus()
GuiMenuBar	removeMenu(menu)
GuiMenuBar	removeMenuItem(menu,menuItem)
GuiMenuBar	setMenuItemBitmap(menu,menuItem,bitmapIndex)
GuiMenuBar	setMenuItemChecked(menu,menuItem,checked)
GuiMenuBar	setMenuItemEnable(menu,menuItem,enabled)
GuiMenuBar	setMenuItemText(menu,menuItem,newMenuItemText)
GuiMenuBar	setMenuItemVisible(menu,menuItem,isVisible)
GuiMenuBar	setMenuText(menu,newMenuText)
GuiMenuBar	setMenuVisible(menu,visible)
GuiMessageVectorCtrl	attach(item)
GuiMessageVectorCtrl	detach()
GuiMLTextCtrl	addText(text,reformat)
GuiMLTextCtrl	forceReflow()
GuiMLTextCtrl	getText()
GuiMLTextCtrl	scrollToBottom()
GuiMLTextCtrl	scrollToTag(tagID)
GuiMLTextCtrl	scrollToTop()
GuiMLTextCtrl	setAlpha()
GuiMLTextCtrl	setCursorPosition(newPos)
GuiMLTextCtrl	setText(text)
GuiPaneControl	setCollapsed(bool)
GuiPlayerView	setModel(raceOrGender,skin)
GuiPlayerView	setSeq(index)
GuiPopUpMenuCtrl	add(name,idNum,scheme=0)
GuiPopUpMenuCtrl	addScheme(id,fontColor,fontColorHL,fontColorSEL)
GuiPopUpMenuCtrl	clear()
GuiPopUpMenuCtrl	findText(text)

continued

Table A.2   continued

Object Class	Method
GuiPopUpMenuCtrl	forceClose()
GuiPopUpMenuCtrl	forceOnAction()
GuiPopUpMenuCtrl	getSelected()
GuiPopUpMenuCtrl	getText()
GuiPopUpMenuCtrl	getTextById(id)
GuiPopUpMenuCtrl	replaceText(doReplaceText)
GuiPopUpMenuCtrl	setEnumContent(class,enum)
GuiPopUpMenuCtrl	setSelected(id)
GuiPopUpMenuCtrl	setText(text)
GuiPopUpMenuCtrl	size()
GuiPopUpMenuCtrl	sort()
GuiScrollCtrl	scrollToBottom()
GuiScrollCtrl	scrollToTop()
GuiSliderCtrl	getValue()
GuiTabBookCtrl	addPage()
GuiTerrPreviewCtrl	getOrigin()
GuiTerrPreviewCtrl	getRoot()
GuiTerrPreviewCtrl	getValue()
GuiTerrPreviewCtrl	reset()
GuiTerrPreviewCtrl	setOrigin(x,y)
GuiTerrPreviewCtrl	setRoot()
GuiTerrPreviewCtrl	setValue()
GuiTextCtrl	setText(newText)
GuiTextCtrl	setTextID(newText)
GuiTextEditCtrl	getCursorPos()
GuiTextEditCtrl	getText()
GuiTextEditCtrl	setCursorPos(newPos)
GuiTextListCtrl	addRow(id,text,index=0)
GuiTextListCtrl	clear()
GuiTextListCtrl	clearSelection()
GuiTextListCtrl	findTextIndex(needle)
GuiTextListCtrl	getRowId(index)
GuiTextListCtrl	getRowNumById(id)
GuiTextListCtrl	getRowText(index)
GuiTextListCtrl	getRowTextById(id)
GuiTextListCtrl	getSelectedId()
GuiTextListCtrl	isRowActive(rowNum)
GuiTextListCtrl	removeRow(index)
GuiTextListCtrl	removeRowById(id)

Table A.2 continued

Object Class	Method
GuiTextListCtrl	rowCount()
GuiTextListCtrl	scrollVisible(rowNum)
GuiTextListCtrl	setRowActive(rowNum,active)
GuiTextListCtrl	setRowById(id,text)
GuiTextListCtrl	setSelectedById(id)
GuiTextListCtrl	setSelectedRow(rowNum)
GuiTextListCtrl	sort(columnID,increasing=false)
GuiTextListCtrl	sortNumerical(columnID,increasing=false)
GuiTheoraCtrl	getCurrentTime()
GuiTheoraCtrl	setFile(filename)
GuiTheoraCtrl	stop()
GuiTickCtrl	setProcessTicks([tick=true])
GuiTreeViewCtrl	addSelection(id)
GuiTreeViewCtrl	buildIconTable(iconListString[csv])
GuiTreeViewCtrl	clear()
GuiTreeViewCtrl	clearSelection()
GuiTreeViewCtrl	deleteSelection()
GuiTreeViewCtrl	editItem(item,newText,newValue)
GuiTreeViewCtrl	expandItem(item,expand=true)
GuiTreeViewCtrl	findItemByName(name)
GuiTreeViewCtrl	getChild(item)
GuiTreeViewCtrl	getFirstRootItem()
GuiTreeViewCtrl	getItemCount()
GuiTreeViewCtrl	getItemText(item)
GuiTreeViewCtrl	getItemValue(item)
GuiTreeViewCtrl	getNextSibling(item)
GuiTreeViewCtrl	getParent(item)
GuiTreeViewCtrl	getPrevSibling(item)
GuiTreeViewCtrl	getSelectedItem()
GuiTreeViewCtrl	getTextToRoot(item,Delimiter=none)
GuiTreeViewCtrl	insertItem(parent,name,value,icon,normal=0,expanded=0)
GuiTreeViewCtrl	lockSelection([id])
GuiTreeViewCtrl	moveItemUp(item)
GuiTreeViewCtrl	open(okToEdit=true)
GuiTreeViewCtrl	removeItem(item)
GuiTreeViewCtrl	removeSelection(id)
GuiTreeViewCtrl	selectItem(item,select=true)
HTTPObject	get(addr,requestURI,query=NULL)

continued

Table A.2 continued

Object Class	Method
HTTPObject	post(ddr,requestURI,query,post)
InteriorInstance	activateLight(lightName)
InteriorInstance	deactivateLight(lightName)
InteriorInstance	echoTriggerableLights()
InteriorInstance	getNumDetailLevels()
InteriorInstance	setAlarmMode(mode)
InteriorInstance	setDetailLevel(level)
InteriorInstance	setSkinBase(basename)
Item	getLastStickyNormal()
Item	getLastStickyPos()
Item	isRotating()
Item	isStatic()
Item	setCollisionTimeout(obj)
LangTable	addLanguage(filename,[languageName])
LangTable	getCurrentLanguage()
LangTable	getLangName(language)
LangTable	getNumLang()
LangTable	getString(filename)
LangTable	setCurrentLanguage(language)
LangTable	setDefaultLanguage(language)
Lightning	strikeObject(id)
Lightning	strikeRandomPoint()
Lightning	warningFlashes()
MessageVector	clear()
MessageVector	deleteLine(deletePos)
MessageVector	dump(filename,header=NULL)
MessageVector	getLineIndexByTag(tag)
MessageVector	getLineTag(line)
MessageVector	getLineText(line)
MessageVector	getLineTextByTag(tag)
MessageVector	getNumLines()
MessageVector	insertLine(insertPos,msg,tag=0)
MessageVector	popBackLine()
MessageVector	popFrontLine()
MessageVector	pushBackLine(msg,tag=0)
MessageVector	pushFrontLine(msg,tag=0)
MissionArea	getArea()
MissionArea	setArea(x,y,width,height)
MissionAreaEditor	centerWorld()

Table A.2 continued

Object Class	Method
MissionAreaEditor	getArea()
MissionAreaEditor	setArea(x,y,w,h)
MissionAreaEditor	updateTerrain()
NetConnection	checkMaxRate()
NetConnection	clearPaths()
NetConnection	connect(remoteAddress)
NetConnection	connectLocal()
NetConnection	getAddress()
NetConnection	getGhostID(realID)
NetConnection	getGhostsActive()
NetConnection	getPacketLoss()
NetConnection	getPing()
NetConnection	resolveGhostID(ghostID)
NetConnection	resolveObjectFromGhostIndex(ghostIdx)
NetConnection	setLogging(bool)
NetConnection	setSimulatedNetParams(packetLoss,delay)
NetConnection	transmitPaths()
NetObject	clearScopeToClient(client)
NetObject	getGhostID()
NetObject	scopeToClient(client)
NetObject	setScopeAlways()
ParticleData	reload()
ParticleEmitterData	reload()
ParticleEmitterNode	setEmitterDataBlock(data)
Path	getPathId()
PathCamera	popFront()
PathCamera	pushBack(transform,speed,type,path)
PathCamera	pushFront(transform,speed,type,path)
PathCamera	reset(speed=0)
PathCamera	setPosition(pos)
PathCamera	setState({forward,backward,stop})
PathCamera	setTarget(pos)
PathedInterior	setPathPosition(pos)
PathedInterior	setTargetPosition(pos)
PhysicalZone	activate()
PhysicalZone	deactivate()
Player	checkDismountPoint(oldPos,pos)
Player	clearControlObject()

continued

Table A.2 continued

Object Class	Method
Player	getControlObject()
Player	getDamageLocation(pos)
Player	getState()
Player	setActionThread(sequenceName,hold,fsp)
Player	setArmThread(sequenceName)
Player	setControlObject(obj)
Precipitation	modifyStorm(Percentage<0.0 to 1.0>,Time<sec>)
Precipitation	setPercentage(percentage,<0.0to1.0>)
SceneObject	getForwardVector()
SceneObject	getObjectBox()
SceneObject	getPosition()
SceneObject	getScale()
SceneObject	getTransform()
SceneObject	getWorldBox()
SceneObject	getWorldBoxCenter()
SceneObject	setScale(scale)
SceneObject	setTransform(T)
ShapeBase	applyDamage(amt)
ShapeBase	applyImpulse(Pos,VectorF vel)
ShapeBase	applyRepair(amt)
ShapeBase	canCloak()
ShapeBase	getAIRepairPoint()
ShapeBase	getCameraFov()
ShapeBase	getControllingClient()
ShapeBase	getControllingObject()
ShapeBase	getDamageFlash()
ShapeBase	getDamageLevel()
ShapeBase	getDamagePercent()
ShapeBase	getDamageState()
ShapeBase	getEnergyLevel()
ShapeBase	getEnergyPercent()
ShapeBase	getEyePoint()
ShapeBase	getEyeTransform()
ShapeBase	getEyeVector()
ShapeBase	getImageAmmo(slot)
ShapeBase	getImageLoaded(slot)
ShapeBase	getImageSkinTag(slot)
ShapeBase	getImageState(slot)
ShapeBase	getImageTrigger(slot)

Table A.2   continued

Object Class	Method
ShapeBase	getMountedImage(slot)
ShapeBase	getMountedObject(slot)
ShapeBase	getMountedObjectCount()
ShapeBase	getMountedObjectNode(node)
ShapeBase	getMountNodeObject(node)
ShapeBase	getMountSlot(db)
ShapeBase	getMuzzlePoint(slot)
ShapeBase	getMuzzleVector(slot)
ShapeBase	getObjectMount()
ShapeBase	getPendingImage(slot)
ShapeBase	getRechargeRate()
ShapeBase	getRepairRate()
ShapeBase	getShapeName()
ShapeBase	getSkinName()
ShapeBase	getSlotTransform(slot)
ShapeBase	getVelocity()
ShapeBase	getWhiteOut()
ShapeBase	isCloaked()
ShapeBase	isDestroyed()
ShapeBase	isDisabled()
ShapeBase	isEnabled()
ShapeBase	isHidden()
ShapeBase	isImageFiring(slot)
ShapeBase	isImageMounted(db)
ShapeBase	isMounted()
ShapeBase	mountImage(image,slot,loaded=true,skinTag=NULL)
ShapeBase	mountObject(object,slot)
ShapeBase	pauseThread(slot)
ShapeBase	playAudio(slot,ap)
ShapeBase	playThread(slot,sequenceName)
ShapeBase	setCameraFov(fov)
ShapeBase	setCloaked(isCloaked)
ShapeBase	setDamageFlash(lvl)
ShapeBase	setDamageLevel(level)
ShapeBase	setDamageState(state)
ShapeBase	setDamageVector(origin)
ShapeBase	setEnergyLevel(level)
ShapeBase	setHidden(show)

continued

Table A.2 continued

Object Class	Method
ShapeBase	setImageAmmo(slot,hasAmmo)
ShapeBase	setImageLoaded(slot,loaded)
ShapeBase	setImageTrigger(slot,isTriggered)
ShapeBase	setInvincibleMode(time,speed)
ShapeBase	setRechargeRate(rate)
ShapeBase	setRepairRate(amt)
ShapeBase	setShapeName(tag)
ShapeBase	setSkinName(tag)
ShapeBase	setThreadDir(slot,isForward)
ShapeBase	setVelocity(vel)
ShapeBase	setWhiteOut(flashLevel)
ShapeBase	startFade(fadeTimeMS,fadeDelayMS,fadeOut)
ShapeBase	stopAudio(slot)
ShapeBase	stopThread(slot)
ShapeBase	unmount()
ShapeBase	unmountImage(slot)
ShapeBase	unmountObject(obj)
ShapeBaseData	checkDeployPos(xform)
ShapeBaseData	getDeployTransform(pos,normal)
SimObject	delete()
SimObject	dump()
SimObject	getClassName()
SimObject	getGroup()
SimObject	getId()
SimObject	getName()
SimObject	getType()
SimObject	save(fileName,<selectedOnly>)
SimObject	schedule(time,command,<arg1. . . argN>)
SimObject	setName(newName)
SimpleNetObject	setMessage1(msg)
SimpleNetObject	setMessage2(msg)
SimSet	add(obj1,. . .)
SimSet	bringToFront(object)
SimSet	clear()
SimSet	getCount()
SimSet	getObject(objIndex)
SimSet	isMember(object)
SimSet	listObjects()

Table A.2 continued

Object Class	Method
SimSet	pushToBack(object)
SimSet	remove(obj1,. . .)
Sky	getWindVelocity()
Sky	realFog(show,max,min,speed)
Sky	setWindVelocity(x,y,z)
Sky	stormClouds(show,duration)
Sky	stormCloudsShow(showClouds)
Sky	stormFog(percent,duration)
Sky	stormFogShow(show)
StaticShape	getPoweredState()
StaticShape	setPoweredState(isPowered)
TCPObject	connect(addr)
TCPObject	disconnect()
TCPObject	listen(port)
TCPObject	send(. . .)
Terraformer	blend(srcA,srcB,dest_register,factor,operation)
Terraformer	canyon(dest_register,frequency,turbulence,seed)
Terraformer	clearRegister(r)
Terraformer	erodeHydraulic(srcreg,dstreg,iterations,arr)
Terraformer	erodeThermal(srcreg,dstreg,slope,materialLoss,iterations)
Terraformer	fBm(r,freq,roughness,detail,seed)
Terraformer	filter(src_register,dst_register,arr)
Terraformer	generateSeed()
Terraformer	getCameraPosition()
Terraformer	loadGreyscale(register,filename)
Terraformer	maskFBm(destreg,freq,rough,seed,arr,distortfactor,distortreg)
Terraformer	maskHeight(srcreg,dstreg,arr,distortfactor,distortreg)
Terraformer	maskSlope(srcreg,dstreg,arr,distortfactor,distortreg)
Terraformer	maskWater(srcreg,dstreg,distortfactor,distortreg)
Terraformer	mergeMasks(srcarray,dstreg)
Terraformer	preview(destination,register)
Terraformer	previewScaled(destination,source)
Terraformer	rigidMultiFractal(r,freq,roughness,detail,seed)
Terraformer	saveGreyscale(register,filename)
Terraformer	saveHeightField(register,filename)
Terraformer	scale(src_register,dst_register,min,max)
Terraformer	setCameraPosition(x,y,z=0)

continued

Table A.2 continued

Object Class	Method
Terraformer	setMaterials(src_array,material_array)
Terraformer	setShift(x,y)
Terraformer	setTerrain(register)
Terraformer	setTerrainInfo(blkSiz,tileSiz,minHgt,hgtRange,waterPercent)
Terraformer	sinus(r,a,seed)
Terraformer	smooth(src_register,dst_register,factor,iterations)
Terraformer	smoothRidges(src_register,dst_register,factor,iterations)
Terraformer	smoothWater(src_register,dst_register,factor,iterations)
Terraformer	terrainData(register)
Terraformer	terrainFile(register,filename)
Terraformer	turbulence(src_register,dst_register,factor,radius)
TerrainBlock	getHeightfieldScript()
TerrainBlock	getSquareSize()
TerrainBlock	getTextureScript()
TerrainBlock	save(fileName)
TerrainBlock	setHeightfieldScript(script)
TerrainBlock	setTextureScript(script)
TerrainEditor	attachTerrain(terrain)
TerrainEditor	buildMaterialMap()
TerrainEditor	clearModifiedFlags()
TerrainEditor	clearSelection()
TerrainEditor	getActionName(num)
TerrainEditor	getBrushPos()
TerrainEditor	getCurrentAction()
TerrainEditor	getNumActions()
TerrainEditor	getNumTextures()
TerrainEditor	getTerrainMaterials()
TerrainEditor	getTextureName(index)
TerrainEditor	markEmptySquares()
TerrainEditor	mirrorTerrain()
TerrainEditor	popBaseMaterialInfo()
TerrainEditor	processAction(action=NULL)
TerrainEditor	pushBaseMaterialInfo()
TerrainEditor	redo()
TerrainEditor	resetSelWeights(clear)
TerrainEditor	setAction(action_name)
TerrainEditor	setBrushPos(x,y)
TerrainEditor	setBrushSize(w,h)

Table A.2 continued

Object Class	Method
TerrainEditor	setBrushType(type)
TerrainEditor	setLoneBaseMaterial(materialListBaseName)
TerrainEditor	setTerraformOverlay(overlayEnable)
TerrainEditor	setTerrainMaterials(matList)
TerrainEditor	undo()
Trigger	getNumObjects()
Trigger	getObject(idx)
TriggerData	onEnterTrigger(trigger,intruder)
TriggerData	onLeaveTrigger(trigger,intruder)
TriggerData	onTickTrigger(trigger)
WaterBlock	toggleWireFrame()
WheeledVehicle	getWheelCount()
WheeledVehicle	setWheelPowered(wheel#,bool)
WheeledVehicle	setWheelSpring(wheel#,spring)
WheeledVehicle	setWheelSteering(wheel#,float)
WheeledVehicle	setWheelTire(wheel#,tire)
WorldEditor	addUndoState()
WorldEditor	canPasteSelection()
WorldEditor	clearIgnoreList()
WorldEditor	clearSelection()
WorldEditor	copySelection()
WorldEditor	deleteSelection()
WorldEditor	dropSelection()
WorldEditor	getMode()
WorldEditor	getSelectedObject(index)
WorldEditor	getSelectionCentroid()
WorldEditor	getSelectionSize()
WorldEditor	hideSelection(hide)
WorldEditor	ignoreObjClass(class_name,...)
WorldEditor	lockSelection(lock)
WorldEditor	pasteSelection()
WorldEditor	redirectConsole(objID)
WorldEditor	redo()
WorldEditor	selectObject(obj)
WorldEditor	setMode(newMode)
WorldEditor	undo()
WorldEditor	unselectObject(obj)

Table A.3 TorqueScript Keywords

Keyword	Description
break	Breaks execution out of a loop.
case	Indicates a choice in a switch block.
continue	Causes execution to continue at the top of a loop.
datablock	Indicates that the following code block defines a data block.
default	Indicates the choice to make in a switch block when no cases match.
do	Indicates the start of a do-while type loop block.
else	Indicates alternative execution path in an if statement.
false	Evaluates to 0, the opposite of true.
for	Indicates the start of a for loop.
function	Indicates that the following code block is a callable function.
if	Indicates the start of a conditional (comparison) statement.
new	Creates a new object data block.
package	Indicates that the following code block encompasses a package.
return	Indicates return from a function.
switch	Indicates the start of a switch selection block.
true	Evaluates to 1, the opposite of false.
while	Indicates the start of a while loop.

Table A.4 TorqueScript Operators

Symbol	Meaning
+	Add.
−	Subtract.
*	Multiply.
/	Divide.
%	Modulus.
++	Increment by 1.
--	Decrement by 1.
+=	Addition totalizer.
−=	Subtraction totalizer.
*=	Multiplication totalizer.
/=	Division totalizer.
%=	Modulus totalizer.
@	String append.
( )	Parentheses—operator precedence promotion.
[ ]	Brackets—array index delimiters.
{ }	Braces—indicate start and end of code blocks.

Table A.4 continued

Symbol	Meaning
SPC	Space append macro (same as @ " " @).
TAB	Tab append macro (same as @ "\t" @).
NL	New line append (same as @ "\n" @).
~	(Bitwise NOT) Flips the bits of its operand.
|	(Bitwise OR) Returns a 1 in a bit if bits of either operand are 1.
&	(Bitwise AND) Returns a 1 in each bit position if bits of both operands are 1s.
^	(Bitwise XOR) Returns a 1 in a bit position if bits of one but not both operands are 1.
<<	(Left-shift) Shifts its first operand in binary representation the number of bits to the left specified in the second operand, shifting in 0s from the right.
>>	(Sign-propagating right-shift) Shifts the first operand in binary representation the number of bits to the right specified in the second operand, discarding bits shifted off.
|=	Bitwise OR with result assigned to the first operand.
&=	Bitwise AND with result assigned to the first operand.
^=	Bitwise XOR with result assigned to the first operand.
<<=	Left-shift with result assigned to the first operand.
>>=	Sign-propagating right-shift with result assigned to the first operand.
!	Evaluates the opposite of the value specified.
&&	Requires both values to be true for the result to be true.
||	Requires only one value to be true for the result to be true.
==	Left-hand value and right-hand value are equal.
!=	Left-hand value and right-hand value are not equal.
<	Left-hand value is less than right-hand value.
>	Left-hand value is greater than right-hand value.
<=	Left-hand value is less than or equal to right-hand value.
>=	Left-hand value is greater than or equal to right-hand value.
$=	Left-hand string is equal to right-hand string.
!$=	Left-hand string is not equal to right-hand string.
//	Comment operator---ignore all text from here to the end of the line.
;	Statement terminator.
.	Object/data block method or property delimiter.

Table A.5 TorqueScript Operator Precedence

High Priority							Low Priority
(	)	*	/	%	+	−	=

Table A.6 TorqueScript Tokens

Token	Description
string literal	A sequence of alphanumeric characters bracketed by single or double quotes.
variable	Prefixed with % for a local variable or $ for a global variable, which is then always followed by a letter character. After the initial letter character, there can be a series of alphanumeric characters, underscores, or colons; a variable cannot end with a colon.
identifier	An initial letter character followed by an optional sequence of alphanumeric characters or underscores.
number	A decimal integer or floating point number. Hexadecimal numbers can be used if the token begins with 0x (zero-x).

Table A.7 TorqueScript String Formatting Codes

Code	Description
\r	Embeds a carriage return character.
\n	Embeds a new line character.
\t	Embeds a tab character.
\x*hh*	Embeds an ASCII character specified by the hex number (*hh*) that follows the x.
\c	Embeds a color code for strings that will be displayed on-screen.
\cr	Resets the display color to the default.
\cp	Pushes the current display color onto a stack.
\co	Pops the current display color off the stack.
\c*n*	Uses *n* as an index into the color table defined by GUIControlProfile.fontColors.

Table A.8 Torque Datablocks

Datablock	Parent
AudioDescription	SimDataBlock
AudioEnvironment	SimDataBlock
AudioProfile	SimDataBlock
AudioSampleEnvironment	SimDataBlock
CameraData	ShapeBaseData
DebrisData	GameBaseData
DecalData	SimDataBlock
ExplosionData	GameBaseData

Table A.8 continued

Datablock	Parent
FireballAtmosphereData	GameBaseData
FlyingVehicleData	VehicleData
fxLightData	GameBaseData
GameBaseData	SimDataBlock
HoverVehicleData	VehicleData
ItemData	ShapeBaseData
LightningData	GameBaseData
MissionMarkerData	ShapeBaseData
ParticleData	SimDataBlock
ParticleEmitterData	GameBaseData
ParticleEmitterNodeData	GameBaseData
PathCameraData	ShapeBaseData
PathedInteriorData	GameBaseData
PlayerData	ShapeBaseData
PrecipitationData	GameBaseData
ProjectileData	GameBaseData
ShapeBaseData	GameBaseData
ShapeBaseImageData	GameBaseData
SimDataBlock	SimObject
SplashData	GameBaseData
StaticShapeData	ShapeBaseData
TriggerData	GameBaseData
TSShapeConstructor	SimDataBlock
VehicleData	ShapeBaseData
WeatherLightningData	GameBaseData
WheeledVehicleData	VehicleData
WheeledVehicleSpring	SimDataBlock
WheeledVehicleTire	SimDataBlock

Table A.9 Torque Console Objects

Object	Parent
ActionMap	SimObject
AIConnection	GameConnection
BanList	SimObject
ConsoleLogger	SimObject
CreatorTree	GuiArrayCtrl

continued

Table A.9   continued

Object	Parent
DbgFileView	GuiArrayCtrl
DebugView	GuiTextCtrl
DecalManager	SceneObject
EditManager	GuiControl
EditTSCtrl	GuiTSCtrl
Explosion	GameBase
FileObject	SimObject
GameConnection	NetConnection
GameTSCtrl	GuiTSCtrl
GuiArrayCtrl	GuiControl
GuiAviBitmapCtrl	GuiControl
GuiBackgroundCtrl	GuiControl
GuiBitmapBorderCtrl	GuiControl
GuiBitmapButtonCtrl	GuiButtonCtrl
GuiBitmapButtonTextCtrl	GuiBitmapButtonCtrl
GuiBitmapCtrl	GuiControl
GuiBorderButtonCtrl	GuiButtonBaseCtrl
GuiBubbleTextCtrl	GuiTextCtrl
GuiButtonBaseCtrl	GuiControl
GuiButtonCtrl	GuiButtonBaseCtrl
GuiCanvas	GuiControl
GuiCheckBoxCtrl	GuiButtonBaseCtrl
GuiChunkedBitmapCtrl	GuiControl
GuiClockHud	GuiControl
GuiColorPickerCtrl	GuiControl
GuiConsole	GuiArrayCtrl
GuiConsoleEditCtrl	GuiTextEditCtrl
GuiConsoleTextCtrl	GuiControl
GuiControl	SimGroup
GuiControlArrayControl	GuiControl
GuiControlListPopUp	GuiPopUpMenuCtrl
GuiControlProfile	SimObject
GuiCrossHairHud	GuiBitmapCtrl
GuiCursor	SimObject
GuiDirectoryFileListCtrl	GuiTextListCtrl
GuiDirectoryTreeCtrl	GuiTreeViewCtrl
GuiEditCtrl	GuiControl
GuiEditorRuler	GuiControl
GuiEffectCanvas	GuiCanvas

Table A.9   continued

Object	Parent
GuiFadeinBitmapCtrl	GuiBitmapCtrl
GuiFilterCtrl	GuiControl
GuiFrameSetCtrl	GuiControl
GuiGraphCtrl	GuiControl
GuiHealthBarHud	GuiControl
GuiInputCtrl	GuiControl
GuiInspector	GuiStackControl
GuiInspectorDatablockField	GuiInspectorField
GuiInspectorDynamicField	GuiInspectorField
GuiInspectorField	GuiControl
GuiInspectorGroup	GuiTickCtrl
GuiInspectorTypeCheckBox	GuiInspectorField
GuiInspectorTypeColor	GuiInspectorField
GuiInspectorTypeColorF	GuiInspectorTypeColor
GuiInspectorTypeColorI	GuiInspectorTypeColor
GuiInspectorTypeEnum	GuiInspectorField
GuiInspectorTypeFileName	GuiInspectorField
GuiInspectorTypeGuiProfile	GuiInspectorTypeEnum
GuiMenuBar	GuiControl
GuiMessageVectorCtrl	GuiControl
GuiMLTextCtrl	GuiControl
GuiMLTextEditCtrl	GuiMLTextCtrl
GuiMouseEventCtrl	GuiControl
GuiNoMouseCtrl	GuiControl
GuiPaneControl	GuiControl
GuiPlayerView	GuiTSCtrl
GuiPopUpMenuCtrl	GuiTextCtrl
GuiProgressCtrl	GuiControl
GuiRadioCtrl	GuiCheckBoxCtrl
GuiScrollCtrl	GuiControl
GuiShapeNameHud	GuiControl
GuiSliderCtrl	GuiControl
GuiSpeedometerHud	GuiBitmapCtrl
GuiStackControl	GuiControl
GuiTabBookCtrl	GuiControl
GuiTabPageCtrl	GuiTextCtrl
GuiTerrPreviewCtrl	GuiControl
GuiTextCtrl	GuiControl

continued

Table A.9 continued

Object	Parent
GuiTextEditCtrl	GuiTextCtrl
GuiTextEditSliderCtrl	GuiTextEditCtrl
GuiTextListCtrl	GuiArrayCtrl
GuiTheoraCtrl	GuiControl
GuiTickCtrl	GuiControl
GuiTreeViewCtrl	GuiArrayCtrl
GuiTSCtrl	GuiControl
GuiVectorFieldCtrl	GuiTickCtrl
GuiWindowCtrl	GuiTextCtrl
HTTPObject	TCPObject
LangTable	SimObject
MaterialPropertyMap	SimObject
MessageVector	SimObject
MirrorSubObject	InteriorSubObject
MissionAreaEditor	GuiBitmapCtrl
NetConnection	SimGroup
NetObject	SimObject
Path	SimGroup
SceneObject	NetObject
ScriptGroup	SimGroup
ScriptObject	SimObject
ShowTSCtrl	GuiTSCtrl
SimChunk	SimGroup
SimGroup	SimSet
SimObject	ConsoleObject
SimSet	SimObject
TCPObject	SimObject
Terraformer	SimObject
TerrainEditor	EditTSCtrl
TextChunk	SimChunk
TorqueObject	ConsoleObject
UnknownChunk	SimChunk
Vehicle	SceneObject
WorldEditor	EditTSCtrl

Table A.10 Torque Net Objects

Datablock	Parent
AIPlayer	Player
AIWheeledVehicle	WheeledVehicle
AudioEmitter	SceneObject
Camera	ShapeBase
ClientAudioEmitter	AudioEmitter
Debris	GameBase
FireballAtmosphere	GameBase
FlyingVehicle	Vehicle
fxFoliageReplicator	SceneObject
fxLight	GameBase
fxShapeReplicatedStatic	TSStatic
fxShapeReplicator	SceneObject
fxSunLight	SceneObject
GameBase	SceneObject
HoverVehicle	Vehicle
InteriorInstance	SceneObject
InteriorMap	SceneObject
Item	ShapeBase
Lightning	GameBase
Marker	SceneObject
MissionArea	NetObject
MissionMarker	ShapeBase
ParticleEmitterNode	GameBase
PathCamera	ShapeBase
PathedInterior	GameBase
PhysicalZone	SceneObject
Player	ShapeBase
Precipitation	GameBase
Projectile	GameBase
ScopeAlwaysShape	StaticShape
ShapeBase	GameBase
SimpleNetObject	NetObject
Sky	SceneObject
SpawnSphere	MissionMarker
Splash	GameBase
StaticShape	ShapeBase
Sun	NetObject

continued

Table A.10 Torque Net Objects

Datablock	Parent
TerrainBlock	SceneObject
Trigger	GameBase
TSStatic	SceneObject
VehicleBlocker	SceneObject
WaterBlock	SceneObject
WayPoint	MissionMarker
WeatherLightning	GameBase
WheeledVehicle	Vehicle

Table A.11 Torque Console Types

Type	Parent
AudioDescription	SimDataBlock
AudioEnvironment	SimDataBlock
AudioProfile	SimDataBlock
AudioSampleEnvironment	SimDataBlock
DebrisData	GameBaseData
DecalData	SimDataBlock
ExplosionData	GameBaseData
FireballAtmosphereData	GameBaseData
fxLightData	GameBaseData
GameBaseData	SimDataBlock
ParticleEmitterData	GameBaseData
PrecipitationData	GameBaseData
ProjectileData	GameBaseData
SplashData	GameBaseData

Table A.12 Torque Engine-Sourced Preference Variables

Variable	Variable
$Pref::backgroundSleepTime	$Pref::OpenGL::force16BitTexture
$Pref::CloudOutline	$Pref::OpenGL::forcePalettedTexture
$Pref::CloudsOn	$Pref::OpenGL::gammaCorrection
$Pref::Decal::decalTimeout	$Pref::OpenGL::lightingAmbientColor
$Pref::Decal::maxNumDecals	$Pref::OpenGL::materialAmbientColor
$Pref::decalsOn	$Pref::OpenGL::materialDiffuseColor

Table A.12 Torque Engine-Sourced Preference Variables

Variable	Variable
$Pref::Editor::visibleDistance	$Pref::OpenGL::maxHardwareLights
$Pref::enableBadWordFilter	$Pref::OpenGL::noDrawArraysAlpha
$Pref::environmentMaps	$Pref::OpenGL::noEnvColor
$Pref::Input::JoystickEnabled	$Pref::OpenGL::textureAnisotropy
$Pref::Input::KeyboardEnabled	$Pref::OpenGL::textureTrilinear
$Pref::Input::MouseEnabled	$Pref::Player::renderMyItems
$Pref::Interior::detailAdjust	$Pref::Player::renderMyPlayer
$Pref::Interior::DynamicLights	$Pref::ResourceManager::excludedDirectories
$Pref::Interior::LightUpdatePeriod	$Pref::SkyOn
$Pref::Interior::lockArrays	$Pref::Terrain::dynamicLights
$Pref::Interior::ShowEnvironmentMaps	$Pref::Terrain::enableDetails
$Pref::Interior::TexturedFog	$Pref::Terrain::enableEmbossBumps
$Pref::Interior::VertexLighting	$Pref::Terrain::screenError
$Pref::Net::LagThreshold	$Pref::Terrain::texDetail
$Pref::Net::PacketRateToClient	$Pref::Terrain::textureCacheSize
$Pref::Net::PacketRateToServer	$Pref::timeManagerProcessInterval
$Pref::Net::PacketSize	$Pref::TS::autoDetail
$Pref::NumCloudLayers	$Pref::TS::detailAdjust
$Pref::OpenGL::allowCompression	$Pref::TS::fogTexture
$Pref::OpenGL::disableARBMultitexture	$Pref::TS::screenError
$Pref::OpenGL::disableARBTextureCompression	$Pref::TS::skipFirstFog
$Pref::OpenGL::disableEXTCompiledVertexArray	$Pref::TS::skipLoadDLs
$Pref::OpenGL::disableEXTFogCoord	$Pref::TS::skipRenderDLs
$Pref::OpenGL::disableEXTPalettedTexture	$Pref::TS::UseTriangles
$Pref::OpenGL::disableEXTTexEnvCombine	$Pref::visibleDistanceMod
$Pref::OpenGL::disableSubImage	

Table A.13 Torque Engine-Sourced Console Variables

Variable	Variable
$Camera::movementSpeed	$mvYawRightSpeed
$cameraFov	$OpenGL::primCount0
$Collision::boxSize	$OpenGL::primCount1
$Collision::depthRender	$OpenGL::primCount2
$Collision::depthSort	$OpenGL::primCount3
$Collision::renderAlways	$OpenGL::triCount0

continued

Table A.13 continued

Variable	Variable
$Collision::testClippedPolyList	$OpenGL::triCount1
$Collision::testDepthSortList	$OpenGL::triCount2
$Collision::testExtrudedPolyList	$OpenGL::triCount3
$Collision::testPolytope	$Player::maxPredictionTicks
$Con::File	$Player::maxWarpTicks
$Con::Root	$Player::minWarpTicks
$debugControlSync	$SB::DFDec
$farDistance	$SB::WODec
$frameSkip	$SceneLighting::lightingProgress
$GameBase::boundingBox	$SceneLighting::terminateLighting
$Interior::DontRestrictOutside	$screenSize
$Item::maxWarpTicks	$showBackwardAction
$Item::minWarpTicks	$showDownAction
$MasterServerAddress	$showForwardAction
$movementSpeed	$showLeftAction
$mvBackwardAction	$showMovementSpeed
$mvDownAction	$showPitch
$mvForwardAction	$showRightAction
$mvFreeLook	$showUpAction
$mvLeftAction	$showYaw
$mvPitch	$specialFog
$mvPitchDownSpeed	$Stats::netBitsReceived
$mvPitchUpSpeed	$Stats::netBitsSent
$mvRightAction	$Stats::netGhostUpdates
$mvRoll	$T2::dynamicTextureCount
$mvRollLeftSpeed	$T2::staticTextureCount
$mvRollRightSpeed	$timeAdvance
$mvUpAction	$timeScale
$mvYaw	$TSControl::frameCount
$mvYawLeftSpeed	$Video::numTexelsLoaded

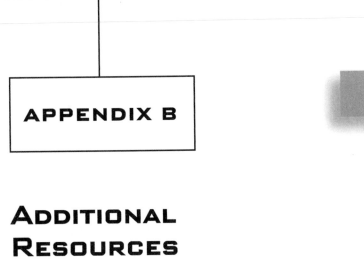

APPENDIX B

ADDITIONAL RESOURCES

Game Development Resources on the Internet

Just about everything you could possibly need to know regarding game development can be found on the Internet. But then, you probably already knew this! Search engines may be your friend, but they can often return a bewildering array of hits that may or may not be appropriate to your game development needs.

I've listed in this appendix every link from my own personal bookmark folder of game development resources, as well as a some more recommended by friends.

Of course, this is certainly not an exhaustive list. However, the sites listed have very long histories on the Web, so most are not likely to succumb to "link rot."

I think you will find these resources useful.

Torque-Related Web Sites

BraveTree Productions
ThinkTanks' home.
http://www.bravetree.com

GarageGames
Home of the Torque Engine.
http://www.garagegames.com

Gnometech
Torque modeling and other resources.
http://www.gnometech.com

Hall of Worlds
Torque development notes and tips.
http://www.hallofworlds.com

Holodeck: Virtual Reality Computing for Design
Torque and QuArK tutorials.
http://holodeck.st.usm.edu/vrcomputing/vrc_t

PlanetTribes—Torque
Source for Torque-related files and content.
http://www.planettribes.com/torque

Prairie Games
Information from the company that created *Minions of Mirth*, an RPG developed using the Torque Game Engine.
http://www.prairiegames.com
http://www.minionsofmirth.com

Realm Wars Development Site
Cooperative game development project.
http://www.realmwarsgame.com

Game Development Web Sites

3D Café
3D models and resources.
http://www.3dcafe.com

3Dup.com
2D and 3D models and resources.
http://www.3dup.com

AngelCode
Game development and more.
http://www.angelcode.com

Art Institute of Toronto
Information on game art and design programs offered in Toronto and various other locations.
http://wherecreativitygoestoschool.ca/artinstitutes/toronto

CFXweb
Game design, tutorials, and resources.
http://www.cfxweb.net

CodeGuru
Programming news, tutorials, and links.
http://www.codeguru.com

Designer Today Magazine
3D modeling tutorials, resources, and articles.
http://3dtoday.com

Dictionary of Algorithms and Data Structures
National Institute of Standards and Technology resource.
http://www.nist.gov/dads

Dr. Dobb's Journal
Programming news, articles, and links.
http://www.ddj.com

flipCode
Archives of game development news and resources.
http://www.flipcode.com

Gamasutra
Game development news, articles, and resources.
http://www.gamasutra.com

Game Developer Magazine
Game development news, articles, and resources.
http://www.gdmag.com

Game Developers Conference
GDC news and promotional information.
http://www.gdconf.com

GameDev.net
Game development news, articles, and resources.
http://www.gamedev.net

Gamer's Technical Resources
Game development news, articles, and resources—by gamers, for gamers.
http://www.gamerstech.org/forum

iDevGames
Macintosh game development news, articles, and resources.
http://www.idevgames.com

insert credit
Gaming news, articles, reviews, and resources.
http://www.insertcredit.com

Linux Game Development Center
Game development news, articles, and resources.
http://lgdc.sunsite.dk

Linux Game Tome
Game development news, articles, and resources.
http://www.happypenguin.org

Machinima.com
Real-time 3D animation resource.
http://www.machinima.com

MathWorld
Math tutorials, articles, and resources.
http://mathworld.wolfram.com

Mesh Factory
Source for 3D models.
http://www.meshfactory.com

NeHe Productions
Game technology articles and tutorials.
http://nehe.gamedev.net

NeXe
Game technology articles and tutorials.
http://nexe.gamedev.net

Oxford Dynamics
FastCar library—fast, precise, and simple library for vehicle simulation in games.
http://www.oxforddynamics.co.uk

Polycount
Game development articles, resources, and tutorials.
http://www.planetquake.com/polycount

Prefabland
Freeware 3D models source.
http://www.ejoop.com/pfl

Programmers Heaven
Programming articles, resources, and tutorials.
http://www.programmersheaven.com

Psionic's 3D Game Resources
3D modeling resources.
http://www.psionic3d.co.uk

SourceForge.net
Open Source software development Web site; large repository of Open Source code.
http://sourceforge.net

Steering Behaviors for Autonomous Characters
Paper by Craig Reynolds.
http://www.red3d.com/cwr/steer

Wotsit's Format
Programming articles, resources, and tutorials.
http://www.wotsit.org

APPENDIX C

GAME DEVELOPMENT TOOL REFERENCE

All of the tools listed in this appendix are for Windows platforms. Some of the listed tools are available also for the Linux and Macintosh systems. For more information on Linux and Macintosh game development tools, see Tables C.1 and C.2.

Note

Quoted prices for tools and their Web sites are accurate at the time of this writing.

Table C.1 Linux Tool Sources on the Web

Site	Link
Linux Game Development Center	http://lgdc.sunsite.dk
Linux Game Tome	http://www.happypenguin.org
Tucows/Linux	http://download.tucows.com/perl/Linux.html

Table C.2 Macintosh Tool Sources on the Web

Site	Link
iDevGames	http://www.idevgames.com
Mac's Heaven	http://www.mac-heaven.com
Tucows/Macintosh	http://download.tucows.com/perl/Mac.html

Shareware and Freeware Tools
Modeling
Blender
3D modeling
Multiplatform: Windows, Linux, Irix, Sun Solaris, FreeBSD, or Mac OS X.
Free software: Open Source/GPL.
http://www.blender3d.org

Hammer/Worldcraft
3D modeling—maps or levels
Worldcraft (later renamed Hammer) was written for creating Half-Life maps.

Free to be used only for creating Half-Life levels or for use by developers using the Torque Engine. Plug-ins available for Torque DIF format. Windows only.

VERC Collective Web site:
http://collective.valve-erc.com

MilkShape 3D
3D modeling
Supports Torque using exporter plug-in. Windows only.
INCLUDED ON COMPANION CD
chUmbaLum sOft:
http://www.swissquake.ch/chumbalum-soft

QuArK
3D modeling—maps or levels
Originally written for creating Quake maps. Supports Torque DIF format. Windows only.
INCLUDED ON COMPANION CD
http://dynamic.gamespy.com/~quark
http://quark.planetquake.gamespy.com/

Image Editing
The Gimp
Image editing
Fully featured image processing, painting, and editing tool.

Free software: Open Source/GPL.
http://www.gimp.org

Programming Editing

Tribal IDE
Text editing and debugging
Integrated debugger-editor written specifically to work with Tribes 2 and Torque. Useful to have around for debugging.
Free software. Hosted at GarageGames.
http://www.garagegames.com

UltraEdit-32
Text editing
Includes project and workspace features as well as macros.
INCLUDED ON COMPANION CD
http://www.ultraedit.com

Audio Editing

Audacity
Audio editing and sound processing
Allows manual editing of sound files, recording, and wave manipulation.
INCLUDED ON COMPANION CD
http://audacity.sourceforge.net

SoundEdit Pro
Audio editing and sound processing
Allows manual editing of sound files and conversion between many types.
$39.95
http://www.rmbsoft.com/sep.asp

UVMapper
3D UV texture-mapping utility
Allows users to completely remap the model textures of a Wavefront (obj) model.
INCLUDED ON COMPANION CD
http://www.uvmapper.com

Retail Tools

3D Studio Max
3D modeling
Popular commercial 3D modeling software for Windows.
$3,000 (Price is approximate—may vary according to reseller and discount eligibility.)
http://www.discreet.com
http://usa.autodesk.com

3D World Studio
3D modeling—maps or levels
Worldcraft/Hammer workalike and compatible CSG modeling tool. Also handles meshes and terrains.
$79.95
http://3dworldstudio.thegamecreators.com

Adobe Photoshop
Image editing
Popular fully featured image processing, painting, and editing tool.
$649
http://www.adobe.com

Corel Painter
Image editing
Popular commercial paint program for Windows.
$199 (Price varies—sometimes lower with special offers.)
http://www.corel.com

Corel Paint Shop Pro
Image editing
Fully featured image processing, painting, and editing tool.
$79.00
http://www.jasc.com
http://www.corel.com/

Deep Paint 3D
Image editing
Popular commercial paint program for Windows.

$995

http://www.righthemisphere.com

Deep UV
3D UV texture-mapping utility
Fully featured commercial product targeted to professionals.
$795

http://www.righthemisphere.com

Maya
3D modeling
Popular commercial 3D modeling software for Windows.
$1,999 to $6,999 (Price depends on product set.)
http://www.alias.com
http://usa.autodesk.com/

Poser
3D animation editing
Fully featured commercial product with rendering and automated tools.
$249.99
http://www.curiouslabs.com
http://www.e-frontier.com/

ZBrush 2
3D modeling and texturing
Uses 3D pixels to create 3D objects much like a sculptor would, working with clay.
$489
http://www.pixologic.com
http://www.zbrush.com

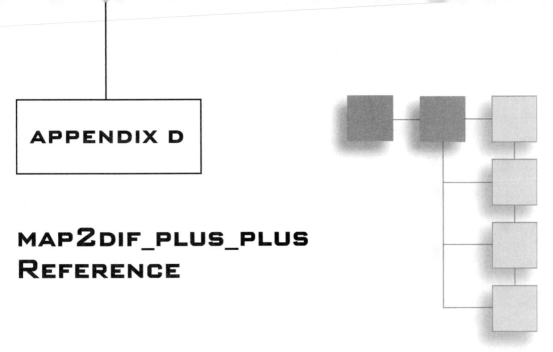

APPENDIX D

MAP2DIF_PLUS_PLUS REFERENCE

The tool we use in Constructor for compiling maps to create DIF structures or interiors is, as we have already seen, map2dif_plus_plus.exe. This program is part of the Torque SDK package.

The tool can be used outside of Constructor by invoking it from the command shell. The syntax for using map2dif_plus is as follows:

```
map2dif_plus [-d][-h][-l][-s][-o outputDirectory][-t textureDirectory]
filename.map
```

Switches:

-d	Process only the detail specified on the command line.
-l	Process as a low-detail shape (implies -d).
-h	Process for final build (exhaustive BSP search).
-s	Don't search for textures in parent directory.
-t *dir*	Location of textures.
-o *dir*	Directory in which to place the DIF file.
file.map	Name of file to be processed.

The program takes a map file, processes it according to the supplied switches, and produces as output a Torque DIF file. The DIF file is deposited in the same directory as the MAP file unless the -o switch is employed to specify the output directory.

The textures used in the map have to be loaded in order to process the map. The map2dif_plus tool needs to load the textures so that it can determine the width and height of each texture. It uses this information to calculate polygon texture mapping information that will be included in the DIF file. If you change the size of a texture, you may need to reprocess any map files that use that texture.

When it runs, map2dif_plus looks in the default directory of the MAP input file; it then recursively looks in its parent directory and on upward until it reaches the root directory or finds the texture in question. If the -t *dir* switch is used in the command line, the program starts searching for the textures in the directory specified by *dir*. The program will load either JPG or PNG forms of the textures specified in the map.

When it runs, the Torque Engine expects textures to be in the same directory as the map files that it uses or in a parent directory. Parent directories are searched all the way to the root main directory (where the Torque Engine executable resides). The root directory itself is never searched.

The map2dif_plus tool uses certain texture names to help identify special brushes. These textures are:

- null.png

- origin.png

- trigger.png

- forcefield.png

Table D.1 contains a list of the entities supported by map2dif_plus and the various entity attribute options.

Table D.1 map2dif_plus Supported Entities

Category	Entity	Attribute	Data Type
Core Entities			
	worldspawn		
	detail_number	int (default is 0)	
	min_pixels	int (default is 250)	
	geometry_scale	int must be a power of 2 (default is 32)	
	light_geometry_scale	int must be a power of 2 (default is 32)	
		ambient_color	color (default is 0,0,0)
		emergency_ambient_color	color (default is 0,0,0)
	detail		
	collision		
	vehicle_collision		
	portal		
	ambient_light	bool: pass ambient light (default is 0)	
	target		
		name	string (default is "")
		origin	pos (default is 0,0,0)
Light Emitters			
	light_emitter_point		
		origin	pos (default is 0,0,0)
		target	
		state_index	
		falloff_type	bool: 0 = distance, 1 = linear (default is false)
		falloff1	float (default is 10)
		falloff2	float (default is 100)
		falloff3	float (default is 0)
	light_emitter_spot		
	origin	pos (default is 0,0,0)	
		target	
		state_index	
		falloff_type	bool: 0=distance, 1=linear (default is false)
		falloff1	int (default is 10)
		falloff2	int (default is 100)
		falloff3	int (default is 0)
		direction	vector (default is 0,0,-1)
		theta	radian: inner angle (default is 0.2)
		phi	radian: outer angle (default is 0.4)
Lights			

continues

Table D.1   Continued

Category	Entity	Attribute	Data Type
	light		
		name	string (default is "")
		origin	pos (default is 0,0,0)
		spawnflags	int: animation flags . . .
		alarm_type	bool (default is 0)
		state	int: state number
		duration	float: state duration
		color	color: state color
Scripted Lights			
	light_omni		
		name	string (default is "")
		origin	pos (default is 0,0,0)
		color	color (default is 1,1,1)
		alarm_type	bool (default is 0)
		falloff1	int (default is 10)
		falloff2	int (default is 100)
	light_spot		
		name	string (default is "")
	origin	pos (default is 0,0,0)	
		target	
		color	color (default is 1,1,1)
		alarm_type	bool (default is 0)
		falloff1	int (default is 10)
		falloff2	int (default is 100)
		distance1	int: inner distance (default is 10)
		distance2	int: outer distance (default is 100)
Animated Lights			
	light_strobe		
		name	string (default is "")
		origin	pos (default is 0,0,0)
		target	
		spawnflags	int: animation flags . . .
		color1	color (default is 0,0,0)
		color2	color (default is 1,1,1)
		alarm_type	bool (default is 0)
		falloff1	int (default is 10)
		falloff2	int (default is 100)
		speed	int
	light_pulse		
		name	string (default is "")

Table D.1 Continued

Category	Entity	Attribute	Data Type
		origin	pos (default is 0,0,0)
		spawnflags	int: animation flags . . .
		color1	color (default is 0,0,0)
		color2	color (default is 1,1,1)
		alarm_type	bool (default is 0)
		falloff1	int (default is 10)
		falloff2	int (default is 100)
		speed	int
	light_pulse2		
		name	string (default is "")
		origin	pos (default is 0,0,0)
		spawnflags	int: animation flags . . .
		color1	color (default is 0,0,0)
		color2	color (default is 1,1,1)
		alarm_type	bool (default is 0)
		falloff1	int (default is 10)
		falloff2	int (default is 100)
		attack	float (default is 1)
		sustain1	float (default is 1)
		sustain2	float (default is 1)
		decay	float (default is 1)
	light_flicker		
		name	string (default is "")
		origin	pos (default is 0,0,0)
		spawnflags	int: animation flags . . .
		color1	color (default is 1,1,1)
		color2	color (default is 0,0,0)
		color3	color (default is 0,0,0)
		color4	color (default is 0,0,0)
		color5	color (default is 0,0,0)
		alarm_type	bool (default is 0)
		falloff1	int (default is 10)
		falloff2	int (default is 100)
		speed	int
	light_runway		
		name	string (default is "")
		origin	pos (default is 0,0,0)
		spawnflags	int: animation flags . . .
		color	color (default is 1,1,1)

continues

Table D.1 Continued

Category	Entity	Attribute	Data Type
	target		
		alarm_type	bool (default is 0)
		falloff1	int (default is 10)
		falloff2	int (default is 100)
		speed	int
		steps	int (default is 0)
		pingpong	bool (default is 0)
Special Entities			
	mirror_surface		
		origin	pos (default is 0,0,0)
		alpha_level	int
	door_elevator		
		name	string (default is "")
		path_name	string
		trigger[0-7]_name	string
	force_field		
		name	string (default is "")
		color	color (default is 0.5,0.8,1.9)
		trigger[0-7]_name	string
	ai_special_node		
		name	string (default is "")
		origin	pos (default is 0,0,0)
Path Entities			
	path_node		
		name	string (default is "")
		next_node	string
		next_time	int
	path_start		
		name	string (default is "")
		next_node	string
		next_time	int
Trigger Entities			
	trigger		
		name	string (default is "")

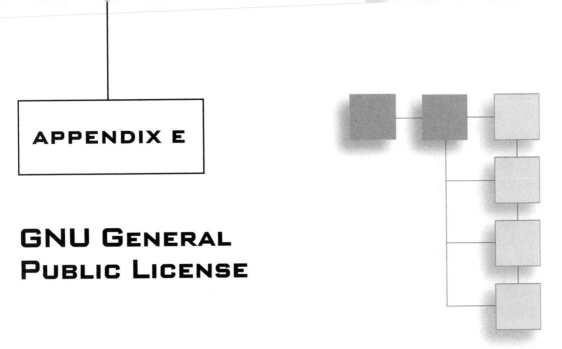

APPENDIX E

GNU GENERAL PUBLIC LICENSE

Several of the software packages listed in these appendices and included on the companion CD—like Audacity and QuArK—are distributed under the terms of the GNU *General Public License* (GPL).

The text of the GPL is as follows:

GNU GENERAL PUBLIC LICENSE

Version 2, June 1991

Copyright © 1989, 1991 Free Software Foundation, Inc.

59 Temple Place, Suite 330, Boston, MA 02111-1307 USA

Everyone is permitted to copy and distribute verbatim copies of this license document, but changing it is not allowed.

Preamble

The licenses for most software are designed to take away your freedom to share and change it. By contrast, the GNU General Public License is intended to guarantee your freedom to share and change free software—to make sure the software is free for all its users. This General Public License applies to most of the Free Software Foundation's software and to any other program whose authors commit to using it. (Some other Free Software Foundation software is covered by the GNU Library General Public License instead.) You can apply it to your programs, too.

When we speak of free software, we are referring to freedom, not price. Our General Public Licenses are designed to make sure that you have the freedom to distribute copies of free software (and charge for this service if you wish), that you receive source code or can get it if you want it, that you can change the software or use pieces of it in new free programs; and that you know you can do these things.

To protect your rights, we need to make restrictions that forbid anyone to deny you these rights or to ask you to surrender the rights. These restrictions translate to certain responsibilities for you if you distribute copies of the software, or if you modify it.

For example, if you distribute copies of such a program, whether gratis or for a fee, you must give the recipients all the rights that you have. You must make sure that they, too, receive or can get the source code. And you must show them these terms so they know their rights.

We protect your rights with two steps: (1) copyright the software, and (2) offer you this license which gives you legal permission to copy, distribute and/or modify the software.

Also, for each author's protection and ours, we want to make certain that everyone understands that there is no warranty for this free software. If the software is modified by someone else and passed on, we want its recipients to know that what they have is not the original, so that any problems introduced by others will not reflect on the original authors' reputations.

Finally, any free program is threatened constantly by software patents. We wish to avoid the danger that redistributors of a free program will individually obtain patent licenses, in effect making the program proprietary. To prevent this, we have made it clear that any patent must be licensed for everyone's free use or not licensed at all.

The precise terms and conditions for copying, distribution and modification follow.

GNU GENERAL PUBLIC LICENSE
TERMS AND CONDITIONS FOR COPYING, DISTRIBUTION AND MODIFICATION

0. This License applies to any program or other work which contains a notice placed by the copyright holder saying it may be distributed under the terms of this General Public License. The "Program", below, refers to any such program or work, and a "work based on the Program" means either the Program or any derivative work under copyright law: that is to say, a work containing the Program or a portion of it, either verbatim or with modifications and/or translated into another language. (Hereinafter, translation is included without limitation in the term "modification".) Each licensee is addressed as "you".

Activities other than copying, distribution and modification are not covered by this License; they are outside its scope. The act of running the Program is not restricted, and the output from the Program is covered only if its contents constitute a work based on the Program (independent of having been made by running the Program). Whether that is true depends on what the Program does.

1. You may copy and distribute verbatim copies of the Program's source code as you receive it, in any medium, provided that you conspicuously and appropriately publish on each copy an appropriate copyright notice and disclaimer of warranty; keep intact all the notices that refer to this License and to the absence of any warranty; and give any other recipients of the Program a copy of this License along with the Program.

   You may charge a fee for the physical act of transferring a copy, and you may at your option offer warranty protection in exchange for a fee.

2. You may modify your copy or copies of the Program or any portion of it, thus forming a work based on the Program, and copy and distribute such modifications or work under the terms of Section 1 above, provided that you also meet all of these conditions:

   a. You must cause the modified files to carry prominent notices stating that you changed the files and the date of any change.

   b. You must cause any work that you distribute or publish, that in whole or in part contains or is derived from the Program or any part thereof, to be licensed as a whole at no charge to all third parties under the terms of this License.

c. If the modified program normally reads commands interactively when run, you must cause it, when started running for such interactive use in the most ordinary way, to print or display an announcement including an appropriate copyright notice and a notice that there is no warranty (or else, saying that you provide a warranty) and that users may redistribute the program under these conditions, and telling the user how to view a copy of this License. (Exception: if the Program itself is interactive but does not normally print such an announcement, your work based on the Program is not required to print an announcement.)

These requirements apply to the modified work as a whole. If identifiable sections of that work are not derived from the Program, and can be reasonably considered independent and separate works in themselves, then this License, and its terms, do not apply to those sections when you distribute them as separate works. But when you distribute the same sections as part of a whole which is a work based on the Program, the distribution of the whole must be on the terms of this License, whose permissions for other licensees extend to the entire whole, and thus to each and every part regardless of who wrote it.

Thus, it is not the intent of this section to claim rights or contest your rights to work written entirely by you; rather, the intent is to exercise the right to control the distribution of derivative or collective works based on the Program.

In addition, mere aggregation of another work not based on the Program with the Program (or with a work based on the Program) on a volume of a storage or distribution medium does not bring the other work under the scope of this License.

3. You may copy and distribute the Program (or a work based on it, under Section 2) in object code or executable form under the terms of Sections 1 and 2 above provided that you also do one of the following:

a. Accompany it with the complete corresponding machine-readable source code, which must be distributed under the terms of Sections 1 and 2 above on a medium customarily used for software interchange; or,

b. Accompany it with a written offer, valid for at least three years, to give any third party, for a charge no more than your cost of physically performing source distribution, a complete machine-readable copy of the corresponding source code, to be distributed under the terms of Sections 1 and 2 above on a medium customarily used for software interchange; or,

c. Accompany it with the information you received as to the offer to distribute corresponding source code. (This alternative is allowed only for noncommercial distribution and only if you received the program in object code or executable form with such an offer, in accord with Subsection b above.)

The source code for a work means the preferred form of the work for making modifications to it. For an executable work, complete source code means all the source code for all modules it contains, plus any associated interface definition files, plus the scripts used to control compilation and installation of the executable. However, as a special exception, the source code distributed need not include anything that is normally distributed (in either source or binary form) with the major components (compiler, kernel, and so on) of the operating system on which the executable runs, unless that component itself accompanies the executable.

If distribution of executable or object code is made by offering access to copy from a designated place, then offering equivalent access to copy the source code from the same place counts as distribution of the source code, even though third parties are not compelled to copy the source along with the object code.

4. You may not copy, modify, sublicense, or distribute the Program except as expressly provided under this License. Any attempt otherwise to copy, modify, sublicense or distribute the Program is void, and will automatically terminate your rights under this License. However, parties who have received copies, or rights, from you under this License will not have their licenses terminated so long as such parties remain in full compliance.

5. You are not required to accept this License, since you have not signed it. However, nothing else grants you permission to modify or distribute the Program or its derivative works. These actions are prohibited by law if you do not accept this License. Therefore, by modifying or distributing the Program (or any work based on the Program), you indicate your acceptance of this License to do so, and all its terms and conditions for copying, distributing or modifying the Program or works based on it.

6. Each time you redistribute the Program (or any work based on the Program), the recipient automatically receives a license from the original licensor to copy, distribute or modify the Program subject to these terms and conditions. You may not impose any further restrictions on the recipients' exercise of the rights granted herein. You are not responsible for enforcing compliance by third parties to this License.

7. If, as a consequence of a court judgment or allegation of patent infringement or for any other reason (not limited to patent issues), conditions are imposed on you (whether by court order, agreement or otherwise) that contradict the conditions of this License, they do not excuse you from the conditions of this License. If you cannot distribute so as to satisfy simultaneously your obligations under this License and any other pertinent obligations, then as a consequence you may not distribute the Program at all. For example, if a patent license would not permit royalty-free redistribution of the Program by all those who receive copies directly or indirectly through you, then the only way you could satisfy both it and this License would be to refrain entirely from distribution of the Program.

If any portion of this section is held invalid or unenforceable under any particular circumstance, the balance of the section is intended to apply and the section as a whole is intended to apply in other circumstances.

It is not the purpose of this section to induce you to infringe any patents or other property right claims or to contest validity of any such claims; this section has the sole purpose of protecting the integrity of the free software distribution system, which is implemented by public license practices. Many people have made generous contributions to the wide range of software distributed through that system in reliance on consistent application of that system; it is up to the author/donor to decide if he or she is willing to distribute software through any other system and a licensee cannot impose that choice.

This section is intended to make thoroughly clear what is believed to be a consequence of the rest of this License.

8. If the distribution and/or use of the Program is restricted in certain countries either by patents or by copyrighted interfaces, the original copyright holder who places the Program under this License may add an explicit geographical distribution limitation excluding those countries, so that

distribution is permitted only in or among countries not thus excluded. In such case, this License incorporates the limitation as if written in the body of this License.

9. The Free Software Foundation may publish revised and/or new versions of the General Public License from time to time. Such new versions will be similar in spirit to the present version, but may differ in detail to address new problems or concerns.

   Each version is given a distinguishing version number. If the Program specifies a version number of this License which applies to it and "any later version", you have the option of following the terms and conditions either of that version or of any later version published by the Free Software Foundation. If the Program does not specify a version number of this License, you may choose any version ever published by the Free Software Foundation.

10. If you wish to incorporate parts of the Program into other free programs whose distribution conditions are different, write to the author to ask for permission. For software which is copyrighted by the Free Software Foundation, write to the Free Software Foundation; we sometimes make exceptions for this. Our decision will be guided by the two goals of preserving the free status of all derivatives of our free software and of promoting the sharing and reuse of software generally.

NO WARRANTY

11. BECAUSE THE PROGRAM IS LICENSED FREE OF CHARGE, THERE IS NO WARRANTY FOR THE PROGRAM, TO THE EXTENT PERMITTED BY APPLICABLE LAW. EXCEPT WHEN OTHERWISE STATED IN WRITING THE COPYRIGHT HOLDERS AND/OR OTHER PARTIES PROVIDE THE PROGRAM "AS IS" WITHOUT WARRANTY OF ANY KIND, EITHER EXPRESSED OR IMPLIED, INCLUDING, BUT NOT LIMITED TO, THE IMPLIED WARRANTIES OF MERCHANTABILITY AND FITNESS FOR A PARTICULAR PURPOSE. THE ENTIRE RISK AS TO THE QUALITY AND PERFORMANCE OF THE PROGRAM IS WITH YOU. SHOULD THE PROGRAM PROVE DEFECTIVE, YOU ASSUME THE COST OF ALL NECESSARY SERVICING, REPAIR OR CORRECTION.

12. IN NO EVENT UNLESS REQUIRED BY APPLICABLE LAW OR AGREED TO IN WRITING WILL ANY COPYRIGHT HOLDER, OR ANY OTHER PARTY WHO MAY MODIFY AND/OR REDISTRIBUTE THE PROGRAM AS PERMITTED ABOVE, BE LIABLE TO YOU FOR DAMAGES, INCLUDING ANY GENERAL, SPECIAL, INCIDENTAL OR CONSEQUENTIAL DAMAGES ARISING OUT OF THE USE OR INABILITY TO USE THE PROGRAM (INCLUDING BUT NOT LIMITED TO LOSS OF DATA OR DATA BEING RENDERED INACCURATE OR LOSSES SUSTAINED BY YOU OR THIRD PARTIES OR A FAILURE OF THE PROGRAM TO OPERATE WITH ANY OTHER PROGRAMS), EVEN IF SUCH HOLDER OR OTHER PARTY HAS BEEN ADVISED OF THE POSSIBILITY OF SUCH DAMAGES.

END OF TERMS AND CONDITIONS

How to Apply These Terms to Your New Programs

If you develop a new program, and you want it to be of the greatest possible use to the public, the best way to achieve this is to make it free software which everyone can redistribute and change under these terms.

To do so, attach the following notices to the program. It is safest to attach them to the start of each source file to most effectively convey the exclusion of warranty; and each file should have at least the "copyright" line and a pointer to where the full notice is found.

<one line to give the program's name and a brief idea of what it does.>
Copyright © 19yy <name of author>

This program is free software; you can redistribute it and/or modify it under the terms of the GNU General Public License as published by the Free Software Foundation; either version 2 of the License, or (at your option) any later version.

This program is distributed in the hope that it will be useful, but WITHOUT ANY WARRANTY; without even the implied warranty of MERCHANTABILITY or FITNESS FOR A PARTICULAR PURPOSE. See the GNU General Public License for more details.

You should have received a copy of the GNU General Public License along with this program; if not, write to the Free Software Foundation, Inc., 59 Temple Place, Suite 330, Boston, MA 02111-1307 USA

Also add information on how to contact you by electronic and paper mail.

If the program is interactive, make it output a short notice like this when it starts in an interactive mode:

Gnomovision version 69, Copyright © 19yy name of author

Gnomovision comes with ABSOLUTELY NO WARRANTY; for details type 'show w'.

This is free software, and you are welcome to redistribute it under certain conditions; type 'show c' for details.

The hypothetical commands 'show w' and 'show c' should show the appropriate parts of the General Public License. Of course, the commands you use may be called something other than 'show w' and 'show c'; they could even be mouse-clicks or menu items—whatever suits your program.

You should also get your employer (if you work as a programmer) or your school, if any, to sign a "copyright disclaimer" for the program, if necessary. Here is a sample; alter the names:

Yoyodyne, Inc., hereby disclaims all copyright interest in the program 'Gnomovision' (which makes passes at compilers) written by James Hacker.

<signature of Ty Coon>, 1 April 1989

Ty Coon, President of Vice

This General Public License does not permit incorporating your program into proprietary programs. If your program is a subroutine library, you may consider it more useful to permit linking proprietary applications with the library. If this is what you want to do, use the GNU Library General Public License instead of this License.

INDEX

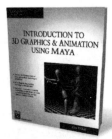

License Agreement/Notice of Limited Warranty

By opening the sealed disc container in this book, you agree to the following terms and conditions. If, upon reading the following license agreement and notice of limited warranty, you cannot agree to the terms and conditions set forth, return the unused book with unopened disc to the place where you purchased it for a refund.

License

The enclosed software is copyrighted by the copyright holder(s) indicated on the software disc. You are licensed to copy the software onto a single computer for use by a single user and to a backup disc. You may not reproduce, make copies, or distribute copies or rent or lease the software in whole or in part, except with written permission of the copyright holder(s). You may transfer the enclosed disc only together with this license, and only if you destroy all other copies of the software and the transferee agrees to the terms of the license. You may not decompile, reverse assemble, or reverse engineer the software.

Notice of Limited Warranty

The enclosed disc is warranted by Thomson Course Technology PTR to be free of physical defects in materials and workmanship for a period of sixty (60) days from end user's purchase of the book/disc combination. During the sixty-day term of the limited warranty, Thomson Course Technology PTR will provide a replacement disc upon the return of a defective disc.

Limited Liability

THE SOLE REMEDY FOR BREACH OF THIS LIMITED WARRANTY SHALL CONSIST ENTIRELY OF REPLACEMENT OF THE DEFECTIVE DISC. IN NO EVENT SHALL THOMSON COURSE TECHNOLOGY PTR OR THE AUTHOR BE LIABLE FOR ANY OTHER DAMAGES, INCLUDING LOSS OR CORRUPTION OF DATA, CHANGES IN THE FUNCTIONAL CHARACTERISTICS OF THE HARDWARE OR OPERATING SYSTEM, DELETERIOUS INTERACTION WITH OTHER SOFTWARE, OR ANY OTHER SPECIAL, INCIDENTAL, OR CONSEQUENTIAL DAMAGES THAT MAY ARISE, EVEN IF THOMSON COURSE TECHNOLOGY PTR AND/OR THE AUTHOR HAS PREVIOUSLY BEEN NOTIFIED THAT THE POSSIBILITY OF SUCH DAMAGES EXISTS.

Disclaimer of Warranties

THOMSON COURSE TECHNOLOGY PTR AND THE AUTHOR SPECIFICALLY DISCLAIM ANY AND ALL OTHER WARRANTIES, EITHER EXPRESS OR IMPLIED, INCLUDING WARRANTIES OF MERCHANTABILITY, SUITABILITY TO A PARTICULAR TASK OR PURPOSE, OR FREEDOM FROM ERRORS. SOME STATES DO NOT ALLOW FOR EXCLUSION OF IMPLIED WARRANTIES OR LIMITATION OF INCIDENTAL OR CONSEQUENTIAL DAMAGES, SO THESE LIMITATIONS MIGHT NOT APPLY TO YOU.

Other

This Agreement is governed by the laws of the State of Massachusetts without regard to choice of law principles. The United Convention of Contracts for the International Sale of Goods is specifically disclaimed. This Agreement constitutes the entire agreement between you and Thomson Course Technology PTR regarding use of the software.